DATA STRUCTURES & OTHER OBJECTS

Using C++

DATA STRUCTURES & OTHER OBJECTS

Using C++

MICHAEL MAIN
Department of Computer Science
University of Colorado at Boulder

WALTER SAVITCH
Department of Computer Science
and Engineering
University of California, San Diego

 ADDISON WESLEY

Reading, Massachusetts • Harlow, England
Menlo Park, California • Berkeley, California • Don Mills, Ontario
Sydney • Bonn • Amsterdam • Tokyo • Mexico City

Acquisitions Editor:	J. Carter Shanklin	Production:	Editorial Services of New England Inc.
Editor:	Susan Hartman	Project Manager:	Penny Stratton
Associate Editor:	Deborah Lafferty	Production Manager:	Karen Wernholm
Cover Designer:	Eileen Hoff	Project Editor:	Lauren Byrne
		Technical Support:	Peter Whitmer

The cover artwork *Saddle World* by Michael Main, copyright © 1997, was produced with the Persistence of Vision Ray Tracer (POV-Ray), and further edited with Fauve Matisse SE. The image is a saddle shape, embossed with a three-dimensional fractal surface. The height of the surface determines the color from the blue sea through the brown mountains. A similar program to generate two-dimensional fractals appears in Chapter 9 of this book.

Reprinted with corrections, August 1998.

Access the latest information about Addison Wesley titles from our World Wide Web page:
`http://www.aw.com/cseng`

Library of Congress Cataloging-in-Publication Data
Main. M. (Michael), 1956–
    Data structures and other objects using C++
    / Michael Main, Walter Savitch
       p.   cm.
    Includes index.
    ISBN 0-8053-7470-1
    1. Data structures (Computer science) 2. C++ (Computer program language)
    I. Savitch, Walter J., 1943–   . II. Title
QA76.9.D35M35 1997
005.7'3—dc20

96-36154
CIP

8 9 10—DOC—01 00 99

Preface

This book is written for a second course in computer science. It can be used for a course based on the ACM CS2 curriculum, or the C102 course in the ACM/IEEE Computing Curricula. The text's emphasis is on the *specification*, *design*, *implementation*, and *use* of the basic data types that are normally covered in a second-semester course. In addition, we cover a range of important programming techniques and provide self-contained coverage of abstraction techniques, object-oriented programming, big-O time analysis of algorithms, and sorting.

We assume that the student has already had an introductory computer science and programming class, but we do include coverage of those topics (such as recursion and pointers) that are not always covered completely in a first course. The text uses C++, but our coverage of C++ classes begins from scratch, so the text may be used by students whose introduction to programming was in C rather than C++. In our experience, such students need a brief coverage of C++ input and output techniques (such as those provided in our Appendix F), and some coverage of C++ parameter types (which we provide in Chapter 2). When C programmers are over the input/output hurdle and the parameter hurdle (and perhaps a small "fear" hurdle), they can readily step into classes and other object-oriented features of C++.

As this indicates, there are several pathways through the text that can be tailored to different student backgrounds. We'll discuss these pathways in detail at the end of this preface, but first we provide an overview of the text's other features.

The design above is a random fractal coastline, embossed onto a saddle shape. A program to generate similar fractals appears in the chapter on recursion (Chapter 9) .

The Five Steps for Each Data Type

The book's core consists of the well-known data types: *sets, bags* (or *multisets*), *sequential lists, ordered lists* (with ordering from a "less than" operator), *stacks, queues, tables, and graphs*. There are also additional supplemental data types such as a priority queue. Each of these data types is introduced following a pattern of five steps:

Step 1: Understand the Data Type Abstractly. At this level, a student gains an understanding of the data type and its operations at the level of concepts and pictures. For example, a student can visualize a stack and its operations of pushing and popping elements. Simple applications are understood and can be carried out by hand, such as using a stack to reverse the order of letters in a word.

Step 2: Write a Specification of the Data Type as a C++ Class. In this step, the student sees and learns how to write a specification for a C++ class that can implement the data type. The specification includes prototypes for the constructors, public member functions, and sometimes other public features (such as an underlying constant that determines the maximum size of a stack). The prototype of each member function is presented along with a precondition/postcondition contract that completely specifies the behavior of the function. At this level, it's important for the students to realize that the specification is not tied to any particular choice of implementation techniques. In fact, this same specification may be used several times for several different implementations of the same data type.

Step 3: Use the Data Type. With the specification in place, students can write small applications or demonstration programs to show the data type in use. These applications are based solely on the data type's specification, as we still have not tied down the implementation.

Step 4: Select Appropriate Data Structures, and Proceed to Design and Implement the Data Type. With a good abstract understanding of the data type, we can select an appropriate data structure, such as a fixed-sized array, a dynamic array, a linked list of nodes, or a binary tree of nodes. For many of our data types, a first design and implementation will select a simple approach, such as a fixed-sized array. Later, we will redesign and reimplement the same data type with a more complicated underlying structure.

Since we are using C++ classes, an implementation of a data type will have the selected data structures (arrays, pointers, etc.) as private member variables of the class. With each implemented class, we stress the necessity for a clear understanding of the rules that relate the private member variables to abstract notion of the data type. We require each student to write these rules in clear English sentences that we call the *invariant of the abstract data type*. Once the invariant is written, students can proceed to implementing various member functions. The invariant helps in writing correct functions because of two facts: (a) Each function (except the constructors) knows that the invariant is true when the function begins its work; and (b) Each function (except the destructor) is responsible for ensuring that the invariant is again true when the function finishes.

Step 5: Analyze the Implementation. Each implementation can be analyzed for correctness, flexibility (such as a fixed size versus dynamic size), and time analysis of the operations (using big-*O* notation). Students have a particularly strong opportunity for these analyses when the same data type has been implemented in several different ways.

Where Will the Students Be at the End of the Course?

At the end of our course, students understand the data types inside out. They know how to use the data types, they know how to implement them several ways, and they know the practical effects of the different implementation choices. The students can reason about efficiency with a big-*O* analysis and argue for the correctness of their implementations by referring to the invariant of the ADT.

One of the important lasting effects of the course is the specification, design, and implementation experience. The improved ability to reason about programs is also important. But perhaps most important of all is the exposure to classes that are easily used in many situations. The students no longer have to write everything from scratch. We tell our students that someday they will be thinking about a problem, and they will suddenly realize that a large chunk of the work can be done with a bag, or a stack, or a queue, or some such. And this large chunk of work is work that they won't have to do. Instead they will pull out the bag or stack or queue or some such that they wrote this semester—using it with no modifications. Or, more likely, they will use the familiar data type from a library of standard data types, such as the proposed C++ *Standard Template Library*. In fact, the behavior of the data types in this text is a cut-down version of the *Standard Template Library*, so when a student takes the step to the real STL, they will be on familiar ground. And at that point of realization, knowing that a certain data type is the exact solution they need, the student graduates to being a real programmer.

the data types in this book are cut-down versions of the standard template library

Other Foundational Topics

Throughout the course, we also lay a foundation for other aspects of "real programming," with coverage of the following topics beyond the basic data structures material:

Object-Oriented Programming. The foundations of object-oriented programming are laid by giving students a strong understanding of C++ classes. The important aspects of classes are covered early: the notion of a member function, the separation into private and public members, the purpose of constructors, and a small exposure to operator overloading. This is enough to get students going and excited about classes.

Further major aspects of classes are introduced when the students first use dynamic memory (Chapter 4). At this point, the need for three additional items is explained: the copy constructor, the overloaded assignment operator, and the destructor. Teaching these OOP aspects with the first use of dynamic memory has the effect of giving the students a concrete picture of dynamic memory as a resource that can be taken and must later be returned.

Conceptually, the largest innovation of OOP is the software reuse that occurs via inheritance. And there are certainly opportunities for introducing inheritance right from the start of a data structures course (such as implementing a set class as a descendant of a bag class). However, an early introduction may also result in juggling too many new concepts at once, resulting in a weaker understanding of the fundamental data structures. Therefore, in our own course we introduce inheritance at the end as a vision of things to come. But, the introduction to inheritance (Sections 14.1 and 14.2) could be covered as soon as copy constructors are understood. With this in mind, some instructors may wish to cover Chapter 14 earlier, just before stacks and queues, so that stacks and queues can be derived from a list class.

Another alternative is to identify students who already know the basics of classes. These students can carry out an inheritance project (such as the ecosystem of Section 14.2), while the rest of the students first learn about classes.

Templates. Template functions and template classes are an important part of the proposed Standard Template Library, allowing a programmer to easily change the type of the underlying item in a container class. Template classes also allow the use of several different instantiations of a class in a single program. As such, we think it's important to learn about and use templates (Chapter 6) prior to stacks (Chapter 7), since expression evaluation is an important application that uses two kinds of stacks.

Iterators. Iterators are another important part of the proposed Standard Template Library, allowing a programmer to easily step through the items in a container object (such as the elements of a set or bag). Such iterators may be *internal* (implemented with member functions of the container class) or *external* (implemented by a separate class that is a friend of the container class). We introduce internal iterators with one of the first container classes (a sequential list in Section 3.2). An internal iterator is added to the bag class when it is needed in Chapter 6. At that point, the more complex external iterators also are discussed, and students should be aware of the advantages of an external iterator. Throughout the text, iterators provide a good opportunity for programming projects, such as implementing an external bag iterator (Chapter 6) or using a stack to implement an internal iterator of a binary search tree (Chapter 10).

Recursion. First-semester courses sometimes introduce students to recursion. But many of the first-semester examples are tail recursion, where the final act of the function is the recursive call. This may have given students a misleading impression that recursion is nothing more than a loop. Because of this, we prefer to avoid early use of tail recursion in a second-semester course. For example, list traversal and other operations on linked lists can be implemented with tail recursion, but the effect may reinforce wrong impressions about recursion (and the tail recursive list operations may need to be unlearned when the students work with real lists of thousands of items, running into potential run-time stack overflow).

So, in our second-semester course, we emphasize recursive solutions that use more than tail recursion. The recursion chapter provides three examples along these lines. Two of the examples—generating random fractals and traversing a maze—are big hits with the students. In our class, we teach recursion (Chapter 9) just before trees (Chapter 10), since it is recursive tree algorithms where recursion becomes vital. However, instructors who desire more emphasis on recursion can move that topic forward, even before Chapter 2.

In a course that has time for advanced tree projects (Chapter 11), we analyze the recursive tree algorithms, explaining the importance of keeping the trees balanced—both to improve worst-case performance, and to avoid potential run-time stack overflow.

Searching and Sorting. Chapters 12 and 13 provide fundamental coverage of searching and sorting algorithms. The searching reviews binary search of an ordered array, which many students will have seen before. Hash tables also are introduced in the search chapter. The sorting chapter reviews simple quadratic sorting methods, but the majority of the chapter focuses on faster algorithms: the recursive merge sort (with worst-case time of $O(n \log n)$), Tony Hoare's recursive quicksort (with average-time $O(n \log n)$), and the tree-based heap sort (with worst-case time of $O(n \log n)$).

Advanced Projects

The text offers good opportunities for optional projects that can be undertaken by a more advanced class or by students with a stronger background in a large class. Particular advanced projects include the following:

- An external iterator for the bag class (Chapter 6 Programming Projects)
- Using a stack to build an internal iterator for the binary search tree (Chapter 10 Programming Projects)
- A priority queue, implemented as an array of ordinary queues (Section 8.4), or implemented using a heap (Section 11.1)
- A set class, implemented with B-trees (Section 11.2). We have made a particular effort on this project to provide information that is sufficient for

students to implement the class without need of another text. In our courses, we have successfully directed advanced students to do this project as independent work.

- An inheritance project, such as the ecosystem of Section 14.2
- A graph class and associated graph algorithms from Chapter 15. This is another case where advanced students may do work on their own.

C++ Language Features

bool type

static constant member variables

C++ is a complex language with many advanced features that will not be touched in a second-semester course. But we endeavor to provide complete coverage for those features that we do touch. In this edition of the text, we have included coverage of two new features that many C++ programmers have not seen, and some compilers do not yet support. These features are the new *bool* data type (Figure 2.1 on page 34), and static constant member variables (see the section on page 93). In both cases, these features can be easily simulated in older compilers that do not yet provide direct support (see Appendix E, "Dealing with Older Compilers").

Flexibility of Topic Ordering

This book was written to allow instructors latitude in reordering the material to meet the specific background of students or to add early emphasis to selected topics. The dependencies among the chapters are shown on page xi. A line joining two boxes indicates that the upper box should be covered before the lower box.

Here are some suggested orderings of the material:

Typical Course. Start with chapters 1–10, skipping parts of Chapter 2 if the students have a prior background in C++ classes. Most chapters can be covered in a week, but you may want more time for Chapter 5 (linked lists), Chapter 6 (templates), Chapter 9 (recursion), or Chapter 10 (trees). Typically, we cover the material in thirteen weeks, including time for exams and extra time for linked lists and trees. Remaining weeks can be spent on a tree project from Chapter 11, or on binary search (Section 12.1) and sorting (Chapter 12).

Heavy OOP emphasis. If students will cover sorting and searching elsewhere, then there is time for a heavier emphasis on object-oriented programming. The first four chapters are covered in detail, and then derived classes (Section 14.1) are introduced. At this point, students can do an interesting OOP project, perhaps based on the ecosystem of Section 14.2). The basic data structures (Chapters 5–8) are then covered, with the queue implemented as a derived class (Section 14.3). Finish up with recursion (Chapter 9) and trees (Chapter 10), placing special emphasis on recursive member functions.

Chapter Dependencies

At the start of the course, students should be comfortable writing functions and using arrays in C++ or C. Those who have used only C should read Appendix F and pay particular attention to the discussion of reference parameters in Section 2.4.

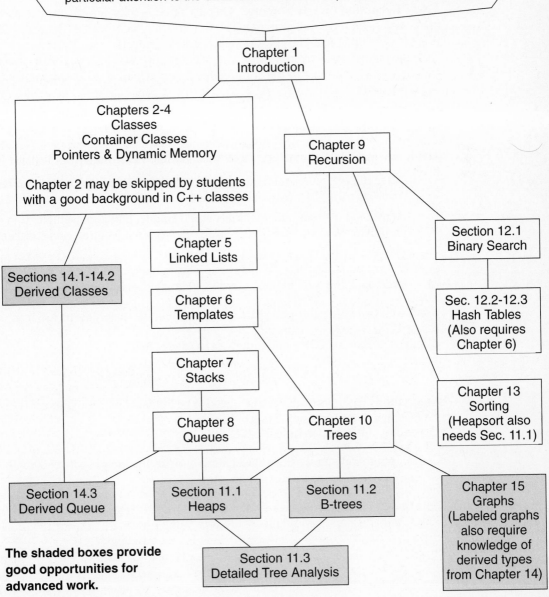

Chapter 1
Introduction

Chapters 2-4
Classes
Container Classes
Pointers & Dynamic Memory

Chapter 2 may be skipped by students
with a good background in C++ classes

Chapter 9
Recursion

Section 12.1
Binary Search

Sections 14.1-14.2
Derived Classes

Chapter 5
Linked Lists

Sec. 12.2-12.3
Hash Tables
(Also requires
Chapter 6)

Chapter 6
Templates

Chapter 7
Stacks

Chapter 13
Sorting
(Heapsort also
needs Sec. 11.1)

Chapter 8
Queues

Chapter 10
Trees

Section 14.3
Derived Queue

Section 11.1
Heaps

Section 11.2
B-trees

Chapter 15
Graphs
(Labeled graphs
also require
knowledge of
derived types
from Chapter 14)

**The shaded boxes provide
good opportunities for
advanced work.**

Section 11.3
Detailed Tree Analysis

Accelerated course. Assign the first three chapters as independent reading in the first week, and start with Chapter 4 (pointers). This will leave two to three extra weeks at the end of the term, so that students may spend more time on searching, sorting, and the advanced topics (shaded on page xi.)

We also have taught the course with further acceleration by spending no lecture time on stacks and queues (but assigning those chapters as reading).

Early Recursion / Early Sorting. One to three weeks may be spent at the start of class on recursive thinking. The first reading will then be Chapters 1 and 9, perhaps supplemented by additional recursive projects.

If the recursion is covered early, you may also proceed to cover binary search (Section 12.1) and most of the sorting algorithms (Chapter 13) before introducing C++ classes.

Supplements Via Internet

The following support material is available via internet from the publishers:

- All textbook figures marked with the symbol FTP have code that can be obtained using FTP or a web browser.

- Additional instructional materials are available, including sample assignments, exam questions, syllabi, Powerpoint lectures, and speaker's notes.

- We are building a library of Java applets to demonstrate some data structures. We will add one or two new applets each month.

Use a web browser. For information on obtaining the materials, please read our World Wide Web home page at:
```
http://www.cs.colorado.edu/~main/dsoc.html
```
or
```
http://www.aw.com/cseng/authors/main/dsoc/dsoc.html
```

Anonymous ftp. Some materials may also be obtained by anonymous ftp from the machine "ftp.aw.com". Start by reading the file:
```
/cseng/authors/main/dsoc/README
```

Contact your Addison Wesley representative for further details, or send email to aw.cse@aw.com or main@colorado.edu

Acknowledgments

We started this book while Walter was visiting Michael at the Computer Science Department of the University of Colorado in Boulder. The work was completed after Walter moved back to the Department of Engineering and Computer Science at the University of California, San Diego. We are grateful to these institutions for providing facilities, wonderful students, and interaction with congenial colleagues.

Our students have been particularly helpful—nearly 1000 students, working through early versions of the material, making suggestions, showing us how they learned. We thank the instructors who used the early material in their data structures courses: Gina Cherry, Patrick Lynn, Evi Nemeth, Karl Winklmann. During this time, the book was also extensively reviewed by Wolfgang W. Bein, Bill Hankley, Michael Milligan, Jeff Parker, Andrew L. Wright, John R. Rose, and Evan Zweifel. We thank these colleagues for their excellent critique and their encouragement.

Our thanks also go to the editors and staff at Addison Wesley. Debbie Lafferty's daily work has dramatically improved the book from front to back. We thank Eileen Hoff for turning our saddle fractal into reality on the cover. Penny Stratton, Lauren Byrne, and Peter Whitmer at Editorial Services of New England helped us at every stage of production, and we offer our thanks. We extend a special thanks to our editors Carter Shankin, who started us off and offered continual support, and Susan Hartman for her support and advice throughout the production process.

In addition to the work and support from those who put the book together, we thank those who offered us daily interest and encouragement. Our deepest thanks go to Lydia Aucoin, David Benson, Steve Brookes, Paul Chadwick, Amy Cronin, Dan Dorman, Andrzej Ehrenfeucht, Paul Eisenbrey, Lloyd Fosdick, Rick Lowell, George Main, Mickey Main, Jim W. Martin Jr., Austin Melton, Michael Milligan, Michael Mislove, Philip Mulry, Evi Nemeth, Cathy Preston, Harry Preston, Grzegorz Rozenberg, David Schmidt, Karl Winklmann, Evan Zweifel, Hannah, Timothy, and Janet.

Michael Main
main@colorado.edu
Boulder, Colorado

Walter Savitch
wsavitch@ucsd.edu
San Diego, California

Chapter List

Contents

5 LINKED LISTS 201

9   RECURSIVE THINKING   387

10 TREES 423

11 TREE PROJECTS 492

12 SEARCHING 533

13   SORTING   570

APPENDIXES

1 Program Specification, Design, and Analysis

Chapter the first which explains how, why, when, and
where there was ever any problem in the first place

NOEL LANGLEY
The Land of Green Ginger

In this chapter we outline the approach to data structures and programming used throughout this book. The approach has three primary components: specification, design, and analysis. The specification indicates what a program, or portion of a program, is meant to accomplish, without regard to precisely how the program is to accomplish its work. During the design phase, a programmer selects and creates specific data structures and algorithms to meet the specification. Our designs have a particular emphasis on the well-known data types that are used by experienced programmers, and on the algorithms that manipulate these data types. Analysis consists of reasoning about the resulting data structures and algorithms, both to increase confidence in correctness and to determine properties such as the efficiency of an algorithm.

three primary components

Specification, design, and analysis all transcend any particular programming language. The techniques and knowledge of data structures that you learn will serve you well in whatever language you happen to use next year, or next century. Nevertheless, when we get down to implementation details, we do need to decide

1

*OOP supports
information
hiding and
component
reuse*

on one particular language. The language we use in this book is C++. The C++ language was designed by Bjarne Stroustrup at AT&T Bell Laboratories as an extension of the C language, with the purpose of supporting **object-oriented programming (OOP)**—a relatively new technique that encourages important strategies of information hiding and component reuse. Throughout the book, we will employ OOP in our designs and implementations.

There are many different C++ compilers that you may successfully use with this text. Each compiler implements the basic C++ language. However, differences arise in the mechanics needed to write, compile, link, and run a program. Appendix D, "Compiling, Linking, and Running Programs," describes how to use two common C++ compilers.

1.1 SPECIFICATION AND DESIGN

One begins with a list of difficult design decisions which are likely to change. Each module is then designed to hide such a decision from the others.

D. L. PARNAS
On the Criteria to Be Used in Decomposing Systems into
Modules

Experienced programmers employ a collection of design principles that make the program-design process less time-consuming and make the final program more reliable. Learning some widely used design principles will be worth the effort. We start with a review of a basic design strategy.

A Basic Design Strategy

Program design is a creative process. We cannot give you a complete formula to follow in this process. Still, there is an outline to follow as well as a number of specific techniques that can help in certain cases. In broad outline, the process is as follows:

Program Design Strategy

1. Specify the input and output.
2. Design the algorithm and data structures.
3. Translate the algorithm into a programming language such as C++.
4. Test and debug the program.

Notice that there is no step that says "write a program." Successful programmers do not simply sit down and write programs—at least not directly. In Step 3 the programmer is writing a program, but the process is not what you might think. Step 3 is a simple translation process. Most of the work comes before that point. Let's briefly go over each of the four steps.

When you set out to write a program, the first task is to specify _precisely_ what the program is supposed to do. If you do not know _exactly_ what you want your program to do, you will probably design a program that does not perform to your satisfaction. Even without analyzing the problem, you do have some idea of what your program is supposed to do. However, you need more than a vague idea. You need to know exactly what the input to your program will be and exactly what information should be in the output. To help clarify and to give you a reference for later use, you should write down precise descriptions of the desired program input and output. This is called the **specification**. The next step is to find a solution.

specification

An **algorithm** is a precise set of instructions that leads to a solution. In other words, an algorithm is a precisely stated method for solving a problem. When we express this method in the C++ language (or any other programming language), we get a program. However, when we are designing an algorithm, the details and limitations of a programming language can be distracting. So, during the algorithm design phase, we generally write in English. We use a rather corrupted kind of English that mixes in a bit of C++ when that's convenient. This mixture of English and a programming language is called **pseudocode**. At the design stage, most algorithms are expressed in pseudocode. When the C++ code for a step is obvious, then the pseudocode may use C++. When a step is difficult to express in C++, the algorithm will be clearer if the pseudocode uses English.

algorithm design

Algorithms are instructions for doing something. **Data** is the information manipulated by these algorithms, including numbers or text or whatever information is used as input, output, and for intermediate calculations. In order to make an algorithm efficient, clear, and correct, we need to structure the algorithm's underlying data. A **data structure** is simply a way to organize data. Even a simple program variable is a data structure, but it is such a simple data structure that we might not bother to use a term as fancy as *data structure* to describe it. A more sophisticated data structure is an array. Data structures are the main topic of this book, but the algorithms that manipulate the structures are equally important. Neither is of much value without the other. Thus, in addition to giving you techniques for designing data structures, we will also give you techniques for designing algorithms. Should you design the algorithm first or the data structure first? It is hard to say. In practice, they are designed together, and in fact part of the purpose of *object-oriented programming* is to combine algorithms and data into one package. In this book, we take an OOP approach that makes the data structures and algorithms an inseparable combination.

the connection between data structures and algorithms

Once you have designed an algorithm and a data structure, you have your program, except that it is expressed in pseudocode rather than C++, so you cannot run this program on a computer. To obtain a program that you can run on a

coding an algorithm in a programming language

computer, the pseudocode is translated into a programming language—in our case C++.

testing and debugging

If you design your algorithm and data structures using the techniques in this text, then your programs will be correct and run perfectly when translated into C++ —in a perfect world. But even in the less-than-perfect world, debugging should not be the most time-consuming part of programming. If you design your algorithms and data structures carefully, your program should require little debugging. However, we are all human and we all do make mistakes. The experienced programmer employs a number of testing techniques to discover and correct errors. In fact, some informal testing should be done at all stages. For example, you can test an algorithm by doing a simple case with pencil and paper. At any stage, you may discover shortcomings in your algorithm, the data structures, or even in the input/output specifications for the program. In such cases, you may need to back up and rethink a previous step. Throughout the book we encourage this kind of informal testing, and we also illustrate a collection of more rigid testing techniques.

Now let's discuss some more specific techniques for designing algorithms and data structures. We'll start by reviewing a simple but fundamentally important technique for designing algorithms.

> **Key Design Concept**
>
> *Break down a task into a few subtasks, then decompose each subtask into smaller subtasks.*

Decomposing Problems

A good technique for designing an algorithm is to break down the problem at hand into a few subtasks, then decompose each subtask into smaller subtasks, then replace the smaller subtasks with even smaller subtasks, and so forth. Eventually the subtasks become so small that they are trivial to implement in C++ or whatever language you are using. When the algorithm is translated into C++ code, each subtask is implemented as a C++ function. In this way the hierarchical design of an algorithm is preserved in the structure of the final C++ program. For example, many programming tasks can be decomposed into these three subtasks:

1. Obtain the input data.
2. Perform some appropriate calculation.
3. Output the result of the calculation in a clear format.

Sometimes each of these subtasks will be small enough to be solved by a simple algorithm, which is then translated into a C++ function. More complex subtasks need to be broken down into smaller sub-subtasks.

easily modified code

Decomposing problems into subtasks is an efficient design method. It also produces a good final program in the sense that the program is easy to understand, and subsequent modifications are relatively easy to make. Easily modified code is vital, because most real-world programs are changed eventually, and some of them are changed continually. For example, a program might be changed to display the output in a different format. If the output subtask is performed by a separate function, then only that function needs to be changed. In fact, you need not even look at the rest of the program. But, for this method to work effectively, the functions need to be genuinely separated from one another. An analogy might help.

Suppose you are moving a heavy bag of gold coins to a safe hiding place. If the bag is too heavy to carry, you might divide the coins into three smaller bags and carry the bags one by one to your hiding place. Unless you are a character in a comedy, you would not try to carry all three bags of coins at once. That would defeat the purpose of dividing the coins into three groups. This strategy only works if you carry the bags one at a time. Something similar happens in problem decomposition. If you divide your programming task into three subtasks and solve these subtasks by writing three functions, then you have traded one hard problem for three easier problems. Your total job has become easier—provided that you design the functions separately. When you are working on one function, you should not worry about how the other functions perform their jobs. But the functions do interact. So when you are designing one function, you need to know something about what the other functions do. The trick is to know *only as much as you need, but no more*. This is called **information hiding.** One technique for incorporating information hiding involves specifying your functions' behavior using *preconditions* and *postconditions*.

information hiding

Preconditions and Postconditions

When you write a complete function definition, you specify how the function performs its computation. However, when you are using a function, you only need to think about *what* the function does. You need not think about *how* the function does its work. For example, consider the function `new_balance` shown in Figure 1.1. It is designed to compute the new balance in a banking account after a year's interest has been added. For instance, suppose you are saving for a trip to Hawaii, and your account starts with $100.00 and an annual interest rate of 4.5%. After one year, the new balance will be $104.50. Using the `new_balance` function, the following code will set `initial_hawaii_fund` to $100.00, then calculate the value of `final_hawaii_fund` as $104.50:

```
initial_hawaii_fund = 100.00;
final_hawaii_fund = new_balance(initial_hawaii_fund, 4.5);
```

But, Figure 1.1 contains *two* different function definitions for the function `new_balance`. When a programmer uses the function `new_balance` in a program, it does not matter which of the two definitions is used. Because it does not matter which definition we use, we can simply forget about the details of the definition. We need to know *what* the function does, but we do not need to know *how* the task is accomplished.

FIGURE 1.1   Two Different Implementations of a Function

One Implementation

```
double new_balance(double balance, double interest_rate)
{
    double interest_fraction, interest;

    // Convert interest_rate from a percent to a fraction.
    interest_fraction = interest_rate/100;
    // Compute the interest, and return the new balance.
    interest = balance * interest_fraction;
    return (balance + interest);
}
```

Another Implementation

```
double new_balance(double balance, double interest_rate)
{
    double interest_fraction, updated_balance;

    // Convert interest_rate from a percent to a fraction.
    interest_fraction = interest_rate/100;
    // Compute the new balance and return this amount.
    updated_balance = balance * (1 + interest_fraction);
    return updated_balance;
}
```

balance.cxx   **FTP**

---

procedural abstraction

When we pretend that we do not know the details of how a function is implemented, we are using a form of information hiding called **procedural abstraction**. This simplifies your reasoning by abstracting away irrelevant details, that is, by hiding the irrelevant details. When programming in C++, it might make more sense to call it functional abstraction, since you are abstracting away irrelevant details about how a function works. However, the term *procedure* is a more general term than *function*. Computer scientists use the term procedure for any "function-like" sequence of instructions, and so they use the term *procedural abstraction*. Procedural abstraction can be a powerful tool. It simplifies your reasoning by allowing you to consider functions one at a time rather than all together.

To make procedural abstraction work for us, we need some techniques for documenting what a function does without indicating how the function works. The documentation should occur in a comment at the start of the function definition. The comment tells a programmer all that he or she needs to know in order to *use* the function. The programmer who uses the function should not need to read anything beyond this comment.

One format for writing these comments is to include two kinds of information called the *precondition* and the *postcondition* of the function, described here:

Preconditions and Postconditions

A **precondition** is a statement giving the condition that is supposed to be true when a function is called. The function is not guaranteed to perform as it should unless the precondition is true.

A **postcondition** is a statement describing what will be true when a function call is completed. If the function is correct and the precondition was true when the function was called, then the function will complete, and the postcondition will be true when the function call is completed.

For example, a precondition/postcondition comment for the function `new_balance` in Figure 1.1 is shown here:

```
double new_balance(double balance, double interest_rate);
// Precondition:  The parameter interest_rate is the annual bank account
// interest rate, for example 5.0 for 5%. The parameter balance is an
// account balance before interest is posted.
// Postcondition: The value returned by the function is the new account
// balance after posting one year of simple interest at the rate given by
// interest_rate.
```

This format of comments might be new to you: The characters `//` indicate the start of a comment that extends to the end of the current line. The other form of C++ comments, starting with `/*` and continuing until `*/` are also permitted.

Preconditions and postconditions are more than a way to summarize a function's actions. Stating these conditions should be the first step in designing any function. Before you start to think about algorithms and C++ code for a function, you should write out the function's **prototype**, which consists of the function's return type, the function's name, and the function's parameter list, all followed by a semicolon. As you are writing the prototype, you should also write the precondition and postcondition as comments. If you later discover that your specification cannot be realized in a reasonable way, you may need to back up and rethink what the function should do. But by clearly specifying what you think the function should do, you will reduce wasted time writing code that does not fit the task at hand.

As a programmer who *uses* `new_balance`, the precondition and postcondition are all you need to know. You do not need to know which of the two different function definitions is actually used; the function could even be implemented in some way other than the two we have given.

programming
teams

Preconditions and postconditions provide a way to keep your reasoning about your own programs clear. Preconditions and postconditions are even more important when a group of programmers work together. In team situations, one programmer often does not know how a function written by another programmer works and, in fact, sharing knowledge about how functions work can be counterproductive. Instead, the combination of the precondition and postcondition provide all the interaction that's needed. In effect, the precondition/postcondition pair forms a contract between the programmer who uses a function and the programmer who writes that function. To aid the explanation of this "contract," we'll give these two programmers names: Judy is the head of a programming team that is writing a large piece of software. Jervis is one of her programmers, who writes various functions for Judy to use in large programs.

The precondition/postcondition contract, illustrated in Figure 1.2, tells Judy precisely what one of Jervis's functions does. The contract states that *if* Judy makes sure that the precondition is met when the function is called, *then* Jervis ensures that the function returns with the postcondition satisfied.

FIGURE 1.2 The Precondition/Postcondition Contract

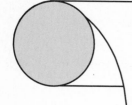

Whereas Jervis Pendleton has written a function (henceforth known as "the function") and Judy Abbott is going to use the function, we hereby agree that:

(i) Judy will never call the function unless she is certain that the precondition is true, and

(ii) Whenever the function is called, and the precondition is true when the function is called, then Jervis guarantees that:

    a. the function will eventually end (infinite loops are forbidden!), and

    b. when the function ends, the postcondition will be true.

Judy Abbott

Jervis Pendleton

As another example, here is the prototype of a function that Jervis wrote, along with the precondition and postcondition. The function determines whether a particular hour of the day has already been reached:

```
int time_check(int hour);
// Precondition:  hour lies in the range 0 <= hour <= 23.
// Postcondition: hour has been interpreted as an hour of the day;
// for example, 0 is midnight, 12 is noon, 14 is 2 P.M. If the given
// hour has been reached today (according to the computer's clock),
// then the function returns 0. Otherwise the value returned is
// the approximate number of minutes until the given hour will
// occur.
```

Even without the knowledge of *how* Jervis writes this function, Judy can still write a program that *uses* Jervis's function. Figure 1.3 shows the pseudocode for Judy's program. The program asks the user to type an hour between 0 and 23. The program then uses `time_check` to see whether that time has been reached, and the program prints an appropriate message. Even though the program is just a quick demonstration, Judy ensures that the precondition of `time_check` is satisfied by refusing to proceed to Step 2 until the user provides valid input.

FIGURE 1.3   Pseudocode for a Demonstration of the Time Check Function

Pseudocode

1. Ask the user to enter an hour between 0 and 23, and read the answer into an integer variable, `user_input`. Don't continue to the next step until the user has typed a valid answer in the range 0 through 23.

2. Using another variable, `time_remaining`, make the function call:
   ```
   time_remaining = time_check(user_input);
   ```

3. Print a message to the user:
   ```
   if (time_remaining == 0)
   ```
   Print a message saying that the time has been reached.
   ```
   else
   ```
   Print a message saying there are `time_remaining` minutes until the user's hour.

PITFALL

Pitfall: Failing to Ensure the Precondition

Consider the function time_check discussed in the previous section. What happens if Judy fails to guarantee that the precondition is true? For example, she might let the user type any integer, and pass this integer to the function time_check without ensuring that the number lies in the range 0 through 23. If the user's number is outside the proper range, then the precondition is violated, and at that point we have *no idea* what the time_check function does—because the precondition/postcondition contract has been violated.

If a function is called and the precondition fails, then the function could do *anything at all*. It is always the responsibility of the programmer who *uses* a function to ensure that the precondition is valid. Nonetheless, the person who writes a function, such as Jervis, makes every effort to avoid the more unpleasant behaviors, even if Judy—or you—neglects to satisfy a precondition. As part of this effort, the first action of a function should be to check that its precondition has been satisfied. If the precondition fails, then the function prints a message and either (a) halts the entire program, or (b) simply returns to the caller with no further actions.

Checking whether a precondition is met can be difficult—or even impossible. So sometimes it is not practical to have a function check its precondition, but a check should be done whenever it is practical. It is easy to check the precondition for the function time_check, as you can see in Figure 1.4. That figure shows the beginning of the time_check function written by Jervis. The assert function called in that code is part of the ANSI C library facilities, which we discuss next.

FIGURE 1.4   Checking the Precondition

The Start of a Function Implementation

```
int time_check(int hour)
// Precondition: hour lies in the range 0 <= hour <= 23.
// Postcondition: hour has been interpreted as an hour of the day; for example, 0 is midnight,
// 12 is noon, 14 is 2 P.M. If the given hour has been reached today (according to the
// computer's clock), then the function returns 0. Otherwise, the value returned is the
// approximate number of minutes until the given hour will occur.
// Library facilities used: assert.h
{
    assert((0 <= hour) && (hour <= 23));
    ...
```

Read about the assert function in the C++ feature on page 11.

C++ Feature: The Library Facilities iostream and assert

In 1989 the American National Standards Institute (ANSI) adopted C compiler requirements called the "ANSI C standards." The standard aids programmers in writing portable code that can be compiled and run with many different compilers on many different machines. Part of the standard is a collection of library facilities. Each of the library facilities provides a group of constants, data types, and functions supporting particular activities such as input/output, mathematical functions, clock functions, and so on.

Most implementations of C++ provide all of the ANSI C library facilities plus additional library facilities that are specific to C++. In order to use a facility, a program places an "include directive" at the top of the file that uses the facility. For example, in order for a program to use the usual C++ input/output facilities, the program should use the include directive:

```
#include <iostream.h>
```

This gives the program access to all of the usual C++ input/output facilities, which are described in detail in Appendix F. (Some compilers require additional steps to use some library facilities; see Appendix D for details.)

A second library facility that you should know about is the `assert` facility, which is obtained by using the include directive:

```
#include <assert.h>
```

The primary function in the `assert` facility is a function named `assert`, which has one argument. The argument may be any integer expression, but usually the argument is a true/false expression (that is, an expression where zero indicates "false" and any nonzero value indicates "true"). The `assert` function will evaluate the expression. If the result is true, then no action is taken. But if the result is false, then a useful error message is printed, and the program is halted.

Now you can see how the `time_check` function of Figure 1.4 uses `assert` to ensure that the precondition is valid. The test is accomplished by the statement:

```
assert((0 <= hour) && (hour <= 23));
```

If the expression (0 <= hour) && (hour <= 23) is true, then hour is valid and the `assert` function will take no action. On the other hand, if the expression is false, then the precondition has been violated, so `assert` will print a message and halt the entire program.

Of course, in order to use `assert`, the proper include directive must appear at the top of the file that contains `time_check`. We have indicated the need for the `assert.h` include directive in a comment that follows the precondition/postcondition contract. Our general suggestion is that you list all necessary library facilities in a comment at the front of each function.

A Documentation Standard

Preconditions and postconditions are one part of a program's documentation. Complete documentation for a program includes other items—enough items to act as an owner's manual for the program. It tells what the program does, how to run the program, and in case changes are needed, it describes how the program works. The documentation also tells who wrote each part of the program, in case you have questions to ask that programmer. A description of how each part of the documentation should be written is called a **documentation standard**.

Fundamental Style Guide

Every group's documentation standard seems to be different from every other group's. Some are formal, some are loose, and maybe the only real guarantee is that there will be some part of the standard that you disagree with (even if you wrote the standard yourself). However, when you are working on a programming project, it is important to agree on a documentation standard and stick to it. If an owner's manual is to be written by a team of people, it would make poor reading if they each wrote in a different style and used a different vocabulary. We will stick to a documentation standard that we call the *Fundamental Style Guide*, which is given in Appendix J.

The Software Life-Cycle

Commercial software systems are much larger than the programs you encounter in most programming classes. One widely used compiler consists of almost 7400 lines of high-level-language code. If written as small as the text of this book, that program would occupy over 130 pages. Programs that large are produced by teams rather than individual programmers. Moreover, in order to keep the software up to date, follow-up work is required after the software is delivered to customers. The entire development and maintenance process for a software system is referred to as the software life-cycle. In this book we will be writing smaller programs, but even small programs experience a similar life-cycle. This life-cycle can be divided into the following six phases:

The Software Life-Cycle

1. Analysis and specification of the task
2. Design of the algorithms and data structures
3. Implementation (coding)
4. Testing
5. Maintenance and evolution of the system
6. Obsolescence

The first four phases are the program design strategy that we have already discussed. However, we should add that during these four phases a large team of programmers must also worry about management and team organization as well as algorithms and data structures. The design phase for a team project includes the design and implementation of an organizational structure so that the programmers work as a team using consistent style, and all team members have well-defined responsibilities.

Even when a software system is released for general use, its life-cycle continues. The software must be maintained and updated. In fact, the typical cost of maintenance far exceeds the cost of producing the original system. A large system is likely to exhibit bugs for some time after it is released. These bugs must be diagnosed and fixed. As new hardware is introduced, the system may be modified to run in new environments. As users' needs change, it is less expensive and quicker to modify the existing system than to produce a totally new system. The majority of systems programmers' time is spent on the maintenance of existing systems, not on designing completely new systems. For this reason, among others, we will always attempt to design programs so that they are easy to understand and easy to change.

maintenance

Perhaps the last step in the software life-cycle should be called "death." However, while all systems eventually become obsolete, they often do not go away. A large system represents such a huge capital investment that it usually seems less expensive to modify the existing system rather than build a completely new system. Often this impression is correct. Large systems are designed to be modified. A system may be productively revised many times. However, even a large program eventually becomes out of date in its basic design. Unless a large program is well written and suitable for the task at hand, then just as in the case of a small program, it is more efficient to write a new program than it is to fix the old one.

obsolescence

Self-Test Exercises

Each section of this book finishes with a few Self-Test Exercises. Answers to these exercises are given at the end of each chapter. The first exercise below refers to a function that Jervis has written for *you* to use. Here is the prototype and precondition/postcondition contract:

```
int date_check(int year, int month, int day);
// Precondition: The three parameters are a legal year, month, and
// day of the month in the 20th or 21st century.
// Postcondition: If the given date has been reached on or before today,
// then the function returns 0. Otherwise, the value returned is the number
// of days until the given date will occur.
```

1. Suppose you call the function `date_check(1999, 7, 29)`. What is the return value if today is July 22, 1999? What if today is July 30, 1999? What about February 1, 2000?

2. One of the ANSI C library facilities is the `math.h` facility, which contains a function with this prototype:

   double `sqrt(`*double* `x);`

   The function returns the square root of x. Write a reasonable precondition and postcondition for this function, and compare your answer to the solution at the end of the chapter.

3. Write the include directive that must appear before using the `sqrt` function from Self-Test Exercise 2.

1.2 RUNNING TIME ANALYSIS

Time analysis consists of reasoning about an algorithm's speed. *Does the algorithm work fast enough for my needs? How much longer does the method take when the input gets larger? Which of several different methods is fastest?* We'll discuss these issues in this section. An example will help start the discussion.

The Stair-Counting Problem

Suppose that you and your friend Judy are standing at the top of the Eiffel Tower. As you gaze out over the French landscape, Judy turns to you and says, "I wonder how many steps there are to the bottom?" You, of course, are the ever-accommodating host, so you reply, "I'm not sure . . . but I'll find out." We'll look at three different methods that you could use and analyze the time requirements of each.

Method 1: Walk down and keep a tally.   In the first method, Judy gives you a pen and a sheet of paper. "I'll be back in a minute," you say as you dash down the stairs. Each time you take a step down, you make a mark on the sheet of paper. When you reach the bottom, you run back up, show Judy the piece of paper, and say "There are this many steps."

Method 2: Walk down, but let Judy keep the tally.   In the second method, Judy is unwilling to let her pen or paper out of her sight. But you are undaunted. Once more you say, "I'll be back in a minute," and you set off down the stairs. But this time you stop after one step, lay your hat on the step, and run back to Judy. "Make a mark on the piece of paper!" you exclaim. Then you run back to your hat, pick it up, take one more step, and lay the hat down on the second step. Then back up to Judy: "Make another mark on the piece of paper!" you say. You run back down the two stairs, pick up your hat, move to the third step, and lay down the hat. Then back up the stairs to Judy: "Make another mark!" you tell her. This continues until your hat reaches the bottom, and you speed back up the steps one more time. "One more mark, please." At this point, you grab Judy's piece of paper and say, "There are this many steps."

Method 3: Jervis to the rescue. In the third method, you don't walk down the stairs at all. Instead, you spot your friend Jervis by the staircase, holding the sign drawn here:

Il y a 2689 marches dans cet escalier

(vraiment!)

The translation is *There are 2689 steps in this stairway (really!)*. So, you take the paper and pen from Judy, write the number 2689, and hand the paper back to her, saying, "There are this many steps."

This is a silly example, but even so, it does illustrate the issues that arise when performing a time analysis for an algorithm or program. The first issue is deciding exactly how you will measure the time spent carrying out the method or executing the program.

At first glance the answer seems easy: For each of the three stair-counting methods, just measure the actual time it takes to carry out the method. You could do this with a stopwatch. But, there are some drawbacks to measuring actual time. Actual time can depend on various irrelevant details, such as whether you or somebody else carried out the method. The actual elapsed time may vary from person to person, depending on how fast each person can run the stairs. Even if we decide that *you* are the runner, the time may vary depending on other factors such as the weather, what you had for breakfast, and what other things are on your mind.

So, instead of measuring the actual elapsed time during each method, we count certain operations that occur while carrying out the methods. In this example, we will count two kinds of operations:

1. Each time you walk up or down one step, that is one operation.

2. Each time you or Judy marks a symbol on the paper, that is also one operation.

Of course, each of these operations takes a certain amount of time, and making a mark may take a different amount of time than taking a step. But this doesn't concern us because we won't measure the actual time taken by the operations. Instead, we will ask: *How many operations are needed for each of the three methods?*

decide what operations to count

In the first method, you take 2689 steps down, another 2689 steps up, and you also make 2689 marks on the paper, for a total of 3×2689 operations—that is 8067 total operations.

In the second method, there are also 2689 marks made on Judy's paper, but the total number of operations is considerably more. You start by going down one step and back up one step. Then down two and up two. Then down three and up three, and so forth. The total number of operations taken is:

Downward steps   = 3,616,705 (which is $1 + 2 + \ldots + 2689$)

Upward steps   = 3,616,705

Marks made   = 2689

Total operations   = Downward steps
    + Upward steps
    + Marks made
    = 7,236,099

The third method is the quickest of all: Only four marks are made on the paper (that is, we're counting one "mark" for each of digit of 2689), and there is no going up and down stairs. The number of operations used by each of the methods is summarized here:

Method 1	8067	operations
Method 2	7,236,099	operations
Method 3	4	operations

Doing a time analysis for a program is similar to the analysis of the stair-counting methods. For a time analysis of a program, we do not usually measure the actual time taken to run the program because the number of seconds can depend on too many extraneous factors—such as the speed of the processor, and whether the processor is busy with other tasks. Instead, the analysis counts the number of operations required. There is no precise definition of what constitutes an **operation**, although an operation should satisfy your intuition of a "small step." An operation can be as simple as the execution of a single program statement. Or we could use a finer notion of operation that counts each arithmetic operation (addition, multiplication, etc.) and each assignment to a variable as a separate operation.

typical operations for program time analysis

dependence on input size

For most programs, the number of operations depends on the program's input. For example, a program that sorts a list of numbers is quicker with a short list than with a long list. In the stairway example, we can view the Eiffel Tower as the input to the problem. In other words, the three different methods all work on the Eiffel Tower, but the methods also work on Toronto's CN Tower, or the stairway to the top of the Statue of Liberty, or any other stairway.

When a method's time depends on the size of the input, then the time can be given as an expression, where part of the expression is the input's size. The time expressions for our three methods are given here:

Method 1 $3n$

Method 2 $n + 2(1 + 2 + \ldots + n)$

Method 3   The number of digits in the number n

The expressions on the right give the number of operations performed by each method when the stairway has n steps.

The expression for the second method is not easy to interpret. It needs to be simplified in order to become a formula that we can easily compare to other formulas. So, let's simplify it. We start with the subexpression:

$$(1 + 2 + \ldots + n)$$

There is a trick that will enable us to find a simplified form for this expression. The trick is to *compute twice the amount of the expression and then divide the result by 2*. Unless you've seen this trick before, it sounds crazy. But it works fine. The trick is illustrated in Figure 1.5. Let's go through the computation of that figure step-by-step.

simplification of the Method 2 time analysis

We write the expression $(1 + 2 + \ldots + n)$ twice and add the two expressions. But as you can see in Figure 1.5, we also use another trick: When we write the expression twice, *we write the second expression backwards*. After we write down the expression twice, we see the following:

$$(1 + 2 + \ldots + n)$$
$$+ (n + \ldots + 2 + 1)$$

We want the sum of the numbers on these two lines. That will give us twice the value of $(1 + 2 + \ldots + n)$, and we can then divide by 2 to get the correct value of the subexpression $(1 + 2 + \ldots + n)$.

Now, rather than proceed in the most obvious way, we instead add pairs of numbers from the first and second lines. We add the 1 and the n to get $n + 1$. Then we add the 2 and the $n - 1$ to again get $n + 1$. We continue until we reach the last pair consisting of an n from the top line and a 1 from the bottom line. All the pairs add up to the same amount, namely $n + 1$. Now that is handy! We get n numbers, and all the numbers are the same, namely $n + 1$. So the total of all the numbers on the above two lines is:

$$n(n + 1)$$

The value of twice the expression is n multiplied by $n + 1$. We are now essentially done. The number we computed is twice the quantity we want. So, to

FIGURE 1.5   Deriving a Handy Formula

$(1 + 2 + \ldots + n)$ can be computed by first computing the sum of twice $(1 + 2 + \ldots + n)$, as shown here:

$$
\begin{array}{ccccccc}
1 & + & 2 & + \ldots + & (n-1) & + & n \\
+ \quad n & + & (n-1) & + \ldots + & 2 & + & 1 \\
\hline
(n+1) & + (n+1) & + \ldots + & (n+1) & + & (n+1) &
\end{array}
$$

The sum is $n\,(n+1)$, so $(1 + 2 + \ldots + n)$ is half this amount:

$$
(1 + 2 + \ldots + n) \; = \; \frac{n\,(n+1)}{2}
$$

obtain our simplified formula, we only need to divide by 2. The final simplification is thus:

$$
(1 + 2 + \ldots + n) \; = \; \frac{n\,(n+1)}{2}
$$

We will use this formula to simplify the Method 2 expression, but you'll also find that the formula occurs in many other situations. The simplification for the Method 2 expression is as follows:

Number of operations for Method 2

$$= n + 2\,(1 + 2 + \ldots + n)$$

$$= n + 2\left(\frac{n\,(n+1)}{2}\right) \qquad \textit{Plug in the formula for } (1 + 2 + \ldots + n)$$

$$= n + n(n+1) \qquad \textit{Cancel the 2's}$$

$$= n + n^2 + n \qquad \textit{Multiply out}$$

$$= n^2 + 2n \qquad \textit{Combine terms}$$

So, Method 2 requires $n^2 + 2n$ operations.

simplification of the Method 3 time analysis

The number of operations for Method 3 is just the number of digits in the integer n when written down in the usual way. The usual way of writing down numbers is called **base 10 notation**. As it turns out, the number of digits in a number *n*, when written in base 10 notation, is approximately equal to another mathematical quantity known as the **base 10 logarithm** of *n*. The notation for the base 10 logarithm of *n* is written:

$$\log_{10} n$$

The base 10 logarithm does not always give a whole number. For example, the actual base 10 logarithm of 2689 is about 3.43 rather than 4. If we want the actual number of digits in an integer *n*, we need to carry out some rounding. In particular, the exact number of digits in a positive integer *n* is obtained by rounding $\log_{10} n$ downward to the next whole number, and then adding 1. The notation for rounding down and adding 1 is obtained by adding some marks to the logarithm notation as follows:

$$\lfloor \log_{10} n \rfloor + 1$$

This is all fine if you already know about logarithms, but what if some of this is new to you? For now, you can simply define the above notation to mean *the number of digits in the base 10 numeral for n*. You can do this because if others use any of the other accepted definitions for this formula, they will get the same answers that you do. You will be right! (And they will also be right.) In Section 11.3 of this book, we will show that the various definitions of the logarithm function are all equivalent. For now, we will not worry about all that detail. We have larger issues to discuss first. The table of the number of operations for each method can now be expressed more concisely as shown here:

Method 1 $3n$

Method 2 $n^2 + 2n$

Method 3 $\lfloor \log_{10} n \rfloor + 1$

Big-*O* Notation

The time analyses we gave for the three stair-counting methods were very precise. They computed the exact number of operations for each method. But such precision is sometimes not needed. Often it is enough to know in a rough manner how the number of operations is affected by the input size. In the stair example, we developed the methods thinking about a particular tower, the Eiffel Tower, with a particular number of steps. We expressed our formulas for the operations in terms of *n*, which stood for the number of steps in the tower. Now suppose that we apply our various stair-counting methods to a tower with ten times as many steps as the Eiffel Tower. If *n* is the number of steps in the Eiffel Tower, then this taller tower will have $10n$ steps. The number of operations needed for Method 1 on the taller tower increases tenfold (from $3n$ to $3 \times (10n) = 30n$); the time for Method 2 increases approximately 100-fold (from about n^2 to about $(10n)^2 = 100n^2$); and Method 3 increases by only one operation (from the number of digits in n to the number of digits in $10n$, or to be very concrete, from the 4 digits in 2689 to the 5 digits in 26,890). We can express this kind of information in a format called **big-O notation**. The symbol O in this notation is the letter O, so big-O is pronounced "big Oh."

We will describe three common examples of the big-O notation. In these examples, we use the notion of "the largest term in a formula." Intuitively, this is the term with the largest exponent on n, or the term that grows the fastest as n itself becomes larger. For now, this intuitive notion of "largest term" is enough. Here are the examples:

quadratic time
$O(n^2)$

Quadratic time. If the largest term in a formula is no more than a constant times n^2, then the algorithm is said to be "**big-O of n^2**," written $O(n^2)$, and the algorithm is called **quadratic**. In a quadratic algorithm, doubling the input size makes the number of operations increase by approximately fourfold (or less). For a concrete example, consider Method 2, requiring $n^2 + 2n$ operations. A 100-step tower requires 10,200 operations (that is, $100^2 + 2 \times 100$). Doubling the tower to 200 steps increases the time by approximately fourfold, to 40,400 operations (that is, $200^2 + 2 \times 200$).

linear time $O(n)$

Linear time. If the largest term in the formula is a constant times n, then the algorithm is said to be "**big-O of n**," written $O(n)$, and the algorithm is called **linear**. In a linear algorithm, doubling the input size makes the time increase by approximately twofold (or less). For example, a formula of $3n + 7$ is linear, so that $3 \times 200 + 7$ is about twice $3 \times 100 + 7$.

logarithmic time
$O(\log n)$

Logarithmic time. If the largest term in the formula is a constant times a logarithm of n, then the algorithm is "**big-O of the logarithm of n**," written $O(\log n)$, and the algorithm is called **logarithmic**. (The base of the logarithm may be base 10, or possibly another base. We'll talk about the other bases in Section 11.3.) In a logarithmic algorithm, doubling the input size will make the time increase by no more than a fixed number of new operations, such as one more operation, or two more operations—or in general by c more operations, where c is a fixed constant. For example, Method 3 for stair-counting has a logarithmic time formula. And doubling the size of a tower (perhaps from 500 stairs to 1000 stairs) never requires more than one extra operation.

Using big-O notation, we can express the time requirements of our three stair-counting methods as follows:

Method 1 $O(n)$
Method 2 $O(n^2)$
Method 3 $O(\log n)$

When a time analysis is expressed with big-O, the result is called the **order** of the algorithm. We want to reinforce one important point: Multiplicative constants are ignored in the big-O notation. For example, both $2n$ and $42n$ are linear formulas, so both are expressed as $O(n)$, ignoring the multiplicative constants 2 and 42. As you can see, this means that a big-O analysis loses some information about relative times. Nevertheless, a big-O analysis does provide some useful information for comparing algorithms. The stair example illustrates the most important kind of information provided by the order of an algorithm:

order of an algorithm

The order of an algorithm generally is more important than the speed of the processor.

For example, using the quadratic method (Method 2) the fastest stair climber in the world is still unlikely to do better than a slowpoke—provided that the slowpoke uses one of the faster methods. In an application such as sorting a list, a quadratic algorithm can be impractically slow on even moderately sized lists, regardless of the processor speed. To see this, notice the comparisons showing actual numbers for our three stair-counting methods, which are shown in Figure 1.6.

Time Analysis of C++ Functions

The principles of the stair-climbing example can be applied to counting the number of operations required by a function written in a high-level language such as C++. As an example, consider the function implemented in Figure 1.7 on page 23. When the function is called, the user is asked to think of a number, and then the function asks a series of questions until the number is found. An

FIGURE 1.6 Number of Operations for Three Methods

Number of stairs (n)	Logarithmic $O(\log n)$ Method 3, with $\lfloor \log_{10} n \rfloor + 1$ operations	Linear $O(n)$ Method 1, with $3n$ operations	Quadratic $O(n^2)$ Method 2, with $n^2 + 2n$ operations
10	2	30	120
100	3	300	10,200
1000	4	3000	1,002,000
10,000	5	30,000	100,020,000

example is shown at the bottom of the figure, where the user is asked to "think of a number between 1 and 100."

As with the stair-climbing example, the first step of the time-analysis is to decide precisely what we will count as a single operation. For C++ functions, a good choice is to count the total number of C++ operations (such as an assignment, the < operation, or the << operation) plus the number of function calls (such as the call to assert). If the functions calls did complex work themselves, then we would also need to count the operations that are carried out there.

With this in mind, let's analyze the guess_game function for the case where the parameter is a positive integer *n,* and (just to be difficult) the user is thinking of the number 1. How many operations does the function carry out in all? Our analysis has three parts:

1. Prior to the for-loop, there are seven operations (one >= comparison, one call to assert, four output operations, and an assignment to answer). Then there is the loop initialization (guess = n). Thus, before the loop body occurs, there are eight operations.

2. We then execute the body of the loop, and because our user is thinking of the number 1, we will execute this body *n* times. How many operations occur during each execution of the loop body? We could count this number, but let's just say that each execution of the loop body requires *k* operations, where *k* is some number around 10 or 20. If necessary, we'll figure out *k* later, but for now it is enough to know that we execute the loop body *n* times, and each execution takes *k* operations, for a total of *kn* operations.

3. After the loop finishes, there are five more operations (three in the test of the if-statement, plus two << operations).

The total number of operations is now $kn + 13$. Regardless of how big *k* is, this formula is always linear time. So, in the case where the user thinks of the number 1, the guess_game function takes linear time. In fact, this is a frequent pattern that we summarize here:

Linear Pattern

A loop that does a fixed amount of operations *n* times requires $O(n)$ time.

Later you will see additional patterns, resulting in quadratic, logarithmic, and other times. In fact, in Chapter 12 you will rewrite the guess_game function in a better way that requires only logarithmic time.

FIGURE 1.7   Guessing Game Function for the Time Analysis Example

A Function Implementation

```
void guess_game(int n)
// Precondition: n > 0.
// Postcondition: The user has been asked to think of a number between 1 and n. The function
// asks a series of questions, until the number is found.
// Library facilities used: assert.h, iostream.h
{
    int guess;
    char answer;

    assert(n >= 1);

    cout << "Think of a whole number between 1 and " << n << "." << endl;
    answer = 'N';
    for (guess = n; (guess > 0) && (answer != 'Y') && (answer != 'y'); guess--)
    {
        cout << "Is your number " << guess << "?" << endl;
        cout << "Please answer Y or N, and press return: ";
        cin >> answer;
    }

    if ((answer == 'Y') || (answer == 'y'))
        cout << "I knew it all along." << endl;
    else
        cout << "I think you are cheating!" << endl;
}
```

Kn

A Sample Dialogue from calling `guess_game(100)`:

```
Think of a whole number between 1 and 100.
Is your number 100?
Please answer Y or N, and press return: N
Is your number 99?
Please answer Y or N, and press return: N
Is your number 98?
Please answer Y or N, and press return: Y
I knew it all along.
```

| guess.cxx | **FTP** |

Worst-case, Average-case, and Best-case Analyses

The guess_game function has another important feature: For any particular value of *n*, the number of required operations can differ depending on the user's input. For example, with *n* equal to 100, the user might think of the number 100, and the loop body executes just one time. On the other hand, when the user is thinking of the number 1, the loop body executes the maximum number of times (*n* times). In other words, for any given *n*, different possible inputs from the user result in a different number of operations. When this occurs, then we usually count the *maximum* number of required operations for inputs of a given size. Counting the maximum number of operations is called the **worst-case** analysis.

worst-case analysis

During a time analysis, you may sometimes find yourself unable to provide an exact count of the number of operations. If the analysis is a worst-case analysis, you may estimate the number of operations, always making sure that your estimate is on the high side. In other words, the actual number of operations must be guaranteed to always be less than the estimate that you use in the analysis.

In Chapter 12, when we begin the study of searching and sorting, you'll see two other kinds of time-analysis: **average-case** analysis, which determines the average number of operations required for a given *n*, and **best-case** analysis, which determines the fewest number of operations required for a given *n*.

Self-Test Exercises

4. Each of the following are formulas for the number of operations in some algorithm. Express each formula in big-*O* notation.

   $O(n^2)$ a. $n^2 + 5n$ $O(n)$ d. $100n + 5$
   $O(n^2)$ b. $3n^2 + 5n$ $O(n^2)$ e. $5n + 3n^2$
   $O(n^2)$ c. $(n + 7)(n - 2)$ $O(\log n)$ f. The number of digits in $2n$.

5. Write code for a function that uses a loop to compute the sum of all integers from 1 to *n*. Do a time analysis, counting each basic operation (such as assignment and ++) as one operation.

1.3 TESTING AND DEBUGGING

> *Always do right. This will gratify some people, and astonish the rest.*
>
> MARK TWAIN
> To the Young People's Society, February 16, 1901

program testing

Program testing occurs when you run a program and observe its behavior. Each time you execute a program on some input, you are testing to see how the program works for that particular input, and you are also testing to see how long the program takes to complete. Part of the science of *software engineering* is the systematic construction of a set of test inputs that is likely to discover errors, and such test inputs are the topic of this section.

Choosing Test Data

To serve as good test data, your test inputs need two properties:

Properties of Good Test Data

1. You must know what output a correct program should produce for each test input.

2. The test inputs should include those inputs that are most likely to cause errors.

Do not take the first property lightly—you must choose test data for which you know the correct output. Just because a program compiles, runs, and produces output that looks about right does not mean the program is correct. If the correct answer is 3278 and the program outputs 3277, then something is wrong. How do you know the correct answer is 3278? The most obvious way to find the correct output value is to work it out with pencil and paper using some method other than that used by the program. To aid you in doing this, you might choose test data for which it is easy to calculate the correct answer, perhaps by using smaller input values or by using input values for which the answer is well known.

Boundary Values

We will focus on two methods for finding test data that is most likely to cause errors. The first method is based on identifying and testing inputs called *boundary values*, which are particularly apt to cause errors. A **boundary value** of a problem is an input that is one step away from a different kind of behavior. For example, recall the `time_check` function from page 9. It has a parameter called `hour`, with a precondition:

Precondition: hour lies in the range 0 <= hour <= 23.

Two boundary values for `time_check` are `hour` equal to 0 (since one step below 0 is illegal) and `hour` equal to 23 (since one step above 23 is illegal). If we expect the function to behave differently for morning hours (0 to 11) than for afternoon hours (12 through 23), then 11 and 12 are also boundary values. If we expect a different behavior for `hour` equal to 0, then 1 is a boundary value. In fact, 0 and 1 have special behavior in so many situations that it is a good idea to consider 0, 1, and even –1 to be boundary values whenever they are legal input.

In general, there is no precise definition of a boundary value, but you should develop an intuitive feel for finding inputs that are "one step away from different behavior."

Test Boundary Values

If you cannot test all possible inputs, at least test the boundary values. For example, if legal inputs range from zero to one million, then be sure to test input 0 and input 1000000. It is a good idea to also consider 0, 1, and −1 to be boundary values whenever they are legal input.

Fully Exercising Code

The second widely used testing technique requires intimate knowledge of how a program has been implemented. The technique, called **fully exercising code**, is simple to state with two rules:

1. Make sure that each line of your code is executed at least once by some of your test data. For example, there might be a portion of your code that is only handling a rare situation. Make sure that this rare situation is included among your set of test data.

2. If there is some part of your code that is sometimes skipped altogether, then make sure that there is at least one test input that actually does skip this part of your code. For example, there might be a loop where the body is sometimes executed zero times. Make sure that there is a test input that causes the loop body to be executed zero times.

profiler

Many compilers have a software tool called a **profiler** to help fully exercise code. A typical profiler will generate a listing indicating how often each statement of your program was executed. This can help you spot parts of your program that were not tested.

Fully Exercising Code

1. Make sure that each line of your code is executed at least once by some of your test data.

2. If there is some part of your code that is sometimes skipped altogether, then make sure that there is at least one test input that actually does skip this part of your code.

Use a software tool called a *profiler* to ensure that you are fully exercising your code.

Programming Tip: **How to Debug**

Finding a test input that causes an error is only half the problem of testing and debugging. After an erroneous test input is found, you still must determine exactly why the "bug" occurs, and "debug the program." When you have found an error, there is an impulse to dive right in and start changing code. It is tempting to look for suspicious parts of your code and change these suspects to something "that might work better."

Avoid the temptation.

An impulsive change to suspicious code almost always makes matters worse. Instead, you must discover *exactly* why a test case is failing and limit your changes to *corrections of known errors*. Once you have corrected a known error, all test cases should be rerun.

Tracking down the exact reason why a test case is failing can be difficult. For large programs, tracking down errors is nearly impossible without the help of a software tool called a **debugger.** A debugger executes your code one line at a time, or it may execute your code until a certain condition arises. Using a debugger, you can specify what conditions should cause the program execution to pause. You can also keep a continuous watch on the location of the program execution and on the values of specified variables.

debugger

Debugging Tips

1. Never start changing suspicious code on the hope that the change "might work better."

2. Instead you should discover *exactly* why a test case is failing and limit your changes to *corrections of known errors*.

3. Once you have corrected a known error, all test cases should be rerun.

Use a software tool called a *debugger* to help track down exactly why an error occurs.

Self-Test Exercises

6. Suppose you write a program that accepts as input any integer in the range −20 through 20, and outputs the number of digits in the input integer. What boundary values should you use as test inputs?

7. Suppose you write a program that accepts a single line as input, and outputs a message telling whether or not the line contains the letter A, and whether or not it contained more than three A's. What is a good set of test inputs?

8. Describe how a profiler and a debugger typically aid in testing and debugging programs.

CHAPTER SUMMARY

- The first step in producing a program is to write down a precise description of what the program is supposed to do.

- One good method for specifying what a function is supposed to do is to provide a *precondition* and *postcondition* for the function. These form a contract between the programmer who uses the function and the programmer who writes the function.

- *Pseudocode* is a mixture of C++ (or some other programming language) and English (or some other natural language). Pseudocode is used to express algorithms so that you are not distracted by details about C++ syntax.

- Before you write a program in the C++ language (or other programming language), first design an algorithm expressed in pseudocode.

- *Time analysis* is an analysis of how many operations an algorithm requires. Often, it is sufficient to express a time analysis in big-O notation, which is the *order* of an algorithm. The order analysis is often enough to compare algorithms and estimate how running time is affected by changing input size.

- Three important examples of big-O analyses are *linear* (i.e., $O(n)$), *quadratic* (i.e., $O(n^2)$), and *logarithmic* (i.e., $O(\log n)$).

- An important testing technique is to identify and test *boundary values*. These are values that lie on a boundary between different kinds of behavior for your program.

- A second important testing technique is to ensure that your test cases are *fully exercising* the code. A software tool called a *profiler* can aid in fully exercising code.

- During debugging, you should discover exactly why a test case is failing and limit your changes to corrections of known errors. Once you have corrected a known error, all test cases should be rerun. Use a software tool called a *debugger* to help track down exactly why an error occurs.

1. The function returns 7 on July 22, 1999. On both July 30, 1999 and February 1, 2000 the function returns 0 (since July 29, 1999 has already passed).

2. Precondition: x >= 0. Postcondition: The value returned is the positive square root of x.

3. `#include <math.h>`
   Some compilers also require additional steps to be taken when the program is compiled or linked.

4. Part d is linear (i.e., $O(n)$); part f is logarithmic (i.e., $O(\log n)$); all of the others are quadratic (i.e., $O(n^2)$).

5. Here is one implementation of the function:
   ```
   int sum(int n)
   // Precondition: n >= 1.
   // Postcondition: The value returned is the
   // sum of all integers from 1 to n.
   {
      int answer, i;

      answer = 0;
      for (i = 1; i <= n; i++)
         answer += i;
      return answer;
   }
   ```
   Our solution uses `answer += i`, which causes the current value of `i` to be added to what's already in `answer`.

   For a time analysis, there are two assignment operations (`answer = 0` and `i = 1`). The `<=` test is executed n + 1 times (the first n times it is true, and the final time, with i equal to n + 1, it is false). The ++ and += operations are each executed n times. The entire code is $O(n)$.

6. As always, 0, 1, and –1 are boundary values. In this problem, –20 (smallest value) and 20 (largest value) are also boundary values. Also 9 and 10 (since the number changes from a single digit to two digits) and –9 and –10. (By the way, this particular problem is small enough that it would be reasonable to test *all* legal inputs, rather than just testing the boundary values.)

7. You should include an empty line (with no characters before the carriage return) and lines with 0, 1, 2, 3 A's. Also include a line with 4 A's (the smallest case with more than three) and a line with more than 4 A's. For the lines with 1 or more A's, include lines that have only the A's, and also include lines that have A's together with other characters. Also test the case where all the A's appear at the front or the back of the line.

8. A profiler can ensure that your code is being fully exercised (by printing the count of how many times each line of your code has been executed). Once an error has been noticed, a debugger can help track down the cause of the error by displaying the values of variables while the code executes one line at a time.

2 Abstract Data Types and C++ Classes

The happiest way to deal with a man is never to tell him anything he does not need to know.

ROBERT A. HEINLEIN
Time Enough for Love

Object-oriented programming ("**OOP**") is an approach to programming where data occurs in tidy packages called *objects*. Manipulation of an object happens with functions called *member functions,* which are part and parcel of their objects.

ADTs emphasize what work is done rather than how the work is done

In C++, the mechanism to create objects and member functions is called a **class**. Classes can support information hiding, which was presented as a cornerstone of program design in Chapter 1. Typically one programming team designs and implements a class, while other programmers use the class. The programmers that *use* the class have no knowledge of *how* the class is implemented. In fact, the implementor of a C++ class can completely hide the knowledge of how the class is implemented—resulting in ideal information hiding.

Such a strong emphasis on information hiding is partly motivated by mathematical research about how programmers can improve their reasoning about data types that are used in programs. These mathematical data types are called **abstract data types,** or "ADTs"—and therefore, programmers sometimes use the term **ADT** to refer to a class that is presented to other programmers with information hiding. This chapter presents two examples of such classes. The examples illustrate the features of C++ classes, with emphasis on information hiding. By the end of the chapter you will be able to implement your own classes in C++. Other programmers could *use* one of your classes without knowing the details of *how* you implemented the class.

2.1 CLASSES AND MEMBERS

A class is a new kind of data type. Each class that you define is a collection of data, such as integers, characters, and so on. In addition, a class has the ability to include special functions, called *member functions.* Member functions are incorporated into the class's definition and are designed specifically to manipulate the class. A programmer who designs a class can even mandate that the *only* way of manipulating the class is through its member functions. But this abstract discussion does not really tell you what a class is. We need some examples. As you read through the first example, concentrate on learning the techniques for implementing a class. Also notice features that allow you to use a class written by another programmer, without knowing details of the class's implementation.

PROGRAMMING EXAMPLE: The Throttle Class

Our first example of a class is a new data type to store and manipulate the status of a simple throttle. Classes such as our throttle class appear in programs that simulate real-world objects. For instance, a flight simulator might include classes for the plane and various parts of the plane such as the engines, the rudder, the altimeter, and even the throttle.

the Throttle class

An object of this new class holds information about a simple throttle, as shown in the picture. The throttle is a lever that can be moved to control fuel flow. The throttle we have in mind has a single shut-off point (where there is no fuel flow) and a sequence of six on positions where the fuel is flowing at progressively higher rates. At the topmost position, the fuel flow is fully on. At the intermediate positions, the fuel flow is proportional to the location of the lever. For example, with six possible positions, and the lever in the fourth position, the fuel flows at $^4/_6$ of its maximum rate.

One of the functions provided with the class permits a program to initialize a throttle to its shutoff position. Once the throttle has been initialized, there is another function to shift the throttle lever by a given amount.

We also have two functions to examine the status of a throttle. The first of these functions returns the amount of fuel currently flowing, expressed as a proportion of the maximum flow. For example, this function will return approximately 0.667 when the six-position throttle is in its fourth position. The other function returns a true-or-false value, telling whether the throttle is currently on (that is, whether the lever is above the zero position). Thus, the throttle has a total of four functions:

four throttle functions

1. A function to set a throttle to its shutoff position.
2. A function to shift a throttle's position by a given amount.
3. A function that returns the fuel flow, expressed as a proportion of the maximum flow.
4. A function to tell us whether the throttle is currently on.

We can define this new data type as a "class" called `Throttle` that includes both data (to store the throttle's current position) and the four functions to modify and examine the throttle. Once the new class is defined, a programmer can declare objects of type `Throttle` and manipulate those objects with the four functions. Here is the class definition we have in mind:

declaring the Throttle class

```
class Throttle
{
public:
    // MODIFICATION MEMBER FUNCTIONS
    void shut_off( );
    void shift(int amount);
    // CONSTANT MEMBER FUNCTIONS
    double flow( ) const;
    bool is_on( ) const;
private:
    int position;
};
```

This class definition defines a new data type called `Throttle`. The new data type is a *class*, meaning that it may have some components that are data and other components that are functions. Let's examine the definition piece by piece.

The class head. The *head* of the definition consists of the C++ keyword *class*, followed by the name of the new class. You may use any legal identifier for the class's name. We chose the name `Throttle`. We will always use a capital letter for the first character of names of new classes—this isn't required by C++, but it's a part of our documentation standard (Appendix J), making it easy to identify class names.

The member list.   The rest of the definition, from the opening bracket to the closing semicolon, is the *member list* of the definition.

The public section.   The first part of the member list is called the *public section*. It begins with the C++ keyword *public* followed by a colon. A list of items appears after the colon. These are items that are made available to anyone who uses the new data type. In this example, the list contains the four functions to manipulate a `Throttle`. Such functions are usually called **member functions** to distinguish them from ordinary functions. When a member function is listed in a class body, we list only the function's prototype (that is, the head followed by a semicolon). For example, one of the throttle function prototypes is:

```
void shift(int amount);
```

The prototype indicates that the function has one parameter (an integer called `amount`). We will use this function to shift a throttle's lever up or down by a given amount. The implementation of the `shift` function does not appear in the class definition; it will appear elsewhere with other function implementations.

One of the other throttle functions has the following prototype:

```
bool is_on( );
```

This function can be used to determine whether a throttle is currently on. The return value of the function has the data type *bool*, which is a built-in data type provided in the latest ANSI C++ standards. The *bool* data type is intended solely for true-or-false values (also called **boolean values** or **logical values**). The important properties of the *bool* type are shown in Figure 2.1. If your compiler does not support the *bool* type, then see Appendix E, "Dealing with Older Compilers," for alternatives.

the bool type

Anyone who declares a variable of type `Throttle` can manipulate that throttle with the four public member functions. In fact, these four functions are the *only* way that a throttle may be manipulated, since there is nothing else available in the public section of the definition.

public member functions

You should notice one other feature: We have classified the public member functions into two kinds of functions. The first two functions, `shut_off` and `shift`, are **modification member functions**. A modification member function can change the value of an object. In the case of a throttle, the modification functions can change the position of the throttle's lever.

modification member functions

On the other hand, the functions `flow` and `is_on` are classified as **constant member functions**. A constant member function may examine the status of an object, but changing the object is forbidden. In our example, the two constant member functions can examine but not change a throttle. The prototypes of the constant member functions have the keyword *const* before the semicolon. Using the *const* keyword tells the compiler and other programmers that the function cannot change the object.

constant member functions

FIGURE 2.1 The Boolean Data Type

C++ Has a New Boolean Data Type

The results of true-or-false tests play an important role in programming. For example, we might test whether two variables are equal (x == y), or compare the relative ordering of two integer variables (i < j). In these cases, and others, the result of the test is either *true* or *false*.

In early versions of C and C++, *false* was represented by the integer 0, and *true* was represented by any nonzero integer. But the 1996 ANSI standard for C++ provided a new built-in data type called *bool*. The data type is intended to store true-or-false values that are generated from various tests. Along with the data type are two new keywords, *true* and *false*, which are *bool* constants.

Here is a summary of the important features of the new *bool* type:

- A *bool* value may be *true* or *false*; no other values are permitted.
- The built-in relational operators (==, !=, <, <=, >, >=) produce a *bool* value.
- The binary "and" operator (&&) combines two *bool* arguments, producing a *true* result only if both arguments are *true*. The binary "or" operator (| |) combines two *bool* arguments, producing a *true* result if either of its arguments is *true*. The "not" operator (!) is applied to a single *bool* argument, producing a *false* result from a *true* argument, and vice versa.
- User-defined functions may also compute and return *bool* values.
- A *bool* value may be used as the controlling expression of an if-statement or a loop.

For example, suppose we write a function with the following specification:

```
bool is_even(int i);
// Postcondition: The return value is true if and only if i is an even number.
```

We could use the is_even function in code that prints a message about a number:

```
if (is_even(j))
    cout << j << " is even." << endl;
else
    cout << j << " is odd." << endl;
```

If your compiler does not support the bool type, then see Appendix E, "Dealing with Older Compilers."

The name "bool" is derived from the name of George Boole, a 19th-century mathematician who developed the foundations for a formal calculus of logical values. Boole was a self-educated scholar with limited formal training. He began his teaching career at the age of 16 as an elementary school teacher and eventually progressed to a professorship at Queen's College in Cork. As a dedicated teacher, he died at the age of only 49—the result of pneumonia brought on by a two-mile trek through the rain to lecture to his students.

The private section. The second part of the member list is called the private section. It begins with the C++ keyword *private* followed by a colon. After the colon is a list of items that are part of the class but are not directly available to programmers who use the class. In our example, the private section contains one integer called position. This component is a **member variable** of the class, in contrast to the other four members which are member *functions*. Member variables may be any data type, such as *int*, *char*, *double*, and so on.

Our intention is to use the private member variable to store the *current position* of a throttle, ranging from 0 to 6. The member variable is private, which means that the programmer who *implements* the Throttle class can access this member. But programmers who *use* the new class have no way to directly read or assign values to the private member variable.

private member variables

A Common Pattern for New Classes

Public member functions permit programmers to modify and examine objects of the new class. You should use the keyword const (after the function's prototype) when a member function examines data without making modifications.

Private member variables of the new class store the information about the status of an object of the new class.

To summarize, we have declared two public member functions that examine our new class without alterations, and these two functions are declared as *const* functions. Two other public member functions actually allow data to be modified. The data itself is declared as a private member of the new class. This follows a pattern that we will generally use for new classes. Later you will see examples that include private member functions (i.e., member functions that are available to the implementor of the new class but forbidden from other programmers), and occasionally public member variables (i.e., member variables that may be used by any programmer). But for now this common pattern will serve you well.

As you have seen, the class body contains prototypes for the member functions but not the full definitions of these functions. The full definitions for the member functions occur after the class definition, in the same place as any other function definition. There are a few peculiarities about the definition of a member function, but before we look at the definitions, we'll tackle another question: How does a programmer use a class such as Throttle?

Using a Class

As with any other data type, you may declare variables of type Throttle. These are called Throttle **objects**, or sometimes Throttle **instances**. They are

programs can declare objects of a class

declared in the same way as variables of any other type. Here are two sample declarations of `Throttle` objects:

```
Throttle my_throttle;
Throttle control;
```

Every `Throttle` object contains the private member variable `position`, but there is no way for a program to access this component directly since it is a *private* member. The only way that a program can use its `Throttle` objects is by using the four public member functions. For example, suppose we have declared the variables shown above, and we want to set `control` to its third notch. We do this by calling the member functions, as shown here:

```
control.shut_off( );
control.shift(3);
```

Calling a member function always involves the four pieces shown in these examples:

1. Start with the name of the object that you are manipulating. In this example, we want to manipulate `control`, so we begin with "`control`". If, instead, we wanted to manipulate `my_throttle`, then we would begin with "`my_throttle`". Always remember that you cannot just call a member function—you must always indicate which object is being manipulated.

how to use a member function

2. After the object name, place a single period.

3. Next, write the name of the member function. In our example, we first call control's `shut_off` function, so we write "`control.shut_off`"—which you can pronounce "control *dot* shut off."

4. Finally, list the parameters for the function call. In our example, `shut_off` has no parameters, so we have an empty parameter list ( ). The second function call, to the function `shift`, requires one parameter, which is the amount (3) that we are shifting the throttle.

```
control.shut_off( );
control.shift(3);
```

Our example made function calls to the `shut_off` and `shift` member functions of `control`. An OOP programmer usually would use slightly different terminology, saying that we **activated** the `shut_off` and `shift` member functions. **Activating a member function** is nothing more than OOP jargon for *making a function call* to a member function.

As another example, here is a sequence of several activations to set a throttle according to user input, and then print the throttle's flow:

```
Throttle control;
int user_input;

control.shut_off( );
cout << "Please type a number from 0 to 6: ";
cin >> user_input;
control.shift(user_input);
if (control.is_on( ))
    cout << "The flow is " << control.flow( ) << endl;
else
    cout << "The flow is now off" << endl;
```

Notice how the return value of `control.flow` is used directly in the output statement. As with any other function, the return value of a member function can be used as part of an output statement or other expression.

Using a `Throttle` is easy because we don't have to worry about how the member functions accomplish their work. We simply activate each member function and wait for it to return, just like any other function. This is information hiding at its best.

A Small Demonstration Program for the Throttle Class

An example of a program using the `Throttle` class is shown in Figure 2.2. The program declares a throttle called `sample` and shifts the throttle upward according to the user's input. The throttle is then moved down one notch at a time, with the flow printed at each notch. A typical dialogue with the program would look like this (with the user's input printed in bold):

```
I have a Throttle with 6 positions.
Where would you like to set the Throttle?
Please type a number from 0 to 6: 3
The flow is now 0.5
The flow is now 0.333333
The flow is now 0.166667
The flow is now off
```

dialogue with the demo program

The only pieces missing from the demonstration program are the complete member function definitions. We'll look at these definitions after we discuss one other feature, the `EXIT_SUCCESS` constant.

FIGURE 2.2	Sample Program for the Throttle Class

A Program

```
// FILE: demo1.cxx
// This small demonstration shows how the Throttle class is used.
#include <iostream.h>        // Provides cout and cin
#include <stdlib.h>          // Provides EXIT_SUCCESS

class Throttle
{
public:
    // MODIFICATION MEMBER FUNCTIONS
    void shut_off( );
    void shift(int amount);
    // CONSTANT MEMBER FUNCTIONS
    double flow( ) const;
    bool is_on( ) const;
private:
    int position;
};
```

These lines are the definition of the Throttle class.

```
int main( )
{
    Throttle sample;
    int user_input;

    // Set the sample Throttle to a position indicated by the user.
    cout << "I have a Throttle with 6 positions." << endl;
    cout << "Where would you like to set the Throttle? " << endl;
    cout << "Please type a number from 0 to 6: ";
    cin >> user_input;
    sample.shut_off( );
    sample.shift(user_input);

    // Shift the Throttle down to zero, printing the flow along the way.
    while (sample.is_on( ))
    {
        cout << "The flow is now " << sample.flow( ) << endl;
        sample.shift(-1);
    }
    cout << "The flow is now off" << endl;
    return EXIT_SUCCESS;
}
```

This is the declaration of a Throttle object called "sample".

See the C++ Feature, "Using EXIT_SUCCESS in a Main Program," page 39.

In the actual program, you would place the implementations of the Throttle's four member functions here, but we haven't yet written these implementations!

| demo1.cxx | **FTP** |

C++ *Feature:* Using EXIT_SUCCESS in a Main Program

When the demonstration program finishes, it prints an ending message and then executes the statement:

```
        o
    return EXIT_SUCCESS;
```

This return statement ends the main program and also sends the value of the constant EXIT_SUCCESS back to your computer's operating system. The operating system is the software that is responsible for running all programs on your computer. Although you may not realize it, the operating system is able to take further actions based on the return value from a main program. For example, the return value of EXIT_SUCCESS tells the operating system that the program ended normally, and the operating system can then proceed with its next task. Other return values tell the operating system about abnormal terminations such as problems opening files or running out of memory. For now, our main programs will always return EXIT_SUCCESS, which is a constant defined in stdlib.h. For most operating systems, this constant is defined as zero (which is why you may have used return 0 in other programming).

By the way, a program can also return another constant, EXIT_FAILURE, as a simple way of indicating non-normal completion.

Implementing Member Functions

Writing the complete definition of a member function is just like writing any other function, with one small difference: In the head of the function definition, the class name must appear before the function name, separated by two colons. In our example, Throttle:: appears in the head, before the function name. This requirement, called the **scope resolution operator**, tells the compiler that the function is a member function of a particular class. For example, the definition of our first member function must include the full name Throttle::shut_off, as shown here:

using the class name with two colons ::

```
void Throttle::shut_off( )
// Precondition: None.
// Postcondition: The Throttle has been turned off.
{
    position = 0;
}
```

implementation of shut_off

The reason for the scope resolution operator is that a function name might be used as the name of another class's member function, or as the name of another ordinary function. By specifying the full name, Throttle::shut_off, we indicate that this is the implementation of the Throttle member function, and not some other shut_off function.

We use the term **function implementation** to describe a full function definition such as this. The function implementation provides all the details of how the function works, as opposed to the mere prototype that appears in the class definition and gives no indication of how the function accomplishes its work.

Our implementation of `shut_off` simply sets the private member variable `position` to zero. But just whose `position` is being used here? Are we assigning to `my_throttle.position`? Or to `control.position`? Or even to some other throttle's `position` member? The answer depends on just which object activates `shut_off`. If `my_throttle.shut_off` is activated, then `position` refers to `my_throttle.position`. If we activate `control.shut_off`, then `position` in the implementation refers to `control.position`.

The Key to Member Variables

Each object keeps its own copies of all member variables.

When a member function's implementation refers to a member variable, then the actual member variable used always comes from the object that activated the member function.

Because each object of a class keeps its own copies of the member variables, it is possible to have several different objects of the same class in a single program. For example, we might have these statements in a program:

```
Throttle big, low;  ⟵──────────── Declare two Throttles.

big.shut_off( );
low.shut_off( );                     Set the positions of the
big.shift(6);                        Throttle's levers.
low.shift(1);                        Print the flows.

cout << "The big flow is: " << big.flow( ) << endl;
cout << "The low flow is: " << low.flow( ) << endl;
```

The first output statement prints `1.0` (which is `big`'s flow). The second output statement prints `0.166667` (which is `low`'s flow).

implementing flow

By now you know enough about member functions to implement the other three member functions of a throttle. For example, `flow` simply returns the current flow as determined by the `position` member variable, shown here:

```
double Throttle::flow( ) const
// Precondition: shut_off has been called at least once to initialize the Throttle.
// Postcondition: The value returned is the current flow as a proportion of
// the maximum flow.
{
    return position / 6.0;
}
```

Divide by 6.0, since
the Throttle has
six positions.

Since flow is a constant member function, we must include the keyword *const* at the end of the function's head. The flow function also has a precondition, requiring that shut_off has been called at least once to initialize the throttle. The precondition is required to ensure that we are not returning just garbage— although this is an example of a precondition that we cannot actually verify.

The shift function changes the position member variable by the amount specified in the parameter. In the implementation, we make sure that the shift doesn't go below 0 or above 6, as shown here:

implementing shift

```
void Throttle::shift(int amount)
// Precondition: shut_off has been called at least once to initialize the
// Throttle.
// Postcondition: The Throttle's position has been moved by amount (but
// not below 0 or above 6).
{
    position += amount;

    if (position < 0)
        position = 0;
    else if (position > 6)
        position = 6;
}
```

using +=

This might be the first time you've seen the += operator. Its effect is to take the amount on the right side (such as amount) and add it to what's already in the variable on the left (such as position). This sum is then stored back in the variable on the left side of +=.

The final Throttle function is called is_on. The function returns a boolean true-or-false value, indicating whether the fuel flow is on. Here is one way to implement is_on so that it returns the correct boolean value:

```
bool Throttle::is_on( ) const
// Precondition: shut_off has been called at least once to initialize the
// Throttle.
// Postcondition: If the Throttle's flow is above 0, then the function
// returns true; otherwise it returns false.
{
    return (flow( ) > 0);
}
```

implementing is_on

Member Functions May Activate Other Members

The implementation of `is_on` illustrates a final important feature of member functions: The implementation of a member function may activate other member functions. For example, our implementation of `is_on` activates the `flow` member function. When `flow` is used within the body of `is_on`, it is used without an object name such as `my_throttle` or `control`. No object name is needed in front of it—we just write `flow( )`; the actual instance of `flow` that will be used is determined by the activation of `is_on`. So when `my_throttle.is_on` is activated, it uses `my_throttle.flow`. On the other hand, when `control.is_on` is activated, it uses `control.flow`.

TIP

Programming Tip: Style for Boolean Values

The return statement in the `is_on` function is important. We simply wrote:

```
return (flow( ) > 0);
```

The test in the parentheses is evaluated, and the true-or-false value of this test is returned by the function. Whenever possible, you should use a true-or-false test (such as >) to return a boolean value. This tip is one of several style issues concerning boolean values.

A second issue for boolean values is that the value can be used to directly control an if-statement or a loop. For example, in Figure 2.2 on page 38 we have the following while-loop:

```
while (sample.is_on( ))
{
    cout << "The flow is now " << sample.flow( ) << endl;
    sample.shift(-1);
}
```

If the return value of the `is_on` function is true, then the loop continues. When `is_on` returns false, the loop will end.

As a final tip, we generally use the word "is" for the first part of the name of a function that returns a boolean value. This increases the readability of statements such as the statement written above that reads "while sample is on …"

Self-Test Exercises

1. What kind of member of a class supports information hiding?
2. Describe the one common place where the scope resolution operator `Throttle::` is used. ↓
3. Write a C++ program that declares a throttle, shifts the throttle halfway up (to the third position), and prints the current flow.

4. What is the purpose of *return* EXIT_SUCCESS in a main program? *tells the operating system that the program ended normaaly*

5. Add a new throttle member function that will return true if the current flow is more than half. The body of your implementation should activate flow and use the guidelines for boolean values listed above.

2.2 CONSTRUCTORS

The Throttle class is complete. It can be used in a program, as we did in Figure 2.2 on page 38. In that program we started with the Throttle class definition, followed by the program that uses the new class, and finally the implementations of the four member functions. This works fine; all of Figure 2.2 can be placed in a single file that is compiled and run like any other program. But there are some improvements to make before leaving the throttle example.

The first improvement deals with initializing a throttle. Three of the member functions have a precondition indicating that "shut_off has been called at least once to initialize the throttle." Without this precondition, the member variable position would contain garbage, and anything might happen. Unfortunately, there is no way to test the precondition to ensure that a throttle has been initialized.

Constructors are a way to solve this problem by providing an initialization function that is *guaranteed* to be called. A **constructor** is a member function with these special properties:

- If a class has a constructor, then the constructor is automatically called whenever a variable of the class is declared. If a constructor has any parameters, then the arguments for the constructor call must be given after the variable name (at the point where the variable is declared).

- The name of the constructor must be the same as the name of the class. In our example, the name of the constructor is Throttle. This seems strange: Normally we *avoid* using the same name for two different things. But it is a requirement of C++ that the constructor use the same name as the class.

- A constructor does not have *any* return value. Because of this, you must *not* write *void* (or any other return type) at the front of the constructor's head. The compiler knows that every constructor has no return value, but a compiler error occurs if you actually write *void* at the front of the constructor's head.

The Throttle's Constructor

Let's make these features concrete by implementing a throttle constructor. The constructor we have in mind will actually make the throttle more flexible by allowing the total number of throttle positions to vary from one throttle to another. We will no longer be restricted to throttles with only six positions. For example, a lawn mower throttle might need only four positions, whereas a forty-position throttle could be used for a rocket that needs finer control.

Our throttle constructor has one parameter, which tells the total number of positions that the throttle contains. We do not need a second parameter for the "current throttle position" because our constructor will always initialize the current position to zero. Here is the prototype for the new constructor, along with its precondition/postcondition contract:

```
Throttle(int size);
// Precondition: 0 < size.
// Postcondition: The Throttle has size positions above the shutoff position,
// and its current position is off.
```

It does look strange, seeing the word `Throttle` used in this way, but we have no choice: The name of the constructor must be the same as the name of the class. Also notice that the word *void* does not appear at the front of the prototype, nor is there any other return type for the function. The constructor's prototype is placed in the `Throttle` class definition along with the other member functions' prototypes, as indicated here:

```
class Throttle
{
public:
    // CONSTRUCTOR
    Throttle(int size);
    // MODIFICATION MEMBER FUNCTIONS
    void shut_off( );
    . . .
```

This is the prototype for the Throttle constructor.

Prototypes for other member functions appear as usual.

We'll look at the implementation of the constructor in a moment, but first let's see some examples of using the constructor in declarations of throttle objects. For example, here are the declarations of two throttles:

```
Throttle mower_control(4), apollo(40);
```

After these declarations, each throttle is shut off. The `mower_control` has four positions, and the `apollo` throttle has forty.

Often it is useful to provide several different constructors, each of which does a different kind of initialization. For instance, suppose many of our throttles require just one on position—a kind of all-or-nothing throttle. Then we could provide a second constructor with no parameters. The second constructor gives the throttle just one on position, and sets the current position to zero. The prototype for this constructor is shown here:

```
Throttle( );
// Precondition: None.
// Postcondition: The Throttle has one position above the shutoff position,
// and its current position is off.
```

A constructor with no parameters is called a **default constructor**. Here is a declaration of two throttles, with the first using the default constructor and the second using the other constructor:

```
Throttle toggle, complicated(100);
```

When `toggle` uses the default constructor, there is no argument list—not even a pair of parentheses. In other words, to use the default constructor, just declare an object with no argument list. The default constructor will be called.

You may declare as many constructors as you like—one for each different way of initializing an object. Each constructor must have a distinct parameter list so that the compiler can tell them apart. Only one default constructor is allowed.

To implement our new constructors we need a new private member variable called `top_position`, which keeps track of the maximum position of the throttle. The default constructor sets `top_position` to 1, and the other constructor sets `top_position` according to the constructor's `size` parameter. The complete new class definition, along with the implementations of the new constructors, is given in Figure 2.3.

Constructors

A **constructor** is a member function that is automatically called to initialize an object when the object is declared. The name of the constructor must be the same as the name of the class. If the constructor has parameters, then the arguments for the constructor call must be given after the object name (at the point where the object is declared).

What Happens If You Write a Class with No Constructors?

If you write a class with no constructors, then the compiler automatically creates a simple default constructor. This **automatic default constructor** doesn't do much work. It just calls the default constructor for the member variables that are objects of some other class. Generally, you should write your own constructors, including your own default constructor, rather than depending on the automatic default constructor.

TIP

Programming Tip: Always Provide Constructors

When you write a class, and you define the constructors, each variable of the class will have one of your constructors called when the variable is declared. This increases the reliability of programs by reducing the chance of using uninitialized variables. We also recommend that you define a default constructor for each of your classes. This allows programmers to declare a variable of your class, without having to provide any arguments for a constructor.

FIGURE 2.3 | Constructors for the Throttle

A Class Definition

```
class Throttle                          prototype for the
{                                       default constructor
public:
    // CONSTRUCTORS
    Throttle( );                        prototype for the
    Throttle(int size);                 other constructor
    // MODIFICATION MEMBER FUNCTIONS
    void shut_off( );
    void shift(int amount);
    // CONSTANT MEMBER FUNCTIONS
    double flow( ) const;
    bool is_on( ) const;
private:                                A new private member
    int top_position;                   variable keeps track of
    int position;                       how many positions the
};                                      Throttle has.
```

Implementations of the Constructors

```
Throttle::Throttle( )            Throttle::Throttle(int size)
{                                // Library facilities used: assert.h
    top_position = 1;            {
    position = 0;                    assert(0 < size);
}                                    top_position = size;
                                     position = 0;
                                 }
```

Revising the Throttle's Member Functions

Because we added a new member variable, `top_position`, we must revise the member functions to use `top_position` rather than the number 6 for the number of throttle positions. For example, here is the revised implementation of `shift`:

```
void Throttle::shift(int amount)
// Postcondition: The Throttle's position has been moved by amount (but
// not below 0 or above the top position).
{
    position += amount;

    if (position < 0)
        position = 0;
    else if (position > top_position)
        position = top_position;
}
```

Use the member variable, top_position, instead of the number 6.

Notice that we no longer need a precondition, because we are guaranteed to have one of the constructors called. When there is no precondition you may omit it, as we have done here, or you may list the precondition as "None."

when there is no precondition

Inline Member Functions

We'll use a new technique to revise the other three member functions. The technique is to place the complete definitions of `shut_off`, `flow`, and `is_on` inside the class definition, as shown in the three highlighted lines of Figure 2.4.

The use of *double* in the definition of `flow` changes `top_position` from an integer to a `double` number (otherwise the division will perform an integer division, throwing away any remainder). The change of data types is called a **type cast**. It is needed whenever you compute the ordinary division of two integers (which includes a fractional part in the result).

The other change we made in the implementations is to have `is_on` merely examine `position`. This seems simpler than our original implementation (which activated the `flow` function).

Placing a function definition inside the class definition is called an **inline member function**. It has two effects:

- You don't have to write the implementation later.
- Each time the inline function is used in your program, the compiler will recompile the short function definition and place a copy of this compiled short definition in your code. This saves some execution time (there is no actual function call and function return), but it may be inefficient in space (you end up with many copies of the same compiled code).

Notice that when you declare an inline member function, there is no semicolon before the opening curly bracket or after the closing curly bracket.

FIGURE 2.4 | Inline Member Functions

A Class Definition

```
class Throttle
{
public:
    // CONSTRUCTORS
    Throttle( );
    Throttle(int size);
    // MODIFICATION MEMBER FUNCTIONS
    void shut_off( ) { position = 0; }
    void shift(int amount);
    // CONSTANT MEMBER FUNCTIONS
    double flow( ) const { return position / double(top_position); }
    bool is_on( ) const { return (position > 0); }
private:
    int top_position;
    int position;
};
```

The highlighted code shows three inline member functions.

The type name "double" changes top_position from an integer to a double number. The change is called a "type cast," and it prevents an unintended integer division.

△ **TIP**

***Programming Tip:* When to Use an Inline Member Function**

Inline functions cause some inefficiency—your compiled code might be longer than it needs to be. Inline functions also result in a messier class definition, which is harder to read and harder to debug. Because of these problems, we recommend using an inline member function only for the simple situation when the function definition consists of a single short statement.

Self-Test Exercises

6. Use an inline function to rewrite the "halfway on" function from Self-Test Exercise 5 on page 43.

7. Write a new throttle constructor with two parameters: the total number of positions for the throttle, and its initial position.

2.3 THE HEADER FILE AND THE IMPLEMENTATION FILE

It makes sense to make our new Throttle class easily available to any program that needs it. (After all, you never know when you might need a throttle.) We'd like to do so without revealing all the details of the new class's implementation—in other words, providing the Throttle class as an *abstract data type* (ADT) that programmers can use without knowing how the member functions are implemented. This is accomplished by writing two separate files that provide your ADT to any program that wants to use it. The two files are the following:

- A **header file** that provides all the information that a programmer needs in order to use the ADT
- An **implementation file** that provides the actual implementations of the class's member functions

This section illustrates our format of the header and implementation files for our throttle ADT, along with an example of how a program can use these files.

The Header File

The **header file** for an ADT provides all the information that a programmer needs to use the ADT. In fact, all the information needed to use the ADT should appear in a **header file comment** at the top of the header file. To use the ADT, a programmer only needs to read this informative comment. The comment should include a list of all the public member functions, along with a precondition/postcondition contract for each function. (If a function has no precondition, then we will usually omit it, listing the postcondition on its own.) The comment does not list any private members, because a programmer who *uses* the new class is not concerned with private members.

a comment in the header file tells how to use the ADT

The class definition for the new class appears after the header file comment. But only the class definition appears—the implementations of the member functions do not appear here (except for inline functions).

There are some problems with putting the class definition in the header file. One problem is that programmers who use the ADT might think that they have to read this definition to use the class. They don't. All the information needed to use the ADT is in the header file comment. But C++ requires the class definition to appear here, so we have no way around this problem.

A second problem arises from the way that header files are sometimes used. As you will see in later chapters, a program sometimes includes a header file more than once. As a result, the class definition appears more than once, and compilation fails because of "duplicate class definition." We can avoid duplicate class definition by placing all the header file's definitions inside a compiler directive called a **macro guard**. The form of the throttle's macro guard is shown here:

avoid duplicate definition by using a macro guard

```
#ifndef THROTTLE_H
#define THROTTLE_H

    class Throttle
    {
        ‖ The usual class definition appears here.
    };

#endif
```

The first line, `#ifndef THROTTLE_H`, indicates the start of the macro guard. All the statements that appear between here and the `#endif` are under the power of the macro guard. These statements will be compiled only if the compiler has not yet seen a definition of the word THROTTLE_H.

So how does this avoid a duplicate definition? At the first appearance of the code, the class definition is compiled, and the word THROTTLE_H is also defined (by the definition `#define THROTTLE_H`). Now, if the code should appear a second time, the class definition is skipped (since THROTTLE_H is now defined).

Our throttle header file, called "throttle.h", is shown in Figure 2.5. Most programmers use ".h" as the end of the header file name.

Header File for an ADT

When you design and implement an abstract data type, you should provide a separate header file.

At the top of the header file, place all of the documentation that a programmer needs to use the ADT.

The class definition for the ADT appears after the documentation. But only the class definition appears and not the implementations of member functions (except inline functions).

Place a "macro guard" around the entire class definition, as described above. The macro guard prevents accidental duplicate definition.

FIGURE 2.5   Header File for the Throttle Class

A Header File

```
// FILE: throttle.h
// CLASS PROVIDED: Throttle (an ADT for a throttle that controls fuel flow)
//
// CONSTRUCTORS for the Throttle class:
//    Throttle( )
//        Postcondition: The Throttle has one position above the shut_off position, and it is
//        currently shut off.
//
//    Throttle(int size)
//        Precondition:  size > 0.
//        Postcondition: The Throttle has size positions above the shut_off position, and it is
//        currently shut off.
```

(continued)

(FIGURE 2.5 continued)

```
//
// MODIFICATION MEMBER FUNCTIONS for the Throttle class:
//     void shut_off( )
//        Postcondition: The Throttle has been turned off.
//
//     void shift(int amount)
//        Postcondition: The Throttle's position has been moved by
//        amount (but not below 0 or above the top position).
//
// CONSTANT MEMBER FUNCTIONS for the Throttle class:
//     double flow( ) const
//        Postcondition: The value returned is the current flow as a
//        proportion of the maximum flow.
//
//     bool is_on( ) const
//        Postcondition: If the Throttle's flow is above 0 then
//        the function returns true; otherwise it returns false.
//
// VALUE SEMANTICS for the Throttle class: (See the discussion on page 52.)
//     Assignments and the copy constructor may be used with Throttle objects.
```

Member functions often have no precondition.

```
#ifndef THROTTLE_H          ← start of the macro guard
#define THROTTLE_H

    class Throttle
    {
    public:
        // CONSTRUCTORS
        Throttle( );
        Throttle(int size);
        // MODIFICATION MEMBER FUNCTIONS
        void shut_off( ) { position = 0; }
        void shift(int amount);
        // CONSTANT MEMBER FUNCTIONS
        double flow( ) const { return position / double(top_position); }
        bool is_on( ) const { return (position > 0); }
    private:
        int top_position;
        int position;
    };
                            ── end of the macro guard
    #endif   ←
```

throttle.h **FTP**

Value Semantics of a Class

The **value semantics** of a class determines how values are copied from one object to another. In C++, the value semantics consists of two operations: the assignment operator and the copy constructor.

The assignment operator. For two objects x and y, an assignment `y = x` copies the value of x to y. Assignments such as this are permitted for any new class that we define. For a new class, C++ normally carries out assignments by simply copying each member variable from the object on the right of the assignment to the object on the left of the assignment. This method of copying is called the **automatic assignment operator.** Later we will see examples where the automatic assignment operator does not work. But for now, our new classes can use the automatic assignment operator.

The copy constructor. A **copy constructor** is a constructor with exactly one argument, and the data type of the argument is the same as the constructor's class. For example, a copy constructor for the throttle has one argument, and that argument is itself a throttle. The usual purpose of a copy constructor is to initialize a new object as an exact copy of an existing object. For example, here is a bit of code that creates a 100-position throttle called x, shifts x to its middle position, and then declares a second throttle called y, which is initialized as an exact copy of x:

```
Throttle x(100);        The throttle y is initialized as a
x.shift(50);            copy of x, so that both throttles
Throttle y(x);          are at position 50 out of 100.
```

The highlighted statement activates the throttle's copy constructor to initialize y as an exact copy of x. After the initialization, x and y may take different actions, ending up with different fuel flows, but at this point, both the throttles are set to position 50 out of 100.

There is also an alternative syntax for calling the copy constructor. Instead of writing `Throttle y(x);`, you may write `Throttle y = x;`. This alternative syntax looks like an assignment statement, but keep in mind that the actual effect is a bit different. The assignment `y = x;` merely copies x to the already existing object, y. On the other hand, the declaration `Throttle y = x;` both declares a new object, y, and calls the copy constructor to initialize y as a copy of x. We will always use the original form `Throttle y(x);`, because this form is less likely to be confused with an ordinary assignment statement.

As the implementor of a class, you may write a copy constructor much like any other constructor—and you will do so for classes in future chapters. But for now we can take advantage of a C++ feature: C++ provides an **automatic copy constructor**. Similar to assignment, the automatic copy constructor initializes a new object by merely copying all the member variables from the existing object.

For example, in the declaration `Throttle y(x);`, the automatic copy constructor will copy the two member variables from the existing throttle x to the new throttle y.

For many classes, the automatic assignment operator and the automatic copy constructor work fine. But as we have warned, we will later see classes where the automatic versions fail. Merely copying member variables is not always sufficient. Because of this, programmers are wary of assignments and the copy constructor. To address this problem, we suggest that your documentation include a comment indicating that the value semantics is safe to use.

Programming Tip: Document the Value Semantics

When you implement an ADT, the documentation should include a comment indicating that the value semantics is safe to use. For example, in our throttle header file we wrote:

```
// VALUE SEMANTICS for the Throttle class:
//      Assignments and the copy constructor may be used with Throttle
//      objects.
```

TIP △

The Implementation File

An **implementation file** for a new class has three items: First, a small comment appears, indicating that the documentation is available in the header file. Second, an include directive appears, causing the compiler to grab the class definition from the header file. In our throttle example, the include directive is:

```
#include "throttle.h"
```

When we list the name of the header file, "throttle.h", we use quotation marks rather than angle brackets. The angle brackets (such as the include directive #include <iostream.h>) are only used to include a standard library facility. Finally, after the include directive, you place the implementations of the class's member functions.

Most compilers require specific endings for the name of an implementation file, such as ".cpp" or ".C". We will use ".cxx" for the endings of our implementation file names, such as the complete implementation file "throttle.cxx" shown in Figure 2.6.

Implementation File for an ADT

Each ADT has a separate implementation file that contains the implementations of the class's member functions.

FIGURE 2.6   Implementation File for the Throttle Class

An Implementation File

```
//  FILE: throttle.cxx
//  CLASS IMPLEMENTED: Throttle (See throttle.h for documentation.)

#include <assert.h>       // Provides assert
#include "throttle.h"

Throttle::Throttle( )
{
    top_position = 1;     // A simple on-off Throttle
    position = 0;
}

Throttle::Throttle(int size)
// Library facilities used: assert.h
{
    assert(size > 0);
    top_position = size;
    position = 0;
}

void Throttle::shift(int amount)
{
    position += amount;

    if (position < 0)
        position = 0;
    else if (position > top_position)
        position = top_position;

}
```

throttle.cxx   **FTP**

How a Program Uses an ADT

Once the header and implementation files are in place, any program can use our new class. At the top of the program, you place an include directive to include the header file, as shown here for our example:

```
#include "throttle.h"
```

Here is the important point for you to remember:

> In order to use an ADT, a program includes *only* the header file, and not the implementation file.

When the complete program is actually compiled, you will need to provide extra information about where to find a compiled version of the implementation file, `throttle.cxx`. This process, called *linking,* varies from compiler to compiler (see Appendix D). Our sample program for the revised throttle appears in Figure 2.7 on page 56.

C++ Feature: **Constant Declarations**

FEATURE ++

The demonstration program in Figure 2.7 uses another C++ feature that may be new to you. Before the main program, we have the definition:

```
const int DEMO_SIZE = 5;
```

To some extent, this is just an ordinary declaration of an integer variable called DEMO_SIZE, which is given an initial value of 5. The keyword `const`, appearing before the declaration, makes DEMO_SIZE more than just an ordinary declaration. It is a **constant declaration**, which means that its value will never be changed while a program is running. In C++, the compiler can take advantage of the "never changed" rule by using the actual value 5 wherever DEMO_SIZE occurs.

There are several advantages to defining DEMO_SIZE in this way. First, the name DEMO_SIZE provides more meaning than the simple number 5. We know that DEMO_SIZE is the size of our demonstration throttle, making the program easier to read. Second, using DEMO_SIZE makes it easy to change the demonstration to a 50-position throttle, or to a 500-position throttle, or to any other size. To make such a change, we need only change the 5 at the one place where DEMO_SIZE is defined, at the top of the program. We don't have to worry about changing the number 5 at many different places. As a third advantage, the compiler provides some extra help with constant declarations by raising a compiler error at any statement that tries to change the value of a declared constant.

Because of these advantages, we suggest that you declare a constant for any meaningful number that appears in your program—especially if the number may need to be changed for a later recompilation. As part of our programming style, we use all upper-case letters for the names of any such constants.

It is fine to declare constants at the top of a file, resulting in a "global" scope that can be used throughout the file. (You would not want to declare an ordinary variable here because of the debugging difficulties caused by global variables.)

| FIGURE 2.7 | Sample Program for the Revised Throttle Class |

A Program

```
// FILE: demo2.cxx
// This small demonstration shows how the revised Throttle class is used.
#include <iostream.h>      // Provides cout and cin
#include <stdlib.h>        // Provides EXIT_SUCCESS
#include "throttle.h"      // Provides the Throttle class

const int DEMO_SIZE = 5;   // Number of positions in a demonstration Throttle
```

←————See the C ++ Feature,
"Constant Declarations,"
on page 55.

```
int main( )
{
    Throttle sample(DEMO_SIZE);   // A Throttle to use for our demonstration
    int user_input;               // The position that we set the Throttle to

    // Set the sample Throttle to a position indicated by the user.
    cout << "I have a Throttle with " << DEMO_SIZE << " positions." << endl;
    cout << "Where would you like to set the Throttle?" << endl;
    cout << "Please type a number from 0 to " << DEMO_SIZE << ": ";
    cin >> user_input;
    sample.shift(user_input);

    // Shift the Throttle down to zero, printing the flow along the way.
    while (sample.is_on( ))
    {
        cout << "The flow is now " << sample.flow( ) << endl;
        sample.shift(-1);
    }
    cout << "The flow is now off" << endl;

    return EXIT_SUCCESS;
}
```

A Sample Dialogue

```
I have a Throttle with 5 positions.
Where would you like to set the Throttle?
Please type a number from 0 to 5: 3
The flow is now 0.6
The flow is now 0.4
The flow is now 0.2
The flow is now off
```

| demo2.cxx | **FTP** |

Self-Test Exercises

8. What would a programmer read to learn how to use a new class?

9. What is the normal action of an assignment `y = x`, if x and y are objects?

10. Suppose that x is a throttle. What is the effect of the declaration `Throttle y(x)`?

11. Write the `#include` directive that must be present for a main program to use the `Throttle` class.

12. Design and implement a class called `CircleLocation` to keep track of the position of a single point that travels around a circle. An object of this class records the position of the point as an angle, measured in a clockwise direction from the top of the circle. Include these public member functions: (1) A default constructor to place the point at the top of the circle; (2) Another constructor to place the point at a specified position; (3) A function to move the point a specified number of degrees around the circle. Use a positive argument to move clockwise, and a negative argument to move counterclockwise. (4) A function to return the current position of the point, in degrees, measured clockwise from the top of the circle. Your solution should include a separate header file, implementation file, and an example of a main program using the new class.

13. Design and implement a class called `Clock`. A `Clock` object holds one instance of a time value such as 9:48 P.M. Have at least these public member functions:

    *   A default constructor that sets the time to midnight

    *   A function to explicitly assign a given time (you will have to give some thought to appropriate parameters for this function)

    *   Functions to retrieve information: the current hour, the current minute, and a boolean function to determine whether the time is at or before noon

    *   A function to advance the time forward by a given number of minutes

14. Write a constant declaration for an integer named `UNIVERSE`, with a value of 42. What would happen if you later tried an assignment statement `UNIVERSE = 0`?

2.4 CLASSES AND PARAMETERS

Every programmer requires an unshakable understanding of functions and parameters. The realm of OOP requires extra understanding because classes can be used as the type of a function's parameter, or as the type of the return value from a function. This section illustrates several such functions, including a review of different kinds of parameters. The examples use a new class called `Point`.

FIGURE 2.8 Three Points in a Plane

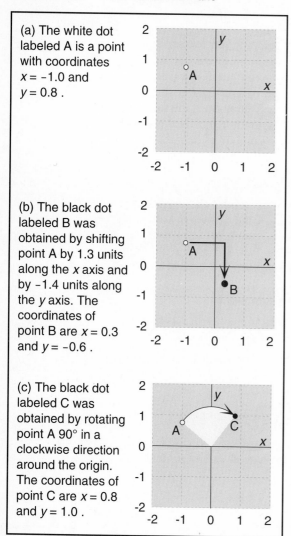

(a) The white dot labeled A is a point with coordinates $x = -1.0$ and $y = 0.8$.

(b) The black dot labeled B was obtained by shifting point A by 1.3 units along the x axis and by -1.4 units along the y axis. The coordinates of point B are $x = 0.3$ and $y = -0.6$.

(c) The black dot labeled C was obtained by rotating point A 90° in a clockwise direction around the origin. The coordinates of point C are $x = 0.8$ and $y = 1.0$.

PROGRAMMING EXAMPLE: **The Point Class**

The new class is a data type to store and manipulate the location of a single point on a plane, as shown in Figure 2.8. The example point in Figure 2.8(a) lies at a location with coordinates $x = -1.0$ and $y = 0.8$. The `Point` class has the member functions listed here:

- There is a constructor to initialize a point. The constructor's parameters use default arguments that we'll discuss in a moment.

- There is a member function to shift a point by given amounts along the x and y axes, as shown in Figure 2.8(b).

- There is a member function to rotate a point by 90° in a clockwise direction around the origin, as shown in Figure 2.8(c).

- There are two constant member functions that allow us to retrieve the current x and y coordinates of a point.

These functions are simple, yet they form the basis for an actual data type that is used in drawing programs and other graphics applications. All the member functions, including the constructor, are listed in the header file of Figure 2.9 on page 59, with an implementation in Figure 2.10 on page 60. After you've looked through the figures, we'll review the implementations, starting with *default arguments*, which are used in an interesting way in the point's constructor.

FIGURE 2.9 Header File for the Point Class

A Header File

```
// FILE: point.h
// CLASS PROVIDED: Point (an ADT for a point on a two-dimensional plane)
//
// CONSTRUCTOR for the Point class:
//    Point(double initial_x = 0, double initial_y = 0)
//    Postcondition: The Point has been set to (initial_x, initial_y).
//
// MODIFICATION MEMBER FUNCTIONS for the Point class:
//    void shift(double x_amount, double y_amount)
//    Postcondition: The Point has been moved by x_amount along the x axis
//     and by y_amount along the y axis.
//
//    void rotate90( )
//    Postcondition: The Point has been rotated clockwise 90° around the origin.
//
// CONSTANT MEMBER FUNCTIONS for the Point class:
//    double get_x( ) const
//    Postcondition: The value returned is the x coordinate of the Point.
//
//    double get_y( ) const
//    Postcondition: The value returned is the y coordinate of the Point.
//
// VALUE SEMANTICS for the Point class:
//     Assignments and the copy constructor may be used with Point objects.

#ifndef POINT_H
#define POINT_H

    class Point
    {
    public:
        // CONSTRUCTOR
        Point(double initial_x = 0, double initial_y = 0);
        // MODIFICATION MEMBER FUNCTIONS
        void shift(double x_amount, double y_amount);
        void rotate90( );
        // CONSTANT MEMBER FUNCTIONS
        double get_x( ) const { return x; }
        double get_y( ) const { return y; }
    private:
        double x; // x coordinate of this Point
        double y; // y coordinate of this Point
    };

#endif
```

point.h **FTP**

FIGURE 2.10 | Implementation File for the Point Class

An Implementation File

```
// FILE: point.cxx
// CLASS IMPLEMENTED: Point (See point.h for documentation.)

#include "point.h"

Point::Point(double initial_x, double initial_y)
{
    x = initial_x;     // Constructor sets the Point to a given position.
    y = initial_y;
}

void Point::shift(double x_amount, double y_amount)
{
    x += x_amount;
    y += y_amount;
}

void Point::rotate90( )
{
    double new_x;
    double new_y;

    new_x = y;    // For a 90 degree clockwise rotation, the new x is the original y,
    new_y = -x;   // and the new y is - 1 times the original x.
    x = new_x;
    y = new_y;
}
```

point.cxx | **FTP**

Default Arguments

A **default argument** is a value that will be used for an argument when a programmer does not provide an actual argument. Default arguments may be listed
in the prototype of any function. For example, here is a modified version of a
function prototype that we used on page 13:

```
int date_check(int year, int month = 1, int day = 1);
```

The exact behavior of date_check is not important. The important thing is that
we have added default arguments for the month and day parameters. As shown
in the shaded part of the example, the default argument appears with an equals

sign after the parameter name. Once a default argument is available, the function can be called with or without certain arguments.

For example, a program can call `date_check` with just the `year` argument:

```
date_check(1999);
```

Since the last two arguments were omitted in this function call, the default arguments (`month = 1` and `day = 1`) will be used. The function call is identical to calling `date_check(1999, 1, 1)`.

The function can also be called with a year and a month, omitting the day, as in this example:

```
date_check(1999, 7);
```

In this example, the default argument will be used for the day, so the function call is identical to calling `date_check(1999, 7, 1)`.

The general rules for providing and using default arguments are reviewed in Figure 2.11 on page 62. Default arguments are especially convenient for constructors, such as the point's constructor in Figure 2.9 on page 59. The constructor's prototype has these two default arguments:

default arguments are especially convenient for constructors

```
Point(double initial_x = 0, double initial_y = 0);
```

Both arguments of the constructor have a default of 0, as shown in these three declarations of point objects:

```
Point a(-1, 0.8);  ←—Uses the usual constructor with two arguments
Point b(-1);  ←————Uses -1 for the first argument and uses the default
Point c;                 argument, initial_y = 0, for the second argument

                    ——— Uses default arguments for both initial_x = 0
                        and initial_y = 0
```

The third use of our constructor—simply `Point c;`—is interesting because defaults are used for both arguments. In effect, we have a constructor with no arguments. A constructor with no argument is a **default constructor**. As we saw with the throttle, it's important to always provide a default constructor. One way to provide a default constructor is to have a constructor with default arguments for all of its arguments.

Programming Tip: A Default Constructor Can Be Provided by Using Default Arguments

TIP △

A good way to provide a default constructor is to have one constructor with default arguments for all of its arguments. Don't forget that default constructors are always used with no argument list; not even the parentheses are present. So to use the point's default constructor, we simply write `Point c;`.

FIGURE 2.11 Default Arguments

Default Arguments

A default argument is a value that will be used for an argument when no actual argument is provided. The usage follows the format and rules listed below.

Syntax in a prototype's parameter list:

    Type_Name var_name = default_value

Example:

    int date_check(int year, int month = 1, int date = 1);

→ default argument
→ default value

1. The default argument is specified only once—in the prototype—and not in the function's implementation.
2. A function with several arguments does not need to specify default arguments for every argument. But if only some of the arguments have defaults, then those arguments must be rightmost in the parameter list.
3. In a function call, arguments with default values may be omitted from the right end of the actual argument list. For example:

            date_check(1999); ←———— *Uses default arguments for month = 1 and date = 1*
            date_check(1999, 7); ←———— *Uses default argument for date = 1*
            date_check(1999, 7, 22); ←———— *Does not use the default arguments at all*

Parameters

review of function parameters

Classes can be used as the type of a function's parameter, just like any other data type. We'll review three different kinds of parameters, with examples that use the new Point class.

Value parameters. The simplest parameters are *value parameters*. To illustrate a value parameter, we'll write a simple function. The function we have in mind has one value parameter, a point that we'll call p. The integer returned by the function is the number of 90° rotations that would be needed to move p into the upper right quadrant, as shown in Figure 2.12.

FIGURE 2.12

This point, p, needs three 90° rotations to move it to the upper right quadrant.

Value Parameter

Here is the function's implementation:

type *variable*

```
int rotations_needed(Point p)
// Postcondition: The value returned is the number of 90 degree
// clockwise rotations needed to move p into the upper right
// quadrant (where x >= 0 and y >= 0).
{
    int answer;

    answer = 0;
    while ((p.get_x( ) < 0) || (p.get_y( ) < 0))
    {
        p.rotate90( );
        answer++;
    }
    return answer;
}
```

# of 90° clockwise rotations to move p to upper right Quad.

In C++, a value parameter is declared by placing the type name followed by the parameter name. So, we have written `Point p` in the parameter list. The effect of a value parameter is that any change made to the parameter within the body of the function does not change the actual argument from the calling program. Let's look at an example in a program:

```
Point sample(6, -4); // Constructor places the Point at x = 6, y = -4.
cout << "  x coordinate is " << sample.get_x( )
     << "  y coordinate is " << sample.get_y( ) << endl;  = argument
cout << "  Rotations: " << rotations_needed(sample) << endl;
cout << "  x coordinate is " << sample.get_x( )
     << "  y coordinate is " << sample.get_y( ) << endl;
```

After the constructor, the code prints a message with the point's coordinates. Then, in the second output statement, `rotations_needed` is called. The function's parameter (p in this case) is referred to as the **formal parameter** to distinguish it from the value that is passed in during the function call. The passed value (`sample` in this case) is the **argument** (sometimes called the **actual argument** or the **actual parameter**).

formal parameters and arguments

With a value parameter, the argument provides the initial value for the formal parameter. To be more precise, the formal parameter is implemented as a local variable of the function, and the class's copy constructor is used to initialize the formal parameter as a copy of the actual argument. This is the only connection between the argument and the formal parameter. So, if the formal parameter p changes in our function body, the argument `sample` remains unchanged in the calling program. In our example, p will rotate three times, ending up at $x = 4$ and $y = 6$. The function returns the number of rotations (3), and `sample` still has its

the effect of a value parameter

original value in the calling program. Therefore, the complete output from the code is:

```
x coordinate is 6   y coordinate is -4
Rotations: 3
x coordinate is 6   y coordinate is -4
```

The value of the argument, `sample`, did not change.

Value Parameters

A **value parameter** is declared by writing the type name followed by the parameter name. With a value parameter, the argument provides the initial value for the formal parameter. The value parameter is implemented as a local variable of the function, so that any changes made to the parameter in the body of the function will leave the argument unaltered.

Example:
```
int rotations_needed(Point p);
```

Reference parameters.   *Reference parameters* are an important kind of parameter in C++. Our example of a reference parameter is similar to the `rotations_needed` function. But this time the point p will be a reference parameter. The new function does not return a value; it merely rotates p into the upper right quadrant, as shown here:

```
void rotate_to_upper_right(Point& p)
// Postcondition: The Point p has been rotated in 90 degree
// increments until p has been moved into the upper right
// quadrant (where x >= 0 and y >= 0).
{
    while ((p.get_x( ) < 0) || (p.get_y( ) < 0))
        p.rotate90( );
}
```

In C++, a reference parameter is declared by placing the type name followed by the symbol & and the parameter name. So, we have written `Point& p` in the parameter list.

the effect of a reference parameter

Here is the key to reference parameters: Any use of the parameter within the body of the function will access the argument in the calling program. Let's look at an example in a program:

```
Point sample(6, -4); // Constructor places Point at x = 6, y = -4.
cout << "  x coordinate is " << sample.get_x( )
     << "  y coordinate is " << sample.get_y( ) << endl;
rotate_to_upper_right(sample);
cout << "  x coordinate is " << sample.get_x( )
     << "  y coordinate is " << sample.get_y( ) << endl;
```

As we did before, the code prints the point's coordinates and then calls the function. The formal parameter is still called p and the argument is still `sample`—but p is now a reference parameter.

Because p is a reference parameter, any use of p within the body of the function will actually access `sample`. Thus it is the argument, `sample`, that is rotated into the upper right quadrant. When the function returns, `sample` has a new value. The complete output from the code is:

```
x coordinate is 6  y coordinate is -4
x coordinate is 4  y coordinate is 6
```

The value of the argument `sample` was changed by the function.

Reference Parameters

A **reference parameter** is declared by writing the type name followed by the character & and the parameter name. With a reference parameter, any use of the parameter within the body of the function will access the argument from the calling program. Changes made to the formal parameter in the body of the function will alter the argument.

Example:
```
void rotate_to_upper_right(Point& p);
```

Pitfall: Using a Wrong Argument Type for a Reference Parameter

PITFALL

In order for a reference parameter to work correctly, the data type of an argument must match exactly with the data type of the formal parameter. For example, suppose we have this reference parameter:

```
void make_int_42(int& i)
// Postcondition: i has been set to 42.
{
    i = 42;
}
```

Suppose we have an integer variable j, and we make the call make_int_42(j).

After the function returns, j will have the value 42. But you might be surprised at the output from this code:

```
double d;
d = 0;              ──── does not change d
make_int_42(d); ←
cout << d; ←──── prints 0
```

This example compiles, but because d is the wrong data type, a separate *integer* copy of d is created to use as the argument. The *double* variable d is never changed to 42.

If the argument's data type does not exactly match the data type of the formal parameter, then the compiler will try to convert the argument to the correct type. If the conversion is possible, then the compiler treats the argument like a value parameter, passing a *copy* of the argument to the function. Fortunately, most compilers provide a warning message such as "Temporary used for parameter 'i' in call to 'make_int_42'"—just make sure that you pay attention to the compiler's warnings!

Const reference parameters. For large data types, value parameters are less efficient than reference parameters. This is because a value parameter must make an extra copy of the argument to use within the body of the function. Hence, we generally prefer to use reference parameters. But often a reference parameter is unattractive because we don't want a programmer to worry about whether the function changes the actual argument. Changes are a definite possibility with a reference parameter, but they cannot occur with a value parameter.

the effect of a const reference parameter

Sometimes there is a solution that provides the efficiency of a reference parameter along with the security of a value parameter. The new parameter type is called a *const reference parameter*, and it may be used whenever a function guarantees that no change will occur to the parameter. For example, we can write a function that computes the distance between two points. The function has two point parameters, and neither parameter is changed by the function. Therefore we can use const reference parameters, as shown in Figure 2.13. The figure shows a function that computes the distance between two points, using this prototype:

```
double distance( const Point& p1, const Point& p2 );
```

The const reference parameter uses the keyword *const* before the parameter's type, and it also uses the symbol & after the type. A const reference parameter is efficient (since it is a reference parameter), but a programmer is guaranteed that the actual argument will not be altered by the function. For example, in our implementation of distance we use only get_x and get_y, both of which are *const* functions and therefore cannot change p1 and p2. It is important that get_x and get_y are actually declared as *const* functions, otherwise the compiler would not permit us to use them with the *const* parameters p1 and p2.

FIGURE 2.13	A Function with Const Reference Parameters

A Function Implementation

```
double distance(const Point& p1, const Point& p2)
// Postcondition: The value returned is the distance between p1 and p2.
// Library facilities used: math.h
{
    double a, b, c_squared;

    // Calculate differences in x and y coordinates.
    a = p1.get_x( ) - p2.get_x( ); // Difference in x coordinates
    b = p1.get_y( ) - p2.get_y( ); // Difference in y coordinates

    // Use Pythagorean Theorem to calculate the square of the distance between the Points.
    c_squared = a*a + b*b;

    return sqrt(c_squared);

}
```

$a^2 + b^2 = c^2$

p1

c   b

p2   a

Pythagorean
Theorem

newpoint.cxx   **FTP**

Const Reference Parameters

A **const reference parameter** is declared by writing the keyword *const* before a reference parameter and placing & after the parameter's type. The parameter is efficient, but unlike an ordinary reference parameter, the programmer is guaranteed that the function cannot change the value of the argument.

Example:
```
    double distance(const Point& p1, ...
```

If you use const reference parameters, be sure to follow the consistency requirements in the Programming Tip on page 68.

TIP

Programming Tip: Use const Consistently

When you define a new class along with functions and member functions to manipulate the class, you should make a consistent use of *const*. In particular:

1. Any member functions that do not change the value of the object should be declared const member functions. This is accomplished by placing the keyword *const* after the parameter list in both the prototype and the head of the function's definition. For example, the prototype of the throttle's `flow` function is:

    double `flow( ) const;`

2. Whenever you use the class as the type of a parameter, and the function does not alter the parameter, use a const reference parameter. This is accomplished by placing the keyword *const* before the parameter's type in the parameter list, and placing the symbol & after the type name. For example, the prototype:

    double `distance(const Point& p1, const Point& p2)`

You should not use *const* unless you intend to use it at every location that meets the requirements listed above.

When the Type of a Function's Return Value is a Class

The type of a function's return value may be a class. Here is a typical example:

```
Point middle(const Point& p1, const Point& p2)
// Postcondition: The value returned is the Point that
// is halfway in-between p1 and p2.
{
    double x_midpoint, y_midpoint;

    // Compute the x and y midpoints.
    x_midpoint = (p1.get_x( ) + p2.get_x( )) / 2;
    y_midpoint = (p1.get_y( ) + p2.get_y( )) / 2;

    // Construct a new Point and return it.
    Point midpoint(x_midpoint, y_midpoint);
    return midpoint;
}
```

Point Returned
By the Middle
Function

p1

p2 midpoint

The function computes a new point in the local variable `midpoint`, and then returns a copy of this point. Often the return value will be stored in a local variable such as `midpoint`, but not always. Here's another example, in which one of the parameters is the return value:

```
      type        name
Throttle slower(const Throttle& t1, const Throttle& t2)
// Postcondition: The value returned is a copy of t1 or t2, whichever
// has the slower flow. If the flows are equal, then t1 is returned.
{
    if (t1.flow( ) <= t2.flow( ))
        return t1;
            parameter
    else
        return t2;
        parameter
}
```

By the way, the C++ return statement uses the copy constructor to copy the function's return value to a temporary location before returning the value to the calling program.

Self-Test Exercises

15. Add default arguments to your throttle constructor from Self-Test Exercise 7 on page 48. Once you have done this, are the other two constructors still needed?

16. Which of these function calls could change the value of a point p:

```
cout << rotations_needed(p);
rotate_to_upper_right(p);
```

17. Suppose a function has a parameter named x, and the body of the function changes the value of x. When should x be a value parameter? When should it be a reference parameter? With this function, could x ever be a const reference parameter?

2.5 OPERATOR OVERLOADING

A **binary function** is a function with two arguments. Often, when you design a new class, there are binary functions to manipulate the class. Sometimes the new binary functions are naturally described using symbols such as == and +, which are symbols that C++ already uses to describe its own operations on numbers and other data types. For example, we might want to test whether two points are equal, and it seems natural to write this code:

```
Point p1, p2;
if ( p1 == p2 )
    cout << "Those points are equal." << endl;
```

Unfortunately, the == operator cannot be used with a new class—unless you define a binary function that tells exactly what == means. In fact, C++ lets you define the meaning of many operators for a new class. Defining a new meaning for an operator is called **overloading** the operator. We'll look at several common overloading examples.

Overloading Binary Comparison Operators

The == operator that "compares for equality" can be overloaded for any new class by defining a function with a rather peculiar name. The name of the new function is "*operator* ==" as shown in this example:

```
bool operator == (const Point& p1, const Point& p2)
// Postcondition: The value returned is true if p1 and p2
// are identical; otherwise false is returned.
{
    return
        (p1.get_x( ) == p2.get_x( ))
        &&
        (p1.get_y( ) == p2.get_y( ));
}
```

In order for this function to return true, both parts of the && expression must be true—in other words, both *x* and *y* coordinates of p1 must be equal to the corresponding coordinate in p2.

operator ==

Apart from the peculiar name, "*operator* ==", the function is just like any other function. It returns a boolean value that can be used as a true-or-false value, such as in an if-statement:

```
if (p1 == p2)...
```

The overloaded operator is used in a program just like any other use of ==, by putting the first argument before == and the second argument after ==.

usual usages of == are still available

When you overload an operator, the usual usages of that operator are still available. For example, we can still use == to test the equality of two integers or two doubles. In fact, in the body of our *operator* ==, we *do* use the ordinary == to compare the doubles p1.get_x( ) and p2.get_x( ). This is fine. For each use of ==, the compiler determines the data type of the objects being compared and uses the appropriate comparison function.

Once you have overloaded one operator, you can sometimes use the overloaded operator to make an easy implementation of another operator. For example, suppose we have defined *operator* == for the Point class. Then we can quickly overload != to be the "not equal" operator:

operator !=

```
bool operator !=(const Point& p1, const Point& p2)
// Postcondition: The value returned is true if p1 and p2
// are not identical; otherwise false is returned.
{
    return !(p1 == p2) ;
}
```

The expression `!(p1 == p2)` deserves some examination. The == operator that we use is the overloaded == that we just defined for points. It returns true if the two points are equal, and false otherwise. We take the result of `(p1 == p2)` and "reverse it" with the usual "not" operator "`!`". So, if `(p1 == p2)` is true, then `!(p1 == p2)` is false, and the `!=` function returns false. On the other hand, if `(p1 == p2)` is false, then `!(p1 == p2)` is true, and the `!=` function returns true.

The *operator* == and *operator* `!=` functions can also be defined as member functions rather than existing on their own. In this case, the p1 in an expression `(p1 == p2)` is the object that actually activates the member function, and the p2 is a parameter. In fact, p2 will be the *only* parameter if we implement == as a member

> **FIGURE 2.14**
>
> Binary Operators that are Often Overloaded as Comparison Functions
>
> | | |
> |---|---|
> | == | != |
> | < | > |
> | <= | >= |

function (since the object that activates a member function is never actually listed in the parameter list). The choice between member function and non-member function is partly an issue of programming style. We prefer the use of the nonmember function since a nonmember function places the two arguments (p1 and p2) on equal footing. There really is no reason to say that p1 activates the operator any more than p2 does. (Later, you will find that non-member functions also provide more flexibility for classes with a feature called "conversions.")

Figure 2.14 shows the six binary operators from C++ that are often overloaded as binary comparison operators for new classes.

other binary comparison operators

Overloading Binary Arithmetic Operators

In addition to the comparison operators, most of the other binary operators of C++ also can be overloaded for a new class. For example, the operators +, -, *, and /, which we normally think of as "arithmetic" operators, can all be overloaded for a new class. As a natural example, physicists often use points as objects that can be "added" by adding their *x* and *y* coordinates. If we could "add" two of our points, then we might write this program:

```
   type   name
Point speed1(5, 7);
Point speed2(1, 2);
Point total;

total = speed1 + speed2;       sets total to
                               the sum of speed1
                               and speed2
cout << total.get_x( ) << endl;  ← prints 6
cout << total.get_y( ) << endl;  ← prints 9
```

In fact, we can define the meaning of + for points by overloading the + operator. The overloaded operator has two parameters, which are the two points being added. And the function returns the sum of these two points, as shown here:

operator +

```
Point operator +(const Point& p1, const Point& p2)
// Postcondition: The sum of p1 and p2 is returned.
{
    double x_sum, y_sum;

    // Compute the x and y of the sum.
    x_sum = (p1.get_x( ) + p2.get_x( ));
    y_sum = (p1.get_y( ) + p2.get_y( ));
    Point sum(x_sum, y_sum);
    return sum;
}
```

As with the binary comparison operators, a binary arithmetic operator can also be defined as a member function rather than a function that stands on its own. The member function would have just one parameter, which is the right-hand argument in an expression such as (p1 + p2). The left-hand argument is the object that activates the member function. Our programming style prefers implementing the binary operators as nonmember functions.

other arithmetic operators

Figure 2.15 shows the five binary operators from C++ that are most often overloaded to perform arithmetic operations.

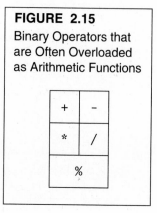

FIGURE 2.15

Binary Operators that are Often Overloaded as Arithmetic Functions

+	-
*	/
%	

Overloading Output and Input Operators

The standard C++ data types can be written and read using the output operator "<<" and the input operator ">>". For example, we can read and write an integer:

```
int i;
cin >> i;      ← reads the value of i from the
                 standard input
cout << i;     ← writes the value of i to
                 the standard output
```

No doubt you would like to do the same with your impressive new Point class:

```
Point p;
cin >> p;      ← reads the x and y coordinates
                 of p from the standard input
cout << p;     ← writes the x and y coordinates
                 of p to the standard output
```

You can provide input/output power to the Point class by overloading the "<<" and ">>" operators. We start by overloading the output operator, which has the mysterious prototype shown here:

[handwritten annotations: "reference return type", "output stream", "type reference", "constant reference"]

```
ostream& operator <<(ostream& outs, const Point& source);
```

Let's demystify this problematic prototype. The function has two parameters: outs (which is an ostream) and source (which is a Point). We use the function by listing the two arguments like this:

The first argument, cout, is an ostream. → *[handwritten: iostream.h]*

```
cout << p;
```
The second argument, p, is a Point

As shown, the data type of cout is ostream, which means "output stream." The ostream class is part of the iostream.h library facility. The facility also defines cout (the **console output device** or "standard output") and provides the ability for programmers to define other output streams (such as output streams connected to a disk file or a printer). In any case, our intention is for the << function to print the Point named source to the ostream named outs. We can now write most of our postcondition:

```
ostream& operator <<(ostream& outs, const Point& source);
// Postcondition: The x and y coordinates of source have been
// written to outs.
```

The outs parameter is a reference parameter, meaning that the function can change the output stream (by writing to it), and the change will affect the actual argument (such as the standard output stream, cout). The source parameter is a constant reference parameter, meaning that the function will not alter the point that it is writing.

One last mystery remains: The return type of the function is ostream&:

```
ostream& operator <<(ostream& outs, const Point& source);
```

For the most part, this return type means that the function returns an ostream. In fact, the function returns the ostream that it has just written to. There is additional meaning of the & symbol (called a **reference return type**). But we won't use that additional meaning in this text, so it is enough to know that the output and input operators both require a reference return type.

With this in mind, we can now write the complete postcondition:

```
ostream& operator <<(ostream& outs, const Point& source);
// Postcondition: The x and y coordinates of source have been
// written to outs. The return value is the ostream outs.
```

The reason that the function returns an ostream is that C++ will then permit the "chaining" of output statements such as the following:

```
cout << "The points are " << p << " and " << q << endl;
```

This example calls five << functions, with each function changing the ostream and passing the result on to the next function call.

ostream
operator <<

The complete implementation of the point's output operator is shown at the top of Figure 2.16. Most of the work is done in the statement:

```
outs << source.get_x( ) << " " << source.get_y( );
```

The statement uses the ordinary << operator to print the coordinates of the point, with a single blank character in between.

The prototype for the point's input function is similar to the output function, but it uses an istream (input stream) instead of an ostream, as shown here:

```
istream& operator >>(istream& ins, Point& target);
// Postcondition: The x and y coordinates of target have been
// read from ins. The return value is the istream ins.
```

istream
operator >>

The implementation of the input function is shown at the bottom of Figure 2.16. The key work is accomplished with the usual >> operator reading two double numbers in the statement shown here:

```
ins >> target.x >> target.y;
```

But hold on! The statement sends input directly to the *private* member variables

---

FIGURE 2.16	Output and Input Operations for the Point

Function Implementations

```
ostream& operator <<(ostream& outs, const Point& source)
// Postcondition: The x and y coordinates of source have been
// written to outs. The return value is the ostream outs.
// Library facilities used: iostream.h
{
    outs << source.get_x( ) << " " << source.get_y( );
    return outs;
}
```

This prints the Point's coordinates with a blank in between.

```
istream& operator >>(istream& ins, Point& target)
// Postcondition: The x and y coordinates of target have been
// read from ins. The return value is the istream ins.
// Library facilities used: iostream.h
// Friend of: Point class
{
    ins >> target.x >> target.y;
    return ins;
}
```

This function must be a friend function since it requires direct access to the private members of the Point class.

newpoint.cxx   **FTP**

x and y of the point. Only *member* functions can access private member variables, and the input function is not a point member function. There are two possible solutions to the problem:

1. We could write new member functions to set a point's coordinates and use these member functions within the input function's implementation.
2. Because we are the implementor of the `Point` class, and we are also writing the input function ourselves, we can grant special permission for the input function to access the private members of the `Point` class.

The second approach is called using a *friend function*, which we'll explain now.

Friend Functions

A **friend function** is a function that is *not* a member function, but that still has access to the private members of its parameters. In order to declare a friend function, the function's prototype is placed in a class definition, preceded by the keyword `friend`.

friend functions can access private members

For example, to declare the point's input function as a friend, we must insert the friend prototype in the class definition, as shown here:

```
class Point
{
public:                        The Point class with a new friend
    ...
    // FRIEND FUNCTIONS
    friend istream& operator >>(istream& ins, Point& target);
private:
    ...
};
```

Once the friend prototype has been placed in the class definition, the body of the function may access private members of its point parameter, as shown here:

```
istream& operator >>(istream& ins, Point& target)
// Postcondition: The x and y coordinates of target have been
// read from ins. The return value is the istream ins.
// Library facilities used: iostream.h
// Friend of: Point class
{
    ins >> target.x >> target.y;
    return ins;
}
```

Notice that a friend function is not a member function, so it is not activated by a particular object of a class. All of the information that the friend function manipulates must be present in its parameters. It would be illegal to simply write *x* or *y* in the body of our function; we must write `target.x` and `target.y`. In our case, the *friend operator* `>>` has one point parameter, and it is the private member variables of this parameter that the function may access.

friendship and information hiding

Friendship may be provided to any function, not just to operator functions. But friendship should be limited to functions that are written by the programmer who implements the class—after all, this programmer is the only one who really knows about the private members. In this way, information hiding about a new class remains intact.

Friend Functions

A **friend function** is a function that is not a member function, but that still needs access to private members of some of its parameters. In order to declare a friend function, the function's prototype is placed in a class definition, preceded by the keyword *friend*.

Friendship should be limited to functions that are written by the programmer who implements the class

---

 TIP

Programming Tip: When to Use a Friend Function

When you are implementing a class, you often implement additional functions to manipulate objects of the class. If a function needs access to private members of the class, then you should first consider providing the access via a member function. However, if a member function is inconvenient or unacceptable for other reasons, then you may grant friendship to a function, giving it access to the class's private members.

The Point Class—Putting Things Together

We have defined quite a few new functions to manipulate points. In all, we now have:

- The constructor
- The two original modification functions (`shift` and `rotate90`), and the two original constant functions (`get_x` and `get_y`)
- Overloaded comparison operators `==` and `!=`
- Overloaded arithmetic operator `+` to add two points
- Overloaded output and input operators
- Functions `middle`, `rotations_needed`, `rotate_to_upper_right`, and `distance` from Section 2.4

We could continue with more point functions, but there is a definite danger of never finishing Chapter 2. So we'll stop here, collecting most of the items into a new, improved point ADT. The header file for the new ADT is `newpoint.h`, shown in Figure 2.17. The implementation should go in a separate file named `newpoint.cxx`. What should be present in `newpoint.cxx`? (See Self-Test Exercise 22.)

When you provide functions or operators to manipulate a class, you should follow these lists for good information hiding:

In the Header File:

- Documentation, including a precondition/postcondition contract for each function
- Class definitions for any new classes
- Prototypes for any other functions that are neither member functions nor friend functions

In the Implementation File:

- An include directive to include the header file
- Implementations for each member function (except for the inline functions)
- Implementations for each friend function and other functions that are not member functions

Summary of Operator Overloading

We have mentioned more than a dozen C++ operators that may be overloaded for your own classes. In all, there are 44 such operators, although we shall only use the ones you have seen in this chapter plus two assignment operators that you'll meet in the next two chapters.

Programming style varies widely for overloading operators. The eventual style you adopt should be clear and consistent. Our own guidelines for operator overloading within this book are listed in Figure 2.18 on page 80.

Self-Test Exercises

18. Overload the < operator for the throttle. The function should return true if the flow of the first throttle is less than the flow of the second.

19. Overload the – operator for the point, as a binary arithmetic operator.

20. Why should friend functions be written only by the programmer who implements a class?

21. Overload the output operator for the throttle so that it prints 100 times the current flow, followed by a % sign.

22. What should be present in the implementation file `newpoint.cxx`?

FIGURE 2.17	Header File for the New Point Class

A Header File

```
//  FILE: newpoint.h (revised from point.h in Figure 2.9 on page 59)
//  CLASS PROVIDED: Point (an ADT for a point on a two-dimensional plane)
//
//  CONSTRUCTOR for the Point class:
//     Point(double initial_x = 0, double initial_y = 0)
//        Postcondition: The Point has been set to (initial_x, initial_y).
//
//  MODIFICATION MEMBER FUNCTIONS for the Point class:
//     void shift(double x_amount, double y_amount)
//        Postcondition: The Point has been moved by x_amount along the x axis
//        and by y_amount along the y axis.
//
//     void rotate90( )
//        Postcondition: The Point has been rotated clockwise 90 degrees.
//
//  CONSTANT MEMBER FUNCTIONS for the Point class:
//     double get_x( ) const
//        Postcondition: The value returned is the x coordinate of the Point.
//
//     double get_y( ) const
//        Postcondition: The value returned is the y coordinate of the Point.
//
//  NONMEMBER FUNCTIONS for the Point class:
//     double distance(const Point& p1, const Point& p2)
//        Postcondition: The value returned is the distance between p1 and p2.
//
//     Point middle(const Point& p1, const Point& p2)
//        Postcondition: The Point returned is halfway between p1 and p2.
//
//     Point operator +(const Point& p1, const Point& p2)
//        Postcondition: The sum of p1 and p2 is returned.
//
//     bool operator ==(const Point& p1, const Point& p2)
//        Postcondition: The return value is true if p1 and p2 are identical.
//
//     bool operator !=(const Point& p1, const Point& p2)
//        Postcondition: The return value is true if p1 and p2 are not identical.
//
```

(continued)

(FIGURE 2.17 continued)

```
//      ostream& operator <<(ostream& outs, const Point& source)
//          Postcondition: The x and y coordinates of source have been
//          written to outs. The return value is the ostream outs.
//
//      istream& operator >>(istream& ins, Point& target)
//          Postcondition: The x and y coordinates of target have been
//          read from ins. The return value is the istream ins.
//
// VALUE SEMANTICS for the Point class:
//      Assignments and the copy constructor may be used with Point objects.

#ifndef NEWPOINT_H
#define NEWPOINT_H
#include <iostream.h> // Provides ostream and istream

    class Point
    {
    public:
        // CONSTRUCTOR
        Point(double initial_x = 0, double initial_y = 0);
        // MODIFICATION MEMBER FUNCTIONS
        void shift(double x_amount, double y_amount);
        void rotate90( );
        // CONSTANT MEMBER FUNCTIONS
        double get_x( ) const { return x; }
        double get_y( ) const { return y; }          ⟵ prototype for a friend function
        // FRIEND FUNCTION
        friend istream& operator >>(istream& ins, Point& target);
    private:
        double x, y; // x and y coordinates of this Point
    };

    // NONMEMBER FUNCTIONS for the Point class
    double distance(const Point& p1, const Point& p2);              prototypes
    Point middle(const Point& p1, const Point& p2);                 for
    Point operator +(const Point& p1, const Point& p2);            nonmember
    bool operator ==(const Point& p1, const Point& p2);            functions
    bool operator !=(const Point& p1, const Point& p2);
    ostream& operator <<(ostream & outs, const Point& source);

#endif
```

newpoint.h **FTP**

FIGURE 2.18 Guidelines for Operator Overloading

Binary comparison operators `== != <= >= < >`	Overload as a nonmember function with two parameters, returning a boolean value	See point example on page 70
Binary arithmetic operators `+ - * / %`	Overload as a nonmember function with two parameters	See point example on page 71
Input and output `>> <<`	Overload as a nonmember function, returning an istream or ostream	See point example on page 72
Auxiliary assignment operators `+= -=` etc.	When the + operator is overloaded, then we will usually also overload `+=` as a member function so that x `+=` y has the same effect as x `=` x `+` y	See bag example on page 92
Assignment operator `=`	Must be overloaded as a member function if we want x `=` y to do more than copy member variables from the object y to the object x	See bag example on page 170

CHAPTER SUMMARY

- Object-oriented programming (OOP) supports information hiding by placing data in packages called *objects*, which are implemented via *classes* in C++. Objects are manipulated through functions called *member functions*, which are defined along with their classes.

- A new data type, together with the functions to manipulate the type is called an *abstract data type* or *ADT*. The term abstract refers to the fact that we emphasize the abstract specification of *what* has been provided, disassociated from any actual implementation.

- *Private member variables* support ADTs by forbidding data components of a class to be accessed outside of the class's member functions. If the implementor of a new class needs other functions to have access to the member variables, then the other functions may be declared as *friend* functions.

- A *constructor* is a member function that is automatically called to initialize a variable when the variable is declared. Defining constructors increases the reliability of your classes by reducing the chance of using an uninitialized variable.

- Place the documentation and class definition for a new class in a separate *header file*. Place the implementations of the member functions in a separate *implementation file*.

- C++ provides three common kinds of parameters: With a *value parameter*, the argument only provides the initial value for the formal parameter. With a *reference parameter*, any use of the parameter within the body of the function will access the argument from the calling program. A *const reference parameter* has the efficiency of an ordinary reference parameter, but there is a guarantee that the argument will not be changed by the function.

- C++ permits you to define the meaning of *operators* such as + and == for your new classes.

Solutions to Self-Test Exercises ?

1. The *private* members.

2. The scope resolution operator is used at the head of each member function implementation. See the example use of the scope resolution operator on page 39.

3. The program should include the following statements:
```
Throttle exercise;
exercise.shut_off( );
exercise.shift(3);
cout << exercise.flow( ) << endl;
```

4. The statement ends a main program and tells the operating system that the program ended normally.

5. The prototype for the new member function is placed in the class definition. The function implementation is:
```
bool Throttle::is_above_half( ) const
// Precondition: shut_off has been called at
// least once to initialize the Throttle.
// Postcondition: The return value is true if
// the current flow is above 0.5.
{
    return (flow( ) > 0.5);
}
```

6. In the public section of the class definition:
```
bool is_above_half( ) const
    { return (flow( ) > 0.5); }
```

7. The prototype for the new constructor is placed in the class definition. The constructor implementation is:

```
Throttle::Throttle
(int size, int initial)
// Precondition: (0 < size) and
// (0 <= initial <= size).
// Postcondition: The Throttle has size
// positions above the shutoff position, and
// it is currently in the position given by the
// parameter initial.
// Libraries used: assert.h
{
    assert(size > 0);
    assert(initial >= 0);
    assert(initial <= size);
    top_position = size;
    position = initial;
}
```

8. All the information needed to use the class is in the comment at the front of the header file.

9. The automatic assignment operator will copy the member variables of x to y.

10. The automatic copy constructor will initialize y as a copy of x (by copying the member variables).

11. #include "throttle.h"

12. Hint: Keep track of the current angle in a private member variable. If the variable goes below zero, or becomes >= 360, then readjust it so that it lies between 0 and 360.

13. You'll find part of a solution in Figure 14.1 on page 621.

14. const int UNIVERSE = 42;
After this, an attempt to assign a new value to UNIVERSE will cause a compiler error.

15. Change the constructor's prototype to this:
Throttle(int size = 1, int initial = 0)
The other two constructors are no longer needed.

16. rotate_to_upper_right can change p because the parameter is a reference parameter. But the call to rotations_needed cannot change p because it uses a value parameter.

17. x should be a value parameter if you want the actual argument to remain unchanged. It should be a reference parameter if you want changes to x to affect the actual argument. It can never be a const reference parameter because the function's body alters the parameter.

18. Here is the implementation:

```
int operator < (
    const Throttle& t1,
    const Throttle& t2
)
// Postcondition: The return value is true if
// the flow of t1 is less than the flow of t2.
{
    return (t1.flow( ) < t2.flow( ));
}
```

19. The solution is the same as the + operator on page 72, but replace each plus sign with a minus.

20. This advice supports information hiding, because the programmer who implements the class is the only one who knows about the private members.

21. Here is the implementation (you fill in the postcondition):

```
ostream& operator << (
    ostream& outs,
    const Throttle& source
)
{
    outs << 100*source.flow( ) << '%';
    return outs;
}
```

22. The top of newpoint.cxx contains a short comment indicating that the documentation for how to use the Point class is in the header file. The function implementations appear after the comment, including all the functions listed in Figure 2.17 on page 78, except for get_x and get_y (which are inline functions).

1 Specify, design, and implement a class that can be used in a program that simulates a combination lock. The lock has a circular knob, with the numbers 0 through 39 marked on the edge, and it has a three-number combination, which we'll call *x, y, z*. To open the lock, you must turn the knob clockwise at least one entire revolution, stopping with *x* at the top; then turn the knob counterclockwise, stopping the *second* time that *y* appears at the top; finally turn the knob clockwise again, stopping the next time that *z* appears at the top. At this point, you may open the lock.

Your Lock class should have a constructor that initializes the three-number combination (use 0, 0, 0 for default arguments). Also provide member functions:

    (a) to alter the lock's combination to a new three-number combination

    (b) to turn the knob in a given direction until a specified number appears at the top

    (c) to close the lock

    (d) to attempt to open the lock

    (e) to inquire the status of the lock (open or shut)

    (f) to tell you what number is currently at the top

2 Specify, design, and implement a class called Statistician. After a statistician is initialized, it can be given a sequence of double numbers. Each number in the sequence is given to the statistician by activating a member function called next_number. For example, we can declare a statistician called s, and then give it the sequence of numbers 1.1, –2.4, 0.8 as shown here:

```
Statistician s;
s.next_number(1.1);
s.next_number(-2.4);
s.next_number(0.8);
```

After a sequence has been given to a statistician, there are various member functions to obtain information about the sequence. Include member functions that will provide the length of the sequence, the last number of the sequence, the sum of all the numbers in the sequence, the arithmetic mean of the numbers (i.e., the sum of the numbers divided by the length of the sequence), the smallest number in the sequence, and the largest number in the sequence. Notice that the length and sum functions can be called at any time, even if there are no numbers in the sequence. In this case of an "empty" sequence, both length and sum will be zero. But the other member functions all have a precondition requiring that the sequence is non-empty.

You should also provide a member function that erases the sequence (so that the statistician can start afresh with a new sequence).

Notes: Do not try to store the entire sequence (because you don't know how long this sequence will be). Instead, just store the necessary information about the sequence: What is the sequence length, what is the sum of the numbers in the sequence, what are the last, smallest, and largest numbers? Each of these pieces of information can be stored in a private member variable that is updated whenever next_number is activated.

3 Overload the + operator to allow you to "add" two statisticians from the previous project. If s1 and s2 are two statisticians, then the result of s1 + s2 should be a new statistician that behaves as if it had all of the numbers of s1 followed by all of the numbers of s2.

4 Specify, design, and implement a class for a card in a deck of playing cards. The object should contain methods for setting and retrieving the suit and rank of a card.

5 Specify, design, and implement a class that can be used to keep track of the position of a point in *three*-dimensional space. For example, consider the point drawn here:

The point shown above has three coordinates: $x = 2.5$, $y = 0$, and $z = 2.0$. Include member functions to set a point to a specified location, to shift a point a given amount along one of the axes, and to retrieve the coordinates of a point. Also provide member functions that will rotate the point by a specified angle around a specified axis.

To compute these rotations, you will need a bit of trigonometry. Suppose you have a point with coordinates x, y, and z. After rotating this point by an angle θ, the point will have new coordinates, which we'll call x', y', and z'. The equations for the new coordinates use the math.h library functions sin and cos, as shown here:

After a θ rotation around the x-axis:

$$x' = x$$
$$y' = y \cos(\theta) - z \sin(\theta)$$
$$z' = y \sin(\theta) + z \cos(\theta)$$

After a θ rotation around the y-axis:

$$x' = x \cos(\theta) + z \sin(\theta)$$
$$y' = y$$
$$z' = -x \sin(\theta) + z \cos(\theta)$$

After a θ rotation around the z-axis:

$$x' = x \cos(\theta) - y \sin(\theta)$$
$$y' = x \sin(\theta) + y \cos(\theta)$$
$$z' = z$$

6 In three-dimensional space, a line segment is defined by its two endpoints. Specify, design, and implement a class for a line segment. The class should have two private member variables that are points from the previous project.

7 Specify, design, and implement a class that can be used to hold information about a musical note. A programmer should be able to set and retrieve the length of the note and the value of the note. The length of a note may be a sixteenth note, eighth note, quarter note, half note, or whole note. A value is specified by indicating how far the note lies above or below the A note that orchestras use in tuning. In counting "how far," you should include both the white and black notes on a piano. For example, the note numbers for the octave beginning at middle C are shown here:

Note numbers for the octave of middle C

The default constructor should set a note to a middle C quarter note. Include member functions to set a note to a specified length and value. Write member functions to retrieve information about a note, including functions to tell you the letter of the note (A, B, C, etc.), whether the note is natural or sharp (i.e., white or black on the piano), and the frequency of a note in hertz. To calculate the frequency, use the formula $440 \times 2^{n/12}$, where n is the note number. Feel free to include other useful member functions.

8 A one-variable **quadratic expression** is an arithmetic expression of the form $ax^2 + bx + c$, where *a, b,* and *c* are some fixed numbers (called the **coefficients**) and *x* is a variable that can take on different values. Specify, design, and implement a class that can store information about a quadratic expression. The default constructor should set all three coefficients to zero, and another member function should allow you to change these coefficients. There should be constant member functions to retrieve the current values of the coefficients. There should also be a member function to allow you to "evaluate" the quadratic expression at a particular value of *x* (i.e., the function has one parameter *x*, and returns the value of the expression $ax^2 + bx + c$).

Also overload the following operators (as nonmember functions) to perform these indicated operations:

```
Quadratic operator +(
    const Quadratic& q1,
    const Quadratic& q2
);
// Postcondition: The return value is the
// quadratic expression obtained by adding
// q1 and q2. For example, the c coefficient
// of the return value is the sum of q1's c
// coefficient and q2's c coefficient.

Quadratic operator *(
    double r,
    const Quadratic& q
);
// Postcondition: The return value is the
// quadratic expression obtained by
// multiplying each of q's
// coefficients by the number r.
```

Notice that the left argument of the overloaded *operator* * is a double number (rather than a quadratic expression). This allows expressions such as 3.14 * q, where q is a quadratic expression.

9 This project is a continuation of the previous project. For a quadratic expression such as $ax^2 + bx + c$, a **real root** is any double number *x* such that $ax^2 + bx + c = 0$. For example, the quadratic expression $2x^2 + 8x + 6$ has one of its real roots at $x = -3$, because substituting $x = -3$ in the formula $2x^2 + 8x + 6$ yields the value:

$$2 \times (-3^2) + 8 \times (-3) + 6 = 0$$

There are six rules for finding the real roots of a quadratic expression:

(1) If *a, b,* and *c* are all zero, then every value of *x* is a real root.

(2) If *a* and *b* are zero, but *c* is nonzero, then there are no real roots.

(3) If *a* is zero, and *b* is nonzero, then the only real root is $x = -c/b$.

(4) If *a* is nonzero and $b^2 < 4ac$, then there are no real roots.

(5) If *a* is nonzero and $b^2 = 4ac$, then there is one real root $x = -b/2a$.

(6) If *a* is nonzero, and $b^2 > 4ac$, then there are two real roots:

$$x = \frac{-b - \sqrt{b^2 - 4ac}}{2a}$$

$$x = \frac{-b + \sqrt{b^2 - 4ac}}{2a}$$

Write a new member function that returns the number of real roots of a quadratic expression. This answer could be 0, or 1, or 2, or infinity. In the case of an infinite number of real roots, have the member function return 3. (Yes, we know that 3 is not infinity, but for this purpose it is close enough!) Write two other member functions that calculate and return the real roots of a quadratic expression. The precondition for both functions is that the expression has at least one real root. If there are two real roots, then one of the functions returns the smaller of the two roots, and the other function returns the larger of the two roots. If every value of *x* is a real root, then both functions should return zero.

10 Specify, design, and implement a class that can be used to simulate a lunar lander, which is a small spaceship that transports astronauts from lunar orbit to the surface of the moon. When a lunar lander is constructed, the following items should be specified, with default values as indicated:

(1) Current fuel flow rate as a fraction of the maximum fuel flow (default zero)

(2) Vertical speed of the lander (default zero meters/sec)

(3) Altitude of the lander (default 1000 meters)

(4) Amount of fuel (default 1700 kg)

(5) Mass of the lander when it has no fuel (default 900 kg)

(6) Maximum fuel consumption rate (default 10 kg/sec)

(7) Maximum thrust of the lander's engine (default 5000 newtons)

Don't worry about other properties (such as horizontal speed).

The lander has constant member functions that allow a program to retrieve the current values of any of the seven items listed above. There are only two modification member functions, described below.

The first modification function changes the current fuel flow rate to a new value ranging from 0.0 to 1.0. This value is expressed as a fraction of the maximum fuel flow.

The second modification function simulates the passage of a small amount of time. This time, called t, is expressed in seconds and will typically be a small value such as 0.1 seconds. The function will update the first four values in the above list, to reflect the passage of t seconds. To implement this function, you will require a few physics formulas listed below. These formulas are only approximate, because some of the lander's values are changing during the simulated time period. But if the time span is kept short, these formulas will suffice.

Fuel flow rate: Normally, the fuel flow rate does not change during the passage of a small amount of time. But there is one exception: If the fuel flow rate is greater than zero, and the amount of fuel left is zero, then you should reset the fuel flow rate to zero (because there is no fuel to flow).

Velocity change: During t seconds, the velocity of the lander changes by approximately this amount (measured in meters/sec):

$$t \times \left(\frac{f}{m} - 1.62 \right)$$

The value m is the total mass of the lander, measured in kilograms (i.e., the mass of a lander with no fuel, plus the mass of any remaining fuel). The value f is the thrust of the lander's engine, measured in newtons. You can calculate f as the current fuel flow rate times the maximum thrust of the lander. The number -1.62 is the downward acceleration from gravity on the moon.

Altitude change: During t seconds, the altitude of the lander changes by $t \times v$ meters, where v is the vertical velocity of the lander (measured in meters/sec, with negative values downward).

Change in remaining fuel: During t seconds, the amount of remaining fuel is reduced by $t \times r \times c$ kilograms. The value of r is the current fuel flow rate, and c is the maximum fuel consumption (measured in kilograms per second).

We suggest that you calculate the changes to the four items in the order listed above. After all the changes have been made, there are two further adjustments. First, if the altitude has dropped below zero, then reset both altitude and velocity to zero (indicating that the ship has landed). Second, if the total amount of remaining fuel drops below zero, then reset this amount to zero (indicating that we have run out of fuel).

11 In this project you will design and implement a class that can generate a sequence of **pseudorandom** integers, which is a sequence that appears random in many ways. The approach uses the **linear congruence method**, explained below.

The linear congruence method starts with a number called the **seed**. In addition to the seed, three other numbers are used in the linear congruence method, called the **multiplier**, the **increment**, and the **modulus**. The formula for generating a sequence of pseudorandom numbers is quite simple. The first number is:

```
(multiplier * seed + increment) % modulus
```

This formula uses the C++ % operator, which computes the remainder from an integer division.

Each time a new random number is computed, the value of the seed is changed to that new number. For example, we could implement a pseudorandom number generator with `multiplier = 40`, `increment = 3641`, and `modulus = 729`. If we choose the seed to be 1, then the sequence of numbers will proceed as shown here:

First number
= (multiplier * seed + increment) % modulus
= (40 * 1 + 3641) % 729
= 36
and 36 becomes the new seed.

Next number
= (multiplier * seed + increment) % modulus
= (40 * 36 + 3641) % 729
= 707
and 707 becomes the new seed.

Next number
= (multiplier * seed + increment) % modulus
= (40 * 707 + 3641) % 729
= 574
and 574 becomes the new seed, and so on.

These particular values for multiplier, increment, and modulus happen to be good choices. The pattern generated will not repeat until 729 different numbers have been produced. Other choices for the constants might not be so good.

For this project, design and implement a class that can generate a pseudorandom sequence in the manner described. The initial seed, multiplier, increment, and modulus should all be parameters of the constructor. There should also be a member function to permit the seed to be changed, and a member function to generate and return the next number in the pseudorandom sequence.

12 Add a new member function to the random number class of the previous project. The new member function generates the next pseudorandom number but does not return the number directly. Instead, the function returns this number divided by the modulus. (You will have to cast the modulus to a double number before carrying out the division; otherwise, the division will be an integer division, throwing away the remainder).

The return value from this new member function is a pseudorandom double number in the range [0..1). (The square bracket, '[', indicates that the range does include 0, but the rounded parenthesis, ')', indicates that the ranges goes up to 1, without actually including 1.)

13 Run some experiments to determine the distribution of numbers returned by the new pseudorandom function from the previous project. Recall that this function returns a *double* number in the range [0..1). Divide this range into ten intervals, and call the function one million times, producing a table such as this:

Range	Number of Occurrences
[0.0..0.1)	99889
[0.1..0.2)	100309
[0.2..0.3)	100070
[0.3..0.4)	99940
[0.4..0.5)	99584
[0.5..0.6)	100028
[0.6..0.7)	99669
[0.7..0.8)	100100
[0.8..0.9)	100107
[0.9..1.0)	100304

Run your experiment for different values of the multiplier, increment, and modulus. With good choices of the constants, you will end up with about 10% of the numbers in each interval. A pseudorandom number generator with this equal-interval behavior is called **uniformly distributed.**

14 This project is a continuation of the previous project. Many applications require pseudorandom number sequences that are *not* uniformly distributed. For example, a program that simulates the birth of babies can use random numbers for the birth weights of the newborns. But these birth weights should have a **Gaussian distribution.** In a Gaussian distribution, numbers are more likely to fall in intervals near the center of the overall distribution. The exact probabilities of falling in a particular interval can be computed from knowing two numbers: (1) the center of the overall distribution (called the *median*), and (2) a number called the *variance*, which indicates how widely spread the distribution appears.

Generating a pseudorandom number sequence with an exact Gaussian distribution can be difficult, but there is a good way to approximate a Gaussian distribution using uniformly distributed random numbers in the range [0..1]. The approach is to generate three pseudorandom numbers r_1, r_2, and r_3, each of which is in the range [0..1]. These numbers are then combined to produce the next number in the Gaussian sequence. The formula to combine the numbers is:

Next number in the Gaussian sequence

$$= \text{median} + (2 \times (r_1 + r_2 + r_3) - 3) \times \text{variance}$$

Add a new member function to the random number class, which can be used to produce a sequence of pseudorandom numbers with a Gaussian distribution.

3 Container Classes

(I am large. I contain multitudes.)

WALT WHITMAN
Song of Myself

The throttle and point classes in Chapter 2 are good examples of abstract data types. But their applicability is limited to a few specialized programs. This chapter begins the presentation of several ADTs with broad applicability in programs large and small. The two particular ADTs in this chapter—bags and lists—are simple, but they provide the basis for more complex ADTs provided with many commercially available compilers.

an ADT in which each object contains a collection of items

Both of the ADTs in this chapter are examples of **container classes**. Intuitively, a container class is a class where each object contains a collection of items. For example, one program might keep track of a collection of integers, perhaps the ages of all the people in your family. Another program, perhaps a cryptography program, can use a collection of characters.

A key feature of a good container class is that it should be easy to change the type of item in the container so that a new application can use the container. With this kind of "easy reuse," many different applications can use the same container class. The same container class can be used by one program for a collection of

easy reuse of the container

integers, and by another program for a collection of characters or some other data type. In this chapter we use **typedef statements** to provide the ability to easily change the type of item in a container class. In Chapter 6, which focuses explicitly on software reusability, we'll use a more sophisticated technique called **templates** to achieve easily changed items.

3.1   THE BAG ADT

This section provides an example of a container class, called a *bag of integers*. To define the new bag data type, think about an actual bag—a grocery bag or a garbage bag—and imagine writing integers on slips of paper and putting them in the bag. A **bag of integers** is similar to this imaginary bag: a container that can hold a collection of integers that we place into it. A bag of integers can be used by any program that needs to store a collection of integers for later use. For example, later we will write a program that keeps track of the ages of your family's members. If you have a large family with ten people, the program keeps track of ten ages—and these ages are kept in a bag of integers.

The Bag ADT—Specification

We've given an intuitive description of a bag of integers, but for a more precise specification of the Bag class, we must describe the collection of functions to manipulate a Bag object. We'll do this by providing a prototype for each of the functions, most of which are member functions. With each prototype we also specify the precise action that the function will perform. These specifications will later become our precondition/postcondition contracts. Let's look at the functions one at a time.

The constructor.   The Bag class has a default constructor to initialize a bag so that it is empty. The name of the constructor must be the same as the name of the class itself, so the prototype for our constructor is the following:

```
Bag( );
```

The insert member function.   This is a member function that places a new integer, called entry, into a bag. Here is the prototype:

```
void insert(int entry);
```

As an example, here is a sequence of function calls for a bag called first_bag:

```
Bag first_bag;
first_bag.insert(8);
first_bag.insert(4);            After these statements, first_bag
first_bag.insert(8);            contains two 8's and a 4.
```

After the above statements are executed, `first_bag` contains three integers: the number 4 and two copies of the number 8. It is important to realize that a bag can contain many copies of the same integer, such as this example which has two copies of 8.

The value semantics. As part of our specification, we require that bag objects can be copied with an assignment statement. Also, a newly declared bag can be initialized as a copy of another bag, using the copy constructor such as:

```
Bag b;
b.insert(42);
Bag c(b);
```

b now contains a 42.

c is initialized with the copy constructor to be a copy of b.

At this point, because we are only specifying which operations can manipulate a bag, we don't need to say anything more about the value semantics.

The size member function. This constant member function returns the total number of integers in a bag. The return value from this function is a data type called `size_t`, which might be new to you. Here is a description of the type:

C++ Feature: The `size_t` Data Type

FEATURE ++

The data type `size_t` is an integer data type that can hold only non-negative numbers. Each C++ implementation guarantees that the values of the `size_t` type are sufficient to hold the size of any variable that can be declared on your machine. Therefore, when you want to describe the size of some array or other variable, the best choice is the `size_t` data type, which you can think of as the "size type." The `size_t` type is part of the standard library facility, `stdlib.h`.

The return value for the bag's `size` member function uses `size_t` as shown in this prototype:

```
size_t size( ) const;
```

As usual, the *const* keyword indicates that the function does not alter the bag. To illustrate the use of the function, suppose `first_bag` contains one copy of the number 4 and two copies of the number 8. Then `first_bag.size( )` returns 3.

The occurrences member function. This is a constant member function that determines how many copies of a *particular* number are in a bag. The prototype uses `size_t`:

```
size_t occurrences(int target) const;
```

The activation of `occurrences(n)` returns the number of occurrences of `n` in a bag. For example, if `first_bag` contains the number 4 and two copies of the number 8, then we will have these values:

```
cout << first_bag.occurrences(1) << endl;     Prints 0
cout << first_bag.occurrences(4) << endl;     Prints 1
cout << first_bag.occurrences(8) << endl;
                                              Prints 2
```

The remove member function. This member function removes a particular number from a bag. The prototype is:

```
void remove(int target);
```

Provided that `target` is actually in the bag, the function removes one copy of `target`. If `target` is not in the bag, attempting to remove `target` has no effect on the bag.

Union operator. The **union** of two bags is a new larger bag that contains all the numbers in the first bag plus all the numbers in the second bag, as shown here:

In the drawing we wrote "+" for "union." To implement the union, we will overload the + operator as a nonmember function with this prototype:

```
Bag operator +(const Bag& b1, const Bag& b2);
```

The function is not a member function because of our guidelines about overloading binary operators (see page 80).

Overloading the += operator. The + operator is defined for bags, so it is sensible to also overload +=. The overloaded += will allow us to add the contents of one bag to the existing contents of another bag in much the same way that += works for integers or real numbers. We intend to use += as shown here:

```
Bag first_bag, second_bag;
first_bag.insert(8);
second_bag.insert(4);          This adds the contents of
second_bag.insert(8);          second_bag to what's
first_bag += second_bag;       already in first_bag.
```

After these statements `first_bag` contains one 4 and two 8's.

Our style preference is to overload += as a member function. The reason is that the first argument (to the left of the +=) has special significance: It is the argument that actually has its value changed. The second argument (to the right of the +=) never has its value changed. By making the operator += into a member function, we place special emphasis on the left argument in a statement such as:

```
first_bag += second_bag;
```

This statement means "activate the += member function of first_bag, and use second_bag as the argument." Here is the prototype of the member function:

```
void operator +=(const Bag& addend);
```

overload += as a member function

There are several points to notice:

- This is a *void* function. It does not return a value. It only alters the contents of the bag that activates the function.
- The function has only one parameter, addend. This is the right-hand bag in an expression such as first_bag += second_bag the left-hand bag is the bag that activates += and that has its contents altered.
- We use the name addend for the parameter, meaning "something to be added," but you may use whatever name you like.

That's the end of our list of functions, and we're almost ready to write the header file. But first, there are two C++ features that we'd like to use.

C++ *Feature:* Static Member Constants

Our plan is for bounded bags that can hold 30 items each. (Later we will remove this restriction, providing an unbounded bag class.) There is nothing magic about the number 30—we just picked it as a conveniently small size for our first bags. Later, we might want to change the size 30, allowing bags that hold 300 or 5000 or some other number of items. In order to make it easy to change the bag's size, and also to make our programs more readable, we will use a name such as CAPACITY rather than simply using the number 30.

The best way to define CAPACITY is as a **static member constant**, as shown in this example with the Bag class:

```
class Bag
{
public:
    static const size_t CAPACITY = 30;
    ...
```

→ has to be positive

The keyword *const* has the same meaning that we have seen with other constant declarations, so that the value of CAPACITY is defined once and cannot be changed while the program is running. (See "Constant Declarations" on page 55.)

The keyword *static* has several meanings in C++. When *static* is used to describe a class member, it means that *all* of the class's objects use the *same value*. This is different! Usually each object has its own copy of each member variable. But with our static member constant, every bag has the same CAPACITY of 30. In fact, the only reason that we can set the CAPACITY to 30 *within* the class definition is because every bag has the same value for CAPACITY. When a program declares a bag b, the program can refer to the capacity with the usual notation for selecting a member: b.CAPACITY. Because every bag has the same capacity, a program can also refer to a bag's capacity using the Bag:: "scope resolution operator," as shown in this example:

```
Bag b;
cout << "The capacity of b is " << b.CAPACITY << endl;
cout << "Every Bag has capacity " << Bag::CAPACITY << endl;
```

As shown in this example, we recommend all upper-case letters for the name of any constant. This makes it easy to recognize which values are constant.

Member constants may also be *nonstatic*, and they may vary from one object to another. A nonstatic member constant requires a more complex technique of initialization (called the member initialization list, which we will see later). For now, though, a static member constant is what we want. We will use static member constants according to the following guideline.

ADTs and Static Member Constants

When an ADT depends on some constant values, then declare these values as **static member constants** in the public part of the class declaration. If a constant does need to be changed, then the declaration can be changed, and the program can be recompiled.

Our documentation standard (Appendix J) requires the names of constants to be all upper-case letters for easy identification.

Example in the Bag class definition:
```
class Bag
{
public:
    static const size_t CAPACITY = 30;
    ...
```

Programs can use a static constant member with the usual member selection notation (e.g., b.CAPACITY), or with the scope resolution operator (e.g., Bag::CAPACITY).

**Older Compilers Do Not Support Initialization of
Static Member Constants**

Our bag's CAPACITY is declared and initialized right inside the Bag class definition, as shown here:

```
class Bag
{
public:
    static const size_t CAPACITY = 30;
    ...
```

The ability to initialize and use a static member constant within the class definition is a relatively new feature. The feature was proposed as part of the February 1995 Draft of the C++ Language Standard. Older C++ compilers are unlikely to support the feature. Even those compilers that do support the feature may restrict it to integral data types.

If you have an older compiler that does not support static constant members, then Appendix E, "Dealing with Older Compilers," provides two alternatives for your programming.

C++ Feature: Typedef Statements within a Class Definition

FEATURE ++

So far we have considered only bags of integers. But programs need bags of many kinds: bags of integers, bags of characters, bags of real numbers, even bags of throttles. None of our functions really requires the bag to contain integers.

So, to be more flexible, we will use the name Item for the data type of the items in a bag. Some programs might need the Item to be an integer; other programs can use a different Item type. In order to allow the flexible Item type, we will place the following statement at the top of the public section of the bag's class definition:

```
class Bag
{
public:
    typedef int Item;
    ...
```

This statement is a **typedef** statement. It consists of the keyword *typedef* followed by a data type (such as *int*) and then a new identifier (such as Item). The effect of this typedef statement is that bag functions can use the name Item as a synonym for the data type *int*. Wherever a bag member function uses the name Item, the compiler will recognize it as simply another name for *int*. Other functions, which are not bag member functions, can use the name Bag::Item as the type of the items in a bag. Moreover, if we want a new kind of bag, we can simply change the word *int* to a new data type and recompile. No other changes will be needed anywhere in our program. For example, to declare a bag of double numbers we would change the typedef statement to the following:

```
class Bag
{
public:
    typedef double Item;
    ...
```

Using the typedef also suggests one other change to some of the bag's prototypes. The Item type might be large, meaning that value parameters will be inefficient. Therefore, wherever possible, we will use const reference parameters instead of value parameters. For example, the prototype for the insert function uses the const reference parameter shown here:

```
void insert(const Item& entry);
```

In Chapter 6 we will use an alternative solution to the changing-item problem. The alternative, called a *template class*, is more cumbersome to use, but it overcomes some drawbacks of the typedef statement.

Container Data Types and Typedef Statements

The simplest way to provide flexible containers is to give a name to the underlying item type by using a typedef statement at the top of the public section of the class definition.

If the underlying item type needs to be changed, then the typedef statement can be changed, and the program can be recompiled.

The Bag ADT—Documentation

We now know enough about the bag ADT to write the documentation of the header file, as shown in Figure 3.1. We've used the name bag1.h for this header file because it is the first of several different kinds of bags that we plan to implement.

The documentation includes information about the two new features: the static member constant and the typedef statement. In particular, notice that we have been very specific about what sort of data type is required for the Item data type. The documentation about the Item data type indicates that Item may be any of the C++ built-in data types (such as *int* or *char*), or it may be a class with a default constructor, an assignment operator, and operators to test for equality (x == y) and non-equality (x != y).

FIGURE 3.1   Documentation for the Bag Header File

Documentation for a Header File

```
//  FILE: bag1.h
//  CLASS PROVIDED: Bag (a container class for a collection of items)
//
//  TYPEDEF and MEMBER CONSTANTS for the Bag class:
//    static const size_t CAPACITY = _____
//       Bag::CAPACITY is the maximum number of items that a Bag can hold.
//
//    typedef _____ Item
//       Bag::Item is the data type of the items in the Bag. It may be any of the C++ built-in
//       types (int, char, etc.), or a class with a default constructor, an assignment operator,
//       and operators to test for equality (x == y) and  non-equality (x != y).
//
//  CONSTRUCTOR for the Bag class:
//    Bag( )
//       Postcondition: The Bag has been initialized as an empty Bag.
//
//  MODIFICATION MEMBER FUNCTIONS for the Bag class:
//    void insert(const Item& entry)
//       Precondition:  size( ) < CAPACITY.
//       Postcondition: A new copy of entry has been added to the Bag.
//
//    void remove(const Item& target)
//       Postcondition: If target was in the Bag, then one copy of target has been removed from
//       the Bag; otherwise the Bag is unchanged.
//
//    void operator +=(const Bag& addend)
//       Precondition:  size( ) + addend.size( ) <= CAPACITY.
//       Postcondition: Each item in addend has been added to this Bag.
//
//  CONSTANT MEMBER FUNCTIONS for the Bag class:
//    size_t size( ) const
//       Postcondition: The return value is the total number of items in the Bag.
//
//    size_t occurrences(const Item& target) const
//       Postcondition: The return value is number of times target is in the Bag.
//
//  NONMEMBER FUNCTIONS for the Bag class:
//    Bag operator +(const Bag& b1, const Bag& b2)
//       Precondition:  b1.size( ) + b2.size( ) <= Bag::CAPACITY.
//       Postcondition: The Bag returned is the union of b1 and b2.
//
//  VALUE SEMANTICS  for the Bag class:
//    Assignments and the copy constructor may be used with Bag objects.
```

bag1.h   **FTP**

97

Documenting the Value Semantics

One of the requirements for the item data type may seem peculiar—why do we require that the item type "must have an assignment operator"? Doesn't every data type permit assignments such as x = y? Won't there always be an automatic assignment operator? No! For example, x = y is forbidden when x and y are arrays. Later we will see other data types that forbid assignments, or at least require care in defining what the assignment operator actually means.

Take a moment to read and understand all of the preconditions in Figure 3.1, such as this precondition for the += operator:

> *Precondition: size( ) + addend.size( ) <= CAPACITY.*

In this precondition, size( ) refers to the size of the bag that activates the function, and CAPACITY refers to the capacity of the bag that activates the function. On the other hand, addend.size( ) refers to the size of the addend, which is a parameter of the function.

The Bag ADT—Demonstration Program

With the documentation in hand, we can write a program that uses a bag. We don't need to know what the private members of a bag are, and we don't need to know how the functions are implemented. As an example, a demonstration program appears in Figure 3.2, which we will discuss after you look through the program.

FIGURE 3.2   Demonstration Program for the Bag Class

A Program

```
// FILE: bag_demo.cxx
// This is a small demonstration program showing how the Bag class is used.
#include <iostream.h>    // Provides cout and cin
#include <stdlib.h>      // Provides EXIT_SUCCESS
#include "bag1.h"        // With Item defined as an int

// PROTOTYPES for functions used by this demonstration program:
void get_ages(Bag& ages);
// Postcondition: The user has been prompted to type in the ages of family members. These
// ages have been read and placed in the ages Bag, stopping when the Bag is full or when the
// user types a negative number.

void check_ages(Bag& ages);
// Postcondition: The user has been prompted to type in the ages of family members again.
// Each age is removed from the ages Bag when it is typed, stopping when the Bag is empty.
```

(continued)

(FIGURE 3.2 continued)

```cpp
int main( )
{
    Bag ages;

    get_ages(ages);
    check_ages(ages);
    cout << "May your family live long and prosper." << endl;
    return EXIT_SUCCESS;
}

void get_ages(Bag& ages)
{
    int user_input;

    cout << "Type the ages in your family.\n";
    cout << "Type a negative number when you are done:" << endl;
    cin >> user_input;
    while (user_input >= 0)
    {
        if (ages.size( ) < ages.CAPACITY)
            ages.insert(user_input);
        else
            cout << "I have run out of room and can't add that age." << endl;
        cin >> user_input;
    }
}

void check_ages(Bag& ages)
{
    int user_input;

    cout << "Type those ages again. Press return after each age:" << endl;
    while (ages.size( ) > 0)
    {
        cin >> user_input;
        if (ages.occurrences(user_input) == 0)
            cout << "No, that age does not occur!" << endl;
        else
        {
            cout << "Yes, I've got that age and will remove it." << endl;
            ages.remove(user_input);
        }
    }
}
```

bag_demo.cxx **FTP**

The demonstration program of Figure 3.2 asks a user about the ages of family members. The user enters the ages followed by a negative number to indicate the end of the input. (Using a special value to end a list is a common technique called a **sentinel value**.) A typical dialogue with the program looks like this:

```
Type the ages in your family.
Type a negative number when you are done:
5   19    47    -1
Type those ages again. Press return after each age:
19
Yes, I've got that age and will remove it.
36
No, that age does not occur!
5
Yes, I've got that age and will remove it.
47
Yes, I've got that age and will remove it.
May your family live long and prosper.
```

we ensure that each precondition is met

The program puts the ages in a bag and then asks the user to type the ages again, as a simple test. Take a look at the activations of `insert`. Have we guaranteed that the precondition is met? (Yes, this was guaranteed in the if-statement that compares `ages.size( )` to the static member constant `ages.CAPACITY`.) As for the `Bag` class itself, we still don't know how the implementation will work, but we're getting there.

The Bag ADT—Design

There are several ways to design the `Bag` class. For now, we'll keep things simple and design a somewhat inefficient data structure using an array. The data structure will be redesigned several times to allow more efficient functions.

We start the design by thinking about the data structure—the actual configuration of private member variables used to implement the ADT. The primary structure for our design is an array that stores the items of a bag. Or, to be more precise, we use *the beginning* part of a large array. Such an array is called a **partially filled array**. For example, if the bag contains the integer 4 and two copies of 8, then the first part of the array could look this way:

use the beginning part of an array

Components of
the partially filled
array contain the
items of the bag.

data

8   4   8

[0] [1] [2] [3] [4] [5]

This array will be one of the private member variables of the Bag class. The length of the array will be determined by the constant CAPACITY, but as the picture indicates, when we are using the array to store a bag with just three items, we don't care what appears beyond the first three components. Starting at index 3, the array might contain all zeros, or it might contain garbage, or our favorite number—it really doesn't matter.

Because part of the array can contain garbage, the Bag class must keep track of one other item: *How much of the array is currently being used?* For example, in the picture above, we are using only the first three components of the array because the bag contains three items. The amount of the array being used can be as small as zero (an empty bag) or as large as CAPACITY (a full bag). The amount increases as items are added to the bag, and it decreases as items are deleted. In any case, we will keep track of the amount in a private member variable called used. With this approach, there are two private members for a bag:

the bag's member variables

```
class Bag
{
public:
    // TYPEDEF and MEMBER CONSTANTS
    static const size_t CAPACITY = 30;
    typedef int Item;
    ‖ The rest of the public members will be listed later.
private:
    Item data[CAPACITY];    // An array to store items
    size_t used;            // How much of the array is used
};
```

two private member variables for the Bag

When we declare the array, we must know the total size of the array, which is obtained from the constant CAPACITY.

Pitfall: The Item Type Must Have a Default Constructor

PITFALL

The item data type is used as the component type of an array in the private member variable shown here:

```
class Bag
{
...
private:
    Item data[CAPACITY];    // An array to store items
...
```

If the item data type is a class with constructors (rather than one of the C++ built-in types), then the compiler must initialize each component of the data array using the item's default constructor. This is why our bag documentation includes the statement that the Bag::Item type may be "a class with a default constructor..."

The key point to remember is that when an array is declared, and the component type is a class with constructors, the compiler uses the default constructor to initialize the array components. Therefore, our bag documentation should mention this requirement.

The Invariant of an ADT

We've defined the bag data structure, and we have a good intuitive idea of how the structure will be used to represent a bag of items. But as an aid in implementing the ADT we should also write down an explicit statement of how the data structure is used to represent a bag. In the case of the bag, we need to state how the member variables of the Bag class are used to represent a bag of items. There are two rules for our bag implementation:

rules that dictate how the member variables are used to represent a value

1. The number of items in the bag is stored in the member variable used.

2. For an empty bag, we do not care what is stored in any of data; for a non-empty bag, the items in the bag are stored in data[0] through data[used-1], and we don't care what is stored in the rest of data.

The rules that dictate how the member variables of a class represent a value (such as a bag of items) are called the **invariant of the ADT**. The knowledge of these rules is essential to the correct implementation of the ADT's functions. With the exception of the constructors, each function depends on the invariant being valid when the function is called. And each function, including the constructors, has a responsibility of ensuring that the invariant is valid when the function finishes. In some sense, the invariant of an ADT is a condition that is an *implicit* part of every function's postcondition. And (except for the constructors) it is also an implicit part of every function's precondition. The invariant is not usually written as an *explicit* part of the preconditions and postconditions because the programmer who uses the ADT does not need to know about these conditions. But to the implementor of the ADT, the invariant is indispensable. In other words, the invariant is a critical part of the implementation of an ADT, but it has no effect on the way the ADT is used.

Key Design Concept

The invariant is a critical part of an ADT's implementation.

The Invariant of an ADT

When you design an abstract data type, always make an explicit statement of the rules that dictate how the member variables are used. These rules are called the **invariant of the ADT**. All of the functions (except the constructors) can count on the invariant being valid when the function is called. Each function also has the responsibility of ensuring that the invariant is valid when the function finishes.

The Bag ADT—Implementation

Once the invariant of an ADT is stated, the implementation of the functions is relatively simple because there is no interaction between the functions—except for their cooperation at keeping the invariant valid. Let's discuss each function along with its implementation.

The constructor. The default constructor initializes a bag as an empty bag, and does no other work. The only task involved is to set the member `used` to zero, which can be accomplished with an inline member function:

implementing the constructor

```
Bag( ) { used = 0; }
```

The value semantics. Our documentation indicates that assignments and the copy constructor may be used with a bag. Our plan is to use the automatic assignment operator and the automatic copy constructor, each of which simply copies the member variables from one bag to another. This is fine because the copying process will copy both the `data` array and the member variable `used`.

For example, if a programmer has two bags x and y, then the statement `y = x` will invoke the automatic assignment operator to copy all of `x.data` to `y.data`, and to copy `x.used` to `y.used`. This is exactly what we want the assignment operator to do, and the automatic copy constructor is also correct.

So, our only "work" for the value semantics is confirming that the automatic operations are correct. Don't you wish all implementations were that easy?

The occurrences member function. To count the number of occurrences of a particular item in a bag, we step through the used portion of the partially filled array. Remember that we are using locations `data[0]` through `data[used-1]`, so the correct loop is shown in this implementation:

```
size_t Bag::occurrences(const Item& target) const
// Library facilities used: stdlib.h
{
    size_t answer;
    size_t i;

    answer = 0;
    for (i = 0; i < used; i++)
        if (target == data[i])
            answer++;
    return answer;
}
```

implementing the occurrences function

This is the implementation of a member function, so we can use the name `Item` in the parameter list. In a nonmember function, we would have to use the full name `Bag::Item`.

The insert member function. The insert function checks that there is room to insert a new item. If so, then the item is placed in the next available location of the array. What is the index of the next available location? For example, if used is 3, then data[0], data[1], and data[2] are already occupied, and the next location is data[3]. In general, the next available location will be data[used]. We can place the new item in data[used], as shown in the highlighted statement of this implementation:

implementing insert

```
void Bag::insert(const Item& entry)     See Self-Test Exercise 5 for
// Library facilities used: assert.h    an alternative approach to
{                                        these steps.
    assert(size( ) < CAPACITY);
    data[used] = entry;
    used++;
}
```

Within a member function we can refer to the static member constant CAPACITY with no extra notation. This refers to the CAPACITY member constant of the bag that activates the insert function.

TIP

Programming Tip: Public Members Make Assertions More Meaningful

At the start of the insert member function we wrote the assertion:

```
    assert(size( ) < CAPACITY);
```

Of course, we could have written "used < CAPACITY" instead, but it is better to write assertions with public members (such as the size function). The public member is better because it has meaning to the programmer who uses our ADT. If the assertion fails, that programmer will understand the message "Assertion failed: size( ) < CAPACITY."

The remove member function. The remove function takes several steps to remove an item named target from a bag. In the first step, we find the index of target in the bag's array, and store this index in a local variable named index. For example, suppose that target is the number 6 in the five-item bag drawn at the top of the next page.

The index of the target is found and placed in a local variable called index.

In this example, `target` is a parameter to the `remove` member function, `index` is a local variable in the `remove` member function, and `used` is the familiar bag member variable. As you can see in the drawing, the first step of `remove` was to locate the target (6) and place the index of the target in the local variable called `index`.

Once the index of the target is found, the second step is to take the *final* item in the bag and copy it to `data[index]`. The reason for this copying is so that all the bag's items stay together at the front of the partially filled array, with no "holes." In our example, the number 8 is copied to `data[index]` as shown here:

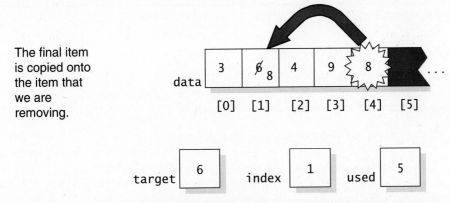

The final item is copied onto the item that we are removing.

The third step is to reduce the value of `used` by one—in effect reducing the used part of the array by one. In our example, `used` is reduced from 5 to 4:

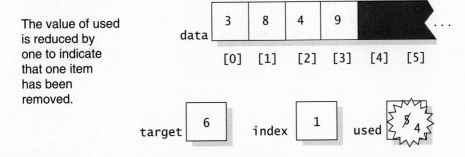

The value of used is reduced by one to indicate that one item has been removed.

The code for the remove function, shown in Figure 3.3, follows these three steps. The only item added is a check that the target is actually in the bag. If we discover that the target is not in the bag, then we do not need to remove anything. Also note that our remove function works correctly for the boundary values of removing the first or last item in the array.

implementing remove

Before we continue, we want to point out some programming techniques. Look at the following for-loop from Figure 3.3:

```
for (index = 0; (index < used) && (data[index] != target); index++)
    // No work is needed in the body of this for-loop.
    ;
```

At the end of the for-loops's three clauses is a semicolon, which means that the body of this loop has no statements; all of the work is accomplished by the loop's three clauses. The first clause initializes index to zero. The second clause indicates that the loop continues as long as index is still a location in the used part of the array (i.e., index < used) and we have not yet found the

---

FIGURE 3.3 Implementation of the Member Function to Remove an Item

A Member Function Implementation

```
void Bag::remove(const Item& target)
// Postcondition: If target was in the Bag, then one copy of target has been
// removed from the Bag; otherwise the Bag is unchanged.
{
    size_t index; // The location of target in the data array

    // First, set index to the location of target in the data array,
    // which could be as small as 0 or as large as used-1.
    // If target is not in the array, then index will be set equal to used.
    for (index = 0; (index < used) && (data[index] != target); index++)
        // No work is needed in the body of this for-loop.
        ;

    if (index == used)
        return; // target isn't in the Bag, so no work to do.

    // When execution reaches here, target is in the Bag at data[index].
    // So, reduce used by 1 and copy the last item onto data[index].
    used--;
    data[index] = data[used]; ⟵——— See Self-Test Exercise 5 for an
                                     alternative approach to this step.
}
```

bag1.cxx   **FTP**

target (i.e., data[index] != target). Each time through the loop, the third clause increments index by one (index++). No other work is needed in the loop, so the body of the loop has no statements.

A second programming technique concerns the boolean expression used to control the loop:

```
for (index = 0; (index < used) && (data[index] != target); index++)
    // No work is needed in the body of this for-loop.
    ;
```

Look at the expression data[index] in the second part of the test. The valid indexes for data range from 0 to used-1. But, if the target is not in the array, then index will eventually reach used, which could be an invalid index. At that point, with index equal to used, we must not evaluate the expression data[index]. In some situations, trying to evaluate data[index] with an invalid index can even cause your program to crash. The general rule: *Never use an invalid index with an array.*

Avoiding the invalid index is the reason for the first part of the logical test (i.e., index < used). Moreover, the test for (index < used) must appear *before* the other part of the test. Placing (index < used) first ensures that only valid indexes are used. The insurance comes from a technique called *short-circuit evaluation,* which C++ uses to evaluate boolean expressions. In **short-circuit evaluation** a boolean expression is evaluated from left to right, and the evaluation stops as soon as there is enough information to determine the value of the expression. In our example, if index equals used, then the first part of the logical expression (index < used) is false, so the entire && expression *must* be false. It doesn't matter whether the second part of the && expression is true or false. Therefore, C++ doesn't bother to evaluate the second part of the expression, and the potential error of an invalid index is avoided.

short-circuit evaluation of logical operations

The operator +=.   The operator += is a member function. Most of the work of this function is accomplished by a loop that copies each of the items from addend.data to the data array of the object that activates +=. We expect an implementation something like this:

```
void Bag::operator +=(const Bag& addend)
{
    ...
    for (i = 0; i < number of items to copy; i++)
    {
        data[used] = addend.data[i];
        used++;
    }
}
```

*implementing
operator +=*

The key assignment statement in the loop is highlighted. On the left of the assignment we have written data[used], which is the next available location of the data array for the object that activated the function. On the right of the assignment we have written addend.data[i], which is item number i from the data array that we are copying.

The operator +.   The operator + is different from our other functions. It is an ordinary function rather than a member function. The function must take two bags, add them together into a third bag, and return this third bag. The "third bag" is declared as a local variable called answer in this implementation:

```
Bag operator +(const Bag& b1, const Bag& b2)
// Library facilities used: assert.h
{
    Bag answer;

    assert(b1.size( ) + b2.size( ) <= Bag::CAPACITY);

    answer += b1;          Add in the items of b1.
    answer += b2;
    return answer;
}                           Add in the items of b2.
```

Notice that this function does not need to be a friend function. Why not? (See the answer to Self-Test Exercise 4.) Also, the function implementation can access the static member constant with the notation Bag::CAPACITY.

The Bag ADT—Putting the Pieces Together

Only the size function remains to be implemented, which we'll do as an inline function of the class definition shown in the completed header file of Figure 3.4 on page 109. Notice that in the header file we also list the prototype of the bag's *operator* + function. This is not a member function, so the prototype appears *after* the end of the Bag class definition.

All the function implementations are collected in the implementation file of Figure 3.5 on page 110.

TIP

Programming Tip: **Document the ADT Invariant in the Implementation File**

We wrote the invariant for the bag ADT at the top of the implementation file in Figure 3.5 on page 110. This is the best place to document the ADT's invariant. In particular, do not write the invariant in the header file, because a programmer who uses the ADT does not need to know about how the invariant dictates the use of private fields. But the programmer who implements the ADT does need to know about the invariant.

A Header File

```
// FILE: bag1.h
// CLASS PROVIDED: Bag (a container class for a collection of items)
```

See Figure 3.1 on page 97 for the other documentation that goes here.

```
#ifndef BAG1_H
#define BAG1_H
#include <stdlib.h>   // Provides size_t

    class Bag
    {
    public:
        // TYPEDEF and MEMBER CONSTANTS
        static const size_t CAPACITY = 30;
        typedef int Item;
        // CONSTRUCTOR
        Bag( ) { used = 0; }
        // MODIFICATION MEMBER FUNCTIONS
        void insert(const Item& entry);
        void remove(const Item& target);
        void operator +=(const Bag& addend);
        // CONSTANT MEMBER FUNCTIONS
        size_t size( ) const { return used; }
        size_t occurrences(const Item& target) const;
    private:
        Item data[CAPACITY];   // The array to store items
        size_t used;           // How much of array is used
    };

    // NONMEMBER FUNCTIONS for the Bag class
    Bag operator +(const Bag& b1, const Bag& b2);

#endif
```

If your compiler does not permit initialization of static constants, see Appendix E.

bag1.h   **FTP**

FIGURE 3.5 | Implementation File for the Bag Class

An Implementation File

```
// FILE: bag1.cxx
// CLASS IMPLEMENTED: Bag (See bag1.h for documentation.)
// INVARIANT for the Bag ADT:
//      1. The number of items in the Bag is in the member variable used.
//      2. For an empty Bag, we do not care what is stored in any of data; for a non-empty Bag,
//         the items in the Bag are stored in data[0] through data[used-1], and we don't care
//         what's in the rest of data.

#include <assert.h>   // Provides assert
#include <stdlib.h>   // Provides size_t
#include "bag1.h"
```

```
void Bag::insert(const Item& entry)
// Library facilities used: assert.h
{
    assert(size( ) < CAPACITY);

    data[used] = entry;
    used++;
}
```

See Self-Test Exercise 5 for an alternative approach to these steps.

```
void Bag::remove(const Item& target)
// Library facilities used: stdlib.h
{
    size_t index;  // The location of target in the data array

    // First, set index to the location of target in the data array,
    // which could be as small as 0 or as large as used-1.
    // If target is not in the array, then index will be set equal to used.
    for (index = 0; (index < used) && (data[index] != target); index++)
        // No work is needed in the body of this for-loop.
        ;

    if (index == used) // target isn't in the Bag, so no work to do
        return;

    // When execution reaches here, target is in the Bag at data[index].
    // So, reduce used by 1 and copy the last item onto data[index].
    used--;
    data[index] = data[used];
}
```

See Self-Test Exercise 5 for an alternative approach to this step.

(FIGURE 3.5 continued)

```cpp
void Bag::operator +=(const Bag& addend)
// Library facilities used: assert.h, stdlib.h
{
    size_t i;
    size_t other_bag_size;

    assert(size( ) + addend.size( ) <= CAPACITY);

    other_bag_size = addend.size( );
    for (i = 0; i < other_bag_size; i++)
    {
        data[used] = addend.data[i];
        used++;
    }
}


size_t Bag::occurrences(const Item& target) const
// Library facilities used: stdlib.h
{
    size_t answer;
    size_t i;

    answer = 0;
    for (i = 0; i < used; i++)
        if (target == data[i])
            answer++;
    return answer;
}


Bag operator +(const Bag& b1, const Bag& b2)
// Library facilities used: assert.h
{
    Bag answer;

    assert(b1.size( ) + b2.size( ) <= Bag::CAPACITY);

    answer += b1;
    answer += b2;
    return answer;
}
```

bag1.cxx   **FTP**

The Bag ADT—Testing

Thus far, we have focused on the design and implementation of new classes, including new member functions and operator overloading. But it's also important to continue practicing the other aspects of software development, particularly testing. Each of the bag's new functions must be tested, including the overloaded operators. As shown in Chapter 1, it is important to concentrate the testing on boundary values. At this point, we will alert you to only one potential pitfall, leaving the complete testing to Programming Project 1 on page 132.

PITFALL

Pitfall: An Object Can Be an Argument to Its Own Member Function

The same variable is sometimes used on both sides of an assignment or other operator. For example, the value of an integer d is doubled by the highlighted statement here:

```
int d = 5;
d += d;
```
Add the current value of d to d, giving it a value of 10.

A similar technique can be used with a bag, as shown here:

```
Bag b;
b.insert(5);
b.insert(2);
b += b;
```
b now contains a 5 and a 2.

Now b contains two 5's and two 2's.

The highlighted statement takes all the items in b (the 5 and the 2) and adds them to what's already in b, so b ends up with two copies of each number.

In the += statement, the bag b is activating the += operator, but this same bag b is the actual argument to the operator. This is a situation that must be carefully tested. As an example of the danger, consider the incorrect implementation of += in Figure 3.6. Do you see what goes wrong with b += b? (See the answer to Self-Test Exercise 6.)

The situation: A member function has a parameter type that is the same as the member function's class. For example, the bag's += operator has a parameter that is itself a bag.

The danger: The member function might fail when an object activates the member function, and the same object is used as the actual argument. For example, a bag b could be used in the statement: b += b.

The solution: Always test this special situation.

FIGURE 3.6 | Wrong Implementation of the Bag's += Operator

A Wrong Member Function Implementation

WARNING!

There is a bug in this implementation. See Self-Test Exercise 6.

```
void Bag::operator +=(const Bag& addend)
// Library facilities used: assert.h, stdlib.h
{
    size_t i; // An array index

    assert(size( ) + addend.size( ) <= CAPACITY);

    for (i = 0; i < addend.used; i++)
    {
        data[used] = addend.data[i];
        used++;
    }
}
```

The Bag ADT—Analysis

We finish this section with a time analysis of the bag's functions. We'll use the number of items in a bag as the input size. For example, if b is a bag containing n integers, then the number of operations required by b.occurrences is a formula involving n. To count the operations, we'll count the number of statements executed by the function, although we won't need an exact count since our answer will use big-O notation. Except for the return statement, all of the work in occurrences happens in this loop:

```
for (i = 0; i < used; i++)
    if (target == data[i])
        answer++;
```

We can see that the body of the loop will be executed exactly n times—once for each item in the bag. The body of the loop also has another important property: The body contains no other loops or calls to functions that contain loops. This is enough to conclude that the total number of statements executed by occurrences is no more than:

$n \times$ (number of statements in the loop) + 1

The extra "+1" at the end is for the return statement. Regardless of how many statements are actually in the loop, the time expression is *always* $O(n)$—so the occurrences function is linear.

A similar analysis shows that `remove` is also linear, although `remove`'s loop sometimes executes fewer than *n* times. However, the fact that `remove` *sometimes* requires less than *n* × (number of statements in the loop) does not change the fact that the function is $O(n)$. In the worst case, the loop does execute a full *n* iterations, therefore the correct time analysis is no better than $O(n)$.

constant time
O(1)

Several of the other bag functions do not contain any loops at all. This is a pleasant situation because the time required for any of these functions does not depend on the number of items in the bag. For example, when an item is added to a bag, the new item is always placed at the end of the array, and the `insert` function never looks at the items that were already in the bag. When the time required by a function does not depend on the size of the input, the procedure is called **constant time**, which is written $O(1)$.

The time analyses of all the functions are summarized in Figure 3.7.

Self-Test Exercises

1. The bag's documentation in Figure 3.1 on page 97 says that the `Item` data type may be a class, but only if it has a default constructor and several operators. Why?

2. Draw a picture of `mybag.data` after these statements:
   ```
   Bag mybag;
   mybag.insert(1);
   mybag.insert(2);
   mybag.insert(3);
   mybag.remove(1);
   ```

3. Write the invariant of the bag ADT.

4. Why isn't the bag's *operator* + function a friend function?

FIGURE 3.7 Time Analysis for the Bag ADT Functions (First Version)

Operation	Time Analysis	
Default constructor	$O(1)$	Constant time
occurrences	$O(n)$	*n* is the size of the Bag
insert	$O(1)$	Constant time
remove	$O(n)$	Linear time

Operation	Time Analysis	
+= another Bag	$O(n)$	*n* is the size of the other Bag
b1 + b2	$O(n_1 + n_2)$	n_1 and n_2 are the sizes of the Bags
size	$O(1)$	Constant time

5. Use the expression --used (with the -- *before* used) to rewrite the last two statements of remove (Figure 3.3 on page 106) as a single statement. (If you are unsure of the difference between used-- and --used, then go ahead and peek at our answer at the back of the chapter.) Use used++ to make a similar alteration to the insert function member.

6. Suppose we implement the += operator as shown in Figure 3.6 on page 113. What goes wrong with `b += b`?

3.2 PROGRAMMING PROJECT: THE LIST ADT

You are ready to tackle a container class implementation on your own. The class is a container class called a **list**. A list is similar to a bag—both contain a bunch of items. But unlike a bag, the items in a list are arranged in a sequence, one after another.

How does this differ from a bag? After all, aren't the bag items arranged one after another in the partially filled array that implements the bag? Yes, but that's a quirk of our particular bag implementation, and the order is just haphazard. Moreover, there is no way that a program using the bag can refer to the bag items by their position in the array.

how a list differs from a bag

In contrast, the items of a list are kept as a sequence, and member functions will allow a program to step through the sequence one item at a time. Member functions also permit a program to control precisely where items are inserted and removed within the sequence.

The List ADT—Specification

Our list is a class that depends on an underlying Item type, and that is limited to no more than 30 items for now. As with our bag, the list's capacity and the Item type will be defined in the public section of the list's class definition. Throughout the discussion, we will use examples in which the items are double numbers, and the list has no more than 30 items. So in the header file we would place the definitions highlighted here:

```
class List
{
public:
    // TYPEDEF and MEMBER CONSTANTS
    static const size_t CAPACITY = 30;
    typedef double Item;
    ...
```

Keep in mind that the capacity and item type can be easily changed and recompiled if we need other kinds of lists. Also, remember the alternatives if your compiler does not support this way of initializing a static constant in a class definition (see Appendix E).

The class that we implement will be called `List`. We'll now specify the member functions of this new class:

Default constructor. The list has just one constructor—a default constructor that creates an empty list.

The size member function. The `size` member function returns the number of items on the list. The prototype is given here along with the postcondition:

```
size_t size( ) const;
// Postcondition: The value returned is the number of items on the List.
```

For example, if `scores` is a list containing the values 10.1, 40.2, and 1.1, then `scores.size( )` returns 3. Throughout our examples, we will draw lists vertically, with the first item of the list on top, as shown in the picture in the margin (where the first item is 10.1).

| 10.1 |
| 40.2 |
| 1.1 |

Member functions to examine a list. We will have member functions to build a list, but it will be easier to first explain the member functions that examine a list which has already been built. Now, with the bag ADT, all that we can do is inquire how many copies of a particular item are in the bag. A list is more flexible, allowing us to examine the items one after another. The items must be examined in order, from the front to the back of the sequence. Three member functions work together to enforce the in-order retrieval rule. The functions' prototypes are given here:

```
void start( );
Item current( ) const;
void advance( );
```

When we want to retrieve the items in a list, we begin by activating `start`. After activating `start`, the `current` function returns the first item on the list. Each time we call `advance`, the `current` function changes so that it returns the next item on the list. For example, if a list named `numbers` contains the four numbers 37, 10, 83, and 42, then we can write the following code to print the first three numbers on the list:

start,
current,
advance

```
numbers.start( );                             ⟋ Prints 37
cout << numbers.current( ) << endl;◀
numbers.advance( );
cout << numbers.current( ) << endl;◀──── Prints 10
numbers.advance( );
cout << numbers.current( ) << endl;  ◀──── Prints 83
```

One other member function cooperates with `current`. The function, called `is_item`, returns a boolean value to indicate whether there actually is another item for `current` to provide, or whether `current` has advanced right off the end of the list. The `is_item` prototype is given here with a postcondition:

```
bool is_item( ) const;
// Postcondition: A true return value indicates that there is a valid
// "current" item that can be obtained from the current member function.
// A false return value indicates that there is no valid current item.
```

Using all four of the member functions in a for-loop, we can print an entire list, as shown here for the `numbers` list:

```
for (numbers.start( ); numbers.is_item( ); numbers.advance( ))
    cout << numbers.current( ) << endl;
```

The insert and attach member functions. There are two member functions to add new items to a list. One of the functions, called `insert`, places a new item before the current item. For example, suppose that we have created the list shown to the right with three items, and that the current item is 8.8. In this example, we want to add 10.0 to our list, immediately before the current item. When 10.0 is inserted before the current item, other items in the list—such as 8.8 and 99.0—will move down the list to make room for the new item. After the insertion, the list has the four items shown in the lower box.

If there is no current item, then `insert` places the new item at the front of the list. In any case, after the `insert` function returns, the newly inserted item will be the current item, as specified in this precondition/postcondition contract:

42.1
8.8
99.0

The list grows by inserting 10.0 before the current item.

42.1
10.0
8.8
99.0

```
void insert(const Item& entry);
// Precondition: size( ) < CAPACITY.
// Postcondition: A new copy of entry has been inserted in the List before
// the current item. If there was no current item, then the new entry has
// been inserted at the front of the List. In either case, the new item is
// now the current item of the List.
```

A second member function, called `attach`, also adds a new item to a list—but the new item is added *after* the current item, as specified here:

```
void attach(const Item& entry);
// Precondition: size( ) < CAPACITY.
// Postcondition: A new copy of entry has been inserted in the List after
// the current item. If there was no current item, then the new entry has been
// attached to the end of the List. In either case, the new item is
// now the current item of the List.
```

If there is no current item, then the attach function places the new item at the end of the list (rather than the front). Either `insert` or `attach` can be used to place the first item on a list.

The remove_current member function. The current item can be removed from a list. The member function for a removal has no parameters:

```
void remove_current( );
// Precondition: is_item returns true.
// Postcondition: The current item has been removed from the List,
// and the item after this (if there is one) is now the new current item.
```

The function's precondition requires that there is a current item; it is this current item that is removed. For example, suppose `scores` is the four-item list shown at the top of the box in the margin, and the highlighted 8.3 is the current item. After activating `scores.remove_current( )`, the 8.3 has been deleted, and the 4.1 is now the current item.

The List ADT—Documentation

The header file for this first version of our `List` class is shown in Figure 3.8 on page 120. The header file includes the class definition with our suggestion for three member variables. We discuss these member variables next.

The List ADT—Design

Our suggested design for the list ADT has three private member variables. The first variable, `data`, is an array that stores the items of the list. Just like the bag, `data` is a partially filled array, and a second member variable, called `used`, keeps track of how much of the `data` array is currently being used. Therefore, the used part of the array extends from `data[0]` to `data[used-1]`. The third member variable, `current_index`, gives the index of the "current" item in the array (if there is one). If there is no valid current item in the list, then `current_index` will be set to the same number as `used` (since this is larger than any valid index). Here is the complete invariant of our ADT, stated as three rules:

1. The number of items in the list is stored in the member variable `used`.
2. For an empty list, we do not care what is stored in any of `data`; for a non-empty list, the items in the list are stored in their sequence order from `data[0]` to `data[used-1]`, and we don't care what is stored in the rest of `data`.
3. If there is a current item, then it lies in `data[current_index]`; if there is no current item, then `current_index` equals `used`.

As an example, suppose that a list contains four numbers, with the current item at data[2]. The member variables of the object might appear as shown here:

In this example, the current item is at data[2], so the current( ) function would return the number 6. At this point, if we called advance( ), then current_index would increase to 3, and current( ) would then return the 9.

Normally, a list has a "current" item, and the member variable current_index contains the location of that current item. But if there is no current item, then current_index contains the same value as used. In the above example, if current_index was 4, then that would indicate that there is no current item. Notice that this value (4) is beyond the used part of the array (which stretches from data[0] to data[3]).

The stated requirements for the member variables form the invariant of the list ADT. You should place this invariant at the top of your implementation file (list1.cxx). We will leave most of this implementation file up to you, but we will offer some hints and a bit of pseudocode.

invariant of the ADT

The List ADT—Pseudocode for the Implementation

The remove_current function. This function removes the current item from the list. First check that the precondition is valid (use is_item( )). Then remove the current item by shifting each of the subsequent items leftward one position. For example, suppose we are removing the current item from the list drawn to the here:

What is the current item in this picture? It is the 1.4 since current_index is 1, and data[1] contains the 1.4.

(text continues on page 122)

FIGURE 3.8 Header File for the List Class

A Header File

```
//  FILE: list1.h
//  CLASS PROVIDED: List (a container class for a List of items,
//  where each List may have a designated item called the current item)
//
//  TYPEDEF and MEMBER CONSTANTS for the List class:
//     static const size_t CAPACITY = ____
//        List::CAPACITY is the maximum number of items that a List can hold.
//
//     typedef ____ Item
//        List::Item is the data type of the items in the List. It may be any of the C++ built-in
//        types (int, char, etc.), or a class with a default constructor, an assignment operator
//        and a copy constructor.
//
//  CONSTRUCTOR for the List class:
//     List( )
//        Postcondition: The List has been initialized as an empty List.
//
//  MODIFICATION MEMBER FUNCTIONS for the List class:
//     void start( )
//        Postcondition: The first item on the List becomes the current item (but if the List is
//        empty, then there is no current item).
//
//     void advance( )
//        Precondition: is_item returns true.
//        Postcondition: If the current item was already the last item on the List, then there is no
//        longer any current item. Otherwise, the new item is the item immediately after the
//        the original current item.
//
//     void insert(const Item& entry)
//        Precondition: size( ) < CAPACITY.
//        Postcondition: A new copy of entry has been inserted in the List before the current
//        item. If there was no current item, then the new entry has been inserted at the front of
//        the List. In either case, the new item is now the current item of the List.
//
//     void attach(const Item& entry)
//        Precondition: size( ) < CAPACITY.
//        Postcondition: A new copy of entry has been inserted in the List after the current item.
//        If there was no current item, then the new entry has been attached to the end of the
//        List. In either case, the new item is now the current item of the List.
//
//     void remove_current( )
//        Precondition: is_item returns true.
//        Postcondition: The current item has been removed from the List, and the
//        item after this (if there is one) is now the new current item.
```

(continued)

(FIGURE 3.8 continued)

```
//
//  CONSTANT MEMBER FUNCTIONS for the List class:
//      size_t size( ) const
//          Postcondition: The return value is the number of items on the List.
//
//      bool is_item( ) const
//          Postcondition: A true return value indicates that there is a valid "current" item that
//          may be retrieved by the current member function (listed below). A false return value
//          indicates that there is no valid current item.
//
//      Item current( ) const
//          Precondition: is_item( ) returns true.
//          Postcondition: The item returned is the current item on the List.
//
//  VALUE SEMANTICS  for the List class:
//      Assignments and the copy constructor may be used with List objects.

#ifndef LIST1_H
#define LIST1_H
#include <stdlib.h>   // Provides size_t

    class List
    {
    public:
        // TYPEDEF and MEMBER CONSTANTS
        static const size_t CAPACITY = 30;
        typedef double Item;
        // CONSTRUCTOR
        List( );
        // MODIFICATION MEMBER FUNCTIONS
        void start( );
        void advance( );
        void insert(const Item& entry);
        void attach(const Item& entry);
        void remove_current( );
        // CONSTANT MEMBER FUNCTIONS
        size_t size( ) const;
        bool is_item( ) const;
        Item current( ) const;
    private:
        Item data[CAPACITY];
        size_t used;
        size_t current_index;
    };

    #endif
```

If your compiler does not permit initialization of static constants, see Appendix E.

The three private member variables are discussed in the section "The List ADT—Design" on page 118.

list1.h   **FTP**

In the case of the bag, we could remove an element such as 1.4 by copying the final item (1.1) onto the 1.4. But this approach won't work for the *list* because the items would lose their sequence order. Instead, each item after the 1.4 must be moved leftward one position. The 6 moves from `data[2]` to `data[1]`; the 9 moves from `data[3]` to `data[2]`; the 1.1 moves from `data[4]` to `data[3]`. This is a lot of movement, but a simple for-loop suffices to carry out all the work. This is the pseudocode:

> *for* (i = the index after the current item; i < used; i++)
>   Move an item from `data[i]` back to `data[i-1]`;

When the loop completes, you should reduce `used` by one. The final result for our example is shown here:

After the removal, the value in `current_index` is unchanged. In effect, this means that the item that was just after the removed item is now the current item. You should check that the function works correctly for boundary values— removing the first item and removing the final item. In fact, both these cases do work fine. When the final item is removed, `current_index` will end up with the same value as `used`, indicating that there is no longer a current item.

The insert function. If there is a current item, then the insert function must take care to insert the new item just before the current position. Items that are already at or after the current position must be shifted rightward to make room for the new item. We suggest that you start by checking the precondition. Then shift items at the end of the array rightward one position each until you reach the position for the new item.

For example, suppose you are inserting 1.4 at the location `data[1]` in the list drawn here:

You would begin by shifting the 1.1 rightward from data[3] to data[4]; then move the 9 from data[2] to data[3]; then the 6 moves from data[1] rightward to data[2]. At this point, the array looks as we've drawn here:

Of course, data[1] actually still contains a 6 since we just copied the 6 from data[1] to data[2]. But we have drawn data[1] as an empty box to indicate that data[1] is now available to hold the new item (that is, the 1.4 that we are inserting). At this point we can place the 1.4 in data[1] and add one to used, as shown here:

The pseudocode for shifting the items rightward uses a for-loop. Each iteration of the loop shifts one item, as shown here:

```
for (i = used;  data[i] is the wrong spot for entry ; i--)
    data[i] = data[i-1];
```

The key to the loop is the test data[i] is the wrong spot for entry. How do we test whether a position is the wrong spot for the new item? A position is wrong if (i > current_index). Can you now write the entire member function in C++? (See the solution to Self-Test Exercise 7, and don't forget to handle the special case when there is no current item.)

Other Member Functions. The other list member functions are straightforward; for example, the attach function is similar to insert. Some additional useful member functions are described in Programming Projects 3 and 4 on page 132. You'll also need to watch out for a pitfall that we describe next.

PITFALL

Pitfall: When to Use the Full Type Name List::Item

When you implement the list's `current` function, you must take care to write the return type as shown here:

```
List::Item List::current( ) const
```

We have used the completely specified type `List::Item` rather than just `Item`. This is because many compilers do not recognize that you are implementing a `List` member function until after seeing `List::current`. In the implementation, after `List::current`, we may use the simpler name `Item`, but before `List::current`, we should use the full type name `List::Item`.

Self-Test Exercises

7. Write the list's insert function.

8. Suppose that a list has 24 items, and there is no current item. According to the invariant of the ADT, what is `current_index`?

9. Suppose g is a list with 10 items and you activate `g.start( )` and then activate `g.advance( )` three times. What value is then in `g.current_index`?

10. What are good boundary values to test the `remove_current` function?

11. Write a demonstration program that asks the user for a list of family member ages, then prints the list in the same order that it was given.

12. Write a new member function to remove a specified item from a list. The function has one parameter (the item to remove).

13. For a list of numbers, suppose that you attach 1, then 2, then 3, and so on up to *n*. What is the big-*O* time analysis for the combined time of attaching all *n* numbers? How does the analysis change if you insert *n* first, then *n*-1, and so on down to 1—always using `insert` instead of `attach`?

14. Which of the ADTs—the bag or the list—*must* be implemented by storing the items in an array? (Hint: We are not beyond asking a trick question.)

3.3 INTERACTIVE TEST PROGRAMS

Your list ADT is a good candidate for an interactive test program that follows a standard format. The format, illustrated by the program of Figure 3.9, can be used with any ADT. The start of the main program declares an object—in this case, a `List` object. The rest of the main program is an interactive loop that continues as long as the user wants. Three things occur inside the loop:

1. A small menu of choices is written for the user. Each choice is printed along with a letter or other meaningful character to allow the user to select the choice.

2. The user's selection from the menu is read.

3. Based on the user's selection, some action is taken on the List object.

Our example interactive test program for the list is shown in Figure 3.9, with part of a sample dialogue in Figure 3.10 on page 128. Some of the techniques used in the test program are familiar. For example, subtasks, such as printing the menu, are accomplished with functions. Two techniques in the test program may be new to you: converting input to upper-case letters, and acting on the input via a *switch* statement. We'll discuss these two techniques after you've looked through the program.

FIGURE 3.9   Interactive Test Program for the List Class

A Program

```
// FILE: listtest.cxx
// An interactive test program for the new List ADT
#include <ctype.h>       // Provides toupper
#include <iostream.h>    // Provides cout and cin
#include <stdlib.h>      // Provides EXIT_SUCCESS and size_t
#include "list1.h"       // With Item defined as double

// PROTOTYPES for functions used by this test program:
void print_menu( );
// Postcondition: A menu of choices for this program has been written to cout.


char get_user_command( );
// Postcondition: The user has been prompted to enter a one-character command.
//  The next character has been read (skipping blanks and newline characters),
//  and this character has been returned.


void show_list(List display);
// Postcondition: The items on display have been printed to cout (one per line).


double get_number( );
// Postcondition: The user has been prompted to enter a real number. The
// number has been read, echoed to the screen, and returned by the function.
```

(continued)

(FIGURE 3.9 continued)

```cpp
int main( )
{
    List test;      // A List that we'll perform tests on
    char choice;    // A command character entered by the user

    cout << "I have initialized an empty List of real numbers." << endl;

    do
    {
        print_menu( );
        choice = toupper(get_user_command( ));
        switch (choice)
        {
            case '!': test.start( );
                      break;
            case '+': test.advance( );
                      break;
            case '?': if (test.is_item( ))
                          cout << "There is an item." << endl;
                      else
                          cout << "There is no current item." << endl;
                      break;
            case 'C': if (test.is_item( ))
                          cout << "Current item is: " << test.current( ) << endl;
                      else
                          cout << "There is no current item." << endl;
                      break;
            case 'P': show_list(test);
                      break;
            case 'S': cout << "List size is " << test.size( ) << '.' << endl;
                      break;
            case 'I': test.insert(get_number( ));
                      break;
            case 'A': test.attach(get_number( ));
                      break;
            case 'R': test.remove_current( );
                      cout << "The current item has been removed." << endl;
                      break;
            case 'Q': cout << "Ridicule is the best test of truth." << endl;
                      break;
            default:  cout << choice << " is invalid." << endl;
        }
    }
    while ((choice != 'Q'));

    return EXIT_SUCCESS;
}
```

(continued)

(FIGURE 3.9 continued)

```cpp
void print_menu( )
// Library facilities used: iostream.h
{
    cout << endl; // Print blank line before the menu
    cout << "The following choices are available: " << endl;
    cout << " !   Activate the start( ) function" << endl;
    cout << " +   Activate the advance( ) function" << endl;
    cout << " ?   Print the result from the is_item( ) function" << endl;
    cout << " C   Print the result from the current( ) function" << endl;
    cout << " P   Print a copy of the entire List" << endl;
    cout << " S   Print the result from the size( ) function" << endl;
    cout << " I   Insert a new number with the insert(...) function" << endl;
    cout << " A   Attach a new number with the attach(...) function" << endl;
    cout << " R   Activate the remove_current( ) function" << endl;
    cout << " Q   Quit this test program" << endl;
}

char get_user_command( )
// Library facilities used: iostream.h
{
    char command;

    cout << "Enter choice: ";
    cin >> command; // Input of characters skips blanks and newline character

    return command;
}

void show_list(List display)
// Library facilities used: iostream.h
{
    for (display.start( ); display.is_item( ); display.advance( ))
        cout << display.current( ) << endl;
}

double get_number( )
// Library facilities used: iostream.h
{
    double result;

    cout << "Please enter a real number for the List: ";
    cin  >> result;
    cout << result << " has been read." << endl;
    return result;
}
```

listtest.cxx   **FTP**

FIGURE 3.10   Part of a Sample Dialogue from the Program of Figure 3.9

A Sample Dialogue

```
I have initialized an empty List of real numbers.

The following choices are available:
 !  Activate the start( ) function
 +  Activate the advance( ) function
 ?  Print the result from the is_item( ) function
 C  Print the result from the current( ) function
 P  Print a copy of the entire List
 S  Print the result from the size( ) function
 I  Insert a new number with the insert(...) function
 A  Attach a new number with the attach(...) function
 R  Activate the remove_current( ) function
 Q  Quit this test program
Enter choice: A
Please enter a real number for the List: 3.14
3.14 has been read.

The following choices are available:
 !  Activate the start( ) function
 +  Activate the advance( ) function
 ?  Print the result from the is_item( ) function
 C  Print the result from the current( ) function
 P  Print a copy of the entire List
 S  Print the result from the size( ) function
 I  Insert a new number with the insert(...) function
 A  Attach a new number with the attach(...) function
 R  Activate the remove_current( ) function
 Q  Quit this test program
Enter choice: S
List size is 1.
```

‖ The dialogue continues until the user types **Q** to stop the program.

C++ *Feature:* Converting Input to Upper-Case Letters

Even small test programs should have some flexibility regarding user input. For example, the program should accept either upper- or lower-case letters for each menu choice. We accomplish this by reading the user's input and then, if necessary, converting a lower-case letter to the corresponding upper-case letter. The conversion is carried out by a function `toupper` with this specification:

```
char toupper(char c);
// Postcondition: If c is a lower-case letter, then the return value is the
// upper-case equivalent of c. Otherwise the return value is just c itself.
```

The `toupper` function is part of the C++ library facility `ctype.h`. In our main program, we use `toupper` to convert the result of the `get_user_command` function, as shown here:

```
choice = toupper(get_user_command( ));
```

After this statement, we don't need to worry about `choice` being a lower-case letter.

C++ *Feature:* The Switch Statement

After the user's choice is read, the main program takes an action. The action depends on the single character that the user typed from the menu. An effective statement to select among many possible actions is the *switch* statement, with the general form:

```
switch (<Control value>)
{
    <Body of the switch statement>
}
```

When the switch statement is reached, the control value is evaluated. The program then looks through the body of the switch statement for a matching case label. For example, if the control value is the character 'A', then the program looks for a case label of the form `case 'A':`. If a matching case label is found, then the program goes to that label and begins executing statements. Statements are executed one after another—but if a **break** statement (of the form `break;`) occurs, then the program skips to the end of the body of the switch statement.

If the control value has no matching case label, then the program will look for a **default label** of the form `default:`. This label handles any control values that don't have their own case label.

If there is no matching case label and no default label, then the whole body of the switch statement is skipped.

For an interactive test program, the switch statement has one case label for each of the menu choices. For example, one of the menu choices is the character 'A' to allow the user to attach a new number to the list. In the switch statement, the 'A' command is handled as shown here:

```
switch (choice)
{
    ...
    case 'A': test.attach(get_number( ));
              break;
    ...
}
```

Self-Test Exercises

15. What are the values of `toupper('a')`, `toupper('A')`, and `toupper('+')`?

16. What situation calls for a switch statement?

17. The `show_list` function on page 127 uses a *value* parameter rather than a *reference* parameter. Why?

CHAPTER SUMMARY

- A *container class* is an ADT where each object contains a collection of items. Bags and lists are two examples of container classes.

- A container class should be implemented in a way that makes it easy to alter the data type of the underlying items. In C++, the simple approach to this problem uses a typedef statement to define the type of the container's item.

- The simplest implementations of container classes use a *partially filled array*. Using a partially filled array requires each object to have at least two member variables: the array itself and a `size_t` variable to keep track of how much of the array is being used.

- When you design an ADT, always make an explicit statement of the rules that dictate how the member variables are used. These rules are called the *invariant of the ADT*, and should be written at the top of the implementation file for easy reference.

- Small ADTs can be effectively tested with an *interactive test program* that follows the standard format of our list test program.

1. The default constructor is required because Item is used as the component type of an array. Each of the required operators (=, ==, and !=) is used with the Item in at least one of the bag's member functions.

2.

3	2

[0] [1]

We don't care what appears beyond data[1].

3. See the two rules on page 102.

4. It does not need to be a friend function because it does not directly access any private members of the bag.

5. The two statements can be replaced by one statement: data[index] = data[--used]; When --used appears as an expression, the variable used is decremented by one, and the resulting value is the value of the expression. (On the other hand, if used-- appears as an expression, the value of the expression is the value of used prior to subtracting one.) Similarly, the last two statements of insert can be combined to data[used++] = entry;

6. If we have activated b += b, then the private member variable used is the same variable as addend.used. Each iteration of the loop adds 1 to used, and hence addend.used is also increasing, and the loop never ends. The correct implementation is in Figure 3.5 on page 110.

7.
```
void List::insert(const Item& entry)
{
    size_t i;

    assert(size( ) < CAPACITY);
    if (!is_item( ))
        current_index = 0;
    for (i = used; i > current_index; i--)
        data[i] = data[i-1];
    data[current_index] = entry;
    used++;
}
```

8. 24

9. g.current_index will be 3 (since the 4th item occurs at data[3]).

10. The remove_current function should be tested when the list's size is just 1, and when the list is at its full capacity. At full capacity you should try removing the first item, and the last item on the list.

11. Your program can be similar to Figure 3.2 on page 98.

12. Here is our function's prototype, with a postcondition:
void remove(*const* Item& target);
// *Postcondition: If target was on the List,*
// *then the first copy of target has been*
// *removed from the List, and the item after*
// *the removed item (if there is one)*
// *becomes the new current item; otherwise*
// *the List remains unchanged.*

The easiest implementation searches for the index of the target. If this index is found, then set current_index to this index, and activate the ordinary remove_current function.

13. The total time to attach 1, 2, ... , n is $O(n)$. The total time to insert n, n-1, ... , 1 is $O(n^2)$. The larger time for the insert is because an insertion at the front of the list requires all of the existing items to be shifted right to make room for the new item. Hence, on the second insertion, one item is shifted. On the third insertion, two items are shifted. And so on to the nth item which needs n-1 shifts.. The total number of shifts is 1+2+...+(n-1), which is $O(n^2)$. (To show that this sum is $O(n^2)$, use a technique similar to Figure 1.5 on page 18.)

14. Neither of the classes *must* use an array. In later chapters we will see both classes implemented without arrays.

15. The first two calls return 'A'. The function call toupper('+') returns '+'.

16. Use a switch statement when a single control value determines which of several possible actions is to be taken.

17. With a reference parameter, the advancing of the current element through the list would alter the actual argument.

PROGRAMMING PROJECTS

1 A **black box** test of a class is a program that tests the correctness of the class's member functions without directly examining the private members of the class. You can imagine that the private members are inside an opaque black box where they cannot be seen, so all testing must occur only through activating the public member functions.

Write a black box test program for the Bag class. Make sure that you test the boundary values, such as an empty bag, a bag with just one item, and a full bag.

2 Implement operators for - and -= for the Bag class from Section 3.1. For two bags x and y, the bag x-y contains all the items of x, with any items from y removed. For example, suppose that x has seven copies of the number 3, and y has two copies of the number 3. Then x-y will have five copies of the number 3 (i.e., 7 - 2 copies of the number 3). In the case where y has more copies of an item than x does, the bag x-y will have no copies of that item. For example, suppose that x has nine copies of the number 8, and y has ten copies of the number 8. Then x-y will have no 8's. The statement x -= y should have the same effect as the assignment x = x-y;

3 Implement the List class from Section 3.2. You may wish to provide some additional useful member functions, such as: (1) a function to add a new item at the front of the list; (2) a function to remove the item from the front of the list; (3) a function to add a new item at the end of the list; (4) a function that makes the last item of the list become the current item; (5) operators for + and +=. For the + operator, a list x + y contains all the items of x, followed by all the items of y. The statement x += y appends all of the items of y to the end of what's already in x.

4 For a list x, we would like to be able to refer to the individual items using the usual C++ notation for arrays. For example, if x has three items, then we want to be able to write x[0], x[1], and x[2] to access these three items. This use of the square brackets is called the **subscript operator**. The subscript operator may be overloaded as a member function, with the prototype shown here as part of the List class:

```
class List
{
public:
    ...
    Item operator [ ] (size_t index) const;
    ...
```

As you can see, the *operator* [ ] is a member function with one parameter. The parameter is the index of the list item that we want to retrieve. The implementation of this member function should check that the index is a valid index (i.e., index is less than the list's size), and then return the specified item.

For this project, specify, design, and implement this new subscript operator for the list.

5 A bag can contain more than one copy of an item. For example, the chapter describes a bag that contains the number 4 and two copies of the number 8. This bag behavior is different from a **set**, which can contain only a single copy of any given item. Write a new container class called Set, which is similar to a bag, except that a set can contain only one copy of any given item. You'll need to change the interface a bit. For example, instead of the bag's occurrences function, you'll want a constant member function such as this:

```
bool Set::contains
(const Item& target) const;
// Postcondition: The return value is true if
// target is in the set; otherwise the return
// value is false.
```

Make an explicit statement of the invariant of the set ADT. Do a time analysis for each operation. At this point, an efficient implementation is not needed. For example, just adding a new item to a set will take linear time because you'll need to check that the new item isn't already present. Later we'll explore more efficient implementations.

You may also want to add additional operations to your set ADT, such as an operator for subtraction.

6 Suppose that you implement a list where the underlying item type has a comparison operator < to determine when one item is "less than" another item. For example, integers, double numbers, and characters all have such a comparison operator (and classes that you implement yourself may also be given such a comparison). Rewrite the list class using a new class name, SortedList. In a sorted list, the insert function always inserts a new item so that all the items stay in order from smallest to largest. There is no attach function. All the other functions are the same as the original list ADT.

7 In this project, you will implement a new class called a **bag with receipts.** This new class is similar to an ordinary bag, but the way that items are added and removed is different. Each time an item is added to a bag with receipts, the insert function returns a unique integer called the

receipt. Later, when you want to remove an item, you must provide a copy of the receipt as a parameter to the remove function. The remove function removes the item whose receipt has been presented, and also returns a copy of that item through a reference parameter.

Here's an implementation idea: A bag with receipts can have *two* private arrays, like this:

```
class BagWithReceipts
{
...
private:
    Item data[CAPACITY];
    bool in_use[CAPACITY];
};
```

Arrays such as these, which have the same size, are called **parallel arrays.** The idea is to keep track of which parts of the data array are being used by placing boolean values in the second array. When in_use[i] is true, then data[i] is currently being used; when in_use[i] is false, then data[i] is currently unused. When a new item is added, we will find the first spot that is currently unused and store the new item there. The receipt for the item is the index of the location where the item is stored.

8 Another way to store a collection of items is called a **keyed bag.** In this type of bag, whenever an item is added, the programmer using the bag also provides an integer called the **key.** Each item added to the keyed bag must have a unique key; two items cannot have the same key. So, the insertion function has the specification shown here:

```
void KeyedBag::insert
(const Item& entry, int key);
// Precondition: size( ) < CAPACITY, and the
// bag does not yet contain any item with
// the given key.
// Postcondition: A new copy of entry has
// been added to the bag, with the given key.
```

When the programmer wants to remove an item from a keyed bag, the key of the item must be specified, rather than the item itself. The keyed bag should also have a boolean member function that can be used to determine whether the bag has an item with a specified key.

A keyed bag differs from the bag with receipts (in the previous project). In a keyed bag, the programmer using the class specifies a particular key when an item is inserted. In contrast, for a bag with receipts, the insert function returns a receipt, and the programmer using the class has no control over what that receipt might be.

For this project, do a complete specification, design, and implementation of a keyed bag.

9 A one-variable **polynomial** is an arithmetic expression of the form:

$$a_0 + a_1 x + a_2 x^2 + \ldots + a_k x^k$$

The highest exponent, k, is called the **degree** of the polynomial, and the constants $a_0, a_1, \ldots$ are the **coefficients.** For example, here are two polynomials with degree three:

$$2.1 + 4.8x + 0.1x^2 + (-7.1)\,x^3$$
$$2.9 + 0.8x + 10.1x^2 + 1.7x^3$$

Specify, design, and implement a class for polynomials. The class may contain a static member constant, MAXDEGREE, which indicates the maximum degree of any polynomial. (This allows you to store the coefficients in an array with a fixed size). Spend some time thinking about operations that make sense on polynomials. For example, you can write an operation that adds two polynomials. Another operation should evaluate the polynomial for a given value of x.

10 Specify, design, and implement a class that can be one player in a game of tic-tac-toe. The constructor should specify whether the object is to be the first player (X's) or the second player (O's). There should be a member function to ask the object to make its next move, and a member function that tells the object what the opponent's next move is. Also include other useful member functions, such as a function to ask whether a given spot of the tic-tac-toe board is occupied, and if so, whether the occupation is with an X or an O. Also,

include a member function to determine when the game is over, and whether it was a draw, an X win, or an O win.

Use the class in two programs: a program that plays tic-tac-toe against the program's user, and a program that has two tic-tac-toe objects that play against each other.

11 Specify, design, and implement a container class that can hold up to five playing cards. Call the class PokerHand, and overload the boolean comparison operators to allow you to compare two poker hands. For two hands x and y, the relation x > y means that x is a better hand than y. If you do not play in a weekly poker game yourself, then you may need to consult a card rule book for the rules on the ranking of poker hands.

12 Specify, design, and implement a class that keeps track of rings stacked on a peg, rather like phonograph records on a spindle. An example with five rings is shown here:

Rings stacked on a peg

The peg may hold up to 64 rings, with each ring having its own diameter. Also, there is a rule that requires each ring to be smaller than any ring underneath it, as shown for the five rings on the peg above. The class's member functions should include: (a) a constructor that places n rings on the peg (where n may be as large as 64); use 64 for a default argument. These n rings have diameters from n inches (on the bottom) to one-inch (on the top). (b) a const member function that returns the number of rings on the peg. (c) a const member function that returns the diameter of the topmost ring. (d) a member function that adds a new ring to the top (with the diameter of the ring as a parameter to the function). (e) a member function that removes the topmost ring. (f) an overloaded output function that prints some clever representation of the peg and its rings. Make sure that all functions have appropriate pre-conditions to guarantee that the rule about ring sizes is enforced. Also spend time designing appropriate private data fields.

13 In this project, you will design and implement a class called `Towers`, which is part of a program that lets a child play a game called Towers of Hanoi. The game consists of three pegs and a collection of rings that stack on the pegs. The rings are different sizes. The initial configuration for a five-ring game is shown here, with the first tower having rings from one-inch (on the top) to five-inches (on the bottom).

Initial configuration for a five-ring game of Towers of Hanoi

The rings are stacked in decreasing order of their size, and the second and third towers are initially empty. During the game, the child may transfer rings one-at-a-time from the top of one peg to the top of another. The object of the game is to move all the rings from the first peg to the second peg. The difficulty is that the child may not place a ring on top of one with a smaller diameter. There is the one extra peg to hold rings temporarily, but the prohibition against a larger ring on a smaller ring applies to it as well as the other two pegs. A solution for a three-ring game is shown at the bottom of the page. The `Towers` class must keep track of the status of all three pegs. You might use an array of three pegs, where each peg is an object from the previous

project. The `Towers` functions are specified here:

```
Towers::Towers(size_t n = 64);
// Precondition: 1 <= n <= 64.
// Postcondition: The towers have been initialized
// with n rings on the first peg and no rings on
// the other two pegs. The diameters of the first
// peg's rings are from one-inch (on the top) to n
// inches (on the bottom).
```

```
size_t Towers::many_rings
(int peg_number) const;
// Precondition: peg_number is 1, 2, or 3.
// Postcondition: The return value is the number
// of rings on the specified peg.
```

```
size_t Towers::top_diameter
(int peg_number) const;
// Precondition: peg_number is 1, 2, or 3.
// Postcondition: If many_rings(peg_number) > 0,
// then the return value is the diameter of the top
// ring on the specified peg; otherwise the return
// value is zero.
```

```
void Towers::move
(int start_peg; int end_peg);
// Precondition: start_peg is a peg number
// (1, 2, or 3), and many_rings(start_peg) > 0;
// end_peg is a different peg number (not equal
// to start_peg), and top_diameter(end_peg) is
// either 0 or more than top_diameter(start_peg).
// Postcondition: The top ring has been moved
// from start_peg to end_peg.
```

Also overload the output operator so that a `Towers` object may be displayed easily.

Use the `Towers` object in a program that allows a child to play Towers of Hanoi. Make sure that you don't allow the child to make any illegal moves.

At game start

After 1 move

After 2 moves

After 3 moves

After 4 moves

After 5 moves

After 6 moves

After 7 moves

4 Pointers and Dynamic Arrays

And bade his messengers ride forth
East and west and south and north
To summon his array

THOMAS BABINGTON
Horatius

The container classes from Chapter 3 still have a vexing limitation. Their capacity is declared as a constant in the class definition. For example, the `Bag::CAPACITY` constant determines the capacity of every bag. If we need bigger bags, then we can increase the constant and recompile, but doing so increases the size of *every* bag. This is wasteful for a program that needs one large bag and many small bags. Even the small bags have the capacity of the largest bag.

the size of each bag will be independent of the other bags

The solution is to provide control over the size of each bag, independent of each of the other bags. This control can come from *dynamic arrays*, which are arrays whose size is determined only after a program is actually running. Dynamic arrays require an understanding of pointers and dynamic memory, which are introduced and developed in the first two sections of this chapter. The dynamic arrays are then used for a new implementation of the bag class in Section 4.3, and for a flexible implementation of a string class in Section 4.4. The understanding of pointers, which you gain in this chapter, also forms the foundation for many ADTs in subsequent chapters.

4.1 POINTERS AND DYNAMIC MEMORY

In order to improve our container class implementations, we need to know about pointers. A **pointer** is the memory address of a variable. To understand this definition, you need a mental picture of the computer's memory as consisting of numbered memory locations (called *bytes*). Each variable in a program is stored in a sequence of adjacent bytes. For example, on some machines each integer variable requires four bytes of memory. On such a machine, an integer declaration such as `int i;` provides four adjacent bytes of memory to store the value of the integer i. The example drawn below provides bytes numbered 990 through 993 for an integer variable i.

An integer variable might require four bytes of memory.

998	
997	
996	
995	
994	
993	
992	
991	
990	
989	
988	

A program might provide these four bytes for an integer i.

The numbers labeling each byte are called the **memory addresses**. When a variable occupies several adjacent bytes, then the memory address of the first byte is also called the memory address of the variable. So in our example, the address of the integer i is 990. The address of a variable is called a **pointer**. These addresses are called pointers because they can be thought of as "pointing" to a variable. The address "points" to the variable because it identifies the variable by telling *where* the variable is, rather than telling what the variable's name is. Our integer i can be pointed out by saying, "It's over there at location 990."

Pointers are much more useful than mere indications of variable locations. To begin to see the utility of pointers, we must look at pointer variables.

Pointer Variables

A pointer can be stored in a variable, but not by using an ordinary integer variable. Instead, a variable to store a pointer must be declared as a special *pointer variable* by placing an asterisk before the pointer variable's name. The complete declaration of a pointer variable must contain three items shown at the top of the next page.

double *my_first_ptr;*

the type of data
that the pointer
variable can
point to

an asterisk

the name of the
newly declared
pointer
variable

declaring
pointer variables

In our example, my_first_ptr is a pointer variable that is capable of pointing to any double variable. In other words, my_first_ptr can hold the memory address of a double variable. The pointer variable my_first_ptr does not actually contain a double number itself—it merely contains the address of a double variable. Also, since we used the double data type in our declaration, my_first_ptr cannot contain a pointer to a variable of some other type, such as *int* or *char*. It may contain only a pointer to a double variable.

If you declare several pointer variables on a single line, then an asterisk must appear before each variable name. For example, to declare two pointers to characters:

```
char *c1_ptr, *c2_ptr;
```
◄—— *Declaring two char pointers*

If you omit the asterisk before c2_ptr, then c2_ptr will be an ordinary character variable rather than a pointer to a character. For additional clarity we often use "_ptr" as the end of a pointer variable's name, or we use "cursor" as part of a pointer variable's name because a "cursor" means a pointer that "runs through a structure."

Pointer Variable Declarations

A variable that is a pointer to other variables of type *Type_Name* is declared in the same way that you declare a variable of type *Type_Name*, except that you place an asterisk at the beginning of the variable name.

Syntax:
```
Type_Name *var_name1;
```

Examples:
```
int *cursor;
char *c1_ptr, *c2_ptr;
```

Of course, a pointer variable is of no use unless there is something for it to point to. For example, consider these two declarations:

```
int *example_ptr;
int i;
```

We can make `example_ptr` contain the address of `i` by using the & operator shown here:

`example_ptr = &i;`   *This statement puts the address of i into the pointer variable example_ptr.*

The & operator, called the **address** operator, provides the address of a variable, for instance &`i` is "the address of the integer variable `i`." So the assignment statement places "the address of `i`" into `example_ptr`. Or we could simply say that `example_ptr` now "points to" `i`.

the & operator

After the assignment, you have two ways to refer to `i`: You can call it `i`, or you can call it "the variable pointed to by `example_ptr`." In C++ "the variable pointed to by `example_ptr`" is written `*example_ptr`. This is the same asterisk notation that we used to declare `*example_ptr`, but now it has yet another meaning. When the asterisk is used in this way, it is called the **dereferencing operator**, and the pointer variable is said to be **dereferenced**. For example:

*the * operator*

```
i = 42;
example_ptr = &i;
cout << i << endl;
cout << *example_ptr << endl;
```
Both statements print 42.
This dereferences example_ptr.

The dereferencing operator can produce some surprising results. Consider the following code:

```
i = 42;
example_ptr = &i;
*example_ptr = 0;
cout << *example_ptr << endl;
cout << i << endl;
```
This prints 0.
This also prints 0.

As long as `example_ptr` contains a pointer to `i`, then `i` and `*example_ptr` refer to the same variable. So when you set `*example_ptr` equal to 0, you are really setting `i` equal to 0.

The symbol & that is used as the address operator is the same symbol that is used in a function's parameter list to specify a reference parameter (see page 64). This is more than a coincidence. The implementation of a reference parameter is accomplished by using the *address* of the actual parameter, rather than making a completely separate copy (as a value parameter does). So, these two usages of the symbol & are much the same. However, the usages are slightly different, and we will consider them to be two different (but closely related) usages of the symbol &.

Using the Assignment Operator with Pointers

You can copy the value of one pointer variable to another with the usual assignment operator. For example:

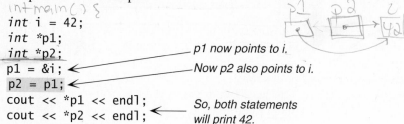

```
int i = 42;
int *p1;
int *p2;
p1 = &i;           p1 now points to i.
p2 = p1;           Now p2 also points to i.
cout << *p1 << endl;
cout << *p2 << endl;    So, both statements
                        will print 42.
```

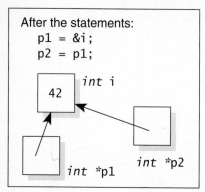

After the statements:
```
p1 = &i;
p2 = p1;
```

The highlighted assignment statement says "make p2 point to the same variable that p1 is already pointing to."

A pointer variable usually is drawn as a box containing an arrow. The arrow points to the variable whose address is stored in the pointer. For example, after the assignment `p2 = p1`, we would draw the picture shown in the margin. There are now three names for the variable i: You can call it i, or you can call it *p1, or you can call it *p2.

When dealing with pointer variables, there is a critical distinction between a pointer variable (such as p1) and the thing it points to (such as *p1). Do not confuse the meaning of these two assignment statements:

$$p2 = p1; \quad \textbf{versus} \quad *p2 = *p1;$$

As we have seen, `p2 = p1` means "make p2 point to the same variable that p1 is already pointing to." On the other hand, the inclusion of the dereferencing asterisks in `*p2 = *p1` gives the statement quite a different meaning. The new meaning is to "copy the value from the variable that p1 points at, to the variable that p2 points at." Here is an example, which starts by declaring two integers and two pointers to integers.

```
int i = 42;
int j = 80;
int *p1;
int *p2;
p1 = &i;
p2 = &j;
```

After the statements, the
pointer variables are as
shown to the right.

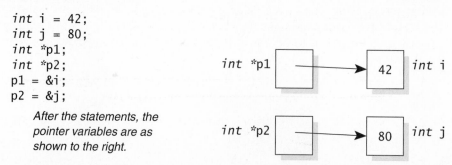

Pointers and Dynamic Memory   **141**

Once the two pointers are initialized, we can see the effect of an assignment statement:

```
*p2 = *p1;
```
After this assignment statement, the pointer variables still point to different locations, but the contents of one of those locations has changed.

The assignment statement has copied the value 42 from the variable that p1 points at, to the variable that p2 points at. In effect, j has changed its contents, but the pointers themselves still point to separate memory locations.

Pointer Variables Used with =

If p1 and p2 are pointer variables, then the assignment p2 = p1 changes p2 so that it points to the same variable that p1 already points to.

On the other hand, the assignment *p2 = *p1 copies the value from the variable that p1 points at, to the variable that p2 points at—but the pointers p1 and p2 still point to the memory locations that they did before the assignment statement.

Dynamic Variables and the *new* Operator

Pointers may point to ordinary variables, such as i in our previous example. But the real power of pointers arises when pointers are used with special kinds of variables called *dynamically allocated variables*, or more simply, *dynamic variables*. **Dynamic variables** are like ordinary variables, with two important differences:

1. Dynamic variables are <u>not declared</u>. A program may use many dynamic variables, but the dynamic variables never appear in any declaration the way an ordinary variable does. Moreover, a dynamic variable has no identifier (such as the identifiers i and j that are used in our examples).

2. Dynamic variables are <u>created during the execution of a program</u>. Only at that time does a dynamic variable come into existence.

In order <u>to create a dynamic variable</u> while a program is running, C++ programs use an operator called <u>*new*</u>, as shown here:

```
double *d_ptr;
d_ptr = new double;
```

In this example, the *new* operator creates a new dynamic variable of type *double* and returns a pointer to this new dynamic variable. The pointer is assigned to the pointer variable d_ptr. The creation of new dynamic variables is called memory **allocation** and the memory is **dynamic memory**, so we may say that "d_ptr points to a newly *allocated* double variable from *dynamic memory*." Here is another example, which allocates a new *int* variable:

```
int *p1;
```
At this point, p1 is declared, but it has nothing to point to.

p1   ?

```
p1 = new int;
```
Now p1 is pointing to a newly allocated integer variable.

A new integer is allocated by the new operator.

```
*p1 = 42;
```
The new integer variable now contains our favorite number, 42.

42

The assignment statement at the end of this example places 42 in the dynamic variable that p1 points to.

Using *new* to Allocate Dynamic Arrays

We have seen the *new* operator allocate one dynamic variable at a time. But in fact, *new* can allocate an entire array at once. When *new* allocates an entire array, it actually returns a pointer to the *first* component of the array. The number of array components is listed in square brackets, immediately after the component data type, as shown here:

```
double *d_ptr;
d_ptr = new double[10];
```
The new operator allocates an array of 10 double components and points d_ptr to the first component.

In this example, the *new* operator allocates an array of 10 *double* components and returns a pointer to the first component of the array. The pointer is assigned to the pointer variable d_ptr. After the allocation, the array can be accessed by *using array notation* with the pointer variable d_ptr. For example, the following statement will place 3.14 in the [9] component of the new array:

d_ptr[9] = 3.14; *Because d_ptr points to an array with 10 components, we can use array notation to access component [9].*

Here is another example, which allocates a new *int* array:

int *p1;

At this point, p1 is declared, but it has nothing to point to.

p1 = new int[4];

Now p1 is pointing to a new array of four integers.

a newly allocated array of four integers

[0] [1] [2] [3]

p1[2] = 42;

The [2] component of the array now contains 42.

42

[0] [1] [2] [3]

The assignment statement at the end of this example places 42 in the [2] component of the array that p1 points to.

All the versions of *new* are summarized in Figure 4.1, including information about which constructor gets called when *new* allocates a new *object* of a class. The array version of *new* is particularly useful because the number of array components does not need to be specified when the program is written. Instead, the number of components can depend on factors such as user input, which are not available until the program is actually running. This is **dynamic** behavior—behavior that is determined when a program is *running*—and the arrays allocated by *new* are called **dynamic arrays.**

As an example of dynamic behavior, consider a program that reads a list of numbers and computes the average of the numbers. After computing the average, the program prints the list with an indication of which numbers are below the average and which are above. We would like this program to work for ten numbers, or a hundred numbers, or however many numbers we happen to have. The

dynamic behavior is determined while a program is running

size of the array can be determined by user input, as shown here:

```
size_t array_size;
int *numbers;

cout << "How many numbers do you have? ";
cin >> array_size;
numbers = new int[array_size];
```

We'll fully develop this example in a moment, but first we need a closer look at memory allocation.

FIGURE 4.1 The *new* Operator

The *new* Operator

The *new* operator allocates memory for a dynamic variable of a specified type and returns a pointer to the newly allocated memory. For example, the following allocates a new dynamic integer variable and sets p to point to this new variable:

```
int *p;
p = new int;
```

If the dynamic variable is an object of a class, then the default constructor will be called to initialize the new class instance. A different constructor will be called if you place the constructor's arguments after the type name in the new statement. For example:

```
Throttle *t_ptr;
t_ptr = new Throttle(50);    ←──── This calls the constructor with
                                    an integer argument.
```

The *new* operator can also allocate a dynamic array of components, returning a pointer to the first element. The size of the array is specified in *square brackets* after the data type of the components:

```
double *d_ptr;
d_ptr = new double[50];    ←──── This allocates a dynamic array of 50 doubles.

d_ptr[3] = 3.14;    ←──── This assigns 3.14 to the [3] component of the
                          array that d_ptr points to.
```

If the data type of the array component is a class, then the default constructor is used to initialize all components of the dynamic array. There is no mechanism to use a different constructor on the array components.

The Heap and the `new_handler` Function

When *new* allocates a dynamic variable or dynamic array, the memory comes from a location called the program's **heap** (also called the **free store**). Some computers provide huge heaps, more than a billion bytes. But even the largest heap can be exhausted by allocating too many dynamic variables. When the heap runs out of room, the *new* operator fails.

the heap

The *new* operator usually indicates its failure by calling a special C++ function called `new_handler`. The normal action of `new_handler` is to "raise an exception"; the exception causes an error message to be printed and the program halts. A programmer can make the exception have different behavior or even rewrite the `new_handler` function itself. But the normal behavior—error message and halt—will be sufficient for us. We will, however, clearly document which functions use *new* so more experienced programmers can deal with the `new_handler` in their own manner.

the new_handler function

You should also know that older versions of C++ deal with *new* failure in a different way, by returning a special pointer value called the *null pointer*. We'll have other uses for the null pointer in the next chapter, but we won't use it to indicate *new* failure.

Failure of the *new* Operator

The *new* operator usually indicates failure by calling a special function called `new_handler`. The new_handler raises an exception that prints an error message and halts the program. (Some C++ implementations use a different mechanism for new failure.)

We clearly document which functions use *new* so experienced programmers can deal with the failure in their own manner.

The *delete* Operator

The size of the heap varies from one computer to another. It could be just a few thousand bytes or more than a billion. Small programs are not likely to use all of the heap. However, even with small programs, it is an efficient practice to release any heap memory that is no longer needed. If your program no longer needs a dynamic variable, the memory used by that dynamic variable can be returned to the heap where it can be reused for more dynamic variables. In C++, the *delete* operator is used to return the memory of a dynamic variable back to the heap. The *delete* operator is called by writing the word *delete*, followed by the pointer variable. An example appears at the top of the next page.

```
int *example_ptr;
example_ptr = new int;
```

// *Various statements that use *example_ptr appear here. When the*
// *program no longer needs the dynamic variable that example_ptr*
// *points to, the memory for that dynamic variable is returned to*
// *the heap with the following statement:*

```
delete example_ptr;
```

After the *delete* statement, the memory that example_ptr was pointing to has been returned to the heap for reuse. Using the *delete* operation is sometimes called **freeing** or **releasing** memory.

A slightly different version of *delete* is used to release a dynamic array. In this case, the square brackets [ ] appear between the word *delete* and the pointer variable's name, as shown here:

```
int *example_ptr;
example_ptr = new int[50];
```

// *Various statements that use the array example_ptr[. . .] appear*
// *here. When the program no longer needs the dynamic array, the*
// *memory for that dynamic array is returned to the heap with*
// *the following statement:*

```
delete [ ] example_ptr;
```

When *delete* [ ] releases a dynamic array, there is no need for the array's size inside the square brackets. C++ automatically keeps track of the array's size and releases the correct amount of memory.

Figure 4.2 on page 147 summarizes the *delete* operator.

Programming Tip: Define Pointer Types

▲ TIP

You can define a name for a pointer type so that pointer variables can be declared like other variables, without placing an asterisk in front of each pointer variable. For example, the following defines a data type called IntPtr, which is the type for pointer variables that point to *int* variables:

```
typedef int* IntPtr;
```

A type definition such as this usually appears in a header file or with the collection of function prototypes that precede a main program. After this type definition, the declaration IntPtr i_ptr; is equivalent to *int* *i_ptr;.

FIGURE 4.2 The *delete* Operator

The *delete* Operator

The *delete* operator frees memory that has been used for dynamic variables. The memory is returned to the heap where it can be reused at a later time. For example, the following allocates an integer dynamic variable, and frees the memory when it is no longer needed:

```
int *p;
p = new int;
```

> // *Various statements that use *p appear here. When the program no longer*
> // *needs the dynamic variable that p points to, the memory for that*
> // *dynamic variable is returned to the heap with the following statement:*

```
delete p;
```

The *delete* operator can also free a dynamic array of components. All of the array's memory is returned to the heap, where it can be reused. To free an entire array, the array brackets [ ] are placed after the word delete, as shown here:

```
int *p;
p = new int[50];
```

> // *Various statements that use the array p[. . .] appear here. When the program no*
> // *longer needs the dynamic array, the memory for that dynamic array is returned*
> // *to the heap with the following statement:*

```
delete [ ] p;
```

The array size does not need to be specified with the *delete* operator.

Self-Test Exercises

1. Describe two different uses of & in a C++ program.
2. Write code that (1) allocates a new array of 1000 integers; (2) places the numbers 1 through 1000 in the components of the new array; and (3) returns the array to the heap.

3. What output is produced by the following?

```
int *p1;
int *p2;

p1 = new int;
p2 = new int;
*p1 = 100;
*p2 = 200;
cout << *p1 << " and " << *p2 << endl;
delete p1;
p1 = p2;
cout << *p1 << " and " << *p2 << endl;
*p1 = 300;
cout << *p1 << " and " << *p2 << endl;
*p2 = 400;
cout << *p1 << " and " << *p2 << endl;
delete p1;
```

4. The previous exercise calls *delete*. Why is this a good idea?

4.2   POINTERS AND ARRAYS AS PARAMETERS

A function parameter may be a pointer or an array—but some care is needed to ensure that the connection between the argument and the formal parameter is the intended connection. We'll look at several common situations.

Value parameters that are pointers. Figure 4.3 shows a silly function to illustrate a value parameter that is a pointer. The function's prototype is:

```
void make_it_42( int* i_ptr );
```

The prototype indicates that the parameter i_ptr has type *int**, that is, a pointer to an integer. The parameter is a value parameter because the reference

---

FIGURE 4.3   A Value Parameter that Is a Pointer

A Function Implementation

```
void make_it_42(int* i_ptr)
// Precondition: i_ptr is pointing to an integer variable.
// Postcondition: The integer that i_ptr is pointing at has been changed to 42.
{
    *i_ptr = 42;
}
```

symbol & does not appear. Within the parameter list, most programmers place the asterisk with the data type (*int*) rather than with the parameter name (i_ptr)—although the compiler will accept the asterisk in either position. The reason for the placement with the data type is to emphasize that the "complete type" of the parameter is "an integer pointer."

most programmers place the * with the data type

The only purpose of make_it_42 is to show what happens when a value parameter is a pointer. Notice that the body of the function does not actually change i_ptr, it only changes the integer that i_ptr points at. Let's examine a program that calls make_it_42. The program declares a pointer to an integer, allocating memory for the pointer to point at and calls make_it_42:

```
int *main_ptr;
main_ptr = new int;
```

Now main_ptr is pointing to a newly allocated integer. Next, we call make_it_42, with main_ptr as the actual parameter.

main_ptr ⟶ a new integer

```
make_it_42(main_ptr);
```

As with any value parameter, the *actual* argument provides the initial value for the *formal* parameter. In the example, main_ptr provides the initial value for the formal parameter i_ptr in the body of the make_it_42 function. This means that the parameter i_ptr will point to the same place that main_ptr is already pointing to. At the start of the function's execution we have this situation:

The argument, main_ptr, provides the initial value for the parameter i_ptr.

main_ptr

a new integer

main_ptr = i-ptr;

i_ptr

Within the make_it_42 function, we have the assignment ***i_ptr = 42**. The assignment places 42 in the location that i_ptr points at, as shown here:

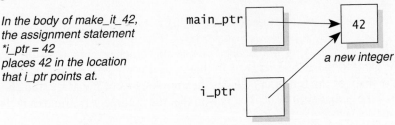

In the body of make_it_42, the assignment statement
*i_ptr = 42
places 42 in the location that i_ptr points at.

main_ptr

42

a new integer

i_ptr

Finally, the function returns and the formal parameter i_ptr is no longer available. However, the pointer variable main_ptr is still around, and it is still pointing to the same location. But the location has a new value of 42, as shown here:

The original argument, main_ptr, is pointing to the same location, but the location has a new value.

a new integer

Value Parameters that Are Pointers

When a value parameter is a pointer, the function may change the value in the location that the pointer points to. The actual argument in the calling program will still point to the same location, but that location will have a new value.

Syntax in the parameter list:
    *Type_Name** var_name

Example:
    void make_it_42(*int** i_ptr);

In ordinary C programming (rather than C++), pointers are frequently used as value parameters. This is because ordinary C does not have reference parameters, so the only convenient way for a function to affect its actual parameters is with a value parameter that is a pointer.

Array Parameters. There is a surprising twist when a parameter is an array. *The parameter is automatically treated as a pointer that points to the first element of the array.* Within the body of the function, the pointer can be used with array notation, which is just like any other pointer that points to the first element of an array. For example, Figure 4.4 shows a function to set the first n elements of an array to the number 42.

a surprising twist for array parameters

Notice that the array parameter is indicated by placing brackets after the parameter name so the function's prototype is:

void make_it_all_42(*double* data[ ], size_t n);

The size of the array is not needed inside the brackets, but usually there is another parameter (such as size_t n) that indicates the size of the array.

If the body of the function changes the components of the array, the changes *do* affect the actual argument. The reason that the argument is affected is that an array parameter is actually a pointer to the first element of the array. Here is an example that calls the function from Figure 4.4:

```
double main_array[10];                 ⟵—— Set all 10 array components to 42.
make_it_all_42(main_array, 10);
cout << main_array[5]; ⟵———— This prints 42.
```

The actual argument of `make_it_all_42` may be a dynamic array, as shown here:

```
double *numbers;                     ⟋— Allocate a dynamic array.
numbers = new double[10]; ⟵
make_it_all_42(numbers, 10); ⟵—— Set all elements to 42.
```

Array Parameters

A parameter that is an array is indicated by placing [ ] after the parameter name, as shown here:

Syntax in the parameter list:
    Type_Name var_name[ ]

Example:
    void make_it_all_42(*double* data[ ], size_t n);

There is usually a separate size_t parameter to indicate the size of the array. Any changes that the function makes to the components of the array *do* affect the actual argument.

FIGURE 4.4 An Array Parameter

A Function Implementation

```
void make_it_all_42(double data[ ], size_t n)
// Precondition: data is an array with at least n components.
// Postcondition: The first n elements of the array data have been set to 42.
// Library facilities used: stdlib.h
{
    size_t i;

    for (i = 0; i < n; i++)
        data[i] = 42;
}
```

Const parameters that are pointers or arrays.   A parameter that is a pointer or an array may also include the *const* keyword, as in these two prototypes:

```
bool is_42(const int* i_ptr);
double average(const double data[ ], size_t n);
```

The *const* keyword in the first prototype indicates that i_ptr is a pointer to a constant integer. In other words, the implementation of is_42 may examine *i_ptr, but may not change the value of *i_ptr. The complete body of is_42 is shown in Figure 4.5, where *i_ptr is compared to the number 42.

The second prototype indicates that data is an array and, because of the *const* keyword, the function cannot change the array entries. The average function may examine all the array entries, but it may not change them. Our intention is for average to return the arithmetic average of all the entries in the data array. You'll see this function written in an example program at the end of this section.

Const Parameters that are Pointers or Arrays

A parameter that is a pointer or array may include the *const* keyword, as shown here:

Syntax in the parameter list:
```
const Type_Name* var_name       → pointer
const Type_Name var_name[ ]     → array
```

Examples:
```
bool is_42(const int* i_ptr);
double sum(const double data[ ], ...
```

The functions may examine the item that is pointed to (or the array), but changing the item (or array) is forbidden.

FIGURE 4.5   A Const Parameter that Is a Pointer

A Function Implementation

```
bool is_42(const int* i_ptr)
// Precondition: i_ptr is pointing to an integer variable.
// Postcondition: The return value is true if *i_ptr is 42.
{
    return (*i_ptr == 42);

}
```

The *const* keyword with a typedef for pointer types. Suppose that you define IntPtr as the data type for a pointer to an integer, as shown here:

```
typedef int* IntPtr;
```

Although it is now legal to use `const IntPtr` as the type of a parameter in a parameter list, the effect is different from `const int*`—and it is unlikely that `const IntPtr` accomplishes what you want. The effect of `const IntPtr` is a *constant pointer* to an integer—in other words, the parameter is a pointer to an ordinary integer variable, and this pointer cannot be altered to point to some other variable. This differs from `const int*`, which is an *ordinary pointer* to a constant integer.

However, there is an alternative to `const int*`, which does use a type definition. The alternative is to define:

```
typedef const int* ConstIntPtr;
```

Now, the name ConstIntPtr can be used in a parameter list for a pointer to a constant integer, for example:

```
bool is_42(ConstIntPtr i_ptr);
```

This prototype is identical to `bool is_42(const int* i_ptr);`.

Reference parameters that are pointers. Sometimes a function will actually *change a pointer parameter so that the pointer points to a new location*, and the programmer needs the change to affect the actual parameter. This is the only situation where a reference parameter will be a pointer. For example, Figure 4.6 shows a function named allocate_doubles that allocates memory for a new dynamic array. Here is the function's prototype:

```
void allocate_doubles(double*& p, size_t& n);
```

The parameter p is a pointer to a *double* (that is, *double**) and it is a reference parameter (indicated by the symbol &). The complete parameter type is thus *double*&*.

In the body of allocate_doubles, the parameter p is changed so that it points to a newly allocated array. In a program we can use allocate_doubles to allocate an array of double values, with the size of the array determined by interacting with the user. Here is an example that calls allocate_doubles:

```
double *numbers;
size_t array_size;
allocate_doubles(numbers, array_size);
```

FIGURE 4.6	A Reference Parameter that Is a Pointer

A Function Implementation

```
void allocate_doubles(double*& p, size_t& n)
// Postcondition: The user has been prompted for a size n, and this size has been read.
// The pointer p has been set to point to a new dynamic array containing n doubles.
// NOTE: If there is insufficient dynamic memory, then new_handler is called.
// Library facilities used: iostream.h, stdlib.h
{
    cout << "How many doubles should I allocate?" << endl;
    cout << "Please type a positive integer answer: ";
    cin >> n;
    p = new double[n];  ←———— Allocate the array of n doubles.
}
```

In this example, the `allocate_doubles` function asks the user how many `double` numbers should be allocated. The user's answer is used to set the argument, `array_size`. The function then allocates an array of the requested size, and the argument called `numbers` is set to point at the first component of the array. Because the function makes its formal parameter p point to a newly allocated array of double numbers, and we want the actual argument `numbers` to point to the newly allocated memory, we are required to use a *reference* parameter.

If you have defined a type definition for a pointer type, then you can avoid the cumbersome syntax of "*&". For example:

```
void allocate_doubles(DoublePtr& p, size_t& n);
```

Reference Parameters that Are Pointers

Sometimes a function will actually *change a pointer parameter so that the pointer points to a new location*, and the programmer needs the change to affect the actual parameter. This is the only situation in which a reference parameter will be a pointer.

Syntax in the parameter list:
   Type_Name*& var_name

Example:
   `void allocate_doubles(double*& p, size_t& n);`

PROGRAMMING EXAMPLE: **Using a Dynamic Array**

Figure 4.7 shows a sample program using dynamic arrays. The program reads a list of numbers, calculates the average, and prints the list of the numbers compared to the average. A sample dialogue is shown at the end of the figure.

Self-Test Exercises

5. What is our favorite number? (Hint: It lies between 41 and 43).

6. When should a pointer parameter be a reference parameter?

7. Suppose that an array is passed as a parameter. How does this differ from the usual use of a value parameter?

8. Write a function with one reference parameter that is a pointer to an integer. The function allocates a dynamic array of n integers, making the pointer point to this new array. It then fills the array with 0 through n - 1.

9. Why do average and compare in Figure 4.7 on page 157 use the keyword *const* with the data array, but fill_array does not?

10. Write a function that copies n elements from the front of one integer array to the front of another. One of the arrays should be a const parameter, and the other should be an ordinary array parameter.

FIGURE 4.7 Demonstration Program for Dynamic Arrays

A Program

```
// FILE: dynademo.cxx
// This is a small demonstration program showing how a dynamic array is used.
#include <iostream.h>    // Provides cout and cin
#include <stdlib.h>      // Provides EXIT_SUCCESS and size_t
#include <assert.h>      // Provides assert

// PROTOTYPES for functions used by this demonstration program
void allocate_doubles(double*& p, size_t& n);
// Postcondition: The user has been prompted for a size n, and this size has been read.
// The pointer p has been set to point to a new dynamic array containing n doubles.
// NOTE: If there is insufficient dynamic memory, then new_handler is called.

void fill_array(double data[ ], size_t n);
// Precondition:  data is an array with at least n components.
// Postcondition: The user has been prompted to type n doubles, and these
// numbers have been read and placed in the first n components of the array.
```

(continued)

(FIGURE 4.7 continued)

```
double average(const double data[ ], size_t n);
```
// *Precondition: data is an array with at least n components, and n > 0.*
// *Postcondition: The value returned is the average of data[0]..data[n-1].*

```
void compare(const double data[ ], size_t n, double value);
```
// *Precondition: data is an array with at least n components.*
// *Postcondition: The values data[0] through data[n - 1] have been printed with a*
// *message saying whether they are above, below, or equal to value.*

```
int main( )
{
    double *numbers;      // Will point to the first component of an array
    size_t array_size;
    double mean_value;

    // Allocate an array of doubles to hold the user's input.
    cout << "This program will compute the average of some numbers. The\n";
    cout << "numbers will be stored in an array of doubles that I allocate.\n";
    allocate_doubles(numbers, array_size);

    // Read the user's input and compute the average.
    fill_array(numbers, array_size);
    mean_value = average(numbers, array_size);

    // Print the output.
    cout << "The average is: " << mean_value << endl;
    compare(numbers, array_size, mean_value);
    cout << "This was a mean program.";

    return EXIT_SUCCESS;
}
```

```
void allocate_doubles(double*& p, size_t& n)
```
‖ See Figure 4.6 on page 154 for the body of this function.

```
void fill_array(double data[ ], size_t n)
```
// *Library facilities used: stdlib.h*
```
{
    size_t i;
    cout << "Please type " << n << " double numbers: " << endl;

    // Read the n numbers one at a time.
    for (i = 0; i < n; i++)
        cin >> data[i];
}
```

(continued)

(FIGURE 4.7 continued)

```
void compare(const double data[ ], size_t n, double value)
{
    size_t i;

    for (i = 0; i < n; i++)
    {
        cout << data[i];
        if (data[i] < value)
            cout << " is less than ";
        else if (data[i] > value)
            cout << " is more than ";
        else
            cout << " is equal to  ";
        cout << value << endl;
    }
}


double average(const double data[ ], size_t n)
// Library facilities used: assert.h, stdlib.h
{
    size_t i;    // An array index
    double sum;  // The sum of data[0] through data[n - 1]

    assert(n > 0);

    // Add up the n numbers and return the average.
    sum = 0;
    for (i = 0; i < n; i++)
        sum += data[i];
    return (sum/n);
}
```

A Sample Dialogue

```
This program will compute the average of some numbers. The
numbers will be stored in an array of doubles that I allocate.
How many doubles should I allocate?
Please type an integer answer: 3
Please type 3 double numbers:
15.1    24.6    86.3
The average is: 42
15.1 is less than 42
24.6 is less than 42
86.3 is more than 42
This was a mean program.
```

| dynademo.cxx | FTP |

4.3   THE BAG ADT WITH A DYNAMIC ARRAY

Pointers enable us to define data structures whose size is determined when a program is actually *running* rather than at *compilation time*. Such data structures are called **dynamic data structures**. This is in contrast to **static data structures,** which have their size determined when a program is compiled.

A class may be a dynamic data structure—in other words, it may use dynamic memory. When a class uses dynamic memory, several new factors come into play. In this section, we'll illustrate these factors by implementing a new bag ADT that contains its items in a *dynamic* array rather than an array of fixed size. Apart from the use of a dynamic array, the new bag is much the same as the original Bag class from Section 3.1.

Pointer Member Variables

The original Bag class in Section 3.1 has a member variable that is a static array containing the bag's items. Our new, dynamic bag has a member variable that is a pointer to a dynamic array. In both cases, the array is a *partially filled* array, containing the bag's items at the front of the array. Here is a comparison of the member variables of the two class definitions:

The Static Bag:

```
// From bag1.h in Section 3.1:
class Bag
{
    ...
private:
    Item data[CAPACITY];
    size_t used;
};
```

The Dynamic Bag:

```
// From bag2.h in this section:
class Bag
{
    ...
private:
    Item *data;
    size_t used;
    ...
};
```

A static bag has a private member variable, data, which is an array that can hold up to CAPACITY items. The static bag can never hold more than CAPACITY items. That's the limit.

On the other hand, a dynamic bag has a private member variable, also called data, which is a *pointer* to an item. The constructor for the dynamic bag will allocate a dynamic array, and point data at the newly allocated array. As a program runs, the size of the dynamic array may increase beyond its initial capacity. Because the size of the dynamic array can change, the dynamic bag actually needs one more private member variable to keep track of how much memory is currently allocated. At the top of the next page, we show the complete private section of the new bag class, including the extra member variable.

```
class Bag
{
public:
    ...
private:
    Item *data;         // Pointer to dynamic array
    size_t used;        // How much of array is being used
    size_t capacity;    // Current capacity of the Bag
};
```

With this much of the class definition in hand, we can now state the invariant of the dynamic bag ADT:

Invariant for the Revised Bag ADT

1. The number of items in the bag is in the member variable used.

2. The actual items of the bag are stored in a partially filled array. The array is a dynamic array, pointed to by the member variable data.

3. The total size of the dynamic array is in the member variable capacity.

Member Functions Allocate Dynamic Memory as Needed

When a class uses dynamic memory, *the class's member functions allocate dynamic memory as needed.* For example, the constructor of the dynamic bag allocates the dynamic array that the member variable data points to. But how big should this array be? Our plan is to have the constructor allocate a dynamic array whose initial size is determined by a parameter to the constructor. As a bag is used in a program, the size of its dynamic array may increase to whatever capacity is needed.

In other words, the parameter to the constructor determines the *initial capacity of the bag*, but even after this initial capacity is reached, more items can be inserted. Whenever items are inserted into a bag—through the insert member function or the += operator—the bag's current capacity is examined. If the current capacity is too small, then the member function allocates a new, larger dynamic array. The user of a bag does not need to do anything special to obtain the increased capacity. The insert and += functions simply increase the capacity as needed.

You might wonder why a programmer needs to be concerned about the initial capacity of a bag. Can't a programmer just start with a small initial capacity and insert items one after another? The insert function will take care of increasing the capacity as needed. Yes, this approach will always work correctly. But if

the importance of the initial capacity

there are many items, then many of the activations of `insert` would need to increase the capacity. This could be inefficient. Each time the capacity is increased, new memory is allocated, the items are copied into the new memory, and the old memory is released. To avoid this repeated allocation of memory, a programmer can request a large initial capacity. With this in mind, here is the documentation for the new bag constructor:

```
Bag(size_t initial_capacity = DEFAULT_CAPACITY);
// Postcondition: The Bag is empty with a capacity given by the parameter.
// The insert function will work efficiently (without allocating new
// memory) until this capacity is reached.
```

For example, suppose that a programmer is going to place 1000 items into a bag named `kilosack`. When the bag is declared, the programmer can specify a capacity of 1000, as shown here:

```
Bag kilosack(1000);  ⟵──── 1000 items can be efficiently added to kilosack.
```

After the initial capacity is reached, the `insert` function continues to work *correctly*, but it might be slowed down by memory allocations.

the constructor serves as a default constructor

Notice that the parameter of the constructor has a default argument, `DEFAULT_CAPACITY`, which will be a constant in our class definition. Because of the default argument, the single constructor actually serves two purposes: It can be used with an argument to construct a bag with a specific capacity, or it can be used as a default constructor (with no argument list). When the constructor is used with no argument list, `DEFAULT_CAPACITY` is used for the initial capacity. Here are two examples, using the default constructor and using the constructor with an argument:

```
Bag ordinary;  ⟵──────── The initial capacity is DEFAULT_CAPACITY.
Bag super(9000);  ⟵────  The initial capacity is 9000.
```

Here is one more example to show how the new constructor works with the other members. The example declares a bag with an initial capacity of 6 and places three items in the bag:

```
Bag sixpack(6);  ⟵────── The constructor creates a bag
sixpack.insert(10);       with an initial capacity of 6.
sixpack.insert(20);
sixpack.insert(30);
```

After these declarations, the bag's private member variables look like this:

The private member variables of the bag include a pointer to a dynamically allocated array of six elements. The first three elements are now being used.

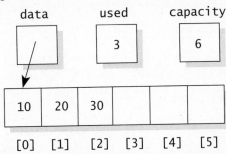

Later, the program could insert more items into this bag, maybe even more than six. If there are more than six items, then the bag's member functions will increase the bag's capacity as needed.

After a bag has been declared and is already in use, a programmer can make an explicit adjustment to the bag's capacity via a new member function called `resize`. Here is the specification of the member function:

```
void resize(size_t new_capacity);
// Postcondition: The Bag's current capacity is changed to the
// new_capacity (but not less than the number of items already in the Bag).
// The insert function will work efficiently (without allocating new memory) until
// the new capacity is reached.
```

To some extent, the `resize` function is a luxury. Programmers can avoid `resize` altogether, allowing the other member functions to adjust the size of a bag as needed. But by using the `resize` member function, the bag's efficiency is improved.

All told, five of the member functions that we have seen so far can allocate new dynamic memory: the constructor, `resize`, `insert`, and the two operators (+= and +). As with any function that allocates dynamic memory, these functions are subject to possible failure—the heap might run out of room. In this case, the function calls the *new* operator, and the *new* operator will fail, calling the `new_handler`. The `new_handler` prints an error message and halts the program. For our programs, the error-message-and-halt will suffice. But part of our ADT documentation will indicate which member functions allocate dynamic memory so that more experienced programmers can deal with the `new_handler` in their own way. You can see this documentation at the bottom of Figure 4.8, which provides the complete documentation for the header file (`bag2.h`) of our new bag ADT.

FIGURE 4.8	Documentation for the Dynamic Bag Header File

Documentation for a Header File

```
//   TYPEDEF and MEMBER CONSTANTS for the Bag class:
//      static const size_t DEFAULT_CAPACITY = _____
//         Bag::DEFAULT_CAPACITY is the initial capacity of a Bag that is created by the default
//         constructor.
//
//      typedef _____ Item
//         Bag::Item is the data type of the items in the Bag. It may be any of the C++ built-in
//         types (int, char, etc.), or a class with a default constructor, an assignment operator,
//         and operators to test for equality (x == y) and non-equality (x != y).
//
//   CONSTRUCTOR for the Bag class:
//      Bag(size_t initial_capacity = DEFAULT_CAPACITY)
//         Postcondition: The Bag is empty with an initial capacity given by the parameter. The
//         insert function will work efficiently (without allocating new memory) until this capacity
//         is reached.
//
//   MODIFICATION MEMBER FUNCTIONS for the Bag class:
//      void resize(size_t new_capacity)          ←————————  The resize member
//         Postcondition: The Bag's current capacity                     function provides
//         is changed to the new_capacity (but not                       efficiency.
//         less than the number of items already in
//         the Bag). The insert function will work efficiently (without allocating
//         new memory) until the new capacity is reached.
//
//      void insert(const Item& entry)
//         Postcondition: A new copy of entry has been inserted into the Bag.
//
//      void remove(const Item& target)
//         Postcondition: If target was in the Bag, then one copy of target has been removed from
//         the Bag; otherwise the Bag is unchanged.
//
//      void operator +=(const Bag& addend)
//         Postcondition: Each item in addend has been added to this Bag.
//
//   CONSTANT MEMBER FUNCTIONS for the Bag class:
//      size_t size( ) const
//         Postcondition: Return value is the total number of items in the Bag.
//
```

(continued)

(FIGURE 4.8 continued)

```
//    size_t occurrences(const Item& target) const
//       Postcondition: Return value is number of times target is in the Bag.
//
// NONMEMBER FUNCTIONS for the Bag class:
//    Bag operator +(const Bag& b1, const Bag& b2)
//    Postcondition: The Bag returned is the union of b1 and b2.
//
// VALUE SEMANTICS for the Bag class:
//    Assignments and the copy constructor may be used with Bag objects.
//
// DYNAMIC MEMORY USAGE by the Bag:
//    If there is insufficient dynamic memory, then the following functions call new_handler:
//    The constructors, resize, insert, operator += , operator +, and the assignment operator.
```

*Extra documentation
tells experienced programmers
about dynamic memory usage.*

bag2.h   **FTP**

Programming Tip: **Provide Documentation about Possible Dynamic Memory Failure**

TIP

When an ADT uses dynamic memory, you should include documentation to indicate which member functions allocate dynamic memory. This will allow experienced programmers to deal with potential failure.

The documentation in Figure 4.8 provides adequate information for a programmer to use our new bag ADT. But before we implement the class there are two extra factors that play an important role whenever a class uses dynamic memory. The first factor is the *value semantics* (i.e., the assignment operator and the copy constructor). The second factor is a requirement for a special member function called a *destructor*. We'll discuss these two factors before completing the implementation.

Value Semantics

The value semantics of the bag class determines how values are copied from one bag to another—in assignment statements and when one bag is initialized as a copy of another. Until now, we have not worried much about value semantics. With all our other classes, it was sufficient to use the automatic assignment operator and the automatic copy constructor. So, in the past, when we wrote y = x, we were content to let the automatic assignment operator copy all the member variables from the object x to the object y.

*the value
semantics
determines
how values are
copied*

Our days of easy contentment are done. The automatic assignment operator fails for the dynamic bag (or for any other class that uses dynamic memory).

Here is an example to show what goes wrong. Suppose we set up a bag called x with an initial capacity of 5, containing the integers 10, 20, and 30—then we copy the private member variables of x to another bag y. The result is that the two pointers, x.data and y.data, both point to the same dynamic array, like this:

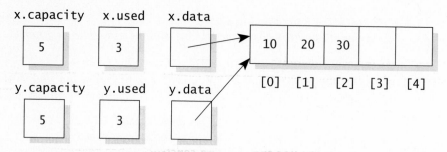

The problem with this arrangement is that a subsequent change to x's array will also change y's array. Normally, this is not what we want; after an assignment y = x, we do not want further changes to one object to directly affect the other.

Instead, when we assign y = x, we want y to have its own dynamic array, completely separate from x's dynamic array. Of course, the dynamic array of y will contain the same values as the x array, but they two arrays will not share the same dynamic memory. The desired situation after the assignment looks like this:

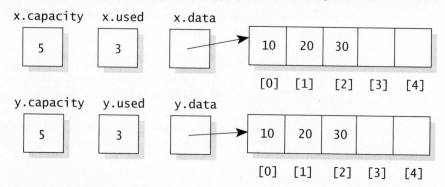

To achieve this situation, we must provide our own assignment operator rather than relying on the automatic assignment operator. We can do this by overloading the assignment operator for the bag class, in roughly the same way that we have overloaded other operators for the bag. The operator will be overloaded as a bag member function with the prototype given here:

```
void Bag::operator =(const Bag& source);
// Postcondition: The Bag that activated this function has the same items
// and capacity as source.
```

In fact, when you overload the assignment operator, C++ requires it to be a member function. In an assignment statement y = x, the bag y is activating the function, and the bag x is the argument for the parameter named source. In a moment we will implement this member function, and you will see how it correctly makes a new dynamic array rather than merely copying the pointer.

The second part of the value semantics is the copy constructor, which is activated when a new object is initialized as a copy of an existing object, such as the declaration:

```
Bag y(x); // Initialize y as a copy of the Bag x.
```

Unless you indicate otherwise, y is initialized using the automatic copy constructor, which merely copies the member variables from x to y. If you want to avoid the simple copying of member variables, then you must provide a copy constructor with the prototype:

```
Bag::Bag(const Bag& source);
// Postcondition: The Bag that is being constructed has been initialized
// with the same items and capacity as source.
```

The parameter of the copy constructor is usually a *const* reference parameter (although C++ also permits an ordinary reference parameter). If a copy constructor is present, then it is used instead of the automatic copy constructor. The copy constructor also has several other uses that we'll discuss on page 177.

Our documentation of the bag in Figure 4.8 on page 162 indicates that the assignment operator and copy constructor are safe to use with the Bag class:

```
// VALUE SEMANTICS for the Bag class:
//     Assignments and the copy constructor may be used with Bag objects.
```

Value Semantics and Dynamic Memory

If a class uses dynamic memory, the automatic assignment operator and the automatic copy constructor fail. The implementor of the class must provide member functions for the assignment operator and the copy constructor. For example:

```
class Bag
{
public:
    Bag(const Bag& source);
    void operator =(const Bag& source);
    ...
```

The documentation of the class should indicate that the value semantics may be used.

One final point about the value semantics: The programmer who uses the bag does not need to know whether the implementor has overriden the automatic value semantics. Such a programmer need know only that there is a valid value semantics. Therefore, the bag documentation indicates that there is a valid value semantics, but does not indicate whether the automatic value semantics was overriden.

The Destructor

The final new factor for a class that uses dynamic memory is a special member function called the **destructor**. The primary purpose of the destructor is to return an object's dynamic memory to the heap when the object is no longer in use. The destructor has three unique features:

- The name of the destructor is always the character ~ followed by the class name. In our example the name of the destructor is ~Bag.

- The destructor has no parameters and no return value. As with the constructor, you must *not* write *void* (or any other return type) at the front of the destructor's head. However, you must list the empty parameter list, as shown in this prototype: `~Bag( );`.

- Programmers who *use* a class should not need to know about the destructor. This is because programs rarely activate the destructor *explicitly*. What good is a destructor that is never activated? The answer is that destructors *are* activated, but the activation is usually *automatic* whenever an object becomes inaccessible.

Several common situations cause automatic destructor activation:

1. Suppose a function has a *local* variable that is an object, like this:
   ```
   void example1( )
   {
       Bag sample1;
       ...
   ```

destructors are automatically activated when an object becomes inaccessible

When the function `example1` returns, the destructor `sample1.~Bag( )` is automatically activated. The general situation: A local variable is an object with a destructor, and the destructor is automatically activated when the function returns.

2. Suppose a function has a *value* parameter that is an object, like this:
   ```
   void example2(Bag sample2)
   // Does some calculation using a Bag
   ```
   As with the previous example, when the function `example2` returns, the destructor `sample2.~Bag( )` is automatically activated. On the other hand, if `sample2` was a reference parameter, then the destructor would not be activated because a reference parameter is actually an object in the calling program, and that object is still accessible.

3. Suppose that a dynamic variable is an object, as shown here:

```
Bag *b_ptr;
b_ptr = new Bag;
...
delete b_ptr;
```

When `delete b_ptr` is executed, the destructor for *b_ptr is automatically activated. The destructor ensures that the dynamic array used by *b_ptr is released.

There are several other situations where a destructor is automatically called, but the three examples you have seen provide the general idea. Because destructors are not directly activated by a program, we omitted the destructor from the *how-to-use-a-Bag* documentation of Figure 4.8 on page 162.

The Destructor

The **destructor** of a class is a member function that is automatically activated when an object becomes inaccessible. The destructor has no arguments and its name must be the character ~ followed by the class name (e.g., ~Bag for the Bag class).

Because the destructor is automatically called, programs rarely make explicit calls to the destructor, and we generally omit the destructor from the documentation that tells how to use the class.

The primary responsibility of the destructor is simply releasing dynamic memory.

The Revised Bag ADT—Class Definition

We can now write the complete class definition for the dynamic bag. As usual, the class definition appears in the header file, surrounded by a macro guard. This definition is shown in Figure 4.9 (where the file is called `bag2.h`).

Notice that the bag's *operator* + function is not a member function, but its implementation will be simplified if it has access to the capacity of its two argument bags. Because the capacity is a *private* member variable, the way to provide this access is to make the *operator* + be a *friend* function. Therefore, the *operator* + prototype is listed as a friend function at the end of the public section of the new Bag class definition. (Remember that a friend function is a nonmember function that has been granted access to the private members of a class.)

FIGURE 4.9	Header File for the Bag Class with a Dynamic Array

A Header File

```
// FILE: bag2.h
// CLASS PROVIDED: Bag (a container class for a collection of items)
//
```

‖ See Figure 4.8 on page 162 for the other documentation that goes here.

```
#ifndef BAG2_H
#define BAG2_H
#include <stdlib.h>   // Provides size_t

    class Bag
    {
    public:
        // TYPEDEF and MEMBER CONSTANTS
        static const size_t DEFAULT_CAPACITY = 30;
        typedef int Item;
        // CONSTRUCTORS and DESTRUCTOR
        Bag(size_t initial_capacity = DEFAULT_CAPACITY);
        Bag(const Bag& source);
        ~Bag( );
        // MODIFICATION MEMBER FUNCTIONS
        void resize(size_t new_capacity);
        void insert(const Item& entry);
        void remove(const Item& target);
        void operator +=(const Bag& addend);
        void operator =(const Bag& source);
        // CONSTANT MEMBER FUNCTIONS
        size_t size( ) const { return used; }
        size_t occurrences(const Item& target) const;
        // FRIEND FUNCTION
        friend Bag operator +(const Bag& b1, const Bag& b2);
    private:
        Item *data;        // Pointer to partially filled dynamic array
        size_t used;       // How much of array is being used
        size_t capacity;   // Current capacity of the Bag
    };

#endif
```

If your compiler does not permit initialization of static constants, see Appendix E.

Prototype for the copy constructor is discussed on page 165.

Prototype for the destructor is discussed on page 166.

Prototype for the overloaded operator = is discussed on page 164.

bag2.h	FTP

The Revised Bag ADT—Implementation

We'll look at the implementation of the new bag member functions. Three functions are particularly important: The copy constructor, the assignment operator, and the destructor. These three member functions are always needed when a class uses dynamic memory.

The constructors. Each of the constructors is responsible for setting up the three private member variables in a way that satisfies the invariant of the dynamic bag ADT. For example, here is the implementation of the first constructor. Notice how all three private member variables are assigned values:

```
Bag::Bag(size_t initial_capacity)
// Library facilities used: stdlib.h
{
    data = new Item[initial_capacity];
    capacity = initial_capacity;
    used = 0;
}
```

The parameter, initial_capacity, tells how many items to allocate for the dynamic array.

The bag's copy constructor is similar, also allocating memory for a dynamic array. In the case of the copy constructor, the capacity of the dynamic array is the same as the capacity of the bag that is being copied. After the dynamic array has been allocated, the items may be copied into the newly allocated array with a small loop, as shown here:

the copy constructor

```
Bag::Bag(const Bag& source)
// Library facilities used: stdlib.h
{
    size_t i;

    data = new Item[source.capacity];
    capacity = source.capacity;
    used = source.used;
    for (i = 0; i < used; i++)
        data[i] = source.data[i];
}
```

The amount of memory allocated for source determines how much memory to allocate for the new dynamic array.

The destructor. The primary responsibility of the destructor is releasing dynamic memory. Sometimes there is other "cleanup" work needed, but not for the bag's destructor, which has only one statement:

```
Bag::~Bag( )
{
    delete [ ] data;
}
```

The private member variable called data points to the dynamic array.

The most formidable aspect of the destructor is getting used to the '~' in the name.

The assignment operator. The implementation of the assignment operator is nearly identical to the copy constructor. There are only small differences:

- The copy constructor is constructing a bag from scratch. It allocates the initial memory for the partially filled array.

- The assignment operator is not constructing a bag from the beginning, meaning that there is already a partially filled array allocated. The size of this array might need to be changed, or we might be satisfied with the array that already exists. If we do end up allocating a new array, then the original array must be returned to the heap.

Except for memory allocation, you will generally find that the overloaded assignment operator is the same as the copy constructor. The first few statements of the assignment operator handle the potential memory allocation as shown here:

```
if (capacity != source.capacity)
{
    Item *new_data;
    new_data = new Item[source.capacity];

    delete [ ] data;

    data = new_data;

    capacity = source.capacity;
}
```

Allocate memory for the new array.

Return the old array to the heap.

The pointer, data, now points to the newly allocated array.

Change capacity to indicate the size of the new array.

Let's trace through the statements of this memory allocation. To trace the statements we assume that `source` is a bag with a capacity of 5. We will execute the assignment assuming that the bag that activated the function has a mere capacity of 2. When the assignment begins, we have this situation:

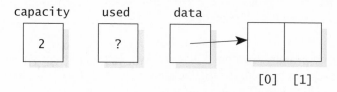

Since the current capacity (2) is not equal to the amount needed (5), the code enters the body of the if-statement. In the body, we have a local variable, `new_data`, which is set to point to a newly allocated array of five items, as shown here:

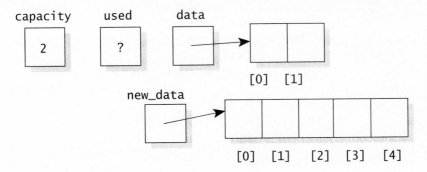

Once the new array has been allocated, we return the old array to the heap and assign `data = new_data`, so that the `data` pointer points to the new array:

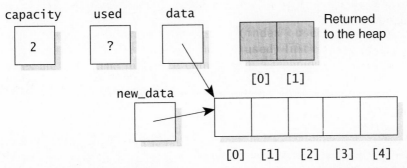

Finally, `capacity` is changed to 5, and we no longer need the local variable `new_data`, as shown here:

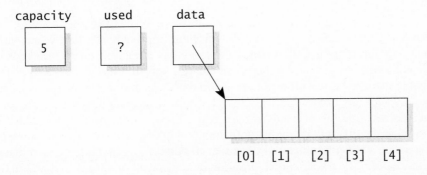

At this point, all that remains is to copy the items from `source`'s array into the newly allocated array, and to correctly set the value of `used`. You can see how this is accomplished in the complete function implementation in Figure 4.10.

FIGURE 4.10   Implementation of the Bag's = Operator

A Member Function Implementation

```
void Bag::operator =(const Bag& source)
// Library facilities used: stdlib.h
{
    size_t i;
    Item *new_data;

    if (capacity != source.capacity)
    {
        new_data = new Item[source.capacity];        If necessary,
        delete [ ] data;                             allocate a
        data = new_data;                             dynamic array of
        capacity = source.capacity;                  a different size.
    }
    used = source.used;
    for (i = 0; i < used; i++)
        data[i] = source.data[i];
}
```

bag2.cxx   **FTP**

It is tempting to implement the new memory allocation without the local variable new_data, using just two statements:

```
delete [ ] data;                     // Release old array
data = new Item[source.capacity];    // Allocate new array
```

This shortcut could cause a headache. If there is insufficient memory, the new_handler is called—but with the shortcut approach, the bag is not valid when new_handler is called (since the array has already been released). With an invalid bag, the usual new_handler can fail before it has a chance to print a sensible error message. The failure occurs because the new_handler calls the destructor for any object that was previously constructed. When the destructor is given an invalid object—such as our invalid bag—the destructor will cause an error message that will be more confusing than the new_handler error message. As a result, your programs will be harder to debug. The invalid bag also makes it impossible for experienced programmers to deal with the new_handler exception in a sensible way.

Because of these problems, we suggest that member functions always ensure that all objects are valid prior to calling *new*. Also, your documentation should always indicate which functions allocate dynamic memory. For the bag, we have already taken care of this documentation in the header file with this comment (from the bottom of Figure 4.8 on page 163):

```
//  DYNAMIC MEMORY USAGE by the Bag:
//    If there is insufficient dynamic memory then the following functions
//    call new_handler: The constructors, resize, insert, operator +=,
//    operator +, and the assignment operator.
```

Programming Tip: How to Allocate Memory in a Member Function

TIP

When a member function allocates memory, it is a good idea to have the invariant of the ADT valid when the call to the *new* operator is made. Also, the documentation should indicate which functions allocate dynamic memory. This approach aids debugging and allows experienced programmers to deal with `new_handler` exceptions in a sensible way.

This tip is not necessary (and often not possible) for constructors that allocate dynamic memory. But it is critical for easy debugging of other member functions.

The `resize` member function. Our design includes a member function called `resize`, which is called to explicitly increase the capacity of a bag. Here is the function's heading with a precondition/postcondition contract:

```
void resize(size_t new_capacity)
// Postcondition: The Bag's current capacity is changed to the
// new_capacity (but not less than the number of items already in the Bag).
// The insert function will work efficiently (without allocating new memory)
// until the new capacity is reached.
```

Figure 4.11 shows our implementation of `resize`. The function first carries out a couple checks. After the checks, the new array is allocated with a new size, the items are copied into the new array, and the original array is released. The private member variable `data` is then pointed at the new array, and `capacity` is set to indicate how much memory is now allocated.

The Revised Bag ADT—Putting the Pieces Together

Several of the other bag member functions need small changes to work correctly with the dynamic array. The most obvious change is that member functions such as `insert` must ensure that there is sufficient capacity before a new item is inserted. If more room is needed, then the function increases the bag's capacity by activating `resize`. The necessary changes to the bag functions are marked in the new implementation file of Figure 4.12 on page 175.

FIGURE 4.11	Implementation of the Bag's Resize Member Function

A Member Function Implementation

```
void Bag::resize(size_t new_capacity)
// Library facilities used: stdlib.h
{
    size_t i;
    Item *larger_array;

    if (new_capacity == capacity)
        return; // The allocated memory is already the right size.

    if (new_capacity < used)
        new_capacity = used; // Can't allocate less than we are using.

    larger_array = new Item[new_capacity];
    for (i = 0; i < used; i++)
        larger_array[i] = data[i];
    delete [ ] data;
    data = larger_array;
    capacity = new_capacity;
}
```

bag2.cxx	FTP

Self-Test Exercises

11. Describe the difference between a dynamic data structure and a static data structure. p.158

12. Suppose that you declare a bag like this: `Bag exercise;`. What is the initial capacity for `exercise`? What will happen if you try to put 31 items in the bag? whatever Default Capacity is ; capacity = 31

13. If a bag is full, then the `insert` function increases the bag's capacity by only one. This could be rather inefficient if we are inserting a sequence of items to a full bag, since each insertion calls `resize`. Rewrite the bag's `insert` function so that when the bag is full, the capacity is always increased by at least 10%.

14. What is the primary responsibility of the destructor? When is the destructor of an object activated? p.156

15. Why does the bag's assignment operator need to be overloaded? Does our implementation work correctly for self-assignment (`x = x`)?

16. Why is bag's the *operator* + function declared as a friend function? p.167

FIGURE 4.12	Implementation File for the Bag Class with a Dynamic Array

An Implementation File

```
// FILE: bag2.cxx
// CLASS implemented: Bag (See bag2.h for documentation.)
// INVARIANT for the Bag ADT:
//    1. The number of items in the Bag is in the member variable used.
//    2. The actual items of the Bag are stored in a partially filled array.
//       The array is a dynamic array, pointed to by the member variable data.
//    3. The size of the dynamic array is in the member variable capacity.

#include <assert.h> // Provides assert
#include <stdlib.h> // Provides size_t
#include "bag2.h"

Bag::Bag(size_t initial_capacity)
// Library facilities used: stdlib.h
{
    data = new Item[initial_capacity];
    capacity = initial_capacity;
    used = 0;
}


Bag::Bag(const Bag& source)
// Library facilities used: stdlib.h
{
    size_t i;

    data = new Item[source.capacity];
    capacity = source.capacity;
    used = source.used;
    for (i = 0; i < used; i++)
        data[i] = source.data[i];
}



Bag::~Bag( )
{
    delete [ ] data;
}
```

The revised bag has two constructors. The first constructor serves as a default constructor since the parameter has a default argument. The second constructor is a copy constructor, which you can read about on page 169.

Read about the destructor on page 169.

(continued)

(FIGURE 4.12 continued)

```
void Bag::resize(size_t new_capacity)
|| See the implementation in Figure 4.11 on page 174.

void Bag::insert(const Item& entry)
// Library facilities used: assert.h
{
    if (used == capacity)
        resize(used+1);
    data[used] = entry;
    used++;
}
```

The first action of the insert function is to ensure that there is room for a new item.

```
void Bag::remove(const Item& target)
|| No change from the original bag: See the implementation in Figure 3.3 on page 106.

void Bag::operator +=(const Bag& addend)
// Library facilities used: assert.h, stdlib.h
{
    size_t i; // An array index
    size_t other_bag_size;

    other_bag_size = addend.used;
    if (used + other_bag_size > capacity)
        resize(used + other_bag_size);
    for (i = 0; i < other_bag_size; i++)
    {
        data[used] = addend.data[i];
        used++;
    }
}
```

The += operator starts by ensuring that there is enough room for the new items.

```
void Bag::operator =(const Bag& source)
|| See the implementation in Figure 4.10 on page 172.

size_t Bag::occurrences(const Item& target) const
|| No change from the original bag: See the implementation in Figure 3.5 on page 110.

Bag operator +(const Bag& b1, const Bag& b2)
{
    Bag answer(b1.capacity + b2.capacity);

    answer += b1;
    answer += b2;
    return answer;
}
```

The function declares a Bag of the correct size.

4.4   PRESCRIPTION FOR A DYNAMIC CLASS

This section summarizes the important factors for a class that uses dynamic memory. We also point out the additional importance of the copy constructor.

Four Rules

When a class uses dynamic memory, you will generally follow these four rules:

1. Some of the member variables of the class are pointers.
2. Member functions allocate and release dynamic memory as needed.
3. The automatic value semantics of the class is overridden (otherwise two different objects end up with pointers to the same dynamic memory). This means that the implementor must write an assignment operator and a copy constructor for the class.
4. The class has a destructor. The primary purpose of the destructor is to return all dynamic memory to the heap.

Special Importance of the Copy Constructor

When a class uses dynamic memory, the programmer who implements the class writes a copy constructor. The copy constructor is used when one object is to be initialized as a copy of another, as in the declaration:

```
Bag y(x); // Initialize y as a copy of x.
```

There are three other common situations where the copy constructor is particularly important. These situations reinforce the need for special value semantics when an object uses dynamic memory.

Alternate syntax.   The first situation is really just an alternate syntax for using the copy constructor to initialize a newly declared object. The alternate syntax is:

```
Bag y = x; // Initialize y as a copy of x.
```

This syntax is an alternative to `Bag y(x);`. Both versions merely activate the copy constructor to initialize y as a copy of x.

Returning an object from a function.   The second situation that uses the copy constructor is when a return value is an object. For example, the bag's *operator* + returns a bag object. The function computes its answer in a local variable, and then has a return statement. When the return statement is executed, here's what actually happens: The value from the local variable is copied to a temporary location called the **return location.** The local variable itself is then destroyed (along with any other local variables), and the function returns to the place where it was called.

Unless you indicate otherwise, the copying into the return location occurs by using the automatic copy constructor, which copies all the member variables from the local variable to the return location. If you want to avoid the simple copying of member variables, then you must provide a copy constructor. If a copy constructor is present, then it is used to copy the return value from a function's local variable to the return location.

When a value parameter is an object. A third situation arises when a value parameter is an object. For example, on page 63 we declared a function to do a calculation on a `Point`, with this prototype:

```
int rotations_needed(Point p);
```

When the function is called, the actual parameter is copied to the formal parameter p. Normally, the copying occurs by using the automatic copy constructor. But, if this is inappropriate (such as when dynamic memory is used), then you can define a copy constructor. When there is a defined copy constructor, then the argument value is copied to the formal parameter by activating the copy constructor to initialize the formal parameter.

PITFALL

Pitfall: Using Dynamic Memory Requires a Destructor, a Copy Constructor, and an Overloaded Assignment Operator

When a member variable of a class is a pointer to dynamic memory, the class should always be given a destructor, and the value semantics should always be defined (that is, a copy constructor and an overloaded assignment operator should be provided).

- The destructor is responsible for returning an object's dynamic memory to the heap. If you forget the destructor, then dynamic memory that is allocated to the object will continue to occupy heap memory, even when the object is no longer needed.

- The copy constructor and the overloaded assignment operator are responsible for correctly copying one object to another. Make sure that the copying process allocates new memory for the new copy, rather than just copying the pointers from one object to another. If you forget the copy constructor, then value parameters and return values from functions will perform incorrectly.

Self-Test Exercise

To construct a new object, just like any other constructor.

17. Name the three situations where a copy constructor is activated.

When a class used dynamic memory
— Alternat syntax
— Return an object from a function
— A value parameter is an object

4.5 PROGRAMMING PROJECT: THE STRING ADT

C programs abound with oversize arrays to hold character sequences of worst-case length. Or they contain ornate logic to allocate and free storage, copy strings about, and get those terminating null characters where they belong.

Little wonder, then, that writing string classes is one of the more popular indoor sports among C++ programmers.

P. J. PLAUGER
The Draft Standard C++ Library

A **string** is a sequence of characters. In C++ strings can be written using quote marks such as the string "Hi Mom!" in this output statement:

```
cout << "Hi Mom!";
```

A string written with quote marks is called a **string constant**. Strings can also be stored in variables, and early versions of C++ provided rudimentary facilities for manipulating string variables. More recent versions of C++ (starting with the 1995 proposed C++ Standard) provide a flexible String class in a standard library.

In this section we'll review the original rudimentary string facilities, and show how the new String class can be implemented using dynamic memory. Much of the implementation of the new String class is left up to you as a programming project. In your future programs, when you need a flexible string, you may use the new standard library (if it is available for your compiler), or you may use the String class that you implement yourself in this section.

String Variables

In C++ a **string variable** is exactly the same as an array of characters. This is natural since a string is a sequence of characters, and an array of characters is just what's needed to store a sequence of characters. Thus, the following array declaration provides us with a string variable capable of storing a string with 9 or fewer characters:

```
char s[10];
```

That is not a mistake. We said that s can hold a string with 9 or fewer characters. The string variable s cannot hold a full 10 characters even though the array does contain 10 components. That is because a string variable is used in a slightly different way than an ordinary array.

A string variable is a partially filled array of characters. A string variable, like any other partially filled array, uses positions starting at index [0] through as many positions as are needed. But, a string variable uses a different technique to remember how much of the partially filled array is used. With a string variable,

the null character marks the end of the string

we do not generally have another variable (of type `size_t`) that remembers how much of the array has been filled. Instead, a string variable places the special symbol `'\0'` in the array immediately after the last character of the string. Thus, if `s` contains the string `"Hi Mom!"` then the array components are filled as shown here:

the longest possible string is one less than the size of the array

The character `'\0'` is used as a sentinel value to mark the end of the string. If you read the characters in the string starting at `s[0]`, and proceed to `s[1]`, and then to `s[2]`, and so on, you know that when you encounter the symbol `'\0'`, then you have reached the end of the string. Since the symbol `'\0'` always occupies one component of the array, the length of the longest possible string is one less than the size of the array.

The character `'\0'` is called the **null character**, and the string itself is called a **null-terminated string**. In a program, the null character is written `'\0'`—the single quote marks are used with all C++ characters such as `'a'`, `'b'`, `'c'`. The `\0` (a backslash followed by a zero) indicates the null character. It looks like two characters, but it is officially a single character, and it occupies just one location in a character array. C++ has several other special characters that are denoted with a backslash, as shown here:

Special Characters

`\0`	null character	`\f`	form feed
`\n`	newline	`\a`	alert (ring bell)
`\b`	backspace	`\\`	backslash
`\t`	horizontal tab	`\'`	single quote
`\v`	vertical tab	`\"`	double quote
`\r`	carriage return		

For example, `'\\'` is the notation for the backslash character itself in a C++ program. Remember that the null *character* is different from the digit zero (which is written `'0'`), and it is different from a blank space (which is written `' '` with a blank between the quote marks).

string variables versus arrays of characters

The only distinction between a string variable and an array of characters is the fact that a string variable must use the null character to mark the end of the string. This is a distinction in how the array is used rather than a distinction about what the array is. *A string variable is a character array, but it is used in a different way.*

Initializing a String Variable

You can initialize a string variable when you declare it, as shown here:

```
char proclaim[20] = "Make it so.";
```

Notice that the string assigned to the string variable need not fill the entire array.

When you initialize a string variable, you can omit the array size and C++ will automatically make the string variable an array that is exactly long enough to hold the string plus the null terminating character. For example:

```
char thought[ ] = "Peace";
```
← *This allocates an array of six characters.*

The special characters written with a backslash can also appear in a string constant such as this string constant that contains the bell character: `"Noise\a."`

String Variables

A **string variable** is declared to be an array of characters in the usual way:

Syntax:
```
char array_name[Maximum string size + 1];
```

Example:
```
char my_string[10];
```

The "+1" is for the null character that terminates any string stored in the array. For example, the string variable `my_string`, in the above example, can hold strings of 9 or fewer characters.

A string variable can be **initialized** with a string constant when it is declared.

Examples:
```
char proclaim[20] = "Make it so.";
char thought[ ] = "Peace";
```

Initializing in this way places the null character in the array at the end of the specified string.

If you omit the size of the array, then the string variable will be given the exact size needed to hold the string plus the null terminating character.

The Empty String

Sometimes a program needs a string that has no characters at all, not even a single blank. This string with no characters is called the **empty string**, and it is specified by two double quotes with nothing in between. For example:

```
char quip[20] = "";
```

There is not even a space between the two double quote marks. The initialization of `quip` will put the null terminator at location `quip[0]`, so there are no characters before the termination. This is a very quiet quip indeed.

Reading and Writing String Variables

C++ supports reading and writing string variables with the usual `>>` and `<<` operators. For example:

```
char message[20] = "Noise\a";
cout << message;    ←──────────── This prints Noise and rings bell.
cin >> message;     ←──────────── This reads a string from
                                  standard input device.
```

The string-reading mechanism begins by skipping any *white space* in the input stream. **White space** consists of any blank, tab, or the return key. The operation then reads characters until some more white space is encountered, placing these characters in the string variable. The white space character itself is not read, but a null terminating character is placed at the end of the string, making it a valid null-terminated string.

PITFALL

Pitfall: Using = and == with Strings

Strings are not like other data types. Many of the usual operations simply do not work for strings. You cannot use a string variable in an assignment statement using `=`. If you use `==` to test strings for equality, you will not get the result you expect. The reason for these problems is that strings are implemented as arrays rather than simple values.

An attempt to assign a value to a string variable will quickly show the problem, as in this example:

```
char greeting[10];          ──── Illegal!
greeting = "Hello";  ←
```

This example results in a compilation error. Although you can use the equals sign to assign a value to a string variable when the variable is declared, you cannot do it any place else in your program.

You also cannot use the operator == in an expression to compare two strings for equality. Things are actually worse than that. You can use == to test two string variables, but it does not test for the strings being equal. A good compiler will warn you that == actually tests to see whether the starting addresses of the arrays are the same. But you will get incorrect results if you think you are testing for string equality.

There are ways around the string problems, which we will discuss next.

The strcpy Function

The easiest way to assign a value to a string variable is with the library function strcpy, as shown here:

```
strcpy(greeting, "Hello");
```
This is legal, using strcpy from string.h.

The above function call will set the value of greeting to "Hello", using the strcpy function from the string.h library. The precise function prototype is:

```
char* strcpy(char target[ ], const char source[ ]);
// Precondition: source is a null-terminated string, and target is an array
//  that is long enough to hold a copy of source.
// Postcondition: source has been copied to target, and the return value is
//  a pointer to the first character of target.
```

Notice that the return value is a pointer to a character, indicated by *char** in the prototype. This pointer points to the first character of the target array.

The strcat Function

Another string.h library function is strcat, which serves to add one string onto the end of another. The "cat" in "strcat" comes from **catenate**, meaning to connect in a series. The strcat function copies its second argument onto the end of its first argument, as shown here:

```
char greeting[20] = "Hello ";
strcat(greeting, "Good-bye");
```
"Good-bye" is added to the end of what's already in greeting.

After the function call, greeting contains "Hello Good-bye". The precise prototype of strcat is:

```
char* strcat(char target[ ], const char source[ ]);
// Precondition: target and source are null-terminated strings,
//  and target is long enough to catenate source on the end.
// Postcondition: source has been catenated to target, and the
//  return value is a pointer to the first character of target.
```

PITFALL

Pitfall: Dangers of `strcpy`, `strcat`, and Reading Strings

Be careful using the `strcpy` and `strcat` functions, and also reading strings. None of these operations check that the string variable actually has sufficient room to hold the copied string. If you try to copy a string with 100 characters into an array of size 50, the result will be the same disaster that occurs whenever you try to access an array beyond its declared bounds. Such behavior usually results in writing to memory locations that are not part of the array, often changing values of other declared variables.

During debugging, if you notice that a variable seems to be changing its value for no apparent reason, then think about the string variables and other arrays that your program uses. Have you accessed a string variable or array beyond its declared size?

The `strlen` Function

A `string.h` library function named `strlen` returns the number of characters in a null-terminated string, as shown here:

```
size_t strlen(const char s[ ]);
// Precondition: s is a null-terminated string.
// Postcondition: The return value is number of characters in s,
// up to (but not including) the null character.
```

For example, `strlen("Hello Good-bye")` is 14. The function returns 0 for the length of the empty string.

The `strcmp` Function

You can use the library function `strcmp` to compare two strings. The function is part of `string.h`, with the prototype given here:

```
int strcmp(const char s1[ ], const char s2[ ]);
// Precondition: s1 and s2 are null-terminated strings.
// Postcondition: The return value indicates the following:
//     The return value is 0 -- s1 is equal to s2;
//     The return value < 0 -- s1 is lexicographically before s2;
//     The return value > 0 -- s1 is lexicographically after s2.
```

As you can see, `strcmp` returns zero if its two string arguments are equal to each other. If the strings are not equal, then they are compared in the **lexicographic order**, which is the normal alphabetical order for ordinary words of all lowercase letters. For example, `strcmp("chaos", "order")` will return some negative number, since "chaos" is alphabetically before "order". On the other hand, `strcmp("order", "chaos")` will return some positive integer.

Strings of all upper-case letters also are handled alphabetically, but strings that mix upper- and lower-case letters have unpredictable results. For example, most compilers use a lexicographic order that places all upper-case letters before any lower-case letters, so that "Order" (with a capital O) is actually before "chaos", but some compilers might reverse this order.

comparing strings with strcmp

The complete string.h library facility has more than a dozen functions for manipulating null-terminated strings. But the four functions, strcpy, strcat, strlen, and strcmp, are enough to start us on our own string ADT project.

The String ADT—Specification

We'd like a String class that avoids the pitfalls of null-terminated strings. In particular, we want our strings to have a proper *value semantics*, allowing assignment statements and other copying of values without problems.

We'd also like to be able to compare strings using the usual six operators to test for equality (==), and various inequalities (!=, >=, <=, >, <). The inequalities should use the familiar lexicographic ordering that we just talked about. For example, "chaos" < "order" will be true because "chaos" is alphabetically before "order". The lexicographic order is an example of a **total order semantics** for the six comparison operators. Intuitively, a total order semantics requires that the different values of a class can all be placed on a single line, proceeding from smaller to larger along the line. This intuition is sufficient for most programming tasks, although you may sometimes need to know the more formal definition of a total order semantics shown in Figure 4.13.

The specification for a simple version of a String class is shown in Figure 4.14, including a total order semantics using the lexicographic order. The specification has a few new features that we'll discuss starting on page 187.

FIGURE 4.13   Total Order Semantics

A **total order semantics** for a class requires the six comparison operators (==, !=, >=, <=, >, <) to be defined, forming a total order that meets these requirements:

1. **Equality:** (x == y) is true if and only if two values are identical.

2. **Totality:** For any two values x and y, exactly one of these three comparisons is true:
    (x < y), (x == y), or (x > y).

3. **Consistency:** For any two values x and y:
    (x > y) is the same as (y < x)
    (x >= y) is the same as ((x > y) || (x == y))
    (x <= y) is the same as ((x < y) || (x == y))
    (x != y) is the same as !(x == y)

4. **Transitivity:** Whenever there are three values (x, y, and z) with (x < y) and (y < z), then (x < z) is also true.

| FIGURE 4.14 | Documentation for the Simple String Class |

Documentation for a Header File

```
//  FILE: mystring.h
//  CLASS PROVIDED: String (a sequence of characters)
//
//  CONSTRUCTOR for the String class:
//    String(const char str[ ] = "") -- default argument is the empty string.
//       Precondition: str is an ordinary null-terminated string.
//       Postcondition: The String contains the sequence of chars from str.
//
//  CONSTANT MEMBER FUNCTIONS for the String class:
//    size_t length( ) const
//       Postcondition: The return value is the number of characters in the String.
//
//    char operator [ ](size_t position) const
//       Precondition: position < length( ).
//       Postcondition: The value returned is the character at the specified position of the
//       String. A String's positions start from 0 at the start of the sequence and go up to
//       length( ) - 1  at the right end.
//
//  MODIFICATION MEMBER FUNCTIONS for the String class:
//    void operator +=(const String& addend)
//       Postcondition: addend has been catenated to the end of the String.
//
//    void operator +=(const char addend[ ])
//       Precondition: addend is an ordinary null-terminated string.
//       Postcondition: addend has been catenated to the end of the String.
//
//    void operator +=(char addend)
//       Postcondition: The single character addend has been catenated to the end of the String.
//
//    void resize(size_t n)
//       Postcondition: All functions will now work efficiently (without allocating new memory)
//       until n characters are in the String.
//
//  NONMEMBER FUNCTIONS for the String class:
//    String operator +(const String& s1, const String& s2)
//       Postcondition: The String returned is the catenation of s1 and s2.
//
```

(continued)

(FIGURE 4.14 continued)

```
//    istream& operator >>(istream& ins, String& target)
//        Postcondition: A String has been read from the istream ins, and the istream ins is then
//        returned by the function. The reading operation skips white space (i.e., blanks, tabs,
//        newlines) at the start of ins. Then the String is read up to the next white space or the end
//        of the file. The white space character that terminates the String has not been read.
//
//    ostream& operator <<(ostream& outs, const String& source)
//        Postcondition: The sequence of characters in source has been written to outs.
//        The return value is the ostream outs.
//
//    void getline(istream& ins, String& target)
//        Postcondition: A String has been read from the istream ins. The reading operation reads
//        all characters (including white space) until a newline or end of file is encountered. The
//        newline character is read and discarded (but not added to the end of the String).
//
// VALUE SEMANTICS for the String class:
//     Assignments and the copy constructor may be used with String objects.
//
// TOTAL ORDER SEMANTICS for the String class:
//     The six comparison operators (==, !=, >=, <=, >, and <) are implemented for the String
//     class, forming a total order semantics, using the usual lexicographic order on Strings.
//
// DYNAMIC MEMORY usage by the String class:
//     If there is insufficient dynamic memory, the following functions call new_handler:
//     the constructors, resize, operator +=, operator +, and the assignment operator.
```

`mystring.h` **FTP**

Constructor for the String Class

The String class has a constructor with one argument, shown in this prototype:

```
String(const char str[ ] = "");
```

The constructor initializes the string to contain the sequence of characters that is in the ordinary null-terminated string called str. For example, if we want to create one of our strings that contains the sequence "Peace", then we may write:

```
char sequence[6] = "Peace";
String greeting(sequence);
```

Without the variable sequence, we could also declare greeting as shown here:

```
String greeting("Peace");
```

Both approaches declare `greeting` to be one of our string objects that contains the sequence of characters `"Peace"`.

The string constructor can also be used with no arguments (that is, as a default constructor). In this case, the `str` argument uses the default argument, which is the empty string. For example, the following declares `jack` to be a `String` object with no characters:

```
String jack;
```

Overloading the *operator* [ ]

One of the string's member functions is an overloaded operator with this specification:

```
char operator [ ](size_t position) const;
// Precondition: position < length( ).
// Postcondition: The value returned is the character at the specified
// position of the String. Note: A String's positions start from 0 at the start
// of the sequence and go up to length( ) - 1 at the right end.
```

This member function allows you to use the syntax of square brackets to examine the individual characters of a `String` object. For example:

```
String greeting("Peace");
cout << greeting[0]; // Prints the P from greeting.
```

The name of this member function, *operator* [ ], is rather peculiar, but other than that it is just like any other overloaded operator.

Some Further Overloading

The string specification introduces another important feature of ADTs. Often, an ADT has several different functions with the same name. In our `String` class, there are three different += member functions with these prototypes:

```
void String::operator +=(const String& addend);
void String::operator +=(const char addend[ ]);
void String::operator +=(const char addend);
```

All three of these functions are called "operator +=" and all three can be used in a program. This is an example of overloading a single function name to carry out several related tasks.

When one of the functions is used, the compiler looks at the type of the argument to determine which of the three functions to call. For example:

```
String jack;
String adjective("nimble");

jack += adjective;
jack += '&';
jack += "quick";
```

(handwritten annotations:) String class → String; Character → '&'; Character array → "quick"

When the compiler sees the first += in the statement `jack += adjective`, the argument `adjective` is seen to be a `String`, so the compiler will call the member function with this prototype:

void String::*operator* +=(*const* String& addend);

On the other hand, in the statement `jack += '&'`, the argument '&' is a character, so the compiler will call the member function with this prototype:

void String::*operator* +=(*char* addend);

Finally, with the third statement `jack += "quick"`, the compiler sees the string constant "quick" as a character array and calls the member function with this prototype:

void String::*operator* +=(*const char* addend [ ]);

At the end of the three statements, the string `jack` contains the phrase "nimble&quick". The three different += functions are easily handled by the compiler. As the implementor of the ADT, you write all three functions just like any other function.

Other Operations for the String Class

In addition to the features that we have already mentioned, our specification indicates that assignments and the copy constructor may be used with `String` objects (that is, a valid *value semantics*). Since the string uses dynamic memory, you cannot rely on the automatic assignment operator and copy constructor. Instead, you must implement your own assignment operator and copy constructor. There are also functions for reading, writing, and comparing strings.

The String ADT—Design

The key point of our design is that a programmer must have the option of using strings with no worries about how long a string becomes. That programmer does not need to think about how a string is stored or what happens when the length of a string increases.

The plan is to have a private member variable that is a dynamic array to hold the null-terminated string. Each member function ensures that the array has sufficient room, increasing the size of the array whenever necessary. A programmer can also explicitly set the size of the dynamic array that holds the null-terminated string, by calling the `resize` function. But, similar to the dynamic bag ADT, explicit resizing is not required—it is just a convenience for efficiency. Let's examine the design considerations that our plan entails. We suggest three private member variables, shown here:

```
class String
{
public:
    ...
private:
    char *sequence;
    size_t allocated;
    size_t current_length;
};
```

The use of the member variables is controlled by the invariant of the ADT:

Invariant for the String ADT

1. The string is stored as a null-terminated string in the dynamic array pointed to by the member variable `sequence`.

2. The total length of the dynamic array is stored in the member variable `allocated`.

3. The total number of characters prior to the null character is stored in `current_length`, which is always less than `allocated`.

Notice that there is a requirement for the current length of the string to always be *less than* the amount of memory allocated for the dynamic array. This allows room for the extra null terminator at the end of the sequence.

The String ADT—Implementation

We'll leave most of the string implementation up to you, but we will discuss a few points including the constructors, the destructor, and some of the operators.

Before the discussion, we should point out a small extravagance in our three member variables. We could manage without `current_length` by using the library function `strlen`, but keeping track of the length ourselves is likely to be more efficient than continually asking `strlen` to recompute the length.

FIGURE 4.15	Implementation of a String Constructor and an Operator

Implementations of a Constructor and an Operator

```
String::String(const char str[ ])
// Library facilities used: string.h
{
    current_length = strlen(str);
    allocated = current_length + 1;
    sequence = new char[allocated];
    strcpy(sequence, str);
}
```

The constructor must provide initial values for the three member variables.

```
bool operator ==(const String& s1, const String& s2)
// Postcondition: The return value is true if s1 is identical to s2.
// Library facilities used: string.h
{
    return (strcmp(s1.sequence, s2.sequence) == 0);
}
```

The boolean operator == must be a friend of the String class.

Constructors. The constructor is responsible for initializing the three private member variables. The initialization occurs by copying a character sequence from an ordinary null-terminated string, as shown in the first part of Figure 4.15. Notice that the constructor makes use of the library function `strcpy` to copy the null-terminated string from the parameter `str` to the dynamic array `sequence`. Within your string implementation, you should make use of the library functions whenever they are needed.

The destructor. We did not list a destructor in the documentation of the `String` class, since programmers typically do not activate a destructor directly. But, since the class uses dynamic memory, you must implement a destructor. Your destructor will return the string's dynamic array to the heap.

Comparison operators. The string class has six comparison operators, forming a total order semantics. The prototypes for the operators are:

```
bool operator ==(const String& s1, const String& s2);
bool operator !=(const String& s1, const String& s2);
bool operator >=(const String& s1, const String& s2);
bool operator <=(const String& s1, const String& s2);
bool operator > (const String& s1, const String& s2);
bool operator < (const String& s1, const String& s2);
```

Each function can be implemented with an appropriate call to the library function. For example, an implementation of == is shown in the second part of Figure 4.15. Notice that our implementation must be a friend function since it accesses sequence, which is a private member variable of the String class.

The resize function. Our design includes a member function called resize, similar to the dynamic bag's resize function. Here is the precondition/postcondition contract:

```
void resize(size_t n);
// Postcondition: All functions will now work efficiently (without allocating
// new memory) until n characters are in the string.
```

Programmers who use our string ADT never need to activate resize, but they may wish to, for better efficiency.

Our own implementations of other member functions can also activate resize whenever a larger array is needed. When a member function activates resize, the activation should occur before any other changes are made to the string. This follows our usual programming guideline of allocating new memory before changing an object. (See "How to Allocate Memory in a Member Function" on page 173.)

The operator >>. Our input operator begins by skipping any *white space* in the input stream. (**White space** is the term for blanks, newlines, and tabs. All the standard >> operators in C++ start by skipping white space.) After skipping the initial white space, our string input operator reads a string—reading up to but not including the next white space character (or until the input stream becomes "bad," which might occur from several causes, such as reaching the end of the file.). The function isspace from the ctype.h library facility can help. This function has one argument (a character); it returns true if its argument is one of the white space characters. With this in mind, we can skip any initial white space with this loop:

```
while (ins && isspace(ins.peek( )))
    ins.ignore( );
```

The loop also uses three istream features: (1) In a boolean expression, the name of the istream (which is ins) acts as a test of whether the input stream is bad. If ins results in a true value, then the stream is okay; a false value indicates a bad input stream. (2) The peek member function returns the next character to be read (without actually reading it). (3) The ignore member function reads and discards the next character.

After skipping the initial white space, you can set the string to the empty string, and then read the input characters one at a time, adding each character to the end of the string. The reading stops when you reach more white space (or the end of file). This idea is implemented by the code at the top of the next page.

```
target = "";  // Set the target to the empty string.
while (ins && !isspace(ins.peek( )))
{
    ins >> c;
    target += c;  // Call the operator += with a char argument.
}
```

Once the target string reaches its current capacity, our approach continues to work correctly, although it is inefficient because `target` is probably resized by the += operator each time that we add another character. Your documentation should warn programmers of this inefficiency so that a programmer can explicitly resize the target before calling the input operator.

The getline function. This function has the following prototype:

```
void getline(istream& ins, String& target);
```

The function is not a member function, nor does it need to be a friend function. Its job is to read all of one line of input (including white space), until the newline character is encountered. All the characters of the line are placed in the string variable, `target`. The newline character is read and discarded, but not placed in the target.

In order to implement `getline`, you'll need the ability to read input characters one at a time, including reading a white space character. The usual >> operator for characters cannot do this (it skips white space), but another istream member function called `get` can read single characters (including white space). For our istream, `ins`, the statement `ins.get(c)` will read the next input character, placing the result in the character variable `c`.

Demonstration Program for the String Class

Figure 4.16 on page 194 shows a short demonstration program for the `String` class. The program asks the user for their first and last name, and then prints some messages. A sample dialogue would go something like this:

```
What is your first name? Timothy
My first name is Demo.
What is your last name? Program
That is the same as my last name!
I am happy to meet you, Timothy Program.
```

The program uses several C++ object features such as an automatic conversion from ordinary strings to our new class. We'll discuss these features now, and you can try them out with your own `String` class.

FIGURE 4.16	Demonstration Program for the String Class

A Program

```
// FILE: str_demo.cxx
// This is a small demonstration program showing how the String class is used.
#include <iostream.h>    // Provides cout and cin
#include <stdlib.h>      // Provides EXIT_SUCCESS
#include "mystring.h"

// PROTOTYPES for functions used by this demonstration program:
void match(const String& variety, const String& mine, const String& yours);
// The two strings, mine and yours, are compared. If they are the same, then a
// message is printed saying they are the same; otherwise mine is printed
// in a message. In either case, the string variety is part of the message.

int main( )
{
    const String BLANK(" ");
    String me_first("Demo"), me_last("Program");
    String you_first, you_last, you;

    cout << "What is your first name? ";
    cin >> you_first;
    match("first name", me_first, you_first);
    cout << "What is your last name? ";
    cin >> you_last;
    match("last name", me_last, you_last);

    you = you_first + BLANK + you_last;
    cout << "I am happy to meet you, " << you << "." << endl;
    return EXIT_SUCCESS;
}


void match(const String& variety, const String& mine, const String& yours)
{
    if (mine == yours)
        cout << "That is the same as my " << variety << '!' << endl;
    else
        cout << "My " << variety << " is " << mine << '.' << endl;
}
```

Constants of type String may be declared. (See page 195.)

See "Constructor-Generated Conversions" on page 195 to read about the use of an ordinary string for the first argument of the match function.

Overloaded operators, such as the + operator, may be used in complex expressions. (See page 196.)

str_demo.cxx	**FTP**

Chaining the Output Operator

Look at the function `match` at the bottom of Figure 4.16. The function has three constant string parameters. Two of the parameters (`mine` and `yours`) are compared using the string's `==` operator. If the strings are equal, then the third parameter (`variety`) is printed as part of a message:

```
cout << "That is the same as my " << variety << '!' << endl;
```

For example, if `variety` is the string `"first name"`, then the output statement prints `"That is the same as my first name!"` The actual output involves a sequence, or "chaining," of four occurrences of the output operator `<<`.

1. The first `<<` prints the string constant: `"That is the same as my "`. This is an ordinary C++ string constant, not a `String` object.
2. The second `<<` prints the `String` object, `variety`, using the `<<` operator of the new `String` class.
3. The third `<<` prints an exclamation point as an ordinary character.
4. The final `<<` prints the end-of-line.

The key point is that the `<<` operator of the `String` class may be chained in combination with other objects to print a series of objects—some `String` objects, some not.

Declaring Constant Objects

The top of the main program in Figure 4.16 declares several strings. The first declaration is:

A single blank is written here between two quote marks.

```
const String BLANK(" ");
```

This declares a *constant* string named BLANK, which is initialized as a sequence that contains just a single blank. Using the name BLANK in this way makes it easier to read statements that use a blank. The use of the keyword *const* forbids the program from actually changing BLANK to a different string. As part of our documentation standard (Appendix J), we use all upper-case letters for the names of declared constants.

Constructor-Generated Conversions

In the main program of Figure 4.16, we have two calls to the `match` function. For example:

```
match("first name", me_first, you_first);
```

Look at the first argument, "first name", which is an ordinary string constant. But the first parameter of match is not an ordinary string; it is a String object from our new String class:

```
void match( const String& variety, ...
```

How can this be? Isn't this an error because the argument is a different type than the formal parameter? The answer is no, because of a special conversion operation that is automatically applied by C++. Here is how the conversion works: When a type mismatch is detected, the compiler attempts to convert the given value into a value of the needed type. In our example, the compiler tries to convert the string constant "first name" into a String object. One of the conversion mechanisms is to find a constructor for the needed type, with a single parameter. In our example, the compiler uses the constructor

```
String(const char[ ]);
```

to convert the ordinary string constant to a String object. The constructed String object is then used for the first argument of match.

Constructor-Generated Conversions

When a type mismatch is detected, the compiler attempts to convert the given value into a value of the needed type. One of the conversion mechanisms, called a **constructor-generated conversion**, is to find a constructor for the needed type, with a single parameter. The compiler will apply the constructor to the given value to create an object of the needed type.

Using Overloaded Operations in Expressions

The String class has overloaded binary + to perform string catenation. The way that + is used in the main program of Figure 4.16 may seem unusual:

```
you = you_first + BLANK + you_last;
```

The compiler treats the expression using ordinary associativity rules for the + operator in an expression. As usual for a series of + operations, the leftmost + is applied first, equivalent to this parenthesized expression, where the highlighted part is evaluated first:

```
you = (you_first + BLANK) + you_last;
```

Our String Class Versus the C++ Library String Class

The new `String` class is implemented with a header file (`mystring.h`) and an implementation file (`mystring.cxx`) that you write. The class has only a handful of operations—enough for us to write some sample programs throughout the rest of the text. With these sample programs, and programs that you write, you may use `mystring.h`. However, if you have a newer compiler that provides a C++ library `String` class, then you may wish to use the library's class instead of our simple class. The library `String` class has all of our operations and more.

Self-Test Exercises

18. Write C++ code that declares a regular C++ null-terminated string that can hold up to 20 characters, reads user-input into the string, appends an exclamation point to the end of the string, and prints the result.

19. Suppose that `strlen` was not part of the `string.h` library. Implement `strlen` yourself, using the prototype on page 184.

20. Describe the major motivation for implementing a `String` class instead of using ordinary string variables.

21. What are the three private member variables for our `String` class? → *char * sequence; size_t allocated; size_t current_length*

22. Why does the `String` class need a destructor? *dynamic memory*

23. Which of the string member functions are likely to activate `resize`?

24. Which of the nonmember functions should be friends of the `String` class?

25. When do constructor-generated conversions take place? *type - mismatch*

CHAPTER SUMMARY

- A *pointer* stores an address of another variable. Pointers are most useful when they are used to point to *dynamically allocated memory*, such as a *dynamic array*. The size of a dynamic array does not need to be determined until a program is running. Such behavior, determined at run time, is called *dynamic behavior*. Dynamic behavior is more flexible than decisions that are made at compile time (i.e., *static behavior*).

- The member variables of classes are frequently arrays or dynamic arrays. Ordinary arrays are simple to program, and are often sufficient. Dynamic arrays provide better flexibility since their size can vary according to need. However, dynamic arrays also involve more complex programming since the necessary memory must be correctly allocated, and freed when it is no longer needed.

- In C++, the *new* operator is used to allocate dynamic memory. The *delete* operator is used to free dynamic memory.

- The *new* operator usually indicates failure by calling a special function called new_handler. Normally the new_handler halts the program with an error message. You should clearly document which functions use *new*, so that experienced programmers can deal with the new_handler in their own way.

- Strings and bags are two examples of ADTs that can be implemented with dynamic arrays.

- Classes that use dynamic memory should always include a copy constructor, an overloaded assignment operator, and a destructor. The copy constructor and assignment operator must each copy an object by making a new copy of the dynamic memory (rather than just copying a pointer). The destructor is responsible for freeing dynamic memory.

? Solutions to Self-Test Exercises

1. One use of & indicates a reference parameter. A second use of & provides the address of a variable.

2.
```
int *exercise;
size_t i;

exercise = new int[1000];
for (i = 1; i <= 1000; i++)
    exercise[i-1] = i;
delete [ ] exercise;
```

3.
```
100 and 200
200 and 200
300 and 300
400 and 400
```

4. We no longer need the memory that p1 points to.

5. 42

6. A parameter that is a pointer must be a reference parameter if the function makes the pointer point to a new location and you want the actual argument to also point to this new location.

7. When an array is passed as a parameter, changes to the array affect the actual argument. This is because the parameter is treated as a pointer that points to the first component of the array. This is different from a value parameter (where changes to the parameter do not affect the actual argument).

8. The critical point is that the pointer parameter must be a reference parameter, as shown here:
```
void exercise(int*& p, size_t n);
```

9. Neither average nor compare changes the contents of the array, so the keyword *const* may be used. The fill_array function does change the array's contents, so *const* must not be used.

10. Here is the function:
```
void copyints(
    int target[ ],
    const int source[ ],
    size_t n
)
// Postcondition: source[0] through
// source[n - 1] have been copied to
// target[0] through target[n - 1].
{
    size_t i;

    for (i = 0; i < n; i++)
        target[i] = source[i];
}
```

11. Typically, the size of a dynamic data structure is not determined until a program is running. But the size of a static data structure is determined at the time of compilation.

12. The initial capacity is DEFAULT_CAPACITY (which is 30). If 31 items are placed in the bag, then the insert function will increase the capacity to 31.

13. In the insert implementation, the call to resize becomes resize(1 + used*1.1); (The extra "+1" causes any fraction to round up.)

14. The primary responsibility of a destructor is to free the dynamic memory used by an object. See the list on page 166 for situations when the destructor is automatically called.

15. Ordinarily, the assignment operator merely copies member variables from one object to another. But since the new bag uses dynamic memory, the assignment operator must make a copy of the dynamic memory rather than just copying the pointer, which is a member variable. The way to get the assignment operator to do the extra work is by overloading the assignment operator.

 Our implementation of the assignment operator does work correctly for a self-assignment.

16. Our implementation of the *operator* + function accesses the private member variable capacity. Therefore, the function must be a friend of the Bag class.

17. The copy constructor can be called to construct a new object, just like any other constructor. It is also called when a value parameter is an object or when a function returns an object.

18.
```
char s[21];
cin >> s;
strcat(s, "!");
cout << s;
```

19. Here is the function:
```
size_t strlen(const char s[ ])
{
    size_t len;

    for (len = 0; s[len] != '\0'; len++)
    // No work in the body of this loop.
    ;
    return len;
}
```

20. Ordinary string variables do not support operations such as assignment and comparisons.

21. Private member variables of the String class are sequence, current_length, and allocated (see the definition on page 190).

22. Any class that uses dynamic memory needs a destructor to return its dynamic memory to the heap.

23. The operators =, +, +=, and >> and the copy constructor.

24. Any nonmember function that accesses a private member variable must be a friend function. In our implementation, the output operator and the six boolean functions were friends, but your implementation might need different friends (depending on where you access private member variables).

25. If there is a type-mismatch, then the compiler tries to take the given value and convert it to the needed type with a constructor-generated conversion.

PROGRAMMING PROJECTS

1 Add more operations to the String class from Section 4.5. Some possibilities are listed here:

(a) A new constructor that has one parameter (a character). The constructor initializes the string to have just this one character.

(b) An insert function that allows you to insert a string at a given position in another string.

(c) A deletion function that allows you to delete a portion of a string.

(d) A replacement function that allows you to replace a single character in a string with a new character.

(e) A replacement function that allows you to replace a portion of a string with another string.

(f) A search function that searches a string for the first occurrence of a specified character.

(g) A search function that counts the number of occurrences of a specified character in a string.

(h) A more complex search function that searches through a string for an occurrence of some smaller string.

2 Revise one of the container classes from Chapter 3, so that it uses a dynamic array. Some choices are: (a) the list from Section 3.2; (b) the set (Project 5 on page 133); (c) the sorted list (Project 6 on page 133); (d) the bag with receipts (Project 7 on page 133); (e) the keyed bag (Project 8 on page 133).

3 Revise the Chapter 3 polynomial class from Project 9 on page 134, so that there is no maximum degree. Include an operation to allow you to multiply two polynomials in the usual way. For example:

$$(3x^2 + 7) \ * \ (2x + 4) \ = \ (6x^3 + 12x^2 + 14x + 28)$$

4 Write a checkbook balancing program. The program will read in the following for all checks that were not cashed as of the last time you balanced your checkbook: the number of each check, the amount of the check, and whether it has been cashed yet. Use a dynamic array of "checks," where each check is an object of a data type called Check that you design and implement yourself. In addition to the checks, the program also reads all the deposits as well as the old and new account balance. You may want a second dynamic array to hold the list of deposits. The new account balance should equal the old balance plus all deposits, minus all checks that have been cashed.

The program also prints several items: the total of the checks cashed, the total of the deposits, what the new balance should be, and how much this figure differs from what the bank says the new account balance is. Also print two lists of checks: the checks cashed since the last time you balanced your checkbook, and a list of checks still not cashed.

5 Write a program that uses a dynamic list of strings to keep track of a list of chores that you have to accomplish today. The user of the program can request several services: (1) Add an item to the list of chores; (2) Ask how many chores are in the list; (3) Have the list of chores printed to the screen; (4) Delete an item from the list; (5) Exit the program.

If you know how to read and write strings from a file, then have the program obtain its initial list of chores from a file. When the program ends, it should write all unfinished chores back to this file.

5 Linked Lists

The simplest way to interrelate or link a set of elements is to line them up in a single list... For, in this case, only a single link is needed for each element to refer to its successor.

NIKLAUS WIRTH
Algorithms + Data Structures = Programs

We begin this chapter with a concrete discussion of a new data structure, *linked lists*, which are used to implement a list of items arranged in some kind of order. The linked list structure uses dynamic memory that shrinks and grows as needed but in a different manner than dynamic arrays. The discussion of linked lists includes the necessary type definitions in C++, together with ten fundamental functions to manipulate linked lists.

Once you understand the fundamentals, linked lists can be used as part of your ADTs, similar to the way that arrays have been used in previous ADTs. For example, linked lists can be used to reimplement the bag and list ADTs from Chapter 3.

linked lists are used to implement a list of items arranged in some kind of order

By the end of the chapter you will understand linked lists well enough to use them in various programming projects (such as the revised bag and list ADTs) and in the ADTs of future chapters. You will also know the advantages and drawbacks of using linked lists versus dynamic arrays for these ADTs.

5.1 FUNDAMENTALS OF LINKED LISTS

A **linked list** is a sequence of items arranged one after another, with each item connected to the next item by a "link." In programming languages, each item is placed together with the link to the next item, resulting in a simple component called a **node**. A node is represented pictorially as a box with the item written inside the box and the link drawn as an arrow pointing out of the box.

Several typical nodes are drawn in Figure 5.1 (in the margin). For example, the topmost node has the number 12.1 as its data. Most of the nodes in the figure also have an arrow pointing out of the node. These arrows, or "links," are used to connect one node to another.

The links are represented as arrows because they do more than simply connect two nodes. The links also place the nodes in a sequence. In Figure 5.1, the five nodes form a sequence from top to bottom. The first node is linked to the second node; the second node is linked to the third node; and so on until we reach the last node. We must do something special when we reach the last node, since the last node is not linked to another node. In this special case, we will replace the link in this node with a note saying "end marker."

Declaring a Class for Nodes

As you might guess from our pictures, the links between nodes are implemented using pointers. But pointers to *what*? Remember that we cannot simply declare a pointer; each pointer must be declared as a pointer to a particular type of data. For example, we have pointers to integers, pointers to characters, pointers to throttles. In the case of a linked list, each link is a pointer to a *node*.

But what exactly is a *node*? To answer this question, look once more at our pictures. Each node is a combination of two things: a piece of data (double numbers in our examples) and a link to the next node. In C++, we can define a new data type for a node that contains these two things, as shown here:

FIGURE 5.1
Linked List
Made of Nodes
Connected
with Links

```
struct Node
{
    double data;
    Node *link;
};
```

The definition uses the C++ keyword *struct*, which is a special kind of class. In fact, if you change the keyword from *struct* to *class*, the definition looks a lot like a class with two member variables: a double number called `data`, and a pointer called `link`. So why have we used a struct rather than a class? The answer lies in a subtle difference between a struct and an ordinary class: Unless you state otherwise, *struct members are public*. Therefore, even without the keyword *public*, our node definition has two *public* member variables named `data` and `link`.

unless you state otherwise, struct members are public

As a kind of programming pact, C++ programmers tend to use a struct only when all the members are public.

Struct

A **struct** is a special kind of class. The special feature is that struct members are all public (unless you state otherwise).

C++ programmers tend to use a struct only when *all* the members are public.

Using a Typedef Statement with Linked List Nodes

Until now we have considered only nodes where the data consists of double numbers. But, in general, other kinds of data are just as useful. Linked lists of integers, or characters, or even strings, are all useful. In other words, the `Node` class depends on an underlying data type—the type of data in each node. To allow for easy changing of the item type, we generally use a typedef statement to define the name `Item` to be a synonym for the type of data in each node. The `Item` type is then used within the node struct, as shown here:

```
struct Node
{
    typedef double Item;
    Item data;
    Node *link;
};
```

This is the same technique that we've used before to define the type of elements in a bag or list. If we need to change the type of items in the nodes, then we will have to change only the `Item` typedef statement. Whenever a program needs to refer to the item type, we can use the expression `Node::Item`.

Head Pointers, Tail Pointers

Usually, programs do not actually declare node variables. Instead, when we build and manipulate a linked list, the list is accessed through one or more *pointers* to nodes. The most common access to a linked list is through the list's first node, which is called the **head** of the list. A pointer to the first node is called the **head pointer**. Sometimes we maintain a pointer to the last node in a linked list. The last node is the **tail** of the list, and a pointer to the last node is the **tail pointer**. We could also maintain pointers to other nodes in a linked list.

Each pointer to a node must be declared as a pointer variable. For example, if we are maintaining a linked list with a head and tail pointer, then we would declare two pointer variables:

```
Node *head_ptr;
Node *tail_ptr;
```

The program could now proceed to create a linked list, always keeping `head_ptr` pointing to the first node and `tail_ptr` pointing to the last node, as shown in Figure 5.2.

Building and Manipulating Linked Lists

Whenever a program builds and manipulates a linked list, the access to the nodes in the list is through one or more pointers to nodes. Typically, a program includes a pointer to the first node (the **head pointer**) and a pointer to the last node (the **tail pointer**).

FIGURE 5.2   Type Declarations in a Program with a Linked List

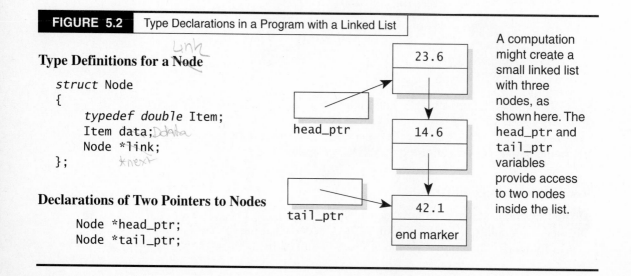

Type Definitions for a Node

```
struct Node
{
    typedef double Item;
    Item data;
    Node *link;
};
```

Declarations of Two Pointers to Nodes

```
Node *head_ptr;
Node *tail_ptr;
```

A computation might create a small linked list with three nodes, as shown here. The head_ptr and tail_ptr variables provide access to two nodes inside the list.

The Null Pointer

Figure 5.3 illustrates a linked list with a head pointer and one new feature. Look at the link member of the final node. Instead of a pointer, we have written the word NULL. The word NULL indicates the **null pointer**, which is a special C++ constant. You can use the null pointer for any pointer value that has no place to point. There are two common situations where the null pointer is used:

- Use the null pointer for the link field of the final node of a linked list.
- When a linked list does not yet have any nodes, use the null pointer for the value of the head pointer and tail pointer. Such a list is called the **empty list**.

In a program, the null pointer may be written as NULL, which is a constant from the standard library facility stdlib.h. You may also see some programmers who write the null pointer as the number 0, but it is clearer style to write it as NULL.

The Null Pointer

The null pointer is a special C++ pointer value that can be used for any pointer that does not point anywhere. It can be written as the constant NULL from stdlib.h.

The null pointer can be assigned to a pointer variable with an ordinary assignment statement. For example:

```
Node *head_ptr;
head_ptr = NULL; // Uses the constant NULL from stdlib.h
```

FIGURE 5.3
Linked List with the Null Pointer at the Final Link

The Meaning of a Null Head Pointer or Tail Pointer

Keep in mind that the head pointer and tail pointer of a linked list may be NULL, which indicates that the list is empty (has no nodes). In fact, this is the way that most linked lists start out. Any functions that you write to manipulate linked lists *must* be able to handle a null head pointer and tail pointer.

The Member Selection Operator

Suppose that a program has built the linked list and head pointer shown in Figure 5.3 (in the margin). Now, head_ptr is a pointer to a Node, so here is a small quiz: Using the dereferencing asterisk, what is the data type of *head_ptr? Remember that *head_ptr means "the thing that head_ptr points to." Looking at the picture you can see that the data type of *head_ptr is Node (i.e., a node object).

As with any object, you can access the two members of *head_ptr. For example, the following writes the data (12.1) from the head node:

```
cout << (*head_ptr).data;
```

The expression (*head_ptr).data means "the data member of the node pointed to by head_ptr." The parentheses are necessary around the first part of the expression, (*head_ptr). The parentheses are needed because unary operations that appear on the right (such as accessing the data member variable) have higher precedence than unary operations that appear on the left (such as the dereferencing asterisk). Without the parentheses, the meaning of *head_ptr.data will cause a syntax error, trying to evaluate head_ptr.data before dereferencing.

Because of the parentheses problem, C++ offers an alternative way to select a member of a class, shown here:

The -> Operator

If p is a pointer to a class (or struct), and m is a member of the class, then p->m means the same as (*p).m.

Example: head_ptr->data is the data member of the node pointed to by head_ptr.

---

the -> operator

The symbol "->" is considered a single operator (rather than two separate symbols "-" and ">"). It is called the **member selection operator** or **component selection operator**. Visually, the p->m operator reminds you of an arrow, leading from the pointer p to the object that contains the member m. Using the member selection operator, we can print the data from the first node of the list in Figure 5.3, as shown here:

```
cout << head_ptr->data;
```

PITFALL

Pitfall: Dereferencing the Null Pointer

One of the most common pointer errors is writing the expression *p or p-> when the value of the pointer p is the null pointer. This must always be avoided because the null pointer does not point to anything. Therefore, when p is the null pointer, *p (which means "the thing that p points to") is meaningless. In this case, p-> is also meaningless. Because the asterisk in *p is called the *dereferencing operator*, we can state this rule: *Never dereference the null pointer.*

Accidental dereferencing of the null pointer is sometimes a hard error to track down. The error does not cause a syntax error. Instead, when the program is running, there will be an attempt to interpret the null pointer as if it were a valid address. Sometimes this will cause an immediate run time error with a message such as "Address protection violation" or "Bus error, core dumped." But on other machines, the null address might be a valid address, causing your program to read or write an unintended memory location. Often this memory location is part of the machine's operating system, resulting in part of the operating system being corrupted. At some later point, perhaps after your program has completed, the corrupted operating system can cause an error. Fortunately, restarting your machine usually writes a fresh copy of the operating system into memory—but even so, *never dereference the null pointer!*

Self-Test Exercises

1. How does a struct differ from an ordinary class in C++?

2. Write the struct definition needed for a node in a linked list. Use the name Item for the type of the data.

3. Describe two common uses for the null pointer.

4. What is the data type of head_ptr in Figure 5.3 on page 205? What is the data type of *head_ptr? What is the data type of head_ptr->data?

5. Suppose that head_ptr points to the first node of a non-empty linked list. Write code to print the word "zero" if the data in the first node is 0.

6. Suppose that b_ptr is a pointer to a bag (from Chapter 3). One of the bag's member functions is size, which returns the number of elements in a bag. Write a statement that prints the number of elements in the bag pointed to by b_ptr. Use the member selection operator.

7. Describe a catastrophe that can occur if you dereference the null pointer.

5.2 A LINKED LIST TOOLKIT

We're now in a position to write programs that use linked lists. Such a program includes the node definition from Figure 5.2 on page 204, and it declares some pointer variables that point to nodes in its linked list. But the program would require many parts to build and manipulate the lists—parts that are not central to the program's main objectives. In fact, many programs might need these same parts, which suggests that we write a collection of linked list functions once and for all, allowing any program to use the functions. This is what we will do, creating a small "toolkit" of ten fundamental linked list functions.

a collection of linked list functions

The toolkit comes in two parts: a header file and an implementation file, similar to the way that we have provided separate files for ADTs in the past. The contents of the two files are discussed in this section.

Linked List Toolkit—Header File

For our first toolkit that manipulates linked lists of double numbers, the header file, link1.h, contains the node definition and prototypes for the toolkit's ten functions. For example, the first prototype is as shown here (in the highlighted line):

```
struct Node
{
    typedef double Item;
    Item data;
    Node *link;
};

size_t list_length(Node* head_ptr);
...
```

The first prototype is for a function that computes the number of nodes in a linked list.

The list_length function computes the number of nodes in a linked list. The one parameter, head_ptr, is a pointer to the first node of the linked list. An empty list is indicated by setting head_ptr to the null pointer.

The ten functions, including list_length, are implemented in a separate implementation file, link1.cxx. Each of the ten functions has one or more parameters that are pointers to nodes in a linked list.

Functions that Manipulate Linked Lists

A function that manipulates linked lists has one or more parameters that are pointers to nodes in the list.

Is a Toolkit an ADT?

The Node class and its ten functions are *not* really an ADT. Effective use of our functions requires knowledge of the details of linked lists and nodes, whereas such "inside information" is never needed to use an ADT. Our ten functions provide only the tools that a programmer needs to write many different ADTs and applications that use linked lists. In this sense, link1.h is similar to the library facility string.h. Both provide a collection of functions that make it easier to write ADTs and other applications.

A collection of useful functions to support a concept is sometimes called a **software toolkit**. The C++ standard libraries provide a string toolkit, and we are about to write our own linked list toolkit.

So, read through our ten functions. Understand how the functions work and how to use the functions, and you will be well on your way to becoming a master linked list programmer.

Computing the Length of a Linked List

Our first toolkit function computes the **length** of a linked list, which is simply the number of nodes. Here is the prototype:

```
size_t list_length(Node* head_ptr);
// Precondition: head_ptr is the head pointer of a linked list.
// Postcondition: The value returned is the number of nodes in
//   the linked list. The list itself is unaltered.
```

list_length

The precondition indicates that the parameter, `head_ptr`, is the head pointer of a linked list. If the list is not empty, then `head_ptr` points to the first node of the list. If the list is empty, then `head_ptr` is the null pointer (and the function returns zero, since there are no nodes).

Our implementation uses a pointer variable to step through the list, counting the nodes one at a time. Here are the three steps of the pseudocode, using a pointer variable named `cursor` to step through the nodes of the list one at a time. (We often use the name `cursor` for such a pointer, since "cursor" means a "pointer that runs through a structure.")

1. Initialize a variable named `answer` to zero (this variable will keep track of how many nodes we have seen so far).

2. Make `cursor` point to each node of the list, starting at the head node. Each time `cursor` points to a new node, add one to `answer`.

3. *return* `answer`.

Both `cursor` and `answer` are local variables in the function.

The first step initializes `answer` to zero, because we have not yet seen any nodes.

The implementation of Step 2 is a for-loop, following a pattern that you should use whenever *all of the nodes of a linked list must be traversed*. The general pattern looks like this:

how to traverse all the nodes of a linked list

```
for (cursor = head_ptr; cursor != NULL; cursor = cursor->link)
{
    ...        Inside the body of the loop, you may
               carry out whatever computation is
               needed for a node in the list.
}
```

In our function, the "computation" inside the loop is simple because we are just counting the nodes. Therefore, in our body we will just add one to `answer`, as shown in the code at the top of the next page.

```
for (cursor = head_ptr; cursor != NULL; cursor = cursor->link)
    answer++;
```

Let's examine the loop on an example. Suppose that the linked list has three nodes containing the numbers 10, 20, and 30. After the loop initializes (with `cursor = head_ptr`), we have this situation:

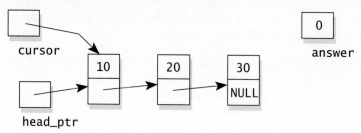

Notice that `cursor` points to the same node that `head_ptr` is pointing to.

Since `cursor` is not NULL, we enter the body of the loop. Each iteration increments `answer` and then executes `cursor = cursor->link`. The effect of `cursor = cursor->link` is to copy the `link` field of the first node into `cursor` itself, so that `cursor` ends up pointing to the second node. In general, the statement `cursor = cursor->link` moves `cursor` to the next node. So, at the completion of the loop's first iteration, the situation is this:

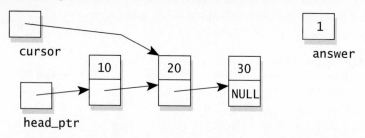

The loop continues. After the second iteration, `answer` is 2, and `cursor` points to the third node of the list, as shown here:

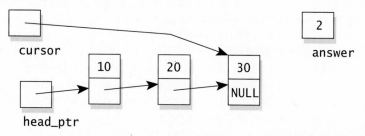

Each time we complete an iteration of the loop, `cursor` points to some location in the list, and `answer` is the number of nodes *before* this location. In our example, we are about to enter the loop's body for the third and last time. During the

FIGURE 5.4	A Function to Compute the Length of a Linked List

A Function Implementation

```
size_t list_length(Node* head_ptr)
// Precondition: head_ptr is the head pointer of a linked list.
// Postcondition: The value returned is the number of nodes in the linked list.
// The list itself is unaltered.
// Library facilities used: stdlib.h
{
    Node *cursor;
    size_t answer;

    answer = 0;
    for (cursor = head_ptr; cursor != NULL; cursor = cursor->link)
        answer++;                             Step 2 of the
                                              pseudocode
    return answer;
}
```

link1.cxx   FTP

last iteration, `answer` is incremented to 3, and `cursor` becomes NULL, as shown here:

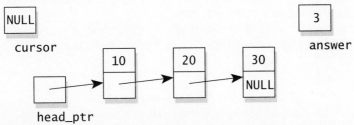

The pointer variable `cursor` has become NULL because the loop control statement `cursor = cursor->link` copied the `link` member of the third node into `cursor`. Since this `link` member is NULL, the value in `cursor` is now NULL.

At this point, the loop's control test `cursor != NULL` is false. The loop ends, and the function returns the answer 3. The complete implementation of the `list_length` function is shown in Figure 5.4.

Programming Tip: **How to Traverse a Linked List**

TIP

You should learn the important pattern for traversing a linked list, as used in the `list_length` function (Figure 5.4). The same pattern can be used whenever you need to step through the nodes of a linked list one at a time.

The first part of the pattern concerns moving from one node to another. Whenever we have a pointer that points to some node, and we want the pointer to point to the next node, we must use the `link` member of the node. Here is the reasoning that we follow:

1. Suppose `cursor` points to some node;

2. Then `cursor->link` points to the next node (if there is one), as shown here:

The pointer in the shaded box is `cursor->link`, and it points to the next node after `cursor`.

3. In order to move `cursor` to the next node, we use the assignment statement:

$$cursor = cursor->link;$$

If there is no next node, then `cursor->link` will be NULL, and therefore our assignment statement will set `cursor` to NULL.

The key is to know that the assignment statement `cursor = cursor->link` moves `cursor` so that it points to the next node. If there is no next node, then the assignment statement sets `cursor` to NULL.

The second part of the pattern shows how to traverse all of the nodes of a linked list, starting at the head node. The pattern of the loop looks like this:

```
for (cursor = head_ptr; cursor != NULL; cursor = cursor->link)
{
    ...        Inside the body of the loop, you may
               carry out whatever computation is
               needed for a node in the list.
}
```

You'll find yourself using this pattern continually in functions that manipulate linked lists.

PITFALL

Pitfall: Forgetting to Test the Empty List

Functions that manipulate linked lists should always be tested to ensure that they have the right behavior for the empty list. When `head_ptr` is NULL (indicating the empty list), our `list_length` function should return 0. Testing this case shows that `list_length` does correctly return 0 for the empty list.

Parameters for Linked Lists

When a function manipulates a linked list, one of the parameters must be a pointer to a node in the list—often the head pointer, but sometimes another pointer is used. These pointers to nodes are generally used as parameters in just two ways, requiring a bit of discussion before we can proceed with our toolkit. (And you thought you *already* knew everything there is to know about parameters!)

how to use a node pointer as a parameter

Value parameters that are node pointers. The first sort of node pointer parameter is a value parameter. The `list_length` function has such a parameter:

```
size_t list_length(Node* head_ptr);
```

The function uses the head pointer to access the list's nodes, but the function does not make the head pointer point to a new node. In general, this is the situation when you should use a value parameter: *A node pointer should be a value parameter when the function needs access to the linked list and does not need to make the pointer point to a new node.*

With a value parameter, a function cannot make the head pointer point to a different node—but it could actually change the contents of the list, perhaps changing the `data` field of one of the nodes, or even adding nodes somewhere down the line. Of course, the well-behaved `list_length` function does not change the contents of the list. Isn't there some way we could indicate in the parameter list that both the head pointer and the rest of the list are *unaltered*? Unfortunately not. Once you have given a function access to the head pointer, you cannot prevent it from altering nodes. This makes the precondition/postcondition contract all the more important: If a function does not alter a list in any way, then this should be stated as part of the postcondition. We include such a statement in the `list_length` postcondition:

```
// Postcondition: The value returned is the number of nodes in
// the linked list. The list itself is unaltered.
```

Reference parameters that are node pointers. Sometimes a function must make the head pointer point to a new node. For example, one of the toolkit functions adds a new node at the front of a linked list, with this prototype and precondition/postcondition contract:

```
void list_head_insert(Node*& head_ptr, const Node::Item& entry);
// Precondition: head_ptr is the head pointer of a linked list.
// Postcondition: A new node containing the given entry
// has been added at the head of the linked list; head_ptr now
// points to the head of the new, longer linked list.
```

The head_ptr is a reference parameter, since the function creates a new head node and makes the head pointer point to this new node. *A node pointer should be a reference parameter when the function needs access to the linked list and the function makes the pointer point to a new node.*

Const node pointers are misleading. Value and reference parameters are the only kinds of node pointer parameters that we will use. The type of the value parameter is written Node* , and the postcondition indicates whether the linked list is altered. The type of the reference parameter is written Node*& . We won't use *const* parameters, because there is no way to prevent a function from changing part of a linked list, even when we use a *const* parameter.

Parameters for Linked Lists

When a function needs access to a linked list, use a Node* parameter and follow these guidelines:

1. Use a value parameter, Node* , when the function needs access to the linked list and the function does not need to make the pointer point to a new node. Have the post-condition indicate whether or not the list is altered.
2. Use a reference parameter, Node*& , when the function needs access to the linked list and the function does make the pointer point to a new node.

Inserting a New Node at the Head of a Linked List

The next function in our toolkit is the list_head_insert function that we mentioned above, with a reference parameter that is a pointer. The function adds a new node at the head of a linked list. This is the easiest place to add a new node. The function prototype with complete documentation is given here:

list_head_insert

```
void list_head_insert(Node*& head_ptr, const Node::Item& entry);
// Precondition: head_ptr is the head pointer of a linked list.
// Postcondition: A new node containing the given entry
// has been added at the head of the linked list; head_ptr now
// points to the head of the new, longer linked list.
// NOTE: If there is insufficient dynamic memory for a new
// node, then new_handler is called before changing the list.
```

As we saw a moment ago, the head pointer is a reference parameter, since the function makes the head pointer point to a new node. Also, the documentation indicates what happens if there is insufficient dynamic memory for a new node.

In order to insert a new node at the head of the linked list, the function uses *new* to allocate a new node. The item is then copied into the new node, and the new node is inserted at the head of the list. Because we will need to refer to the new node before it is actually part of the list, we use a local pointer variable to point to this new node. The local pointer variable is called `insert_ptr`, since it points to the node that will be inserted into the list. The complete insertion process can be summarized with this pseudocode:

1. Allocate a new node pointed to by `insert_ptr`.
2. Place the new item in the `data` member of the new node.
3. Make the `link` member of the new node point to the head (first node) of the original list.
4. Make `head_ptr` point to the new node that we just created.

Let's step through an example insertion. Suppose that the linked list originally has three nodes containing the numbers 10, 20, and 30, and we will insert a new item number 5. After the first two steps, we have allocated a new node (pointed to by `insert_ptr`) and placed the new item 5 into the data member of the new node, as shown here:

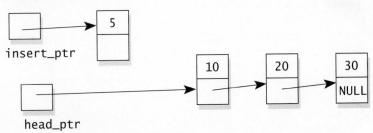

The C++ code for these two steps is shown here:

```
insert_ptr = new Node;
insert_ptr->data = entry;
```

In the call *new* `Node`, you must remember that we are allocating a `Node` *object*. Any time we allocate an object of a class (or a struct), the call to *new* first allocates memory for the new object, and then *calls the default constructor to initialize the object*. But we didn't define a default constructor for the node. That is okay. C++ automatically provides a default constructor, provided that you have not defined any constructors at all. The automatic default constructor doesn't do much work—it just calls the default constructor for any member variables of the object. In the case of the node, the action of the automatic default constructor depends on the type of the underlying `Item` type. If this underlying type is a class with a default constructor, then the node's automatic default constructor calls the default constructor for the member `Item data`. This is fortunate because the `Item` data type *might* be a complicated class that requires its default constructor to carry out some initialization.

In Step 3, we make the link member of the new node point to the current head of the list. In C++, this will be implemented as:

```
insert_ptr->link = head_ptr;
```

What does our example look like after Step 3? The link member of the new node (which is shaded in the diagram below) has now been set:

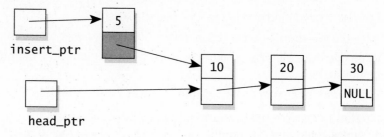

Finally, in Step 4, we change the head pointer to point to the newly allocated node. In C++, the change to the head pointer is an assignment statement:

```
head_ptr = insert_ptr;
```

You can read this statement to yourself as saying "make the head pointer point to the same thing that `insert_ptr` points to." After Step 4, our example is finished:

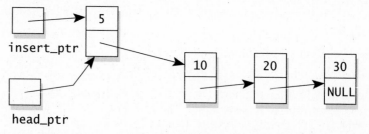

At this point, the function returns, and the local variable `insert_ptr` disappears. But the `head_ptr` remains, pointing to the longer linked list, with one extra node at the front, as shown here:

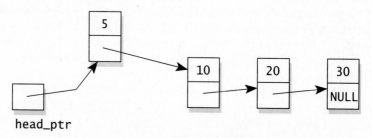

| **FIGURE 5.5** | A Function to Insert at the Head of a List |

A Function Implementation

pass by reference

```
void list_head_insert(Node*& head_ptr, const Node::Item& entry)
// Precondition: head_ptr is the head pointer of a linked list.
// Postcondition: A new node containing the given entry has been added at the head of the linked
// list; head_ptr now points to the head of the new, longer linked list. NOTE: If there is insufficient
// dynamic memory for a new node, then new_handler is called before changing the list.
{
    Node *insert_ptr;

    insert_ptr = new Node;            Allocate a new node.
    insert_ptr->data = entry;         Put the item in the new node.
    insert_ptr->link = head_ptr;      Connect the new node at
                                      the front of the list.
    head_ptr = insert_ptr;            Move the head pointer to
                                      point to the new node.
}
```

| link1.cxx | **FTP** |

The complete implementation of list_head_insert is shown in Figure 5.5.

Also, the four steps of list_head_insert work correctly even if we are adding the first node to a previously empty list. In this case, head_ptr starts out as NULL and ends up pointing to the one new node of the linked list.

Pitfall: Unintended Calls to *delete* and *new*

PITFALL

Both list_head_insert and list_length use local variables that are pointers. The local variable in list_head_insert is called insert_ptr. When the function finishes, insert_ptr is no longer needed, and it will go away, just like any other local variable. But watch out! A common error is to think "insert_ptr is no longer needed, so I should write the statement *delete* insert_ptr at the end of the list_head_insert function." *Don't!*

The effect of *delete* insert_ptr is to get rid of *the node* that insert_ptr points to. In other words, you will get rid of the node at the front of the list—the very node that you worked so hard to insert. The general rule is this: *Never call delete unless you are actually reducing the number of nodes.*

A similar error might occur with the local variable cursor in the list_length function. You might be tempted to write cursor = *new* Node to try to initialize this pointer variable. *Don't!*

The effect of cursor = *new* Node is to create a new node that was not previously part of the linked list. But cursor does not need to point to a new node; it merely steps through the existing nodes of the linked list. The general rule is this: *Never call new unless you are actually increasing the number of nodes.*

Inserting a New Node That Is Not at the Head

New nodes are not always inserted at the head of a linked list. They may be inserted in the middle or at the tail of a list. For example, suppose you want to insert the number 42 after the 20 in this list:

After the insertion, the new, longer list has these four nodes:

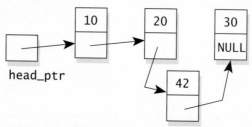

Whenever an insertion is not at the head, the insertion process requires a pointer to the node that is just *before* the intended location of the new node. In our example, we would require a pointer to the node that contains 20, since we want to insert the new node after this node. We use the name previous_ptr for the pointer to the node that is just before the location of the new node. So to insert an item after the 20, we would first have to set up previous_ptr as shown here:

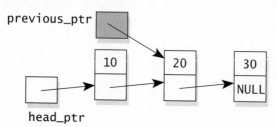

Once a program has calculated previous_ptr, the insertion can proceed. Our third toolkit function carries out the insertion, as indicated by this prototype:

list_insert

```
void list_insert(Node* previous_ptr, const Node::Item& entry);
// Precondition: previous_ptr points to a node in a linked list.
// Postcondition: A new node containing the given entry
// has been added after the node that previous_ptr points to.
// NOTE: If there is insufficient dynamic memory for a new
// node, then new_handler is called before changing the list.
```

The steps required by `list_insert` are similar to inserting at the head of a list. Here is the pseudocode:

1. Allocate a new node pointed to by `insert_ptr`.
2. Place the new item in the `data` member of the new node.
3. Make the `link` member of the new node point to the node after the new node's location (or NULL if there are no nodes after the new location).
4. Make `previous_ptr->link` point to the new node that we just created.

Let's follow the four steps for the example of inserting 42 after the second node of a small list. After the first two steps, the new node has been created, containing the number 42, as shown here:

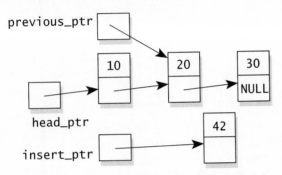

We have drawn the head pointer in this picture, though the function does not actually use the head pointer. Steps 3 and 4 make use of only `previous_ptr`. For example, Step 3 sets the `link` member of the new node to point to the node that's after the new node's location. What is the node after the new location? It is not `previous_ptr`, since `previous_ptr` points to the node *before* the new location. But the pointer named `previous_ptr->link` does point to the node that's after the location of the new node. The pointer `previous_ptr->link` is shaded in this picture, to show you that it points to the spot that's after the new node's location:

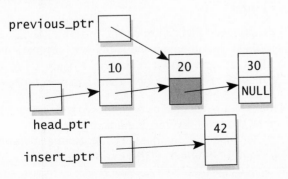

An assignment statement, `insert_ptr->link = previous_ptr->link`, now carries out Step 3. After the assignment, we have this situation:

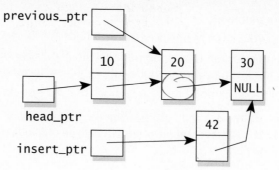

Another assignment statement, `previous_ptr->link = insert_ptr`, completes Step 4, as shown here:

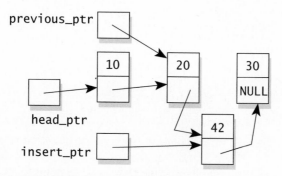

After inserting the new node containing 42, you can step through the complete linked list, starting at the head node 10, then 20, then 42, and finally 30. The `list_insert` function implementation is shown as the first of three functions in Figure 5.6. Notice that `previous_ptr` is not a reference parameter, since we are not making `previous_ptr` point to a new node.

Searching for an Item in a Linked List

In C++, functions may return pointers. Hence, when the job of a subtask is to find a single node, it makes sense to implement the subtask as a function that returns a pointer to that node. Our next toolkit operation is such a function, returning a pointer to a node that contains a specified item. The prototype is:

```
Node* list_search(Node* head_ptr, const Node::Item& target);
// Precondition: head_ptr is the head pointer of a linked list.
// Postcondition: The return value is a pointer to the first node containing
//   the specified target in its data member. If there is no such node,
//   the null pointer is returned. The list itself is unaltered.
```

(text continues on page 222)

Three Function Implementations

```
void list_insert(Node* previous_ptr, const Node::Item& entry)
// Precondition: previous_ptr points to a node in a linked list.
// Postcondition: A new node containing the given entry has been added after the node that
// previous_ptr points to. NOTE: If there is insufficient dynamic memory for a new
// node, then new_handler is called before changing the list.
{
    Node *insert_ptr;

    insert_ptr = new Node;
    insert_ptr->data = entry;
    insert_ptr->link = previous_ptr->link;
    previous_ptr->link = insert_ptr;
}
```

(handwritten annotations: A, B, C circled; "current →next = last →next;")

```
Node* list_search(Node* head_ptr, const Node::Item& target)
// Precondition: head_ptr is the head pointer of a linked list.
// Postcondition: The return value is a pointer to the first node containing the specified target in its
// data member. If there is no such node, the null pointer is returned. The list itself is unaltered.
// Library facilities used: stdlib.h
{
    Node *cursor;

    for (cursor = head_ptr; cursor != NULL; cursor = cursor->link)
        if (target == cursor->data)
            return cursor;
    return NULL;
}
```

```
Node* list_locate(Node* head_ptr, size_t position)
// Precondition: head_ptr is the head pointer of a linked list, and position > 0.
// Postcondition: The pointer returned points to the node at the specified position in the list.
// (The head node is position 1, the next node is position 2, and so on.) If there is no such
// position then the null pointer is returned. The list itself is unaltered.
// Library facilities used: assert.h, stdlib.h
{
    Node *cursor;
    size_t i;

    assert(0 < position);
    cursor = head_ptr;
    for (i = 1; (i < position) && (cursor != NULL); i++)
        cursor = cursor->link;
    return cursor;
}
```

link1.cxx | FTP

As indicated by the return type of Node*, the function returns a pointer to a node in a linked list. The node is specified by a parameter named target, which is the item that appears in the sought-after node. For example, with the linked list from Figure 5.7, the function list_search(head_ptr, -4.8) will return a pointer to the shaded node.

Sometimes, the specified target might not appear in the list. In this case, the function returns the null pointer.

The implementation of list_search is shown in the middle of Figure 5.6 on page 221. Most of the work is carried out with the usual traversal pattern, using a local pointer variable called cursor to step through the nodes one at a time:

```
for (cursor = head_ptr; cursor != NULL; cursor = cursor->link)
{
    if (target == the data in the node that cursor points to)
        return cursor;
}
```

As the loop executes, cursor points to the nodes of the list, one after another. The test inside the loop determines whether we have found the sought-after node, and if so, then a pointer to the node is immediately returned with the return statement *return cursor*. When a return statement occurs like this, inside a loop, the function returns without ado—the loop is not run to completion.

On the other hand, should the loop actually complete by eventually setting cursor to NULL, then the sought-after node is not on the list. According to the function's postcondition, the function returns NULL when the node is not on the list. This is accomplished with one more return statement—*return NULL*—at the end of the function's implementation.

Finding a Node by Its Position in a Linked List

Our toolkit has a second function that returns a pointer to a node in a linked list. Here is the prototype:

```
Node* list_locate(Node* head_ptr, size_t position);
// Precondition: head_ptr is the head pointer of a linked list, and position > 0.
// Postcondition: The pointer returned points to the node at the specified
// position in the list. (The head node is position 1, the next node is position
// 2, and so on.) If there is no such position, then the null pointer is
// returned. The list itself is unaltered.
```

FIGURE 5.7
Example for
list_search
and
list_locate

In this function, a node is specified by giving its position in the list, with the head node at position 1, the next node at position 2, and so on. For example, with the linked list from Figure 5.7, the function list_locate(head_ptr, 3) will return a pointer to the shaded node. Notice that the first node is number 1, not number 0 as in an array. The specified position might also be larger than the length of the list. In this case, the function returns the null pointer.

The implementation of `list_locate` is shown at the bottom of Figure 5.6 on page 221. It uses a variation of the list traversal technique that we have already seen. The variation is useful when we want to move to a particular node in a linked list and we know the ordinal position of the node (such as position number 1, position number 2, and so on). We start by pointing a pointer variable, `cursor`, to the head node of the list. A loop then moves the `cursor` forward the correct number of spots, as shown here:

```
cursor = head_ptr;
for (i = 1; (i < position) && (cursor != NULL); i++)
    cursor = cursor->link;
```

moving to a specified position in a linked list

Each iteration of the loop executes `cursor = cursor->link` to move the `cursor` forward one node. Normally, the loop stops when i reaches `position`, and `cursor` points at the correct node. The loop can also stop if `cursor` becomes `NULL`, indicating that `position` was larger than the number of nodes on the list.

Copying a Linked List

Our next linked list function makes a copy of a linked list, providing both head and tail pointers for the newly created copy. Here is the prototype:

```
void list_copy(Node* source_ptr, Node*& head_ptr, Node*& tail_ptr);
// Precondition: source_ptr is the head pointer of a linked list.
// Postcondition: head_ptr and tail_ptr are the head and tail pointers for
// a new list that contains the same items as the list pointed to by
// source_ptr. The original list is unaltered. NOTE: If there is insufficient
// dynamic memory to create the new list, then new_handler is called.
```

list_copy

For example, suppose that `source_ptr` points to the following list:

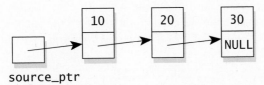

source_ptr

The `list_copy` function creates a completely separate copy of the three-node list. The copy of the list has its own three nodes, which also contain the numbers 10, 20, and 30. Through the parameter list, the `list_copy` function returns pointers to the head and tail of the newly created list. The original list remains intact.

The pseudocode begins by setting the new head and tail pointers to `NULL`, then handling one special case—the case where the original list is the empty list (so that `source_ptr` is the null pointer). In this case the function simply returns (since the head and tail pointers have already been set to `NULL`). The complete pseudocode appears at the top of the next page.

1. Set head_ptr and tail_ptr to NULL.
2. *if* (source_ptr == NULL), then return with no further work.
3. Allocate a new node for the head node of the new list that we are creating. Make both head_ptr and tail_ptr point to this new node, and copy data from the head node of the original list to our new node.
4. Make source_ptr point to the second node of the original list, then the third node, then the fourth node, and so on until we have traversed all of the original list. At each node that source_ptr points to, add one new node to the tail of the new list, and move the tail pointer forward to the newly added node, as follows:
   4.1 list_insert(tail_ptr, source_ptr->data);
   4.2 tail_ptr = tail_ptr->link;

The fourth step of the pseudocode is implemented by this loop:

```
for (source_ptr = source_ptr->link; source_ptr != NULL; source_ptr = source_ptr->link)
{
    list_insert(tail_ptr, source_ptr->data);
    tail_ptr = tail_ptr->link;
}
```

The for-loop starts by setting source_ptr to the second node of the original list with the assignment statement source_ptr = source_ptr->link. If there is no second node of the original list, then this assignment will set source_ptr to the null pointer, which is fine since we require the test source_ptr != NULL in order for the loop to continue. Each time through the loop, we move source_ptr to the next node in the original list with the assignment statement source_ptr = source_ptr->link.

The two statements in the body of the for-loop are Steps 4.1 and 4.2 in our pseudocode. Step 4.1 inserts a new node at the tail end of the newly created list. Step 4.2 moves the tail pointer of the new list forward, to the new end of the list.

As an example, consider again the three-node list with data 10, 20, and 30. The first two steps of the pseudocode are carried out and then the for-loop is initialized with the statement source_ptr = source_ptr->link. At this point, the function's pointers look like this:

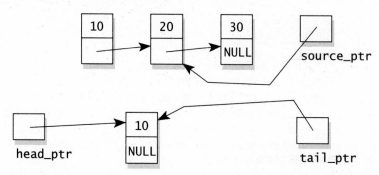

Notice that we have already copied the first node of the linked list. During the first iteration of the for-loop, we will copy the second node of the linked list—the node that is pointed to by `source_ptr`. The first part of copying the node is a call to one of our other tools, `list_insert`, as shown here:

```
list_insert(tail_ptr, source_ptr->data);
```

This function call adds a new node to the end of the list that we are creating (i.e., *after* the node pointed to by `tail_ptr`), and the data in the new node is the number 20 (i.e., the data from `source_ptr->data`). Immediately after the insertion, the function's pointers look like this:

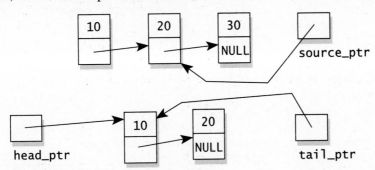

The second statement in the for-loop body moves `tail_ptr` forward to the new tail of the new list, as shown here:

```
tail_ptr = tail_ptr->link;
```

This is the usual way that we make a pointer "move to the next node," as we have seen in other functions such as `list_search`. After moving the tail pointer, the function's pointers look like this:

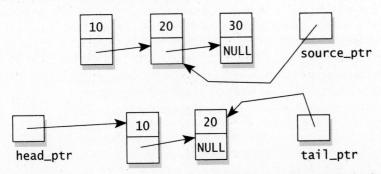

In this example, `source_ptr` will move to the third node, and the body of the for-loop will execute one more time to copy the third node to the new list. Then the loop will end.

The complete implementation of `list_copy` is shown in Figure 5.8.

FIGURE 5.8	Functions for Copying a List and Copying Part of a List

Two of the Toolkit's Functions

```
void list_copy(Node* source_ptr, Node*& head_ptr, Node*& tail_ptr)
// Precondition: source_ptr is the head pointer of a linked list.
// Postcondition: head_ptr and tail_ptr are the head and tail pointers for
// a new list that contains the same items as the list pointed to by
// source_ptr. The original list is unaltered. NOTE: If there is insufficient
// dynamic memory to create the new list, then new_handler is called.
// Library facilities used: stdlib.h
{
    head_ptr = NULL;
    tail_ptr = NULL;

    // Handle the case of the empty list.
    if (source_ptr == NULL)
        return;

    // Make the head node for the newly created list, and put data in it.
    list_head_insert(head_ptr, source_ptr->data);
    tail_ptr = head_ptr;

    // Copy the rest of the nodes one at a time, adding at the tail of new list.
    for (source_ptr = source_ptr->link; source_ptr != NULL; source_ptr = source_ptr->link)
    {
        list_insert(tail_ptr, source_ptr->data);        Loop for Step 4
        tail_ptr = tail_ptr->link;
    }
}
```

Prototype and precondition/postcondition contract for list_piece.
See Self-Test Exercise 15 on page 231 for the implementation.

```
void list_piece(Node* start_ptr, Node* end_ptr, Node*& head_ptr, Node*& tail_ptr);
// Precondition: start_ptr and end_ptr are pointers to nodes on the same
// linked list, with the start_ptr node at or before the end_ptr node.
// Postcondition: head_ptr and tail_ptr are the head and tail pointers for a
// new list that contains the items from start_ptr to end_ptr. The original
// list is unaltered. NOTE: If there is insufficient dynamic memory to
// create the new list, then new_handler is called.

}
```

link1.cxx	**FTP**

Copying Part of a Linked List

Sometimes a program needs to copy only part of a linked list rather than the entire list. Our toolkit provides a function, `list_piece`, which copies part of a list, from a given start node to another given ending node. The prototype and precondition/postcondition contract for `list_piece` are given at the bottom of Figure 5.8 on page 226, leaving the implementation for Self-Test Exercise 15.

Removing a Node at the Head of a Linked List

Our toolkit has three more functions, all of which remove nodes from a linked list. The first removal function removes the head node, as specified here:

```
void list_head_remove(Node*& head_ptr);
// Precondition: head_ptr is the head pointer of a linked list,
// with at least one node.
// Postcondition: The head node has been removed and returned to the
// heap; head_ptr is now the head pointer of the new, shorter linked list.
```
list_head_remove

As with `list_head_insert`, the head pointer is a reference parameter, since the function makes the head pointer point to a different node.

At first glance, it seems that the head node can be removed with just two steps: (1) Move the head pointer to the next node of the list; and (2) Return the original head node to the heap. There is a small flaw with these steps: After we move the head pointer in Step 1, we no longer have any contact with the original head node. So, our complete pseudocode requires three steps:

1. Set a pointer named `remove_ptr` to point to the head node. (This is how we maintain contact with the original head node.)
2. Move the head pointer so that it points to the second node (or it becomes NULL if there is no second node).
3. *delete* `remove_ptr`. (This returns the original head node to the heap.)

These three steps are implemented in the top of Figure 5.9 on page 230.

Removing a Node That Is Not at the Head

Our second removal procedure removes a node that is not at the head of a linked list. The approach is similar to inserting a node in the middle of a linked list. In order to remove a midlist node, we must set up a pointer to the node that is just *before* the node that we are removing. For example, in order to remove the 42 from the following list, we would need to set up `previous_ptr` as shown at the top of the next page.

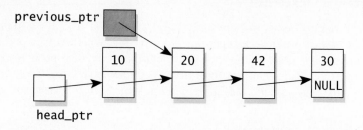

As you can see, `previous_ptr` does not actually point to the node that we are deleting (the 42); instead it points to the node that is before the condemned node. This is because the link field of the *previous* node must be reassigned, hence we need a pointer to this previous node. The removal function's prototype, using `previous_ptr`, is shown here:

list_remove

```
void list_remove(Node* previous_ptr);
// Precondition: previous_ptr points to a node in a linked list,
// and this is not the tail node of the list.
// Postcondition: The node after previous_ptr has been removed
// from the linked list.
```

The steps required by `list_remove` are similar to removing at the head of a list. Here is the pseudocode:

1. Set a pointer named `remove_ptr` to point to the condemned node. (This is the node after the one pointed to by `previous_ptr`.)

2. Move the `previous_ptr->link` so that it points to the node after the condemned node (or `NULL` if the condemned node is the tail node).

3. *delete* `remove_ptr`. (This returns the condemned node to the heap.)

As an example, let's remove the node 42 from the list that is drawn above. The `previous_ptr` is set to point to the previous node, and then Step 1 of the removal pseudocode is executed. After Step 1, the pointers look like this:

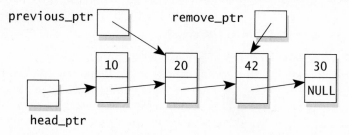

Step 2 of the pseudocode needs to make `previous_ptr->link` point to the node that's after the node we are removing. This is carried out with an assignment statement `previous_ptr->link = remove_ptr->link`. The assignment changes the shaded pointer in the drawing at the top of the next page.

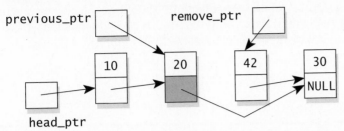

At this point, the node containing 42 is no longer part of the linked list. The list's first node contains 10, the next node has 20, and following the pointers we arrive at the third and last node containing 30. All that remains is Step 3, `delete remove_ptr`, which returns the deleted node to the heap.

The complete implementation is shown in the middle part of Figure 5.9 on page 230. You should check that the function works properly, even if the removed node is the last node of the list. In this case, the link member, `previous_ptr->link`, should be set to NULL, which occurs without any need for special code.

Clearing a Linked List

Our final linked list function removes all the nodes from a linked list, returning them to the heap, and setting the head pointer to NULL. Here is the prototype:

```
void list_clear(Node*& head_ptr);
// Precondition: head_ptr is the head pointer of a linked list.
// Postcondition: All nodes of the list have been returned to
// the heap, and the head_ptr is now NULL.
```

list_clear

The simplest implementation is a loop that repeatedly calls `list_head_remove` until all the nodes are gone. This implementation is shown in the bottom of Figure 5.9 on page 230. Notice that when `list_head_remove` removes the final node of the list, the head pointer will be the null pointer, and this stops the loop in `list_clear`. Also, the head pointer is a reference parameter, so that when the function returns, the actual head pointer in the calling program will be NULL.

Linked List Toolkit—Putting the Pieces Together

The ten functions of the toolkit are complete. A header file should be provided for the toolkit. Figure 5.10 on page 232 shows our header file, called `link1.h`. In addition to the documentation, the header file provides the type definitions for the Node, plus prototypes for the ten functions. In our header, we have defined the type of an Item to be a *double*, but as the documentation indicates, Item may be changed to another data type.

The implementations of the ten functions should be placed in a separate implementation file called link1.cxx. We do not provide a listing of this file, but you can build it with the implementations from Figures 5.4 through 5.9.

Go over in class temorrow

| FIGURE 5.9 | Functions for Removing Nodes from a Linked List |

Three Function Implementations

```
void list_head_remove(Node*& head_ptr)
// Precondition: head_ptr is the head pointer of a linked list, with at least one node.
// Postcondition: The head node has been removed and returned to the heap;
// head_ptr is now the head pointer of the new, shorter linked list.
{
    Node *remove_ptr;                        This statement
                                             causes head_ptr
    remove_ptr = head_ptr;                   to point to the
    head_ptr = head_ptr->link; <------       second node (or it
    delete remove_ptr;                       becomes NULL if there
}                                            is no second node).
```

```
void list_remove(Node* previous_ptr)
// Precondition: previous_ptr points to a node in a linked list, and this is not the tail node of the list.
// Postcondition: The node after previous_ptr has been removed from the linked list.
{
    Node *remove_ptr;              ⌐ assert(previous_ptr -> link != NULL);

    remove_ptr = previous_ptr->link; Ⓐ
    previous_ptr->link = remove_ptr->link; Ⓑ
    delete remove_ptr; Ⓒ
}
```

```
void list_clear(Node*& head_ptr)
// Precondition: head_ptr is the head pointer of a linked list.
// Postcondition: All nodes of the list have been returned to the heap, and head_ptr is now
// NULL.
// Library facilities used: stdlib.h
{
    while (head_ptr != NULL)
        list_head_remove(head_ptr);

}
```

| link1.cxx | **FTP** |

Using the Linked List Toolkit

Any program can use our toolkit. The programmer defines the Item type according to his or her need and places the include directive

```
#include "link1.h"
```

in the program. The program can then use the ten functions to build and manipulate linked lists.

However, the programmer must have an understanding of linked lists and our specific nodes. From the standpoint of information hiding, it would be better if we use the toolkit ourselves to build various abstract versions of lists. The different list ADTs that we build can be used by any programmer with no knowledge of our underlying implementation. This is what we will do in the rest of the chapter, providing two ADTs that use the linked list toolkit.

Self-Test Exercises

8. Suppose you want to use a linked list where the items are strings from our String class in Chapter 4. How would the toolkit's header file need to be changed?

9. Suppose that locate_ptr is a pointer to a node in a linked list (and it is not the null pointer). Write an assignment statement that will make locate_ptr move to the next node in the list. What does your assignment statement do if locate_ptr was already pointing to the last node in the list?

10. Why don't we use const node pointers as parameters?

11. Suppose that head_ptr is a head pointer for a linked list of numbers. Write a few lines of code that will insert the number 42 as the second item of the list. (If the list was originally empty, then 42 should be added as the first node instead of the second.)

12. Which of the ten functions use *new* to allocate a new node? Which use *delete* to return a node to the heap?

13. Suppose that head_ptr is a head pointer for a linked list of numbers. Write a few lines of code that will remove the second item of the list. (If the list originally had only one item, then remove that item instead; if it had no items, then leave the list empty.)

14. Suppose that head_ptr is a head pointer for a linked list with just one node. What will head_ptr be after list_head_remove(head_ptr)?

15. Implement list_piece from the bottom of Figure 5.8 on page 226.

| FIGURE 5.10 | Header File for the Linked List Toolkit |

A Header File

```
// FILE: link1.h
// PROVIDES: A toolkit of ten functions for manipulating linked lists. Each node of the list
// contains a piece of data and a pointer to the next node. The type of the data is defined as
// Node::Item in a typedef statement. The complete type definitions used by the toolkit are:
//
//    struct Node
//    {
//        typedef _____ Item;
//        Item data;
//        Node *link;
//    };
//
```

Item may be any of the C++ built-in types (int, char, etc.), or a class with a default constructor, an assignment operator, and a test for equality (x == y).

```
// FUNCTIONS in the linked list toolkit:
//    size_t list_length(Node* head_ptr)
//        Precondition: head_ptr is the head pointer of a linked list.
//        Postcondition: The value returned is the number of nodes in the linked list. The list
//        itself is unaltered.
//
//    void list_head_insert(Node*& head_ptr, const Node::Item& entry)
//        Precondition: head_ptr is the head pointer of a linked list.
//        Postcondition: A new node containing the given entry has been added at the head of
//        the linked list; head_ptr now points to the head of the new, longer linked list.
//
//    void list_insert(Node* previous_ptr, const Node::Item& entry)
//        Precondition: previous_ptr points to a node in a linked list.
//        Postcondition: A new node containing the given entry has been added after the node
//        that previous_ptr points to.
//
//    Node* list_search(Node* head_ptr, const Node::Item& target)
//        Precondition: head_ptr is the head pointer of a linked list.
//        Postcondition: The pointer returned points to the first node containing the specified
//        target in its data member. If there is no such node, the null pointer is returned. The list
//        itself is unaltered.
//
//    Node* list_locate(Node* head_ptr, size_t position)
//        Precondition: head_ptr is the head pointer of a linked list, and position > 0.
//        Postcondition: The pointer returned points to the node at the specified position in the
//        list. (The head node is position 1, the next node is position 2, and so on.) If there is no
//        such position, then the null pointer is returned. The list itself is unaltered.
//
```

(continued)

(FIGURE 5.10 continued)

```
//    void list_head_remove(Node*& head_ptr)
//        Precondition: head_ptr is the head pointer of a linked list, with at least one node.
//        Postcondition: The head node has been removed and returned to the heap;
//        head_ptr is now the head pointer of the new, shorter linked list.
//
//    void list_remove(Node* previous_ptr)
//        Precondition: previous_ptr points to a node in a linked list, and this is not the tail node of
//        the list.
//        Postcondition: The node after previous_ptr has been removed from the linked list.
//
//    void list_clear(Node*& head_ptr)
//        Precondition: head_ptr is the head pointer of a linked list.
//        Postcondition: All nodes of the list have been returned to the heap, and the head_ptr is
//        now NULL.
//
//    void list_copy(Node* source_ptr, Node*& head_ptr, Node*& tail_ptr)
//        Precondition: source_ptr is the head pointer of a linked list.
//        Postcondition: head_ptr and tail_ptr are the head and tail pointers for a new list that
//        contains the same items as the list pointed to by source_ptr. The original list is
//        unaltered.
//
//    void list_piece
//        (Node* start_ptr, Node* end_ptr, Node*& head_ptr, Node*& tail_ptr)
//        Precondition: start_ptr and end_ptr are pointers to nodes on the same
//        linked list, with the start_ptr node at or before the end_ptr node.
//        Postcondition: head_ptr and tail_ptr are the head and tail pointers for a new linked list
//        that contains the items from start_ptr to end_ptr. The original list is unaltered.
//
// DYNAMIC MEMORY usage by the toolkit:
//    If there is insufficient dynamic memory, then the following functions call new_handler
//    before any changes are made to the list that head_ptr points to : list_head_insert,
//    list_insert, list_copy, list_piece.

#ifndef LINK1_H
#define LINK1_H
#include <stdlib.h> // Provides size_t

    struct Node
    {
        typedef double Item;
        Item data;
        Node *link;
    };
```

(continued)

(FIGURE 5.10 continued)

```
// FUNCTIONS for the linked list toolkit
size_t list_length(Node* head_ptr);
void list_head_insert(Node*& head_ptr, const Node::Item& entry);
void list_insert(Node* previous_ptr, const Node::Item& entry);
Node* list_search(Node* head_ptr, const Node::Item& target);
Node* list_locate(Node* head_ptr, size_t position);
void list_head_remove(Node*& head_ptr);
void list_remove(Node* previous_ptr);
void list_clear(Node*& head_ptr);
void list_copy(Node* source_ptr, Node*& head_ptr, Node*& tail_ptr);
void list_piece(Node* start_ptr, Node* end_ptr, Node*& head_ptr, Node*& tail_ptr);

#endif
```

link1.h   **FTP**

5.3   THE BAG ADT WITH A LINKED LIST

We're ready to write an ADT that is implemented with a linked list. We'll start with the familiar bag ADT, which we have previously implemented with an array (Section 3.1) and a dynamic array (Section 4.3). So this is our third bag implementation. At the end of this chapter we'll compare the advantages and disadvantages of these different implementations. But first, let's see how a linked list is used in our third bag implementation.

Our Third Bag—Specification

The advantage of using a familiar ADT is that you already know the specification. The documentation for the header file is nearly identical to our previous bag. The major difference is that our new bag has no worries about capacity: There is no default capacity and no need for a "resize" function that increases capacity. This is because our planned implementation—storing the bag's items on a linked list—can easily grow and shrink by adding and removing nodes from the linked list. Of course, the programmer who uses the new bag ADT does not need to know about linked lists, and the documentation of our new header file will make no mention of linked lists.

The new bag will also have one other minor change. Just for fun, we'll add a new member function called grab, which returns a randomly selected item from a bag. In Programming Project 1 on page 258 we'll use the grab function in a program that generates some silly sentences.

Our Third Bag—Class Definition

Our plan has been laid. We will implement the new bag by storing the items on a linked list. The class will have two private member variables: (1) a head pointer that points to the head of a linked list that contains the items of the bag; and (2) a size_t variable that keeps track of the length of the list. The second member variable isn't really needed since we could call list_length to determine the length of the list. But perhaps you remember the string ADT from Chapter 4, where we also kept the length of the string in a separate member variable that wasn't really needed. Our motivation is the same in both cases: When we keep the length in a member variable, then the length can be quickly determined by examining the variable (a constant time operation). This is in contrast to actually counting the length by traversing the string or list (a linear time operation). In any case, the private members of our class are shown here:

```
class Bag
{
public:
    | Prototypes of public member functions go here.
private:
    Node *head_ptr;        // Head pointer for the list of items
    size_t many_nodes;     // Number of nodes on the list
};
```

Keep in mind that our design is not the only way to implement a bag. In fact, we have already seen two other implementations. To avoid confusion over how we are using our linked list, we now make an explicit statement of the invariant for our third design of the bag ADT:

Invariant for the Third Bag ADT

1. The items in the bag are stored on a linked list.

2. The head pointer of the list is stored in the member variable head_ptr.

3. The total number of items in the list is stored in the member variable many_nodes.

Having decided on our class definition, we can write the header file for the third bag. (See Figure 5.11 on page 236.) In this header file, we use the Node data type from the linked list toolkit. Therefore, before the bag's class definition we need the include directive #include "link1.h". This allows us to use the Node type within our bag class definition.

| **FIGURE 5.11** | Header File for Our Third Bag Class |

A Header File

```
// FILE: bag3.h
// CLASS PROVIDED: Bag (a container class for a collection of items)
//
// TYPEDEF for the Bag class:
//    typedef _____ Item
//       Bag::Item is the data type of the items in the Bag. It may be any of the C++ built-in
//       types (int, char, etc.), or a class with a default constructor, a copy constructor, an
//       assignment operator, and a test for equality (x == y).
//
// CONSTRUCTOR for the Bag class:
//    Bag( )
//       Postcondition: The Bag is empty.
//
// MODIFICATION MEMBER FUNCTIONS for the Bag class:
//    void insert(const Item& entry)
//       Postcondition: A new copy of entry has been inserted into the Bag.
//
//    void remove(const Item& target)
//       Postcondition: If target was in the Bag, then one copy of target has been removed from
//       the Bag; otherwise the Bag is unchanged.
//
//    void operator +=(const Bag& addend)
//       Postcondition: Each item in addend has been added to this Bag.
//
// CONSTANT MEMBER FUNCTIONS for the Bag class:
//    size_t size( ) const
//       Postcondition: Return value is the total number of items in the Bag.
//
//    size_t occurrences(const Item& target) const
//       Postcondition: Return value is number of times target is in the Bag.
//
//    Item grab( ) const
//       Precondition: size( ) > 0.
//       Postcondition: The return value is a randomly selected item from the Bag.
//
// NONMEMBER FUNCTIONS for the Bag class:
//    Bag operator +(const Bag& b1, const Bag& b2)
//       Postcondition: The Bag returned is the union of b1 and b2.
//
// VALUE SEMANTICS for the Bag class:
//    Assignments and the copy constructor may be used with Bag objects.
//
```

(FIGURE 5.11 continued)

```
// DYNAMIC MEMORY USAGE by the Bag:
//    If there is insufficient dynamic memory, then the following functions call new_handler:
//    The constructors, insert, operator +=, operator +, and the assignment operator.

#ifndef BAG3_H
#define BAG3_H
#include <stdlib.h>      // Provides size_t and NULL
#include "link1.h"       // Provides Node struct

    class Bag
    {
    public:
        // TYPEDEF
        typedef Node::Item Item;
        // CONSTRUCTORS and DESTRUCTOR
        Bag( );
        Bag(const Bag& source);
        ~Bag( );
        // MODIFICATION MEMBER FUNCTIONS
        void insert(const Item& entry);
        void remove(const Item& target);
        void operator +=(const Bag& addend);
        void operator =(const Bag& source);
        // CONSTANT MEMBER FUNCTIONS
        size_t size( ) const { return many_nodes; }
        size_t occurrences(const Item& target) const;
        Item grab( ) const;
    private:
        Node *head_ptr;      // Head pointer for the list of items
        size_t many_nodes;   // Number of nodes on the list
    };

    // NONMEMBER FUNCTIONS for the Bag class:
    Bag operator +(const Bag& b1, const Bag& b2);

#endif
```

Prototype for the copy constructor

Prototype for the destructor

Prototype for the overloaded operator =

bag3.h **FTP**

How to Make the Bag Item Match the Node Item

The bag's class definition also depends on the data type of the items in the bag. This data type, called Node::Item, is already defined in link1.h, so there is no absolute need for a second definition of Item in the bag's class definition. However, the programmers who use our bag don't know about the linked list toolkit, so for their benefit it's reasonable to go ahead and define Item as part of the Bag, too. So, the beginning of the Bag's definition looks this way:

```
#include "link1.h" // Provides Node struct
class Bag
{
public:
    typedef Node::Item Item;
    . . .
```

The highlighted definition makes Bag::Item the same as Node::Item, so that a programmer who uses the bag can write Bag::Item without having to know about the implementation details of nodes and linked lists.

If we need a different type of item, we can change Node::Item to the required new type and recompile. The Bag::Item will then match the new Node::Item. For example, suppose we want a bag of strings using our own string ADT (from Section 4.5). In order to obtain the bag of strings, the start of our node definition will be:

```
#include "mystring.h" // Provides String class, from Section 4.5
class Node
{
public:
    typedef String Item;
    . . .
```

In this case, the Node::Item is defined as the String class, so that Bag::Item will also be a string. By the way, when we get to the implementation details, we will use examples where the items are strings, but keep in mind that the underlying item type could be easily changed.

Following the Rules for Dynamic Memory Usage in a Class

Our new bag is a class that uses dynamic memory, therefore it must follow the four rules that we outlined in "Prescription for a Dynamic Class" on page 177. Let's review these rules:

1. Some of the member variables of the class are pointers. In particular, our new bag has a member variable, head_ptr, which is a pointer to the first node of a linked list.

2. Member functions allocate and release dynamic memory as needed. We will see this when the bag's member functions are implemented. For example, the bag's `insert` function will allocate a new node.

3. The automatic value semantics of the class is overriden. In other words, the class must implement a copy constructor and an assignment operator that correctly copy one bag to another. You can see that the bag's class definition in Figure 5.11 on page 237 accounts for this by including the prototypes for the copy constructor and the assignment operator

4. The class has a destructor. Again, the bag's class definition in Figure 5.11 provides for this with the destructor's prototype.

Also notice that the bag's documentation does not list a destructor, since the programmer who uses the ADT does not normally make explicit calls to the destructor. But our planned implementation uses dynamic memory, so a destructor will be part of the class.

The Third Bag Class—Implementation

With our invariant in mind, we can implement each of the member functions, starting with the constructors. The key to simple implementations is to use the linked list toolkit whenever possible.

Constructors. The default constructor sets `head_ptr` to be the null pointer (indicating the empty list) and sets `many_nodes` to zero. The copy constructor uses `list_copy` to make a separate copy of the source list, and `many_nodes` is then copied from the source to the newly constructed bag. Only a few statements are needed for the copy constructor, as shown here:

```
Bag::Bag(const Bag& source)
// Library facilities used: link1.h
{
    Node *tail_ptr; // Needed for argument to list_copy

    list_copy(source.head_ptr, head_ptr, tail_ptr);
    many_nodes = source.many_nodes;
}
```

constructors

Overloading the Assignment Operator. The overloaded assignment operator needs to change an existing bag so that it is the same as some other bag. The only difference between this and the copy constructor is that we must remember that when the assignment operator begins, the bag already has a linked list, and *this linked list must be returned to the heap*. With this in mind, you might write the implementation on the top of the next page, with the highlighted statement returning the existing linked list to the heap.

```
void Bag::operator =(const Bag& source)
// Library facilities used: link1.h
{
    Node *tail_ptr; // Needed for argument to list_copy

    list_clear(head_ptr);
    many_nodes = 0;
    list_copy(source.head_ptr, head_ptr, tail_ptr);
    many_nodes = source.many_nodes;
}
```

WARNING!
Can you find
the bug?

In fact, we actually did write this implementation for our first attempt on the assignment operator. Then we remembered the pitfall from Chapter 3: "An Object Can Be an Argument to Its Own Member Function" on page 112. For a bag b, it is possible for a programmer to write b = b. Perhaps you think this is a pointless assignment statement, but nevertheless the operator should work correctly, assigning b to be equal to its current value—that is, leave the bag unchanged. But instead, when the buggy assignment operator is activated with b = b, the first thing that happens is that the bag b (which activated the operator) is cleared. Once that list is cleared, there is no hope of leaving the bag unchanged.

The solution is to check for this special "self-assignment" at the start of the operator. If we find that an assignment such as b = b is occurring, then we will return immediately. We can check for this condition by determining whether source.head_ptr is pointing to the same node as the head pointer of the bag that activated the operator, as shown in the highlighted statement in this correct implementation:

the correct
assignment
operator

```
void Bag::operator =(const Bag& source)
// Library facilities used: link1.h
{
    Node *tail_ptr; // Needed for argument to list_copy

    if (source.head_ptr == head_ptr)
        return;

    list_clear(head_ptr);
    many_nodes = 0;

    list_copy(source.head_ptr, head_ptr, tail_ptr);
    many_nodes = source.many_nodes;
}
```

Notice that the test (source.head_ptr == head_ptr) checks whether the two pointers point to exactly the same node. This would indicate that the two lists have the same head node, and hence they are the same list.

One other point about the implementation: After we clear the linked list, we also set `many_nodes` to zero. The reason for this is that we want the bag to be valid before calling `list_copy`. In general, we will ensure that the bag is valid before calling any function that allocates dynamic memory; otherwise debugging is difficult (see "How to Allocate Memory in a Member Function" on page 173).

Pitfall: The Assignment Operator Causes Trouble with Linked Lists

PITFALL

When an ADT uses a linked list, you must take care with the assignment operator. Part of the care is checking for the special situation of "self-assignment" such as `b = b`. The easiest way to handle self-assignment is to check for it at the start of the assignment operator and simply return with no work if self-assignment is discovered.

Care is also needed before allocating dynamic memory. Before calling a function that allocates dynamic memory, make sure that the invariant of your ADT is valid.

The Destructor. Our documentation, which is meant for other programmers, never mentioned a destructor, but a destructor is needed because our particular implementation uses dynamic memory. The destructor is responsible for returning all dynamic memory to the heap. The job is accomplished by `list_clear`, as shown here:

```
Bag::~Bag( )
// Library facilities used: link1.h
{
    list_clear(head_ptr);
    many_nodes = 0;
}
```

This returns all nodes to the heap and sets head_ptr to NULL.

destructor

There is no absolute need for the second statement, `many_nodes = 0`, since the bag is not supposed to be used after the destructor has been called. But setting `many_nodes` to zero does no harm and in some ways makes it clear that we are "zeroing out the list."

The remove member function. There are two approaches to implementing the `remove` function. The first approach uses the toolkit's removal functions—using `list_head_remove` if the removed item is at the head of the list, and using the ordinary `list_remove` to remove an item that is farther down the line. This first approach is fine, although it does require a bit of thought because `list_remove` requires a pointer to the node that is just *before* the item that you want to remove. We could certainly find this "before" node, but not by using the toolkit's `list_search` function.

The second approach actually uses `list_search` to obtain a pointer to the node that contains the item to be deleted. For example, suppose our target is the string mynie in the bag shown here:

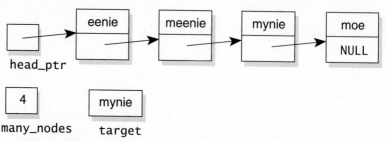

Our approach begins by setting a local variable named `target_ptr` to point to the node that contains our target. This is accomplished with the function call `target_ptr = list_search(head_ptr, target)`. After the function call, the `target_ptr` is set this way:

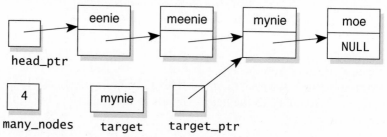

Now we can remove the target from the list with two more steps: (1) Copy the data from the head node to the target node, as shown here:

After this step, we have certainly removed the target, but we are left with two eenies. So, we proceed to a second step: (2) Use `list_head_remove` to remove the head node (that is, one of the copies of eenie). These steps are all implemented in the `remove` function shown in Figure 5.12. The only other steps in the implementation are a test to ensure that the target is actually in the bag and subtracting one from `many_nodes`.

FIGURE 5.12 | A Function to Remove an Item from a Bag

A Function Implementation

```
void Bag::remove(const Item& target)
// Library facilities used: link1.h, stdlib.h
{
    Node *target_ptr;

    target_ptr = list_search(head_ptr, target);
    if (target_ptr == NULL)
        return; // target isn't in the Bag, so no work to do
    target_ptr->data = head_ptr->data;
    list_head_remove(head_ptr);
    many_nodes--;
}
```

bag3.cxx | FTP

***Programming Tip:* How to Choose Between Different Approaches**

 TIP

We had two possible approaches for the remove function. How do we select the best approach? Normally, when two different approaches have equal efficiency, we will choose the approach that makes the best use of the toolkit. This saves us work and also reduces the chance of new errors from writing new code to do an old job. In the case of remove we choose the second approach because it made better use of list_search.

The occurrences member function. Two possible approaches come to mind for the occurrences member function. One of the approaches simply steps through the linked list one node at a time, checking each piece of data to see whether it is the sought-after target. We count the occurrences of the target and return the answer. The second approach uses list_search to find the first occurrence of the target, then uses list_search again to find the next occurrence, and so on until we have found all occurrences of the target. Our second approach for occurrences makes better use of the toolkit, so that is the approach we will take.

As an example of the second approach to the `occurrences` function, suppose we want to count the number of occurrences of meenie in this bag:

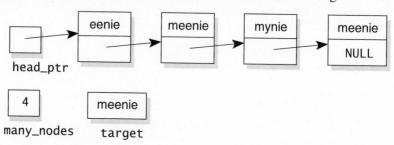

We'll use two local variables: `answer`, which keeps track of the number of occurrences that we have seen so far, and `cursor`, which is a pointer to a node in the list. We initialize `answer` to zero, and we use `list_search` to make `cursor` point to the first occurrence of the target (or to be `NULL` if there are no occurrences). After this initialization, we have this situation:

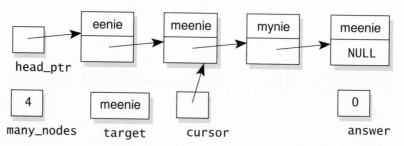

Next, we enter a loop. The loop stops when `cursor` becomes `NULL`, indicating that there are no more occurrences of the target. Each time through the loop we do two steps: (1) Add one to `answer`, and (2) Move `cursor` to point to the next occurrence of the target (or to be `NULL` if there are no more occurrences). Can we use the toolkit to execute Step 2? At first, it might seem that the toolkit is of no use, since `list_search` finds the *first* occurrence of a given target. But there is an approach that will use `list_search` together with the `cursor` to find the *next* occurrence of the target. The approach begins by moving cursor to the next node in the list, using the statement `cursor = cursor->link`. In our example, this results in the following situation:

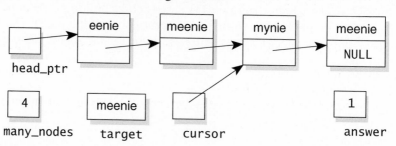

As you can see, `cursor` now points to a node in the middle of a linked list. But, any time that a pointer points to a node in the middle of a linked list, we can pretend that the pointer is a head pointer for a smaller linked list. In our example, `cursor` is a head pointer for a two-item list containing the strings mynie and meenie. Therefore, we can use `cursor` as an argument to `list_search` in the assignment statement `cursor = list_search(cursor, target)`. This assignment moves `cursor` to the next occurrence of the target. This occurrence could be at the cursor's current spot, or it could be farther down the line. In our example, the next occurrence of meenie is farther down the line, so `cursor` is moved as shown here:

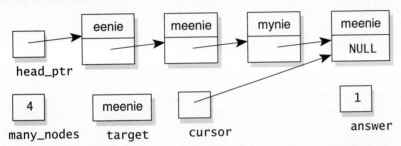

Eventually there will be no more occurrences of the target and `cursor` becomes NULL, ending the loop. At that point the function returns `answer`. The complete implementation of `occurrences` is shown at the top of Figure 5.13 on page 247.

Finding the Next Occurrence of an Item

The situation: A pointer named `cursor` points to a node in a linked list that contains a particular item called `target`.

The task: Make `cursor` point to the next occurrence of `target` (or NULL if there are no more occurrences).

The solution:
```
cursor = cursor->link;
cursor = list_search(cursor, target);
```

The grab member function. The bag has a new grab function, specified here:

```
Item grab( ) const;
//   Precondition: size( ) > 0.
//   Postcondition: The return value is a randomly selected item from the Bag.
```

The implementation will start by generating a random integer between 1 and the size of the bag. The random integer can then be used to select a node from the bag, and we'll return the data from the selected node. So, the body of the function will look something like this:

```
i = some random integer between 1 and the size of the bag;
cursor = list_locate(head_ptr, i);
return cursor->data;
```

Of course the trick is to generate "some random integer between 1 and the size of the bag." The C++ standard library can help us. Within stdlib.h is a function that (sort of) generates random integers, with this specification:

the rand function

```
int rand( );
// Postcondition: The value returned is a pseudorandom
// integer that is greater than or equal to 0.
```

The values returned by rand are not truly random. They are generated by a simple rule (which is discussed in Chapter 2 Programming Project 11 on page 86). But the numbers *appear* random and so the function is referred to as a **pseudorandom number generator**. For most applications, a pseudorandom number generator is a close enough approximation to a true random number generator. In fact, a pseudorandom number generator has one advantage over a true random number generator: The sequence of numbers it produces is repeatable. If run twice with the same initial conditions, a pseudorandom number generator will produce exactly the same sequence of numbers. This is handy when you are debugging programs that use these sequences. When an error is discovered, the corrected program can be tested with the *same* sequence of pseudorandom numbers that produced the original error.

But at this point we don't need a complete memoir on pseudorandom numbers. All we need is a way to use the rand function to generate a number between 1 and the size of the bag. The following assignment statement does the trick:

```
i = (rand( ) % size( )) + 1; // Set i to a random number from
                             // 1 to the size of the Bag.
```

the % operator

Let's look at how the expression works. When x >= 0 and y > 0 are integers, then x % y is the remainder when x is divided by y. The remainder could be as small as 0 or as large as y - 1. Therefore, the expression `rand( ) % size( )` lies somewhere in the range from 0 to size( ) - 1. Since we want a number from 1 to size( ), we add one, resulting in `i = (rand( ) % size( )) + 1`. This assignment statement is used in the complete grab implementation shown at the bottom part of Figure 5.13.

Pitfall: Forgetting to Use the Scope Resolution Operator

The bag's grab function returns an `Item`. In grab's implementation (Figure 5.13), don't forget to use the complete name `Bag::Item` for the return type, as shown here:

```
Bag::Item  Bag::grab( ) const
```

This full return type is needed because some compilers do not recognize the simpler name `Item` until *after* seeing the member function name (`Bag::grab`).

FIGURE 5.13	Implementations of Two Bag Member Functions

Two Function Implementations

```
size_t Bag::occurrences(const Item& target) const
// Library facilities used: stdlib.h, link1.h
{
    size_t answer;
    Node *cursor;

    answer = 0;
    cursor = list_search(head_ptr, target);
    while (cursor != NULL)
    {
        // Each time that cursor is not NULL, we have another occurrence of target, so we
        // add one to answer and then move cursor to the next occurrence of the target.
        answer++;
        cursor = cursor->link;
        cursor = list_search(cursor, target);
    }
    return answer;
}

Bag::Item Bag::grab( ) const
// Library facilities used: assert.h, stdlib.h, link1.h
{
    size_t i;
    Node *cursor;

    assert(size( ) > 0);
    i = (rand( ) % size( )) + 1;
    cursor = list_locate(head_ptr, i);
    return cursor->data;
}
```

bag3.cxx **FTP**

The Third Bag Class—Putting the Pieces Together

The four remaining member functions are straightforward. For example, the size function just returns many_nodes; this is implemented as an inline member function in the header file of Figure 5.11 on page 236. The other bag functions all are implemented in the complete implementation file of Figure 5.14.

Take particular notice of how the bag's += operator is implemented. The implementation makes a copy of the linked list for the bag that's being added. This copy is then attached at the front of the linked list for the bag that's being added to. The bag's + operator is implemented by way of the += operator.

TIP

Programming Tip: Increase Clarity with Include Directives

Our implementation file, bag3.cxx in Figure 5.14, has the include directive

```
#include "link1.h"
```

This include directive is not really needed because link1.h is already included in bag3.h. However, we suggest that you place the include directive in the implementation file anyway. There is no harm in doing so, and it results in extra clarity by indicating that the implementation file really does use link1.h.

Self-Test Exercises

16. Suppose you want to use a bag where the items are strings from our string class in Chapter 4. How would you do this?

17. Write a few lines of code to declare a bag of strings and place the strings squash and handball in the bag. Then grab a random string from the bag, printing it. Finally, print the number of items in the bag.

18. In general, which is preferable: an implementation that uses the linked list toolkit, or an implementation that manipulates a linked list directly?

19. Suppose that p is a pointer to a node in a linked list and that p->data has a copy of an item called d. Write two lines of code that will move p to the next node that contains a copy of d (or set p to NULL if there is no such node). How can you combine your two statements into just one?

20. Describe the steps taken by occurrences if the target is not in the bag.

21. Describe one of the boundary values for testing the remove function.

22. Write an expression that will give a random integer between –10 and 10.

23. Do big-*O* time analyses of the bag's functions.

24. Suppose that a_ptr and b_ptr are node pointers. When will the expression (a_ptr == b_ptr) be true? Which of the bag's member functions use such a test for equality?

FIGURE 5.14	Implementation File for Our Third Bag Class

An Implementation File

```
// FILE: bag3.cxx
// CLASS implemented: Bag (See bag3.h for documentation.)
// INVARIANT for the Bag ADT:
//    1. The items in the Bag are stored on a linked list.
//    2. The head pointer of the list is stored in the member variable head_ptr.
//    3. The total number of items in the list is stored in the member variable
//       many_nodes.

#include <assert.h> // Provides assert
#include <stdlib.h> // Provides NULL, rand, size_t
#include "link1.h"   // Provides Node and the ten linked list functions
#include "bag3.h"

Bag::Bag( )
// Library facilities used: stdlib.h
{
    head_ptr = NULL;
    many_nodes = 0;
}

Bag::Bag(const Bag& source)
// Library facilities used: link1.h
{
    Node *tail_ptr;   // Needed for argument of list_copy

    list_copy(source.head_ptr, head_ptr, tail_ptr);
    many_nodes = source.many_nodes;
}

Bag::~Bag( )
// Library facilities used: link1.h
{
    list_clear(head_ptr);
    many_nodes = 0;
}

void Bag::remove(const Item& target)
```
|| See the implementation in Figure 5.12 on page 243.

```
size_t Bag::occurrences(const Item& target) const
```
|| See the implementation in Figure 5.13 on page 247.

(continued)

(FIGURE 5.14 continued)

```
void Bag::insert(const Item& entry)
// Library facilities used: link1.h
{
    list_head_insert(head_ptr, entry);
    many_nodes++;
}

void Bag::operator +=(const Bag& addend)
// Library facilities used: stdlib.h
{
    Node *copy_head_ptr;
    Node *copy_tail_ptr;

    if (addend.many_nodes > 0)
    {
        list_copy(addend.head_ptr, copy_head_ptr, copy_tail_ptr);
        copy_tail_ptr->link = head_ptr;
        head_ptr = copy_head_ptr;
        many_nodes += addend.many_nodes;
    }
}

void Bag::operator =(const Bag& source)
// Library facilities used: link1.h
{
    Node *tail_ptr; // Needed for argument to list_copy

    if (source.head_ptr == head_ptr)
        return;

    list_clear(head_ptr);
    many_nodes = 0;

    list_copy(source.head_ptr, head_ptr, tail_ptr);
    many_nodes = source.many_nodes;
}

Bag::Item Bag::grab( ) const
```
See the implementation in Figure 5.13 on page 247.

```
Bag operator +(const Bag& b1, const Bag& b2)
{
    Bag answer;

    answer += b1;
    answer += b2;
    return answer;
}
```

bag3.cxx **FTP**

5.4 PROGRAMMING PROJECT: THE LIST ADT WITH A LINKED LIST

In Section 3.2 on page 115 we gave a specification for a list ADT which was implemented using an array. Now you can reimplement this ADT using a *linked list* as the data structure rather than an array. Start by rereading the ADT's specification on page 115, then return here for some implementation suggestions.

The Revised List ADT—Design Suggestions

Using a linked list to implement the list ADT seems natural. We'll keep the items stored on a linked list, in their sequence order. The "current" item on the list can be maintained by a member variable that points to the node that contains the current item. When the start function is activated, we set this "current pointer" to point to the first node of the linked list. When advance is activated, we move the "current pointer" to the next node on the linked list.

With this in mind, we propose five private member variables for the new List class. The first variable, many_nodes, keeps track of the number of nodes in the list. The other four member variables are node pointers:

- head_ptr and tail_ptr—the head and tail pointers of the linked list. If the list has no items, then these pointers are both NULL. The reason for the tail pointer is the attach function. Normally this function adds a new item immediately after the current node. But if there is no current node, then attach places its new item at the tail of the list, so it makes sense to keep a tail pointer around.
- cursor—points to the node with the current item (or NULL if there is no current item).
- precursor—points to the node before current item (or NULL if there is no current item, or the current item is the first node). Can you figure out why we propose a *pre*cursor? The answer is the insert function, which normally adds a new item immediately *before* the current node. But the linked list toolkit has no way of inserting a new node before a specified node. We can only add new nodes after a specified node. Therefore, the insert function will work by adding the new item *after* the precursor node—which is also just *before* the cursor node.

For example, suppose that a list contains four strings, with the current item at the third location. The member variables of the object might appear as shown in the drawing at the top of the next page.

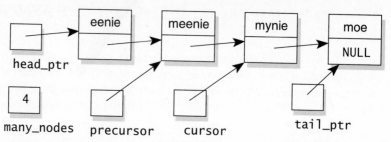

Notice that `cursor` and `precursor` are *pointers* to nodes rather than actual nodes.

what is the invariant of the new list ADT?

Start your implementation by writing the header file and the invariant for the new list ADT. You might even write the invariant in large letters on a sheet of paper and pin it up in front of you as you work. Each of the member functions count on that invariant being true when the function begins. And each function is responsible for ensuring that the invariant is true when the function finishes.

Keep in mind the four rules for an ADT that uses dynamic memory:

1. Some of your member variables are pointers. In fact, for your `List` class, four member variables are pointers.

2. Member functions allocate and release memory as needed. Don't forget to write documentation indicating which member functions allocate dynamic memory so that an experienced programmer can deal with failures.

3. You must override the automatic copy constructor and the automatic assignment operator. Otherwise two different lists end up with pointers to the same linked list. Some hints on these implementations are given in the "value semantics" section below.

4. The class requires a destructor, which is responsible for returning all dynamic memory to the heap.

The Revised List ADT—Value Semantics

The value semantics of your new list ADT consists of a copy constructor and an assignment operator. The primary job of both these functions is to make one list equal to a new copy of another. The list that you are copying is called the "source list," and we suggest that you handle the copying in these three cases:

1. If the source list has no current item, then simply copy the source's linked list with `list_copy`. Then set both `precursor` and `cursor` to the null pointer.

2. If the current item of the source list is its first item, then copy the source's linked list with `list_copy`. Then set `precursor` to null, and set `cursor` to point to the head node of the newly created linked list.

3. If the current item of the source list is after its first item, then copy the source's linked list in two pieces using `list_piece`: The first piece goes from the head pointer to the precursor; the second piece goes from the cursor to the tail pointer. Put these two pieces together by making the link field of the precursor node point to the cursor node. The reason for copying in two separate pieces is to easily set the precursor and cursor of the newly created list.

After copying the linked list, be sure to set `many_nodes` to equal the number of nodes in the source list. Also, beware of the potential pitfalls that accompany the implementation of your assignment operator (see "The Assignment Operator Causes Trouble with Linked Lists" on page 241).

To test the new list ADT, you can use the same interactive test program that you used to test your original list ADT (see "Interactive Test Programs" on page 124).

Self-Test Exercises

25. Suppose a list contains your three favorite strings, and the current item is the first item on the list. Draw the member variables of this list using our implementation.
26. Write a new member function to remove a specified item from a list. The function has one parameter (the item to remove). After the removal, the current item should be the item after the removed item (if there is one). You may assume that the `Item` type has `==` and `!=` operators defined.
27. Which of the list member functions allocate dynamic memory?
28. Which of the list member functions use `list_piece` from the toolkit?

5.5 DYNAMIC ARRAYS VS. LINKED LISTS VS. DOUBLY LINKED LISTS

Many ADTs can be implemented with either dynamic arrays or linked lists. Certainly the bag, our string, and the list ADT could each be implemented with either approach.

Which approach is better?

There is no absolute answer. But there are certain operations that are better performed by dynamic arrays and others where linked lists are preferable. Here are some guidelines:

Arrays are better at random access. The term **random access** refers to examining or changing an arbitrary element that is specified by its position in a list. For example: *What is the 42nd item in the list?* Or another example: *Change the item at position 1066 to a 7.* These are constant time operations for an array (or dynamic array). But, in a linked list, a search for item i must begin at the head and will take $O(i)$ time. Sometimes there are ways to speed up the process, but even improvements remain linear time.

If an ADT makes significant use of random access operations, then a dynamic array is better than a linked list.

Linked lists are better at insertions/deletions at a cursor. Our list ADT maintains a *cursor* that points to a "current element." Typically, a cursor moves through a list one item at a time without jumping around to random locations. If all operations occur at the cursor, then a linked list is preferable to an array. In particular, insertions and deletions at a cursor generally are linear time for an array (since items that are after the cursor must *all* be shifted up or back to a new index in the array). But these operations are constant time operations for a linked list. Also remember that effective insertions and deletions in a linked list generally require maintaining both a cursor and a *precursor* (which points to the node before the cursor).

If an ADT's operations take place at a cursor, then a linked list is better than a dynamic array.

Doubly linked lists are better for a two-way cursor. Sometimes list operations require a cursor that can move forward and backward through a list—a kind of **two-way cursor**. This situation calls for a **doubly linked list**, which is like a simple linked list, except that each node contains two pointers: one pointing to the next node and one pointing to the previous node. An example of a doubly linked list of integers is shown in Figure 5.15 (in the margin). A possible set of definitions for a doubly linked list of items is the following:

```
struct DNode
{
    typedef _____ Item;      Fill in the Item type
    Item data;               however you like.
    DNode *backlink;
    DNode *forelink;
};
```

The `backlink` points to the previous node, and the `forelink` points to the next node in the list.

If an ADT's operations take place at a two-way cursor, then a doubly linked list is the best implementation.

Resizing Can Be Inefficient for a Dynamic Array. A container ADT that uses a dynamic array generally provides a "resize function" to allow a programmer to adjust the capacity as needed. But resizing an array can be inefficient. The new memory must be allocated, the items are then copied from the old memory to the new memory, and then the old memory is deleted. If a program can predict the necessary capacity ahead of time, then resizing is not a big problem, since the object can be given sufficient capacity from the outset. But sometimes the even-

FIGURE 5.15
Doubly Linked List

tual capacity is unknown and a program must continually adjust the capacity. In this situation, a linked list has advantages. When a linked list grows, it grows one node at a time, and there is no need to copy items from old memory to new larger memory.

If an ADT is frequently adjusting its size, then a linked list may be better than a dynamic array.

Making the Decision

Your decision on what kind of implementation to use is based on your knowledge of which operations occur in the ADT, which operations you expect to be performed most often, and whether you expect your containers to require frequent resizing. Figure 5.16 summarizes these considerations.

Self-Test Exercises

29. What underlying data structure is quickest for random access?

30. What underlying data structure is quickest for insertions/deletions at a cursor?

31. What underlying data structure is best if a cursor must move both forward and backward?

32. What is the typical worst-case time analysis for a resizing operation on a container class that is implemented with a dynamic array?

33. Write a function to add a new item at the head of a doubly linked list. Use the DNode struct from page 254.

FIGURE 5.16   Guidelines for Choosing Between a Dynamic Array and a Linked List

Frequent random access operations	Use a dynamic array
Operations occur at a cursor	Use a linked list
Operations occur at a two-way cursor	Use a doubly linked list
Frequent resizing may be needed	A linked list avoids resizing inefficiency

CHAPTER SUMMARY

- A *linked list* consists of nodes; each *node* contains some data and a pointer to the next node in the list. The pointer field of the final node contains the null pointer.

- Typically, a linked list is accessed through a *head pointer* that points to the *head node* (i.e., the first node). Sometimes a linked list is accessed elsewhere, such as through the *tail pointer* that points to the last node.

- A *toolkit* provides a collection of functions to support a concept such as linked lists. You should be familiar with our linked list toolkit, which provides ten fundamental functions. These functions follow basic patterns that every programmer uses.

- Our linked list toolkit can be used to implement ADTs. Such an ADT will have one or more private member variables that are pointers to nodes in a linked list. The member functions of the ADT will use the linked list toolkit to manipulate the linked list, which is accessed through private member variables.

- You have seen two ADTs implemented with the linked list toolkit: a bag and a list. You will see more in the chapters that follow.

- ADTs often can be implemented in many different ways, such as by using a dynamic array or using a linked list. In general, arrays are better at *random access*; linked lists are better at insertions/removals at a *cursor*.

- A *doubly linked list* has nodes with two pointers: one to the next node and one to the previous node. Doubly linked lists are a good choice for supporting a cursor that moves forward and backward.

? Solutions to Self-Test Exercises

1. Unless you state otherwise, struct members are public, whereas class members are private.

2. See the struct definition on page 203.

3. The null pointer is used for the link field of the final node of a linked list; it is also used for the head and tail pointers of a list that doesn't yet have any nodes.

4. `head_ptr` is a pointer to a node. On the other hand, `*head_ptr` is a `Node`, and the type of `head_ptr->data` is `Node::Item`.

5. `if (head_ptr->data == 0)`
   `        cout << "zero";`

6. `cout << b_ptr->size( );`

7. The portions of the operating system that are currently in the computer's memory can be overwritten.

8. The `#include "mystring.h"` directive must be added to the other include directives in the toolkit's header file. Then we can change the typedef statement to:
   `typedef String Item;`

9. `locate_ptr = locate_ptr->link;`
If `locate_ptr` is already pointing to the last node before this assignment statement, then the assignment will set `locate_ptr` to the null pointer.

10. A const node pointer is misleading because it does not prevent the function from changing the linked list that the pointer points to.

11. Using functions from our toolkit:
```
if (head_ptr == NULL)
    list_head_insert(head_ptr, 42);
else
    list_insert(head_ptr, 42);
```

12. The *new* operator is used in the functions: `list_insert`, `list_copy`, `list_piece`, and `list_head_insert`. The *delete* operator is used in the functions `list_head_remove`, `list_remove`, and `list_clear`.

13. Using functions from our toolkit:
```
if (head_ptr != NULL)
{
    if (head_ptr->link == NULL)
        list_head_remove(head_ptr);
    else
        list_remove(head_ptr);
}
```

14. It will be the null pointer.

15. The implementation is nearly the same as `list_copy`, but the copying must stop when the end node has been copied.

16. The item type in the linked list toolkit would need to be changed to `String` (as in the answer to Self-Test Exercise 8).

17. Assuming that we have set the bag's item to a string, we would write this code:
```
Bag exercise;
exercise.insert("squash");
exercise.insert("handball");
cout << exercise.grab( ) << endl;
cout << exercise.size( ) << endl;
```

18. Generally we will choose the approach that makes the best use of the toolkit. This saves us work and also reduces the chance of new errors from writing new code to do an old job. The preference would change if the non-toolkit approach offered better efficiency.

19. The two lines of code that we have in mind:
```
p = p->link;
p = list_search(p, d);
```
These two lines are the same as the single line:
```
p = list_search(p->link, d);
```

20. When the target is not in the bag, the first assignment statement to `cursor` will set it to the null pointer. This means that the body of the loop will not execute at all, and the function returns the answer zero.

21. Test the case where you are removing the last item from the bag.

22. `(rand( ) % 21) - 10;`

23. All the functions are constant time except for `remove`, `grab`, and `occurrences` (which all are linear); the copy constructor and operator = (which are $O(n)$, where n is the size of the bag being copied); the operator += (which is $O(n)$, where n is the size of the addend); and the operator + (which is $O(m+n)$, where m and n are the sizes of the two bags).

24. The expression is true if the two pointers point to exactly the same node. This kind of test is used in the operator = to protect against self-assignment.

25. `many_nodes` is 3, and these are the other member variables:

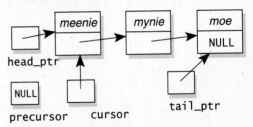

26. First check that the item occurs somewhere in the list. If it doesn't, then return with no work. If the item is in the list, then set the current item to be equal to this item, and call the ordinary remove function.

27. The `insert` and `attach` functions both allocate dynamic memory, as do the copy constructor and assignment operator.

28. The copy constructor and assignment operator use `list_piece`.

29. Arrays are quickest for random access.

30. Linked lists are quickest for insertions/deletions at a cursor.

31. A doubly linked list

32. *O(n)*, where *n* is the size of the array prior to resizing

33. You'll need to write an appropriate precondition/postcondition contract for this solution:

```
void dlist_head_insert(
    DNode*& head_ptr,
    const DNode::Item& entry
)
{
  DNode *insert_ptr;
  insert_ptr = new DNode;
  insert_ptr->data = entry;
  insert_ptr->forelink = head_ptr;
  insert_ptr->backlink = NULL;
  if (head_ptr != NULL)
  head_ptr->backlink = insert_ptr;
  head_ptr = insert_ptr;
}
```

PROGRAMMING PROJECTS

1 For this project, you will use the bag ADT with the item being a string from our string ADT in Section 3.4. The bag ADT should include the `grab` function from Figure 5.13 on page 247. Use this ADT in a program that does the following:

1. Asks the user for a list of ten nouns.
2. Asks the user for a list of ten verbs.
3. Prints some random sentences using the provided nouns and verbs.

For example, if two of the nouns were "monkey" and "piano," and two of the verbs were "eats" and "plays," then we can expect any of these sentences:

```
The monkey eats the piano.
The monkey plays the piano.
The piano eats the monkey.
The piano plays the monkey.
```

Needless to say, the sentences are not entirely sensible. Your program will need to declare two bag variables: one to store the nouns and one to store the verbs. Use an appropriate top-down design.

2 Write a function that takes a linked list of items and deletes all repetitions from the list. In your implementation, assume that items can be compared for equality using ==.

3 Write a function with three parameters. The first parameter is a head pointer for a linked list of items, and the next two parameters are items x and y. The function should write to the screen all items in the list that are between the first occurrence of x and the first occurrence of y. You may assume that items can be compared for equality using ==.

4 Write a function with one parameter that is a head pointer for a linked list of items. The function reverses the order of the nodes so that the last node is first, the first node is last, and so forth. The head pointer is a reference parameter, so that after the function completes, this same pointer variable is pointing to the head of the reversed list.

5 Write a function that has two linked list head pointers as parameters. Assume that linked lists items are ordered by the < operator. On each list, every item is less than the next item on the same list. The function should create a new linked list that contains all the items on both lists, and the new linked list should also be ordered (so that every item is less than the next item on the list). The new linked list should also eliminate duplicate items (i.e., if the same item appears on both input lists, then only one copy is placed in the newly constructed linked list). In order to eliminate duplicate items, you may assume that two items can be compared for equality using ==. The function should return a head pointer for the newly constructed linked list.

6 Write a function that starts with a single linked list of items and a special value called the *splitting value*. Two item values can be compared using the < operator—but the items of the original linked list are in no particular order. The procedure divides the nodes into two linked lists: one containing all the nodes that contain an item less than the splitting value and one that contains all the other nodes. If the original linked list had any repeated integers (i.e., any two or more nodes with the same item in them) then the new linked list that has this item should have the same number of nodes that repeat this item. It does not matter whether you preserve the original linked list or destroy it in the process of building the two new lists, but your comments should document what happens to the original linked list.

7 Write a function that takes a linked list of integers and rearranges the nodes so that the integers stored are sorted into the order smallest to largest, with the smallest integer in the node at the head of the list. Your function should preserve repetitions of integers. If the original list had any integers occurring more than once, then the changed list will have the same number of each integer. For concreteness you will use lists of integers, but your function should still work if you replace the integer type with any other type for which the less than operation is part of a total order semantics. Use

the following function prototype and specification:

```
void sort_list(Node*& head_ptr);
// Precondition: head_ptr is a head pointer of
// a linked list of items, and these items can be
// compared with a less-than operator that is
// part of a total order semantics.
// Postcondition: head_ptr points to the head
// of a linked list with exactly the same entries
// (including repetitions if any), but the entries
// in this list are sorted from smallest to
// largest. The original linked list is no longer
// available.
```

Your procedure will implement the following algorithm (which is often called **selection sort**): The algorithm removes nodes one at a time from the original list and adds the nodes to a second list until all the nodes have been moved to the second list. The second list will then be sorted.

```
// Pseudocode for selection sort
while (the first list still has some nodes)
{
```
    1. Find the node *with the largest item* of all the nodes in the first list.
    2. Remove this node from the first list.
    3. Insert this node at the head of the second list.
```
}
```

After all the nodes are moved to the second list, the pointer, head_ptr, can be moved to point to the head of the second list. Note that your function will move entire nodes, not just items, to the second list. Thus, the first list will get shorter and shorter until it is an empty list. Your function should not need to call the *new* operator since it is just moving nodes from one list to another (not creating new nodes).

8 Write a program for keeping a course list for each student in a college. The information about each student should be kept in an object that contains the student's name and a list of courses completed by the student. The courses taken by a student are stored as a linked list in which each node contains the name of a course, the number of units for the course, and the course grade. The program gives a menu with choices that include adding a student's record, deleting a student's record, adding a single course record to a student's record, deleting a single course record from a student's record, and printing a student's record to the screen. The program input should accept the student's name in any combination of upper- and lower-case letters. A student's record should include the student's GPA (grade point average) when displayed on the screen. When the user is through with the program, the program should store the records in a file. The next time the program is run, the records should be read back out of the file and the list should be reconstructed. (Ask your instructor if there are any rules about what type of file you should use.)

9 Implement operators for - and -= for the Bag class from Section 5.3. See Chapter 3 Programming Project 2 on page 132 for details about how the operations work with a bag.

10 Implement operators for + and += for your List class from Section 5.4. For two lists x and y, the list x+y contains all the items of x, followed by all the items of y. The statement x += y appends all of the items of y to the end of what's already in x.

11 You can represent an integer with any number of digits by storing the integer as a linked list of digits. A more efficient representation will store a larger integer in each node.

Design and implement a unit for an ADT for whole number arithmetic in which a number is implemented as a linked list of integers. Each node will hold an integer less than or equal to 999. The number represented is the concatenation of the numbers in the nodes. For example, if there are four nodes with the four integers 23, 7, 999, and 0, then this represents the number 23,007,999,000. Note that the number in a node is always considered to be three digits long. If it is not three digits long, then leading zeros are added to make it three digits long. Overload all the usual integer operators to work with your new class.

12 Revise one of the container classes from Chapter 3 or 4, so that it uses a linked list. Some choices are: (a) the string from Section 4.5; (b) the set (Project 5 on page 133); (c) the sorted list (Project 6 on page 133); (d) the bag with receipts (Project 7 on page 133); (e) the keyed bag (Project 8 on page 133).

13 Revise the Chapter 3 polynomial class from Project 9 on page 134, so that the coefficients are stored in a linked list and there is no maximum degree. Include an operation to allow you to multiply two polynomials in the usual way. For example:

$$(3x^2 + 7) \quad * \quad (2x + 4) \quad = \quad (6x^3 + 12x^2 + 14x + 28)$$

6 Software Reuse with Templates

The goal of software reuse is to build systems of systems by putting together independently developed software components.

JEANNETTE WING
Address to the 12th MFPS Workshop, June 1996

Professional programmers try to write functions and ADTs that have general applicability in many settings. To some extent, our ADTs do this already. Certainly, the bag and list ADTs can be used in many different settings. However, both our bag and our list suffer from the fact that they require the underlying Item type to be fixed. A single program cannot easily use both a bag of integers and a bag of strings.

This chapter provides a better approach to writing code that is meant to be reused in a variety of settings. The approach, called **templates**, is applicable to individual functions and to classes. By the end of the chapter you will know how to write **template functions** that can easily be used in a variety of settings. You will also know how to use **template classes** to implement container classes, such as the bag and the list, in a way that allows better flexibility for the underlying item type.

6.1 TEMPLATE FUNCTIONS

Sometimes it seems that programmers intentionally make extra work for themselves. For example, suppose we write a function to find the larger of two integers:

```
int maximal(int a, int b)
// Postcondition: The return value is the larger of a and b.
{
    if (a > b)
        return a;
    else
        return b;
}
```

This is a fine function, reliably returning the larger of two integers. But suppose that tomorrow you have another program that needs to compute the larger of two double numbers. Then you'll write a new function:

```
double maximal(double a, double b)
// Postcondition: The return value is the larger of a and b.
{
    if (a > b)
        return a;
    else
        return b;
}
```

The next day, you need a third function that returns the larger of two strings, using the > relationship for our String class from Chapter 4. You'll write a third function:

```
String maximal(String a, String b)
// Postcondition: The return value is the larger of a and b.
{
    if (a > b)
        return a;
    else
        return b;
}
```

In fact, a single program can use all three of the maximal functions. When one of the functions is used, the compiler looks at the type of the arguments and selects the appropriate version of the maximal function. But, with this approach, you do need to write a new function for each type of values that you want to compare.

Of course, you could write just one function, along with a typedef statement, like this:

```
typedef _____ Item;
Item maximal(Item a, Item b)
// Postcondition: The return value is the larger of a and b.
{
    if (a > b)
        return a;
    else
        return b;
}
```

Now, a programmer can fill in the typedef statement with any data type that has the > operator defined and also has a copy constructor. The copy constructor is needed because the function returns an Item, and in C++ the function return mechanism uses the copy constructor (see "Returning an Object from a Function" on page 177).

But the typedef approach has a problem. Suppose that a single program needs to use several different versions of the maximal function. The typedef approach does not allow this, since the program can only define one data type for the Item.

The solution is a more flexible mechanism called a **template function**, which is similar to an ordinary function with one important difference: The definition of a template function can depend on an underlying data type. The underlying data type is given a name—such as Item—but Item is not pinned down to a specific type anywhere in the function's implementation. When a template function is *used*, the compiler examines the types of the arguments and at that point the compiler automatically determines the data type of Item. Moreover, in a single program, several different usages of a template function can result in several different underlying data types.

We avoided introducing template functions right away because the typedef has a simpler syntax. Also, extra pitfalls and cryptic compilation errors can arise from templates. Nevertheless, the advantages of templates make it worthwhile to use them. So, let's dive into the cumbersome syntax that we've been avoiding.

Syntax for a Template Function

As an example of a template function, we will alter the maximal function. The template function requires one change from the typedef approach, as shown at the top of the next page.

<table>
<tr><td>

Using a Typedef Statement:

```
typedef int Item;
Item maximal(Item a, Item b)
{
    if (a > b)
        return a;
    else
        return b;
}
```

</td><td>

Defining a Template Function:

```
template <class Item>
Item maximal(Item a, Item b)
{
    if (a > b)
        return a;
    else
        return b;
}
```

</td></tr>
</table>

With the typedef approach on the left, the maximal function compares two integers. Of course, we can change the underlying type of the compared elements by changing the typedef statement. On the other hand, the single definition of the template function allows a program to use the maximal function with two integers, or with two doubles, or with two of our strings—with any data type that has the > operator and a copy constructor.

The expression *template <class Item>* is called the **template prefix**. It warns the compiler that the following definition will use an unspecified data type called Item. In our example, the template prefix precedes the template function's definition. In effect, the template prefix says, "Item is a data type that will be filled in later; don't worry about it for now, just use it inside the function definition!" The "unspecified type" is called the **template parameter**.

Notice that the template parameter is preceded by the keyword *class* and is surrounded by *angle* brackets (which are the same as the less-than and greater-than signs). We used the name Item for this template parameter, but we could have used any legal identifier.

Using a Template Function

A program can use a template function with any Item type that has the necessary features. In the case of the maximal function, the Item type can be any of the C++ built-in types (such as *int* or *char*), or it may be a class with the > operator and a copy constructor. For example, a program with the maximal template function can have the statement:

```
cout << maximal(1000, 2000);  ←——— Print the larger integer.
```

When the compiler sees this function call, it determines that the type of Item must be *int*, and it automatically uses the maximal function with Item defined as *int*. A C++ programmer says, "The maximal function has been **instantiated** with Item equal to *int*."

The same program can use the template function to compare two strings, using our String class from Chapter 4, as shown at the top of the next page.

```
String s1("frijoles");
String s2("beans");
cout << maximal(s1, s2);
```

Print the string that is lexicographically larger.

A demonstration program using the `maximal` template function is shown in Figure 6.1. This program begins with the `maximal` template function that we have discussed. We have placed the function at the start of the file because some compilers require that the entire template function appears before its use (rather than just a prototype). The `maximal` function itself is used twice in the main program—once to compare two strings and once to compare two integers.

Keep in mind that neither the prototype nor the implementation of the template function actually causes the compiler to compile anything. It is only when the function is instantiated by using it in the main program (or elsewhere), that the compiler takes action to compile a certain version of the template function, using the specified type for the template parameter. In the case of our `maximal` function, the program in Figure 6.1 has one implementation of the `maximal` template function, and the one implementation is *instantiated* in two different ways (that is, with `String` class as the item type and with *int* as the item type).

Pitfall: Failed Unification Errors

PITFALL

There is a special rule for template functions: *The template parameter must appear in the parameter list of the template function.* Without this rule, the compiler cannot figure out how to instantiate the template function when it is used. Violating this rule will likely result in cryptic error messages such as "Failed unification." The term **unification** is the compiler's term for determining the correct way to instantiate a template function.

A Template Function to Swap Two Values

Here is a definition of another template function. The function swaps the values of two variables, as shown here:

```
template <class Item>
void swap(Item& x, Item& y);
// Postcondition: The values of x and y have been interchanged, so that y
// now has the original value of x, and vice versa. Note: Item may be any of
// the C++ built-in types (int, char, etc.), or a class with an assignment
// operator and a default constructor.
{
    Item temp;

    temp = x;
    x = y;
    y = temp;
}
```

(text continues on page 267)

FIGURE 6.1	Demonstration Program for Template Functions

A Program

```
// FILE: maximal.cxx
// A demonstration program for a template function called maximal.

#include <iostream.h>    // Provides cout
#include <stdlib.h>      // Provides EXIT_SUCCESS
#include "mystring.h"    // If available, this could be changed to the standard String class.

// TEMPLATE FUNCTION used in this demonstration program:
// Note that some compilers require the entire function definition to appear before its use
// (rather than a mere prototype).
template <class Item>
Item maximal(Item a, Item b)
// Postcondition: Returns the larger of a and b.
// Note: Item may be any of the C++ built-in types (int, char, etc.), or a class with
// the > operator and a copy constructor.
{
    if (a > b)
        return a;
    else
        return b;
}

int main( )
{
    String s1("frijoles");
    String s2("beans");

    cout << "Larger of frijoles and beans: " << maximal(s1, s2) << endl;
    cout << "Larger of 10 and 20 : " << maximal(10, 20) << endl;
    cout << "It's a large world." << endl;

    return EXIT_SUCCESS;
}
```

Not function calls
They are template instantiation

The main program has two different uses of the maximal template function.

A Sample Dialogue

```
Larger of frijoles and beans: frijoles
Larger of 10 and 20: 20
It's a large world.
```

maximal.cxx	**FTP**

In this example, the values of x and y are interchanged by the usual three assignment statements that use an intermediary temporary variable (`temp`). The example shows two new features. First, notice that the function uses a local variable, `temp`, whose type is `Item`. This is fine, so long as the `Item` type has a default constructor (and we have indicated this requirement in the documentation).

The second feature of the function is that the underlying data type, `Item`, is used as a *reference* parameter. Thus, when `swap` is called, the actual parameters will have their values interchanged, as shown in this string example:

```
String name1("Castor");  // Using String from Section 4.5
String name2("Pollux");
                              The two values are
swap(name1, name2);           interchanged so that
cout << name1;                "Pollux" is printed.
```

Parameter Matching for Template Functions

Our next template function searches an array for the biggest item and returns the index of that item. For example, the array could be an array of six integers, shown here:

10	20	30	1	2	3
[0]	[1]	[2]	[3]	[4]	[5]

The biggest value, 30, appears at location [2], so with this array as the argument, our function returns 2. Here is the template function's complete specification:

```
template <class Item>
size_t index_of_maximal(const Item data[ ], size_t n);
// Precondition: data is an array with at least n items, and n > 0.
// Postcondition: The return value is the index of a maximal item from
// data[0] ... data[n – 1]. Note: Item may be any of the C++ built-in types
// (int, char, etc.), or any class with the > operator defined.
```

Actually, this specification is not exactly what we want. To explain the problem, we need to know a bit more about how the compiler uses template functions.

When a template function is instantiated, the compiler tries to select the underlying data type so that the type of each argument results in an *exact match* with the type of the corresponding formal parameter. For example, suppose that d is a *double* variable. You cannot write `maximal(d, 1)`, since there is no way for the compiler to have `Item` be an exact match with the type of the first argument (*double*) and also be an exact match with the type of the second argument (*int*). Unlike an ordinary function, the compiler does not convert arguments for a template function. The arguments must have an exact match, with no type conversion.

The requirement of an exact match applies to *all* parameters of a template function. For example, consider the `index_of_maximal` prototype:

```
template <class Item>
size_t index_of_maximal(const Item data[ ], size_t n);
```

When we call the function, the second argument must be a `size_t` value. Many compilers won't accept any deviation: not an *int*, not a *const* `size_t`, only a `size_t` value. On such a strict compiler, the following will fail:

```
const size_t SIZE = 5;
double data[SIZE];
...                                These won't work
cout << index_of_maximal(data, SIZE);    with many
cout << index_of_maximal(data, 5);       compilers.
```

The first function call, with `SIZE` as the second argument, fails on many compilers because `SIZE` is declared as **const size_t** rather than a mere **size_t**. The second function call, with 5 as the second argument, fails because the compiler takes 5 to be an **int** rather than a **size_t** value.

A Template Function to Find the Biggest Item in an Array

For the `index_of_maximal` function, we can deal with the problem by slightly changing the specification. The new specification uses two template parameters—one for the data type of the array's components, and a second for the data type of the size of the array, as shown here:

```
template <class Item, class SizeType>
size_t index_of_maximal(const Item data[ ], SizeType n);
// Precondition: data is an array with at least n items, and n > 0.
// Postcondition: The return value is the index of a maximal item from
// data[0] ... data[n - 1]. Note: Item may be any of the C++ built-in types
// (int, char, etc.), or any class with the > operator defined.
// SizeType may be any of the integer or const integer types.
```

With this template function, we have more flexibility. Both these are okay:

```
const size_t SIZE = 5;               SizeType will be
double data[SIZE];                   const size_t.
...
cout << index_of_maximal(data, SIZE);
cout << index_of_maximal(data, 5);   SizeType will
                                     be int.
```

Now we can implement the template function. The function uses a local variable, answer, to keep track of the index of the biggest item that has been seen so far. Initially, answer is set to zero, meaning that the biggest item seen so far is at data[0]. Then we step through the rest of the array: data[1], data[2], and so on. If we spot an item that is bigger than data[answer], then we change answer to the index of that bigger item. Here is the code:

```
template <class Item, class SizeType>
size_t index_of_maximal(const Item data[ ], SizeType n)
// Library facilities used: assert.h, stdlib.h
{
    size_t answer;
    size_t i;

    assert(n > 0);
    answer = 0;

    for (i = 1; i < n; i++)
    {
        if (data[answer] < data[i])
            answer = i;
        // data[answer] is now biggest from data[0]...data[i].
    }

    return answer;
}
```

Pitfall: Mismatches for Template Function Arguments

PITFALL

Each argument to a template function must be an exact match to the data type of the formal parameter, with no type conversions. C++ compilers provide a little leeway on the meaning of "exact match." For example with an *int* argument, the formal parameter may be any of the following:

int (a value parameter)
int& (a reference parameter)
const int& (a const reference parameter)

But for many compilers, an *int* argument does *not* provide an exact match to size_t. With this in mind, we generally will use an extra template parameter for the data type of an integer or size_t argument. For example:

```
template <class Item, class SizeType>
size_t index_of_maximal(const Item data[ ], SizeType n);
```

A Template Function to Insert an Item into a Sorted Array

Our next example defines a template function to insert a new entry into an array that is already sorted from small to large. The insertion must keep all the items in order from small to large. Here is the function's specification:

```
template <class Item, class SizeType>
void ordered_insert(Item data[ ], SizeType n, Item entry);
// Precondition: data is a partially filled array containing n items sorted
//   from small to large. The array size is large enough to hold at least one
//   more item.
// Postcondition: data is a partially filled array containing the n original items
//   plus the new entry. These items are still sorted from small to large.
// Note: Item may be any of the C++ built-in types (int, char, etc.), or a
//   class with the < operator, an assignment operator, and a copy
//   constructor. SizeType may be any of the integer or const integer types.
```

For example, suppose that `data` is this partially filled array of integers, sorted from small to large:

We can use the `ordered_insert` function to insert a new number, as shown here:

```
ordered_insert(data, 3, 15);
```

The compiler will call `ordered_insert`, with both `Item` and `SizeType` instantiated as *int*. After the insertion, the partially filled array contains four items, which are still sorted from small to large:

The function must take care to insert the new entry at the correct position so that everything stays sorted. We suggest that you shift items at the end of the array rightward one position each until you find the correct position for the new entry.

For example, suppose you are inserting 3 in this partially filled, sorted array:

You would begin by shifting the 11 rightward from `data[3]` to `data[4]`; then move the 9 from `data[2]` to `data[3]`; then the 6 moves from `data[1]` to `data[2]`. At this point, the array looks like this:

Of course, `data[1]` actually still contains a 6 since we just copied the 6 from `data[1]` to `data[2]`. But we have drawn `data[1]` as an empty box to indicate that `data[1]` is now available to hold the new entry (i.e., the 3 that we're inserting). At this point we can place the 3 in `data[1]`, as shown here:

The pseudocode for shifting the items rightward uses a for-loop. Each iteration of the loop shifts one item, as shown here:

for (i = n; `data[i]` is the wrong spot for `entry` ; i--)
    `data[i] = data[i-1];`

The key to the loop is the test "`data[i]` is the wrong spot for `entry` ." A position is wrong if (i > 0) and the item at `data[i-1]` is greater than the new entry. We know that such a position must be wrong because placing the new entry at this position would end up with `data[i-1] > data[i]`. Can you now write the loop's test in C++? (See the answer to Self-Test Exercise 4).

Self-Test Exercises

1. Describe the main purpose of a template function.
2. What is the template prefix, and where is it used in a template function?

3. Write a template function that compares two items. If the items are equal, then the message "Those are the same" is printed. Otherwise the message "Those are different" is printed. The function has two parameters. The parameter type may be any type that has the == operator defined.

4. Write an implementation of the ordered_insert template function.

5. Suppose that an actual argument to a template function is an *int*. Which type of formal parameter could be handled by all C++ compilers? (a) *int* (b) *int&* (c) *const int&* (d) *double* (e) size_t.

6.2   TEMPLATE FUNCTIONS IN A TOOLKIT

A summary of how to write template functions is shown in Figure 6.2. When you define some useful template functions, you can give them to other programmers in a "toolkit," similar to the linked list toolkit from Section 5.2. A programmer who wants to use your fabulous functions can include the header file

FIGURE 6.2   Template Functions

How to Write a Template Function

When a function depends on another underlying data type, you should implement a template function rather than an ordinary function. The template function depends on yet-to-be-specified data types, such as the Item type in our examples. The template function differs from an ordinary function in these ways:

1. Place the template prefix immediately before the function prototype and immediately before the function implementation. For example:

```
template <class Item>
Item maximal(Item a, Item b)
{
    if (a > b)
        return a;
    else
        return b;
};
```

The template prefix begins with the keyword *template*, followed by a list of one or more data types that the function depends on. Each data type in the list is preceded by the keyword *class*, and the list itself is enclosed in angle brackets.

2. If the template function is part of a toolkit, put the documentation and prototypes for the functions in a header file. Use an "include" directive at the end of the header file to include the implementation file.

of your toolkit, gaining access to all your riches. As an example, we'll place the four template functions from Section 6.1 in a toolkit.

The Toolkit's Header File and Implementation File

As with any toolkit, the "Item template toolkit" comes in two parts: a header file that provides documentation and prototypes for the functions, and an implementation file. But in the case of template functions, the header/implementation split runs into one annoying requirement: In the header file, you place the documentation and the prototypes of the functions—*then you must include the actual implementations of all the functions.* This is annoying because we try to *avoid* revealing our implementations, and suddenly all is revealed! The reason for the requirement is to make the compiler's job simpler. We recommend that you meet the requirement in a back-door manner: Keep the implementations in a separate implementation file, but place an include directive at the bottom of the header file to pick up these implementations, as shown at the bottom of our item toolkit's header file (`itemtool.h`) shown in the first part of Figure 6.3 on page 274. Near the end of the header file, on page 275, we have the following line, which causes the inclusion of the implementation file:

```
#include "itemtool.template"   // Include the implementation.
```

The file `itemtool.template` is where the four implementations of the template functions will appear. The file name `itemtool.template` (rather than `itemtool.cxx`) reminds a programmer that the implementations cannot be compiled on their own. On some computers, the name must be shortened to `itemtool.tem`.

Our implementation file for the "Item template toolkit" is given in the second part of Figure 6.3 beginning near the middle of page 275, and an expanded version of this toolkit is in Appendix I. Any program can use the functions in this toolkit by including the header file, just like any other toolkit.

Pitfall: Default Arguments in Template Functions

Template functions may have default arguments. But some compilers require the values of these arguments to be placed in both the prototype and the function implementation.

Self-Test Exercise

6. What is a major difference between the header file for a toolkit of template functions and the header file for a toolkit of ordinary functions? Why is this difference needed?

| FIGURE 6.3 | Header File and Implementation File for the Item Toolkit |

A Header File for Template Functions

```
// FILE: itemtool.h
// PROVIDES: A toolkit of four template functions for manipulating items.
//
// TEMPLATE FUNCTIONS in the linked list toolkit:
//     template <class Item>
//     Item maximal(Item a, Item b)
//         Postcondition: Returns the larger of a and b.
//         Note: Item may be any of the C++ built-in types (int, char, etc.), or a class with
//         the > operator and a copy constructor.
//
//     template <class Item>
//     void swap(Item& x, Item& y)
//         Postcondition: The values of x and y have been interchanged, so that y now has the
//         original value of x, and vice versa. Note: Item may be any of the C++ built-in types (int,
//         char, etc.), or a class with an assignment operator and a default constructor.
//
//     template <class Item, class SizeType>
//     size_t index_of_maximal(const Item data[ ], SizeType n)
//         Precondition: data is an array with at least n items, and n>0.
//         Postcondition: The return value is the index of a maximal item from
//         data[0] . . . data[n – 1].
//         Note: Item may be any of the C++ built-in types (int, char, etc.), or any class with
//         the > operator defined. SizeType may be any of the integer or const integer types.
//
//     template <class Item, class SizeType>
//     void ordered_insert(Item data[ ], SizeType n, Item entry)
//         Precondition: data is a partially filled array containing n items sorted from small to
//         large. The array size is large enough to hold at least one more item.
//         Postcondition: data is a partially filled array containing the n original items plus the new
//         entry. These items are still sorted from small to large. Note: Item may be any of the C++
//         built-in types (int, char, etc.), or a class with the < operator, an assignment operator,
//         and a copy constructor. SizeType may be any of the integer or const integer types.
```

(continued)

(FIGURE 6.3 continued)

```
#ifndef ITEMTOOL_H
#define ITEMTOOL_H

    // FUNCTIONS for the item toolkit
    template <class Item>
    Item maximal(Item a, Item b);

    template <class Item>
    void swap(Item& x, Item& y);

    template <class Item, class SizeType>
    size_t index_of_maximal(const Item data[ ], SizeType n);

    template <class Item, class SizeType>
    void ordered_insert(Item data[ ], SizeType n, Item entry);

#include "itemtool.template"   // Include the implementation.

#endif
```

> Most compilers require the implementation file to be included in the header file for template functions.

An Implementation File for Template Functions

```
// FILE: itemtool.template
// IMPLEMENTS: The four template functions of a small toolkit to manipulate items
// (see itemtool.h). Note that this file is not compiled on its own. Instead, this file is included
// with an include directive at the bottom of itemtool.h.

#include <assert.h>    // Provides assert
#include <stdlib.h>    // Provides size_t

template <class Item>
Item maximal(Item a, Item b)
{
    if (a > b)
        return a;
    else
        return b;
}
```

(continued)

(FIGURE 6.3 continued)

```
template <class Item>
void swap(Item& x, Item& y)
{
    Item temp;

    temp = x;
    x = y;
    y = temp;
}


template <class Item, class SizeType>
size_t index_of_maximal(const Item data[ ], SizeType n)
// Library facilities used: assert.h, stdlib.h
{
    size_t answer;
    size_t i;

    assert(n > 0);
    answer = 0;
    for (i = 1; i < n; i++)
    {
        if (data[answer] < data[i])
            answer = i;
        // data[answer] is now biggest from data[0]...data[i].
    }
    return answer;
}


template <class Item, class SizeType>
void ordered_insert(Item data[ ], SizeType n, Item entry)
// Library functions used: stdlib.h
{
    size_t i;

    for (i = n; (i > 0) && (data[i-1] > entry); i--)
        data[i] = data[i-1];
    data[i] = entry;
}
```

itemtool.h and itemtool.template **FTP**

6.3 TEMPLATE CLASSES

A template function is a function that depends on an underlying data type. In a similar way, when a class depends on an underlying data type, the class can be implemented as a **template class**—resulting in the same advantages that you have seen for template functions. For example, with the bag as a template class, a single program can use a bag of integers, and a bag of characters, and a bag of strings, and a bag of whatever else is needed. In fact, this is exactly what we'll do for our first example: Implement a bag as a template class that depends on the underlying data type of the items in the bag.

Syntax for a Template Class

Our original approach to the bag used a typedef statement to define the underlying data type. Implementing a bag as a template class requires three changes from this original approach. The changes are outlined below.

1. The template class definition. The first change is to the class definition itself. We omit the typedef statement and instead put the template prefix `template <class Item>` immediately before the bag's class definition. This template syntax is compared to the typedef approach here:

Using a Typedef Statement:

```
class Bag
{
    typedef int Item;
    . . .
};
```

Using a Template Class:

```
template <class Item>
class Bag
{

    . . .
};
```
> Omit the typedef statement.

The expression `template <class Item>` is the same template prefix that we have used with template functions. It warns the compiler that the following definition will use an unspecified data type called Item. We are telling the compiler "Item is a data type that will be filled in later; don't worry about it now, just use it inside the bag class!"

2. Functions for the template class. All of the functions that manipulate bags are now dependent upon the Item type. If Item is an integer, then the functions will manipulate bags of integers; if Item is a frijole (whatever that is!), then the functions will manipulate bags of frijoles.

Within the template class definition, the compiler already knows about the dependency on the Item data type. But, *outside of the template class definition* (that is, after the closing semicolon of the definition), some rules must be followed to tell the compiler about the dependency on the Item data type:

- The template prefix `template <class Item>` is placed immediately before each function prototype and implementation. This occurs for member functions and also other functions that manipulate bags. In other words, each of these functions is now a template function, dependent on the data type of the items.

- Each use of the class name (such as `Bag`) as the name of a class is changed to the template class name (such as `Bag<Item>`). This tells the compiler that the class is a template class, rather than an ordinary class.

- Each use of the complete underlying type name (such as `Bag::Item`) may now be shortened to just the type name without the "scope resolution operator" (for example, simplify `Bag::Item` to just `Item`). The reason for this simplification is that the use of the underlying type name is now under the scope of the template prefix, so that `Item` correctly refers to the template parameter.

Some examples can illustrate how these rules are applied outside the template class definition. As a first example, recall that the bag has overloaded the + operator as a nonmember function. For our original `Bag` class, the function's implementation began this way:

```
Bag operator +(const Bag& b1, const Bag& b2)...
```

For the template class, the start of the implementation is changed, as shown here:

```
template <class Item>
Bag<Item> operator +(const Bag<Item>& b1, const Bag<Item>& b2)...
```

One warning: The name `Bag` is changed to `Bag<Item>` *only* when it is used as a class name. In particular, the name `Bag` is also used as the name of the bag's constructor, and that usage remains simply `Bag`.

As a second example of these rules, the new bag template class includes the `grab` member function from Chapter 5. The implementation of the original `grab` function began as shown here:

```
Bag::Item Bag::grab( ) const ...
```

The function's return type is specified as the complete name `Bag::Item`, since the compiler does not recognize the name `Item` on its own. But with the bag template class, the `grab` function's return type is merely `Item`, as shown here:

```
template <class Item>
Item Bag<Item>::grab( ) const ...
```

This uses the simpler return type, `Item`, since `Item` is defined by the template parameter.

3. Make the implementation visible.   The third change is the same annoying requirement that we had with template functions: The implementations of the bag functions must be present in the header file. We recommend the same technique that we used with a toolkit of template functions: Keep the implementations in a separate implementation file, but place an "include" directive at the bottom of the header file to pick up these implementations. With this approach, our new bag has a header file (called `bag4.h` since this is our fourth bag) and an implementation file (`bag4.template`). These two files are in Figures 6.4 and Figure 6.5.

The new bag template class has a few other features that we'll discuss after you look through the header and implementation files.

More about the Template Implementation File

The implementation file for the `Bag` template class (Figure 6.5) stretches over several pages. Which of the different methods of implementing the bag have we used here? Did we use a *static array*, a *dynamic array*, or a *linked list*? We could have used any of them. The actual approach that we used in the new template class is an implementation with a dynamic array.

Keep in mind that the `Bag` template class has only a little new code. Except for the template prefix (which precedes each function) and the use of `Bag<Item>` (instead of just `Bag`), the implementation of the template class is no different than an ordinary `Bag` class with a dynamic array.

Actually, there are two other small changes. One of the small changes we have already mentioned: The implementation of the `grab` function specifies its return value as simply `Item` rather than `Bag::Item`. The second change is that there is no longer a need for `#include "bag4.h"` in the implementation file (since the implementation file itself is included in the header file).

A third small change may be needed for some compilers because one of the bag's constructors has a default argument. Some compilers require this default argument to be listed in both the prototype and the implementation for a template function (although we have followed the more usual standard of listing it only in the prototype).

Parameter Matching for Member Functions of Template Classes

In the implementation of a template function, we are careful to help the compiler by providing a template parameter for each of the function's parameters. (See "Mismatches for Template Function Arguments" on page 269.) However, this help is not needed for *member* functions of a template class. For example, we can use a simple `size_t` parameter for the bag's `resize` function. Unlike an ordinary template function, the compiler is able to match a `size_t` parameter of a member function with any of the usual integer arguments (such as *int* or *const int*). If b is a bag object of our new template class, then we may call `b.resize(42)`, with the actual argument being the integer 42. The compiler will convert this integer to the equivalent `size_t` value.

FIGURE 6.4 Header File for the Bag Template Class

A Header File

```
// FILE: bag4.h
// TEMPLATE CLASS PROVIDED: Bag<Item> (a container template class for a collection of items)
//     The template parameter, Item, is the data type of the items in the Bag. It may be any of the
//     C++ built-in types (int, char, etc.), or a class with a default constructor, a copy constructor,
//     an assignment operator, and operators to test for equality (x == y) and non-equality (x != y).
//
// MEMBER CONSTANT for the Bag<Item> template class:
//     static const size_t DEFAULT_CAPACITY = _____
//        This constant is the initial capacity of a Bag that is created by the default constructor.
//
// CONSTRUCTOR for the Bag<Item> template class:
//     Bag(size_t initial_capacity = DEFAULT_CAPACITY)
//        Postcondition: The Bag is empty with a the specified initial capacity. The insert
//        function works efficiently (without allocating new memory) until this capacity is reached.
//
// MODIFICATION MEMBER FUNCTIONS for the Bag<Item> template class:
//     void resize(size_t new_capacity)
//        Postcondition: The Bag's current capacity is changed to new_capacity (but not less
//        than the number of items currently in the Bag). The insert function will work efficiently
//        without allocating new memory) until the capacity is reached.
//
//     void insert(const Item& entry)
//        Postcondition: A new copy of entry has been added to the Bag.
//
//     void remove(const Item& target)
//        Postcondition: If target was in the Bag, then one copy of target has been removed from
//        the Bag; otherwise the Bag is unchanged.
//
//     void operator +=(const Bag<Item>& addend)
//        Postcondition: Each item in addend has been added to this Bag.
//
// CONSTANT MEMBER FUNCTIONS for the Bag<Item> template class:
//     size_t size( ) const
//        Postcondition: Return value is the total number of items in the Bag.
//
//     size_t occurrences(const Item& target) const
//        Postcondition: Return value is number of times target is in the Bag.
//
//     Item grab( ) const
//        Postcondition: The return value is a randomly selected item from the Bag.
//
// NONMEMBER FUNCTIONS for the Bag<Item> template class:
//     template <class Item>
//     Bag<Item> operator +(const Bag<Item>& b1, const Bag<Item>& b2)
//        Postcondition: The Bag returned is the union of b1 and b2.
```

(continued)

(FIGURE 6.4 continued)

```
//
// VALUE SEMANTICS for the Bag<Item> template class:
//     Assignments and the copy constructor may be used with Bag<Item> objects.
//
// DYNAMIC MEMORY USAGE by the Bag<Item> template class:
//     If there is insufficient dynamic memory, then the following functions call new_handler:
//     the constructors, resize, insert, operator += , operator +, and the assignment operator.


#ifndef BAG4_H
#define BAG4_H
#include <stdlib.h>  // Provides size_t
```

The template prefix is used instead of a typedef.

```
    template <class Item>
    class Bag
    {
    public:
        // MEMBER CONSTANTS -- See Appendix E if this fails to compile
        static const size_t DEFAULT_CAPACITY = 30;
        // CONSTRUCTORS and DESTRUCTOR
        Bag(size_t initial_capacity = DEFAULT_CAPACITY);
        Bag(const Bag& source);
        ~Bag( );
        // MODIFICATION MEMBER FUNCTIONS
        void resize(size_t capacity);
        void insert(const Item& entry);
        void remove(const Item& target);
        void operator +=(const Bag& addend);
        void operator =(const Bag& source);
        // CONSTANT MEMBER FUNCTIONS
        size_t size( ) const { return used; }
        size_t occurrences(const Item& target) const;
        Item grab( ) const;
        // FRIEND FUNCTION
        friend Bag<Item> operator +(const Bag<Item>& b1, const Bag<Item>& b2);
    private:
        Item *data;          // Pointer to partially filled dynamic array
        size_t used;         // How much of array is being used
        size_t capacity;     // Current capacity of the Bag
    };


#include "bag4.template"   // Include the implementation.

#endif
```

Most compilers require the implementation file to be included in the header file for a template class.

bag4.h **FTP**

| **FIGURE 6.5** | Implementation File for the Bag Template Class |

An Implementation File

```
//  FILE: bag4.template
//  TEMPLATE CLASS IMPLEMENTED: Bag<Item> (see bag4.h for documentation)
//  This file should be included in the header file and not compiled separately.
//  INVARIANT for the Bag ADT:
//    1. The number of items in the Bag is in the member variable used.
//    2. The actual items of the Bag are stored in a partially filled array.
//       The array is a dynamic array, pointed to by the member variable data.
//    3. The size of the dynamic array is in the member variable capacity.

#include <assert.h>   // Provides assert
#include <stdlib.h>   // Provides size_t, rand

template <class Item>
Bag<Item>::Bag(size_t initial_capacity)
// Library facilities used: stdlib.h
{
    data = new Item[initial_capacity];
    capacity = initial_capacity;
    used = 0;
}


template <class Item>
Bag<Item>::Bag(const Bag<Item>& source)
// Library facilities used: stdlib.h
{
    size_t i;   // An array index

    data = new Item[source.capacity];
    capacity = source.capacity;
    used = source.used;
    for (i = 0; i < used; i++)
        data[i] = source.data[i];
}


template <class Item>
Bag<Item>::~Bag( )
// Library facilities used: assert.h
{
    delete [ ] data;
}
```

Outside of the class definition, the use of Bag as a type name is changed to Bag<Item>.

(continued)

(FIGURE 6.5 continued)

```
template <class Item>
void Bag<Item>::resize(size_t new_capacity)
// Library facilities used: stdlib.h
{
    size_t i;
    Item *larger_array;

    if (new_capacity == capacity)
        return;  // The allocated memory is already the right size.

    if (new_capacity < used)
        new_capacity = used; // Can't allocate less than we are using.

    larger_array = new Item[new_capacity];
    for (i = 0; i < used; i++)
        larger_array[i] = data[i];
    delete [ ] data;
    data = larger_array;
    capacity = new_capacity;
}



template <class Item>
void Bag<Item>::insert(const Item& entry)
{
    if (used == capacity)
        resize(used+1);
    data[used] = entry;
    used++;
}



template <class Item>
Item Bag<Item>::grab( ) const
// Library facilities used: assert.h, stdlib.h
{
    size_t i;

    assert(size( ) > 0);
    i = (rand( ) % size( )); // i is in the range of 0 to size( ) - 1.
    return data[i];
}
```

(continued)

(FIGURE 6.5 continued)

```
template <class Item>
void Bag<Item>::remove(const Item& target)
{
    size_t index;  // The location of target in the data array

    // First, set index to the location of target in the data array,
    // which could be as small as 0 or as large as used - 1.
    // If target is not in the array, then index will be set equal to used.
    for (index = 0; (index < used) && (data[index] != target); index++)
        // No work is needed in the body of this for-loop.
        ;

    if (index == used)
        return;  // target isn't in the Bag, so no work to do.

    // When execution reaches here, target is in the Bag at data[index].
    // So, reduce used by 1 and copy the last item onto data[index].
    used--;
    data[index] = data[used];
}


template <class Item>
void Bag<Item>::operator +=(const Bag<Item>& addend)
// Library facilities used: assert.h, stdlib.h
{
    size_t i;  // An array index
    size_t other_bag_size = addend.used;

    if (used + other_bag_size < capacity)
        resize(used + other_bag_size);
    for (i = 0; i < other_bag_size; i++)
    {
        data[used] = addend.data[i];
        used++;
    }
}
```

(continued)

(FIGURE 6.5 continued)

```
template <class Item>
void Bag<Item>::operator =(const Bag<Item>& source)
// Library facilities used: stdlib.h
{
    size_t i;
    Item *new_data;

    if (capacity != source.capacity)
    {
        new_data = new Item[source.capacity];
        delete [ ]data;
        data = new_data;
        capacity = source.capacity;
    }
    used = source.used;
    for (i = 0; i < used; i++)
        data[i] = source.data[i];
}


template <class Item>
size_t Bag<Item>::occurrences(const Item& target) const
// Library facilities used: stdlib.h
{
    size_t answer;   // Number of times target occurs
    size_t i;        // An array index

    answer = 0;
    for (i = 0; i < used; i++)
        if (target == data[i])
            answer++;
    return answer;
}


template <class Item>
Bag<Item> operator +(const Bag<Item>& b1, const Bag<Item>& b2)
{
    Bag<Item> answer(b1.capacity + b2.capacity);

    answer += b1;
    answer += b2;
    return answer;
}
```

bag4.template   FTP

Programming Tip: Implement the typedef Version First

Whenever you implement a template class, you should first implement a version with a typedef. Debug this simple version, and after debugging you can easily convert the definition to a template class. This will save much debugging time.

Using the Template Class

Using the Bag template class is easy. The program includes the bag4.h header file, and then any kind of bag can be declared. To declare a bag, you write the class name, Bag, followed by the name of the data type for the template parameter (in angle brackets). For example, if a program needs one bag of characters and one bag of double numbers, then the program uses these two declarations:

```
Bag<char> letters;
Bag<double> scores;
```

When an actual bag is declared, as in these examples, the template parameter is said to be **instantiated**. In the letters bag, the template parameter is instantiated as a character; in the scores bag, the template parameter is instantiated as a double number. A program that includes the mystring.h header file (from Chapter 4) can even instantiate the template parameter as a string, creating a bag of strings, as shown here:

```
Bag<String> verbs;
```

Figure 6.6 on page 288 shows a demonstration program that uses a bag of integers and two bags of strings. The program asks the user to type several adjectives, numbers, and names. These items are placed in the bags, and then items are grabbed out of the bags in order for the program to write a silly story called "Life."

The bags are declared in the demonstration program as you would expect:

```
Bag<String> adjectives;  // Contains adjectives typed by user
Bag<int>    ages;        // Contains ages in the teens
Bag<String> names;       // Contains names typed by user
```

After these declarations, the program can use the bags adjectives and names just like any other bag of strings, whereas ages can be used just like any other bag of integers. Let's discuss the details of the story-writing program.

Details of the Story-Writing Program

The story-writing program uses a function, `get_items`, which is actually a template function with this specification:

```
template <class Item, class SizeType, class MessageType>
void get_items(Bag<Item>& collection, SizeType n, MessageType description);
// Postcondition: The string description has been written as a prompt to the
// screen. Then n items have been read from cin and added to the collection.
```

The function uses the third parameter, `description`, as part of a prompt that asks the user to type n items. For example, if `description` is the string constant `"first names"` and n is 4, then the `get_items` function writes this prompt:

```
Please type 4 first names, separated by spaces.
Press the <return> key after the final entry:
```

The function then reads n items and places them in the bag by activating the member function `collection.insert`. Because the function is a template function that depends on the `Item` data type, we can use the function with any kind of bag—with a bag of strings, or a bag of integers, or even some other kind of bag.

In fact, the template prefix indicates that the function depends upon *three* data types:

- `class Item`: This is the type of the item in the bag.
- `class SizeType`: This is the type of the second parameter, n. It may be any integer data type such as *int* or `size_t`.
- `class MessageType`: This may be any printable data type such as a string constant or even a string from our `mystring.h`.

The literary merit of the program's story is debatable, but the ability to use several different kinds of bags in the same program clearly is important.

Self-Test Exercises

7. When you write a template class, where does the template prefix occur?
8. Name two places in the bag template class where the name `Bag` is not changed to `Bag<Item>`.
9. How long would it take you to convert an ordinary bag implementation to a template class?
10. Write declarations for three bags with three different item types. Can you use all three bags in a single program?

FIGURE 6.6 | Demonstration Program for the Bag Template Class

A Program

```
// FILE: author.cxx
// The program reads some words into Bags of Strings, and some numbers into
// a Bag of integers. Then a silly story is written using these words.

#include <iostream.h> // Provides cout and cin
#include <stdlib.h>   // Provides EXIT_SUCCESS
#include "bag4.h"      // Provides the Bag template class
#include "mystring.h" // If available, this could be changed to the standard String class
const int ITEMS_PER_BAG = 4;   // Number of items to put into each Bag
const int MANY_SENTENCES = 3;  // Number of sentences in the silly story

// PROTOTYPE for a function used by this demonstration program
template <class Item, class SizeType, class MessageType>
void get_items(Bag<Item>& collection, SizeType n, MessageType description);
// Postcondition: The string description has been written as a prompt to the
// screen. Then n items have been read from cin and added to the collection.

int main( )
{
    Bag<String> adjectives;  // Contains adjectives typed by user
    Bag<int>    ages;        // Contains ages in the teens typed by user
    Bag<String> names;       // Contains names typed by user
    int line_number;          // Number of the output line

    // Fill the three Bags with items typed by the program's user.
    cout << "Help me write a story.\n\n";
    get_items(adjectives, ITEMS_PER_BAG, "adjectives that describe a mood");
    get_items(ages,       ITEMS_PER_BAG, "integers in the teens");
    get_items(names,      ITEMS_PER_BAG, "first names");
    cout << "Thank you for your kind assistance.\n\n";

    // Use the items to write a silly story.
    cout << "LIFE\n";
    cout << "by A. Computer\n\n";
    for (line_number = 1; line_number <= MANY_SENTENCES; line_number++)
        cout << names.grab( )
             << " was only "
             << ages.grab( )
             << " years old, but he/she was "
             << adjectives.grab( )
             << ".\n";
    cout << "Life is " << adjectives.grab( ) << ".\n\n";
    cout << "The (" << adjectives.grab( ) << ") end\n\n";

    return EXIT_SUCCESS;
}
```

(continued)

(FIGURE 6.6 continued)

```
template <class Item, class SizeType, class MessageType>
void get_items(Bag<Item>& collection, SizeType n, MessageType description)
// Library facilities used: iostream.h, bag4.h
{
    Item user_input; // An item typed by the program's user
    size_t i;

    cout << "Please type " << n << " " << description;
    cout << ", separated by spaces.\n";
    cout << "Press the <return> key after the final entry:\n";
    for (i = 1; i <= n; i++)
    {
        cin >> user_input;
        collection.insert(user_input);
    }
    cout << endl;
}
```

A Sample Dialogue

```
Help me write a story.

Please type 4 adjectives that describe a mood, separated by spaces.
Press the <return> key after the final entry:
joyous  happy  sad  glum

Please type 4 integers in the teens, separated by spaces.
Press the <return> key after the final entry:
19  16  13  16

Please type 4 first names, separated by spaces.
Press the <return> key after the final entry:
Mike  Walt  Cathy  Harry

Thank you for your kind assistance.

LIFE
by A. Computer

Cathy was only 13 years old, but he/she was happy.
Walt was only 19 years old, but he/she was happy.
Mike was only 16 years old, but he/she was joyous.
Life is glum.

The (sad) end.
```

author.cxx   FTP

6.4   USING TEMPLATES IN THE LINKED LIST TOOLKIT

In "A Linked List Toolkit" on page 207, we implemented a toolkit of ten functions for manipulating linked lists. Each linked list consists of a sequence of nodes, and each node contains a data item of some type.

As you might guess, these functions will be more useful if we implement the Node as a template class that depends on the underlying Item data type. Each of the toolkit functions can then be implemented as a template function that also depends on the Item.

Here is a comparison of the original toolkit's Node definition to our new plan:

Original Linked List Toolkit:

```
struct Node
{
    typedef double Item;
    Item data;
    Node *link;
};
```

New Linked List Toolkit:

```
template <class Item>
struct Node
{
    Item data;
    Node *link;
};
```

With the definition on the right, the Node is now a template class, or perhaps "template struct" would be a better description. Each of the ten toolkit functions can be changed to a template function by using the template prefix, changing the name Node to Node<Item>, and replacing occurrences of Node::Item by the template parameter name Item. For example, here is the original prototype for the ordinary list_insert function:

```
void list_insert(Node* previous_ptr, const Node::Item& entry);
```

The new prototype for the list_insert template function is:

```
template <class Item>
void list_insert(Node<Item>* previous_ptr, const Item& entry);
```

The implementation of list_insert is shown here:

```
template <class Item>
void list_insert(Node<Item>* previous_ptr, const Item& entry)
{
    Node<Item> *insert_ptr;

    insert_ptr = new Node<Item>;
    insert_ptr->data = entry;
    insert_ptr->link = previous_ptr->link;
    previous_ptr->link = insert_ptr;
}
```

Notice that we have changed each occurrence of the type name `Node` to `Node<Item>`, and the original type `Node::Item` is now simply `Item`.

One of the toolkit's functions, `list_locate`, needs some extra care. The original prototype has a `size_t` parameter, as shown here:

```
Node* list_locate(Node* head_ptr, size_t position);
```

As we explained in the pitfall "Mismatches for Template Function Arguments" on page 269, the presence of the `size_t` parameter can cause mismatches for an argument type. The solution is the same approach that we used before: Add a second template parameter. The result is this prototype:

```
template <class Item, class SizeType>
Node<Item>* list_locate(Node<Item>* head_ptr, SizeType position);
```

Apart from the use of the templates, the implementation of `list_locate` is the same as our original implementation:

```
template <class Item, class SizeType>
Node<Item>* list_locate(Node<Item>* head_ptr, SizeType position)
// Library facilities used: assert.h, stdlib.h
{
    Node<Item> *cursor;
    size_t i;

    assert(position > 0);

    cursor = head_ptr;
    for (i = 1; (i != position) && (cursor != NULL); i++)
        cursor = cursor->link;
    return cursor;
}
```

Prototypes for the ten template functions appear in the header file for the template version of the toolkit in Figure 6.7. We call this file `link2.h`, since it is our second linked list toolkit. The implementations differ little from the original toolkit, so we leave them for you to work out yourself. When you work them out, you should place them in an implementation file `link2.template`.

Self-Test Exercises

11. Suppose one of the toolkit functions has a local variable called `insert_ptr`, which is a pointer to a `Node`. How will you declare this variable in the template version of the toolkit?

12. Why is it a bad idea to have a `size_t` parameter for a template function?

13. Write the implementation of the template version of `list_head_remove`.

FIGURE 6.7	Header File for the Template Version of the Linked List Toolkit

A Header File

```
// FILE: link2.h
// PROVIDES: A toolkit of ten template functions for manipulating linked lists. Each node of the
// list contains a piece of data and a pointer to the next node, as shown in this template struct:
//
//    template <class Item>          Item may be any of the C++ built-in types
//    struct Node                    (int, char, etc.), or a class with a default
//    {                              constructor, an assignment operator,
//        Item data;                 and a test for equality (x == y).
//        Node *link;
//    };
//
// FUNCTIONS in the linked list toolkit:
//    template <class Item>
//    size_t list_length(Node<Item>* head_ptr)
//       Precondition: head_ptr is the head pointer of a linked list.
//       Postcondition: The value returned is the number of nodes in the linked list. The list
//       itself is unaltered.
//
//    template <class Item>
//    void list_head_insert(Node<Item>*& head_ptr, const Item& entry)
//       Precondition: head_ptr is the head pointer of a linked list.
//       Postcondition: A new node containing the given entry has been added at the head of
//       the linked list; head_ptr now points to the head of the new, longer linked list.
//
//    template <class Item>
//    void list_insert(Node<Item>* previous_ptr, const Item& entry)
//       Precondition: previous_ptr points to a node in a linked list.
//       Postcondition: A new node containing the given entry has been added after the node
//       that previous_ptr points to.
//
//    template <class Item>
//    Node<Item>* list_search(Node<Item>* head_ptr, const Item& target)
//       Precondition: head_ptr is the head pointer of a linked list.
//       Postcondition: The pointer returned points to the first node containing the specified
//       target in its data member. If there is no such node, the null pointer is returned. The list
//       itself is unaltered.
//
```

(continued)

(FIGURE 6.7 continued)

```
//      template <class Item, class SizeType>
//      Node<Item>* list_locate(Node<Item>* head_ptr, SizeType position)
//         Precondition: head_ptr is the head pointer of a list, and position > 0.
//         Postcondition: The pointer returned points to the node at the specified position in the
//         list. (The head node is position 1, the next node is position 2, and so on.) If there is no
//         such position, then the null pointer is returned. The list itself is unaltered.
//
//      template <class Item>
//      void list_head_remove(Node<Item>*& head_ptr)
//         Precondition: head_ptr is the head pointer of a linked list, with at least one node.
//         Postcondition: The head node has been removed and returned to the heap;
//         head_ptr is now the head pointer of the new, shorter linked list.
//
//      template <class Item>
//      void list_remove(Node<Item>* previous_ptr)
//         Precondition: previous_ptr points to a node in a linked list, and this is not the tail node
//         of the list.
//         Postcondition: The node after previous_ptr has been removed.
//
//      template <class Item>
//      void list_clear(Node<Item>*& head_ptr)
//         Precondition: head_ptr is the head pointer of a linked list.
//         Postcondition: All nodes of the list have been returned to the heap, and the head_ptr is
//         now NULL.
//
//      template <class Item>
//      void list_copy
//         (Node<Item>* source_ptr, Node<Item>*& head_ptr, Node<Item>*& tail_ptr)
//         Precondition: source_ptr is the head pointer of a linked list.
//         Postcondition: head_ptr and tail_ptr are the head and tail pointers for a new list that
//         contains the same items as the list pointed to by source_ptr.
//
//      template <class Item>
//      void list_piece
//         (Node<Item>* source_ptr, Node<Item>* end_ptr,
//          Node<Item>*& head_ptr, Node<Item>*& tail_ptr)
//         Precondition: source_ptr and end_ptr are pointers to nodes on the same
//         linked list, with the source_ptr node at or before the end_ptr node.
//         Postcondition: head_ptr and tail_ptr are the head and tail pointers for a new linked list
//         that contains the items from source_ptr to end_ptr. The original list is unaltered.
```

(continued)

(FIGURE 6.7 continued)

```
#ifndef LINK2_H
#define LINK2_H
#include <stdlib.h> // Provides size_t

    template <class Item>
    struct Node
    {
        Item data;
        Node *link;
    };

    // FUNCTIONS for the linked list toolkit
    template <class Item>
    size_t list_length(Node<Item>* head_ptr);

    template <class Item>
    void list_head_insert(Node<Item>*& head_ptr, const Item& entry);

    template <class Item>
    void list_insert(Node<Item>* previous_ptr, const Item& entry);

    template <class Item>
    Node<Item>* list_search(Node<Item>* head_ptr, const Item& target);

    template <class Item, class SizeType>
    Node<Item>* list_locate(Node<Item>* head_ptr, SizeType position);

    template <class Item>
    void list_head_remove(Node<Item>*& head_ptr);

    template <class Item>
    void list_remove(Node<Item>* previous_ptr);

    template <class Item>
    void list_clear(Node<Item>*& head_ptr);

    template <class Item>
    void list_copy(Node<Item>* source_ptr, Node<Item>*& head_ptr, Node<Item>*& tail_ptr);

    template <class Item>
    void list_piece
        (Node<Item>*  source_ptr, Node<Item>*  end_ptr,
         Node<Item>*& head_ptr,   Node<Item>*& tail_ptr);

#include "link2.template"   // Include the implementation.
#endif
```

link2.h **FTP**

6.5   THE BAG TEMPLATE CLASS WITH A LINKED LIST

We can use the template version of the linked list toolkit to implement another Bag template class. This new version of the Bag template class will store the items on a linked list, just like the Bag class in Section 5.3. But our new version will be a *template* class, making use of the template version of the linked list toolkit. Here is the declaration of the new Bag template class, which includes all of the previous bag member functions. The new definition also includes five new functions (start, advance, current, remove_current, and is_item) and one new private member variable (current_ptr) that we'll discuss in a moment:

```cpp
#include "link2.h" // Provides the linked list toolkit
template <class Item>
class Bag
{
public:
    // CONSTRUCTORS and DESTRUCTOR
    Bag( );
    Bag(const Bag& source);
    ~Bag( );
    // MODIFICATION MEMBER FUNCTIONS
    void insert(const Item& entry);
    void remove(const Item& target);
    void operator +=(const Bag& addend);
    void operator =(const Bag& source);
    void start( );
    void advance( );
    void remove_current( );
    // CONSTANT MEMBER FUNCTIONS
    size_t size( ) const { return many_nodes; }
    size_t occurrences(const Item& target) const;
    Item grab( ) const;
    Item current( ) const;
    bool is_item( ) const;
private:
    Node<Item> *head_ptr;       // Head pointer for the list
    Node<Item> *current_ptr;    // Points to node of internal iterator
    size_t many_nodes;          // Number of nodes on the list
};
```

Within the bag's class definition we can refer to the class Bag on its own, with no need to specify the Item. However, when we use the Node class in the definition Node<Item> *head_ptr, we must use the full name Node<Item>. This indicates that we are using a node, and that the data in the node is the same data type as the bag's items. For example, consider this declaration:

```
Bag<char> vowels;
```

This declares a bag with the item instantiated as a *char*. This bag has a private member variable, `head_ptr`, which is a pointer to a `Node<char>`. And, of course, all of this bag's member functions (such as `insert` and `remove`) will deal with characters, too.

As an example, here is the implementation of the new template bag's `grab` function:

```
template <class Item>
Item Bag<Item>::grab( )
// Library facilities used: assert.h, stdlib.h, link2.h
{
    size_t i;
    Node<Item> *cursor;

    assert(size( ) > 0);

    i = (rand( ) % size( )) + 1;
    cursor = list_locate(head_ptr, i);
    return cursor->data;
}
```

This implementation has three differences from the original implementation in Figure 5.13 on page 247. First, this is a template function, so the template prefix `template <class Item>` precedes the function implementation. Second, whenever Bag or Node appears as a data type, we must now use `Bag<Item>` or `Node<Item>` instead, indicating that both the bag and the node are template classes. Third, the return type of the function is now merely `Item`, rather than `Bag::Item` (since the name `Item` is defined from the template parameter).

An Internal Iterator

Our new bag definition includes five new functions: `start`, `advance`, `current`, `remove_current`, and `is_item`. The purpose of these functions is to allow a programmer to step through the items of a bag one at a time, in a manner that is similar to the list ADT. However, unlike the list ADT, we cannot add items at particular spots as we are stepping through the bag's items. But we can step through the bag, get a copy of each item, and then process these items in some way.

The capability to step through the items of a container class is called an **iterator** for the class. Because we have provided the capability via member functions, the iterator is sometimes called an **internal iterator.** Here are the precise specifications for our five internal iterator functions:

```
template <class Item>
void Bag<Item>::start( );
// Postcondition: The Bag's internal iterator has been started, so that a
// programmer may step through the Bag's items one at a time.

template <class Item>
void Bag<Item>::advance( );
// Precondition: is_item returns true.
// Postcondition: If there are more items for the internal iterator to step
// through, then the internal iterator moves to a new item, and is_item
// still returns true. Otherwise, is_item now returns false.

template <class Item>
Item Bag<Item>::current( ) const;
// Precondition: is_item returns true.
// Postcondition: The return value is the current item of the internal iterator.

template <class Item>
void remove_current( );
// Precondition: is_item returns true.
// Postcondition: The current item of the internal iterator has been
// removed from the bag. If there are more items for the internal iterator,
// the internal iterator has also been moved to a new item, and is_item still
// returns true. Otherwise, is_item now returns false.

template <class Item>
bool Bag<Item>::is_item( ) const;
// Postcondition: A true return value indicates that the internal iterator
// has a valid current item that may be retrieved by the current member
// function. A false return value indicates that there is no valid current item.
```

For example, the following code uses the internal iterator of a bag b to print all of the items in b:

```
for (b.start( ); b.is_item( ); b.advance( ))
    cout << b.current( ) << endl;
```

You may be wondering whether the iterator has provided some kind of order to the bag's items. After all, doesn't the iterator step through the items in some kind of order? The answer is both yes and no. The iterator certainly does step through the bag's items one after another, but the programmer who uses the bag has no control over what this order might be. In fact, depending on our implementation, the iterator might even change its ordering so that a programmer who uses the bag cannot even count on the same order occurring during a second use of the iterator.

Invalidating the Iterator

You have seen how to use the proposed bag iterator. You should also realize that some operations will automatically invalidate the bag iterator. For example, a programmer might start the iterator, examine a few items, and then insert a new item into the bag. We suggest that the act of inserting a new item, or making certain other changes to the bag, should immediately invalidate the iterator (so that is_item returns false). After the invalidation, the iterator may be restarted (by activating the start function), and all the items of the revised bag may be traversed. But the key point about our iterator is that changing the bag in any way will invalidate its iterator. The rule that "changes invalidate the iterator" is a common rule for container classes, and a note about the potential invalidation should be included in your class documentation.

For our new bag, this complete documentation is shown in Figure 6.8. This header file, called bag5.h, is our fifth approach to the bag. Most of the new bag implementation (bag5.template) is left up to you. But we will make a few comments about implementing the internal iterator.

FIGURE 6.8	Header File for the Bag Template Class with an Internal Iterator

A Header File

```
// FILE: bag5.h
// TEMPLATE CLASS PROVIDED:  Bag<Item> (a container template class for a collection of items)
//     The template parameter, Item, is the data type of the items in the Bag.
//     It may be any of the C++ built-in types (int, char, etc.), or a class with a default
//     constructor, an assignment operator, a copy constructor, and operators to test for
//     equality (x == y) and non-equality (x != y).
//
// CONSTRUCTOR for the Bag<Item> template class:
//   Bag( )
//       Postcondition: The Bag is empty.
//
// MODIFICATION MEMBER FUNCTIONS for the Bag<Item> template class:
//     void insert(const Item& entry)
//       Postcondition: A new copy of entry has been added to the Bag.
//
//     void remove(const Item& target)
//       Postcondition: If target was in the Bag, then one copy of target has been removed from
//       the Bag; otherwise the Bag is unchanged.
//
//     void operator +=(const Bag<Item>& addend)
//       Postcondition: Each item in addend has been added to this Bag.
//
```

(continued)

(FIGURE 6.8 continued)

```
//     void start( )
//         Postcondition: The Bag's internal iterator has been started, so that a
//         programmer may step through the Bag's items one at a time.
//
//     void advance( )
//         Precondition: is_item returns true.
//         Postcondition: If there are more items for the internal iterator to step through, then
//         the internal iterator moves to a new item, and is_item still returns true. Otherwise,
//         is_item now returns false.
//
//     void remove_current( )
//         Precondition: is_item returns true.
//         Postcondition: The current item of the internal iterator has been removed from the bag
//         If there are more items for the internal iterator, the internal iterator has also been
//         moved to a new item, and is_item still returns true. Otherwise, is_item now returns false.
//
// CONSTANT MEMBER FUNCTIONS for the Bag<Item> template class:
//     size_t size( ) const
//         Postcondition: Return value is the total number of items in the Bag.
//
//     size_t occurrences(const Item& target) const
//         Postcondition: Return value is number of times target is in the Bag.
//
//     Item grab( ) const
//         Postcondition: The return value is a randomly selected item from the Bag.
//
//     Item current( ) const
//         Precondition: is_item returns true.
//         Postcondition: The return value is the current item of the internal iterator.
//
//     bool is_item( ) const
//         Postcondition: A true return value indicates that the internal iterator
//         has a valid current item that may be retrieved by the current member
//         function. A false return value indicates that there is no valid current item.
//
// NONMEMBER FUNCTIONS for the Bag<Item> template class:
//     template <class Item>
//     Bag<Item> operator +(const Bag<Item>& b1, const Bag<Item>& b2)
//         Postcondition: The Bag returned is the union of b1 and b2.
//
// VALUE SEMANTICS for the Bag<Item> template class:
//     Assignments and the copy constructor may be used with Bag<Item> objects.
//
// DYNAMIC MEMORY USAGE by the Bag<Item> template class:
//     If there is insufficient dynamic memory, then the following functions call new_handler:
//     the constructors, insert, operator += , operator +, and the assignment operator.
```

(continued)

(FIGURE 6.8 continued)

```
//
//  INTERNAL ITERATOR:
//     Calling insert, remove, or += will invalidate the internal iterator (so that is_item returns
//     false).

#ifndef BAG5_H
#define BAG5_H
#include <stdlib.h> // Provides NULL and size_t
#include "link2.h"   // Provides the linked list toolkit

    template <class Item>
    class Bag
    {
    public:
        // CONSTRUCTORS and DESTRUCTOR
        Bag( );
        Bag(const Bag& source);
        ~Bag( );
        // MODIFICATION MEMBER FUNCTIONS
        void insert(const Item& entry);
        void remove(const Item& target);
        void operator +=(const Bag& addend);
        void operator =(const Bag& source);
        void start( );
        void advance( );
        void remove_current( );
        // CONSTANT MEMBER FUNCTIONS
        size_t size( ) const { return many_nodes; }
        size_t occurrences(const Item& target) const;
        Item grab( ) const;
        Item current( ) const;
        bool is_item( ) const;
    private:
        Node<Item> *head_ptr;      // Head pointer for the list
        Node<Item> *current_ptr;   // Points to node of internal iterator
        size_t many_nodes;         // Number of nodes on the list
    };

    // NONMEMBER FUNCTIONS for the Bag class
    template <class Item>
    Bag<Item> operator +(const Bag<Item>& b1, const Bag<Item>& b2);

#include "bag5.template"          // Include the implementation

#endif
```

bag5.h **FTP**

Implementing the Internal Iterator

The iterator is implemented by using an extra private member variable, current_ptr, which is a pointer to a node. When the iterator has a valid current item, then current_ptr points to the node containing this item. When there is no valid current item, then current_ptr is NULL. Any of the functions that invalidate the iterator can simply set current_ptr to NULL.

Some care is needed to correctly implement the copy constructor and assignment operator. For example, suppose that x and y are bags, and that y's iterator has already stepped through three of its items. Then, after the assignment statement x = y, the bag x should have the same items as y, and x's iterator should have stepped through the same three items. In other words, whenever an assignment is carried out, or the copy constructor is used, *all* features of the bag must be copied—including the current state of the internal iterator.

The remove_current member function also needs some thought. Removing the current item would be easy if we maintained an extra pointer to the node *before* the current item. But we have no such "precursor." Instead, the current item can be removed with these three steps: (1) Copy the data from the head node to the current node. At this point we now have two copies of the item at the head of the linked list, but we no longer have the item that we are removing. (2) Advance current_ptr to the next node. (3) Get rid of the extra copy of the data from the head node by calling list_head_remove.

External Iterators

Internal iterators are a simple solution to the problem of stepping through the items of a container class. But internal iterators also have a problem. Suppose that your program needs to step through the items of a bag in two different ways. With an internal iterator, the two traversals of the bag items must occur sequentially—stepping through all the items for the first time, then restarting the iterator, and finally stepping through all the items for the second time. However, sometimes you would like to have the two different traversals occurring simultaneously. The first traversal could start, stepping through part of the items, but before the first traversal is finished, the second traversal starts its work. Simultaneous traversals are not easily handled with internal iterators.

The solution is to implement a separate class, called an *external* iterator for the bag. The external iterator class could be called BagIterator, and one of the BagIterator member functions attaches the BagIterator to a specified bag. Now, if we need to step through the items of a bag x two different times, then we can declare two separate BagIterator objects, attaching both of these external iterators to x.

We won't use external iterators until late in this text, but Programming Project 5 on page 305 does provide details if you want to implement an external iterator for the bag.

Summary of the Five Bag Implementations

If nothing else, you should now know how to program your way out of a paper bag, using one of the five bag classes of Figure 6.9. The bag class is a good example to show all these different approaches to implementing a simple container class, but keep in mind that the same approaches can be used for any container class.

Self-Test Exercises

14. Within the definition of the Bag template class, can we write Bag on its own, or do we need Bag<Item>? Can we write Node on its own, or do we need Node<Item>?

15. What is the primary difference between the Bag template class suggested in this section, and the Bag template class from Section 6.3?

16. What is the primary difference between the Bag template class suggested in this section, and the Bag class from Chapter 5?

17. What is the primary purpose of an internal iterator? When might you need to use an external iterator instead?

FIGURE 6.9 Our Five Bag Classes (with template classes shaded).

Approach	Define Item with...	Files
Store the items in an array with a fixed size.	typedef	bag1.h and bag1.cxx in Section 3.1
Store the items in a dynamic array.	typedef	bag2.h and bag2.cxx in Section 4.3
Store the items in a linked list, using the linked list toolkit.	typedef	bag3.h and bag3.cxx in Section 5.3
Store items in a dynamic array.	template parameter	bag4.h and bag4.template in Section 6.3
Store items in a linked list, using the template version of the linked list toolkit. This implementation also has an internal iterator.	template parameter	bag5.h and bag5.template left up to you in Section 6.5

CHAPTER SUMMARY

- A **template function** is similar to an ordinary function with one important difference: The definition of a template function can depend on an underlying data type. The underlying data type is given a name—such as `Item`—but `Item` is not pinned down to a specific type anywhere in the function's implementation.

- When a template function is *used*, the compiler examines the types of the arguments. At that point, the compiler automatically determines the data type of `Item`.

- In a single program, several different usages of a template function can result in several different underlying data types.

- When a class depends on an underlying data type, the class can be implemented as a **template class**.

- A toolkit, such as the linked list toolkit, can be implemented as a collection of template functions, providing more flexibility than an ordinary toolkit.

- An **iterator** allows a programmer to easily step through the items of a container class. Iterators may be **internal** (implemented as member functions of the container class) or **external** (implemented as a separate class). Internal iterators are easier to implement and use, but external iterators allow the flexibility of several traversals to occur simultaneously.

- We have seen many approaches to implementing a container class such as the bag. Both the underlying data structure (fixed array, dynamic array, or linked list) and the method of defining an item (typedef or template parameter) can be varied.

Solutions to Self-Test Exercises   **?**

1. A single template function serves to implement many functions that are identical except for a different underlying data type.

2. The template prefix defines the list of underlying data types that a template function depends upon, for example:
   ```
   template <class Item>
   ```
   It appears immediately before the prototype and immediately before the implementation of the template function.

3. Here is one implementation:
   ```
   template <class Item>
   void compare(const Item& a, const Item& b)
   // Postcondition: A message has
   // been printed indicating whether
   // a and b are different or the same.
   // Note: The Item type must have the
   // == operator defined.
   // Library facilities used: iostream.h
   ```
   (continued)

3. *(continued)*
```
{
    if (a == b)
        cout << "Those are the same";
    else
        cout << "Those are different";
}
```

4. See the solution with a for-loop in Figure 6.3 on page 276. Or you might write a while-loop as shown here:
```
{
    size_t i;
    i = n;

    while (i > 0 && data[i-1] > entry)
    {
        data[i] = data[i-1];
        i--;
    }
    data[i] = entry;
}
```

5. `int`, `int&`, and `const int&` all match the `int` argument type in a template function, but `size_t` and `double` do not match.

6. In a header file for a toolkit of template functions, there is an include statement to include the implementation file. This makes the compiler's job simpler.

7. For a template class, the template prefix occurs before the template class definition and before each member function implementation. It also must appear before the prototype and implementation of any other template functions that manipulate the template class.

8. Within the class definition, `Bag` is not changed to `Bag<Item>`. Also, the name of the constructor is simply `Bag` (not `Bag<Item>`), and the name of the destructor is simply `~Bag`.

9. The time for the conversion depends on how quick you are at using an editor program. It took us about ten minutes to add the needed template prefixes and convert most occurrences of `Bag` to `Bag<Item>`.

10. All three of these definitions can appear in the same program:
```
Bag<char> vowel;
Bag<int> ages;
Bag<double> weights;
```

11. In a template function the declaration is:
```
Node<Item> *insert_ptr;
```

12. See "Mismatches for Template Function Arguments" on page 269.

13. Start with the template prefix, then use the implementation from Figure 5.9 on page 230, changing each `Node` to `Node<Item>`.

14. Within the bag's template class `Bag` is correct on its own, but `Node<Item>` is required.

15. In Section 6.3 we used a dynamic array; now we are using a linked list.

16. In Chapter 5, we used a typedef to define the item; now we are using a template parameter.

17. The primary purpose is to allow a programmer to easily step through the items of a container class. An external iterator is needed when two or more traversals are needed simultaneously.

 PROGRAMMING PROJECTS

1 Rewrite the selection sort (Programming Project 7 on page 259) so that it is a template function, with the template parameter specifying the type of data in each node. Your new selection sort function will use the template version of the linked list toolkit.

2 Add an internal iterator to one of the container classes from Chapter 3, 4, or 5. Some choices are: (a) any of the bags; (b) the set (Project 5 on page 133); (c) the bag with receipts (Project 7 on page 133); (d) the keyed bag (Project 8 on page 133).

3 Revise one of the container classes from Chapter 3, 4, or 5, so that it becomes a template class. Some choices are: (a) the set (Project 5 on page 133); (b) one of the list ADTs (Section 3.2 or Section 5.4); (c) the sorted list (Project 6 on page 133); (d) the bag with receipts (Project 7 on page 133); (e) the keyed bag (Project 8 on page 133). Include an internal iterator in your class.

4 Write a program that uses a bag of strings to keep track of a list of chores that you have to accomplish today. The user of the program can request several services: (1) Add an item to the list of chores; (2) Ask how many chores are in the list; (3) Use the internal iterator to print the list of chores to the screen; (4) Delete an item from the list; (5) Exit the program.

If you know how to read and write strings from a file, then have the program obtain its initial list of chores from a file. When the program ends, it should write all unfinished chores back to this file.

5 An **external iterator** for the bag is a separate class called `BagIterator`. One of the `BagIterator` member functions attaches the `BagIterator` to a specified bag. After the attachment, the other `BagIterator` member functions may be used to step through the items of the attached bag. Such a class might have a public definition shown here:

```
template <class Item>
class BagIterator
{
public:
    // CONSTRUCTOR
    BagIterator( );
    // MODIFICATION MEMBER FUNCTIONS
    void attach
      (const Bag<Item>& attached_bag);
    void advance( );
    // CONSTANT MEMBER FUNCTIONS
    Item current( ) const;
    bool is_item( ) const;
    ...
```

For example, suppose that x is a bag of integers. We can declare an external iterator that steps through the items of x, as shown here:

```
BagIterator<int> iterator;

for (
    iterator.attach(x);
    iterator.is_item( );
    iterator.advance( )
    )
        cout << iterator.current( )
            << endl;
```

Implement the bag iterator described above, using one private member variable (which is a pointer to a node in the attached bag). Make sure that you document which operations on the attached bag will invalidate the iterator. (However, unlike the internal iterator, the invalidation does not set the iterator's pointer to NULL.) In the `attach` function, you will need to initialize the iterator's pointer so that it points to the head node of the bag's linked list. To accomplish this, the bag iterator needs access to the private member variables of the bag. This access is granted by making the bag iterator a friend class of the bag, using the following line in the Bag<Item> class definition:

```
friend class BagIterator<Item>;
```

This line in the Bag<Item> class definition permits the member functions of BagIterator<Item> to access any private members of the bag.

7 Stacks

The pushdown store is a "first in-last out" list. That is, symbols may be entered or removed only at the top of the list.

JOHN E. HOPCROFT AND JEFFREY D. ULLMAN
Formal Languages and Their Relation to Automata

7.1 INTRODUCTION TO STACKS

7.2 STACK APPLICATIONS

7.3 IMPLEMENTATIONS OF THE STACK ADT

7.4 MORE COMPLEX STACK APPLICATIONS

CHAPTER SUMMARY

SOLUTIONS TO SELF-TEST EXERCISES

PROGRAMMING PROJECTS

This chapter introduces a data structure known as a *stack*, or as it is sometimes called, a *pushdown store*. It is a simple structure, even simpler than a list. Yet it turns out to be one of the most useful data structures known to computer science.

7.1 INTRODUCTION TO STACKS

The drawings to the left depict some stacks. There is a stack of pancakes, some stacks of coins, and a stack of books. A *stack* is an ordered collection of entries that can only be accessed at one end. That may not sound like what you see in these drawings, but think for a moment. Each of the stacks is ordered from top to bottom; you can identify any item in a stack by saying it is the top item, second from the top, third from the top, and so on. Unless you mess up one of the neat stacks, you can only access the top item. To remove the bottom book from the stack, you must first remove the two books that are on top of it. The abstract definition of a stack reflects this intuition.

Stack Definition

A **stack** is a data structure of ordered entries such that entries can only be inserted and removed at one end (called the **top**).

When we say that the entries in a stack are *ordered,* all we mean is that there is one that can be accessed first (the one on top), one that can be accessed second (just below the top), a third one, and so forth. We do *not* require that the entries can be compared using the < operator. The entries may be of any type.

Stack entries must be removed in the reverse order to that in which they are placed on the stack. For example, you can create a stack of books by first placing a dictionary, placing a thesaurus on top of the dictionary, and placing a novel on top of those, so the stack has the novel on top. When the books are removed, the novel must come off first (since it is on top), and then the thesaurus, and finally the dictionary. Because of this property, a stack is called a "Last-In/First-Out" data structure (abbreviated **LIFO**).

LIFO

A stack is a Last-In/First-Out data structure. Entries are taken out of the stack in the reverse order of their insertion.

Of course, a stack that is used in a program stores information rather than physical entries, such as books or pancakes. Therefore, it may help to visualize a stack as a pile of papers on which information is written. In order to place some information on the stack, you write the information on a new sheet of paper and place this sheet of paper on top of the stack. Getting information out of the stack is also accomplished by a simple operation, since the top sheet of paper can be removed and read. There is just one restriction: Only the top sheet of paper is accessible. In order to read the third sheet from the top, for example, the top two sheets must be removed from the stack.

A stack is analogous to a mechanism that is used in a popular candy holder called a *Pez® dispenser*, shown in the margin. The dispenser stores candy in a slot underneath an animal head figurine. Candy is loaded into the dispenser by pushing each piece into the hole. There is a spring under the candy with the tension adjusted so that when the animal head is tipped backward, one piece of candy pops out. If this sort of mechanism were used as a stack data structure, then the data would be written on the candy (which may violate some health laws, but it still makes a good analogy). Using this analogy, you can understand why adding an entry to a stack is called a **push** operation, and removing an entry from a stack is called a **pop** operation.

Pushing

Popping

The Stack ADT—Specification and Documentation

The specification of a stack ADT is given in Figure 7.1. Later we will implement this ADT in several different ways. As usual for a container class, the stack is specified as a *template* class, allowing us to have stacks of integers, or stacks of strings, or stacks of whatever. There is also a static member constant, CAPACITY, which is the maximum number of entries that a stack can hold. Our first implementation needs this constant because it uses a fixed-size array to hold the items of the stack. Later implementations will use dynamic memory instead.

Our specification lists a stack constructor and five member functions. The most important member functions are push (to add an entry at the top of the stack) and pop (to remove the top entry). Another function, called peek, allows a programmer to examine the top entry without actually removing it. There are no functions that allow a program to access entries other than the top entry. To access any entry other than the top one, the program must remove entries one at a time from the top until the desired entry is reached.

If a program attempts to pop an item off an empty stack, then it is asking for the impossible; this error is called **stack underflow**. In order to help you avoid a stack underflow, the ADT provides a member function to test whether a stack is empty. If a program attempts to push an item onto a full stack, the result is an error called **stack overflow**. To avoid stack overflow, a programmer compares the CAPACITY constant to the stack's current size (obtained with the size function).

Stack Errors

Stack Underflow: The condition resulting from trying to pop (remove) an item from an empty stack.

Stack Overflow: The condition resulting from trying to push an item onto (add an item to) a full stack.

We could have other operations, such as an explicit boolean function that tests for a full stack, but this first version is enough to teach you about stacks.

FIGURE 7.1   Documentation for the Stack Header File

Documentation for a Header File

```
// FILE: stack1.h
// TEMPLATE CLASS PROVIDED: Stack<Item> (a stack of items)
//     The template parameter, Item, is the data type of the items in the Stack.
//     It may be any of the C++ built-in types (int, char, etc.), or a class with a default
//     constructor, a copy constructor, and an assignment operator.
//
// MEMBER CONSTANT for the Stack<Item> template class:
//     static const size_t CAPACITY = _____
//        Stack<Item>::CAPACITY is the maximum number of items that a Stack can hold.
//
// CONSTRUCTOR for the Stack<Item> template class:
//     Stack( )
//        Postcondition: The Stack has been initialized as an empty Stack.
//
// MODIFICATION MEMBER FUNCTIONS for the Stack<Item> template class:
//     void push(const Item& entry)
//        Precondition: size( ) < CAPACITY.
//        Postcondition: A new copy of entry has been pushed onto the Stack.
//
//     Item pop( )
//        Precondition: size( ) > 0.
//        Postcondition: The top item of the Stack has been popped and returned.
//
// CONSTANT MEMBER FUNCTIONS for the Stack<Item> template class:
//     size_t size( ) const
//        Postcondition: Return value is the total number of items in the Stack.
//
//     bool is_empty( ) const
//        Postcondition: Return value is true if the Stack is empty.
//
//     Item peek( ) const
//        Precondition: size( ) > 0.
//        Postcondition: Return value is the top item on the Stack (but the Stack is unchanged).
//
// VALUE SEMANTICS for the Stack<Item> template class:
//     Assignments and the copy constructor may be used with Stack<Item> objects.
```

stack1.h   **FTP**

uses for stacks   Stacks are very intuitive—even cute—but are they good for anything besides toy problems? Surprisingly, they have many applications. Most compilers use stacks to analyze the syntax of a program. Stacks are used to keep track of local variables when a program is run. Stacks can be used to search a maze or a family tree or other types of branching structures. In this book, we will discuss examples related to each of these applications. But before we present any complicated applications of the stack ADT, let us first practice with a simple "toy" problem, so that we can see how a stack is used.

PROGRAMMING EXAMPLE: Reversing a Word

Suppose you want a program to read in a word and then write it out backwards. If the program reads in NAT, then it will output TAN. If it reads in TAPS it will output SPAT. The author Roald Dahl wrote a book called ESIOTROT, which our program converts to TORTOISE. One way to accomplish this task is to read the input one letter at a time and place each letter in a stack. After the word is read, the letters in the stack are written out, but because of the way a stack works, they are written out in reverse order. The pseudocode is shown below:

> // *Reversing the spelling of a word*
> Declare a stack of characters;
>
> *while* (there are more characters of the word to read)
>   Read a character, and push the character onto the stack.
>
> *while* (the stack is not empty)
>   Pop a character off the stack, and write that character to the screen.

This computation is illustrated in Figure 7.2. At all times in the computation, the only available entry is the entry on "top." Figure 7.2 suggests another intuition for thinking about a stack. You can view a stack as a hole in the ground and view the data entries as being placed in the hole one on top of the other. To retrieve a data entry, you must first remove the entries on top of it.

FIGURE 7.2   Using a Stack to Reverse Spelling.

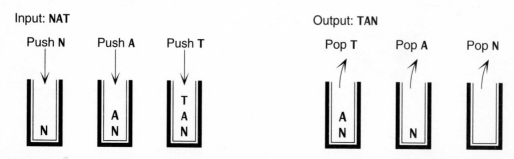

Self-Test Exercises

1. Suppose a program uses a stack of characters to read in a word and then write the word out backwards, as described in this section. Now suppose the input word is DAHL. List all the activations of the push and pop functions. List them in the order in which they will be executed and indicate the character that is pushed or popped. What is the output?

2. Consider the Stack class given in Figure 7.1 on page 309. The peek member function lets you look at the top entry in the stack without changing the stack. Describe how you can define a new member function that returns the second entry from the top of the stack without changing the stack. Your description will be in terms of peek, pop, and push. Give your solution in pseudocode, not in C++.

7.2 STACK APPLICATIONS

In order to write programs that use the stack ADT, we will assume that the documentation of Figure 7.1 on page 309 has been implemented with a header file called stack1.h. We will give the actual header and implementation files later. In order to use the class, you only need to know the information given in the documentation.

PROGRAMMING EXAMPLE: Balanced Parentheses

Later in this chapter we will describe how stacks can be used to evaluate arithmetic expressions. At the moment, we will describe a short function that does a much simpler but closely related task. The function, called is_balanced, appears in Figure 7.3, and checks expressions to see if the parentheses match correctly. It checks nothing else. Any symbol other than a right or left parenthesis is simply ignored.

For example, consider the string "((X + Y*(Z + 7))*(A + B))". Each of the left parentheses has a corresponding right parenthesis. Also, as the string is read from left to right, there is never an occurrence of a right parenthesis that cannot be matched with a corresponding left parenthesis. Therefore the function call is_balanced("((X + Y*(Z + 7))*(A + B))") returns true.

On the other hand, consider the string "((X + Y*(Z + 7)*(A + B))". The parentheses around the subexpression Z + 7 match each other, as do the parentheses around A + B. And the second left parenthesis in the expression matches the final right parenthesis. But the first left parenthesis has no matching right parenthesis. Hence, is_balanced("((X + Y*(Z + 7)*(A + B))") returns false.

The algorithm used by is_balanced is simple: The function scans the characters of the string from left to right. Every time the function sees a left parenthesis, it is pushed onto the stack. Every time the program reads a right parenthesis, the program pops a matching left parenthesis off the stack. All symbols other than parentheses are ignored. If all goes smoothly and the stack is empty at the end of the expression, then the parentheses match. If the stack is empty when the algorithm needs to pop a symbol, or if symbols are still in the stack after all the input has been read, then the parentheses do not match. Now let us see why the algorithm works.

Let us start with some examples. Since no symbols other than parentheses can affect the results, we will use expressions of just parentheses symbols. All of the

---

FIGURE 7.3 A Function to Check for Balanced Parentheses

A Function Implementation

```
bool is_balanced(const String& expression)
// Postcondition: A true return value indicates that the parentheses in the given expression
// are balanced. Otherwise the return value is false.
// Library facilities used: assert.h, stack1.h, stdlib.h, mystring.h.
// NOTE: mystring.h (from Section 4.5) provides a String class. If a standard library String
// class is available, then that could be used instead.
{
    // Meaningful names for constants
    const char LEFT_PARENTHESIS = '(';
    const char RIGHT_PARENTHESIS = ')';

    Stack<char> store;      // Stack to store the left parentheses as they occur
    size_t i;               // An index into the String
    char next;              // The next character from the String
    char discard;           // A char popped off the stack and thrown away
    bool failed = false;    // Becomes true if a needed parenthesis is not found

    for (i = 0; !failed && (i < expression.length( )); i++)
    {
        next = expression[i];
        if (next == LEFT_PARENTHESIS)
        {
            assert(store.size( ) < store.CAPACITY);
            store.push(next);
        }
        else if ((next == RIGHT_PARENTHESIS) && (!store.is_empty( )))
            discard = store.pop( );
        else if ((next == RIGHT_PARENTHESIS) && (store.is_empty( )))
            failed = true;
    }

    return (store.is_empty( ) && !failed);
}
```

parens.cxx   FTP

following are balanced (shading and arrows help find matching parentheses):

If you think about these examples, you can begin to understand the algorithm. In the first example, the parentheses match because they have the same number of left and right parentheses, but the algorithm does more than just count parentheses. The algorithm actually matches parentheses. Every time it encounters a ')', the symbol it pops off the stack is the matching '('. The parenthesis popped is not just any '(', but the one that matches.

The middle example is the same as the first example followed by another pair of matching parentheses. Since the two subexpressions match by themselves, the combination still matches.

The third example is even more revealing. The complete sequence of stack configurations from an execution of the function, using the input "(()())", is shown in Figure 7.4. The stacks shown in the figure show the configuration after processing each character of the expression.

In general the stack works by keeping a stack of the unmatched left parentheses. Every time the program encounters a right parenthesis, the corresponding left parenthesis is deleted (popped) from the stack. If the parentheses in the input match correctly, things work out perfectly, and the stack is empty at the end of the input line.

Our function assumes the input has only one kind of parentheses, but the same technique can be used to check expressions with different kinds of parentheses, such as ( ), [ ], and { }. With different kinds of parentheses, the symbol popped off the stack must match the symbol in the input. For example, when the program encounters a ']' as the next symbol, there must be a '[' on top of the stack. We leave this more general problem as an exercise.

different kinds of parentheses

FIGURE 7.4   Stack Configurations for a Call to is_balanced.

Input: (( ) ( ))

| Initial empty stack | Read and push first (| Read and push second (| Read first) and pop matching (| Read and push third (| Read second) and pop matching (| Read third) and pop the last (|

PROGRAMMING EXAMPLE: **Evaluating Arithmetic Expressions**

In this programming example we will design and write a calculator program. This will be an example of a program that uses two stacks—one is a stack of characters, and the other is a stack of double numbers.

Evaluating Arithmetic Expressions—Specification

input to the calculator program

The program takes as input a fully parenthesized numeric expression such as the following:

```
((((12 + 9)/3) + 7.2)*((6 - 4)/8))
```

The expression consists of integers or double numbers, together with the operators +, -, *, and /. In order to focus on the use of the stack (rather than on input details), we require that each input number is non-negative (otherwise it is hard to distinguish the subtraction operator from a minus sign that is part of a negative number). We will assume that the expression is formed correctly so that each operation has two arguments. Finally, we will also assume that the expression is fully parenthesized, meaning that each operation has a pair of matched parentheses surrounding its arguments. We can later enhance our program so that these assumptions are no longer needed.

output of the calculator program

The output will simply be the value of the arithmetic expression.

Evaluating Arithmetic Expressions—Design

Most of the program's work will be carried out by a function that reads one line of input and evaluates that line as an arithmetic expression. To get a feel for the problem, let's start by doing a simple example by hand.

do an example by hand

Consider the following expression:

```
(((6 + 9)/3)*(6 - 4))
```

If we were to evaluate this expression by hand, we might first evaluate the innermost expressions, (6 + 9) and (6 - 4), to produce the smaller expression:

```
((15/3)*2)
```

Next we would evaluate the expression (15/3) and replace this expression with its value of 5. That would leave us with the expression (5*2). Finally, we would evaluate this last operation to get the final answer of 10.

To convert this intuitive approach into a fully specified algorithm that can be implemented, we need to do things in a more systematic way: We need a specific way to find the expression to be evaluated next and a way to remember the results of our intermediate calculations.

First let us find a systematic way of choosing the next expression to be evaluated. (After that, we can worry about how we will keep track of the intermediate results.) We know that the expression to be evaluated first must be one of the innermost expressions—which is a subexpression that has just one operation. Let's decide to evaluate the leftmost of these innermost expressions. For instance, in our example of

    (((6 + 9)/3)*(6 - 4))

the innermost expressions are (6 + 9) and (6 - 4), and the leftmost one of these is (6 + 9). If we evaluate this *leftmost of the innermost expressions*, we obtain

    ((15/3)*(6 - 4))

We could now go back and evaluate the other innermost expression (6 - 4), but why bother? There is a simpler approach that spares us the trouble of remembering any other expressions. After we evaluate the leftmost of the innermost expressions, we are left with another simpler arithmetic expression, namely ((15/3)*(6 - 4)), so we can simply repeat the process with this simpler expression: We again evaluate the leftmost of the innermost expressions of our new simpler expression. The entire process will look like the following:

1. Evaluate the leftmost of the innermost expressions in

       (((6 + 9)/3)*(6 - 4))

   to produce the simpler expression ((15/3)*(6 - 4)).

2. Evaluate the leftmost of the innermost expressions in

       ((15/3)*(6 - 4))

   to produce the simpler expression (5*(6 - 4)).

3. Evaluate the leftmost of the innermost expressions in

       (5*(6 - 4))

   to produce the simpler expression (5*2).

4. Evaluate the leftmost of the innermost expressions in

       (5*2)

   to obtain the final answer of 10.

translating the hand method to an algorithm

This method works fine with pencil and paper, but the function must read the input one character at a time from left to right. How does the function find *the leftmost of the innermost expressions*? Look at the example on page 315. The end of the expression to be evaluated is always a right parenthesis ')', and moreover, it is always the *first* right parenthesis. After evaluating one of these innermost expressions, there is no need to backup; to find the next right parenthesis we can just keep reading left to right from where we left off. The next right parenthesis will indicate the end of the next expression to be evaluated.

Now we know how to find the expression to be evaluated next, but how do we keep track of our intermediate values? For this we use two stacks. One stack will contain numbers; there will be numbers from the input as well as numbers that were computed when subexpressions were evaluated. The other stack will hold symbols for the operations that still need to be evaluated. Because a stack processes data in a Last-In/First-Out manner, it will turn out that the correct two numbers are on the top of the number stack at the same time that the appropriate operation is at the top of the stack of operations. To better understand how the process works, let's evaluate our sample expression one more time, this time using the two stacks.

We begin by reading up to the first right parenthesis; the numbers we encounter along the way are pushed onto the number stack, and the operations we encounter along the way are pushed onto the operation stack. When we reach the first right parenthesis, our two stacks look like this:

Characters read so far (shaded):
`(((6 + 9) / 3) * (6 - 4))`

Whenever we reach a right parenthesis, we combine the top two numbers (on the number stack) using the topmost operation (on the character stack). In our example, we compute 6 + 9, yielding 15, and this number 15 is pushed back onto the number stack:

Characters read so far (shaded):
`(((6 + 9) / 3) * (6 - 4))`

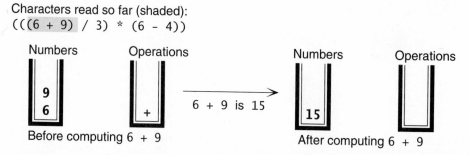

Notice that the leftmost operand (6 in this example) is the *second* number popped off the stack. For addition, this does not matter—who cares whether we have added 6 + 9 or 9 + 6? But the order of the operands does matter for subtraction and division.

Next we simply continue the process: by reading up to the next right parenthesis, pushing the numbers we encounter onto the number stack and pushing the operations we encounter onto the operation stack. When we reach the next right parenthesis, we combine the top two numbers using the topmost operation. Here's what happens in our example when we reach the second right parenthesis:

Characters read so far (shaded):
(((6 + 9) / 3) * (6 - 4))

Again, the leftmost operand (15) is the second number popped off the stack, so the correct evaluation is 15/3, not 3/15. Continuing the process, we obtain:

Characters read so far (shaded):
(((6 + 9) / 3) * (6 - 4))

Finally, continuing the process one more time does not add anything to the stacks, but it does read the last right parenthesis and does combine two numbers from the numbers stack with an operation from the operation stack:

Characters read so far (shaded):
(((6 + 9) / 3) * (6 - 4))

At this point there is no more input, and there is exactly one number in the number stack, namely 10. That number is the answer. Notice that when we used the two stacks we performed the exact same evaluations as we did when we first evaluated this expression in a simple pencil and paper fashion.

cases for evaluating an arithmetic expression

To evaluate our expression we only need to repeatedly handle each input item according to the following cases:

Numbers. When a number is encountered in the input, the number is read and pushed onto the numbers stack.

Operation characters. When one of the four operation characters is encountered in the input, the character is read and pushed onto the operations stack.

Right parenthesis. When a right parenthesis is read from the input, an "evaluation step" takes place. The step pops the top two numbers from the number stack and pops the top operation from the operation stack. The two numbers are combined using the operation (with the second number popped as the left operand). The result of the operation is pushed back onto the numbers stack.

Left parenthesis or blank. The only other characters that appear in the input are left parentheses and blanks. These are read and thrown away, not affecting the computation. A more complete algorithm would need to process the left parentheses in some way to ensure that each left parenthesis is balanced by a right parenthesis, but for now we are assuming that the input is completely parenthesized in a proper manner.

The processing of input items halts when the end of the input line occurs, indicated by '\n' in the input. At this point, the answer is the single number that remains in the number stack.

We now have our algorithm, which we plan to implement as a function meeting this specification:

```
double read_and_evaluate(istream& ins);
// Precondition: The next line of characters in the istream ins is a fully
// parenthesized arithmetic expression formed from non-negative
// numbers and the four operations +, -, *, and /.
// Postcondition: A line has been read from the istream ins, and this line
// has been evaluated as an arithmetic expression. The value of the
// expression has been returned by the function.
```

The implementation of this function appears as part of a complete program in Figure 7.5.

Evaluating Arithmetic Expressions—Implementation

The implementation of `read_and_evaluate` in Figure 7.5 benefits from three of the `istream` functions:

- The name of the `istream`, `ins`, is used as part of the boolean expression that controls the loop. As we have seen before, the expression `ins` remains true so long as `ins` has not encountered bad input (such as the end of the file).
- The function call `ins.peek()` returns the next character of the `ins` input stream (without actually reading it).
- The function call `ins.ignore()` reads and discards the next character from the `ins` input stream.

Our implementation also uses three other functions, which we discuss starting on page 321 (after the figure).

FIGURE 7.5 Basic Calculator Program

A Program

```
// FILE: calc.cxx
// Basic calculator program to evaluate a fully parenthesized arithmetic expression.
// The purpose is to illustrate a fundamental use of stacks.

#include <ctype.h>      // Provides isdigit
#include <iostream.h>   // Provides cout, cin, peek, ignore
#include <stdlib.h>     // Provides EXIT_SUCCESS
#include <string.h>     // Provides strchr
#include "stack1.h"     // Provides the Stack template class

// PROTOTYPES for functions used by this demonstration program:
double read_and_evaluate(istream& ins);
// Precondition: The next line of characters in the istream ins is a fully parenthesized
// expression formed from non-negative numbers and the four operations +, -, *, and /.
// Postcondition: A line has been read from the istream ins, and this line has been evaluated
// as an arithmetic expression. The value of the expression has been returned by the function.

void evaluate_stack_tops(Stack<double>& numbers, Stack<char>& operations);
// Precondition: The top of the operations stack contains +, -, *, or /, and the numbers stack
// contains at least two numbers.
// Postcondition: The top two numbers have been popped from the number stack, and the top
// operation has been popped from the operation stack. The two numbers have been combined
// using the operation (with the second number popped as the left operand). The result of the
// operation has then been pushed back onto the numbers stack.
```

(continued)

(FIGURE 7.5 continued)

```cpp
int main( )
{
    double answer;

    cout << "Type a fully parenthesized arithmetic expression:" << endl;
    answer = read_and_evaluate(cin);
    cout << "That evaluates to " << answer << endl;

    return EXIT_SUCCESS;
}

double read_and_evaluate(istream& ins)
// Library facilities used: iostream.h, stack1.h, string.h
{
    const char DECIMAL = '.';
    const char RIGHT_PARENTHESIS = ')';

    Stack<double> numbers;
    Stack<char> operations;
    double number;
    char symbol;

    // Loop continues while istream is not "bad" (tested by ins) and next character isn't newline.
    while (ins && ins.peek( ) != '\n')
    {
        if (isdigit(ins.peek( )) || (ins.peek( ) == DECIMAL))
        {
            ins >> number;
            numbers.push(number);
        }
        else if (strchr("+-*/", ins.peek( )) != NULL)
        {
            ins >> symbol;
            operations.push(symbol);
        }
        else if (ins.peek( ) == RIGHT_PARENTHESIS)
        {
            ins.ignore( );
            evaluate_stack_tops(numbers, operations);
        }
        else
            ins.ignore( );
    }

    return numbers.pop( );
}
```

(continued)

(FIGURE 7.5 continued)

```
void evaluate_stack_tops(Stack<double>& numbers, Stack<char>& operations)
// Library facilities used: stack1.h
{
    double operand1, operand2;

    operand2 = numbers.pop( );
    operand1 = numbers.pop( );
    switch (operations.pop( ))
    {
        case '+': numbers.push(operand1 + operand2);
                break;
        case '-': numbers.push(operand1 - operand2);
                break;
        case '*': numbers.push(operand1 * operand2);
                break;
        case '/': numbers.push(operand1 / operand2);
                break;
    }
}
```

A Sample Dialogue

```
Type a fully parenthesized arithmetic expression:
( ( (60 + 40)/50) * (16 - 4) )
That evaluates to 24
```

calc.cxx	FTP

Functions Used in the Calculator Program

The other three functions used in our implementation are listed here:

- The `isdigit` function (from the facility `ctype.h`) with the prototype:

    ```
    bool isdigit(char c);
    ```

    The function returns true if its argument is one of the digits `'0'` through `'9'`. Otherwise it returns false.

- The `strchr` function (from `string.h`) with the prototype:

    ```
    char* strchr(const char s[ ], char c);
    ```

    The function scans the string s for an occurrence of the character c. If the character c is found, then the function returns a pointer to the first occurrence of the character in s. Otherwise, the null pointer is returned.

- A function called `evaluate_stack_tops` appears as part of Figure 7.5 on page 321. The function pops two numbers off the number stack, combines them with an operation from the operations stack, and pushes the result back on the numbers stack.

Evaluating Arithmetic Expressions—Testing and Analysis

testing

As usual, you should test your program on boundary values that are most likely to cause problems. For this program, one kind of boundary value consists of the simplest kind of expressions: those that combine only two numbers. In order to test that operations are performed correctly, you should test simple expressions for each of the operations +, −, *, and /. These simple expressions should have only one operation. Be sure to test the division and subtraction operations carefully to ensure that the operations are performed in the correct order. After all, 3/15 is not the same as 15/3, and 3 − 15 is not the same as 15 − 3. These are perhaps the only boundary values. But it is important to also test some cases with nested parentheses. And you can test an illegal division such as 15/0. What does the program do? It probably crashes with a division by zero error. Can you place an assertion in the program that will catch this error, rather than allowing the division by zero to take place?

time analysis

Let's estimate the number of operations that our program will use on an input of length n. We will count each of the following as one program operation: reading or peeking at a symbol, performing one of the arithmetic operations (+, −, *, or /), pushing an entry onto one of the stacks, and popping an entry off of one of the stacks. We consider each kind of operation separately.

Time spent reading characters. There are only n symbols in the input, so the program can read at most n symbols. No character is "peeked" at more than once either, so this part of the program has no more than $2n$ operations.

Time spent evaluating arithmetic operations. Each arithmetic operation performed by the program is the evaluation of an operation symbol in the input. Because there are no more than n arithmetic operations in the input, there are at most n arithmetic operations performed. In actual fact, there are far fewer than n operations, since many of the input symbols are digits or parentheses. But there are certainly no more than n arithmetic operation symbols, so it is safe to say that there are no more than n arithmetic operations performed.

Number of push operations. Since there are no more than n arithmetic operation symbols, we know that there are at most n operation symbols pushed onto the operation stack. The number stack may contain input numbers and numbers obtained from evaluating arithmetic expressions. Again, an upper bound will suffice: There are at most n input numbers and at most n arithmetic operations evaluated. Thus, at most, $2n$ numbers are pushed onto the number stack. This gives an upper bound of $3n$ total push operations onto the stacks.

Number of pop operations.   Once we know the total number of entries that are pushed onto the two stacks, we have a bound on how many things can be popped off of the two stacks. After all, you cannot pop off an entry unless it was first pushed onto the stack. Thus, there is an upper bound of $3n$ pop operations from any of the stacks.

Total number of operations.   Now, let's total things up. The total number of operations is no more than $2n$ reads/peeks, plus n arithmetic operations performed, plus $3n$ entries pushed onto a stack, plus $3n$ entries popped off of a stack—for a grand total of $9n$. The actual number of operations will be less than this because we have used generous upper bounds in several estimates, but $9n$ is enough to let us conclude that the algorithm for this program is $O(n)$; this is a linear algorithm.

Evaluating Arithmetic Expressions—Enhancements

The program in Figure 7.5 on page 319 is a fine example of how to use stacks. As a computer scientist, you will find yourself using stacks in this manner in many different situations. However, the program is not a fine example of a finished program. Before we can consider it to be a finished product, we need to add a number of enhancements to make the program more robust and friendly.

Some enhancements are easy. It is useful (and easy) to add a loop to the main program that will let the user evaluate more expressions until there is an indication that the user is finished with the calculator. Other enhancements are a bit harder. One nice enhancement would be to permit expressions that are not fully parenthesized, and to use the C++ precedence rules to decide the order of operations when parentheses are missing. We will discuss topics related to this enhancement in Section 7.4, where (surprise!) we'll see that a stack is useful for this purpose too.

Self-Test Exercises

3. How would you modify the calculator program in Figure 7.5 on page 319 to allow the symbol ∧ to be used for exponentiation? Describe the changes; do not write out the code.

4. How would you modify the calculator program in Figure 7.5 on page 319 to allow for comments in the calculator input? Comments appear at the end of the expression, starting with a double slash // and continuing to the end of the line. Describe the changes; do not write out the code.

5. What possible errors could cause a stack underflow in the calculator program in Figure 7.5 on page 319?

6. What can cause a stack overflow in the calculator program in Figure 7.5 on page 319?

7.3 IMPLEMENTATIONS OF THE STACK ADT

We will give two implementations of our stack ADT: a static implementation using a fixed-sized array, and a dynamic implementation using a linked list. Except for the presence of the CAPACITY constant, our application programs will run the same with either implementation.

Array Implementation of a Stack

Figure 7.6 gives the complete header file for a Stack template class that meets our earlier specification (from Figure 7.1 on page 309). The class definition uses two private member variables for the stack:

1. An array, called data, that can hold up to CAPACITY items (where CAPACITY is a static constant of the Stack class). This is a partially filled array, holding the stack's items in locations data[0], data[1], data[2], and so on.

2. A single member variable, used, that indicates how much of the partially filled array is currently being used. The entry at data[0] is at "the bottom" of the stack. The entry at data[used-1] is at "the top" of the stack. If the value of used is zero, this will indicate an empty stack.

the stack entries are stored in a partially filled array

In other words, our stack implementation is simply a partially filled array implemented in the usual way: an array and a variable to indicate the index of the last array position used. This description is the invariant of our ADT, so that each member function (except the constructor) may assume that the stack is represented in this way when the operation is activated. Each operation has the responsibility of ensuring that the stack is still represented in this manner when the operation finishes.

Invariant of the Stack ADT (Array Version)

1. The number of items in the stack is stored in the member variable used.

2. The items in the stack are stored in a partially filled array called data, with the bottom of the stack at data[0], the next entry at data[1], and so on to the top of the stack at data[used-1].

---

implementing the stack operations

The member functions that operate on our stack are now straightforward. To initialize the stack, set the private member variable used to zero, indicating an empty array and hence an empty stack. To add an entry to the stack (in the push function), we store the new entry in data[used], and then we increment used by one. To look at the top entry in the stack (function peek), we simply look at the entry in array position data[used-1]. To remove an entry from the stack (in the pop function), we decrement used and then return the value of data[used] (which is the value that was on top prior to the pop operation). The member functions to test for emptiness and to return the size are simple inline implementations that examine the value of used.

The complete implementation file for our stack is given in Figure 7.7 on page 326.

FIGURE 7.6 | Header File for the Array Version of the Stack Template Class

---

A Header File

```
// FILE: stack1.h
// TEMPLATE CLASS PROVIDED: Stack<Item> (a stack of items)
// See Figure 7.1 on page 309 for the other documentation that goes here.

#ifndef STACK1_H
#define STACK1_H
#include <stdlib.h> // Provides size_t

    template <class Item>
    class Stack
    {
    public:
        // MEMBER CONSTANT -- See Appendix E if this fails to compile.
        static const size_t CAPACITY = 30;
        // CONSTRUCTOR
        Stack( ) { used = 0; }
        // MODIFICATION MEMBER FUNCTIONS
        void push(const Item& entry);
        Item pop( );
        // CONSTANT MEMBER FUNCTIONS
        size_t size( ) const { return used; }
        bool is_empty( ) const { return (used == 0); }
        Item peek( ) const;
    private:
        Item data[CAPACITY];    // Partially filled array
        size_t used;            // How much of array is being used
    };

    #include "stack1.template" // Include the implementation.

    #endif
```

stack1.h | FTP

| FIGURE 7.7 | Implementation File for the Array Version of the Stack Template Class |

An Implementation File

```
// FILE: stack1.template
// TEMPLATE CLASS IMPLEMENTED: Stack<Item> (See stack1.h for documentation.)
// This file is included in the header file and not compiled separately.
// INVARIANT for the Stack ADT:
//     1. The number of items in the Stack is in the member variable used.
//     2. The items in the Stack are stored in a partially filled array called
//        data, with the bottom of the stack at data[0], the next entry at
//        data[1], and so on to the top of the stack at data[used – 1].

#include <assert.h>   // Provides assert
#include <stdlib.h>   // Provides size_t

template <class Item>
void Stack<Item>::push(const Item& entry)
// Library facilities used: assert.h
{
    assert(size( ) < CAPACITY);
    data[used] = entry;
    used++;
}

template <class Item>
Item Stack<Item>::pop( )
// Library facilities used: assert.h
{
    assert(!is_empty( ));
    used--;
    return data[used];
}

template <class Item>
Item Stack<Item>::peek( ) const
// Library facilities used: assert.h
{
    assert(!is_empty( ));
    return data[used-1];
}
```

stack1.template   **FTP**

Linked List Implementation of a Stack

A linked list is a natural way to implement a stack as a dynamic structure whose size can grow and shrink during execution, without a predefined limit that is determined at compilation. The head of the linked list serves as the top of the stack. Figure 7.8 on page 328 contains the header file for a `Stack` template class that is implemented with a linked list. Here is a precise statement of the invariant of this version of the new stack ADT:

Invariant of the Stack ADT (Linked List Version)

1. The items in the stack are stored in a linked list, with the top of the stack stored at the head node, down to the bottom of the stack at the final node.

2. The member variable `top_ptr` is the head pointer of the linked list of items.

As usual, all member functions (except the constructors) assume that the stack is represented in this way when the function is activated, and all functions ensure that the stack continues to be represented in this way when the function finishes.

Because we are using a linked list, there is no predetermined limit to the number of items we can place in our stack. Thus, in the header file we have omitted the constant `CAPACITY`, but we have added documentation indicating that some of the functions allocate dynamic memory and will call `new_handler` when dynamic memory is exhausted.

As a further consequence of using a linked list, it makes sense to utilize the linked list toolkit from Section 6.4. Thus, in Figure 7.8 you will find this include directive:

```
#include "link2.h"   // Linked list toolkit
```

By using the toolkit, many of the stack member functions can be implemented with just a line or two of code, as shown in Figure 7.9 on page 330.

Discussion of the Linked List Implementation of the Stack

The default constructor, the destructor, `size`, and `is_empty` are all simple enough to implement as inline member functions in Figure 7.8 on page 329. Since the first node of the list is the top of the stack, the implementation of `peek` is easy: `peek` just returns the data from the first node. The operations `push` and `pop` work by inserting and deleting nodes, always working at the head of the linked list. Inserting and deleting nodes at the head of the linked list is a straightforward use of `list_head_insert` and `list_head_remove` from the linked list toolkit. Both the copy constructor and the assignment operator make use of `list_copy` to copy the source stack to the stack that activates the member function. The assignment operator must check for the potential of a self-assignment (such as s = s), and the assignment operator is also responsible for calling `list_clear` to release the memory that is currently used by the stack.

Self-Test Exercises

7. For the array version of the stack, write a new member function that returns the maximum number of items that can be added to the stack without stack overflow.

8. Describe a simple way to reimplement the array version of the stack without the need for a CAPACITY constant.

9. Give the full implementation a constant member function that returns the second element from the top of the stack without actually changing the stack. Write separate solutions for the two different stack versions.

10. Do a time analysis of the `size` function for the linked list version of the stack. If the function is not constant time, then can you think of a different approach that is constant time?

FIGURE 7.8	Header File for the Linked List Version of the Stack Template Class

A Header File

```
//  FILE: stack2.h
//  TEMPLATE CLASS PROVIDED: Stack<Item> (a stack of items)
//     The template parameter, Item, is the data type of the items in the Stack.
//     It may be any of the C++ built-in types (int, char, etc.) or a class with a default
//     constructor, a copy constructor, and an assignment operator.
//
//  CONSTRUCTOR for the Stack<Item> template class:
//     Stack( )
//        Postcondition: The stack has been initialized as an empty Stack.
//
//  MODIFICATION MEMBER FUNCTIONS for the Stack<Item> template class:
//     void push(const Item& entry)
//        Postcondition: A new copy of entry has been pushed onto the Stack.
//
//     Item pop( )
//        Precondition: size( ) > 0.
//        Postcondition: The top item of the stack has been popped and returned.
//
//  CONSTANT MEMBER FUNCTIONS for the Stack<Item> template class:
//     size_t size( ) const
//        Postcondition: Return value is the total number of items in the Stack.
```

(continued)

(FIGURE 7.8 continued)

```
//
//      bool is_empty( ) const
//          Postcondition: Return value is true if the Stack is empty.
//
//      Item peek( ) const
//          Precondition: size( ) > 0.
//          Postcondition: Return value is the top item on the Stack (but the Stack is unchanged).
//
// VALUE SEMANTICS for the Stack<Item> template class:
//      Assignments and the copy constructor may be used with Stack<Item> objects.
//
// DYNAMIC MEMORY USAGE by the Stack<Item> template class:
//      If there is insufficient dynamic memory, then the following functions call new_handler:
//      the copy constructor, push, and the assignment operator.

#ifndef STACK2_H
#define STACK2_H
#include <stdlib.h>    // Provides NULL and size_t
#include "link2.h"     // Linked list toolkit from Figure 6.7 on page 292

    template <class Item>
    class Stack
    {
    public:
        // CONSTRUCTORS and DESTRUCTOR
        Stack( ) { top_ptr = NULL; }
        Stack(const Stack& source); // Copy constructor
        ~Stack( ) { list_clear(top_ptr); }
        // MODIFICATION MEMBER FUNCTIONS
        void push(const Item& entry);
        Item pop( );
        void operator =(const Stack& source);
        // CONSTANT MEMBER FUNCTIONS
        size_t size( ) const { return list_length(top_ptr); }
        bool is_empty( ) const { return (top_ptr == NULL); }
        Item peek( ) const;
    private:
        Node<Item> *top_ptr;   // Points to top of stack
    };

#include "stack2.template" // Include the implementation

#endif
```

stack2.h   FTP

| **FIGURE 7.9** | Implementation File for the Linked List Version of the Stack Template Class |

An Implementation File

```
// FILE: stack2.template
// TEMPLATE CLASS IMPLEMENTED: Stack<Item> (See stack2.h for documentation.)
// This file is included in the header file and not compiled separately.
// INVARIANT for the Stack ADT:
//     1. The items in the Stack are stored in a linked list, with the top of the Stack stored at the
//        head node, down to the bottom of the Stack at the final node.
//     2. The member variable top_ptr is the head pointer of the linked list.

#include <assert.h> // Provides assert
#include <stdlib.h> // Provides size_t
#include "link2.h"   // Linked list toolkit from Figure 6.7 on page 292

template <class Item>
Stack<Item>::Stack(const Stack<Item>& source)
// Library facilities used: link2.h
{
    Node<Item> *tail_ptr; // Needed for argument of list_copy

    list_copy(source.top_ptr, top_ptr, tail_ptr);
}


template <class Item>
void Stack<Item>::push(const Item& entry)
// Library facilities used: link2.h
{
    list_head_insert(top_ptr, entry);
}


template <class Item>
Item Stack<Item>::pop( )
// Library facilities used: assert.h, link2.h
{
    Item answer;

    assert(!is_empty( ));
    answer = top_ptr->data;
    list_head_remove(top_ptr);
    return answer;
}
```

(continued)

(FIGURE 7.9 continued)

```
template <class Item>
void Stack<Item>::operator =(const Stack<Item>& source)
// Library facilities used: link2.h
{
    Node<Item> *tail_ptr;  // Needed for argument of list_copy

    if (source.top_ptr == top_ptr) // Handle self-assignment
        return;

    list_clear(top_ptr);
    list_copy(source.top_ptr, top_ptr, tail_ptr);
}


template <class Item>
Item Stack<Item>::peek( ) const
// Library facilities used: assert.h
{
    assert(!is_empty( ));
    return top_ptr->data;
}
```

| stack2.template | **FTP** |

7.4 MORE COMPLEX STACK APPLICATIONS

Evaluating Postfix Expressions

We normally write an arithmetic operation between its two arguments, for example, the + operation occurs between the 2 and the 3 in the arithmetic expression 2 + 3. This is called *infix notation*. There is another way of writing arithmetic operations that places the operation in front of the two arguments, for example + 2 3 evaluates to 5. This is called **Polish prefix notation** or simply **prefix notation**.

infix versus prefix notation

A **prefix** is something attached to the front of an expression. You may have heard about similar prefixes for words, such as the prefix *un* in *unbelievable*. Thus, it makes sense to call this notation *prefix notation*. But why *Polish*? It is called Polish because it was devised by the Polish mathematician Jan Łukasiewicz. It would be more proper to call it *Łukasiewicz notation*, but apparently non-Polish-speaking people have trouble pronouncing *Łukasiewicz* (lü-kä-**sha**-vēch).

the origin of the notation

Using prefix notation, parentheses are completely avoided. For example, the expression (2 + 3) * 7 when written in this Polish prefix notation is:

$$\underbrace{* + 2\ 3\ 7}$$

The curved lines under the expression indicate groupings of subexpressions (but the lines are not actually part of the prefix notation).

postfix notation

If we prefer, we can write the operations after the two numbers being combined. This is called **Polish postfix notation**, or more simply **postfix notation** (or sometimes **reverse Polish notation**). For example, the expression (2 + 3) * 7 when written in Polish postfix notation is:

$$\underbrace{2\ 3\ +\ 7\ *}$$

Once again, the curves merely clarify the groupings of subexpressions, and these curves are not actually part of the postfix notation.

Here's a longer example. The postfix expression 7 3 5 * + 4 - is equivalent to the infix expression (7 + (3*5)) - 4.

Do not intermix prefix and postfix notation. You should consistently use one or the other and not mix them together in a single expression.

our goal: evaluation of postfix expressions

Postfix notation is handy because it does not require parentheses and because it is particularly easy to evaluate (once you learn to use the notation). In fact, postfix notation often is used internally for computers because of the ease of expression evaluation. We will describe an algorithm to evaluate a postfix expression. When converted to a C++ program, the postfix evaluation is similar to the calculator program (Figure 7.5 on page 319)—although, from our comments you might guess that the postfix evaluation is actually simpler than the infix evaluation required in the calculator program.

There are two input format issues that we must handle. When entering postfix notation we will require a space between two consecutive numbers so that you can tell where one number ends and another begins. For example, the input

    35 6

consists of two numbers, 35 and 6, with a space in between. This is different from the input

    356

which is just a single number, 356. A second input issue: You probably want to restrict the input to non-negative numbers in order to avoid the complication of distinguishing the negative sign of a number from a binary subtraction operation.

postfix evaluation algorithm

Our algorithm for evaluating a postfix expression uses only one stack, which is a stack of numbers. There is no need for a second stack of operation symbols, because *each operation is used as soon as it is read*. In fact, the reason why postfix evaluation is easy is precisely because each operation symbol is immediately used as soon as it is read. In the algorithm we assume that each input entry is either a number or an operation. For simplicity, we will assume that all the operations take two arguments. The complete evaluation algorithm is given in Figure 7.10, along with an example computation.

Let's study the example to see how the algorithm works. Each time an operation appears in the input, the operands for the operation are the two most recently seen numbers. For example, in Figure 7.10(c), we are about to read the * symbol. Since we have just pushed 3 and 2 onto the stack, the * causes a multiplication of 3*2, resulting in 6. The result of 6 is then pushed onto the stack, as shown in Figure 7.10(d).

Sometimes the "most recently seen number" is not actually an input number, but instead it is a number that we computed and pushed back onto the stack. For example, in Figure 7.10(d), we are about to read the first +. At this point, 6 is on top of the stack (as a result of multiplying 3*2). Below the 6 is the number 5. So, the "two most recently seen numbers" are the 6 (that we computed) and the 5 (underneath the 6). We add these two numbers, resulting in 11 (which we push onto the stack, as shown in 7.10(e)).

And so the process continues: Each time we encounter an operation, the operation is immediately applied to the two most recently seen numbers, which always reside in the top two positions of the stack. When the input is exhausted, the number remaining in the stack is the value of the entire expression.

Translating Infix to Postfix Notation

infix expression

↓

postfix expression

Because it is so easy to evaluate a postfix expression, one strategy for evaluating an ordinary infix expression is to first convert it to postfix notation and then evaluate the postfix expression. This is what compilers often do. In this section, we will present an algorithm to translate an infix expression to a postfix expression. The algorithm's input is an expression in infix notation, and the output is an equivalent expression in postfix notation. We will develop the algorithm as pseudocode and will not specify any precise form of input or output.

Until now we have assumed that the operands in our arithmetic expressions were all numbers. That need not be true. For example, an arithmetic expression may also contain variables. In this example, we will assume that the arithmetic expression can also contain variables. In fact, the operands may be anything at all, so long as we have a way of recognizing an operand when our algorithm encounters one. However, in our examples we will assume that the operands are either numbers or variables. We will also assume that all the operations are **binary operations** (which have two operands), such as addition and subtraction. There will be no **unary operations** (which have only one operand), such as `sqrt` for the square root function. We will present two algorithms, one for fully parenthesized expressions and one for more realistic expressions that omit some parentheses. Our algorithms apply to any sort of operations working on any sort of operands; so, in particular, our algorithms will work on boolean expressions as

FIGURE 7.10   Evaluating a Postfix Expression

Pseudocode

1. Initialize a stack of double numbers.
2. *do*

   >   *if* (the next input is a number)
   >   Read the next input and push it onto the stack.
   >   *else*
   >   {
   >
   >   Read the next character, which is an operation symbol.
   >   Pop two numbers off the stack.
   >   Combine the two numbers with the operation (using the *second* number popped as the *left* operand), and push the result onto the stack.
   >   }
   >   *while* (there is more of the expression to read);

3. At this point, the stack contains one number, which is the value of the expression.

Example

Evaluate the postfix expression
    5   3   2   *   +   4   −   5   +

(a) Input so far (shaded):
5 3 2 * + 4 − 5 +

| |
| 5 |

(b) Input so far (shaded):
5 3 2 * + 4 − 5 +

| |
| 3 |
| 5 |

(c) Input so far (shaded):
5 3 2 * + 4 − 5 +

| |
| 2 |
| 3 |
| 5 |

(d) Input so far (shaded):
5 3 2 * + 4 − 5 +

| |
| 6 |
| 5 |

(e) Input so far (shaded):
5 3 2 * + 4 − 5 +

| |
| 11 |

(f) Input so far (shaded):
5 3 2 * + 4 − 5 +

| |
| 4 |
| 11 |

(g) Input so far (shaded):
5 3 2 * + 4 − 5 +

| |
| 7 |

(h) Input so far (shaded):
5 3 2 * + 4 − 5 +

| |
| 5 |
| 7 |

(i) Input so far (shaded):
5 3 2 * + 4 − 5 +

| |
| 12 |

The result of
the computation
is 12.

well as arithmetic expressions. However, in order to keep matters uncluttered, we will only consider arithmetic expressions in our examples.

algorithm for fully parenthesized expressions

If the infix expression is fully parenthesized, the algorithm is simple. All that's needed to convert from infix to postfix notation is to move each operation symbol to the location of the right parenthesis corresponding to that operation and then remove all parentheses. For example, the following infix expression will have its operation symbols moved to the location indicated by the arrows:

The result is the postfix expression:

```
A 7 + B C / * 2 D * -
```

This process of moving each operation to the location of its corresponding right parenthesis is more of an idea than a complete algorithm. A complete algorithm should read the expression from left to right and must somehow remember the operations and then determine when the corresponding right parenthesis has been found. We have some work to do before this idea becomes an algorithm.

First, observe that the operands (that is, the numbers and variables) in the equivalent postfix expression are in the same order as the operands in the corresponding infix expression that we start out with. So our algorithm can simply copy the infix expression operands, omitting parentheses, and inserting the operations, such as +, *, and so forth, at the correct locations. The problem is finding the location for inserting the operations in the postfix expression. How do we save the operations, and how do we know when to insert them? Look back at our example. If we push the operations onto a stack, then the operations we need will always be on top of the stack. When do we insert an operation? We insert an operation into the output whenever we encounter a right parenthesis in the input. Hence, the heart of the algorithm is to push the operations onto a stack and to pop an operation every time we encounter a right parenthesis. The algorithm is given in Figure 7.11. The algorithm does some checking to ensure that the input expression is fully parenthesized with balanced parentheses, although there is no checking to ensure that each operation appears between its operands (rather than before or after its operands).

Using Precedence Rules in the Infix Expression

So far we have been assuming that our infix expression is fully parenthesized. However, in practice, infix expressions are usually not fully parenthesized, and the computer must rely on precedence rules to determine the order of operations for the missing parentheses. This adds a significant complication.

FIGURE 7.11	Converting a Fully Parenthesized Infix Expression to a Postfix Expression

Pseudocode

1. Initialize a stack of characters to hold the operation symbols and parentheses.

2. *do*

   if (the next input is a left parenthesis)
   Read the left parenthesis and push it onto the stack.
   else if (the next input is a number or other operand)
   Read the operand and write it to the output.
   else if (the next input is one of the operation symbols)
   Read the operation symbol and push it onto the stack.
   else
   {

   Read and discard the next input symbol (which should be a right parenthesis). There should be an operation symbol on top of the stack, so pop this symbol and write it to the output. (If there is no such symbol, then print an error message indicating that there were too few operations in the infix expression, and halt.) After popping the operation symbol, there should be a left parenthesis on the top of the stack, so pop and discard this left parenthesis.
   (If there was no left parenthesis, then the input did not have balanced parentheses, so print an error message and halt.)

   }
   while (there is more of the expression to read) ;

3. At this point, the stack should be empty. Otherwise print an error message indicating that the expression was not fully parenthesized.

Let's start with an example. We will use the usual C++ precedence rules in our example. Consider the following expression:

    2 * (A - B) + 3 + C

In this case the subtraction is performed first, then the multiplication, and finally the two additions are performed from left to right. The subtraction is first because the parentheses indicate that (A - B) must be evaluated before combining the result with any other operands. The multiplication is performed next—before the additions—because multiplication has *higher precedence* than addition. The two additions are of equal precedence and there are no parentheses to tell us which addition to perform first. Operations of equal precedence are performed in left to right order (when parentheses do not indicate some other order). Thus, the left-hand addition occurs before the right-hand addition. This order of evaluation means the expression is the same as this fully parenthesized expression:

    (((2 * (A - B)) + 3) + C)

In order to help determine the order of evaluation for arithmetic expressions, we have been referring to the *precedence* of operations, such as +, -, and *. A **precedence** is just an ordering from high to low for the operations. Operations with a higher precedence are evaluated before operations with a lower precedence. Sometimes, two different operations, such as + and - have equal precedence, in which case we must specify whether the operations are to be evaluated left-to-right or right-to-left. We only need to know when one operation has higher precedence than another, and the direction of evaluation (left-to-right or right-to-left) for operations with equal precedence. For example, in C++, * and / have equal precedence; + and - also have equal precedence, but * and / have higher precedence than + and -. That is why we perform multiplication before addition (when there are no parentheses indicating otherwise.)

Just to make sure they are fresh in our minds, let us review the C++ rules for evaluating arithmetic expressions that are not fully parenthesized:

rules for using precedence

1. Parentheses, when they are present, determine the order of operations. Everything inside a pair of matching parentheses is evaluated, and that value is then combined with things outside the parentheses.
2. If the order is not indicated by parentheses, operations of higher precedence are performed before operations of lower precedence.
3. Arithmetic operations of equal precedence are performed in left to right order, unless parentheses indicate otherwise.

In Figure 7.11 we gave an algorithm to convert a fully parenthesized infix expression to an equivalent postfix expression. Now we can make our algorithm more general. The new version (Figure 7.12 on page 339) does not require full parentheses for the input; the algorithm uses precedence to decide which operation to perform first. In other words, the expressions can be written as we normally write them with parentheses omitted in some cases. Figure 7.13 on page 340 contains an example computation of our algorithm as it translates an infix expression into the corresponding postfix expression. Study the example now, then return here to read the details of the algorithm.

Correctness of the Conversion from Infix to Postfix

In order for the conversion algorithm to be correct, we need to check these items:

1. The postfix expression contains the correct operands in the correct order.
2. The postfix expression evaluates subexpressions in the way indicated by the parentheses in the infix expression.
3. The postfix expression handles operations of differing precedence according to the precedence rules.
4. A string of operations of equal precedence in the infix expression is handled correctly when translated into the postfix expression.

1. The operands are in the right order

Let's consider each of these four issues. First we need to know that the operands (the numbers and variables) in the postfix expression are in the same order as they were in the input infix expression, but this is easy to see. Because operands are written out as soon as they are read in, they are clearly in the same order as in the input infix expression.

2. The parentheses are done correctly

Parentheses are a way of grouping subexpressions. Everything inside a pair of matching parentheses is treated as a single unit by anything outside the parentheses. The parentheses give the following message to the operations outside of the parentheses: *Don't look inside these parentheses. We will work things out among ourselves and deliver a single value for you to combine with other operands.* This means that all operations between a set of matching parentheses in the infix expression should form a subexpression of the postfix expression, and with this algorithm they do just that. To see that they do form a subexpression, we will show the following:

**How the Infix to Postfix Algorithm
Translates Subexpressions**

Claim: All of the operations between a pair of matching parentheses (and no other operations) are output in the time between reading the opening parenthesis and the time that the algorithm reads the closing parenthesis.

Once we show that this claim is true, we will know that all the operations between a pair of matching parentheses in the infix expression will be together in a group within the output postfix notation, and so they will form a subexpression of the postfix expression. So, let's see exactly why the claim is valid.

The algorithm keeps track of expressions within matching parentheses by using the stack. When the algorithm encounters an opening parenthesis, that is, a '(', it pushes this parenthesis onto the stack. Now consider what happens between pushing the opening parenthesis and encountering the matching closing parenthesis, i.e., the matching ')'. The algorithm will never output an operation from the stack that is below the opening parenthesis, '('. Thus, it only outputs operations that are within the pair of matching parentheses in the input (infix) expression. Moreover, it outputs all of these operations. When it encounters the matching closing parenthesis, it outputs all the remaining operations on the stack all the way down to that matching opening parenthesis.

3. The precedence is handled correctly

When the infix expression contains an operation with low precedence followed by an operation with a higher precedence, then the algorithm should output these operations in reverse order. In other words, the higher precedence operation must be written first. A check of the algorithm will show that the operations are indeed output in reverse order.

When the infix expression contains a sequence of operations of equal precedence, they represent an evaluation that goes from left to right. That means the operations should be output from left to right. If you check the algorithm, you will see that this is true. Operations are pushed onto the stack, but when the next operation of equal precedence is encountered, the operation in the stack is output and the new operation is pushed onto the stack. To confirm this, first check the algorithm in the case where the stack is empty at the time that the operations are encountered. That is the easiest case to see. After that, the other cases will be clearer, because they are similar.

4. operations of equal precedence are handled correctly

| **FIGURE 7.12** | Converting an Infix Expression to a Postfix Expression (General Case) |

Pseudocode

1. Initialize a stack of characters to hold the operation symbols and parentheses.

2. *do*

   if (the next input is a left parenthesis)
   Read the left parenthesis and push it onto the stack.
   else if (the next input is a number or other operand)
   Read the operand and write it to the output.
   else if (the next input is one of the operation symbols)
   {

   > Pop and print operations off the stack until one of three things occurs: (1) The stack becomes empty, or (2) The next symbol on the stack is a left parenthesis, or (3) The next symbol on the stack is an operation with lower precedence than the next input symbol. When one of these situations occurs, stop popping, read the next input symbol, and push this symbol onto the stack.

   }
   else
   {

   > Read and discard the next input symbol (which should be a right parenthesis). Pop and print operations off the stack until the next symbol on the stack is a left parenthesis. (If no left parenthesis is encountered, then print an error message indicating unbalanced parentheses, and halt.) Finally, pop and discard the left parenthesis.

   }
   while (there is more of the expression to read) ;

3. Pop and print any remaining operations on the stack. (There should be no remaining left parentheses, otherwise the input expression did not have balanced parentheses.)

FIGURE 7.13	Example Computation for the Algorithm of Figure 7.12

Example

Convert the infix expression:

3 * X + (Y - 12) - Z

(a) Input so far (shaded):

3 * X + (Y - 12) - Z
The operand 3 is printed.

Output so far:
3

(b) Input so far (shaded):
3 * X + (Y - 12) - Z
The * is pushed.

Output so far:
3

(c) Input so far (shaded):
3 * X + (Y - 12) - Z
The operand X is printed.

Output so far:
3 X

(d) Input so far (shaded):
3 * X + (Y - 12) - Z
Pop and print the * since it has higher precedence than the +; then push the +.

Output so far:
3 X *

(e) Input so far (shaded):
3 * X + (Y - 12) - Z
Push the parenthesis.

Output so far:
3 X *

(f) Input so far (shaded):
3 * X + (Y - 12) - Z
The operand Y is printed.

Output so far:
3 X * Y

(g) Input so far (shaded):
3 * X + (Y - 12) - Z
The - is pushed.

Output so far:
3 X * Y

(h) Input so far (shaded):
3 * X + (Y - 12) - Z
The operand 12 is printed.

Output so far:
3 X * Y 12

(i) Input so far (shaded):
3 * X + (Y - 12) - Z
Pop until left parenthesis.

Output so far:
3 X * Y 12 -

(j) Input so far (shaded):
3 * X + (Y - 12) - Z
Pop and print the + since it has precedence equal to the -; then push the -.

Output so far:
3 X * Y 12 - +

(k) Input so far (shaded):
3 * X + (Y - 12) - Z
The operand Z is printed.

Output so far:
3 X * Y 12 - + Z

(l) Input so far (shaded):
3 * X + (Y - 12) - Z
Pop any remaining operations.

Output so far:
3 X * Y 12 - + Z -

Self-Test Exercises

11. Evaluate the postfix expression 2 3 - 43 +.

12. Trace the algorithm from Figure 7.10 on page 334 to evaluate the postfix expression 15 9 6 * + 12 - 15 +. Draw the stack after each push or pop.

13. Trace the algorithm from Figure 7.12 on page 339 to create a postfix expression from 3 / A + (B + 12) - C.

CHAPTER SUMMARY

- A stack is a Last-In/First-Out data structure.

- Adding an entry to a stack is called a *push* operation. Removing an entry from a stack is called a *pop* operation.

- Attempting to push an entry onto a full stack is an error known as a *stack overflow*. Attempting to pop an entry off an empty stack is an error known as a *stack underflow*.

- A stack can be implemented as a partially filled array.

- A stack can be implemented as a linked list.

- An advantage of a linked list implementation of a stack over an array implementation is that with the linked list there is no preset limit on the number of entries you can add to the stack.

- Stacks have many uses in computer science. The evaluation and translation of arithmetic expressions are two common uses.

Solutions to Self-Test Exercises ?

1. Push a 'D'; Push an 'A'; Push an 'H'; Push an 'L'; Pop an 'L'; Pop an 'H'; Pop an 'A'; Pop a 'D'; The output is LHAD.

2. Pop one item, storing it in a local variable called top. Then peek at the next item, storing it in another local variable called result. Push the top back on the stack, and return the result.

3. Within read_and_evaluate, there is a call to strchr to determine whether the next character is one of the operators. This call should add the symbol '^' to its list of operators. Also,

add a new case to the switch statement within the function evaluate_stack_tops. The new case is for the exponentiation operator. This calculates operand1 raised to the power of operand2 and pushes the result back onto the numbers stack.

4. The modification is most easily accomplished in the function read_and_evaluate. Within this function, you can add a bit of code after the line ins >> symbol; This is the line that reads an operator symbol. After reading such a symbol, check whether the symbol is a slash ('/'), and peek ahead to see whether the next

symbol is also a slash. If so, then read and discard the rest of the line (instead of pushing the operator onto the stack).

5. Any pop operation has the potential for a stack underflow. In the evaluation algorithm, the pops occur in `evaluate_stack_tops`, which is called whenever a right parenthesis is encountered. If the input expression is correctly formed, then at the point of the right parenthesis there will always be at least one operation on the character stack and at least two operands on the numbers stack—and therefore there can be no stack underflow. But if one of the operations is omitted from the input expression, then when the right parenthesis occurs, there can be a stack underflow on the character stack. And if one of the operands is omitted from the input expression, then when the right parenthesis occurs, there can be a stack underflow on the numbers stack.

6. A stack overflow can occur if the input expression has parentheses that are nested too deeply. For example, consider the input expression (1 + (2 + (3 + (4 + 5)))). By the time the 5 is read and pushed on the stack, the 1, 2, 3 and 4 are already on the numbers stack. Thus, there is a limit to how deeply we can nest this kind of subexpression. In the example above, there are four nested

subexpressions, and we need to push five numbers onto the numbers stack. So, the limit to this kind of nesting is one less than the stack capacity.

7. The function should return CAPACITY minus used.

8. Use a dynamic array.

9. Here is one solution:
```
template <class Item>
Item Stack<Item>::second( ) const
// Libraries used: assert.h
{
    assert(size( ) >= 2);
    return top_ptr->link->data;
}
```

10. Our `size` implementation calls `list_size`, which is linear time. For a constant time implementation, you could maintain another private member variable to continually keep track of the list length.

11. 42

12. The trace is the same as the computation at the bottom of Figure 7.8 on page 328, except that the numbers are three times as large.

13. The trace is much the same as the computation in Figure 7.13 on page 340, except that the operations are different.

PROGRAMMING PROJECTS

1 In our first case study on evaluating arithmetic expressions we used two stacks that held different types of data. In some other applications, we might need two stacks with the same type of data. If we implement the stacks as arrays, there is a chance that one array (and hence one stack) will become filled causing our computation to end prematurely. This might be a shame, since the other array (stack) might have plenty of room. One way around this problem is to implement two stacks

as one large array rather than two smaller arrays. Write an ADT for a pair of stacks. A pair of stacks is simply an object with two stacks. Call these stacks *StackA* and *StackB*. There should be separate operations for each stack, e.g., pop_a and pop_b. Implement the stack pair as a single array. The two stacks will grow from the two ends of the array, so for example one stack could fill up one quarter of the array while the other fills up three quarters of the array.

2 Choose one of the stack implementations and implement a general version of the `peek` member function with this specification:

```
Item peek(size_t n = 1);
// Precondition: n > 0 and n <= stack size.
// Postcondition: The return value is the
// item that is n from the top (with the top at
// n = 1, the next at n = 2, and so on). The
// stack is not changed.
```

3 In this exercise you will need the version of `peek` from the previous programming project.
Write a program that prints all strings with at most *n* letters, where the letters are chosen from a range `first...last`, which is a subrange of the type *char*. Below is an outline for an algorithm to do this using a stack. Your program should use a stack to implement this algorithm:

```
// Writing all strings of 1 to n letters:
Push first onto the stack.
while (the stack is not empty)
{
    Print the contents of the stack using peek.
    if (the stack contains fewer than n letters)
        Push first onto the stack.
    else
    {
        Pop characters off the stack, until the
        stack is empty, or there is a character
        other than last on the top. (Note: if the
        top character is not last, then nothing is
        popped off the stack.)
        if (the stack is not empty)
            Pop a character c off the stack, and
            push c+1 (i.e., the next letter) onto
            the stack.
    }
}
```

4 Enhance the calculator program given in Figure 7.5 on page 319 so that it has all of the following features: After one expression is evaluated, the user is asked if he or she wants to evaluate another expression and is allowed to choose between evaluating another expression and quitting the program. Expressions need not be fully parenthesized, and when parentheses are missing, the usual C++ precedence rules are followed. If the arithmetic expression entered is not well-formed, then the user is told it is not well-formed and asked to reenter the expression.

5 In Figure 7.5 on page 319 we presented a program to evaluate arithmetic expressions.
In this exercise you will write a similar program to evaluate boolean expressions. Rather than arithmetic operations, the input expressions for this program will use the operations && (the "and" operation), || (the "or" operation), and !(the "not" operation). Rather than combining numbers, the input expression will combine simple boolean comparisons of numbers such as (1 < 2) and (6 < 3). Assume all the numbers in these simple comparisons are integers. Allow the following comparison operations: <, >, <=, >=, ==, and !=. At first assume that all boolean expressions are fully parenthesized and well-formed. Be sure to note that "not" is a unary operation. You can assume that the argument to "not" (which follows the !) is enclosed in parentheses. Your program should allow the user to evaluate additional expressions until the user says he/she wishes to end the program.
For a more difficult assignment, enhance your program by adding any or all of the following features: (a) The numbers need not be integers; (b) The expression need not be fully parenthesized and if parentheses are missing, then the C++ precedence rules apply. (Note that innermost expressions such as (1 < 2) are still assumed to be in parentheses.) (c) The expression need not be well-formed and if it is not well-formed, then the user is asked to reenter the expression.

6 Write a program that evaluates an arithmetic expression in postfix notation. The basic algorithm is contained in "Evaluating Postfix Expressions" on page 331. Assume the input contains numbers (but no variables) as well as the arithmetic operations +, -, *, and /. Your program should allow the user to evaluate additional expressions until the user wants to end the program. You might also enhance your program so that the expression need not be well-formed, and if it is not well-formed, then the user must reenter the expression.

7 Write a program that takes as input an infix expression and outputs the equivalent postfix expression. The basic algorithm is contained in "Translating Infix to Postfix Notation" on page 333. Assume that the input may contain numbers, variables, arithmetic operations +, -, *, and /, as well as parentheses. However, the expression need not be fully parenthesized, and when parentheses are missing, the usual C++ precedence rules are used to determine the order of evaluation. Your program should allow the user to enter additional expressions until the user says he/she wishes to end the program. For a more difficult assignment, enhance your program so that the expression need not be well-formed and if it is not well-formed, then the user is asked to reenter the expression.

8 Redo the calculator program given in Figure 7.5 on page 319, but this time implement it in a different way. To evaluate the arithmetic expression, your program will first convert the expression to postfix notation. After that, it will evaluate the postfix expression. Pseudocode for both of these subtasks is given in this chapter. For this exercise, you should not assume that expressions are fully parenthesized. When parentheses are missing, the usual C++ precedence rules are used to determine the order of evaluation. Your program should allow the user to evaluate additional expressions until the user wants to end the program.

9 Suppose that you have n queens from a chess game, and that you also have an n by n chess board. Is it possible to place all n queens on the board so that no two queens are in the same row, no two queens are in the same column, and no two queens are on the same diagonal? For example, a solution with $n=5$ is shown here:

Solution to the
5-queens problem

This problem is called the n-queens problem. For this project, you are to write a function that has one integer parameter, n, and determines whether there is a solution to the n-queens problem. If a solution is found then the procedure prints the row and column of each queen. Your program should solve the problem by making a sequence of choices, such as "Try placing the row 1 queen in column 1," or "Try placing the row 7 queen in column 3." Each time a choice is made, the choice is pushed onto a stack that already contains all the previously made choices. The purpose of the stack is to make it easy to fix incorrect choices, following the pseudocode, using a stack, s, and a boolean variable, success:

Push information onto the stack indicating the first choice is a queen in row 1, column 1.

```
success = false;
while (!success && !s.is_empty( ))
{
```
   Check whether the most recent choice (on top of the stack) is in the same row, same column, or same diagonal as any other choices (below the top). If so, then we say there is a conflict; otherwise there is no conflict.

   `if` (there is a conflict)
       Pop elements off the stack until the stack becomes empty, or the top of the stack is a choice that is not in column n. If the stack is now not empty, then increase the column number of the top choice by 1.

   `else if` (no conflict, and the stack size is n)
       Set success to true because we have found a solution to the n-queens problem.

   `else`
       Push information onto the stack indicating that the next choice is to place a queen at row number s.size( )+1, and column number 1.
```
}
```

This technique is called **backtracking** since we keep our choices on a stack and *back-up* to correct any mistakes that are made. Notice that when you check for a conflict, you will need access to the entire stack (not just the top), so that you should use the extended version of peek from Programming Project 2 on page 343.

8 Queues

He who comes first, eats first.

Eike von Repkow
Sachsenspiegel

A *queue* is a First-In/First-Out data structure similar to a line of people at a ticket window. It can be used whenever you need a data structure that allows entries to "wait their turn." In this chapter we discuss applications of the queue data structure, give two implementations of a queue ADT, and discuss the differences between queues and stacks. We also discuss and implement a more flexible kind of queue called a *priority queue*.

8.1   INTRODUCTION TO QUEUES

The word *queue* is pronounced as if you were saying the letter Q; the word *queue* means the same thing as the word *line* when used in phrases like "waiting in a line." Every time you get in line at a supermarket or in a bank or at a ticket window, you are adding yourself to a queue. If everybody is polite, then people add themselves to the rear of the queue (the rear of the line), and the person at the front of the queue is always the person who is served first. The queue data structure works in exactly the same way, and the abstract definition of a queue reflects this intuition.

Queue Definition

A **queue** is a data structure of ordered entries such that entries can only be inserted at one end (called the **rear**) and removed at the other end (called the **front**). The entry at the front end of the queue is called the **first entry**.

When we say that the entries in a queue are *ordered,* all we mean is that there is a first one (the front one), a second one, a third one, and so forth. We do *not* require that the entries can be compared using the < operator. The entries may be of any type. In this regard, the situation is the same as it was for a stack.

stacks versus queues

Because entries must be removed in exactly the same order that they were added to the queue, a queue is called a "First-In/First-Out" data structure (abbreviated **FIFO**). This differs from a stack, which is a Last-In/First-Out data structure, but apart from this difference, a stack and a queue are very similar data structures. They differ only in the rule that determines which entry is removed from the list first. The contrast between stacks and queues is illustrated in Figure 8.1. In either structure the entries depicted are entered in the order A, B, C, and D. With a queue, they are removed in the same order: A, B, C, D. With a stack, they are removed in the reverse order: D, C, B, A.

FIFO

A queue is a First-In/First-Out data structure. Items are taken out of the queue in the same order that they were put into the queue.

FIGURE 8.1   Contrasting a Stack and a Queue.

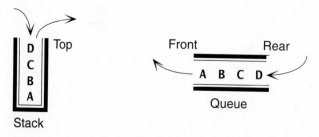

The Queue ADT

In Figure 8.2 we specify an abstract data type for a queue. Later we will implement it as a C++ class. The specification for the queue ADT follows the same general pattern as the generic stack ADT of Chapter 7. As with our stack, the queue is a template class that depends on a template parameter for the type of the items in the queue. Our specification also indicates a member constant, CAPACITY to determine how many items the queue can hold. As you will see

---

FIGURE 8.2	Documentation for the Queue Header File

A Header File

```
// FILE: queue1.h
// TEMPLATE CLASS PROVIDED: Queue<Item> (a queue of items)
//     The template parameter, Item, is the data type of the items in the Queue.
//     It may be any of the C++ built-in types (int, char, etc.), or a class with a default
//     constructor, a copy constructor, and assignment operator.
//
// MEMBER CONSTANT for the Queue<Item> template class:
//     static const size_t CAPACITY = _____
//         Queue<Item>::CAPACITY is the maximum number of items that a Queue can hold.
//
// CONSTRUCTOR for the Queue<Item> template class:
//     Queue( )
//         Postcondition: The Queue has been initialized as an empty Queue.
//
// MODIFICATION MEMBER FUNCTIONS for the Queue<Item> template class:
//     void insert(const Item& entry)
//         Precondition: size( ) < CAPACITY.
//         Postcondition: A new copy of entry has been inserted at the rear of the Queue.
//
//     Item get_front( )
//         Precondition: size( ) > 0.
//         Postcondition: The front item of the Queue has been removed and returned.
//
// CONSTANT MEMBER FUNCTIONS for the Queue<Item> template class:
//     size_t size( ) const
//         Postcondition: The return value is the total number of items in the Queue.
//
//     bool is_empty( ) const
//         Postcondition: The return value is true if the Queue is empty.
//
// VALUE SEMANTICS for the Queue<Item> template class:
//     Assignments and the copy constructor may be used with Queue<Item> objects.
```

queue1.h	FTP

later, only one of our two queue implementations actually requires a capacity. By now you should be able to guess that the implementation that requires a capacity will use a fixed size array, whereas the second implementation will use dynamic memory to avoid a predetermined capacity. The queue's member functions include operations to remove the entry from the front of the queue, to add an entry to the rear of the queue, and so on.

The procedure for adding an entry to the queue is often called an **enqueue** operation (pronounced *en-q*), which is a shortening of "*en*tering the *queue*." But for adding an entry, we will use the simpler name `insert`. The procedure for removing an entry from the queue is often called a **dequeue** operation (pronounced *de-q*), which means "*de*leting from the *queue*," but we will use the simpler name `get_front`.

queue overflow and queue underflow

If a program attempts to add an entry to a queue that is already at its capacity, this is, of course, an error. This error is called **queue overflow**. If a program attempts to remove an entry from an empty queue, that is another kind of error, called **queue underflow**. To help you avoid these errors, the abstract data type provides a boolean function to test for an empty queue and a second function to return the current number of items in the queue. (The function `is_empty` is redundant, since the function `size` can be used to test for an empty queue. However, using the function `is_empty` can make the meaning of your code clearer.)

We could add other operations, such as a procedure to look at the front entry of the queue without removing it from the queue, but this minimal set of operations will be enough for our purposes.

Uses for Queues

Uses for queues are easy to find—we often use queues in our everyday affairs, such as when we wait in line at a bank. To get a feel for using a queue in an algorithm we will first consider a simple example.

copying a word

Suppose you want a program to read a word and then write the word. This is so simple that you may wonder why we bother to consider this task, but it is best to start with a simple example. One way to accomplish this task is to read the input one letter at a time and place each letter in a queue. After the word is read, the letters in the queue are written out. Because a queue is a First-In/First-Out data structure, the letters are written in the same order in which they were read.

The pseudocode for this approach to copying a word is as follows:

```
// Echoing a word
```
1. Declare a queue of characters.
2. *while* (there are more characters of the word to read)
   {
       Read a character.
       Insert the character into the queue.
   }

3. *while* (the queue is not empty)
   {
         Get the front character from the queue.
         Write the character to the screen.
   }

simulation programs

Because queues occur so frequently in real life situations, they are frequently used in simulation programs. For example, a program to simulate the traffic at an intersection might use a software queue to simulate the real-life situation of a growing line of automobiles waiting for a traffic light to change from red to green.

input/output buffering

Queues also appear in computer system software, such as the operating system that runs on your PC. For example, consider a program that reads input from the keyboard. We think of a program as directly reading its input from the keyboard. However, if you think of what actually happens when you give a line of input to a program, you will realize that the program does not necessarily read a character when the corresponding keyboard key is pressed. This allows you to type input to the program, and that input is saved in a queue by software that is part of the operating system. When the program asks for input, the operating system provides characters from the front of its queue. This is called **buffering** the input, and is controlled by the PC's operating system software. In reality, a more sophisticated data structure is used rather than a queue, allowing you to back up and retype part of the line. Also, this form of buffering data in a queue is often used when one computer component is receiving data from another faster computer component. For example, if your fast CPU (central processor unit) is sending data to your printer, which is slow by comparison, then the data is buffered in a queue. By using the queue in this way, the CPU need not wait for the printer to finish printing the first character before the CPU sends the next character.

In a computer system in which more than one process or component uses a single resource, a queue is often used so that the processes or components wait in line and are served on a "first-come, first-served" basis, just like customers in a bank line. For example, if several computers are networked so that they all use the same printer, then a queue would be used to let them "wait in line" whenever more than one computer wants to use the printer at the same time.

Self-Test Exercises

1. Suppose a program uses a queue of characters to read in a word and then echo it to the screen, as described in the pseudocode on page 348. Now suppose the input word is LINE. Trace the algorithm, giving all the calls to the operations `insert` and `get_front`.

2. Name some common situations where a PC's operating system uses some kind of a queue.

3. Write pseudocode for an algorithm that reads an even number of characters. The algorithm then prints the first character, third character, fifth character, and so on. On a second output line, the algorithm prints the second character, fourth character, sixth character, and so on. Use two queues to store the characters.

8.2 QUEUE APPLICATIONS

Before we actually implement the queue class, we'll show two applications that use the queue specified in Figure 8.2 on page 347. We'll assume that the header file for this queue is called `queue1.h`. Since the queue is a template class, our two applications can use different kinds of queues. The first application uses a queue of characters, while the second uses a queue of integers.

PROGRAMMING EXAMPLE: Recognizing Palindromes

A **palindrome** is a string that reads the same forward and backward; that is, the letters are the same whether you read them from right to left or from left to right. For example, the one-word string "radar" is a palindrome. A more complicated example of a palindrome is the following sentence:

```
Able was I ere I saw Elba
```

Palindromes are fun to make up, and they even have applications in at least one area—the analysis of genetic material.

Suppose we want a program to read a line of text and tell us if the line is a palindrome. We can do this by using both a stack and a queue. We will read the line of text into both a stack and a queue, and then write out the contents of the stack and the contents of the queue. The line that is written using the queue is written forward, and the line that is written using the stack is written backward. Now, if those two output lines are the same, then the input string must be a palindrome. Of course, the program need not actually write out the contents of the stack and the queue. The program can simply compare the contents of the stack and the queue character-by-character to see if they would produce the same string of characters.

A program that checks for palindromes in the way we just outlined is given in Figure 8.3. This program uses the stack class defined in Figure 7.1 on page 309 as well as the queue class from Figure 8.2 on page 347. In this program we treat both the upper-case and lower-case versions of a letter as being the same character. This is because we want to consider a sentence as reading the same forward and backward even though it might start with an upper-case letter and end with a lower-case letter. For example, the string "Able was I ere I saw Elba" when written backwards reads "ablE was I ere I saw elbA". The two strings match, provided we agree to consider upper- and lower-case versions of a letter as being

FIGURE 8.3 | A Program to Recognize Palindromes

A Program

```
// FILE: pal.cxx
// A program to test whether an input line is a palindrome. The program ignores spaces,
// punctuation, and the difference between upper- and lower-case letters.

#include <assert.h>    // Provides assert
#include <ctype.h>     // Provides isalpha, toupper
#include <iostream.h>  // Provides cout, cin, peek
#include <stdlib.h>    // Provides size_t, EXIT_SUCCESS
#include "queue1.h"    // Provides the Queue template class
#include "stack1.h"    // Provides the Stack template class

int main( )
{
    Queue<char> q;
    Stack<char> s;
    char letter;               // A character in the input string
    size_t mismatches = 0;     // How often the queue does not match the stack

    cout << "Enter a line and I will see if it's a palindrome:" << endl;

    while (cin.peek( ) != '\n')
    {
        cin >> letter;
        if (isalpha(letter))
        {
            assert(q.size( ) < q.CAPACITY);
            assert(s.size( ) < s.CAPACITY);
            q.insert(toupper(letter));
            s.push(toupper(letter));
        }
    }

    while ((!q.is_empty( )) && (!s.is_empty( )))
    {
        if (q.get_front( ) != s.pop( ))
            mismatches++;
    }

    if (mismatches == 0)
        cout << "That is a palindrome." << endl;
    else
        cout << "That is not a palindrome." << endl;
    return EXIT_SUCCESS;
}
```

pal.cxx | FTP

the toupper function converts lower-case letters to upper-case letters

equal. The treatment of the letters' cases is accomplished with a useful function called `toupper`, from the `ctype.h` library facility. This function has one character as an argument. If this character is a lower-case letter, then the function converts it to the corresponding upper-case letter and returns this value. Otherwise, the function returns the character unchanged.

Our program also ignores spaces and punctuation, requiring only that the *letters* on the line read the same forward and backward. This way we can find more palindromes. If we look only at letters, discarding both spaces and punctuation, then there are many more palindromes. However, they are not always easy to spot. For example, you might not immediately recognize the following as a palindrome:

```
Straw? No, too stupid a fad. I put soot on warts.
```

the isalpha function determines which characters are letters

Depending on your current frame of mind, you may think that discovering such sentences is also a stupid fad, but nevertheless, our program ignores blanks and punctuation. Therefore, according to our program, the above is a palindrome. The determination of whether a character is a letter is accomplished with another function from `ctype.h`. The function, called `isalpha`, returns true if its single argument is one of the alphabetic characters.

Two sample dialogues from the palindrome program are shown in Figure 8.4. As we often do, we have presented a minimal program to concentrate on the new material being presented. Before the program is released to users, it should be enhanced in a number of ways to make it more robust (such as better handling of a possible stack or queue overflow) and more friendly (such as allowing more than one sentence to be entered).

FIGURE 8.4   Sample Dialogues from the Palindrome Program

First Sample Dialogue

```
Enter a line and I will see if it's a palindrome:
Straw? No, too stupid a fad. I put soot on warts.
That is a palindrome.
```

Second Sample Dialogue

```
Enter a line and I will see if it's a palindrome:
Able were you ere you saw Elba.
That is not a palindrome.
```

Self-Test Exercises

4. How would you modify the palindromes program so that it indicates the first position in the input string that violates the palindrome property? For example, consider the input "Able were you ere you saw Elba." This looks like a palindrome until you see the first "e" in "were," so a suitable output would be

   ```
   That is not a palindrome.
   Mismatch discovered at: Able we
   ```

5. How would you modify the palindromes program so that upper-case and lower-case versions of letters are considered different? In the modified program the string "able was I ere I saw elba" would still be considered a palindrome, but the string "Able was I ere I saw Elba" would no longer be considered a palindrome, since, among other things, the first and last letters, "A" and "a," are not the same under these changed rules.

PROGRAMMING EXAMPLE: Car Wash Simulation

The *Handy-Dandy Hand Car Wash Company* has decided to modernize and change its image. It has installed a fast, fully automated car-washing mechanism that can wash a car in one to ten minutes. It will soon reopen under its new name *The Automatic Auto Wash Emporium*. The company wants to know the most efficient way to use its new car-washing mechanism. If the mechanism is used on the fast setting, it can wash a car in one minute, but because of the high pressure required to operate at such speed, the mechanism uses a great deal of water and soap at this setting. At slower settings, it takes longer to wash a car but uses less soap and water. The company wants to know how many customers will be served and how long customers will have to wait in line when the washing mechanism is used at one of the slower speeds. The company also wants to know whether its new motto, "You Ought to Autowash your Auto," will be effective. We respectfully refuse comment on the motto, but we agree to write a program that will simulate automobiles waiting in line for a car wash. This way the manager of the car wash can see how the speed of the car wash, the length of the line, and various other factors interact.

Car Wash Simulation—Specification

The precise program specifications are given by the following input/output descriptions:

Input. The program has three input items: (1) The amount of time needed to wash one car (in total seconds); (2) The probability that a new customer arrives during any given second (we assume that, at most, one customer arrives in a second); and (3) The total length of time to be simulated (in seconds).

Output.   The program produces two pieces of output information: (1) The number of customers serviced in the simulated time; and (2) The average time that a customer spent in line during the simulation (in seconds).

Car Wash Simulation—Design

We will carry out a design of the program in a way that is common for many simulation tasks. The approach is to propose a collection of related object types that correspond to real-world objects in the situation that we are simulating. There are many possibilities—our particular approach focuses on the use of our queue class, which will be used to simulate a line of customers waiting to have their cars washed. We first discuss the queue and then go on to propose the other objects needed for the simulation.

the queue

We need to simulate a queue of customers, but we do not have real live customers, so we must decide how we will represent them. There are many ways to represent customers: We could use their names and place them in a queue of names; we could assign an arbitrary number to each customer and store that number in a queue of numbers; we could represent each customer by the make and year of the customer's automobile, or even by how dirty the automobile is. However, none of those representations has any relevance to the specified simulation. For this simulation, all we need to know about a customer is how long the customer waits in the queue. Hence, a good way to represent a customer is to use a number that represents the time that the customer entered the queue. Thus, our queue will be a queue of numbers. In a more complex simulation, it would be appropriate to implement the customers as objects, and one of the customer's member functions would be a function that returns the customer's arrival time.

> **Key Design Concept**
>
> *Determine which properties of a real-world object are relevant to the problem at hand.*

The numbers that record the times that customers entered the queue are called **time stamps**. Our simulation works in seconds, so a time stamp is just the number of simulated seconds that have passed since the start of the simulation. When the customer (represented by the time stamp) is removed from the queue, we can easily calculate the time the customer spent waiting: The time spent waiting is the total number of seconds simulated so far minus the time stamp.

propose a list of related object types

Now let us propose and discuss other objects that will be useful in the simulation program. In addition to the queue, we propose three other object types, listed here:

Washer.   A washer is an object that simulates the automatic car washing mechanism.

BooleanSource.   An object of this class provides a sequence of boolean values. Some of the elements in the sequence are true, and some are false. During the simulation, we will have one `BooleanSource` object that we query once per simulated second. If the query returns true as its response, this indicates that a new customer has arrived during the simulated second; a false return value indicates that no customer has arrived during the simulated second.

Averager. An averager computes the average of a sequence of numbers. For example, we might send the following four numbers into an averager: 10, 20, 2, and 12. The averager could then tell us that the average of these numbers is 11.0. The averager can also tell us how many numbers it has processed—in our example the averager processed four numbers. We'll use an averager to keep track of the average waiting time and the total number of cars washed.

A good way to design a simulation program is to first write pseudocode illustrating how the proposed objects will be used. From this pseudocode, we then extract the necessary member functions for each object. The simulation program that we have in mind will carry out the simulation using one-second intervals, and to make the simulation simpler, we assume that at most one customer arrives during any particular second. The simulation contains a loop that is iterated once for each simulated second. In each loop iteration, all the activities that take place in one second, such as the possible arrival of a new customer or the removal of a customer from the queue, will be simulated. When the loop terminates, the simulation is over and the needed output values are obtained from the averager. The basic pseudocode for the simulation is shown in Figure 8.5.

write pseudocode indicating how the objects are used

Let's examine the pseudocode and catalog the various actions of the objects one at a time. From this catalog we can later determine the list of member functions for each class.

determine the actions of each object

BooleanSource. During each simulated second, the `BooleanSource` provides us with a single boolean value indicating whether a new customer has arrived during that second. A true value indicates that a customer has arrived; a false indicates that no customer arrived. With this in mind, we propose two functions, described below.

The first function is a constructor for the `BooleanSource`. This constructor has one argument, which is the probability that the `BooleanSource` returns true to a query. The probability is expressed as a decimal value between 0 and 1. For example, suppose that our program uses the name `arrival` for its `Boolean-Source`, and we want to simulate the situation where a new customer arrives during 1% of the simulated seconds. Then our program would have the declaration:

```
BooleanSource arrival(0.01);
```

The argument to this constructor should have a default argument, perhaps 0.5, so that the constructor can also be used as a default constructor.

The second function is a member function that can be called to obtain the next value in the `BooleanSource`'s sequence of values. Here is the prototype:

```
bool BooleanSource::query( ) const;
// Postcondition: The return value is either true or false, with the probability
// of a true value being determined by the argument to the constructor.
```

There are several ways of generating random boolean values, but at this specification stage we don't need to worry about such implementation details.

FIGURE 8.5	The Car Wash Simulation

Pseudocode

1. Declare a queue of unsigned integers, which will be used to keep track of arrival times of customers who are waiting to wash their cars; these integers are unsigned integers, which is the data type used in C++ for numbers that can never be negative. We also declare the following objects:

   (a) A Washer: The washer's constructor has an argument indicating the amount of time (in seconds) needed by the washer to wash one car.

   (b) A BooleanSource: The constructor has an argument that specifies how frequently the BooleanSource returns true (indicating how often customers arrive).

   (c) An Averager.

2. *for* (current_second = 1; current_second <= the simulation length; current_second++)
   {

   > Each iteration of this loop simulates the passage of one second of time, as follows:
   > Ask the BooleanSource whether a new customer arrives during this second, and if so, enter the current_second into the queue.
   > *if* (the Washer is not busy and the queue is not empty)
   > {
   >
   > > Remove the next integer from the queue, and call this integer next.
   > > This integer is the arrival time of the customer whose car we will now wash.
   > > So, compute how long the customer had to wait (current_second - next), and send this value to the Averager. Also, tell the Washer that it should start washing another car.
   >
   > }
   > Indicate to the Washer that another simulated second has passed. This allows the Washer to correctly determine whether it is still busy.

   }

3. At this point, the simulation is completed. So we can get and print two items of information from the Averager: (1) how many numbers the Averager was given (i.e., the number of customers whose cars were washed); and (2) the average of all the numbers that it was given (i.e., the average waiting time for the customers, expressed in seconds).

Averager.   The averager has a default constructor that resets the averager so that it is ready to accept a sequence of numbers. The sequence will be given to the averager one number at a time through a member function called next_number. For example, suppose that our averager is named wait_times, and the next number in the sequence is 10. Then we will activate wait_times.next_number(10); The averager also has two member functions to retrieve its results: One function returns the average of all the numbers that have been given to the averager, and the other function returns the count of how many numbers the averager has been given. Here are the four prototypes:

```
Averager::Averager( );
// Postcondition: The Averager has been initialized so that it is ready to
// accept a sequence of numbers to average.

void Averager::next_number(double value);
// Postcondition: The Averager has accepted value as the next number in
// the sequence of numbers that it is averaging.

size_t Averager::how_many_numbers( ) const;
// Postcondition: The value returned is a count of how many times
// next_number has been activated.

double Averager::average( ) const;
// Precondition: how_many_numbers( ) > 0.
// Postcondition: The value returned is the average of all the numbers that
// have been given to the Averager.
```

Notice that the argument to `next_number` is actually a double number rather than an integer. This will allow us to use the averager in situations where the sequence is more than just whole numbers.

Washer. The simulation program requires one washer object. This washer is initialized with the constructor, and each time another second passes, the simulation program indicates the passage of a second to the washer. This suggests the following constructor and member function:

```
Washer::Washer(unsigned int s);
// Precondition: The value of s is the number of seconds needed to
// complete one wash cycle.
// Postcondition: The Washer has been initialized so that all other member
// functions may be used.

void Washer::one_second( );
// Postcondition: The Washer has recorded (and simulated) the passage of
// one more second of time.
```

Notice that the constructor argument is an *unsigned* integer, which is a data type that forbids negative values. Throughout our simulation, we will use unsigned integers for time values that cannot be negative. As usual, we should provide a default value for this argument (perhaps 60 seconds), so that the constructor can be used as a default constructor.

The other two responsibilities of a washer are to tell the simulation program whether the washing mechanism is currently available and to begin the washing of a new car. These responsibilities are accomplished with two additional member functions:

```
bool Washer::is_busy( ) const;
// Postcondition: The return value is true if the Washer is busy (in a wash
// cycle); otherwise the return value is false.
```

```
void Washer::start_washing( );
// Precondition: The Washer is not busy.
// Postcondition: The Washer has started simulating one wash cycle.
// Therefore, is_busy( ) will return true until the required number of
// simulated seconds has passed.
```

Car Wash Simulation—Implementing the Car Wash Classes

We have completed a specification for the three new classes that will be used in the car wash simulation. We'll define these three types with a header file called washing.h (Figure 8.6, starting on page 359) and an implementation file called washing.cxx (Figure 8.7, starting on page 362). The implementations are straightforward, but we'll provide a little discussion.

Implementation of the BooleanSource. The BooleanSource class has one member variable, probability, which stores the probability that an activation of query will return true. The implementation of the query member function first uses the rand function to generate a random number between 0 and RAND_MAX (including the end points), where RAND_MAX is a constant defined in stdlib.h. (See the discussion of rand on page 246.) Hence, if the member variable probability is the desired probability of returning true, then query should return true provided the following relationship holds:

```
rand( ) < probability * RAND_MAX
```

For example, suppose we want a 10% chance that query returns true, so that probability is 0.1. If rand returns a value less than 0.1*RAND_MAX, then query will return true. The chance that rand returns a value less than 0.1*RAND_MAX is approximately 10%, since 0.1*RAND_MAX marks a point that is approximately 10% of the way through rand's output range. Therefore, there is about a 10% chance that the expression rand( ) < 0.1 * RAND_MAX will be true. It is this boolean expression that is used in the return statement of query.

Implementation of the Averager. The implementation of the averager is a direct implementation of the definition of "average" and some straightforward details. The class has two member variables: one to keep track of how many numbers the averager has been given, and another to keep track of the sum of all those numbers. When the average member function is activated, the function returns the average calculated as the sum of all the numbers divided by the count of how many numbers the averager was given.

Notice that the averager does *not* need to keep track of all the numbers individually. It is sufficient to keep track of the sum of the numbers and the count of how many numbers there were.

Implementation of the Washer. The `Washer` class has two member variables. The first member variable, `seconds_for_wash`, is the number of seconds needed for one complete wash cycle. This variable is set by the constructor and remains constant thereafter. The second member variable, `wash_time_left`, keeps track of how many seconds until the current wash is completed. This value can be zero if the washer is not currently busy.

The washer's `one_second` member function simulates one second of washing time. In our simulation, the only piece of information that might need to change is the number of seconds until the washer is no longer busy. So, the `one_second` function checks whether a car is currently being washed. And if there is a car being washed, then the function subtracts one from `wash_time_left`.

The washer's `is_busy` function simply checks whether `wash_time_left` is greater than zero. If so, then there is a car in the washing mechanism. Otherwise, the washing mechanism is ready for another car.

When the car-washing mechanism is not busy, the `start_washing` member function may be activated to start another car through the washer. The function starts the wash by setting `wash_time_left` equal to `seconds_for_wash`.

FIGURE 8.6   Header File for the Car Wash Classes

A Header File

```
// FILE: washing.h
// CLASSES PROVIDED: BooleanSource, Averager, Washer.
//
// CONSTRUCTOR for the BooleanSource class:
//    BooleanSource(double p = 0.5)
//       Precondition: 0 <= p <= 1.
//       Postcondition: The BooleanSource has been initialized so that p is the approximate
//       probability of returning true in any subsequent activation of the query member function.
//
// CONSTANT MEMBER FUNCTION for the BooleanSource class:
//    bool query( ) const
//       Postcondition: The return value is either true or false, with the probability of a true
//       value being approximately p (from the constructor).
//
// CONSTRUCTOR for the Averager class:
//    Averager( )
//       Postcondition: The Averager has been initialized so that it is ready to accept a
//       sequence of numbers to average.
```

(continued)

(FIGURE 8.6 continued)

```
//
//   MODIFICATION MEMBER FUNCTION for the Averager class:
//     void next_number(double value)
//        Postcondition: The Averager has accepted value as the next number in the sequence of
//        numbers that it is averaging.
//
// CONSTANT MEMBER FUNCTIONS for the Averager class:
//     size_t how_many_numbers( ) const
//        Postcondition: The value returned is a count of how many times next_number has been
//        activated.
//
//     double average( ) const
//        Precondition: how_many_numbers > 0.
//        Postcondition: The value returned is the average of all the numbers that have been
//        given to the Averager.
//
// CONSTRUCTOR for the Washer class:
//     Washer(unsigned int s = 60)
//        Precondition: The value of s is the number of seconds needed for the completion of one
//        wash cycle.
//        Postcondition: The Washer has been initialized so that all other member functions may
//        be used.
//
// MODIFICATION MEMBER FUNCTIONS for the Washer class:
//     void one_second( )
//        Postcondition: The Washer has recorded (and simulated) the passage of one more
//        second of time.
//
//     void start_washing( )
//        Precondition: The Washer is not busy.
//        Postcondition: The Washer has started simulating one wash cycle. Therefore, is_busy( )
//        will return true until the required number of simulated seconds has passed.
//
// CONSTANT MEMBER FUNCTIONS for the Washer class:
//     bool is_busy( ) const
//        Postcondition: Return value is true if the Washer is busy (in a wash cycle);
//        otherwise the return value is false.
//
// VALUE SEMANTICS for the BooleanSource, Averager, and Washer classes:
//     Assignments and the copy constructor may be used with objects of the three classes.
```

(continued)

(FIGURE 8.6 continued)

```cpp
#ifndef WASHING_H
#define WASHING_H

#include <stdlib.h> // Provides size_t

    class BooleanSource
    {
    public:
        // CONSTRUCTOR
        BooleanSource(double p = 0.5);
        // CONSTANT MEMBER FUNCTION
        bool query( ) const;
    private:
        double probability; // Probability of query( ) returning true
    };

    class Averager
    {
    public:
        // CONSTRUCTOR
        Averager( );
        // MODIFICATION MEMBER FUNCTION
        void next_number(double value);
        // CONSTANT MEMBER FUNCTIONS
        size_t how_many_numbers( ) const { return count; }
        double average( ) const;
    private:
        size_t count; // How many numbers have been given to the Averager
        double sum;   // Sum of all the numbers given to the Averager
    };

    class Washer
    {
    public:
        // CONSTRUCTOR
        Washer(unsigned int s = 60);
        // MODIFICATION MEMBER FUNCTIONS
        void one_second( );
        void start_washing( );
        // CONSTANT MEMBER FUNCTION
        bool is_busy( ) const { return (wash_time_left > 0); }
    private:
        unsigned int seconds_for_wash; // Seconds for a single wash
        unsigned int wash_time_left;   // Seconds until Washer no longer busy
    };

#endif
```

washing.h FTP

FIGURE 8.7 Implementation File for the Car Wash Classes

An Implementation File

```
// FILE: washing.cxx
// CLASSES implemented: BooleanSource, Averager, Washer
//
// INVARIANT for the BooleanSource ADT:
//    1. The member variable probability is the approximate probability that query( ) returns
//       true.
//
// INVARIANT for the Averager ADT:
//    1. The member variable count indicates how many numbers the Averager has been given.
//    2. The member variable sum is the sum of all the numbers that the Averager has been
//       given.
//
// INVARIANT for the Washer class:
//    1. The member variable seconds_for_wash is the number of seconds required for one wash.
//    2. The member variable wash_time_left is 0 if the Washer is not busy;
//       otherwise it is the number of seconds until the Washer is free.

#include <assert.h>      // Provides assert
#include <stdlib.h>      // Provides rand, RAND_MAX, size_t
#include "washing.h"     // Provides BooleanSource, Averager, Washer definitions

BooleanSource::BooleanSource(double p)
// Library facilities used: assert.h
{
    assert(p >= 0);
    assert(p <= 1);
    probability = p;
}

bool BooleanSource::query( ) const
// Library facilities used: stdlib.h
{
    return (rand( ) < probability * RAND_MAX);
}

Averager::Averager( )
{
    count = 0;
    sum = 0;
}
```

(continued)

(FIGURE 8.7 continued)

```cpp
void Averager::next_number(double value)
{
    count++;
    sum += value;
}

double Averager::average( ) const
// Library facilities used: assert.h
{
    assert(how_many_numbers( ) > 0);
    return sum/count;
}

Washer::Washer(unsigned int s)
{
    seconds_for_wash = s;
    wash_time_left = 0;
}

void Washer::one_second( )
{
    if (is_busy( ))
        wash_time_left--;
}

void Washer::start_washing( )
// Library facilities used: assert.h
{
    assert(!is_busy( ));
    wash_time_left = seconds_for_wash;
}
```

washing.cxx   **FTP**

Car Wash Simulation—Implementing the Simulation Function

We can now implement the simulation pseudocode from Figure 8.5 on page 356. The implementation is shown as a function in Figure 8.8. The function has three parameters, taken from our original specification: (1) An unsigned integer, wash_time, which is the amount of time needed to wash one car; (2) A double number, arrival_prob, which is the probability that a customer arrives during any particular second; and (3) Another unsigned integer, total_time, which is the total number of seconds to be simulated. The function writes a copy of its parameters to the screen and then runs the simulation.

Most of the simulation work is carried out in the large for-loop, where the local variable `current_second` runs from 1 to `total_time`. This loop parallels the large loop from the original pseudocode (Step 2 in Figure 8.5 on page 356).

After the loop finishes, the simulation function obtains two pieces of information from the averager and writes these items to `cout`.

Self-Test Exercises

6. Can a single program use both a stack and a queue?

7. Describe at least one assumption we made about the real-world car wash in order to make the simulation more manageable.

8. How is potential queue overflow handled by the implementation in Figure 8.8 on page 364?

9. Use short sentences to describe the three main actions that occur during each second of simulated time in the car wash simulation.

10. When the car wash simulation finishes, there could still be some numbers in the queue. What do these numbers represent from the real world? (For a method of handling these leftover numbers, see Programming Project 8 on page 386.)

FIGURE 8.8	Implementation of the Car Wash Function

A Function Implementation

```
void car_wash_simulate
(unsigned int wash_time, double arrival_prob, unsigned int total_time)
// Precondition: 0 <= arrival_prob <= 1.
// Postcondition: The function has simulated a car wash where wash_time is the number of
// seconds needed to wash one car, arrival_prob is the probability of a customer arriving in
// any second, and total_time is the total number of seconds for the simulation. Before the
// simulation, the function has written its three parameters to cout. After the simulation, the
// function has written two pieces of information to cout: (1) The number of cars washed, and
// (2) The average waiting time of a customer.
// Library facilities used: iostream.h, queue1.h, washing.h
{
    Queue<unsigned int> arrival_times;   // Time stamps of the waiting customers
    unsigned int next;                   // A value taken from the queue
    BooleanSource arrival(arrival_prob);
    Washer machine(wash_time);
    Averager wait_times;
    unsigned int current_second;
```

(continued)

(FIGURE 8.8 continued)

```
    // Write the parameters to cout.
    cout << "Seconds to wash one car: " << wash_time << endl;
    cout << "Probability of customer arrival during a second: ";
    cout << arrival_prob << endl;
    cout << "Total simulation seconds: " << total_time << endl;

    for (current_second = 1; current_second <= total_time; current_second++)
    {   // Simulate the passage of one second of time.

        // Check whether a new customer has arrived.
        if (arrival.query( ))
        {
            if (arrival_times.size( ) < arrival_times.CAPACITY)
                arrival_times.insert(current_second);
            else
            {
                cout << "WARNING: Queue overflow during simulation." << endl;
                cout << "Simulation results will not be accurate." << endl;
            }
        }

        // Check whether we can start washing another car.
        if ((!machine.is_busy( ))  &&  (!arrival_times.is_empty( )))
        {
            next = arrival_times.get_front( );
            wait_times.next_number(current_second - next);
            machine.start_washing( );
        }

        // Tell the Washer to simulate the passage of one second.
        machine.one_second( );
    }

    // Write the summary information about the simulation.
    cout << "Customers served: " << wait_times.how_many_numbers( ) << endl;
    if (wait_times.how_many_numbers( ) > 0)
        cout << "Average wait: " << wait_times.average( ) << " sec" << endl;
}
```

Sample Output from the Car Wash Simulation Function

```
Seconds to wash one car: 240
Probability of customer arrival during a second: 0.0025
Total simulation seconds: 6000
Customers served: 14
Average wait: 38.2857 sec
```

carwash.cxx **FTP**

8.3 IMPLEMENTATIONS OF THE QUEUE ADT

A queue seems conceptually simpler than a stack because we notice queues in our everyday lives. However, the implementation of a queue, while similar to that of a stack, is more complicated than the implementation of a stack. As was the case with the stack ADT, we will give two implementations of our queue ADT: a static implementation using a a fixed-sized array, and a dynamic implementation using a linked list. As usual, our application programs will run with either implementation (although the static version imposes a predetermined capacity on the size of the queue).

Array Implementation of a Queue

As we did with the stack ADT, we will implement the queue ADT as a partially filled array. With a queue, we add entries at one end of the array and remove them from the other end. Hence, we will be accessing the used portion of the array at both ends, increasing the size of the used portion at one end and decreasing the size of the used portion at the other end. This differs from our use of a partially filled array for a stack, in that the stack accessed just one end of the partially filled array.

keeping track of both ends of the partially filled array

Because we now need to keep track of both ends of the used portion of the array, we will have *two* variables to keep track of how much of the array is used: One variable, called `front`, indicates the first index currently in use, and one variable, called `rear`, indicates the last index currently in use. If `data` is the array name, then the queue entries will be in the array components:

```
data[front], data[front + 1], ... data[rear].
```

To add an entry we increment `rear` by one, and then store the new entry in the component `data[rear]`, where `rear` is now one larger than it was before. To get the next entry from the queue, we retrieve `data[front]` and then increment `front` by one, so that `data[front]` is then the entry that used to be second.

There is one problem with the above plan. The variable `rear` is incremented but never decremented. Hence, it will quickly reach the end of the array. At that point, we will not be able to add any more entries to the queue. Yet, there is likely to be room in the array. In a normal application, the variable `front` would also be incremented from time to time (when entries are removed from the queue). This will free up the array locations with index values less than `front`. There are several ways to reuse these freed locations.

One straightforward approach for using the freed array locations is to maintain all the queue entries so that `front` is always equal to 0 (the first index of the array). When `data[0]` is removed, we move all the entries in the array down one location so the value of `data[1]` is moved to `data[0]`, and then all other entries are also moved down one. This approach will work, but it is inefficient. Every time we remove an entry from the queue, we must move every entry in the queue. Fortunately, there is a better approach.

We do not need to move all the array elements. When the `rear` index reaches the end of the array, we can simply start using the available locations at the front of the array. One way to think of this arrangement is to think of the array as being bent into a circle so that the first component of the array is immediately after the last component of the array. In this way, the successor of the last array index is the first array index. In this circular arrangement, the free index positions are always "right after" `data[rear]`.

For example, suppose that we have a queue of characters with a capacity of 5, and the queue currently contains three entries 'A', 'B', and 'C'. Perhaps these values are stored with `front` equal to 0 and `rear` equal to 2, as shown here:

The question marks indicate unused spots in the array.

Let's remove two entries (the 'A' and 'B'), and add two more entries to the rear of this queue, perhaps the characters 'D' and 'E'. The result is shown here:

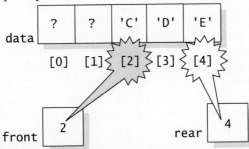

At this point, `front` is 2, `rear` is 4, and the queue elements range from `data[2]` to `data[4]`. Suppose that now we add another character, 'F', to the queue. The new entry cannot go after `rear`, since we have hit the end of the array. Instead, we go to the front of the array, adding the new 'F' at location `data[0]`, as shown here:

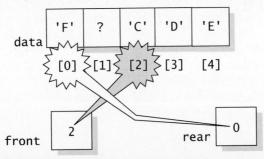

This may look peculiar, with the rear index of 0 being *before* the front index of 2. But keep in mind the *circular* view of the array. With this view, the queue's entries start at data[front] and continue forward. If you reach the end of the array, then come back to data[0], and keep going until you find the rear. It may help to actually view the array as bent into a circle, with the final array element attached back to the front, as shown here:

An array used in this way is called a **circular array**.

We now turn to a detailed implementation of our queue using the idea of a circular array. The header file for our queue is given in Figure 8.9. The queue's entries are held in the array, data, which is a private member variable. The private member variables front and rear hold the indexes for the front and the rear of the queue, as we have discussed. Whenever the queue is non-empty, the entries begin at the location data[front], continuing forward in the array. If the entries reach the end of the array, then they continue at the first location, data[0]. In any case, data[rear] is the last entry in the queue. One other private member variable, count, records the number of items that are in the queue. We will use count to check whether the queue is empty or full, and also to produce the value returned by the size member function.

The Queue class definition also has a new feature: a *private* member function called next_index. This is a function that we think will be useful for the implementation, but it is not part of the public interface. We don't want other programmers to use this function; it is just for our own use in implementing a specific kind of queue. A private function such as this is called a **helper function.**

The next_index helper function allows us to step easily through the array one index after another with wraparound at the end. The function call next_index(i) usually returns i+1, with one exception. When i is equal to the last index of the array, next_index(i) returns the first index of the array (zero).

By the way, you may be wondering, why bother defining `next_index` at all? After all, we could simply use the formula "`(i+1) % CAPACITY`" directly instead of calling `next_index`. The reason for declaring `next_index` is to make the other implementations easier to read. The name `next_index` suggests the purpose it serves, which is to "move to the next index." On the other hand, the formula on its own requires some thought as to its purpose.

FIGURE 8.9	Header File for the Array Version of the Queue Template Class

A Header File

```
// FILE: queue1.h
// TEMPLATE CLASS PROVIDED: Stack<Item> (a stack of items)
   See Figure 8.2 on page 347 for the other documentation that goes here.

#ifndef QUEUE1_H
#define QUEUE1_H
#include <stdlib.h> // Provides size_t

    template <class Item>
    class Queue
    {
    public:
        // MEMBER CONSTANTS -- See Appendix E if this fails to compile.
        static const size_t CAPACITY = 30;
        // CONSTRUCTOR
        Queue( );
        // MODIFICATION MEMBER FUNCTIONS
        void insert(const Item& entry);
        Item get_front( );
        // CONSTANT MEMBER FUNCTIONS
        size_t size( ) const { return count; }
        bool is_empty( ) const { return (count == 0); }
    private:
        Item data[CAPACITY];   // Partially filled array
        size_t front;          // Index of item at front of the queue
        size_t rear;           // Index of item at rear of the queue
        size_t count;          // Total number of items in the queue
        // HELPER MEMBER FUNCTION → For our use only → used to implement a specific
        size_t next_index(size_t i) const { return (i+1) % CAPACITY; }    kind of
    };                                                                    queue

#include "queue1.template" // Include the implementation.

#endif
```

queue1.h	FTP

Programming Tip: Use Small Helper Functions to Improve Clarity

When an ADT requires some small operation that is implemented as a formula, consider implementing the formula with a helper function (that is, a private member function). This will improve the clarity of your other code.

We're almost ready to implement the queue, but first we'll make an explicit statement of the invariant of the ADT:

Invariant of the Queue ADT (Array Version)

1. The number of items in the queue is stored in the member variable `count`.
2. For a non-empty queue, the items are stored in a circular array beginning at `data[front]` and continuing through `data[rear]`. The total capacity of the array is CAPACITY.
3. For an empty queue, `rear` is some valid index, and `front` is always equal to `next_index(rear)`.

Discussion of the Circular Array Implementation of a Queue

The implementation file for the `Queue` class is shown in Figure 8.10. Most of the details are a straightforward implementation of a circular array, so we'll limit ourselves to a brief discussion. Once you understand the `next_index` helper function, it is easy to see that `insert` and `get_front` implement adding and removing items from a queue in the way we outlined for a circular array.

One point that may seem counterintuitive is the implementation of the queue's constructor. It initializes `rear` to the final index of the array (that is, CAPACITY - 1). This may seem peculiar, but the reason relates a requirement that we have imposed on an empty queue. If you examine the invariant of the array version of the queue ADT, you will see this requirement: *For an empty queue,* `rear` *is some valid index, and* `front` *is always equal to* `next_index(rear)`. The queue constructor ensures that this requirement is met by setting `rear` to the final index of the array and setting `front` to the first index of the array.

Of course, you may also wonder *why* we imposed this requirement on an empty queue. The answer involves how the insert function works on an empty array. When the first item is inserted into the queue for an empty array, the insert function moves the `rear` value to the next available index with the assignment statement `rear = next_index(rear)`. After this assignment, the new item is placed at `data[rear]`. Therefore, by requiring an empty queue to have `front` equal to `next_index(rear)`, we have ensured that the first item placed in the queue will reside at `data[front]`.

An Implementation File

```
// FILE: queue1.template
// TEMPLATE CLASS IMPLEMENTED: Queue<Item> (See queue1.h for documentation.)
// This file is included in the header file and not compiled separately.
// INVARIANT for the Queue ADT:
//    1. The number of items in the Queue is in the member variable count.
//    2. For a non-empty Queue, the items are stored in a circular array beginning at data[front]
//       and continuing through data[rear]. The total capacity of the array is CAPACITY.
//    3. For an empty array, rear is some valid index, and front is always equal to
//       to next_index(rear).

#include <assert.h>   // Provides assert
#include <stdlib.h>   // Provides size_t

template <class Item>
Queue<Item>::Queue( )
{
    count = 0;
    front = 0;
    rear = CAPACITY - 1;
}

template <class Item>
void Queue<Item>::insert(const Item& entry)
// Library facilities used: assert.h
{
    assert(size( ) < CAPACITY);
    rear = next_index(rear);
    data[rear] = entry;
    count++;
}

template <class Item>
Item Queue<Item>::get_front( )
// Library facilities used: assert.h
{
    size_t answer_index;

    assert(!is_empty( ));
    answer_index = front;
    front = next_index(front);
    count--;
    return data[answer_index];
}
```

queue1.template   **FTP**

Linked List Implementation of a Queue

A queue can also be implemented as a linked list. One end of the linked list is the front, and the other end is the rear of the queue. The approach uses two pointers: One points to the first node (front_ptr), and the other points to the last node (rear_ptr), as diagrammed here for a queue with three items:

Figure 8.11 shows a header file for a Queue template class that is implemented in this way. The linked list version has no CAPACITY constant, but otherwise the documentation is the same as the array version. Our proposed invariant for the new queue ADT is shown just after the figure, at the top of page 374.

FIGURE 8.11	Header File for the Linked List Version of the Queue Template Class

A Header File

```
//  FILE: queue2.h
//  TEMPLATE CLASS PROVIDED: Queue<Item> (a queue of items)
//     The template parameter, Item, is the data type of the items in the Queue.
//     It may be any of the C++ built-in types (int, char, etc.), or a class with a default
//     constructor, a copy constructor, and assignment operator.
//
//  CONSTRUCTOR for the Queue<Item> template class:
//     Queue( )
//        Postcondition: The Queue has been initialized as an empty Queue.
//
//  MODIFICATION MEMBER FUNCTIONS for the Queue<Item> template class:
//     void insert(const Item& entry)
//        Postcondition: A new copy of entry has been inserted at the rear of the Queue.
//
//     Item get_front( )
//        Precondition: size( ) > 0.
//        Postcondition: The front item of the Queue has been removed and returned.
//
//  CONSTANT MEMBER FUNCTIONS for the Queue<Item> template class:
//     size_t size( ) const
//        Postcondition: The return value is the total number of items in the Queue.
```

(continued)

(FIGURE 8.11 continued)

```
//
//      bool is_empty( ) const
//          Postcondition: The return value is true if the Queue is empty.
//
// VALUE SEMANTICS for the Queue<Item> template class:
//      Assignments and the copy constructor may be used with Queue<Item>
//      objects.
//
// DYNAMIC MEMORY USAGE by the Queue<Item> template class:
//      If there is insufficient dynamic memory, then the following functions
//      call new_handler: the constructors, insert, and the assignment operator.

#ifndef QUEUE2_H
#define QUEUE2_H
#include <stdlib.h>    // Provides size_t
#include "link2.h"     // Linked list toolkit from Figure 6.7 on page 292

    template <class Item>
    class Queue
    {
    public:
        // CONSTRUCTORS and DESTRUCTOR
        Queue( );
        Queue(const Queue& source);
        ~Queue( );
        // MODIFICATION MEMBER FUNCTIONS
        void insert(const Item& entry);
        Item get_front( );
        void operator =(const Queue& source);
        // CONSTANT MEMBER FUNCTIONS
        size_t size( ) const { return count; }
        bool is_empty( ) const { return (count == 0); }
    private:
        Node<Item> *front_ptr;   // Points to front of queue
        Node<Item> *rear_ptr;    // Points to rear of queue
        size_t count;            // Total number of items in the queue
    };

#include "queue2.template" // Include the implementation.

#endif
```

queue2.h **FTP**

Invariant of the Queue ADT (Linked List Version)

1. The number of items in the queue is stored in the member variable `count`.

2. The items in the queue are stored in a linked list, with the front of the queue stored at the head node, and the rear of the queue stored at the final node.

3. The member variable `front_ptr` is the head pointer of the linked list of items. For a non-empty queue, the member variable `rear_ptr` is the tail pointer of the linked list; for an empty list, we don't care what's stored in `rear_ptr`.

Implementation Details

Each of the queue member functions (except the constructors) may assume that the invariant is valid when the member function is activated, and each member function (except the destructor) must ensure that the invariant is valid when the member function finishes its work. Notice that the invariant includes a member variable called `count` to keep track of the total number of items in the queue. We could get by without `count`, but its presence makes the `size` function quicker.

Most of the member functions' work will be accomplished with the linked list tools that are included from Figure 6.7 on page 292. We'll look at the implementations of two functions—`insert` and `get_front`—in some detail.

The `insert` member function. The `insert` operation adds a node at the rear of the queue. For example, suppose we start with three items shown here:

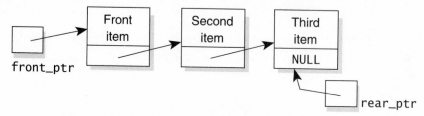

After adding a fourth item, the list would look like this:

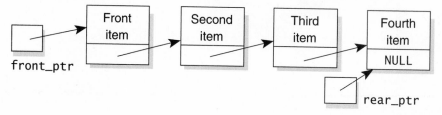

The item for the new fourth entry is placed in a newly created node at the end of the list. Normally, this is accomplished by a function call and an assignment:

```
list_insert(rear_ptr, entry);
rear_ptr = rear_ptr->link;
```

To add the first item, we need a slightly different approach because the empty list has no rear pointer. In this case we should add the new entry at the head of the list, and then assign `rear_ptr` to also point to the new node, as shown in this segment of code:

```
if (is_empty( ))
{    // Insert first entry.
     list_head_insert(front_ptr, entry);
     rear_ptr = front_ptr;
}
else
{    // Insert an entry that is not the first.
     list_insert(rear_ptr, entry);
     rear_ptr = rear_ptr->link;
}
```

In fact, this code is most of the insert function. The only other work is to add one to the `count` member variable.

The `get_front` member function.   The `get_front` operation removes a node from the front of the queue. For example, suppose we start with this queue:

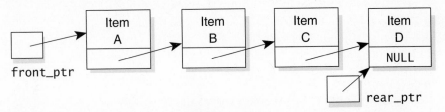

In this example, the `get_front` function will return the item that is labeled "Item A." This item will also be removed from the queue, so that when `get_front` returns, the list will have only three items shown here:

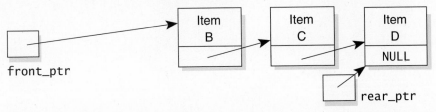

The implementation of `get_front` uses `list_head_remove`. This implementation is part of the complete queue implementation file in Figure 8.12.

| FIGURE 8.12 | Implementation File for the Linked List Version of the Queue Template Class |

An Implementation File

```
// FILE: queue2.template
// TEMPLATE CLASS IMPLEMENTED: Queue<Item> (see queue2.h for documentation)
// This file is included in the header file and not compiled separately.
// INVARIANT for the Queue ADT:
//    1. The number of items in the Queue is stored in the member variable count.
//    2. The items in the queue are stored in a linked list, with the front of the queue stored at
//       the head node and the rear of the queue stored at the final node.
//    3. The member variable front_ptr is the head pointer of the linked list of items. For a
//       non-empty queue, the member variable rear_ptr is the tail pointer of the linked list;
//       for an empty list, we don't care what's stored in rear_ptr.

#include <assert.h>    // Provides assert
#include <stdlib.h>    // Provides size_t
#include "link2.h"     // Linked list toolkit from Figure 6.7 on page 292

template <class Item>
Queue<Item>::Queue( )
// Library facilities used: stdlib.h
{
    count = 0;
    front_ptr = NULL;
}


template <class Item>
Queue<Item>::Queue(const Queue<Item>& source)
// Library facilities used: link2.h
{
    count = source.count;
    list_copy(source.front_ptr, front_ptr, rear_ptr);
}


template <class Item>
Queue<Item>::~Queue( )
{
    list_clear(front_ptr);
}
```

(continued)

(FIGURE 8.12 continued)

```
template <class Item>
void Queue<Item>::operator =(const Queue<Item>& source)
// Library facilities used: link2.h
{
    if (source.front_ptr == front_ptr) // Handle self-assignment
        return;

    list_clear(front_ptr);
    count = source.count;
    list_copy(source.front_ptr, front_ptr, rear_ptr);
}


template <class Item>
void Queue<Item>::insert(const Item& entry)
// Library facilities used: link2.h
{
    if (is_empty( ))
    {   // Insert first entry.
        list_head_insert(front_ptr, entry);
        rear_ptr = front_ptr;
    }
    else
    {   // Insert an entry that is not the first.
        list_insert(rear_ptr, entry);
        rear_ptr = rear_ptr->link;
    }

    count++;
}


template <class Item>
Item Queue<Item>::get_front( )
// Library facilities used: assert.h
{
    Item answer;

    assert(!is_empty( ));
    answer = front_ptr->data;
    list_head_remove(front_ptr);
    count--;
    return answer;
}
```

queue2.template **FTP**

TIP

***Programming Tip:* Make Note of "Don't Care" Situations**

There are often special situations in which we don't care about the value of a member variable. For example, in the special situation of an empty queue, the rear pointer is not used. With some compilers, you may get better error messages if you set such a pointer to NULL. (These compilers provide a message such as "Null pointer access" if you accidentally try to dereference the null pointer.) But in any case—whether you decide to set the rear pointer to NULL or not—you should document the fact that your implementation doesn't care about the value of the rear pointer for an empty queue. In particular, the invariant of the ADT should include an explicit statement of the "don't care" attitude—otherwise we might inadvertently assume that the rear pointer has some valid value for an empty queue.

PITFALL

***Pitfall:* Forgetting Which End Is Which**

We implemented our queue with the front of the queue at the head of the list and the rear of the queue at the tail of the list. As it turns out, this was not an arbitrary choice. Can you see why? What would happen if we had tried to do things the other way around, as shown in this wrong diagram?

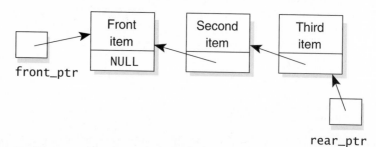

With this wrong arrangement of the queue's front and rear, we can still implement the insert operation, adding a new node at the rear of the queue. We also have easy access to the front item. But it will be difficult to actually *remove* the front item. After the removal, the `front_ptr` must be positioned so that it points to the next node in the queue, and there is no easy way to accomplish that (without starting at the rear and moving through the whole list).

So, keep in mind that it's easy to insert and remove at the head of a linked list, but insertion is the only easy operation at the tail.

Self-Test Exercises

11. Write a new constant member function that returns a copy of the item at the front of the queue. Use the array version of the queue.

12. A programmer who sees our array implementation of a queue shown in Figure 8.10 on page 371 gives us the following suggestion: "Why not eliminate the count member variable, since the number of elements in

the queue can be determined from the values of `front` and `rear`?" Is there a problem with the suggestion?

13. Write a new constant member function that returns a copy of the item at the front of the queue. Use the linked list version of the queue.

14. Write another constant member function that returns a copy of the item at the *rear* of the queue. Use the linked list version of the queue.

15. For our implementation, what is the value of the `rear_ptr` in an empty queue?

16. For our implementation, the `front_ptr` must be `NULL` for an empty queue. Which member functions rely on this requirement?

17. What goes wrong if we try to put the front of the queue at the tail of the linked list?

8.4 PRIORITY QUEUES

Using a queue ensures that customers are served in the exact order in which they arrive. However, we often want to assign priorities to customers and serve the higher priority customers before those of lower priority. For example, a hospital emergency room will handle the most severely injured patients first, even if they are not "first in line." A computer operating system that keeps a queue of programs waiting to use some resource, such as a printer, may give interactive programs a higher priority than batch processing programs that will not be picked up by the user until the next day, or it might give higher priority to short programs and lower priority to longer programs. A **priority queue** is a data structure that stores entries along with a priority for each entry. Entries are removed in order of priorities. The highest priority entry is removed first. If there are several entries with equally high priorities, then the one that was placed in the priority queue first is the one removed first.

For example, suppose the following customer names and priorities are entered into a priority queue in the order given:

higher numbers indicate a higher priority

Ginger Snap, priority 0
Natalie Attired, priority 3
Emanual Transmission, priority 2
Gene Pool, priority 3
Kay Sera, priority 2

The higher numbers indicate a higher priority. The names would be removed in the following order: first Natalie Attired (with the highest priority), then Gene Pool, then Emanual Transmission, then Kay Sera, and finally Ginger Snap (with the lowest priority). Note that both Natalie Attired and Gene Pool have priority 3, which is the highest priority, but Natalie Attired entered the priority queue before Gene Pool, so Natalie Attired is removed before Gene Pool.

Priority Queue ADT—Specification

Figure 8.13 gives the documentation for a priority queue template class. When an entry is added to a priority queue it is entered with a specified priority, which is an unsigned integer in the range 0...HIGHEST, where HIGHEST is a static constant member of the priority queue class. Entries are removed from the queue in order of priority. For example, suppose HIGHEST is 2. In that case, entries of priority 2 are removed first. When there are no entries of priority 2 left, then entries of priority 1 are removed. When there are no entries of priority 1 left, then entries of priority 0 are removed. Entries with the same priority are removed in the order in which they were entered into the priority queue.

Priority Queue ADT—An Implementation That Uses an Ordinary Queue

You may have noticed that the priority queue specification has a lot in common with the ordinary queue. We used the same names for the member functions, and only insert has a different parameter list (since the priority queue's insert function has an extra parameter to specify the priority of the new entry). This suggests that much of the priority queue work has already been accomplished in the queue implementation—but what is the best way to take advantage of this?

One possibility is to provide the priority queue with an array of ordinary queues. For example, suppose HIGHEST is 2. In this case, a priority queue can be implemented using three ordinary queues: one to hold the entries with priority 0, another queue for the entries of priority 1, and a third queue for the lofty entries with priority 2. Using this idea, we could implement a priority queue by defining a private member variable that is an array of ordinary queues, as shown in the highlighted line here:

```
#include "queue2.h" // Provides an ordinary Queue
template <class Item>
class PriorityQueue
{
    public:
        // MEMBER CONSTANTS -- See Appendix E if this fails.
        static const unsigned int HIGHEST = 2;
        ...
    private:
        Queue<Item> queues[HIGHEST+1];        ← an array
};                                              of ordinary
                                                queues
```

In this implementation, the entries with priority 0 are stored in the ordinary queue called queues[0]. Entries with priority 1 are stored in queues[1]. And so on, up to the ordinary queue called queues[HIGHEST]. To enter an entry into the priority queue with a given priority, all we need to do is enter the entry into

FIGURE 8.13	Documentation for the Priority Queue Header File

A Header File

```
//  TEMPLATE CLASS PROVIDED: PriorityQueue<Item> (a priority queue of items)
//      The template parameter, Item, is the data type of the items in the Priority Queue.
//      It may be any of the C++ built-in types (int, char, etc.), or a class with a default
//      constructor, a copy constructor, and assignment operator.
//
//  MEMBER CONSTANT for the PriorityQueue<Item> template class:
//      static const unsigned int HIGHEST = ____
//          The possible priorities of a PriorityQueue Item range from 0 to the constant
//          PriorityQueue<Item>::HIGHEST.
//
//  CONSTRUCTOR for the PriorityQueue<Item> template class:
//      PriorityQueue( )
//          Postcondition: The PriorityQueue has been initialized with no Items.
//
//  MODIFICATION MEMBER FUNCTIONS for the PriorityQueue<Item> template class:
//      void insert(const Item& entry, unsigned int priority)
//          Precondition: priority <= HIGHEST.
//          Postcondition: A new copy of entry has been inserted with the specified priority.
//
//      Item get_front( )
//          Precondition: size( ) > 0.
//          Postcondition: The highest priority item has been returned and has been removed from
//          the PriorityQueue. (If several items have equal priority, then the one that entered first
//          will come out first.)
//
//  CONSTANT MEMBER FUNCTIONS for the PriorityQueue<Item> template class:
//      size_t size( ) const
//          Postcondition: Return value is the total number of items in the PriorityQueue.
//
//      bool is_empty( ) const
//          Postcondition: Return value is true if the PriorityQueue is empty.
//
//  VALUE SEMANTICS for the PriorityQueue<Item> template class:
//      Assignments and the copy constructor may be used with PriorityQueue<Item> objects.
```

the correct ordinary queue. For example, suppose that HIGHEST is 3 and that entries are put into the priority queue in the following order:

Ginger Snap, priority 0
Natalie Attired, priority 3
Emanual Transmission, priority 2
Gene Pool, priority 3
Kay Sera, priority 2

each entry of the priority queue is placed in one of the ordinary queues

After these entries, the array of ordinary queues looks like this:

queues[3]: Natalie Attired (at the front), followed by Gene Pool;
queues[2]: Emanual Transmission (at the front), followed by Kay Sera;
queues[1]: empty;
queues[0]: Ginger Snap;

When an item needs to be removed, we move down through the ordinary queues, starting with the highest priority, until we find a non-empty queue. We then remove the front item from this non-empty queue.

With this approach, we can implement a priority queue as an array of ordinary queues and do not need to duplicate a lot of the previous work. In fact, it is possible to implement the priority queue with no member variables other than the queues array. However, some efficiency is gained by adding two other member variables.

The first is a number, total_size, which keeps track of the total number of entries in all of the queues. Without this member variable, the size function must call the size function from each ordinary queue and add their results.

The second extra member variable is an unsigned integer, which keeps track of the highest priority that is currently in the priority queue. This makes get_front more efficient, since without the extra member variable, we must always search from HIGHEST downward until we find a non-empty queue. With the extra private member variable, get_front can go straight to the correct queue and remove an entry. (Of course, this extra member variable also must be correctly maintained so that its value is always the priority of the highest entry.) We leave the remainder of the details of writing this array-based implementation for Programming Project 4 on page 385.

Priority Queue ADT—A Direct Implementation

If the number of possible priorities is large, then an array of queues might be impractical. In this case, you might think of several alternatives. One possibility is to implement the priority queue as an ordinary linked list, where the data in each node contains two things: the item from the queue, and the priority of that item. This implementation works regardless of how large the priority range is. We will leave the details of the implementation as another exercise (Programming Project 5 on page 385).

Self-Test Exercises

18. Implement the insert member function of the priority queue. Use the implementation that has an array called `queues` of ordinary queues.

19. Suppose you knew that the number of priorities that will be used in a priority queue application is small, but you do not know what the actual priorities will be. For example, suppose you know that the priorities can be any integer values in the range 0 to 10,000, but you also know that there will be at most 25 different numbers used. How might you implement the priority queue as an array of ordinary queues in such a way that the array size is much smaller than 10,000?

CHAPTER SUMMARY

- A queue is a First-In/First-Out data structure.
- A queue can be used to buffer data that is being sent from a fast computer component to a slower component. Queues also have many other applications: in simulation programs, operating systems, and elsewhere.
- A queue can be implemented as a partially filled circular array.
- A queue can be implemented as a linked list.
- When implementing a stack, you need only keep track of one end of the list of entries, but when implementing a queue, you need to keep track of both ends of the list.
- A priority queue can be implemented as an array of ordinary queues or in various ways as a linked list.

Solutions to Self-Test Exercises

1. The operations are insert `'L'`, insert `'I'`, insert `'N'`, insert `'E'`, followed by four get_front operations that return `'L'`, then `'I'`, then `'N'`, then `'E'`.

2. Reading input from a keyboard, and sending output to a printer.

3. Read the characters two at a time. Each pair of characters has the first character placed in queue number 1 and the second character placed in queue number 2. After all the reading is done, print all characters from queue number 1 on one line, and print all characters from queue number 2 on a second line.

4. A straightforward approach is to use a second queue, called `line`. As the input is being read, each character is placed in the `line` queue (as well as being placed in the original stack and queue). During the comparison phase, we also keep track of how many characters correctly matched. If a mismatch occurs, we can then print an appropriate amount of the `line` queue as part of the error message.

5. Do not apply the `toupper` function.

6. Yes

7. We assumed that no more than one customer arrives during any particular second.

8. The queue size is checked before entering a new item. If the queue is full, then an error message is printed and the item is not entered.

9. (a) Sometimes add a new customer to the arrivals queue; (b) Sometimes start a new car through the washer; (c) Tell the washer that another second has passed.

10. These are cars that arrived during the simulation, but they are still waiting in line at the end of the simulation.

11. The body of your function should assert that `size( ) > 0`, and then return `data[front]`.

12. The main problem is that you cannot tell the difference between an empty queue (which has `front` equal to `next_index(rear)`) and a full queue (which also has `front` equal to `next_index(rear)`).

13. The body of your function should assert `size( ) > 0`, and then return with:
    return `front_ptr->data;`

14. The body of your function should assert `size( ) > 0`, and then return with:
    return `rear_ptr->data;`

15. It could be any value. Our implementation does not care.

16. The `insert` member function requires that `front_ptr` is NULL for an empty queue. Otherwise the call to `list_head_insert` does not work.

17. Removals will be hard to implement.

18. The implementation should assert that the priority is valid. Then activate the member function `queues[priority].insert[entry]`. If you are keeping track of other items (such as the current highest priority and the total size), then those items should be updated, too.

19. Since you know that there are at most 25 different priorities, you could get by with an array of only 25 ordinary queues, plus a second array of unsigned integers called `value`. The number in `value[i]` would be the priority of all the entries in `queues[i]`. It might make sense to also keep the arrays sorted according to priorities.

PROGRAMMING PROJECTS

1 In Figure 8.3 on page 351 we presented a program that checks a string to see if the letters in the string read the same forward and backward. These strings are called palindromes. Another kind of palindrome is one in which we look at words, rather than letters. A **word-by-word palindrome** is a string of words such that the words read the same forward and backward. For example, the quote "You can cage a swallow, can't you, but, you can't swallow a cage, can you?" is a word-by-word palindrome. Write a program to test an input string and tell whether or not it is a word-by-word palindrome. Consider upper- and lower-case letters to be the same letter. Define a word as any string

consisting of only letters or an apostrophe, and bounded at each end with one of the following: a space, a punctuation mark, the beginning of the line, or the end of the line. Your program should have a friendly interface and allow the user to check more lines until the user says he or she wishes to quit the program.

2 In Figure 8.3 on page 351 we presented a program that checks a string to see if the letters in the string read the same forward and backward. The previous exercise performed a similar check using words in place of letters. In this exercise, you are to write a program that runs a similar check using lines rather than words or letters. Write a program that reads in several lines of text and decides if the passage reads the same whether you read the lines top-to-bottom or bottom-to-top; this is yet another kind of palindrome. For example, the following poem by J.A. Lindon, reads the same whether you read the lines from top-to-bottom or from bottom-to-top:

> *As I was passing near the jail*
> *I met a man, but hurried by.*
> *His face was ghastly, grimly pale.*
> *He had a gun. I wondered why.*
> *He had. A gun? I wondered...why,*
> *His face was ghastly! Grimly pale,*
> *I met a man but hurried by,*
> *As I was passing near the jail.*

Consider upper- and lower-case versions of a letter to be the same letter. Consider word boundaries to be significant, so for example, the words in the first line must read the same as the words in the last line in order to pass the test (as opposed to just the letters reading the same); however, consider all word delimiters as being equivalent, i.e., a punctuation, any number of spaces, the beginning or end of a line, or any combination of these are all considered to be equivalent. The end of the passage should be marked by a line containing only the word "end," spelled with any combination of upper- and lower-case letters, and possibly with blanks before and/or after it. Your program should have a friendly interface and allow the user to check more passages until the user says he or she wishes to quit the program. Note that to test your program, you need not use such well-constructed poems. Your program will check any passage, regardless of its literary merit.

3 Enhance the car-wash simulation procedure in Figure 8.8 on page 364 so that it has the following additional property. There is an additional parameter, which is a maximum length for the queue. When the queue gets as long as this maximum, any customer who arrives will leave without entering the queue (because she or he does not want to wait that long). There should also be one additional simulation result that is printed. In addition to the output shown in Figure 8.8, the function

also prints the number of simulated customers who left because the queue was too long. Embed the function in a program that allows the user to repeat simulations with different arguments until the user says she or he wishes to quit the program.

4 Give a complete implementation of a priority queue using an array of ordinary queues. For your ordinary queue, use the version from `queue2.h` in Figure 8.11 on page 372.

5 Give a complete implementation of a priority queue, using the idea from the direct implementation on page 382.

6 In this chapter we gave a linked list implementation of a queue. This implementation used two named pointers called `front_ptr` and `rear_ptr` to point to the front and the rear nodes of the queue (linked list). A **circular linked list** is similar to a regular linked list, except that the pointer field in the "last node" points back to the "first node." (Of course, after this change it is no longer clear which node, if any, is intrinsically "first.") If we use a circular linked list, then we only need one pointer to implement a queue, since the front node and the rear node are adjacent nodes, as shown by the following diagram:

In the diagram we have called the single pointer `rear_ptr`, because it points to the last node in the queue. It turns out that this gives a more efficient implementation than having it point to the first node in the queue. Redo the queue ADT using a circular linked list.

7 A **double-ended queue** is a list that allows the addition and removal of entries from either end. One end is arbitrarily called the **front** and the other the **rear**, but the two ends behave identically. Specify, design, and implement a template class for a double-ended queue. Include operations to check if it is empty or full. For each end, include operations for adding and deleting entries. Implement the double-ended queue as a doubly linked list. Call your class `Deque` (which is pronounced "deck").

8 Make improvements to the car-wash simulation program from Section 8.2. One particular improvement that you should make is to handle the customers who are still in the queue at the end of the simulation. These customers should have their cars washed one after another, but no new customers should be allowed to join the queue during this time. The wait times of these leftover customers should be counted along with all the other customers.

9 Write a simulation program for a small airport that has only one runway. There will be a queue of planes waiting to land and a queue of planes waiting to takeoff. However, only one plane can use the runway at a time. So there can be only one takeoff or one landing in progress at any one time. Assume that all takeoffs take the same amount of time. Assume that all landings take the same amount of time, but this need not be the same as the takeoff time. Assume that planes arrive for landing at random times, but with a specified probability of a plane arriving during any given minute. Similarly, assume that planes arrive at the takeoff queue at random times, but with a (possibly different) specified probability of a departure. (Despite the fact that takeoffs and landings are scheduled, delays make this a reasonable assumption.) Since it is more expensive and more dangerous to keep a plane waiting to land than it is to keep a plane waiting to take off, landings will have priority over takeoffs. Thus, as long as some plane is waiting to land, no plane can take off. Use a clock that is an unsigned integer variable that counts the number of minutes simulated. Use the `stdlib.h` random number generator to simulate arrival and departure times of airplanes.

This simulation can be used, among other things, for deciding when the air traffic has become so heavy that a second runway must be built. Hence, the simulation will simulate conditions that would be a disaster in which planes crash because they run out of fuel while waiting too long in the landing queue. By examining the simulated situation, the airport authority hopes to avoid the real tragedy. Assume all planes can remain in the queue the same amount of time before they run out of fuel. If a plane runs out of fuel, your simulation will not discover this until the simulated plane is removed from the queue; at that point, the fact that the plane crashed is recorded, that plane is discarded, and the next plane is processed. A crashed plane is not considered in the calculation of waiting time. At the end of the simulated time, the landing queue is examined to see whether any of the planes in the simulated queue have crashed. You can disregard the planes left in the queue at the end of the simulation, other than those that crashed for lack of sufficient fuel. Use the following input and output specification:

Input: (1) The amount of time needed for one plane to land; (2) The amount of time needed for one plane to takeoff; (3) The average amount of time between arrival of planes to the landing queue; (4) The average amount of time between arrival of planes to the takeoff queue; (5) The maximum amount of time that a plane can stay in the landing queue without running out of fuel and crashing; (6) The total length of time to be simulated.

Output: (1) The number of planes that took off in the simulated time; (2) The number of planes that landed in the simulated time; (3) The number of planes that crashed because they ran out of fuel before they could land; (4) The average time that a plane spent in the takeoff queue; (5) The average time that a plane spent in the landing queue.

10 Do an airplane simulation that is more complex than the previous project. In this version, planes arrive for landing with a random amount of fuel, which determines how long they can remain in the air. A plane will crash unless it lands within the time assigned to it. Your simulation will keep planes in a priority queue, where the priority of a plane is equal to the number of minutes before midnight that the plane will crash.

9 Recursive Thinking

"Well," said Frog, "I don't suppose anyone ever is completely self-winding. That's what friends are for." He reached for the father's key to wind him up again.

RUSSELL HOBAN
The Mouse and His Child

9.1 **RECURSIVE FUNCTIONS**

9.2 **STUDIES OF RECURSION: FRACTALS AND MAZES**

9.3 **REASONING ABOUT RECURSION**

    CHAPTER SUMMARY

    SOLUTIONS TO SELF-TEST EXERCISES

    PROGRAMMING PROJECTS

Often, during top-down design, you'll meet a remarkable situation: One of the subtasks to be solved is nothing more than a simpler version of the same problem you are trying to solve in the first place. In fact, this situation occurs so frequently that experienced programmers start *expecting* to find simpler versions of a large problem during the design process. This expectation is called **recursive thinking**. Programming languages, such as C++, support recursive thinking by permitting a function implementation to contain a call to itself. In such cases, the function is said to use **recursion**.

one of the subtasks is a simpler version of the same problem you are trying to solve in the first place

In this chapter, we start encouraging you to recognize situations where recursive thinking is appropriate. We also discuss recursion in C++, both how it is used to implement recursive designs and the mechanisms that occur during the execution of a recursive function.

9.1 RECURSIVE FUNCTIONS

A First Example of Recursive Thinking

We start with an example. Consider the task of writing a non-negative integer to the screen with its decimal digits stacked vertically. For example, the number 1234 should be written as:

```
1
2
3
4
```

a case with an easy solution . . . and a case that needs more work

There is one version of this problem that is quite easy: If the integer has only one digit, then we can just print that digit. But if the number has more than one digit, the solution is not immediately obvious, so we might break the problem into two subtasks: (1) First print all digits except the last digit, stacked vertically. (2) Then print the last digit. For example, if the number is 1234, then the first step will write:

```
1
2
3
```

and the second step will output the last digit, 4.

Several factors influenced our selection of these two steps. One factor is the ease of providing the necessary data for these two steps. For example, with our input number 1234, the first step needs the digits of 123, which is easily expressed as 1234/10 (since dividing an integer by 10 results in the quotient, with any remainder discarded). In general, if the integer is called number, and number has more than one digit, then the first step prints the digits of number/10, stacked vertically. The second step is equally easy: It requires us to print the last digit of number, which is easily expressed as number % 10 (this is the remainder upon dividing number by 10). Simple expressions, such as number/10 and number % 10, are not so easy to find for other ways of breaking down the problem (such as printing only the first digit in the first step, then printing the rest of the digits in the second step).

The pseudocode for our solution is as follows:

```
// Printing the digits of a non-negative number, stacked vertically
if (the number has only one digit)
    Write that digit.
else
{
    Write the digits of number/10 stacked vertically.
    Write the single digit of number % 10.
}
```

At this point, your recursive thinking cap should be glowing: One of the steps —*write the digits of* number/10 *stacked vertically*—is a simpler instance of the same task of writing a number's digits vertically. It is simpler because number/10 has one fewer digits than number. This step can be implemented by making a recursive call to the function that writes a number vertically. The implementation, with a recursive call, is shown in Figure 9.1. With this function we use the data type *unsigned int* instead of an ordinary *int*. The difference is that an *unsigned int* can never be negative, which is what we want for this function that prints the digits of a *non-negative* integer.

one of the steps is a simpler instance of the same task

In a moment we'll look at the exact mechanism that occurs for a function call such as write_vertical(1234), but first there are two notions to explain:

1. The Stopping Case. If the problem is simple enough, it is solved without recursive calls. In write_vertical, this occurs when number has only one digit. The case without any recursion is called the **stopping case** or **base case**. In Figure 9.1, the stopping case of write_vertical is implemented with the two lines:

```
if (number < 10)
    cout << number << endl; // Write the one digit.
```

FIGURE 9.1 The write_vertical Function

A Function Implementation

```
void write_vertical(unsigned int number)
// Postcondition: The digits of the number have been written, stacked vertically.
// Library facilities used: iostream.h
{
    if (number < 10)
        cout << number << endl; // Write the one digit.
    else
    {
        write_vertical(number/10);      // Write all but the last digit.
        cout << number % 10 << endl;    // Write the last digit.
    }
}
```

Sample Results of write_vertical(1234)

```
1
2
3
4
```

vertical.cxx **FTP**

2. The Recursive Call. In Figure 9.1, the function `write_vertical` makes a recursive call. The recursive call is the highlighted statement here:

```
else
{
    write_vertical(number/10);    // Write all but the last digit.
    cout << number % 10 << endl; // Write the last digit.
}
```

This is an instance of the `write_vertical` function calling itself to solve the simpler problem of writing all but the last digit.

Tracing Recursive Calls

During a function call, such as `write_vertical(3)`, what actually occurs? The first step is that the argument 3 is copied to function's formal parameter, `number`. This is the way that all value parameters are handled in a function call: The argument provides an initial value for the formal parameter.

Once the formal parameter has its initial value, the function's code is executed. Since 3 is less than 10, the boolean expression in the if-statement is true. So, in this case, it is easy to see that the function just prints 3 and does no more work.

Next, let's try an argument that causes the function to enter the else-part, such as the function call:

```
write_vertical(37);
```

When the function is called, the value of `number` is set equal to 37, and the code is executed. Since 37 is not less than 10, the two statements of the else-part are executed. Here is the first statement:

```
write_vertical(number/10);    // Write all but the last digit.
```

example of a recursive call

In this statement, (number/10) is (37/10), which is 3. So, this function call is `write_vertical(3)`. We already know the action of `write_vertical(3)`: Print 3 on a single line of output. After this call to `write_vertical` is completely finished, the second line in the else-part executes:

```
cout << number % 10 << endl;
```

This just writes `number % 10`. In our example, `number` is 37, so the statement prints the digit 7. The total output of the two lines in the else-part is:

```
3
7
```

The function `write_vertical` uses recursion. Yet we did nothing new or different in evaluating the function call `write_vertical(37)`. We treated it just like any other function call. We simply substituted the actual argument for number and then executed the code. When we reached the recursive call write_vertical(3), we simply repeated this process one more time.

PROGRAMMING EXAMPLE: An Extension of write_vertical

Suppose we want to extend write_vertical to a more powerful function, called super_write_vertical, which handles all integers including negative integers. With a negative input, the new function prints the negative sign on the first line of output, above any of the digits. For example,

```
super_write_vertical(-361)
```

produces this output with a minus sign on the first line:

```
-
3
6
1
```

How do we handle a negative number? The first step seems clear enough: Print the negative sign. After this, we must print the digits of number, which are the same as the digits of abs(number). (The abs function is the "absolute value" function from math.h. It leaves positive numbers unchanged and removes the negative sign from negative numbers.) So, the pseudocode for super_write_vertical is an extension of our original pseudocode:

```
if (the number is negative)
{
        Write a negative sign.
        Write the digits of abs(number) stacked vertically.
}
else if (the number has only one digit)
        Write that digit.
else
{
        Write the digits of number/10 stacked vertically.
        Write the single digit of number % 10.
}
```

If you think recursively, you will recognize that the step *write the digits of* abs(number) *stacked vertically* is a simpler version of our original problem (simpler because the negative sign does not need to be written). This suggests the implementation in Figure 9.2, with two recursive calls: one for the new case that writes the digits of abs(number) and a second call for the original case that writes the digits of number/10. We also have added comments in the margin, identifying two particular locations "Spot #1" and "Spot #2" to aid in taking a closer look at recursion.

FIGURE 9.2   The super_write_vertical Function

A Function Implementation

```
void super_write_vertical(int number)
// Postcondition: The digits of the number have been written, stacked vertically.
// If number is negative, then a negative sign appears on top.
// Library facilities used: iostream.h, math.h
{
    if (number < 0)
    {
        cout << '-' << endl;                    // Print a negative sign.
        super_write_vertical(abs(number));      // abs computes absolute value.
        ‖ This is Spot #1 referred to in the text.
    }
    else if (number < 10)
        cout << number << endl;                 // Write the one digit.
    else
    {
        super_write_vertical(number/10);        // Write all but the last digit.
        ‖ This is Spot #2 referred to in the text.
        cout << number % 10 << endl;            // Write the last digit.
    }
}
```

Sample Results of super_write_vertical(-361)

```
-
3
6
1
```

---

vertical.cxx   **FTP**

A Closer Look at Recursion

The computer keeps track of function calls in the following way: When a function call is encountered, the computer temporarily stops the execution. Before actually making the function call, some information is saved that will allow the computation to return to the correct location after the function call is completed. The computer also provides memory for the called function's formal parameters and any local variables that the called function uses. Next, the actual arguments are plugged in for the formal parameters, and the code of the called function begins to execute.

If the execution should encounter *another* function call—recursive or otherwise—then the first function's computation is temporarily stopped. This is because the second function call must be executed before the first function call can continue. Information is saved that indicates precisely where the first function call should resume when the second call is completed. The second function is given memory for its own parameters and local variables. The execution then proceeds to the second function call. When the second function call is completed, the execution returns to the correct location within the first function. And the first function resumes its computation.

This mechanism is used for both recursive and nonrecursive function calls. As an example of the function-call mechanism in a recursive function, let's completely trace the function call `super_write_vertical(-36)`. Initially, we call `super_write_vertical` with number set to -36. The actual argument, -36, is copied to the formal parameter, `number`, and we start executing the code with `number` having the value -36. At the moment when the function's execution begins, all of the important information that the function needs to work is stored in a special memory block called the function's **activation record.** The activation record contains information as to where the function should return when it is done with its computation, and it also contains the values of the function's local variables and parameters. For example, if our `super_write_vertical` function was called from a main program, then the activation record might contain this information:

> Activation record for first call to
> super_write_vertical
> _____
>
> Number: –36
>
> When the function returns, the
> computation should continue at
> line 57 of the main function.

The "return location" specified in a real activation record does not actually refer to lines of code in the main function, but when you're imagining an activation record you can think of a return location in this manner.

With the activation record in place, the function starts executing. Because the `number` is negative, the boolean test of the if-statement is true, and the negative sign is printed. At this point, the computation is about to make a recursive call, indicated here:

```
if (number < 0)
{
    cout << '-' << endl;
    super_write_vertical(abs(number));
    || This is Spot #1 referred to in the text.
}
```

A recursive call is made in the super_write_vertical function.

This function call generates its own activation record with its own value of number (which will be 36) and its own return location. The new activation record is placed on top of the other activation record, like this:

Activation record for first call to super

Number: –36

When the full computation line 57 of the

Activation record for second call to super_write_vertical

Number: 36

When the function returns, the computation should continue at Spot #1 in Figure 9.2 on page 392.

In fact, the collection of activation records is stored in a *stack* data structure called the **run-time stack.** Each function call pushes the next activation record on top of the run-time stack.

In our example, the second call of super_write_vertical executes with its own value of number equal to 36. The function's code executes, taking the last branch of the if-else control structure, arriving at another recursive call shown here:

Another recursive call is made in the super_write_vertical function.

```
else
{
    super_write_vertical(number/10);
    ‖ This is Spot #2 referred to in the text.
    cout << number % 10 << endl;
}
```

To execute this recursive call, another activation record is created (with number now set to 3), and this activation record is pushed onto the run-time stack:

Activation record for first call to super

Number: –36

When the full computation line 57 of the

Activation record for second call to sup

Number: 3

When the computati Spot #1 in

Activation record for second call to super_write_vertical

Number: 3

When the function returns, the computation should continue at Spot #2 in Figure 9.2 on page 392.

The `super_write_vertical` function begins executing once more. With number set to 3, the function enters the section to handle a one-digit number. At this point, the digit 3 is printed, and no other work is done during this function call.

When the third function call ends, its activation record is popped off the stack. But just before it is popped, the activation record provides one last piece of information—telling where the computation should continue. In our example, the third activation record is popped off the stack, and the computation continues at Spot #2 in Figure 9.2 on page 392. At this point we have the two remaining activation records shown here:

As we said, the computation is now at Spot #2 in Figure 9.2 on page 392. This is the highlighted location shown here:

```
else
{
    super_write_vertical(number/10);
    |  This is Spot #2 referred to in the text.
    cout << number % 10 << endl;
}
```

The next statement is an output statement. What does it print? From the activation record on top of the stack, we see that number is 36, so the statement prints 6 (which is 36 % 10). The second function call then finishes, returning to Spot #1 in Figure 9.2 on page 392. But there is no more work to do after Spot #1, so the first function call also returns. The total effect of the original function call was to print three characters: a minus sign, and then 3, and finally 6. The tracing was all accomplished with the usual function call mechanism—no special treatment was needed to trace recursive calls. In the example there are two levels of recursive calls:

1. `super_write_vertical(-36)` made a recursive call to
   `super_write_vertical(36);`

2. `super_write_vertical(36)` made a recursive call to `super_write_vertical(3)`.

In general, function calls may be much deeper than this, but even at the deepest levels the function call mechanism remains the same as the example that we have traced.

General Form of a Successful Recursive Function

Key Design Concept

Find smaller versions of a problem within the larger problem itself.

C++ places no restrictions on how recursive calls are used in function definitions. However, in order for a recursive function definition to be useful, any call of the function must ultimately terminate with some piece of code that does not depend on recursion—in other words, there must be a *stopping case*. The function may call itself, and that recursive call may call the function again. The process may be repeated any number of times. However, the process will not terminate unless eventually one of the recursive calls does not itself make a recursive call. The general outline of a recursive function definition is as follows:

Recursive Thinking

Suppose that a problem has one or more cases in which some of the subtasks are simpler versions of the same problem you are trying to solve in the first place. These subtasks are solved by recursive calls.

A function that makes recursive calls must also have one or more cases in which the entire computation is accomplished without recursion. These cases without recursion are called **stopping cases** or **base cases**.

Often a series of if-else statements determines which of the cases will be executed. A typical scenario is for the original function call to execute a case that includes a recursive call. That recursive call may in turn execute a case that requires another recursive call. For some number of times each recursive call produces another recursive call, but eventually one of the stopping cases applies. Every call of the function must eventually lead to a stopping case or else the function call will never end because of an infinite sequence of recursive calls. (In practice a call that includes infinite recursion will terminate abnormally rather than actually running forever because the computation no longer has enough memory for the run-time stack of activation records.)

Self-Test Exercises

1. What is the output produced by the function call `exercise(3)`, for each of the following three definitions?

```
void exercise(int n)
{
    cout << n << endl;
    if (n > 1)
        exercise(n-1);
}
```

```
void exercise(int n)
{
    if (n > 1)
        exercise(n-1);
    cout << n << endl;
}
```

```
void exercise(int n)
{
    cout << n << endl;
    if (n > 1)
        exercise(n-1);
    cout << n << endl;
}
```

2. What is the output of the following function with an argument of 3?

```
void cheers(int n)
{
    if (n <= 1)
        cout << "Hurrah" << endl;
    else
    {
        cout << "Hip" << endl;
        cheers(n-1);
    }
}
```

3. Modify the `cheers` function from the previous exercise so that it first prints "Hurrah" followed by n-1 "Hip"s. Make a further modification so that n-1 "Hip"s occur both before and after the "Hurrah". Make another modification so that approximately half of the "Hip"s occur before the "Hurrah", and half appear after.

4. Write a recursive function that has one parameter which is a non-negative integer. The function writes out that number of asterisks `'*'` to the screen, followed by that number of exclamation points `'!'`. Do not use any loops or local variables.

9.2   STUDIES OF RECURSION: FRACTALS AND MAZES

Recursive thinking makes its biggest impact on problems in which one of the *subtasks* is a simpler version of the *same* problem that you are working on. For example, when we write the digits of a long `number`, our first step is to write the digits of the smaller number, `number/10`. This section provides additional examples of recursive thinking and the functions that recursion leads to.

FIGURE 9.3
The First Few Steps in Generating a Random Fractal

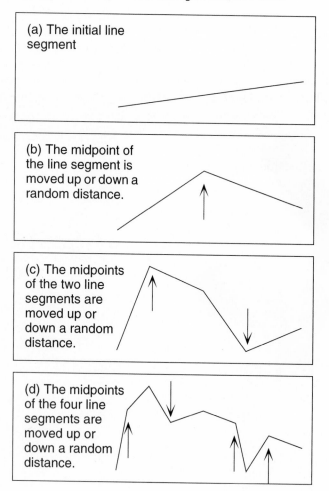

(a) The initial line segment

(b) The midpoint of the line segment is moved up or down a random distance.

(c) The midpoints of the two line segments are moved up or down a random distance.

(d) The midpoints of the four line segments are moved up or down a random distance.

PROGRAMMING EXAMPLE:
Generating Random Fractals

Fractals are one of the tools that graphics programmers use to artificially produce remarkably natural scenes of mountains, clouds, trees, and other objects. We'll explain fractals in a simple setting and develop a recursive function to produce a certain kind of fractal.

To understand fractals, think about a short line segment, as shown in Figure 9.3(a). Imagine grabbing the middle of the line and moving it vertically a random distance. The two endpoints of the line stay fixed, so the result might look like Figure 9.3(b). This movement has created two smaller line segments: the left half of the original segment and the right half. For each of these smaller line segments, we'll grab the midpoint and move it up or down a random distance. Once again, the endpoints of the line segments remain fixed, so the result of this second step might look like Figure 9.3(c). One more step might produce Figure 9.3(d). The process continues as long as you like, with each step creating a slightly more jagged line.

After several more steps, the line could appear as shown here:

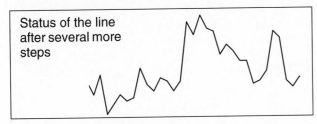

Status of the line
after several more
steps

Perhaps you can imagine that this jagged line is the silhouette of a mountain skyline.

The line that we're generating has an interesting property. Suppose that we carry out thousands of steps to create our line and then magnify a small portion of the result, as shown here:

Magnifying a
portion of the line

The magnified portion is not identical to the entire line, but there is a lot of similarity. **Fractal** is the term coined by the mathematician Benoit Mandelbrot to describe objects, such as our line, that exhibit some kind of similarity under magnification. In fact, the first fractals studied were mathematically defined sets that remain *completely unchanged* when magnified to certain powers. In nature, objects don't generally remain completely unchanged under magnification, but magnified views commonly exhibit similarities with the larger object (such as our line, or a cloud, or a fern). Also, in nature (and our line), the powers of magnification where the similarities occur are limited, so nature's fractals are really rough approximations to the more formal mathematical fractals. Even so, the term *fractal* is often applied to any object that exhibits similarities under some magnification. The jagged line that we have described is called a **random fractal** because of the randomness in its generation.

fractals, nature's fractals, and random fractals

A Function for Generating Random Fractals—Specification

We wish to write a function that can draw or otherwise represent the random fractal that we have described. The input to this function includes the height of the two endpoints of the original line, measured from a fixed baseline, and the horizontal width from the left endpoint to the right endpoint. For example, consider the line segment shown here:

The height of the left endpoint is exactly at the baseline, and the height of the right endpoint is 0.25 inches above the same baseline. The horizontal width of the line is 2.0 inches. The heights of both endpoints and the width of the line segment will be three of the parameters to the fractal-generating function. The function also has a fourth parameter that we call epsilon. Once the width of the line segment becomes less than or equal to epsilon, we will stop the process of grabbing and moving midpoints. (We use the name *epsilon* because that is the Greek letter that mathematicians use for a small positive quantity.)

We can now write the prototype of the fractal generator as shown here:

```
void random_fractal(
    double left_height,
    double right_height,
    double width,
    double epsilon
);
```

Now we must consider the function's behavior. Let's look at an example using the initial line segment drawn in above and an epsilon of 0.6 inches. Here is one possible result of the process, which divides the total 2.0" line into four pieces, each spanning a width of ½":

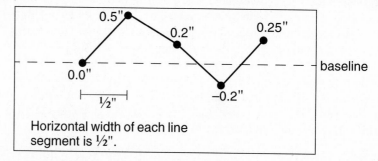

The process stops when the width of a line segment reaches ½", since ½" is less than our specified epsilon of 0.6". The endpoints of each ½" segment have heights above or below the baseline. Our function will be responsible for generating and displaying the height of the right endpoint of each tiny line segment. So, in this example, we expect `random_fractal` to display the four heights 0.5", 0.2", -0.2", and 0.25". For the moment we won't pin down the actual method of displaying these heights—a graphical program might display the heights by actually drawing the random fractal, whereas a simpler program might simply print each height as a *double* number.

Design and Implementation of the Fractal Function

Sometimes, generating a random fractal is simple. In particular, suppose that we call `random_fractal` with the line segment's width less than or equal to epsilon. For example, we might use a 2.0" initial line segment, with epsilon set to 3.0", as in this function call:

```
random_fractal(0.0, 0.25, 2.0, 3.0);
```

This is simple because when `width <= epsilon`, we don't continue dividing the segment. Instead, we simply "display the heights of the right endpoints of each segment." Moreover, we have only *one* segment (which we won't divide anymore), and the height of the right endpoint of that one segment is just the parameter `right_height`. So, we have the first step of our algorithm:

```
if (width <= epsilon)
    display right_height;
```

As with our previous recursive functions, this first step of the design is vital to recursive thinking. You must be able to identify a *stopping case* of the problem that can be solved with little or no work. In `random_fractal`, the stopping case occurs when `width` is no more than `epsilon`.

stopping case for the random fractal function

Now for the larger problem. We must design an algorithm to handle a `width` that is larger than `epsilon`. Our first step is to find the current height of the midpoint of the segment and move it up or down a random amount. We'll call the height of the displaced point the `mid_height`, as shown here:

The value of `mid_height` will be computed in two steps:

1. Compute the average of `left_height` and `right_height` with the assignment:
   ```
   mid_height = (left_height + right_height)/2;
   ```

2. Add a random real number to `mid_height`, as shown here:
   `mid_height += random_real(-width, width);`

The function `random_real` is one that we have written as part of a small toolkit of useful functions. This toolkit does not have to do with recursion, so we have placed it in an appendix (`useful.h` and `useful.cxx` in Appendix H) rather than giving the details here. At the moment we just need to know what value is returned by the function call `random_real(-width, width)`. The function returns a random real number that lies in the range defined by its two arguments. In particular, `random_real(-width, width)` provides a random value from the range `-width` to `width`. We chose this particular range so that the random fractal does not take huge jumps when the width gets smaller.

After computing the height of the displaced midpoint, we have two segments: (a) from the left endpoint of the original segment to the displaced midpoint, and (b) from the displaced midpoint to the right endpoint of the original segment. The horizontal width of each smaller line segment is `width/2`. And what work do we have left to do? *We must generate a random fractal for each of these two smaller line segments*. This work can be accomplished with two recursive calls:

```
random_fractal(left_height, mid_height,  width/2, epsilon);
random_fractal(mid_height,  right_height, width/2, epsilon);
```

*two recursive
calls solve two
smaller versions
of the original
problem*

The first of these recursive calls generates a random fractal for the leftmost smaller line segment. Let's examine the arguments of the first recursive call: The first two arguments are the heights of the endpoints of the leftmost segment (`left_height` and `mid_height`), and the third argument is the horizontal width of the leftmost segment (`width/2`). When we generate the random fractal for this smaller segment, we use the same value of `epsilon` that we were given originally. The second recursive call handles the rightmost line segment in a similar way.

The entire `random_fractal` function is implemented in Figure 9.4. Let's discuss its method of displaying numbers.

How the Random Fractals Are Displayed

In the `random_fractal` function we have called a function named `display` to display the actual numbers. The `display` function (also part of `useful.h` in Appendix H) displays a number with a simple bar drawn out of stars. For example, here are several sample function calls with their output:

```
display(8)   prints:                    |********
display(-4)  prints:              ****|
display(-3)  prints:               ***|
display(0)   prints:                   |
display(2)   prints:                    |**
```

As a general rule, each call of display(x) prints one line of output with a vertical bar in the middle of the line. If x is positive, then approximately x stars are printed to the right of the vertical bar. If x is negative, then approximately x stars are printed to the left of the vertical bar.

Figure 9.5 on page 404 shows a complete sample output from the call:

```
random_fractal(10.0, 10.0, 16.0, 1.0);
```

If you tip your head right 90 degrees, you'll see a nice random fractal landscape.

FIGURE 9.4	A Function to Generate a Random Fractal

A Function Implementation

```
void random_fractal(
    double left_height,
    double right_height,
    double width,
    double epsilon
)
// Precondition: width and epsilon are both positive.
// Postcondition: The function has generated a random fractal from a line segment. The
// parameters left_height and right_height are the heights of the line segment, and the
// parameter width is the segment's width. The generation of the random fractal stops when
// the width of the line segments reaches epsilon or less.
// Method of displaying the output: The height of the right endpoint of each line segment in
// the random fractal is displayed by calling the function display(...).
// Library facilities used: assert.h, useful.h (from Appendix H)
{
    double mid_height;    // Height of the midpoint of the line segment

    assert(width > 0);
    assert(epsilon > 0);

    if (width <= epsilon)
        display(right_height);
    else
    {
        mid_height = (left_height + right_height) / 2;
        mid_height += random_real(-width, width);
        random_fractal(left_height, mid_height,  width/2, epsilon);
        random_fractal(mid_height,  right_height, width/2, epsilon);
    }
}
```

fractal.cxx	FTP

FIGURE 9.5 | Sample Output of the Random Fractal Function

A Sample Result of `random_fractal(10.0, 10.0, 16.0, 1.0)`

```
                    |************
                    |*************
                    |**************
                    |**********
                    |*****
                    |***
                    |
                 ***|
                  **|
               *****|
                ****|
                   *|
                    |*
                    |***
                    |********
                    |**********
```

PROGRAMMING EXAMPLE: Traversing a Maze

Suppose that your friend Jervis has a maze in his backyard. One day, Jervis mentions two facts about the maze:

1. Somewhere in the maze is a magic tapestry that contains the secret of the universe.

2. You may keep this tapestry (and its secret) if you can enter the maze, find the tapestry, and return to the maze's entrance. (So far, many have entered, but none has returned.)

The maze is built on a rectangular grid. At each point of the grid, there are four directions to move: north, east, south, or west. Some directions, however, may be blocked by an impenetrable wall. You decide to accept Jervis's challenge and enter the maze—but only with the help of your portable computer and a function that we'll write to guide you into the maze *and back out*.

Traversing a Maze—Specification

We plan to write a function, `traverse_maze`, which you can execute on a portable computer that you will carry through the maze. The function will give you directions and ask you questions to take you to the magic tapestry and back out. The complete specification appears at the top of the next page.

```
bool traverse_maze( );
```
// Precondition: The user of the program is facing an unblocked spot in the
// maze, and this spot has not previously been visited by the user.
// Postcondition: The function has asked a series of queries and provided
// various directions to the user. The queries and directions have led the
// user through the maze and back to the exact same position that the
// user started at. The return value of the function is a true/false value
// indicating whether the user found a magic tapestry in the maze.

Figure 9.6 shows a drawing of what the maze might look like, along with a sample dialogue. A sample dialog written at this point—before we've written the function—is called a **script**, and it can help clarify a loose specification. As you might suspect, Jervis's actual maze is rather more complex than this sample dialog might suggest, but simplicity often results in the best scripts.

FIGURE 9.6	Script for the Maze Traversal Function

A Sample Dialogue

```
Step forward & write your name on the ground.
Have you found the tapestry? [Yes or No]
No
Please turn left 90 degrees.
Are you facing a wall? [Yes or No]
No
Is your name written ahead of you? [Yes or No]
No
Step forward & write your name on the ground.
Have you found the tapestry? [Yes or No]
No
Please turn left 90 degrees.
Are you facing a wall? [Yes or No]
Yes
Please turn right 90 degrees.
Are you facing a wall? [Yes or No]
No
Is your name written ahead of you? [Yes or No]
No
Step forward & write your name on the ground.
Have you found the tapestry? [Yes or No]
Yes
Pick up the tapestry, and take a step backward.
Please turn right 90 degrees.
Please turn right 90 degrees.
Please step forward, then turn 180 degrees.
Please turn right 90 degrees.
Please turn right 90 degrees.
Please turn right 90 degrees.
Please step forward, then turn 180 degrees.
```

This dialogue supposes that the user starts at the entrance to the maze drawn below. The starting point of the user is represented by the arrow in a circle, with the arrow pointing in the direction that the user is facing. The large X is the magic tapestry.

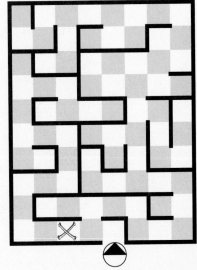

Traversing a Maze—Design

The traverse_maze function appears to perform a pretty complex task. When the function starts, all that's really known is that the user of the program is facing some spot in the maze, and that spot has not been previously visited. The function must take the user into the maze, eventually leading the user back to the exact starting spot. Hopefully, along the way the user will find the magic tapestry. Recursive thinking can make the task easier.

We'll call the program's user Judy. We'll always start by asking Judy to take a step forward onto the spot that she hasn't visited before. We'll also ask her to write her name on the ground so that later we can tell whether she's been to this spot before. After these two steps we will ask her whether she has found the tapestry at this new spot and place her true or false answer in a local variable named found.

the stopping case

Now there is one easy case: If the tapestry is at this spot, then we will have Judy pick up the tapestry and ask her to take a step backward to her starting spot. This is the stopping case, and the function returns true to indicate that the tapestry was found.

But what if Judy does not find the tapestry at this spot? In this case, there are three possible directions for Judy to explore: going forward, leftward, or rightward. We won't worry about exploring backward because that is the direction that Judy just came from. Also, sometimes we do not need to explore all three directions (forward, left, and right). A direction is a "dead end" if (a) There is a wall blocking that direction, or (b) Judy's name is written on the ground in that direction (indicating she has already been there)—and there is no need to explore dead ends. We also don't need to explore a direction if Judy already found the tapestry in one of the other directions.

This description suggests the following steps if the user has not found the tapestry at this spot:

1. Have the user face left (the first direction to explore).

2. *for* each of the three directions
   {
       if (!found && the direction that is now being faced isn't a dead end)
       {
           Explore the direction that is now being faced, returning to this exact spot after the exploration and setting found to true if the tapestry was found.
       }
       Have the user turn 90 degrees to the right (the next direction).
   }

3. The user is now facing the direction she came from, so ask her to step forward and turn around (so that she is facing this spot, as she was before this function was called).

Are you thinking recursively? The highlighted step "Explore the direction that is now being faced. . ." is a simpler instance of the problem that we are trying to solve. The instance is simpler because one spot in the maze has been eliminated from consideration—namely, the spot that the user is at does not contain the tapestry. In our implementation, we'll solve this simpler problem with a recursive call.

Traversing a Maze—Implementation

Our implementation will benefit from some functions to carry out various subtasks. Figure 9.7 on page 408 shows the first function we have in mind. The other two functions deal with input, and are part of our toolkit of useful functions (`useful.h` in Appendix H). The three functions are listed here:

- `dead_end`: This function (from Figure 9.7 on page 408) determines whether the direction in front of the user is a "dead end." Remember that "dead ends" are caused by a wall or by a direction that the user has already explored. The function returns true (for a dead end) or false (for no dead end).
- `eat_line`: This function (from `useful.h`) reads characters from standard input until a newline character is encountered.
- `inquire`: This function (from `useful.h`) asks the user a yes/no question; it returns true if the user answers "yes," and returns false if the user answers "no."

The implementation of the `dead_end` function is short and interesting, as shown here:

```
return inquire("Are you facing a wall?")
       ||
       inquire("Is your name written in front of you?");
```

This implementation of `dead_end` makes two calls of the `inquire` function and returns the "or" of the results (using the `||` operation). When the "or" expression is evaluated, the `inquire` function is called to ask the user "Are you facing a wall?" If the user answers "yes," then the `inquire` function returns true, and the rest of the "or" expression will not be executed. This follows the general rule of **short-circuit evaluation** that we have seen before—meaning that the evaluation of a logical expression stops when there is enough information to determine whether the expression is true or false. On the other hand, if the user answers "no" to the first query, then the `inquire` function returns false, and the rest of the "or" expression will be executed (asking the second question "Is your name written in front of you?").

In all, the function returns true if the user answers "yes" to the first question, or if the user first answers "no" to the first question (there is no wall) and then answers "yes" to the second question (the user's name is written in front of herself).

The actual `traverse_maze` function is given in Figure 9.8. It follows our pseudocode quite closely. You might enjoy knowing that the magic tapestry really does exist in a book called *Castle Roogna* (Ballantine Books) by Piers Anthony. The hero of the book actually becomes part of the tapestry, whereupon his quest leads him to a *smaller* version of the *same* tapestry.

Self-Test Exercises

5. Suppose you call `random_fractal` with a width of 8 and an epsilon of 1. Then `random_fractal` will make two recursive calls, and each of those will make two more calls, and so on until `width` is less than or equal to `epsilon`. How many total calls will be made of `random_fractal`, including the original call?

6. Draw a copy of the maze from Figure 9.6 on page 405, moving the magic tapestry to a more difficult location. Run the `traverse_maze` function, pretending that you are in this maze and following the function's directions. (Do not peek over the walls.)

7. Revise the `random_fractal` function so that the movements of the midpoints are no longer random. Instead, the first midpoint should be moved upward by the amount `width`, the midpoints at the next level of recursion should be moved down by the amount `width`, the next level will move up again, then down, and so on.

8. Suppose that you are exploring a rectangular maze containing ten rows and twenty columns. What is the maximum number of recursive calls that can be generated if you start at the entrance of the maze and call `traverse_maze`?

FIGURE 9.7 The dead_end Function Used in the Maze Traversal

A Function Implementation

```
bool dead_end( )
// Postcondition: The return value is true if the direction directly in front
// is a dead end (that is, a direction that cannot contain the tapestry).
// Library facilities used: useful.h (from Appendix H)
{
    return inquire("Are you facing a wall?")
           ||
           inquire("Is your name written in front of you?");
}
}
```

maze.cxx **FTP**

FIGURE 9.8 A Function to Traverse a Maze

A Function Implementation

```
bool traverse_maze( )
// Precondition: The user of the program is facing an unblocked spot in the maze that has not
// previously been visited by the user.
// Postcondition: The function has asked a series of questions and provided various directions
// to the user. The questions and directions have led the user through the maze and back to
// the exact same position that the user started at. The return value of the function is a
// true/false value indicating whether the user found a magic tapestry in the maze.
// Library facilities used: iostream.h, useful.h (from Appendix H)
// Also uses dead_end from Figure 9.7 on page 408.
{
    int direction;   // Counts 1, 2, 3 for the three directions to explore
    bool found;      // Will be set to true if we find the tapestry

    cout << "Step forward & write your name on the ground." << endl;
    found = inquire("Have you found the tapestry?");

    if (found)
    {   // Pick up the tapestry and step back from whence you came.
        cout << "Pick up the tapestry and take a step backward." << endl;
    }
    else
    {   // Explore the three directions (not counting the one that you just
        // came from). Start with the direction on your left, and then
        // turn through each of the other possible directions one at a time.

        cout << "Please turn left 90 degrees." << endl;
        for (direction = 1; direction <= 3; direction++)
        {
            if ( !found && !dead_end( ) )
                found = traverse_maze( );
            cout << "Please turn right 90 degrees." << endl;
        }

        // You're now facing the direction from whence you came, so step
        // forward and turn around. This will put you in the exact
        // spot that you were at when the function call began.
        cout << "Please step forward, then turn 180 degrees." << endl;
    }
    return found;
}
```

maze.cxx **FTP**

9.3 REASONING ABOUT RECURSION

After a lecture on cosmology and the structure of the solar system, William James was accosted by a little old lady.

"Your theory that the sun is the center of the solar system, and the earth is a ball which rotates around it has a very convincing ring to it, Mr. James, but it's wrong. I've got a better theory," said the little old lady.

"And what is that, madam?" inquired James politely.

"That we live on a crust of earth which is on the back of a giant turtle."

Not wishing to demolish this absurd little theory by bringing to bear the masses of scientific evidence he had at his command, James decided to gently dissuade his opponent by making her see some of the inadequacies of her position.

"If your theory is correct, madam," he asked, "what does this turtle stand on?"

"You're a very clever man, Mr. James, and that's a very good question," replied the little old lady, "but I have an answer to it. And it is this: the first turtle stands on the back of a second, far larger, turtle, who stands directly under him."

"But what does this second turtle stand on?" persisted James patiently.

To this the little old lady crowed triumphantly. "It's no use, Mr. James—it's turtles all the way down."

J. R. Ross
Constraints on Variables in Syntax

In all our examples of recursive thinking, the series of recursive calls eventually reached a call that did not involve further recursion (that is, it reached a *stopping case*). If, on the other hand, every recursive call produces another recursive call, then a recursive call will, in theory, run forever. This is called **infinite recursion**. In practice, such a function will run until the computer runs out of memory for the activation records and terminates the program abnormally. Phrased another way, a recursive declaration should not be "recursive all the way down." Otherwise, like the lady's explanation of the solar system, a recursive call will never end, except perhaps in frustration.

In this section, we will show you how to reason about recursive functions, both to show that there is no infinite recursion, and to show that a recursive function's results are correct. As an example, we'll start with a new recursive function called power which computes powers of the form x^n, where x is any double number and n is an integer. So, power(3.0, 2) is 3.0^2 (which is 9.0), and power(4.2, 3) is 4.2^3 (which is 74.088). For any nonzero value of x, the value of x^0 is defined to be 1, so for example power(9.1, 0) is 1. For a negative exponent, $-n$, the value returned is defined by:

$$x^{-n} = 1/x^n \quad \{ x \text{ is any real number, and } -n \text{ is a negative integer} \}$$

For example, power(3.0, -2) is $1/3.0^2$ (which is 1/9). The only forbidden power is taking 0^n when n is not positive. Here is the function's complete specification:

```
double power(double x, int n);
// Precondition: If x is zero, then n must be positive.
// Postcondition: The value returned is x raised to the power n.
```

Our implementation begins by checking the precondition, and then deals with several cases. The first case, when n is non-negative, is easy. This case is computed by setting a local variable, product, to 1, and then repeatedly multiplying product by x. The repeated multiplication occurs n times, in the for-loop shown here:

```
if (n >= 0)
{
    product = 1;
    for (count = 1, count <= n; count++)
        product = product * x;
    return product;
}
```

To understand what is needed for a negative exponent, let's consider a concrete case. Suppose that we are computing power(3.0, -2), which must return the value 3.0^{-2}. But this value is equal to $1/3.0^2$. Negative powers are the same as positive powers in the denominator. This means that if we know that the function returns the correct answer when n is positive, then we can calculate the correct value for power(3.0, -2) by the expression 1/power(3.0, 2). By thinking recursively, whenever n is negative, power can compute its answer with a recursive call, like this:

```
return 1/power(x, -n); // When n is negative (and so -n is positive)
```

Remember, in this statement, n is negative (such as -2), so that -n is positive, and therefore, the recursive function call in the expression 1/power(x, -n) has a positive second argument. With a positive second argument, our power function makes no further recursive calls (i.e., a stopping case), and so the recursion ends.

This brings us to our first general technique for reasoning about recursion, which can be applied to the complete power function of Figure 9.9:

One Level Recursion

Suppose that every case is either a stopping case or it makes a recursive call that is a stopping case. Then the deepest recursive call is only one level deep, and therefore no infinite recursion occurs.

FIGURE 9.9 Implementation of the power Function with Only One Level of Recursion

---

A Function Implementation

```
double power(double x, int n)
// Precondition: If x is zero, then n must be positive.
// Postcondition: The value returned is x raised to the power n.
// Library facilities used: assert.h
{
    double product;  // The product of x with itself n times
    int count;

    if (x == 0)
        assert(n > 0);

    if (n >= 0)
    {
        product = 1;
        for (count = 1; count <= n; count++)
            product = product * x;
        return product;
    }
    else
        return 1/power(x, -n);
}
```

Sample Results of the Function

Call with these arguments		Return value of function call
x	n	
3.0	2	9.0
2.0	-3	0.125
4.1	0	1.0
-2.0	3	-8.0

powers.cxx **FTP**

How to Ensure That There is No Infinite Recursion In the More General Case

In general, recursive calls don't stop at just one level deep. A recursive call does not need to reach a stopping case immediately. Programmers have developed methods to reason about recursive calls that go beyond one level deep, based on the principles of *mathematical induction*. The reasoning can increase your confidence that a recursive function avoids infinite recursion. As an example to show that there is no infinite recursion, let's rewrite the function power so that it uses more recursion. The revision is based on the observation that for any number x and any positive integer n, the following relation holds:

$$x^n = x(x^{n-1})$$

This formula means that an alternative way to define x^n is as follows:

The value of x^n

The value is undefined when $n \le 0$ and $x = 0$;

otherwise the value is 0 when $x = 0$;

otherwise the value is 1 when $n = 0$;

otherwise the value is x times x^{n-1} when $n > 0$;

otherwise the value is $1/x^{-n}$ when $n < 0$.

The C++ version of a recursive function that computes in this way is given in Figure 9.10. To avoid confusion, we have used a slightly different name, pow, for this version of the function.

an alternative algorithm for computing powers

Tracing a recursive function such as pow can quickly overwhelm you, but there are relatively simple ways of showing that there is no infinite recursion without actually tracing through the execution. The most common way to ensure that a stopping case is *eventually* reached is to define a numeric quantity called the *variant expression*. This quantity must associate each legal recursive call to a single number. In a moment we'll discuss the properties that the variant expression should have; but first let's look at the kind of quantity we have in mind for the variant expression of the pow function. The value of the variant expression for pow is:

The Variant Expression for pow

The variant expression is abs(n) + 1 (when n is negative), and the variant expression is n (when n is non-negative).

FIGURE 9.10   Alternate Implementation of a Function to Compute Powers

---

A Function Implementation

```
double pow(double x, int n)
// Precondition: If x is zero, then n must be positive.
// Postcondition: The value returned is x raised to the power n.
// Library facilities used: assert.h
{
    if (x == 0)
    {   // x is zero, and n should be positive.
        assert(n > 0);
        return 0;
    }
    else if (n == 0)
        return 1;
    else if (n > 0)
        return x * pow(x, n-1);
    else // x is nonzero, and n is negative.
        return 1/pow(x, -n);
}
```

powers.cxx   **FTP**

With this definition we can examine a sequence of recursive pow calls, beginning with pow(2.0, -3):

A Sequence of Recursive Calls

pow(2.0, -3) has a variant expression abs(n) + 1, which is 4; it makes a recursive call of pow(2.0, 3).

pow(2.0, 3) has a variant expression n, which is 3; it makes a recursive call of pow(2.0, 2).

pow(2.0, 2) has a variant expression n, which is 2; it makes a recursive call of pow(2.0, 1).

pow(2.0, 1) has a variant expression n, which is 1; it makes a recursive call of pow(2.0, 0).

pow(2.0, 0) has a variant expression n, which is 0; this is the stopping case.

There are two important points to this example: (a) Each time a recursive call is made, the variant expression is reduced by at least one; and (b) When the variant expression reaches zero, there is a stopping case which terminates with no further recursive calls.

In general, a **variant expression** is a numeric quantity which is decreased by at least some fixed amount on each recursive call. And, once the variant expression reaches a small enough value, then a stopping case occurs. The "small enough value," which guarantees a stopping case, is called the **threshold**. In the pow example, the threshold is zero, and each recursive call reduces the variant expression by one. Here's a summary of the general technique for proving that a recursive call terminates:

variant expression and threshold

Ensuring That There Is No Infinite Recursion

To prove that a recursive call does not lead to infinite recursion, it is enough to find a *variant expression* and a *threshold* with the following properties:

1. Between one call of the function and any succeeding recursive call of that function, the value of the variant expression decreases by at least some fixed amount.

2. If the function is called and the value of the variant expression is less than or equal to the threshold, then the function terminates without making any recursive calls.

It is important that the reduction is at least a fixed amount. Otherwise, the variant expression might start at 1, then decrease to one-half, then to one-quarter, then to one-eighth, and so on, decreasing by ever-smaller amounts and never reaching the threshold. In the most common case, such as pow, the variant expression always decreases by at least one, and the threshold is zero.

To see that these two conditions guarantee no infinite recursion, reason as follows: Suppose the two conditions hold. Since Condition 1 is true, every recursive call will decrease the variant expression. This means that either the function will terminate, which is fine, or else the variant expression will decrease until it reaches the threshold. But if Condition 2 holds, then once the variant expression reaches the threshold, the function will terminate. That covers all the cases.

Inductive Reasoning about the Correctness of a Recursive Function

In addition to checking that a recursive function terminates, you should also check that it always behaves correctly—in other words that it meets its precondition/postcondition contract. The usual method for showing correctness of a recursive function is called **induction**. (And, in fact, the technique is the same

induction

as *mathematical induction* which you may have used in math classes.) The induction method requires a programmer to demonstrate the following facts about the function's behavior:

**Induction Method
To Show That a Recursive Function Is Correct**

To show that a recursive function meets its precondition/postcondition contract, first show that there is no infinite recursion (by showing Conditions 1 and 2, written above), and then show that the following two conditions are also valid:

3. Whenever the function makes no recursive calls, then it meets its precondition/postcondition contract. (This is called the **base step**.)

4. Whenever the function is called *and* all the recursive calls it makes meet their precondition/postcondition contract, then the original call will also meet its precondition/postcondition contract. (This is called the **induction step**.)

The conditions are numbered 3 and 4 to emphasize that they only ensure correctness if you know that there is no infinite recursion. You must also ensure that Conditions 1 and 2 hold for an appropriate variant expression and threshold.

Let's return to the function pow defined in Figure 9.10 on page 414. To complete our demonstration that it performs as desired, we must show that 3 and 4 hold.

It is easy to see that Condition 3 holds. The only way that the function can terminate without a recursive call is if the value of x is zero or n is zero. If x is zero the function returns 0, which is the correct answer; and if n is zero (and x is not zero) the function returns 1, which is also correct.

To see that Condition 4 holds we need only recall the algebraic identities:

$$x^n = x(x^{n-1}) \quad \text{and} \quad x^n = 1/x^{-n}$$

To summarize how to reason about recursion: First check that the function always terminates (no infinite recursion); next make sure that the stopping cases work correctly; finally, for each recursive case, pretend that you know the recursive calls will work correctly, and use this to show that each recursive case works correctly.

Self-Test Exercises

9. Write a recursive function that computes the number of digits in an integer *n*. (You might recall from page 19 that this is $\lfloor \log_{10} n \rfloor + 1$.) Do not use any local variables in your function declaration. Find a variant expression and threshold to show that your function has no infinite recursion.

10. Use inductive reasoning to show that your function from the previous exercise is always correct.

11. Find variant expressions and thresholds to show that the functions `random_fractal` and `traverse_maze` (Section 9.2) never result in infinite recursion.

12. Use induction to show that `random_fractal` meets its precondition/postcondition contract.

CHAPTER SUMMARY

- If a problem can be reduced to smaller instances of the same problem, then a recursive solution is likely to be easy to find and implement.

- A recursive algorithm for a function implementation contains two kinds of cases: one or more cases that include a *recursive call* and one or more *stopping cases* in which the problem is solved without the use of any recursive calls.

- When writing recursive functions, always check to see that the function will not produce infinite recursion. This can be done by finding an appropriate *variant expression* and *threshold*.

- *Inductive reasoning* can be used to show that a recursive function meets its precondition/postcondition contract.

Solutions to Self-Test Exercises ❓

1. The top left function prints 3, then 2, then 1. The top right function prints 1, then 2, then 3. The bottom function prints 3, then 2, then 1, then 1 again, then 2 again, then 3 again.

2. The output is `Hip`, then `Hip`, then `Hurrah`, on three separate lines.

3. For the first modification, change the two lines in the else-block to:
```
cheers(n-1);
cout << "Hip" << endl;
```

For the second modification, change the lines to:
```
cout << "Hip" << endl;
cheers(n-1);
cout << "Hip" << endl;
```

For the third modification, change the lines to:
```
if (n % 2 == 0)
    cout << "Hip" << endl;
cheers(n-1);
if (n % 2 == 1)
    cout << "Hip << endl";
```

4. The function implementation is:
```
void exercise4(unsigned int n).
{
    if (n > 0)
    {
        cout << '*';
        exercise4(n-1);
        cout << '!';
    }
}
```

5. The original call makes two calls with a width of 4. Each of those calls makes two calls with a width of 2, so there are four calls with a width of 2. Each of those four calls makes two more calls, again cutting the width in half, so there are eight calls with a width of 1. These eight calls do not make further calls since width has reached epsilon. The total number of calls, including the original call, is 1 + 2 + 4 + 8, which is 15 calls.

6. Did you peek?

7. The easiest solution requires an extra parameter, called level, which indicates how deep the recursion has proceeded. When the revised function is called from a program, the value of level should be given as zero. Each recursive call increases the level by one. When the level is an even number, then the midpoint is moved upward; when the level is odd, then the midpoint is moved downward. The code to do the movement is as follows:
```
if (level % 2 == 0)
    mid_height += width;
else
    mid_height -= width;
```

8. Each recursive call steps forward into a location that has not previously been visited. Therefore, the number of calls can be no more than the number of locations in the maze, which is 200.

9. The function implementation is:
```
int digits(int n)
{
    if (n < 10) && (n > -10))
        return 1;
    else
        return 1 + digits(n/10);
}
```

A good variant expression is "the number of digits in n, with the threshold of 1.

10. The base case includes numbers that are less than ten and more than negative ten. All these numbers have one digit, and the function correctly returns the answer 1. For the induction case, we have a number *n* with more than one digit. The number of digits will always be one more than *n*/10 (using integer division), so if we assume that the recursive function call digits(n/10) returns the right answer, then 1 + digits(n/10) is the correct number of digits in *n*.

11. For random_fractal, a good variant expression is the ratio width/epsilon. When this ratio is greater than one, each recursive call cuts width in half, which subtracts at least 0.5 from the ratio. When the ratio reaches 1 (or less), the recursion stops since width is then no more than epsilon. Therefore, 1 is the threshold.

The function traverse_maze has a variant expression that is expressed in English as "the number of locations in the maze that do not yet have your name written on the ground." This value is reduced by at least one during each recursive call, and when this value reaches zero, there can be no further recursive calls. Therefore, 0 is the threshold.

12. We have already found a variant expression and threshold for Conditions 1 and 2, showing that random_fractal does not result in infinite recursion. For Condition 3, we must show that the function has correct behavior for the stopping case. In this case, width is no more than epsilon, and therefore the line segment does not need further dividing. We only need to output the height of the right endpoint of the current line segment, which is what the function does. In Condition 4 of the inductive reasoning, we assume that the two recursive calls correctly generate a random fractal for the two smaller line segments that we have created. Putting these two smaller random fractals together correctly gives us the larger random fractal.

1 Write a function that produces the following output:

```
This was written by call number 1.
 This was written by call number 2.
  This was written by call number 3.
   This was written by call number 4.
   This ALSO written by call number 4.
  This ALSO written by call number 3.
 This ALSO written by call number 2.
This ALSO written by call number 1.
```

In this example, the recursion stopped when it reached four levels deep, but your function should be capable of continuing to any specified level.

2 Write a function with two parameters, prefix (a string, using our string ADT from Chapter 4) and levels (an unsigned integer). The function prints the string prefix followed by "section numbers" of the form 1.1., 1.2., 1.3., and so on. The levels argument determines how many levels the section numbers have. For example, if levels is 2, then the section numbers have the form x.y. If levels is 3, then the section numbers have the form x.y.z. The digits permitted in each level are always '1' through '9'. As an example, if prefix is the string "BOX:" and levels is 2, then the function would start by printing

```
BOX:1.1.
BOX:1.2.
BOX:1.3.
```

and finish by printing

```
BOX:9.7.
BOX:9.8.
BOX:9.9.
```

The stopping case occurs when levels reaches zero. The primary string manipulation technique that you will need is the ability to create a new string which consists of prefix followed by a digit and a period. If s is the string you want to create and i is the digit (an integer in the range 1 to 9), then the following statements will perform this task:

```
s = prefix;
s += '.';
s += ('0' + i);
```

The third statement puts the character ('0' + i) on the end of the string, and this character is the ASCII value for the digit that corresponds to the integer i. This new string, s, can be passed as a parameter to recursive calls of the function.

3 Write a recursive function that has two inputs, first and second, which are both strings (from our string ADT of Chapter 4). The function should print all rearrangements of the letters in first, followed by second. For example, if first is the string "CAT" and second is the string "MAN", then the function would print the strings CATMAN, CTAMAN, ACTMAN, ATCMAN, TACMAN, and TCAMAN. The stopping case of the function occurs when the length of first has zero characters. We'll leave the recursive thinking up to you, but we should mention that two extra string member functions will make things go smoother. These member functions are:

```
void String::insert
(size_t position, char c);
// Postcondition: A copy of character c has
// been inserted into the string at the
// indicated position. Existing characters
// that used to be at or after the given
// position have been shifted right one spot.
```

```
void String::remove
(size_t position, size_t n);
// Precondition: position + n <= length( ).
// Postcondition: n characters have been
// removed from the string, beginning at the
// specified position.
```

If you are using the new standard String class, then these two functions are already present, but if you are using our String class, then you'll have to implement the two functions.

4 Write an interactive program to help you count all of the boxes in a room. The program should begin by asking something like *How many unnumbered boxes can you see?* Then the program will have you number those boxes from 1 to *m*, where *m* is your answer. But, remember that each box might have smaller boxes inside, so once the program knows you can see *m* boxes, it should ask you to open box number 1 and take out any boxes you find, numbering those boxes 1.1, 1.2, and so on. It will also ask you to open box number 2 and take out any boxes you find there, numbering those boxes 2.1, 2.2, and so on. This continues for box 3, 4, up to *m*. And, of course, each time you number a box 1.1 or 3.8 or something similar, *that* box might have more boxes inside. Boxes that reside inside of 3.8 would be numbered 3.8.1, 3.8.2, and so on. At the end, the program should print a single number telling you the total number of boxes in the room.

5 Write a recursive function called `sumover` that has one argument *n*, which is an unsigned integer. The function returns a double value, which is the sum of the reciprocals of the first *n* positive integers. (The reciprocal of *x* is the fraction $1/x$.) For example, `sumover(1)` returns `1.0` (which is 1/1); `sumover(2)` returns `1.5` (which is 1/1 + 1/2); `sumover(3)` returns approximately `1.833` (which is 1/1 + 1/2 + 1/3). Define `sumover(0)` to be zero. Do not use any local variables in your function.

6 The formula for computing the number of ways of choosing *r* different things from a set of *n* things is the following:

$$C(n, r) = \frac{n!}{r! \, (n - r)!}$$

In this formula, the factorial function is represented by an exclamation point (!), and defined as the product:

$$n! = n \times (n - 1) \times (n - 2) \times \ldots \times 1$$

Discover a recursive version of the $C(n, r)$ formula and write a recursive C++ function that computes the value of the formula. Embed the function in a program and test it.

7 Write a recursive function that has as arguments an array of characters and two bounds on array indices. The function should reverse the order of those entries in the array whose indices are between the two bounds. For example, suppose that the array is:

```
a[0] = 'A'   a[1] = 'B'   a[2] = 'C'
a[3] = 'D'   a[4] = 'E'
```

and the bounds are 1 and 4. Then after the function is run the array elements should be:

```
a[0] = 'A'   a[1] = 'D'   a[2] = 'C'
a[3] = 'B'   a[4] = 'e'
```

Embed the function in a program and test it.

8 Write a recursive function to produce a pattern of *n* lines of asterisks. The first line contains one asterisk, the next line contains 2, and so on up to the nth line which contains *n* asterisks. Line number *n*+1 again contains *n* asterisks, the next line has *n*-1 asterisks, and so on until line number 2*n* which has just one asterisk.

9 Examine this pattern of asterisks and blanks, and write a recursive function that can generate exactly this pattern:

```
*
*  *
   *
*  *  *  *
      *
      *  *
         *
*  *  *  *  *  *  *  *
      *
      *  *
         *
      *  *  *  *
         *
         *  *
            *
```

With recursive thinking, the function needs only seven or eight lines of code (including two recursive calls). How is this pattern a fractal? Your function should also be capable of producing larger or smaller patterns of the same variety. Hint: Have two parameters. One parameter indicates the indentation of the leftmost line in the pattern; the other parameter indicates the number of stars in the longest line.

10 Write a program that asks the user to think of an integer between 1 and 1,000,000, and then guesses the number through a series of yes/no questions. In order to guess the number, the program calls a recursive function `guess` that has two parameters, `low` and `high`. The precondition for the function requires that the user's number lie in the range `low...high`, so that the program's initial call is to `guess(1, 1000000)`. What is a good base case for `guess`, when it can guess the user's number with little or no work? Answer: If (`low == high`) then there is only one possible number, and the function can guess that number. On the other hand, if (`low < high`) then the function should calculate a point near the middle of the range:

```
midpoint = (low + high) / 2;
```

Then the function asks the user whether the midpoint is the correct number. If so, then the function is finished. On the other hand, if the midpoint is not the user's number, then the function asks whether the correct number is larger than `midpoint`. If so, then the function knows that the user's number lies in the range `midpoint + 1` to `high`, and a recursive call can be made to solve the smaller problem of finding a user's number in the range `midpoint + 1` to `high`. On the other hand, if the user's number is not larger than `midpoint`, then a recursive call can be made to solve the smaller problem of finding a user's number in the range `low` to `midpoint - 1`. This method of searching is called **binary search**, which we will explore further in Chapter 12.

11 For this project, you are to write a recursive function that prints all of the objects in a bag. Use the bag specification from Figure 5.11 on page 236, and assume that the `Item`

data type can be printed to cout with the usual output operator. The items are to be printed in a random order—without using any of the bag private fields. For an empty bag, the function has no work to do (that is, the stopping case). For a non-empty bag, the function carries out four steps: (a) grab a random item from the bag, storing it in a local variable `one_item`; (b) print `one_item`; (c) print any items that remain in the bag; (d) put `one_item` back in the bag. You'll need to identify which of these steps is the "simpler version of the same problem."

12 This project uses the `Towers` class from Chapter 3's Programming Project 13 on page 135. For the project, write a recursive function that computes and prints a solution to the Towers of Hanoi game. The function should meet this specification:

```
void Hanoi(
    Towers& t,
    size_t n,
    int start,
    int target,
    int spare
);
// Precondition: start, target, and spare are
// three different peg numbers of the game.
// Also, the n smallest rings currently are on
// the top of the start peg.
// Postcondition: The function has activated
// a sequence of moves for the tower t, so
// that the total effect of these moves is to
// shift the top n rings from the start peg to
// the target peg, using spare as the extra
// peg. None of the other rings has been
// disturbed. Each time a move is made,
// a message describing the move is
// printed.
```

Your solution should have a simple stopping case: When *n* is zero, there is no work to do. When *n* is more than zero, use a recursive call to move *n*−1 rings from the start peg to the spare peg. Then call the `move` member function to move one ring from the start peg to the target peg. Finally, make another recursive call to move *n*−1 rings from the spare peg to the target peg.

13 This is a number puzzle project. Here are the rules: Your instructor is going to give you a certain number of floppy disks. The number of disks is called `initial`. You then have two choices: (a) you ask for (and receive) 53 more disks, or (b) if you have an even number of disks, then you may give half of them back to your instructor. Each time you do (a) or (b), that is called a *step* in the game. Your goal is to end up with exactly 91 disks in n steps or fewer. For example, if `initial` is 99 and n is 4, then the following sequence of steps will reach the goal of 91:

$$99 \quad \underset{\text{step a}}{\rightarrow} \quad 152 \quad \underset{\text{step b}}{\rightarrow} \quad 76 \quad \underset{\text{step b}}{\rightarrow} \quad 38 \quad \underset{\text{step a}}{\rightarrow} \quad 91$$

For this project, write a recursive function, `goal`, which determines whether it is possible to reach the goal (91) starting with some `initial` number, and allowing no more than n steps. The base cases occurs when `initial` is 91 (since in this case, the answer is yes), or when n is zero and `initial` is not 91 (since in this case, the answer is no). If you do not have a base case, then solve the problem by making one or two recursive calls (one to `goal(initial+53, n-1)` and the other to `goal(initial/2, n-1)`—although this second call is only made if `initial` is an even number).

14 Let's think about your computer science class for a moment. You might know several students, perhaps Judy, Jervis, Walter and Michael. Each of those students knows several other students, and each of those knows more students and so on. Now, there is one particular student named Dor that you would like to meet. One way to meet Dor would be if you had a mutual acquaintance: For example, you know Judy, and Judy knows Dor, so Judy could introduce you to Dor. Or, there might be a longer path of acquaintances: For example, you know Judy, and Judy knows Harry, and Harry knows Cathy, and Cathy knows Dor. In this case, Judy can introduce you to Harry, Harry can introduce you to Cathy, and Cathy can introduce you to Dor.

Write an interactive program to help you figure out whether there is a path-of-acquaintances from you to Dor. The program should include a recursive function that has one argument, `person`, which is the name of a person in your class. The function determines whether there is a path of acquaintances from `person` to Dor. Hint: This problem is similar to the maze problem in Section 9.2. But beware of potential infinite recursion! One way to avoid infinite recursion is to include a bag of student names, which keeps track of the names of the students you have already visited on your search for a path to Dor.

15 A *pretty print* program takes a program, which may not be indented in any particular way, and produces a copy with the same program indented so that bracket pairs (`{` and `}`) line up with inner pairs indented more than outer pairs, so that if-else statements are indented as we have been doing, and so that other indenting is as we have been doing. Write a program that reads a C++ program from one text file and produces a pretty print version of the program in a second text file. To make it easier, simply do this for the body of the program, ignoring the declarations, and assume that all substatements of complex statements (other than compound statements themselves) are compound statements (that is, are enclosed by brackets).

10 Trees

Some people call it the Tree of Heaven. No matter where its seed fell, it made a tree which struggles to reach the sky.

BETTY SMITH
A Tree Grows in Brooklyn

This chapter presents a new data structure, a tree, which is our first example of a **nonlinear structure**. In a nonlinear structure the components do not form a simple sequence of first entry, second entry, third entry, and so on. Instead, there is a more complex linking between the components; this is why they are called *non*linear. The nonlinear structure often allows dramatic improved efficiency for container classes such as the bag.

nonlinear structures

The chapter starts with definitions of various kinds of trees and their applications. We then show how to represent trees and implement a toolkit for building and manipulating trees. The toolkit is useful for many ADTs such as the binary search tree in the last section of this chapter.

423

10.1 INTRODUCTION TO TREES

Binary Trees

Before I left my bed in the morning, little Adèle came running in to tell me that the great horse-chestnut at the bottom of the orchard had been struck by lightning in the night, and half of it split away.

CHARLOTTE BRONTË
Jane Eyre

a real tree. . .

. . .and a computer scientist's tree

The first kind of tree that we'll look at is a *binary tree*, which is the most commonly used tree data structure. A binary tree is not too different from a real tree. The real tree starts at its root, growing upward. At some point, the trunk splits into two smaller branches. Each of the smaller branches continues, perhaps splitting into two still smaller branches, and so forth until each branch ends with some leaves.

If you take that tree, pull it out of the ground, and stick its root in the air, you will have a computer scientist's tree. You see, a computer scientist draws a tree with the root at the top, branches below that, and leaves at the very bottom. And, of course, a computer scientist's tree contains data of one kind or another. Let's be more specific, with a concrete example of a binary tree of integers, shown in Figure 10.1.

Each of the boxes in the Figure 10.1 is called a **node** of the tree, and each node contains some data—in this case each piece of data is an integer, but we might also have trees of double numbers, trees of strings, even trees where each node's data is a complex type like a stack or a queue. The node at the top of the diagram, which has the number 14, is called the **root**. Each node in a binary tree may have up to two nodes below it, one linked on its left and one linked on its right. These are called the node's **left child** and **right child**. For example, the root's left child is the node containing 17, and its right child contains 11. Some nodes have only a left child, some have only a right child, and some have no children at all.

FIGURE 10.1 A Binary Tree of Integers

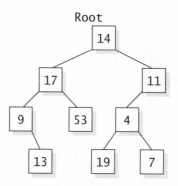

A node with no children is called a **leaf**. In more general kinds of trees, a node may have more than two children, but for the **binary** trees that we're discussing, each node is limited to at most two children. One other point: With the exception of the root, each node is the child of just one node; the root is not the child of any node.

Much of the terminology for trees comes from family relations, such as the word "child." Perhaps you can guess the meaning of some other terms: *parent, sibling, ancestor, descendant*. These definitions are given below, but first we'll provide a complete definition of a binary tree:

Binary Trees

A **binary tree** is a finite set of "nodes." The set might be empty (no nodes, which is called the **empty tree**). But if the set is not empty, it follows these rules:

1. There is one special node, called the root.

2. Each node may be associated with up to two other different nodes, called its **left child** and its **right child**. If a node c is the child of another node p, then we say that "p is c's **parent**."

3. Each node, except the root, has exactly one parent; the root has no parent.

4. If you start at a node and move to the node's parent (provided there is one), then move again to that node's parent, and keep moving upward to each node's parent, you will eventually reach the root.

Here are some other terms used with trees, with examples selected from Figure 10.1 on page 424 and Figure 10.2 on page 426.

tree terminology

Parent. The **parent** of a node is the node linked above it. More precisely, if a node c is the child of another node p, then we say that "p is c's **parent**." Except for the root, every node has just one parent, and the root has no parent. In Figure 10.1, the node containing 17 is the parent of the nodes containing 9 and 53.

Sibling. Two nodes are **siblings** if they have the same parent. In Figure 10.1, the nodes containing 9 and 53 are siblings.

Ancestor. A node's parent is its first ancestor. The parent of the parent is the next ancestor. The parent of the parent of the parent is the next ancestor . . . and so forth, until you reach the root. The root is an ancestor of each other node.

FIGURE 10.2 More Examples of Binary Trees

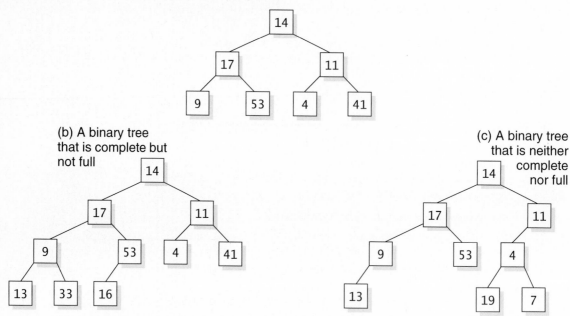

(a) A full binary tree

(b) A binary tree that is complete but not full

(c) A binary tree that is neither complete nor full

Descendant. A node's children are its first descendants. The children's children are its next descendants. The children of the children of the children are... well, you get the idea.

Subtree. Any node in a tree also can be viewed as the root of a new, smaller tree. This smaller tree contains the node that we've picked as the new root and all of the new root's descendants. This is called a **subtree** of the original tree. In Figure 10.2(a), we may choose 17 as the root of a new subtree, and that subtree has three nodes: the nodes containing 17, 9, and 53.

Left and Right Subtrees of a Node. For a node in a binary tree, the nodes beginning with its left child and below are its **left subtree.** The nodes beginning with its right child and below are its **right subtree.**

Depth of a Node. Suppose you start at a node *n* and move upward to its parent. We'll call this "one step." Then move up to the parent of the parent—that's a second step. Eventually, you will reach the root, and the number of steps taken is called the **depth of the node** *n*. The depth of the root itself is zero; a child of the root has depth one. In Figure 10.2(b), the node containing 13 has depth three.

Depth of a Tree. The **depth of a tree** is the maximum depth of any of its leaves. In Figure 10.2(b), the leaf containing 13 has depth three, and there is no deeper leaf. So the depth of the example tree is three. If a tree has only one node, the root, then its depth is zero (since the depth of the root is zero). The empty tree doesn't have any leaves, so we use −1 for its depth. Just to confuse things, you'll often see the term *height* of a tree used instead of *depth*, but they both mean the same thing.

Full Binary Trees. In a **full binary tree**, every leaf has the same depth, and every non-leaf has two children. Figure 10.1 on page 424 is not a full tree because it has leaves at different depths—some with depth two and some with depth three. Also, some of the non-leaves have only one child. In Figure 10.2, part (a) is full, but parts (b) and (c) are not full.

Complete Binary Trees. Suppose you take a full binary tree and start adding new leaves at a new depth from left to right. All the new leaves have the same depth—one more than where we started—and we always add leftmost nodes first. For example, if you add three nodes to Figure 10.2(a), then one possible result is Figure 10.2(b). The tree is no longer a full tree because some leaves are a bit deeper than others. Instead, we call this a **complete binary tree**. In order to be a complete tree, every level except the deepest must contain as many nodes as possible; and at the deepest level, all the nodes are as far left as possible.

Binary Taxonomy Trees

Binary trees are useful in many situations. We'll look at one example, **binary taxonomy trees**, which can be used to store certain kinds of knowledge. The particular example we have in mind stores information about a collection of animals. Each leaf in a binary taxonomy tree contains the name of an animal, and each non-leaf node contains a question about animals.

binary taxonomy trees store knowledge about a collection of animals

For example, suppose that we want a taxonomy tree for four animals: a kangaroo, a mouse, a trout, and a robin. The tree might look like Figure 10.3. To use a binary taxonomy tree, you start at the root and ask the question that is written there. If the answer is "yes," you move to the left child, and if the answer is "no,"

FIGURE 10.3 A Small Binary Taxonomy Tree

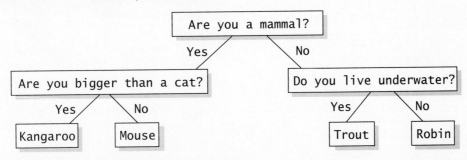

you move to the right child. Eventually, you will reach a leaf, and the name at the leaf tells you which animal you have been examining—or at least it does if the animal is one of the animals that the tree knows about.

General Trees

Each node in a binary tree has at most two children. In fact, that's why the word "binary'" is used. But in general, a node in a tree may have any number of children. Figure 10.4 shows an example where some nodes have one child, some have two, and some have three. A node in a general tree might even have more than three children (although three is the most in Figure 10.4). In Figure 10.4 we have not written any data at the nodes—but we could have written integers or strings or whatever data type we were interested in storing.

Trees

A **tree** is a finite set of "nodes." The set might be empty (no nodes, which is called the **empty tree**). But if the set is not empty, then it must follow these rules:

1. There is one special node, called the **root**.
2. Each node may be associated with one or more different nodes, called its **children**. If a node *c* is the child of another node *p*, then we say that "*p* is *c*'s **parent**."
3. Each node except the root has exactly one parent; the root has no parent.
4. If you start at any node and move to the node's parent (provided there is one), then move again to that node's parent (provided there is one), and keep moving upward to each node's parent, you will eventually reach the root.

FIGURE 10.4 A General Tree

There are other special kinds of trees. For example, Section 11.2 uses B-trees, which are trees where the number of children of each node must lie between a certain minimum and a certain maximum.

Self-Test Exercises

1. Draw a binary tree with 12 nodes. Circle the root, and put asterisks at each leaf. Find two nodes that are siblings, and connect them with a wiggly line. Choose one of the leaves, and shade all of its ancestors.

2. Draw a tree that contains members of your family. The root should contain your mother's mother. Her children nodes contain her actual children, and those nodes contain her children's children, and so on.

3. What is the depth of the tree from Exercise 2? What is the depth of the node that contains *you*. Draw a circle around all nodes that are your ancestor nodes. Do each of these nodes contain one of your real-life ancestors? Draw a big square around all nodes that are descendants of your mother. Does each of these nodes contain one of her real-life descendants?

4. Create a binary taxonomy tree with 16 animals. Is your tree full? Is it complete?

10.2 TREE REPRESENTATIONS

This section discusses two kinds of trees and how they typically are represented in a data structure. For the most part, if you understand these two representations, you can also manage other kinds of trees.

Array Representation of Complete Binary Trees

Complete binary trees have a simple representation using arrays. The representation can use a fixed-sized array (as in the ADTs of Chapter 3), which means that the size of the data structure is fixed during compilation, and during execution it does not grow larger or smaller. Or the representation can use a dynamic array (as in the ADTs of Chapter 4), allowing the representation to grow and shrink as needed during the execution of a program.

Remember that in a complete binary tree, all of the depths are full, except perhaps for the deepest. At the deepest depth, the nodes are as far left as possible. For example, here is a complete binary tree with ten nodes where the item contained in each node is a character.

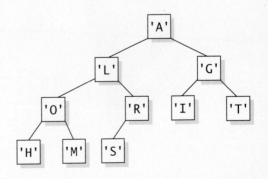

In this example, the first seven nodes completely fill the levels at depth zero (the root), depth one (the root's children), and depth two. There are three more nodes at depth three, and these nodes are as far left as possible.

The ten characters that the tree contains can be stored in an array of characters, starting with the root's character in the [0] location of the array, as shown here:

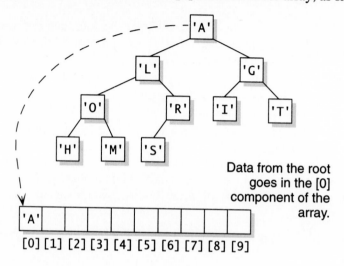

Data from the root goes in the [0] component of the array.

After the root, the two nodes with depth one are placed in the array, as shown here:

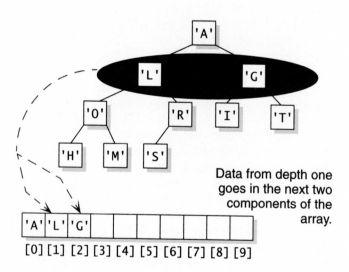

Data from depth one goes in the next two components of the array.

We continue in this way, placing the four nodes of depth two next and finishing off with the nodes of depth three. The entire representation of the tree by an array is shown here:

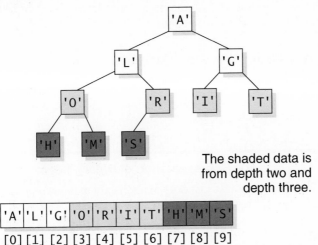

The shaded data is
from depth two and
depth three.

'A''L''G''O''R''I''T''H''M''S'
[0] [1] [2] [3] [4] [5] [6] [7] [8] [9]

There are several reasons why the array representation is convenient:

formulas for storing data from a complete binary tree in the components of an array

1. The data from the root always appears in the [0] component of the array.

2. Suppose that the data for a nonroot node appears in component [i] of the array. Then the data for its parent is always at location [(i-1)/2] (using integer division).

3. Suppose that the data for a node appears in component [i] of the array. Then its children (if they exist) always have their data at these locations:

   Left child at component [2i+1];

   Right child at component [2i+2].

These formulas make it easy to implement algorithms that traverse the tree, moving from node to node in various ways, processing data along the way.

the ADT can use a dynamic array or a static array

Before long you will implement some ADTs that store data in a tree. If the tree is a complete binary tree, then the ADT can store the complete binary tree in a fixed-sized array, using the formulas that we have written. Such a class will have at least two private member variables: (1) The array itself is one member variable, and (2) a second member variable keeps track of how much of the array is used. The actual links between the nodes are not stored. Instead, these links exist only via the formulas that determine where an item is stored in the array based on the item's position in the tree.

As an alternative to a fixed-sized array, the implementation can use a dynamic array. Using a dynamic array entails a third member variable to keep track of the complete size of the dynamic array.

Noncomplete binary trees can also be implemented using an array, although a problem arises in determining which children of a node actually exist. We'll address this problem in the Programming Project 4 on page 490. But for now, let's look at the other alternative: a dynamic implementation of binary trees that allocates and releases nodes as needed.

Representing a Binary Tree with a Struct for Nodes

A binary tree can be represented by its individual nodes, where each node is stored in a *struct*, similar to the way that we used a node *struct* to build linked lists. Here is the basic idea:

Node Representation of Binary Trees

Each node of a tree is stored in an instance of a *struct*. The *struct* contains pointers that link it to other nodes in the tree. An entire tree is represented as a pointer to the root node.

For a binary tree, we'll link each node to its left child and right child. The node also has a member variable to hold some data. The type of the data can be declared with a typedef statement or as a template parameter, as shown here:

Using a typedef statement:

```
struct BinaryTreeNode
{
    typedef char Item;
    Item data;
    BinaryTreeNode *left;
    BinaryTreeNode *right;
};
```

Using a template parameter:

```
template <class Item>
struct BinaryTreeNode
{
    Item data;
    BinaryTreeNode *left;
    BinaryTreeNode *right;
};
```

In the typedef version, we have chosen the item to be *char*, but we could have used any data type. In both versions, the data member variable of a node holds some information that occurs in the node. Each binary tree node also contains two pointers, left and right, which point to the left and right children of the node. When a child pointer is NULL, it indicates that the particular child does not exist. We could include other links in a binary tree node: perhaps a pointer to the node's parent, or to the root of the entire tree, or even to siblings. But many applications need only the children links.

We can draw a boxes-and-arrows representation of a small tree, as in Figure 10.5. Each node is stored in one *struct* of type BinaryTreeNode, and the entire tree is accessed through a pointer that points to the root node of the tree. Within the diagram, a null pointer is drawn as a slash. The pointer to the root node is similar to the head pointer of a linked list, providing a starting point to access all the nodes in the tree. If the tree was empty (with no nodes), then the root pointer would be null.

FIGURE 10.5   A Binary Tree Represented with BinaryTreeNode Structs

(a) Example binary
tree of characters

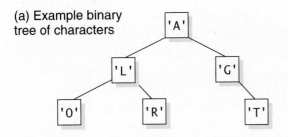

(b) Representation
of the binary tree
using
BinaryTreeNode
structs. Each large
box is a
BinaryTreeNode
struct, and each of
the small shaded
boxes is a pointer to
a BinaryTreeNode.

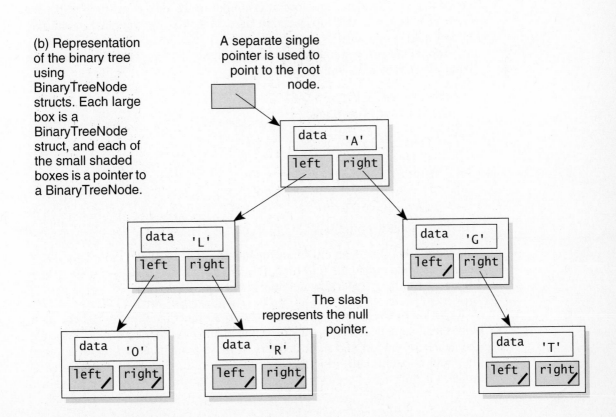

Self-Test Exercises

5. Consider a complete binary tree with exactly 10,000 nodes, implemented with an array. Suppose that a node has its value stored in location 4999. Where is the value stored for this node's parent? Where is the value stored for its left child? What can you say about its right child?

6. Draw a representation of a small binary tree with three nodes containing integers. Put 10 in the root, 20 in the left child of the root, and 30 in the right child of the root. Use the binary tree node definition from this section.

7. Write a new node definition that could be used for a tree where each node has up to four children, and each node also has a pointer to its parent. Store the pointers to the children in an array of four pointers.

10.3 A TOOLKIT FOR BINARY TREE NODES

With the BinaryTreeNode definition in hand, we can define a small toolkit of functions for creating and manipulating binary tree nodes. Primarily, the toolkit functions are meant to help a programmer who is writing an ADT that uses a binary tree to store data. The toolkit is similar to the linked list toolkit that we wrote in Chapter 5 and subsequently used in linked list versions of the bag ADT, list ADT, stack ADT, and queue ADT.

To attain the best generality, our toolkit will use the template definition of the BinaryTreeNode class shown here:

```
template <class Item>
struct BinaryTreeNode
{
    Item data;
    BinaryTreeNode *left;
    BinaryTreeNode *right;
};
```

The Four Toolkit Functions

The toolkit will start with only four functions, but we will add more later. We'll specify and implement the four toolkit functions one at a time, then collect them all together with a header file and implementation file.

A Function to Create a New Node. The first function creates a new node with specified data. When the node is created, the programmer may also specify the values of the left and right pointers. If these pointers aren't specified, then they will be NULL, indicating that the child doesn't exist. The default value of NULL is obtained by specifying a default argument in the prototype, as shown here along with a postcondition:

```
template <class Item>
BinaryTreeNode<Item>* create_node(
    const Item& entry,
    BinaryTreeNode<Item>* l_ptr = NULL,
    BinaryTreeNode<Item>* r_ptr = NULL
);

// Postcondition: The value returned is a pointer to a newly allocated node
// with its data equal to entry and its child pointers equal to l_ptr and
// r_ptr. Note: If there is insufficient dynamic memory, then the
// new_handler is called.
```

The implementation uses *new* to allocate a new node, and then fills in the three member variables from the values of the three parameters, as shown here:

```
template <class Item>
BinaryTreeNode<Item>* create_node(
    const Item& entry,
    BinaryTreeNode<Item>* l_ptr = NULL,
    BinaryTreeNode<Item>* r_ptr = NULL
)
// Library facilities used: stdlib.h
{
    BinaryTreeNode<Item> *result_ptr;

    result_ptr = new BinaryTreeNode<Item>;
    result_ptr->data  = entry;
    result_ptr->left  = l_ptr;
    result_ptr->right = r_ptr;

    return result_ptr;
}
```

Since this is a template function, some compilers require that the default arguments for l_ptr and r_ptr are listed in both the prototype and the implementation. Therefore, we have listed these default arguments in our implementation. (See "Default Arguments in Template Functions" on page 273.)

Testing Whether a Node Is a Leaf.   Our second function tests whether a node is a leaf. You can write the postcondition yourself. Here is our implementation:

```
template <class Item>
bool is_leaf(const BinaryTreeNode<Item>& node)
{
    return (node.left == NULL) && (node.right == NULL);
}
```

Notice that the parameter (node) is actually a BinaryTreeNode rather than a *pointer* to a node. Therefore we use the notation node.left and node.right rather than node->left and node->right.

Returning Nodes to the Heap.   Our third function returns the nodes of a tree to the heap. The function has one parameter, which is the root pointer of the tree. Here is the specification:

```
template <class Item>
void tree_clear(BinaryTreeNode<Item>*& root_ptr);
// Precondition: root_ptr is the root pointer of a binary tree (which may be
// NULL for the empty tree).
// Postcondition: All nodes at the root or below have been returned to the
// heap, and root_ptr has been set to NULL.
```

The implementation is easier than it seems—the ease comes from recursive thinking. First notice that there is one easy case: When root_ptr is NULL, the function does no work. On the other hand, if the root pointer is not null, then there are four steps:

1. Clear the left subtree, returning all its nodes to the heap.
2. Clear the right subtree, returning all its nodes to the heap.
3. Return the root node to the heap.
4. Set the root pointer to null.

Steps 1 and 2 are both examples of "smaller versions of the problem that we are trying to solve in the first place." Think recursively, and you will quickly write this implementation:

```
template <class Item>
void tree_clear(BinaryTreeNode<Item>*& root_ptr)
{
    if (root_ptr != NULL)
    {
        tree_clear(root_ptr->left);
        tree_clear(root_ptr->right);
        delete root_ptr;
        root_ptr = NULL;
    }
}
```

The base case (when the root pointer is null) does no work.

Copying a Tree. Our fourth function also has a simple recursive implementation. The function copies a tree, as specified here:

```
template <class Item>
BinaryTreeNode<Item>* tree_copy(BinaryTreeNode<Item>* root_ptr);
// Precondition: root_ptr is the root pointer of a binary tree (which may be
// NULL for the empty tree).
// Postcondition: A copy of the binary tree has been made, and the return
// value is a pointer to the root of this copy.
```

Once again, there is a simple base case: When `root_ptr` is NULL, the function simply returns NULL. On the other hand, if the root pointer is not null, then the tree has at least one node. The tree can be copied with these three steps (using local variables `l_ptr` and `r_ptr`, which are both pointers to nodes):

1. Make `l_ptr` point to a copy of the left subtree (which might be empty).

2. Make `r_ptr` point to a copy of the right subtree (which might be empty).

3. `return create_node(root_ptr->data, l_ptr, r_ptr);`

Once again, the first two steps of the pseudocode are "smaller versions of the problem we are solving in the first place." Therefore these two steps can be solved with recursive calls. The complete implementation of `tree_copy` appears in our implementation file along with the other three functions (see the file `bintree1.template` in Figure 10.7 on page 440). The toolkit's header file (`bintree1.h`) is also shown in a figure (Figure 10.6 on page 438), providing full documentation for the functions.

Pitfall: Not Connecting All the Links

PITFALL

Any time you are implementing a dynamic structure with pointers, there is a potential pitfall: forgetting to set all of the pointer fields of a node. With a linear structure, such as a list or a stack, the pitfall is not so common, since each node has only one pointer field. But as the structures become more complex, such as our binary tree node, the potential for forgetting to correctly set a pointer becomes more likely.

For example, the `create_node` function must set both the left and right pointers of a newly created node. When you allocate a node that is part of a dynamic structure, any unused pointers should immediately be set to the null pointer. This will prevent you from mistakenly thinking that unused pointers are pointing to a valid node.

FIGURE 10.6   First Version of the Header File for the Binary Tree Toolkit

A Header File

```
// FILE: bintree1.h
// PROVIDES: A toolkit of four template functions for manipulating binary trees. Each node of
// tree contains a piece of data and pointers to its left and right children as shown here:
//
//     template <class Item>          Item may be any of the C++ built-in types
//     struct BinaryTreeNode          (int, char, etc.), or a class with a default
//     {                              constructor, and an assignment operator.
//         Item data;
//         BinaryTreeNode *left;
//         BinaryTreeNode *right;
//     };
//
// The left and right pointers may be NULL to indicate no child. Each tree is accessed through
// a pointer to its root. A NULL root pointer indicates an empty tree.
//
// FUNCTIONS in the binary tree toolkit:
//     template <class Item>
//     BinaryTreeNode<Item>* create_node(
//         const Item& entry,
//         BinaryTreeNode<Item>* l_ptr = NULL,
//         BinaryTreeNode<Item>* r_ptr = NULL
//     )
//       Postcondition: The value returned is a pointer to a newly allocated node with its data
//       equal to entry and its child pointers equal to l_ptr and r_ptr. Note: If there is
//       insufficient dynamic memory, then the new_handler is called.
//
//     template <class Item>
//     bool is_leaf(const BinaryTreeNode<Item>& node)
//       Postcondition: The return value is true if node is a leaf; otherwise the return value is
//       false.
//
//     template <class Item>
//     void tree_clear(BinaryTreeNode<Item>*& root_ptr)
//       Precondition: root_ptr is the root pointer of a binary tree (which may be NULL for the
//       empty tree).
//       Postcondition: All nodes at the root or below have been returned to the heap, and
//       root_ptr has been set to NULL.
//
```

(continued)

(FIGURE 10.6 continued)

```
//    template <class Item>
//    BinaryTreeNode<Item>* tree_copy(BinaryTreeNode<Item>* root_ptr)
//        Precondition: root_ptr is the root pointer of a binary tree (which may be NULL for the
//        empty tree).
//        Postcondition: A copy of the binary tree has been made, and the return value is a
//        pointer to the root of this copy.

#ifndef BINTREE1_H
#define BINTREE1_H
#include <stdlib.h> // Provides NULL

    template <class Item>
    struct BinaryTreeNode
    {
        Item data;
        BinaryTreeNode *left;
        BinaryTreeNode *right;
    };

    // Functions for the binary tree toolkit
    template <class Item>
    BinaryTreeNode<Item>* create_node(
        const Item& entry,
        BinaryTreeNode<Item>* l_ptr = NULL,
        BinaryTreeNode<Item>* r_ptr = NULL
    );

    template <class Item>
    bool is_leaf(const BinaryTreeNode<Item>& node);

    template <class Item>
    void tree_clear(BinaryTreeNode<Item>*& root_ptr);

    template <class Item>
    BinaryTreeNode<Item>* tree_copy(BinaryTreeNode<Item>* root_ptr);

#include "bintree1.template"   // Include the implementation.
#endif
```

FIGURE 10.7   First Version of the Implementation File for the Binary Tree Toolkit

---

A Template Implementation File

```
// FILE: bintree1.template
// IMPLEMENTS: The four template functions of the first version of the binary tree toolkit
// (see bintree1.h for documentation). Note that this file is not compiled on its own. Instead,
// this file is included by an include directive at the bottom of bintree1.h.

#include <stdlib.h>   // Provides NULL, size_t

template <class Item>
BinaryTreeNode<Item>* create_node(
    const Item& entry,
    BinaryTreeNode<Item>* l_ptr = NULL,
    BinaryTreeNode<Item>* r_ptr = NULL
)
// Library facilities used: stdlib.h
{
    BinaryTreeNode<Item> *result_ptr;

    result_ptr = new BinaryTreeNode<Item>;
    result_ptr->data  = entry;
    result_ptr->left  = l_ptr;
    result_ptr->right = r_ptr;

    return result_ptr;
}


template <class Item>
bool is_leaf(const BinaryTreeNode<Item>& node)
// Library facilities used: stdlib.h
{
    return (node.left == NULL) && (node.right == NULL);
}


template <class Item>
void tree_clear(BinaryTreeNode<Item>*& root_ptr)
// Library facilities used: stdlib.h
{
    if (root_ptr != NULL)
    {
        tree_clear(root_ptr->left);
        tree_clear(root_ptr->right);
        delete root_ptr;
        root_ptr = NULL;
    }
}
```

Notice that some compilers require that the default arguments of a template function are listed with both the prototype and the implementation.

(continued)

(FIGURE 10.7 continued)

```
template <class Item>
BinaryTreeNode<Item>* tree_copy(BinaryTreeNode<Item>* root_ptr)
// Library facilities used: stdlib.h
{
    BinaryTreeNode<Item> *l_ptr;
    BinaryTreeNode<Item> *r_ptr;
    if (root_ptr == NULL)
        return NULL;
    else
    {
        l_ptr = tree_copy(root_ptr->left);
        r_ptr = tree_copy(root_ptr->right);
        return create_node(root_ptr->data, l_ptr, r_ptr);
    }
}
```

bintree1.template   **FTP**

PROGRAMMING EXAMPLE: Animal Guessing

Now we'll write a small program that uses the binary tree toolkit. The program is a simple guessing game: You pretend that you are an animal, and the program asks questions to try to guess what animal you are. If the program guesses correctly, another round of the game is started. And if the program can't figure out what you are, you provide some more knowledge to the program so that the next time the game is played, the program is a bit smarter.

As an example, suppose you are pretending to be a raccoon. The program might start by asking "*Are you a mammal?*" and you answer, "Yes." Next, the program wants to know "*Are you bigger than a cat?*" and again you answer, "Yes." Finally, the program guesses: "*Are you a kangaroo?*" and with a smug smile you reply, "No, don't be ridiculous."

an animal guessing program that gets smarter and smarter

At this point, the program says, "*I give up. What are you?*" You explain that you are a raccoon. You then provide the program with a question that the program can use in the future to distinguish a kangaroo from a raccoon—perhaps "*Are you a marsupial?*"—and you tell the program that the answer to this question is "yes" for a kangaroo but "no" for a raccoon. The next time that you are a raccoon, the program will have enough information to guess correctly. A sample dialogue with the program is given in Figure 10.8 on page 442.

FIGURE 10.8　Part of a Sample Dialogue with the Animal Guessing Program

---

A Sample Dialogue

```
Are you a mammal? Please answer [Yes or No]
Yes
Are you bigger than a cat? Please answer [Yes or No]
Yes
My guess is Kangaroo. Am I right? [Yes or No]
No
I give up. What are you?
Raccoon
Please type a yes/no question that will distinguish a Raccoon from a Kangaroo.
Your question:
Are you a marsupial?
As a Raccoon, Are you a marsupial? Please answer [Yes or No]
No
Shall we play again? [Yes or No]
No
Thank you for teaching me a thing or two.
```

As you might guess, the data used by the program is stored in a binary taxonomy tree, as described on page 427, with each non-leaf node containing a question. When the program begins, it will only know about four animals, and the taxonomy tree will look like this:

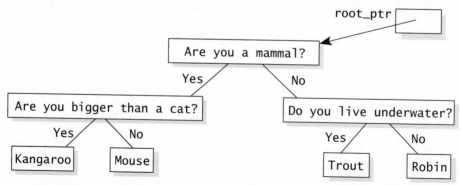

The program maintains a root pointer that always points to the root of the binary taxonomy tree. As the game is being played, the program also maintains a second pointer called `current_ptr`. The current pointer starts at the root and travels down the tree according to the answers that the user provides.

For example, suppose that the user answers "yes" to the first question "*Are you a mammal?*" Then the program will move its current pointer to the left subtree, as shown here:

In the drawing we have hidden part of the tree to indicate that only the left subtree is now relevant to the game. The rest of the tree and the root pointer are still present, but they are not needed at this point in the game.

The program continues asking questions. Each time the user answers "yes" to a question, the current pointer is moved left. Each "no" answer moves the current pointer right. This continues until the program reaches a leaf. When a leaf is reached, the program guesses that you are the animal whose name is stored at the leaf. If the leaf contains the correct animal, then all is well. But if the guess is wrong, then the program elicits information from the user, and that information is used to update the taxonomy tree.

In the example above, where you were a raccoon, the program would use the information to modify the taxonomy tree, resulting in the larger taxonomy tree of Figure 10.9(a). After playing several rounds of the game, the taxonomy tree might contain quite a few animals. Figure 10.9(b) shows what the tree could look like with seven animals. As an exercise, pretend you are a squid, and follow the route that would be taken from the root to the squid leaf in this tree.

Animal Guessing Program—Design and Implementation

Now that we have a general idea of how the program works, let's carry out a top-down design. The main program has three steps, shown in this pseudocode:

1. Print the instructions for the user.
2. Create a small initial taxonomy tree with four animals; the pointer variable `taxonomy_root_ptr` points to the root of this initial tree.
3. Repeat the following steps as often as the user wants:

   a. Play one round of the game, perhaps adding information to the bottom of the tree.

   b. Ask the user, "Shall we play again?" and read the answer.

FIGURE 10.9 Two Possible Taxonomy Trees

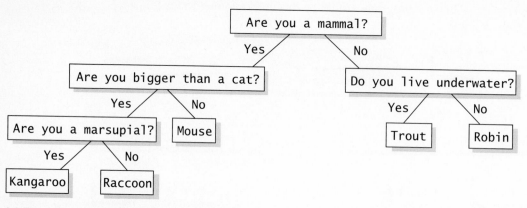

(a) Taxonomy tree after adding a raccoon

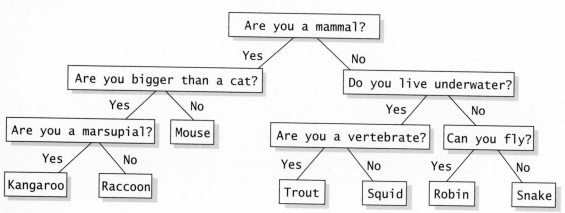

(b) Taxonomy tree with seven animals

The first two steps from our outline will be accomplished by functions that we call `instruct` and `beginning_tree`. For Step 3a, we'll design a function called `play`. Step 3b can be accomplished with the `inquire` function, which is part of the toolkit of useful functions that we have used before (`useful.h` from Appendix H). That function asks a yes/no question, returning true if the user replies "Yes," and returning false if the user replies "No."

Putting these steps together, we can write the main function, using a root pointer to the binary taxonomy tree, as shown at the top of the next page.

```
int main( )
{
    BinaryTreeNode<String> *taxonomy_root_ptr;

    instruct( );
    taxonomy_root_ptr = beginning_tree( );
    do
         play(taxonomy_root_ptr);
    while (inquire("Shall we play again?"));

    cout << "Thanks for teaching me a thing or two." << endl;
    return EXIT_SUCCESS;
}
```

Notice that the type of the data in each node is a String object. This can be our
String class (from mystring.h in Figure 4.14 on page 186), or if you have a
newer compiler, you may use the String class provided by your compiler.

*the data at each
node is a string*

Below, we discuss the functions instruct, beginning_tree, and play.

The instruct function. This is a function with output to the screen to explain
the game. You can write it yourself with the prototype: *void* instruct( );

The beginning_tree function. This function creates the initial binary taxonomy tree and returns a pointer to the root of this tree, as shown in this outline:

```
BinaryTreeNode<String>* beginning_tree( )
// Postcondition: The function has created a small taxonomy tree.
// The return value is the root pointer of the new tree.
{
    BinaryTreeNode<String> *root_ptr;
    BinaryTreeNode<String> *child_ptr;
```

   1. Make root_ptr point to a new node with the data "Are you a
      mammal?" Both child pointers are initially null.
   2. Make child_ptr point to a new node with the data "Are you bigger
      than a cat?" Give it two leaves as children with the data "Kangaroo"
      on the left and "Mouse" on the right. Then assign
      root_ptr->left = child_ptr;
   3. Make child_ptr point to a new node with the data "Do you live
      underwater?" Give it two leaves as children with the data "Trout" on
      the left and "Robin" on the right. Then assign
      root_ptr->right = child_ptr;
   4. *return* root_ptr;
```
}
```

The complete implementation will be shown as part of a program in a moment. For now, you should notice that the operations of `beginning_tree` can be accomplished with `create_node` from the binary tree toolkit. When the `beginning_tree` finishes, the root pointer in the main program will point to the root node of our initial taxonomy tree.

The `play` function. The `play` function has one parameter, which initially is the root pointer of the binary taxonomy tree, as shown in this prototype:

> `void play(BinaryTreeNode<String>* current_ptr);`

The function causes the current pointer to move down the tree in response to the user's replies. (The root pointer, back in the main program, will stay pointing at the root since `current_ptr` is an ordinary value parameter.) When the current pointer reaches a leaf, an animal is guessed.

We'll use two other functions to carry out most of `play`'s work. The first function, named `ask_and_move`, asks the question that's contained at the current node of the tree and then shifts the current pointer to the left or right child, based on the user's answer. Here is the specification for `ask_and_move`:

specification of the `ask_and_move` function

> `void ask_and_move(BinaryTreeNode<String>*& current_ptr);`
> `// Precondition: current_ptr points to a non-leaf node in a binary taxonomy`
> `// tree.`
> `// Postcondition: The question at the current node has been asked. The`
> `// current pointer has been shifted left (if the user answered yes) or right`
> `// (for a no answer).`

The second important function used by `play` is called `learn`. The `learn` function is used after the game reaches a leaf and the animal at the leaf is wrong. The function elicits information from the user and thereby improves the tree, as specified here:

specification of the learn function

> `void learn(BinaryTreeNode<String>* leaf_ptr);`
> `// Precondition: leaf_ptr is a pointer to a leaf in a taxonomy tree.`
> `// This leaf contains a wrong guess that was just made.`
> `// Postcondition: Information has been elicited from the user,`
> `// and the tree has been improved.`

Using the two functions, the implementation of `play` is relatively short, as shown at the top of the next page.

```
void play(BinaryTreeNode<String>* current_ptr)
// Precondition: current_ptr points to the root of a binary taxonomy tree
// with at least two leaves.
// Postcondition: One round of the animal game has been played,
// and maybe the tree has been improved.
// Library facilities used: bintree1.h, useful.h (from Appendix H)
{
    cout << "Think of an animal, then press the return key.";
    eat_line( );

    while (!is_leaf(*current_ptr))
        ask_and_move(current_ptr);

    cout << ("My guess is " + current_ptr->data + ". ");
    if (!inquire("Am I right?"))
        learn(current_ptr);
    else
        cout << "I knew it all along!" << endl;
}
```

Within this implementation we used the familiar `inquire` function to ask the question *"Am I right?"* A function named `eat_line` is also used to read and throw away all characters up to the next newline character. Both of these functions are part of our toolkit of useful functions (see Appendix H).

So what's left to do? Implement the two functions `ask_and_move` and `learn`, which we'll do now.

The ask_and_move function. This function has one argument, which is the current pointer to a node in the taxonomy tree. The function asks the question at this node and shifts the current pointer down to a subtree based on the user's answer. Using the inquire function from `useful.h`, the implementation is short:

```
void ask_and_move(BinaryTreeNode<String>*& current_ptr)
// Library facilities used: mystring.h, useful.h
{
    cout << current_ptr->data;
    if (inquire(" Please answer"))
        current_ptr = current_ptr->left;
    else
        current_ptr = current_ptr->right;
}
```

The learn function. This function is called when the game reaches a leaf and makes a wrong guess. The function takes several steps to improve the taxonomy tree. The function's argument is a pointer to the node that contains the incorrect guess, as shown in this prototype:

```
void learn(BinaryTreeNode<String>* leaf_ptr);
```

For example, suppose we just made an incorrect guess of a kangaroo from this tree:

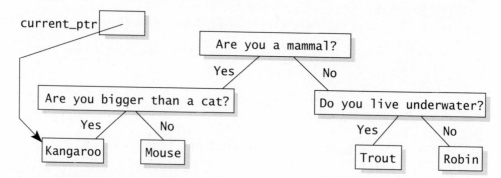

The learn function first sets three local String variables:

1. What animal was guessed? This is obtained from current_ptr->data and stored in a local variable called guess_animal. For this example, the guess_animal is "Kangaroo."

2. What is the correct animal? The user's answer to this question is read into a local String variable called correct_animal. To read the answer, we use the getline function from mystring.h (Figure 4.14 on page 186). This function reads an entire line of input, including blanks, and places this line in a string. For this example, suppose that the user's answer is "Raccoon."

3. What is a yes/no question that can distinguish the right animal from the animal that was guessed? In our example, we need a question that can distinguish a kangaroo from a raccoon. The user might provide the question "Are you a marsupial?" and we'll store this question in another local string variable called new_question.

With the three strings set, we need one more piece of information. In particular, we need to know whether the correct animal answers "yes" or "no" to the question that the user has just provided. In our example, we need to know whether a raccoon answers "yes" or "no" to the question "Are you a marsupial?" Of course, a raccoon is not a marsupial, so based on this "no" answer, we can proceed as follows:

- Copy the distinguishing question into current_ptr->data.
- Copy the *guessed* animal into a new leaf, which is created to be the left child of the current node.
- Copy the *correct* animal into a new leaf, which is created to be the right child of the current node.

In our example, these steps improve the taxonomy tree as shown here:

The other possibility is that the new animal has a "Yes" answer to the new question. For example, the question to distinguish a raccoon from a kangaroo could be "Do you have a ringed tail?" In this case, the new animal (raccoon) would be added as the left child of the new question, and the old animal (kangaroo) added on the right.

As an exercise, you should implement the learn function and add it to the complete program from Figure 10.10 on page 450.

Animal Guessing Program—Improvements

Our animal program suffers from one problem: Each time the program is executed, it starts out by knowing only four animals. An improvement will allow it to store the current taxonomy tree in a file and read that file whenever the program starts. This way it remembers all the animals that you have taught it about.

Self-Test Exercises

8. Implement the learn function from the animal guessing program.

9. Add a new function to the toolkit to compute the number of children that a node has.

10. Add a new function to the toolkit to compute the number of nodes in a binary tree. Add another function to compute the depth of a binary tree. Both functions have one argument, which is the tree's root pointer. Think recursively.

| FIGURE 10.10 | The Animal Guessing Program |

A Program

```
// FILE: animal.cxx
// This animal-guessing program illustrates the use of the binary tree toolkit.

#include <iostream.h>    // Provides cout
#include <stdlib.h>      // Provides EXIT_SUCCESS
#include "bintree1.h"    // Provides the binary tree node functions
#include "mystring.h"    // If available, this could be changed to the standard String class
#include "useful.h"      // Provides eat_line, inquire (from Appendix H)

// PROTOTYPES for functions used by this game program:
void instruct( );
// Postcondition: Instructions for playing the game have been printed to the screen.

BinaryTreeNode<String>* beginning_tree( );
// Postcondition: The function has created a small taxonomy tree. The return value is the root
// pointer of the new tree.

void learn(BinaryTreeNode<String>*& leaf_ptr);
// Precondition: leaf_ptr is a pointer to a leaf in a taxonomy tree. The leaf contains a wrong
// guess that was just made.
// Postcondition: Information has been elicited from the user, and the tree has been improved.

void ask_and_move(BinaryTreeNode<String>*& current_ptr);
// Precondition: current_ptr points to a non-leaf node in a binary taxonomy tree.
// Postcondition: The question at the current node has been asked. The current pointer has
// been shifted left (if the user answered yes) or right (for a no answer).

void play(BinaryTreeNode<String>* current_ptr);
// Precondition: current_ptr points to the root of a binary taxonomy tree with at least two leaves.
// Postcondition: One round of the animal game has been played, and maybe the tree has
// been improved.

int main( )
{
    BinaryTreeNode<String> *taxonomy_root_ptr;

    instruct( );
    taxonomy_root_ptr = beginning_tree( );
    do
        play(taxonomy_root_ptr);
    while (inquire("Shall we play again?"));
    cout << "Thank you for teaching me a thing or two." << endl;
    return EXIT_SUCCESS;
}
```

(continued)

(FIGURE 10.10 continued)

```
void instruct( )
   The implementation of this function is omitted—write it yourself!

BinaryTreeNode<String>* beginning_tree( )
// Library facilities used: mystring.h, bintree1.h
{
    BinaryTreeNode<String> *root_ptr;
    BinaryTreeNode<String> *child_ptr;

    const String root_question("Are you a mammal?");
    const String left_question("Are you bigger than a cat?");
    const String right_question("Do you live underwater?");
    const String animal1("Kangaroo");
    const String animal2("Mouse");
    const String animal3("Trout");
    const String animal4("Robin");

    // Create the root node with the question "Are you a mammal?"
    root_ptr = create_node(root_question);

    // Create and attach the left subtree.
    child_ptr = create_node(left_question);
    child_ptr->left = create_node(animal1);
    child_ptr->right = create_node(animal2);
    root_ptr->left = child_ptr;

    // Create and attach the right subtree.
    child_ptr = create_node(right_question);
    child_ptr->left = create_node(animal3);
    child_ptr->right = create_node(animal4);
    root_ptr->right = child_ptr;

    return root_ptr;
}


void learn(BinaryTreeNode<String>*& leaf_ptr)
   The implementation of this function is Self-Test Exercise 8.

void ask_and_move(BinaryTreeNode<String>*& current_ptr)
// Library facilities used: mystring.h, useful.h
{
    cout << current_ptr->data;
    if (inquire(" Please answer"))
        current_ptr = current_ptr->left;
    else
        current_ptr = current_ptr->right;
}
```

(continued)

(FIGURE 10.10 continued)

```
void play(BinaryTreeNode<String>* current_ptr)
// Library facilities used: iostream.h, mystring.h, bintree1.h, useful.h
{
    cout << "Think of an animal, then press the return key.";
    eat_line( );

    while (!is_leaf(*current_ptr))
        ask_and_move(current_ptr);

    cout << ("My guess is " + current_ptr->data);
    if (!inquire(". Am I right?"))
        learn(current_ptr);
    else
        cout << "I knew it all along!" << endl;
}
```

animal.cxx **FTP**

10.4 TREE TRAVERSALS

And then he got up, and said: "And the only reason for making honey is so as I can eat it." So he began to climb the tree.

He climbed and he climbed and he climbed, and as he climbed he sang a little song to himself.

A.A. MILNE
Winnie-the-Pooh

Traversals of Binary Trees

Programs that use tree structures often need to process all of the nodes in a tree, applying the same operation to each node. This processing is called a **tree traversal.** For example, suppose we have a tree where each node contains an integer, and we need to print a list of all the integers in the tree. For a binary tree, there are three common ways of doing this kind of processing: **pre-order traversal, in-order traversal,** and **post-order traversal.** This section defines and implements the three traversal methods for binary trees. We also implement an unusual fourth traversal method (a **backward in-order traversal**), which is useful for printing a tree. We start with a description of each method:

pre-order: the root is processed prior to its two subtrees

Pre-order traversal. The word "pre-order" refers to when the root is processed; it is processed *prev*ious to its two subtrees. So, a pre-order traversal has these three steps for a non-empty tree:

1. Process the root.
2. Process the nodes in the left subtree with a recursive call.
3. Process the nodes in the right subtree with a recursive call.

At the end of this section we'll give an extremely general implementation of these three steps, which will allow you to do any kind of processing on each node. For now, let's look at a simpler case, where we just want to print the contents of each node. In this case we would add this template function to the binary tree toolkit of Section 10.2:

```
template <class Item>
void preorder_print(BinaryTreeNode<Item>* node_ptr)
// Precondition: node_ptr is a pointer to a node in a binary tree (or
// node_ptr may be NULL to indicate the empty tree).
// Postcondition: If node_ptr is non-NULL, then the data of *node_ptr and
// all its descendants have been written to cout with the << operator, using
// a pre-order traversal.
// Library facilities used: iostream.h, stdlib.h
{
    if (node_ptr != NULL)
    {
        cout << node_ptr->data << endl;
        preorder_print(node_ptr->left);
        preorder_print(node_ptr->right);
    }
}
```

Notice how the processing of the two subtrees is accomplished with recursive calls. It's also important to see that pointers to the roots of the left and right subtrees of the original node are passed as arguments to the recursive calls.

Let's look at an execution of the pre-order traversal in more detail. We'll trace `preorder_print`, applied to the binary tree shown here:

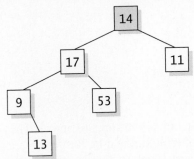

Suppose that our `node_ptr` points to the shaded root in the diagram. The function's first step is to print the number at the root, so after this step, the only number printed is 14 (from the root).

The function's second step makes a recursive call, with a pointer to the root node of the left subtree. In effect, the recursive call says "do a pre-order traversal of the left subtree." To illustrate that we are now doing a traversal of a subtree, we will temporarily hide everything except the left subtree, as shown here:

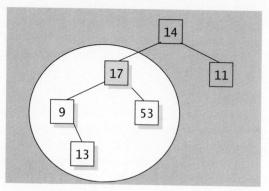

In this recursive call, the `node_ptr` points to the shaded node containing 17. The first step of the recursive call is to print the number at the `node_ptr`, so after that step the total output contains two numbers:

    14
    17

The second step of the recursive call is to make yet another recursive call, with the argument being its own `node_ptr->left`. In other words, this second recursive call will begin at the shaded node containing 9 in this drawing:

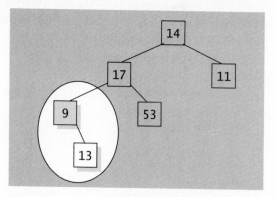

We now have three function calls that are active: The original function call with the pointer to the root (containing 14), the first recursive call with a pointer to the left child of the root (containing 17), and the second recursive call with a pointer to the shaded node shown above (containing 9). This second recursive call carries out its appointed task by first printing a 9. After this, the total output consists of these three lines:

14
17
9

Once again, the function makes a recursive call. But this time the argument node_ptr->left is NULL, indicating that there is no left subtree of the current node_ptr, so the function call returns. Where does it return to? It returns to the place where it was called, with the node_ptr pointing to the node with 9, and executing the code at the spot marked here with an arrow:

```
if (node_ptr != NULL)
{
    cout << node_ptr->data << endl;
    preorder_print(node_ptr->left);
    preorder_print(node_ptr->right);
}
```

At this point in the recursive call, we have already printed the 9 and processed the empty left subtree. So the next step will make another recursive call to process the right subtree. The node_ptr in this recursive call points to the node with 13, in this drawing:

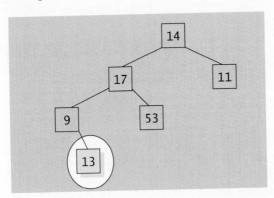

This function call prints the number 13, so that the entire output now has four numbers:

14
17
9
13

Both the left and right subtrees are empty for the node containing 13. So the recursive calls made at this level, to process those two empty subtrees, will do no work. The recursive call, which printed 13, returns. Where do matters go from there? Can you finish tracing the pre-order traversal? By the time the last recursive call has returned, we've "visited" every node in the tree, and the numbers have been printed out, in this order:

```
14
17
9
13
53
11
```

In-order traversal. The only change for an in-order traversal is that the root is processed *in* between the processing of its two subtrees. Here are the three steps for a non-empty tree:

1. Process the nodes in the left subtree with a recursive call.
2. Process the root.
3. Process the nodes in the right subtree with a recursive call.

The implementation of an in-order print function is a rearrangement of the pre-order print:

```
template <class Item>
void inorder_print(BinaryTreeNode<Item>* node_ptr)
// Precondition: node_ptr is a pointer to a node in a binary tree (or
// node_ptr may be NULL to indicate the empty tree).
// Postcondition: If node_ptr is non-NULL, then the data of *node_ptr and
// all its descendants have been written to cout with the << operator, using
// an in-order traversal.
// Library facilities used: iostream.h, stdlib.h
{
    if (node_ptr != NULL)
    {
        inorder_print(node_ptr->left);
        cout << node_ptr->data << endl;
        inorder_print(node_ptr->right);
    }
}
```

*post-order:
the root is
processed
after its two
subtrees*

Post-order traversal. And in a post-order traversal, the processing of the root is *post*poned until last in a non-empty tree:

1. Process the nodes in the left subtree with a recursive call.
2. Process the nodes in the right subtree with a recursive call.
3. Process the root.

We'll leave the implementation as an exercise in rearrangement.

Can you work out the order of the output numbers for the in-order and post-order traversals on an example such as Figure 10.5 on page 433? You'll be asked to work that out in Self-Test Exercise 11 at the end of this section.

A Useful Backward In-Order Traversal

A backward in-order traversal works like an ordinary in-order traversal, except that the *right* subtree is processed first, then the root, and finally the *left* subtree:

1. Process the nodes in the right subtree with a recursive call.
2. Process the root.
3. Process the nodes in the left subtree with a recursive call.

This is backward from the usual in-order traversal, but it is particularly useful for quickly printing the nodes of a tree in an easily understandable form. For example, consider the small tree shown here, along with the output from the backward in-order traversal:

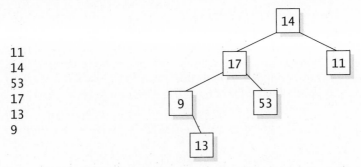

```
11
14
53
17
13
 9
```

There's a small trick that will make the output more useful. The trick is to indent each number according to its depth in the tree. Each number will have an indentation of 4 times the depth of the node, as shown here:

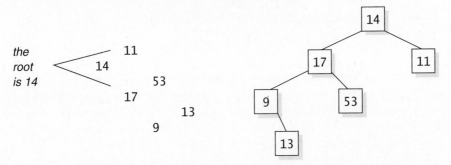

Why is this output useful? Turn your head to the left 90 degrees, and use a pencil to connect each node to the nodes on its left and right on the next level. The result is a cute representation of the tree, drawn at the top of the next page.

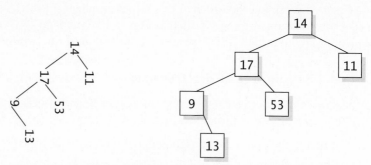

You can see how this representation looks a lot like the drawing of the tree.

The function that prints the backward in-order traversal can't easily draw the pencil lines for you, but it can produce the useful indentation by keeping track of the level of each node and increasing the level at each recursive call, as shown here:

```
template <class Item, class SizeType>
void print(BinaryTreeNode<Item>* node_ptr, SizeType depth)
// Precondition: node_ptr is a pointer to a node in a binary tree (or
// node_ptr may be NULL to indicate the empty tree). If the pointer is not
// NULL, then depth is the depth of the node pointed to by node_ptr.
// Postcondition: If node_ptr is non-NULL, then the contents of *node_ptr and
// all its descendants have been written to cout with the << operator, using
// a backward in-order traversal. Each node is indented 4 times its depth.
// Library facilities used: iomanip.h, iostream.h, stdlib.h
{
    if (node_ptr != NULL)
    {
        print(node_ptr->right, depth+1);
        cout << setw(4*depth) << "";       // Indent 4*depth spaces
        cout << node_ptr->data << endl;
        print(node_ptr->left,  depth+1);
    }
}
```

The statement `cout << setw(4*depth) << "";` prints the empty string (that is, ""), with a "field width" of 4*depth to print this empty string. The result is that 4*depth spaces are printed before printing the node's data. (The setw function from `iomanip.h` sets the field width of the next item that is printed.)

TIP

Programming Tip: Quick and Easy Printing of a Tree

Someday you'll be manipulating trees and need a quick output for debugging purposes—remember the trick of the backward in-order traversal.

The Problem with Our Traversals

The different binary tree traversals visit each node in a tree, and processing is done at each node. For the specific traversals that we have seen, the "processing" was simply printing the value of the contents of the node. But in general, we'd like to be able to do *any* kind of processing—not just printing. On the surface, this is not difficult. We can just replace the cout statement with some other form of processing (or perhaps we could get our efficient friend Jervis to do this). But there are two problems with the replacement strategy:

1. Suppose that our boss Judy wants to do three different kinds of processing, or worse yet, three thousand different kinds of processing. Jervis would need to write three thousand different functions, each of which is nearly the same as all the others.

2. The writer of the binary tree ADT should not have to anticipate every kind of processing that a user may desire. In fact, the writer of the ADT often will have no contact with the programmer (Judy) who uses the ADT. Even if there is contact, Judy might not want to tell the ADT programmer about this processing. "Mind your own business," Judy would say to the ADT programmer. "Just give me *one* function that is capable of doing any kind of processing."

In C++, it is possible to write just one function that is capable of doing a tree traversal and carrying out virtually any kind of processing at the nodes. The solution uses a new kind of parameter, which is actually a function itself. A few examples can help explain how a parameter can be a function.

A Parameter Can Be a Function

Here is the interesting idea that will lead us to a solution to the traversal problem:

> *A parameter of a function may be a function itself.*

The idea underlies the fact that some problems cannot be solved by any algorithm. If you want to pursue that startling result you might read Douglas Hofstadter's book *Gödel, Escher, Bach: An Eternal Golden Braid*. But our own use for the idea is more mundane. We merely want to write some simple functions where some of the parameters are other functions.

As a first example, we'll write a function called apply, with three arguments:

- The first argument is actually a *void* function that we'll call f. The function f has one integer reference parameter of its own.
- The second argument is an array of integers called data.
- The third argument is a size_t value called n, indicating the number of components in the array.

You can see these three parameters in the prototype of the `apply` function. We have highlighted the first parameter:

```
void apply( void f(int&) , int data[ ], size_t n);
```

The first parameter of our `apply` function is no ordinary parameter. We list this first parameter as *void* `f(int&)`, which means that the first parameter, `f`, must be a *void* function with one reference parameter (an integer). The key syntactic feature is that the parameter name, `f`, is followed by parentheses. Inside these parentheses we give the types of `f`'s own parameters.

When a *parameter is a function,* we list that parameter as shown here:

Parameters That are Functions

A parameter to a function may be a function itself. Such a parameter is declared by writing the name of the function's return type (or *void*), then the name of the parameter, and finally a pair of parentheses ( ). Inside the parentheses, is a list of the parameter types that the function needs.

Example:
```
void apply( void f(int&), ...
```

Within the implementation of the `apply` function, the parameter `f` can be used like any other *void* function with a single integer argument. Our intention is for the `apply` function to take the parameter `f`, and apply it to each of the data elements `data[0]`, `data[1]`, and so on up to `data[n-1]`. Here is the implementation:

```
void apply( void f(int&) , int data[ ], size_t n)
// Precondition: data is an array with at least n components.
// Postcondition: The function f has been applied to the first
//  n components of the data array.
{
    size_t i;

    for (i = 0; i < n; i++)
        f(data[i]);
}
```

f can be used just like any other function.

As an example of how `apply` is used, suppose we have this function:

```
void seven_up(int& i)
// Postcondition: i has had 7 added to its value.
{
    i += 7;
}
```

The `seven_up` function adds 7 to its reference parameter `i`. Now suppose that `numbers` is an array of ten integers. How can we easily add 7 to each of the ten integers in the `numbers` array? Here's the solution using `apply`:

```
apply(seven_up, numbers, 10);
```

This use of the `apply` function will execute `seven_up(data[0])`, and then `seven_up(data[1])`, and so on through `seven_up(data[9])`, causing 7 to be added to each of the components of the `numbers` array.

The power of the `apply` function comes from the fact that its first argument can be any *void* function with a single integer reference parameter. For example, suppose we have a function with this prototype:

```
void triple(int& i);
// Postcondition: i has been multiplied by three.
```

Then the call `apply(triple, numbers, 10)` will multiply each of the components of `numbers` by three.

A Template Version of the `apply` Function

At the moment, the `apply` function applies a function to every component in an array of integers. The function becomes more useful if we write it as a template function where the component type of the array is specified by the template parameter. Here is one way to write the new version of `apply`:

```
template <class Item, class SizeType>
void apply(void f(Item&), Item data[ ], SizeType n)
// Precondition: data is an array with at least n components.
// Postcondition: The function f has been applied to the first
// n components of the data array.
// Note: Item may be any type. SizeType may be any of the
// integer or const integer types.
{
    size_t i;

    for (i = 0; i < n; i++)
        f(data[i]);
}
```

In this template function we have used the template parameter `Item` as the component type of the array, and a second template parameter `SizeType` is the data type of the argument that specifies the array size. (See the Pitfall on page 269 for the reason to use a template parameter instead of simply using `size_t`.)

The new `apply` function works fine. For example, suppose we have a function with this prototype:

```
void convert_to_upper(char& c);
// Postcondition: If c was a lower-case letter, then it has been converted to
//   the corresponding upper-case letter; otherwise c is unchanged.
```

Now suppose that name is an array of ten characters. We can convert all these characters to upper case with a single call to the apply template function:

```
apply(convert_to_upper, name, 10);
```

This statement instantiates the apply function with the Item type as a character and the SizeType as an integer. The function call then applies convert_to_upper to each of the ten characters of name.

More Generality for the apply Template Function

Compatibility with Different C++ Compilers

Some C++ compilers don't support the use of a template function with a parameter that is a function itself. Templates still seem to be a sticky point in compatibility between different compilers.

There's another improvement we can make to the apply function. At the moment, the first argument to the apply function must have the form:

```
void f(Item&);
```

This strict form precludes many functions that we might want to use. For example, f cannot have a value parameter (it must have a *reference* parameter). As another example, f cannot have a *const* reference parameter (it must have an ordinary reference parameter). To obtain more generality with the function f, we can add a third template parameter, as shown in the highlights here:

```
template <class Process, class Item, class SizeType>
void apply(Process f, Item data[ ], SizeType n)
// Precondition: data is an array with at least n components.
// Postcondition: The function f has been applied to the first
//   n components of the data array.
// Note: Process is the type of a function f that may be called with a
//   single Item argument. Item may be any type. SizeType may be any of
//   the integer or const integer types.
{
    size_t i;

    for (i = 0; i < n; i++)
        f(data[i]);
}
```

We now have an extra template parameter, Process, which is used as the type of the first argument f. Using a template parameter in this way allows the type of the actual first argument to vary. In particular, the first argument to apply can be any function that "may be called with a single Item argument." Here are some common examples using the numbers array of ten integers:

```
void triple(int& i); // Postcondition: i has been multiplied by three.

// Multiply each number in the array by three:
apply(triple, numbers, 10);
```

As a second example, the function may have a value parameter (instead of a reference parameter):

```
void print(int i); // Postcondition: i has been printed to cout.

// Print all the numbers to cout:
apply(print, numbers, 10);
```

As one last example, consider an array called words containing ten strings (from our own String class, or from the new C++ String class facility):

```
void print(const String& s); // Postcondition: s has been printed to cout.

// Print all the words to cout:
apply(print, words, 10);
```

Template Functions for Tree Traversals

Our apply function applies a specified function to each of the components of an array. We can use the same technique to apply a specified function to every item in a binary tree. For example, this template function will apply a function f to all the items in a binary tree, using a pre-order traversal:

```
template <class Process, class Item>
void preorder(Process f, BinaryTreeNode<Item>* node_ptr)
// Precondition: node_ptr is a pointer to a node in a binary tree (or
// node_ptr may be NULL to indicate the empty tree).
// Postcondition: If node_ptr is non-NULL, then the function f has been
// applied to the contents of *node_ptr and all of its descendants, using a
// pre-order traversal.
// Note: Process is the type of a function f that may be called with a single
// Item argument. Item may be any type.
// Library facilities used: stdlib.h
{
    if (node_ptr != NULL)
    {
        f(node_ptr->data);
        preorder(f, node_ptr->left);
        preorder(f, node_ptr->right);
    }
}
```

Within the implementation of preorder, we can use f just like any other function that needs a single Item argument. In particular, look at the statement:

```
f(node_ptr->data);
```

This statement passes the data from one node to the function f. We don't even need to know exactly what f does. Perhaps it is a function to simply print the data, or maybe it does a more complicated computation. As the writer of the preorder function, we don't need to worry about those details. We have truly managed to provide just *one* function that is capable of doing *any* kind of processing.

We can add our new preorder function to the binary tree toolkit from Section 10.3. We can also add similar inorder and postorder functions, plus the nice print function that we developed with a backward in-order traversal. All these items are collected together in a new version of the toolkit in Figure 10.11 (bintree2.h) and Figure 10.12 (bintree2.template). We also added a function called tree_size to compute the number of nodes in a binary tree.

Self-Test Exercises

11. Look at the tree in Figure 10.5 on page 433. In what order are the letters printed for an in-order traversal? What about a post-order traversal? What about a backward in-order traversal?

12. Suppose we do a traversal of the tree in Figure 10.1 on page 424, printing out the numbers in the order 13, 9, 53, 17, 19, 7, 4, 11, 14. What kind of traversal did we do? What order are the numbers printed for the other kinds of traversals?

13. Suppose that you have a tree where the left subtree contains 3000 nodes, and the right subtree contains 100 nodes. For each of the different kinds of traversals, how many nodes are processed before the root node?

14. Write a function with the prototype *void* stars(*int* i); . The function prints a line of i stars. How can you easily apply the stars function to every node in a binary tree using an in-order traversal?

15. Here is an output from the tree-printing function for a tree of characters:

```
              54
      54
              53
    45
              3
  9
      17
        20
```

For this exercise, draw pencil lines to show the links between the nodes in this tree.

16. Which of the traversal methods make sense for general trees where there is no limit to the number of children that a node may have?

FIGURE 10.11   Second Version of the Header File for the Binary Tree Toolkit

A Header File

```
// FILE: bintree2.h
// PROVIDES: An expanded toolkit of nine template functions for manipulating
// binary trees. Each node of the tree contains a piece of data and pointers
// to its left and right children as shown here:
//
//      template <class Item>            Item may be any of the C++ built-in types
//      struct BinaryTreeNode            (int, char, etc.), or a class with a default
//      {                                constructor, and an assignment operator.
//          Item data;
//          BinaryTreeNode *left;
//          BinaryTreeNode *right;
//      };
//
// The left and right pointers may be NULL to indicate no child. Each tree is accessed through
// a pointer to its root. A NULL root pointer indicates an empty tree.
//
// FUNCTIONS in the binary tree toolkit:
//      template <class Item>
//      BinaryTreeNode<Item>* create_node(
//          const Item& entry,
//          BinaryTreeNode<Item>* l_ptr = NULL,
//          BinaryTreeNode<Item>* r_ptr = NULL
//      )
//      Postcondition: The value returned is a pointer to a newly allocated node with its data
//      equal to entry, and its child pointers equal to l_ptr and r_ptr. Note: If there is
//      insufficient dynamic memory, then the new_handler is called.
//
//      template <class Item>
//      bool is_leaf(const BinaryTreeNode<Item>& node)
//      Postcondition: The return value is true if node is a leaf; otherwise the return value is
//      false.
//
//      template <class Item>
//      void tree_clear(BinaryTreeNode<Item>*& root_ptr)
//      Precondition: root_ptr is the root pointer of a binary tree (which may be NULL for the
//      empty tree).
//      Postcondition: All nodes at the root or below have been returned to the heap, and
//      root_ptr has been set to NULL.
//
```

(continued)

(FIGURE 10.11 continued)

```
// template <class Item>
// BinaryTreeNode<Item>* tree_copy(BinaryTreeNode<Item>* root_ptr)
//    Precondition: root_ptr is the root pointer of a binary tree (which may be NULL for the
//    empty tree).
//    Postcondition: A copy of the binary tree has been made, and the return value is a
//    pointer to the root of this copy.
//
// template <class Process, class Item>
// void preorder(Process f, BinaryTreeNode<Item>* node_ptr)
//    Precondition: node_ptr is a pointer to a node in a binary tree (or node_ptr may be NULL
//    to indicate the empty tree).
//    Postcondition: If node_ptr is non-NULL, then the function f has been applied to the
//    contents of *node_ptr and all of its descendants, using a pre-order traversal.
//    Note: Process is the type of a function f that may be called with a single Item
//    argument; Item may be any type.
//
// template <class Process, class Item>
// void postorder(Process f, BinaryTreeNode<Item>* node_ptr)
//    Same as the pre-order function, except with a post-order traversal.
//
// template <class Process, class Item>
// void inorder(Process f, BinaryTreeNode<Item>* node_ptr)
//    Same as the pre-order function, except with an in-order traversal.
//
// template <class Item, class SizeType>
// void print(BinaryTreeNode<Item>* node_ptr, SizeType depth)
//    Precondition: node_ptr is a pointer to a node in a binary tree (or node_ptr may be NULL
//    to indicate the empty tree). If the pointer is not NULL, then depth is the depth of
//    the node pointed to by node_ptr.
//    Postcondition: If node_ptr is non-NULL, then the contents of *node_ptr and all its
//    descendants have been written to cout with the << operator, using a backward
//    in-order traversal. Each node is indented four times its depth.
//
// template <class Item>
// size_t tree_size(BinaryTreeNode<Item>* node_ptr)
//    Precondition: node_ptr is a pointer to a node in a binary tree (or node_ptr may be
//    NULL to indicate the empty tree).
//    Postcondition: The return value is the number of nodes in the tree.
```

(continued)

(FIGURE 10.11 continued)

```
#ifndef BINTREE2_H
#define BINTREE2_H
#include <stdlib.h> // Provides NULL

    template <class Item>
    struct BinaryTreeNode
    {
        Item data;
        BinaryTreeNode *left;
        BinaryTreeNode *right;
    };

    // Functions for the binary tree toolkit
    template <class Item>
    BinaryTreeNode<Item>* create_node(
        const Item& entry,
        BinaryTreeNode<Item>* l_ptr = NULL,
        BinaryTreeNode<Item>* r_ptr = NULL
    );

    template <class Item>
    BinaryTreeNode<Item>* tree_copy(BinaryTreeNode<Item>* root_ptr);

    template <class Item>
    void tree_clear(BinaryTreeNode<Item>*& root_ptr);

    template <class Item>
    bool is_leaf(const BinaryTreeNode<Item>& node);

    template <class Process, class Item>
    void preorder(Process f, BinaryTreeNode<Item>* node_ptr);

    template <class Process, class Item>
    void postorder(Process f, BinaryTreeNode<Item>* node_ptr);

    template <class Process, class Item>
    void inorder(Process f, BinaryTreeNode<Item>* node_ptr);

    template <class Item, class SizeType>
    void print(BinaryTreeNode<Item>* node_ptr, SizeType depth);

    template <class Item>
    size_t tree_size(BinaryTreeNode<Item>* node_ptr);

#include "bintree2.template"   // Include the implementation.
#endif
```

bintree2.h   FTP

| FIGURE 10.12 | Second Version of the Implementation File for the Binary Tree Toolkit |

An Implementation File

```
//  FILE: bintree2.template
//  IMPLEMENTS: The nine template functions of the expanded version of the binary tree toolkit
//  (see bintree2.h for documentation). Note that this file is not compiled on its own. Instead,
//  this file is included by an include directive at the bottom of bintree2.h.

#include <assert.h>    // Provides assert
#include <iomanip.h>   // Provides setw
#include <iostream.h>  // Provides cout
#include <stdlib.h>    // Provides NULL, size_t
```

```
template <class Item>
BinaryTreeNode<Item>* create_node(
    const Item& entry,
    BinaryTreeNode<Item>* l_ptr = NULL,
    BinaryTreeNode<Item>* r_ptr = NULL
)
```
See the implementation in Figure 10.7 on page 440.

Notice that some compilers require that the default arguments of a template function are listed with both the prototype and the implementation.

```
template <class Item>
bool is_leaf(const BinaryTreeNode<Item>& node)
```
See the implementation in Figure 10.7 on page 440.

```
template <class Item>
void tree_clear(BinaryTreeNode<Item>*& root_ptr)
```
See the implementation in Figure 10.7 on page 440.

```
template <class Item>
BinaryTreeNode<Item>* tree_copy(BinaryTreeNode<Item>* root_ptr)
```
See the implementation in Figure 10.7 on page 441.

```
template <class Process, class Item>
void preorder(Process f, BinaryTreeNode<Item>* node_ptr)
//  Library facilities used: stdlib.h
{
    if (node_ptr != NULL)
    {
        f(node_ptr->data);
        preorder(f, node_ptr->left);
        preorder(f, node_ptr->right);
    }
}
```

(continued)

(FIGURE 10.12 continued)

```
template <class Process, class Item>
void postorder(Process f, BinaryTreeNode<Item>* node_ptr)
// Library facilities used: stdlib.h
{
    if (node_ptr != NULL)
    {
        postorder(f, node_ptr->left);
        postorder(f, node_ptr->right);
        f(node_ptr->data);
    }
}

template <class Process, class Item>
void inorder(Process f, BinaryTreeNode<Item>* node_ptr)
// Library facilities used: stdlib.h
{
    if (node_ptr != NULL)
    {
        inorder(f, node_ptr->left);
        f(node_ptr->data);
        inorder(f, node_ptr->right);
    }
}

template <class Item, class SizeType>
void print(BinaryTreeNode<Item>* node_ptr, SizeType depth)
// Library facilities used: iomanip.h, iostream.h, stdlib.h
{
    if (node_ptr != NULL)
    {
        print(node_ptr->right, depth+1);
        cout << setw(4*depth) << ""; // Indent 4*depth spaces.
        cout << node_ptr->data << endl;
        print(node_ptr->left,  depth+1);
    }
}

template <class Item>
size_t tree_size(BinaryTreeNode<Item>* node_ptr)
// Library facilities used: stdlib.h
{
    if (node_ptr == NULL)
        return 0;
    else
        return 1 + tree_size(node_ptr->left) + tree_size(node_ptr->right);
}
```

bintree2.template **FTP**

10.5 BINARY SEARCH TREES

*Lucy looked very hard between the trees and could just see
in the distance a patch of light that looked like daylight.
"Yes," she said, "I can see the wardrobe door."*

C.S. LEWIS
The Lion, the Witch and the Wardrobe

Perhaps you thought that you would never see another bag after Chapter 3 (the bounded bag), Chapter 4 (the bag with a dynamic array), Chapter 5 (the linked list bag), and Chapter 6 (the bag as a template class). But binary trees offer yet another way to improve our bag ADT, so we will have one last look at bags (the *last* look, we promise).

The Binary Search Tree Storage Rules

Binary trees offer an improved way of implementing the bag ADT. The improvement generally performs faster than our previous bags. Or at least *sometimes* the improved approach may be taken. The improved implementation requires that the bag's entries can be compared with the usual comparison operators <, >, ==, and so on. These operators must form a *total order semantics*. As we've seen before (Figure 4.13 on page 185), a total order semantics means that all the items in the class can be placed on a single line, proceeding from smaller to larger along the line. Apart from requiring a total order semantics, the new bag ADT has a specification that is identical to our earlier bags. Therefore, a programmer who is using the bag ADT may switch to the new, improved bag without difficulty.

So, what good do we obtain from the total order semantics? We'll take advantage of the order to store the items in the nodes of a binary tree, using a strategy that will make it easy to find items. The strategy is to follow a collection of rules called the **binary search tree storage rules,** defined here:

Binary Search Tree Storage Rules

In a **binary search tree**, the entries of the nodes can be compared with a total order semantics. These two rules are followed for every node *n*:

1. Every entry in *n*'s left subtree is less than or equal to the entry in node *n*.

2. Every entry in *n*'s right subtree is greater than the entry in node *n*.

For example, suppose we want to store the numbers {3, 9, 17, 20, 45, 53, 53, 54} in a binary search tree. Figure 10.13(a) shows a binary search tree with these numbers. You can check that each node follows the Binary Search Tree Storage Rules. Binary search trees also can store a collection of strings, or real numbers, or *anything* that can be compared using some sort of total order semantics.

Can you see an advantage to storing a bag in a binary search tree rather than in an array or a linked list? The previous implementations of the bag ADT, using an array or a linked list, have a striking inefficiency: When we count the number of occurrences of an entry in the bag, it is necessary to examine *every* entry of the bag. Even if we are only interested in whether or not an entry appears in the bag, we will often look at many entries before we stumble across the one we seek.

With a binary search tree, searching for an entry is often much quicker. For example, suppose we're looking for the number 16 in the tree of Figure 10.13(a). We'll start at the root and compare 16 to the root's number. Since 16 is less than the root's number (45),

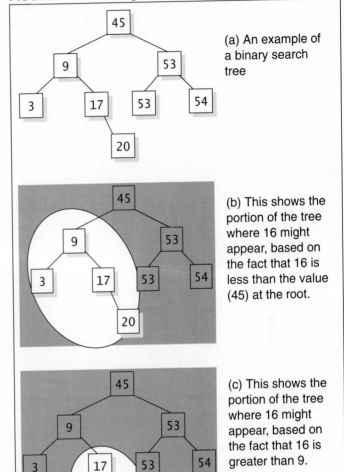

FIGURE 10.13   Using a Binary Search Tree

(a) An example of a binary search tree

(b) This shows the portion of the tree where 16 might appear, based on the fact that 16 is less than the value (45) at the root.

(c) This shows the portion of the tree where 16 might appear, based on the fact that 16 is greater than 9.

we immediately know that 16 can appear only in the left subtree—if it appears at all. In Figure 10.13(b), we show the area where 16 might appear, based on knowing that 16 is less than the value at the root. Next we'll compare 16 with the root of the left subtree. Since 16 is greater than 9, this eliminates another portion of the tree, as shown in 10.13(c).

The number 16 is smaller than the next point on the tree (17), so we should continue to the left. . . but we've run out of tree. At this point, we can stop and conclude that 16 is nowhere in the binary search tree even though we only looked at the three numbers 45, 9, and 17. In fact, the most we'll ever have to look at is the depth of the tree plus one—four entries in this case.

This efficiency is the motivation for representing bags with a binary search tree. In order for the idea to work, the comparisons between entries must form a total order according to the rules of Figure 4.13 on page 185. In the remainder of this section, we'll use binary search trees to implement the bag ADT, as specified in the header file of Figure 10.14. This is the same specification we have used before, but we have added a restriction on the item type, requiring that the comparison operators form a total order.

FIGURE 10.14 | Header File for Our Sixth Bag Class

A Header File

```
// FILE: bag6.h
// TEMPLATE CLASS PROVIDED: Bag<Item> (a container template class for a collection of items)
//     The template parameter, Item, is the data type of the items in the bag.
//     It may be any of the C++ built-in types (int, char, etc.), or a class with a default
//     constructor, a copy constructor, an assignment operator, and the six comparison
//     operators forming a total order.
//
// CONSTRUCTOR for the Bag<Item> template class:
//     Bag( )
//         Postcondition: The Bag is empty.
//
// MODIFICATION MEMBER FUNCTIONS for the Bag<Item> template class:
//     void insert(const Item& entry)
//         Postcondition: A new copy of entry has been added to the Bag.
//
//     void remove(const Item& target)
//         Postcondition: If target was in the bag, then one copy of target has been removed from
//         the bag; otherwise the Bag is unchanged.
//
//     void operator +=(const Bag<Item>& addend)
//         Postcondition: Each item in addend has been added to this Bag.
//
// CONSTANT member functions for the Bag<Item> template class:
//     size_t size( ) const
//         Postcondition: The value returned is the total number of items in the Bag.
//
//     size_t occurrences(const Item& target) const
//         Postcondition: The return value is number of times target is in the Bag.
//
```

(continued)

(FIGURE 10.14 continued)

```
// NONMEMBER functions for the Bag<Item> template class:
//     template <class Item>
//     Bag<Item> operator +(const Bag<Item>& b1, const Bag<Item>& b2)
//         Postcondition: The Bag returned is the union of b1 and b2.
//
// VALUE SEMANTICS for the Bag<Item> template class:
//     Assignments and the copy constructor may be used with Bag<Item> objects.
//
// DYNAMIC MEMORY USAGE by the Bag<Item> template class:
//     If there is insufficient dynamic memory, then the following functions call new_handler:
//     the constructors, insert, operator +=, operator +, and the assignment operator.

#ifndef BAG6_H
#define BAG6_H
#include <stdlib.h>      // Provides size_t
#include "bintree2.h"    // Provides BinaryTreeNode and related functions

    template <class Item>
    class Bag
    {
    public:
        // CONSTRUCTORS and DESTRUCTOR
        Bag( );
        Bag(const Bag& source);
        ~Bag( );
        // MODIFICATION MEMBER FUNCTIONS
        void insert(const Item& entry);
        void remove(const Item& target);
        void operator +=(const Bag& addend);
        void operator =(const Bag& source);
        // CONSTANT MEMBER FUNCTIONS
        size_t size( ) const;
        size_t occurrences(const Item& target) const;
    private:
        BinaryTreeNode<Item> *root_ptr; // Root pointer of binary search tree
        Other private members may be added if you need them.
    };

    // NONMEMBER functions for the Bag<Item> template class
    template <class Item>
    Bag<Item> operator +(const Bag<Item>& b1, const Bag<Item>& b2);

#include "bag6.template" // Include the implementation.

#endif
```

bag6.h **FTP**

Our Sixth Bag—Class Definition

The second part of Figure 10.14 on page 473 shows the class definition for our sixth and final bag. In our definition, the bag's only member variable is a root pointer for the binary search tree. This tree's nodes contain the entries of the bag. If the bag is empty, then the root pointer will be NULL. We could add other member variables—for example, a count of the number of nodes would be convenient. But limiting ourselves to only the root pointer will allow us to clearly focus on the necessary tree algorithms. So, the bag definition in Figure 10.14 looks like this:

```
template <class Item>
class Bag
{
public:
    Prototypes of public member functions go here.
private:
    BinaryTreeNode<Item> *root_ptr; // Root pointer
};
```

Here's a formal statement of the invariant of our new bag:

Invariant for the Sixth Bag ADT

1. The items in the bag are stored in a binary search tree.
2. The root pointer of the binary search tree is stored in the member variable root_ptr (which may be NULL for an empty tree).

Our Sixth Bag—Implementation of Some Simple Functions

Now we're ready to dive into the implementations of the bag functions. For the most part, we will provide only pseudocode that you can implement yourself. Keep in mind that you should use the binary tree toolkit functions as much as possible.

Constructors. The default constructor sets the root pointer to NULL. The copy constructor needs to make a new copy of the source's tree, and point root_ptr to the root of this copy. Which toolkit function can carry out the copying? (Use the tree_copy function.)

The destructor. The destructor needs to return all nodes to the heap. Again, you should make use of an appropriate function from the binary tree toolkit.

Overloading the assignment operator. Since our bag uses dynamic memory, we must overload the assignment operator. The assignment operator works like the copy constructor with two preliminary steps: (1) First check for the possibility of a self-assignment by comparing (`root_ptr == source.root_ptr`). If these two pointers are equal, then we have a self-assignment such as `b = b`. In this case, the function returns with no further work. (2) If the assignment operator is not doing a self-assignment, then before we copy the source tree we must release all memory used by the nodes of the current tree. Use `tree_clear` from the toolkit to carry out the release of memory.

The `size` member function. The `size` member function simply returns the answer from `tree_size(root_ptr)` using the `tree_size` function from the toolkit.

Counting the Occurrences of an Item in a Binary Search Tree

The `occurrences` member function counts the number of occurrences of an item called `target`. We'll keep track of these occurrences in a local variable called `count` (which is initialized to zero). The important point to keep in mind is that we will not look at every entry in the binary search tree. Instead, we'll have a local pointer called `cursor`, which is initialized to the root pointer. We'll use a loop to move the cursor down through the tree, always moving along the path where the target might occur. At each point in the tree we have four possibilities:

1. The cursor can become `NULL`, indicating that we've moved off the bottom of the tree. In this case, we have counted all the occurrences of the target. So the loop can end, and we should return the current count.

2. The target might be smaller than the data at the cursor node. In this case, the target can only appear in the left subtree. For example, suppose we are counting occurrences of the string `Denver` in a binary search tree of strings (using the lexicographic order on our string class). The cursor's data might be `Pittsburgh`, and the situation looks like this:

In this situation, we'll continue our search by assigning:

```
cursor = cursor->left;
```

3. The target might be larger than the data at the cursor node. This is similar to the previous case, except that we must continue our search to the right instead of the left, using the assignment:

```
cursor = cursor->right;
```

4. The target might equal the data at the cursor node. In this case we add one to the count and continue the search to the left (since items to the left are less than *or equal to* the item at the cursor node).

The implementation of these steps is straightforward using a while-loop.

Inserting a New Item into a Binary Search Tree

The `insert` member function adds a new item to a binary search tree, using this prototype:

```
void insert(const Item& entry);
```

We suggest that you handle one special case first: When the first entry is inserted, simply call `root_ptr = create_node(entry)`.

The other case is when there are already some other entries in the tree. In this case, we'll set a `cursor` equal to the current root pointer, then we will pretend to search for the exact entry that we are trying to insert. But the search runs a bit differently than a real search. The main difference is that we stop the search just before the cursor falls off the bottom of the tree, and we insert the new entry at the spot where the cursor was about to fall off. For example, consider the task of inserting 16 into this binary search tree:

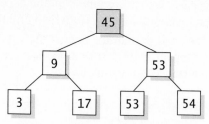

The cursor starts at the shaded node (with 45). If we were searching for the 16, we would continue the search to the left. So, we move our cursor to the left, resulting in the cursor pointing to the node that contains 9:

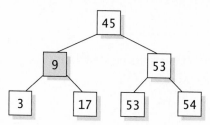

Again pretend that you are searching for the 16 instead of inserting it, so that now the cursor moves right to the node containing 17:

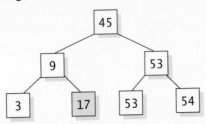

At this point, an ordinary search would continue to the left, stepping off the bottom of the tree. But instead, we insert the new entry at this position, resulting in this tree:

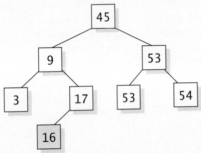

To implement the scheme, we suggest a boolean variable called done, which is initialized to false. We then have a loop that continues until done becomes true. Each iteration of the loop handles these two cases:

1. Suppose the new entry is less than or equal to the data at the cursor node. In this case, check the left pointer. If cursor->left is NULL, then create a new node containing the entry, make cursor->left point to this new node, and set done to true. On the other hand, if the left pointer is not NULL, then move the cursor to the left and continue the search with the single assignment statement:

        cursor = cursor->left;

2. Suppose the new entry is greater than the data at the cursor node. In this case, follow the same procedure as Case 1, but use the right pointer instead of the left pointer.

After the loop ends, the function returns.

Removing an Item from a Binary Search Tree

The remove member function allows us to remove a specified item from a binary search tree, with this prototype:

    void remove(const Item& target);

It is possible to implement the remove function on its own, but the direct solution deals with many special cases and must also maintain a precursor similar to the precursor for removing a node from a linked list. Because of these complications, we prefer an indirect method that uses two auxiliary functions with these specifications:

```
template <class Item>
void bst_remove(
    BinaryTreeNode<Item>*& root_ptr,
    const Item& target
);
// Precondition: root_ptr is a root pointer of a binary search tree (or may
// be NULL for the empty tree).
// Postcondition: If target was in the tree, then one copy of target has been
// removed, and root_ptr now points to the root of the new (smaller) binary
// search tree. Otherwise, if target was not in the tree, then the tree is
// unchanged.

template <class Item>
void bst_remove_max(
    BinaryTreeNode<Item>*& root_ptr,
    Item& removed
);
// Precondition: root_ptr is a root pointer of a non-empty binary search
// tree.
// Postcondition: The largest item in the binary search tree has been
// removed, and root_ptr now points to the root of the new (smaller) binary
// search tree. The reference parameter, removed, has been set to a copy
// of the removed item.
```

You will need to implement these two functions at the top of your implementation file, bag6.template. The only purpose of these functions is for *your* use, making the bag's removal function easier. Since you don't intend for other programmers to use these functions, there is no need to mention them in your header file. Instead, you should list their precondition/postcondition contracts with their implementations.

With these two functions in place, the bag's removal function is simply implemented with a function call bst_remove(root_ptr, target). Now we can turn to our two auxiliary functions.

The bst_remove function. The bst_remove function has a recursive implementation to remove the target. Here are the cases:

1. The binary search tree could be empty, indicated by a root pointer that is NULL. If there's nothing in the tree, then there's nothing to remove, and the function returns with no work.

2. The tree could be non-empty, with the target *less than* the root entry. In this case, make a recursive call to delete the target from the left subtree, like this:

```
bst_remove(root_ptr->left, target);
```

This recursive call works correctly because `root_ptr->left` is the root pointer for a smaller binary search tree (that is, the left subtree).

3. The tree could be non-empty, with the target *greater than* the root entry. Again, make a recursive call, using the pointer to the right subtree.

4. The tree could be non-empty, with the target *equal to* the root entry. We have found a copy of the target and must somehow remove it from the tree. But be careful! We can't simply delete this node because it may have children, and we don't want those children to be disconnected from the rest of the tree. To avoid orphaning those children, we'll deal with Case 4 in two separate cases:

Case 4a: The root node has no left child.

Case 4b: The root node does have a left child.

The pseudocode for these two cases is described below.

Case 4a. In this case of the `bst_remove` function, `root_ptr->data` is equal to the target, and the root node has no left child. For example, we might be deleting Pittsburgh from this subtree:

The left subtree is empty.

In this case, we can delete the root entry and make the right child (Seattle) the new root node. To actually implement this root shift requires three steps:

```
oldroot_ptr = root_ptr;
root_ptr = root_ptr->right;
delete oldroot_ptr;
```

The variable `oldroot_ptr` is a local variable that we make point to the old root (the root that we are about to get rid of). We then move the actual root pointer down to its right child. And finally we execute `delete old_root_ptr`, which returns the old root node to the heap.

Does this scheme work correctly even if there is no right child? Yes, it does. With no right child, the statement `root_ptr = root_ptr->right` will set the root pointer to NULL, indicating that there are no nodes left in this particular tree.

Case 4b. In this case, the root node does have a left child, so we can't simply move the root pointer to the right (as we did in case 4a). We could check whether there is a right child, and if not, we could certainly move the root pointer left—but we have a more general plan in mind. The plan is to find some entry in the non-empty left subtree, and move this entry up to the root. But which entry? Here's an example to help you figure out which entry should be taken from the left subtree to replace the root entry. In this example, we are deleting Pittsburgh from this subtree:

By the way, we don't really have any grudge against Pittsburgh—it's just that it seems like we could delete it without much complaint. Anyway, the plan is to replace the root with one of the three entries from the left subtree. Which of these entries can safely be moved to the root? Not Atlanta, because the remaining entries in the left subtree (Chicago and Denver) would be larger than the new root (Atlanta). Not Chicago, because that would leave the larger string Denver in the left subtree. What about Denver? Yes, that will do, since none of the entries that remain in the left subtree are larger than Denver. Here is the resulting subtree after removing Denver from the left subtree and placing it at the root:

The string Denver is the correct choice because it is the *largest entry in the left subtree.* Any other choice from the left subtree will violate the binary search tree storage rules. So, how do we delete the largest item from the left subtree, and place this same item at the root? We can use our own `bst_remove_max` function with the call:

```
bst_remove_max(root_ptr->left, root_ptr->data);
```

Now you know why we proposed the `bst_remove_max` function. Used in this way, it removes the largest item from the tree with `root_ptr->left` as its root pointer, and it places this largest item in the location `root_ptr->data`.

The `bst_remove_max` function. The `bst_remove_max` function remains to be implemented. We'll leave that as an exercise in recursive thinking, with just two cases: (1) The base case occurs if there is no right child. In this case, the largest item is at the root, so you can set `removed` equal to the data from the root, move the root pointer down to the left, and delete the root node. (2) On the other hand, if there is a right child, then there are larger items in the right subtree. In this case, make a recursive call to delete the largest item from the right subtree.

The Union Operators for Binary Search Trees

The last two operations for the bag are the += and + operators.

The operator +=. The operator += has this prototype:

```
template <class Item>
void operator +=(const Bag<Item>& addend);
```

This is another example of a function that will benefit from an auxiliary function. The auxiliary function that we propose is actually another bag member function, with this specification:

```
template <class Item>
void Bag::insert_all(BinaryTreeNode<Item>* addroot_ptr);
// Precondition: addroot_ptr is the root pointer of a binary search tree that
// is separate from the binary search tree of the bag that activated this
// method.
// Postcondition: All the items from the addroot_ptr's binary search tree
// have been added to the binary search tree of the bag that activated this
// method.
```

Our intention is that this method is a new *private* member function of the bag. Since the function is private, the specification can use private information, such as the fact that the bag is implemented with a binary search tree. As a private method, the prototype for `insert_all` must be placed with other private members in the bag's definition, as shown here:

```
template <class Item>
class Bag
{
public:
    ...
private:
    BinaryTreeNode<Item>* root_ptr; // Root pointer
    void insert_all(BinaryTreeNode<Item>* addroot_ptr);
};
```

A private member function is sometimes called a **helper function** because it will help the other member functions do their work. In the case of the bag, the operator += can be easily implemented by using insert_all, as shown here:

```
template <class Item>
void Bag<Item>::operator +=(const Bag& addend)
{
    BinaryTreeNode<Item> *addroot_ptr;

    if (root_ptr == addend.root_ptr)
    {
        addroot_ptr = tree_copy(addend.root_ptr);
        insert_all(addroot_ptr);
        tree_clear(addroot_ptr);
    }
    else
        insert_all(addend.root_ptr);
}
```

Notice that we do have a bit of complication when the addend is the same bag as the bag that activated the operator += (as in the statement b += b). In this case we must make a second copy of the addend's tree and call insert_all, using the second copy rather than using the addend's tree directly. The reason for this complication is the restriction of insert_all's precondition, which requires that the tree that's being added "is separate from the binary search tree of the bag that activated this method."

Now we can look at the implementation of the private member function insert_all. The approach is to traverse the tree that we are adding, inserting a copy of each traversed item into the bag that activated the operator. For example, if we use a preorder traversal, then the pseudocode for insert_all is:

```
if (addroot_ptr != NULL)
{
    insert(addroot_ptr->data);
    Make a recursive call to insert all of addroot_ptr's left subtree.
    Make a recursive call to insert all of addroot_ptr's right subtree.
}
```

Our pseudocode explicitly uses a pre-order traversal of the nodes. If you wish, you may use a post-order traversal instead. But avoid an in-order traversal. The problem with an in-order traversal is that the nodes of the addend tree will be processed in order from smallest to largest. Therefore, these nodes will be inserted into the other bag from smallest to largest. This is a bad way to build a binary search tree. The resulting tree ends up with a single long narrow path, with only right children. Sometimes such long narrow trees are hard to avoid. But do avoid such trees when you can, because searching and other algorithms are inefficient when the trees lose their branching structure. In the next chapter we will examine some specific ways to ensure that long narrow trees are not created.

The operator +. This is an ordinary function (not a member function) with the prototype:

```
Bag<Item> operator +(const Bag& b1, const Bag& b2);
```

The function is easy to implement by using the operator +=. Look back at the operator + from a previous bag implementation if you are uncertain.

Time Analysis and an Internal Iterator

With the descriptions that we've given, you can put together the implementation file for the new bag. We'll carry out a time analysis of the operations after we've seen a few more trees (see Section 11.3).

You might also want to add an internal iterator to the new bag, to allow a programmer to step through the items of the bag one at a time. One method for implementing an internal iterator utilizes a stack and is described in Programming Project 7 on page 490.

Self-Test Exercises

17. Add a new member function to the bag. The function should print all items in the bag from smallest to largest. (Hint: Use a traversal.)

18. Write a bag friend function called `join` with this prototype:
    ```
    template <class Item>
    void join(
        Bag<Item>& top,
        Bag<Item>& left,
        Bag<Item>& right
    );
    ```
    The precondition of the function requires that `top` has just one item, that everything in `left` is less than or equal to the item in `top`, and that everything in `right` is greater than the item in `top`. The postcondition requires that `top` now contains everything from `left` and `right`, and that `left` and `right` are now both empty. Your function should take constant time.

CHAPTER SUMMARY

- *Trees* are a nonlinear structure, with many applications including organizing information (such as taxonomy trees) and implementing an efficient version of the bag ADT (using binary search trees). The Programming Projects and the next chapter provide more examples of tree applications.

- Trees may be implemented with either fixed-sized arrays or dynamic data structures. An array is particularly appropriate for *complete binary trees* because of the conditions that require the nodes of a complete tree to occur in specific locations.

- A *tree traversal* consists of processing a tree by applying some action to each node. Three common traversal methods—pre-order traversal, in-order traversal, and post-order traversal—differ only in the order in which the nodes are processed. A backward in-order traversal is a quick and convenient way to print the data from a tree in a readable format.

- A parameter of a function may be a function itself.

- Using parameters that are functions, we can write extremely flexible tree traversals, where the action applied to each node is determined by a parameter to the traversal function.

- Binary search trees are one common application of trees, which permit us to store a bag of ordered items in a manner where adding, deleting, and searching for entries is potentially much faster than with a linear structure.

- Operations on trees are good candidates for recursive thinking. This is because many tree operations include a step to process one or more subtrees, and this step is "a smaller version of the same problem."

? Solutions to Self-Test Exercises

1. Here is one possible solution:

2 and 3. Here is a solution. The depth of this tree is 3. The node containing me has a depth of 2. My ancestors are circled, and my mother's descendants have a big square around them.

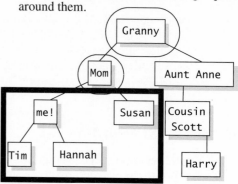

4. This solution is both full and complete. "Yes" answers move left, and "no" answers move right.

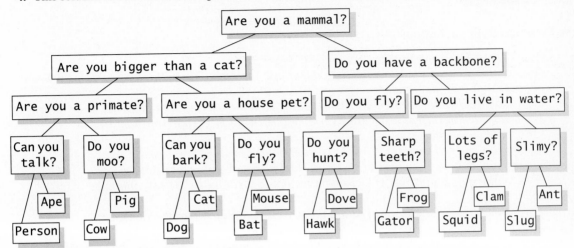

5. We use the formulas from page 431. The parent is stored at index 2499, which is (4999-1)/2. The left child is stored at index 9999, which is (2*4999)+1. If there was a right child, it would be stored at index 10,000 (which is (2*4999)+2). But since the last index is 9999, there is no right child.

6. A separate single pointer is used to point to the root node.

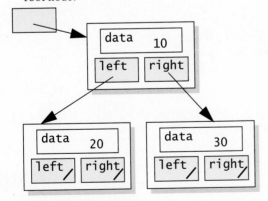

7.
```
typedef char Item;
struct TreeNode
{
    Item data;
    TreeNode *parent_ptr;
    TreeNode *links[4];
};
```

8. See Figure 10.15 on page 486.

9. Here is one solution:
```
template <class Item>
int kids(BinaryTreeNode<Item> node)
// Postcondition: The return value is
// the number of children of node.
// Libraries used: stdlib.h
{
    int answer = 0;
    if (node->left != NULL) answer++;
    if (node->right != NULL) answer++;
    return answer;
}
```

10. The node counting function is `tree_size` from the bottom of Figure 10.12 on page 469. The depth function has a similar recursive implementation.

11. The in-order traversal prints O, L, R, A, G, T. The post-order traversal prints O, R, L, T, G, A. The backward in-order traversal prints T, G, A, R, L, O.

12. This would be a post-order traversal. For in-order: 9, 13, 17, 53, 14, 19, 4, 7, 11. For pre-order: 14, 17, 9, 13, 53, 11, 4, 19, 7. The backward in-order is exactly reversed from the in-order.

13. Pre-order: zero. Post-order: 3100. In-order: 3000. Backward in-order: 100.

FIGURE 10.15 The learn Function for the Solution to Self-Test Exercise 8

A Function Implementation

```
void learn(BinaryTreeNode<String>*& leaf_ptr)
// Precondition: leaf_ptr is a pointer to a leaf in a taxonomy tree. This leaf contains a wrong
// guess that was just made.
// Postcondition: Information has been elicited from the user, and the tree has been improved.
// Library facilities used: iostream.h, mystring.h, useful.h (from Appendix H)
{
    String guess_animal;      // The animal that was just guessed
    String correct_animal;    // The animal that the user was thinking of
    String new_question;      // A question to distinguish the two animals

    // Set strings for the guessed animal, correct animal and a new question.
    guess_animal = leaf_ptr->data;
    cout << "I give up. What are you? " << endl;
    getline(cin, correct_animal);
    cout << "Please type a yes/no question that will distinguish a" << endl;
    cout << correct_animal << " from a " << guess_animal << "." << endl;
    cout << "Your question: " << endl;
    getline(cin, new_question);

    // Put the new question in the current node, and add two new children.
    leaf_ptr->data = new_question;
    cout << "As a " << correct_animal << ", " << new_question << endl;
    if (inquire("Please answer"))
    {
        leaf_ptr->left  = create_node(correct_animal);
        leaf_ptr->right = create_node(guess_animal);
    }
    else
    {
        leaf_ptr->left  = create_node(guess_animal);
        leaf_ptr->right = create_node(correct_animal);
    }
}
```

animal.cxx **FTP**

14.
```
void stars (int i)
{
    int j;
    for (j = i; j > 0; j--);
        cout << '*';
    cout << endl;
}
```
To apply the function to every node in a tree: `in_order(stars, r)`, where `r` is the root pointer.

15.

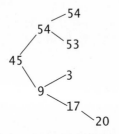

16. Pre-order would process a node before any of its children are processed. Post-order would process a node after all of its children are processed. In-order doesn't really make sense for a general tree.

17. The body of your function should call:
```
inorder(print_item, root_ptr);
```
where `print_item` is a function that you write to print one item.

18. The function needs four assignment statements, as shown here:
```
top.root_ptr->left
    = left.root_ptr;
left.root_ptr = NULL;
top.root_ptr->right
    = right.root_ptr;
right.root_ptr = NULL;
```

PROGRAMMING PROJECTS

1 This project deals with a simple kind of *expression tree*, where there are two kinds of nodes:

(a) Leaf nodes, which contain a real number as their entry;

(b) Non-leaf nodes which contain either the character '+' or the character '*' as their entry, and have exactly two children.

For this project, implement a class for expression trees, including operations for building expression trees. Also include a recursive function to "evaluate" a non-empty expression tree using these rules:

(a) If the tree has only one node (which must be a leaf), then the evaluation of the tree returns the real number which is the node's entry;

(b) If the tree has more than one node, and the root contains '+', then first evaluate the left subtree, then evaluate the right subtree, and add the results. If the root contains '*', then evaluate the two subtrees and multiply the results.

For example, consider the small expression tree shown to the right. The left subtree evalu-

ates to 3+7, which is 10.
The right subtree evaluates to 14. So the entire tree evaluates to 10*14, which is 140.

2 Design and implement an ADT for binary trees, following the specification of Figure 10.15 on page 486. Your design should use the node struct from our binary tree toolkit. If you wish, you may also add other member functions, such as a function to remove a node. However, the collection of functions in Figure 10.15 is sufficient for many applications, such as writing a version of the animal guessing program from Section 10.3.

3 Specify, design, and implement an ADT for *complete* binary trees using the array representation from Section 10.2. You should have only one member function that adds a new node (since there is only one place where a node may be added), and one member function that removes the last node of the tree.

| FIGURE 10.16 | Specification of a Binary Tree Class for Programming Project 2 on page 487 |

Documentation for a Header File

```
// FILE: bt_class.h
// TEMPLATE CLASS PROVIDED: BinaryTree<Item> (a binary tree where each node has an item)
//     The template parameter, Item, is the data type of the items in the tree's nodes.
//     It may be any of the C++ built-in types (int, char, etc.), or a class with a default
//     constructor, a copy constructor and an assignment operator.
//
// NOTE: Each non-empty tree always has a "current node." The location of the current node is
// controlled by three member functions: shift_up, shift_to_root, shift_left, and shift_right.
//
// CONSTRUCTOR for the BinaryTree<Item> template class:
//     BinaryTree( )
//         Postcondition: The Binary Tree has been initialized as an empty tree (with no nodes).
//
// MODIFICATION MEMBER FUNCTIONS for the BinaryTree<Item> template class:
//     void create_first_node(const Item& entry)
//         Precondition: size( ) is zero.
//         Postcondition: The tree now has one node (a root node), containing the specified entry.
//         This new root node is the "current node."
//
//     void shift_to_root( )
//         Precondition: size( ) > 0.
//         Postcondition: The "current node" is now the root of the tree.
//
//     void shift_up( )
//         Precondition: has_parent( ) returns true.
//         Postcondition: The "current node" has been shifted up to the parent of the old current
//         node.
//
//     void shift_left( )
//         Precondition: has_left_child( ) returns true.
//         Postcondition: The "current node" been shifted down to the left child of the original
//         current node.
//
//     void shift_right( )
//         Precondition: has_right_child( ) returns true.
//         Postcondition: The "current node" been shifted down to the right child of the original
//         current node.
//
```

(continued)

(FIGURE 10.16 continued)

```
//      void change(const Item& new_entry)
//         Precondition: size( ) > 0.
//         Postcondition: The data at the "current node" has been changed to the new entry.
//
//      void add_left(const Item& entry)
//         Precondition: size( ) > 0, and has_left_child( ) returns false.
//         Postcondition: A left child has been added to the current node, with the given entry.
//
//      void add_right(const Item& entry)
//         Precondition: size( ) > 0, and has_right_child( ) returns false.
//         Postcondition: A right child has been added to the current node, with the given entry.
//
// CONSTANT MEMBER FUNCTIONS for the BinaryTree<Item> template class:
//      size_t size( ) const
//         Postcondition: The return value is the number of nodes in the tree.
//
//      Item retrieve( ) const
//         Precondition: size( ) > 0.
//         Postcondition: The return value is the data from the "current node."
//
//      bool has_parent( ) const
//         Postcondition: Returns true if size( ) > 0, and the "current node" has a parent.
//
//      bool has_left_child( ) const
//         Postcondition: Returns true if size( ) > 0, and the "current node" has a left child.
//
//      bool has_right_child( ) const
//         Postcondition: Returns true if size( ) > 0, and the "current node" has a right child.
//
// VALUE SEMANTICS for the BinaryTree<Item> template class:
//      Assignments and the copy constructor may be used with BinaryTree objects.
//
// DYNAMIC MEMORY USAGE by the BinaryTree<Item> template class:
//      If there is insufficient dynamic memory, then the following functions call new_handler:
//      create_first_node, add_left, add_right, the copy constructor, and the
//      assignment operator.
```

bt_class.h **FTP**

4 Design and implement an ADT for binary trees, following the specification of Figure 10.15 on page 486. Your design should use a dynamic array to hold the data from the nodes in the same way that a complete binary tree is usually represented. However, these binary trees do *not* need to be complete. Instead, you should have a second private member variable that is a dynamic array of boolean values called is_present. The is_present array indicates which nodes actually exist in the tree. For example, if the tree has a root node, then location is_present[0] is true. If the root has a left child, then is_present[1] is true. If the root has a right child, then is_present[2] is true.

5 Revise the animal guessing program from Figure 10.10 on page 450 so that the initial knowledge tree is obtained by reading information from a file. Also, when the program ends, the knowledge tree at that point is written to the same file. You must carefully specify the format of the data in this file. The format should make it easy to do two things: (a) read the file and set the initial tree, and (b) write the knowledge tree to the file, using some kind of traversal.

6 This project requires that you know how to determine the actual time taken for a function to execute. Write a test program for the bag ADT from Section 10.5. The program should allow the user to specify an integer, *n*. The program then adds *n* randomly selected integers to a bag and then counts the number of occurrences of each integer between 1 and *n*, keeping track of the amount of time needed for the entirety of these operations. Also use the test program to test one of the earlier bag implementations. Graph the results of your tests on a plot that has elapsed time on the y-axis and *n* on the x-axis. (In the next chapter, we will do an analysis to explain these times.)

7 One of our previous bags had an *internal iterator* that allows a programmer to step through the items of a bag one at a time (see bag5.h from Figure 6.8 on page 298). The internal iterator consists of three member functions: start, advance, and current. For this project, add an internal iterator to the bag from Section 10.5. The implementation technique is to use a private member variable called s. The member variable s is a stack of pointers to nodes.

Each of the pointers in the stack points to a node whose entry has not yet been processed by the internal iterator. The current item of the internal iterator is always in the node at the top of the stack. The pseudocode for the internal iterator functions is given here:

The start function: Clear the stack. For an empty tree, there is no more work. For a non-empty tree, do an in-order traversal of the tree's nodes, pushing a pointer to each node onto the stack.

The current function: Check the precondition (the stack must be non-empty). Then peek at the top pointer on the stack (without removing it). Return the data item from the node that this top pointer points to.

The advance function: Check the precondition (the stack must be non-empty). Then pop the top pointer off the stack.

Calling insert, remove, or += should invalidate the internal iterator (by clearing the stack).

When the internal iterator is started, we used an in-order traversal to push node pointers onto the stack. As we pop the stack, these pointers come off in reverse order so that the iterator will advance through the items from largest to smallest. If you prefer a smallest-to-largest order, you could start with a backward in-order traversal, or you could use a queue instead of a stack.

8 Write a function that takes a binary search tree as input, and produces a linked list of the entries, with the entries sorted (smallest entries at the front of the list and largest entries at the back). Hint: In-order traversal.

9 Binary search trees have their best performance when they are *balanced*, which means that at each node, n, the size of the left subtree of n is within one of the size of the right subtree of n. Write a function which takes a sorted linked list of entries and produces a balanced binary search tree. If useful, you may add extra parameters to the procedure, such as the total number of entries in the list. Hint: First build the left subtree of the root, then the right subtree of the root, then put the pieces together with the join function from Self-Test Exercise 18 on page 483. Think recursively!

11 Tree Projects

The great, dark trees of the Big Woods stood all around the house, and beyond them were other trees and beyond them were more trees.

LAURA INGALLS WILDER
The Little House in the Big Woods

This chapter describes two programming projects involving trees. The projects are improvements of ADTs that we've seen before: the priority queue ADT (Section 8.4) and the set ADT (which is like a bag, but does not allow more than one copy of an item). Both projects take advantage of *balanced* trees, in which the different subtrees below a node are guaranteed to have nearly the same height. We also analyze the time performance of tree algorithms, concentrating on a connection between trees and logarithms, and explaining the advantages obtained from balanced trees.

11.1 HEAPS

The Heap Storage Rules

In some ways, a **heap** is like a binary search tree: It is a binary tree where the six comparison operators form a *total order semantics* that can be used to compare the nodes' entries. (For a reminder of the rules of a total order semantics, see Figure 4.13 on page 185.) But the arrangement of the elements in a heap follows some new rules that are different from a binary search tree:

Heap Storage Rules

A **heap** is a binary tree where the entries of the nodes can be compared with a total order semantics. In addition, these two rules are followed:

1. The entry contained by a node is greater than or equal to the entries of the node's children.

2. The tree is a complete binary tree, so that every level except the deepest must contain as many nodes as possible; and at the deepest level, all the nodes are as far left as possible (see "Complete Binary Trees" on page 427).

As an example, suppose that entries are integers. Here are three trees with six entries. Only one is a heap—which one?

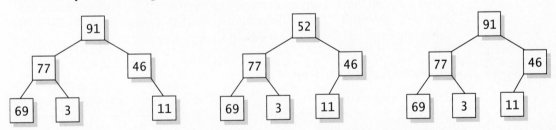

The tree on the left is not a heap because it is not complete—a complete tree must have the nodes on the bottom level as far left as possible. The middle tree is not a heap because one of the nodes (containing 52) has a value that is smaller than its child (which contains 77). The tree on the right *is* a heap.

A heap could be implemented with the binary tree nodes from the toolkit of Chapter 10. But wait! A heap is a *complete* binary tree, and a complete binary tree is more easily implemented with an array than with the node toolkit (see "Array Representation of Complete Binary Trees" on page 429). If we know the maximum size of a heap in advance, then the array implementation can use a *implement heaps with a fixed array or with a dynamic array*

fixed-sized array. If we are uncertain about the heap's maximum size, then the array implementation can use a dynamic array that grows and shrinks as needed.

In Self-Test Exercise 1, you'll be asked to write definitions that would support each of these implementations. The rest of this section will show how heaps can be used to implement an efficient priority queue—and we won't worry much about which heap implementation we are using.

The Priority Queue ADT with Heaps

Priority queues were introduced in Section 8.4. A priority queue behaves much like an ordinary queue: Entries are placed in the queue and later taken out. But unlike an ordinary queue, each entry in a priority queue has an associated number called its priority. When entries leave a priority queue, the highest priority entries always leave first. We have already seen an implementation of a priority queue in Section 8.4. Now we'll give an alternative implementation that uses a heap.

an alternative way to implement priority queues

In the heap implementation of a priority queue, each node of the heap contains one entry along with the entry's priority, and the tree is maintained so that it follows the heap storage rules using the entries' priorities to compare nodes. Therefore:

1. The entry contained by a node has a priority that is greater than or equal to the priority of the entries of the node's children.
2. The tree is a complete binary tree.

We'll focus on two priority queue operations: adding a new entry (along with its priority), and removing the entry with the highest priority. In both operations, we must ensure that the structure remains a heap when the operation concludes. Also, both operations can be described without worrying about precisely how we've implemented the underlying heap.

Adding an Entry to a Heap

Let's start with the operation that adds a new entry. As an example, suppose that we already have nine entries that are arranged in a heap with the following priorities:

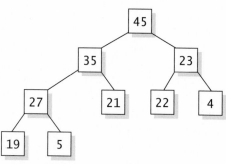

In this diagram, we have shown only the entries' priorities. In an actual priority queue, each entry would also have some additional data in each node.

Suppose that we are adding a new entry with a priority of 42. The first step is to add this entry in a way that keeps the binary tree complete. In this case the new entry will be the left child of the entry with priority 21:

add the new entry in a way that keeps the binary tree complete

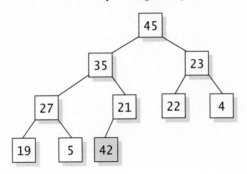

But now the structure is no longer a heap, since the node with priority 21 has a child with a higher priority. The algorithm for the insertion operation fixes this by causing the new entry (with priority 42) to rise upward until it reaches an acceptable location. This is accomplished by swapping the new entry with its parent:

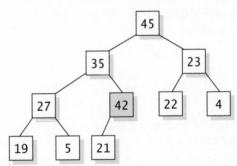

The new entry is *still* bigger than its parent, so a second swap is done:

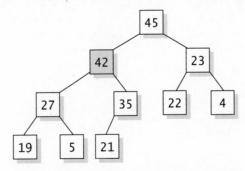

FIGURE 11.1 | Adding an Entry to a Priority Queue

Pseudocode for Adding an Entry

The priority queue has been implemented as a heap.

1. Place the new entry in the heap in the first available location. This keeps the structure as a complete binary tree, but it might no longer be a heap since the new entry might have a higher priority than its parent.

2. `while` (the new entry has a priority that is higher than its parent)
   Swap the new entry with its parent.

Notice that the process in Step 2 will stop when the new entry reaches the root, or when the new entry's parent has a priority that is at least as high as the new entry's priority.

---

reheapification upward

Now the new entry stops rising, because its parent (with priority 45) has a higher priority than the new entry. In general, the "new entry rising" stops when the new entry has a parent with a higher or equal priority, or when the new entry reaches the root. The rising process is called **reheapification upward**.

The steps for adding an entry are outlined in Figure 11.1. Some of the details depend on how the underlying heap is implemented. For example, if the heap is implemented with a fixed-sized array, then the first step must check that there is room for a new entry. With a dynamic array, the first step might need to increase the size of the array.

Removing an Entry from a Heap

When an entry is removed from a priority queue, we must always remove the entry with the highest priority—the entry that stands "on top of the heap." For example, suppose the priority queue contains the ten priorities drawn below. The entry at the root, with priority 45, will be removed, and this is the entry that is returned by the operation:

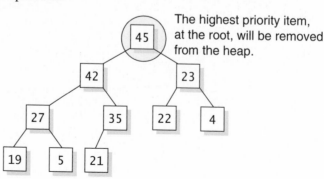

The highest priority item, at the root, will be removed from the heap.

But here we are ignoring a potential problem: There might be several entries with the highest priority. As described in Section 8.4, when several entries have equal priority, the entries should leave the priority queue in first-in/first-out (FIFO) order. Our adding and deleting mechanisms do not provide a way to determine which of several entries arrived first. So, in this discussion we will suspend the requirement that entries with equal priority be treated in FIFO order. We will address this problem in Programming Project 1 on page 532.

The problem of removing the root from a heap remains. During the removal, we must ensure that the resulting structure remains a heap. If the root entry is the only entry in the heap, then there is really no more work to do except to decrement the member variable that is keeping track of the size of the heap. But if there are other entries in the tree, then the tree must be rearranged because a heap is not allowed to run around without a root. The rearrangement begins by moving the last entry in the last level up to the root, like this:

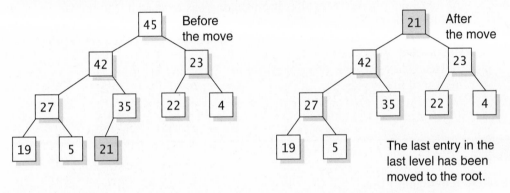

The structure is now a complete tree, but it is not a heap because the root is smaller than its children. To fix this, we can swap the root with its larger child, as shown here:

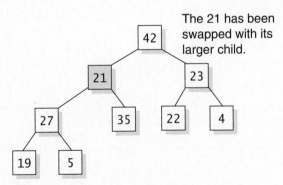

The structure is not yet a heap, so again we swap the out-of-place node with its larger child, giving this tree:

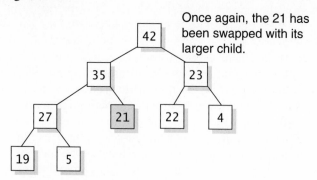

Once again, the 21 has been swapped with its larger child.

reheapification downward

At this point, the node that has been sinking has reached a leaf, so we can stop and the structure is a heap. The process would also stop when the sinking node no longer has a child with a higher priority. This process, called **reheapification downward**, is summarized in Figure 11.2.

Heaps have several other applications, including a sorting algorithm that is discussed in Chapter 13.

FIGURE 11.2   Removing an Entry from a Priority Queue

Pseudocode for Removing an Entry

The priority queue has been implemented as a heap.

1. Copy the entry at the root of the heap to the variable that is used to return a value.
2. Copy the last entry in the deepest level to the root, and then take this last node out of the tree. This entry is called the "out-of-place" entry.
3. `while` (the out-of-place entry has a priority that is lower than one of its children)
   Swap the out-of-place entry with its highest-priority child.
4. Return the answer that was saved in Step 1.

Notice that the process in Step 3 will stop when the out-of-place entry reaches a leaf or when the out-of-place entry has a priority that is at least as high as its children.

Self-Test Exercises

1. Write a C++ class definition that would be appropriate for a priority queue that is implemented as a heap with up to 100 entries. Write a second definition that does not have any predefined limit to the number of entries in the heap. Use a dynamic array for the second class.

2. Start with an empty heap, and enter ten items with priorities 1 through 10. Draw the resulting heap.

3. Remove three entries from the heap that you created in the previous exercise. Draw the resulting heap.

4. In the description of reheapification downward, we specified that the out-of-place entry must be swapped with the larger of its two children. What goes wrong if we swap with the smaller child instead?

11.2 B-TREES

Binary search trees were used in Section 10.5 to implement a bag ADT. But the efficiency of binary search trees can go awry. This section explains the potential problem and shows one way to fix it. Most of the presentation is not tied to any particular programming language.

The Problem of Unbalanced Trees

Let's create a troublesome binary search tree of integers. The first number is 1, then we add 2, then 3, 4, and 5, in that order. The result appears in Figure 11.3(a). Perhaps you've spotted the problem. Suppose next we add 6, 7, 8, 9, and 10, in that order, ending up with Figure 11.3(b). The problem is that the levels of the tree are only sparsely filled, resulting in long, deep paths and defeating the purpose of binary trees in the first place. For example, if we are searching Figure 11.3(b) for the number 12, then we'll end up looking at every node in the tree. In effect, we are no better off than the linked list implementation. Similar problems arise for adding and deleting entries.

FIGURE 11.3 Two Troublesome Search Trees

(a) A Troublesome Search Tree

(b) A More Troublesome Search Tree

The problem has several possible solutions, all of which involve trees where the depth of the leaves remains small. For example, one solution is to periodically balance the search trees, as described in Programming Project 9 in Chapter 10 (page 491). Another solution uses a particular kind of tree called a B-tree, where leaves cannot become too deep (relative to the number of nodes). These trees were proposed by R. Bayer and E.M. McCreight in 1972 (see "Organization and Maintenance of Large Ordered Indexes" in *Acta Informatica,* Volume 1, Number 3 [1972], pages 173–189). The rest of this section provides a B-tree implementation.

The B-tree Rules

B-trees are <u>not</u> binary trees

A B-tree is a special kind of tree, similar to a binary search tree, where each node holds entries of some type. As with binary search trees, the implementation requires the ability to compare two entries via a total order semantics. But a B-tree is not a binary search tree—in fact, a B-tree is not even a *binary* tree because *B-tree nodes have many more than two children.* Another important property of B-trees is that *each node contains more than just a single entry.* The rules for a B-tree make it easy to search for a specified entry, and the rules also ensure that leaves do not become too deep.

B-tree rules may be formulated for either a bag or a set

The precise B-tree rules may be formulated so that the B-tree stores a bag of entries similar to the bag implementations that we have seen before. Alternatively, a B-tree may be formulated to store a *set* of entries. The difference between a set and a bag is that a given entry can occur many times in a bag but only once in a set. We'll look at the "set formulation" of the B-tree rules, but keep in mind that a "bag formulation" is also possible.

The entries in a B-tree node. Every B-tree depends on a positive constant integer called MINIMUM. The purpose of the constant is to determine how many entries are held in a single node, as shown in the first two B-tree rules:

> **B-tree Rule 1:** The root may have as few as one entry (or even no entries if it also has no children); every other node has at least MINIMUM entries.

> **B-tree Rule 2:** The maximum number of entries in a node is twice the value of MINIMUM.

Although MINIMUM may be as small as 1, in practice much larger values are used—perhaps several hundred, or even a couple thousand.

The many entries of a B-tree node are stored in an array, so that we can talk about "the entry at index 0," or "the entry at index 1," and so on. Within the array, the entries must be sorted from smallest to largest. This provides our third B-tree rule:

> **B-tree Rule 3:** The entries of each B-tree node are stored in a partially filled array, sorted from the smallest entry (at index 0) to the largest entry (at the final used position of the array).

The subtrees below a B-tree node. The number of subtrees below a node depends on how many entries are in the node. Here is the rule:

> **B-tree Rule 4:** The number of subtrees below a non-leaf node is always one more than the number of entries in the node.

For example, suppose a node has 42 entries. Then this node will have 43 children. We will refer to the many subtrees of a node from left to right as "subtree number 0, subtree number 1, . . ." and so on up to the last subtree.

The entries in each subtree are organized in a way that makes it easy to search the B-tree for any given entry. Here is the rule for that organization:

> **B-tree Rule 5:** For any non-leaf node: (a) An entry at index i is greater than all the entries in subtree number i of the node, and (b) An entry at index i is less than all the entries in subtree number $i + 1$ of the node.

Let's look at an example to illustrate Rules 4 and 5. Suppose that a non-leaf node contains two integer entries, the numbers 93 and 107. This node must have three subtrees, organized as follows:

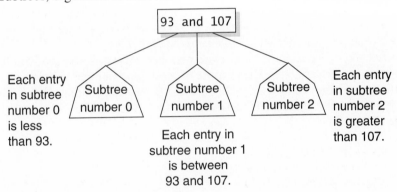

A B-tree is balanced. The final B-tree rule ensures that a B-tree avoids the problem of an unbalanced tree:

> **B-tree Rule 6:** Every leaf in a B-tree has the same depth.

An Example B-Tree

As another example, here is a complete B-tree of ten integers (with MINIMUM set to 1). Can you verify that all six B-tree rules are satisfied?

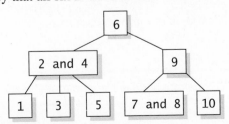

The Set ADT with B-trees

The rest of this section discusses the algorithms for implementing a set class using B-trees. The class is a template class that depends on the underlying type of the items in the set. There are public member functions for adding and removing items, and also for checking whether a given item is in the set. As you can see in our complete header file (Figure 11.4), there are also several private member functions that will simplify the implementations of the other member functions. We'll discuss these "helper" functions at the point where they are used, but first let's examine the private member variables and member constants that we have in mind.

The set class has two private member constants, shown here with a selection of 200 for MINIMUM:

```
static const size_t MINIMUM = 200;
static const size_t MAXIMUM = 2 * MINIMUM;
```

two private member constants of the set

These constants are *private* because a programmer who *uses* the set class does not need to know about their existence. Access to these private values is needed only by the programmer who *implements* the set class.

After the declaration of the private member constants, the set class has four private member variables. The purpose of these four member variables is to store all the information about the root node of the B-tree that contains the set's entries. Here are the first three member variables from the set class in Figure 11.4 on page 504:

member variables store information about the root of the B-tree

```
size_t data_count;
Item data[MAXIMUM+1];
size_t child_count;
```

Keep in mind that the member variables store information about the *root* node. For example, data_count stores the number of entries in the B-tree's root (not in the entire B-tree). The root's entries are stored in the partially filled array called data, ranging from data[0] through data[data_count-1]. The complete size of the data array is MAXIMUM + 1, which allows space for one extra entry beyond the usual maximum number. You'll see the benefit of this extra space when we discuss the implementations of the member functions.

The number of children of the root node is stored in the member variable child_count. The children of the root have an important property that will allow us to use *recursive thinking* in our implementations. Here is the property that you should burn into your memory:

Every child of the root node is also the root of a smaller B-tree.

(text continues on page 505)

FIGURE 11.4   Header File for the Set Template Class

A Header File

```
// FILE: set.h
// TEMPLATE CLASS PROVIDED: Set<Item> (a container class for a set of items)
//   The template parameter, Item, is the data type of the items in the Set.
//   It may be any of the C++ built-in types (int, char, etc.), or a class with a default
//   constructor, a copy constructor, an assignment operator, and the six comparison
//   operators forming a total order.
//
// CONSTRUCTOR for the Set<Item> class:
//   Set( )
//     Postcondition: The Set is empty.
//
// MODIFICATION MEMBER FUNCTIONS for the Set<Item> class:
//   void clear( )
//     Postcondition: The Set is empty.
//
//   void insert(const Item& entry)
//     Postcondition: If entry was already in the Set, then the Set is unchanged.
//     Otherwise, entry has been added to the Set.
//
//   void remove(const Item& target)
//     Postcondition: If target was in the Set, then it has been removed from the Set.
//     Otherwise the set is unchanged.
//
// CONSTANT MEMBER FUNCTIONS for the Set<Item> class:
//   bool contains(const Item& target) const
//     Postcondition: If target is in the Set, then the return value is true.
//     Otherwise the return value is false.
//
//   bool is_empty( ) const
//     Postcondition: If the Set is empty, then the return value is true.
//     Otherwise the return value is false.
//
// VALUE SEMANTICS for the Set<Item> class:
//   Assignments and the copy constructor may be used with Set<Item> objects.
//
// DYNAMIC MEMORY USAGE by the Set<Item> class:
//   If there is insufficient dynamic memory, then the following functions call new_handler:
//   The constructors, insert, and the assignment operator.
```

(continued)

(FIGURE 11.4 continued)

```
#ifndef SET_H
#define SET_H

#include <stdlib.h>    // Provides size_t

    template <class Item>
    class Set
    {
    public:
        // CONSTRUCTORS and DESTRUCTOR
        Set( );
        Set(const Set& source);
        ~Set( ) { clear( ); }
        // MODIFICATION MEMBER FUNCTIONS
        void operator =(const Set& source);
        void clear( );
        void insert(const Item& entry);
        void remove(const Item& target);
        // CONSTANT MEMBER FUNCTIONS
        bool contains(const Item& target) const;
        bool is_empty( ) const { return (data_count == 0); }
    private:
        // MEMBER CONSTANTS
        static const size_t MINIMUM = 200;
        static const size_t MAXIMUM = 2 * MINIMUM;
        // MEMBER VARIABLES
        size_t data_count;
        Item data[MAXIMUM+1];
        size_t child_count;
        Set *subset[MAXIMUM+2];
        // HELPER MEMBER FUNCTIONS
        bool is_leaf( ) const { return (child_count == 0); }
        void loose_insert(const Item& entry);
        void loose_remove(const Item& target);
        void remove_biggest(Item& removed_entry);
        void fix_excess(size_t i);
        void fix_shortage(size_t i);
    };

#include "set.template" // Include the implementation.

#endif
```

If your compiler does not permit initialization of static constants, see Appendix E.

The private member functions are discussed in the text.

The programmer who implements the class may wish to add further private member functions.

Let's look at an example to illustrate the rule "Every child of the root node is also the root of a smaller B-tree." For the example, consider the following B-tree (with MINIMUM equal to 1):

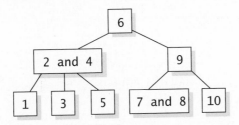

The root of this B-tree has two children, and each of these children is also the root of a smaller B-tree. These two smaller B-trees are clearly shown here:

Each of the smaller B-trees also contains a set of entries. We will call these two smaller sets "subset number 0" and "subset number 1." If there were more children, we would continue with "subset number 2," and so on. The last subset is "subset number child_count-1."

Now consider how to store the subsets. The best solution is to store each subset as *an actual Set object*. In the root node itself, we will store *pointers* to these smaller Set objects. These pointers are stored in the fourth member variable of the set class, declared here:

```
Set *subset[MAXIMUM+2];
```

The member variable subset is a partially filled array of pointers to smaller subsets. It is able to hold up to MAXIMUM + 2 such pointers—which is one more than the maximum number of children that a B-tree node may have. As with the entries, the benefit of this "space for one extra" will become evident shortly.

As an example, suppose a B-tree root has two children. Then subset[0] is a pointer to "subset number 0," and subset[1] is a pointer to "subset number 1." With this in mind, let's again consider the following B-tree:

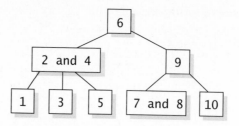

The root contains one entry and two children, so the member variables of the set object for this B-tree will look like this:

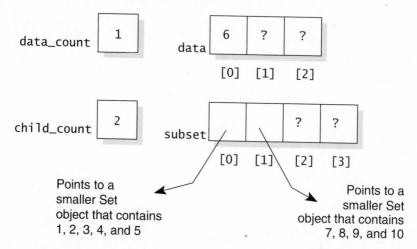

The important idea is that each subset[i] is a pointer to another Set object. We will be able to use all of the Set member functions with these objects in various recursive calls. Here is the complete invariant for our Set class:

Invariant for the Set ADT Implemented with a B-tree

1. The items of the set are stored in a B-tree, satisfying the six B-tree rules.

2. The number of entries in the tree's root is stored in the member variable data_count, and the number of subtrees of the root is stored in the member variable child_count.

3. The root's entries are stored in data[0] through data[data_count-1].

4. If the root has subtrees, then these subtrees are stored in sets pointed to by the pointers subset[0] through subset[child_count-1].

Searching for an Item in a B-tree

The set class has a member function, `contains`, that determines whether an item called `target` appears in the set. Searching for an item in a B-tree follows the same idea as searching a binary search tree, although there's more work needed to handle nodes that contain many entries instead of just one. The basic idea: Start with the entire B-tree, checking to see whether the target is in the root. If the target does appear in the root, the search is done—the function can return true to indicate that it found the target. A second possibility is that the target is not in the root, and the root has no children. In this case, the search is also done—the function can return false to indicate that the target is not in the set. The final possibility is that the target is not in the root, but there are subtrees below. In this case, there is only one possible subtree where the target can appear, so the function makes a recursive call to search that one subtree for the target.

The entire function can benefit from one preliminary step, shown as the first step of this pseudocode:

// Searching for a target in a Set

1. Make a local variable, `i`, equal to the first index such that `data[i] >= target`. If there is no such index, then set `i` equal to `data_count`, indicating that none of the entries is greater than or equal to the target.

2. *if* (we found the target at `data[i]`)
        return true;
    else if (the root has no children)
        return false;
    else
        return `subset[i]->contains(target);`

Be careful how you test the condition at the start of Step 2. In order to "find the target at `data[i]`," you must ensure that `i < data_count` and also that the target is actually equal to `data[i]`.

The recursive call in the pseudocode is highlighted. Notice the form that the activation requires, using the member selection operator (`->`) rather than a simple dot. The reason is that `subset[i]` is a *pointer* to a set (rather than an actual set). The recursive call works well in this situation because the subset is *smaller* than the entire set. Thus, the recursive call is solving a *smaller* version of the original problem.

As an example of executing the pseudocode, suppose we are searching for 10 in this B-tree:

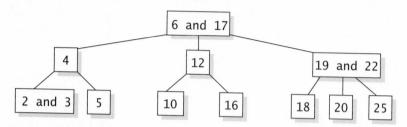

The search begins by finding the first item in the root that is greater than or equal to the target 10. This is the item 17, which occurs at `data[1]` in the root, so Step 1 sets `i` to the index 1. In Step 2 we notice that we have not found the target at `data[1]`, but the root does have children. So, we make a recursive call, searching subtree number 1 for the target 10. You can visualize the recursive call `subtree[1]->contains(10)` as searching for a 10 in this part of the tree:

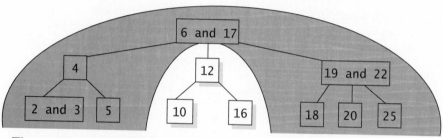

The recursive call of the `contains` member function has its own copy of the local variable `i`. This variable `i` is set to 0 in Step 1 of the recursive call (since `data[0]` of the subtree is greater than or equal to the target 10). Again, we have not found the target, so the recursion continues, activating the `contains` member function for the still smaller subtree shown here:

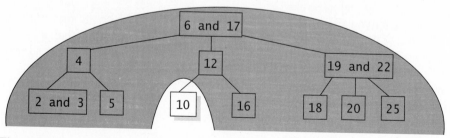

The recursive call finds the target, returning true to the previous recursive call. That previous recursive call then returns true to the original call, and the original call can also return true, indicating that the target was found somewhere in the set.

There are several parts of the pseudocode for you to clarify in your implementation. How do you determine whether the target was found at `data[i]`? How do you determine whether the root has children? The implementation of the first step of the pseudocode benefits from a toolkit of template functions that we wrote in Chapter 6. Appendix I provides an expanded version of this toolkit. Can you look through the documentation of the toolkit to find a function that will be useful for Step 1 of the pseudocode?

Programming Tip: Use Previously Written Functions

TIP △

Much of the B-tree implementation deals with partially filled arrays. Therefore, many of the functions in the toolkit of Appendix I will be useful. As you implement the B-tree, ask yourself, "Is this an operation that deals with a partially filled array?" If so, then try to find and use a function from the toolkit rather than starting from scratch.

Inserting an Item into a B-tree

The `insert` member function of the set class adds a new item to the B-tree. It is easier to add a new entry to a B-tree if we relax one of the B-tree rules. In particular, we will allow a somewhat "loose insertion" function to complete its work with the possibility that there is one entry too many in the root node of the B-tree. In other words, a loose insertion might result in MAXIMUM + 1 entries in the root. For example, consider this B-tree where MAXIMUM is 2:

Suppose that we want to add 18 to the tree. The end result of a loose insertion could be the following illegal B-tree:

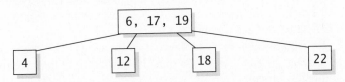

The B-tree is illegal because the root node has three entries, which is one more than the definition of MAXIMUM. Notice that *only the root* may have an extra entry after the "loose insertion." Our plan is for the insert member function to begin by calling another member function that carries out a loose insertion. After the loose insertion, the usual insert member function will examine the root node. If the root node has too many entries, then the insert member function will fix that problem in a way that we'll describe later. For now, though, we'll turn our attention to the design of the loose insertion function.

The Loose Insertion into a B-tree

From our previous discussion, you can design a specification for a loose insertion. The function will be a private member function called `loose_insert`. The specification is given here:

```
template <class Item>
void Set<Item>::loose_insert(const Item& entry);
// Precondition: The entire B-tree is valid.
// Postcondition: If entry was already in the set, then the set is unchanged.
// Otherwise, entry has been added to the set, and the entire B-tree is still
// valid EXCEPT that the number of entries in the root of this set might be
// one more than the allowed maximum.
```

Since this is a *private* member function, it may violate the usual invariant for the set ADT. As you can see, the precondition does satisfy the usual invariant, but the postcondition allows for a violation of the invariant. This precondition/postcondition contract will not appear in the set's header file. It is present only in the implementation file, as an aid to the programmer who implements the class.

The first step of our approach for the loose insertion is identical to the first step of the searching function. This step finds the first location in the root's entries that is greater than or equal to the new entry. Once we have this location, there are three possibilities listed in Step 2 of the pseudocode:

```
// Inserting a new entry in a Set
```

1. Make a local variable, `i`, equal to the first index such that `data[i] >= entry`. If there is no such index, then set `i` equal to `data_count`, indicating that none of the entries is greater than or equal to the target.

2. `if` (we found the new entry at `data[i]`)

pseudocode for the loose insert

    2a. Return with no further work (since the new entry is already in the set, and we may not have two copies of the same entry).

    `else` `if` (the root has no children)

    2b. Add the new entry to the root at `data[i]`. (The original entries at `data[i]` and afterwards must be shifted right to make room for the new entry).

    `else`
    {   2c.
    `subset[i]->loose_insert(entry);`
    If the root of `subset[i]` now has an excess entry, then fix that problem before returning.
    }

Looking through the pseudocode, Steps 2a and 2b are fairly easy. You'll find a function in the Appendix I toolkit to help with 2b.

The more interesting work occurs in Step 2c, where we have not found the new entry, nor are we ready to insert the new entry. In this case, we make a recursive call to do a loose insertion of the new entry in the appropriate subset. Since the recursive call is a *loose* insertion, we may end up with one excess entry in the root of our subset. This excess entry must be dealt with before returning because the postcondition does not allow subsets to have nodes with extra entries.

As an example of executing the pseudocode, suppose we are making a loose insertion of 18 into this B-tree (with MAXIMUM set to 2):

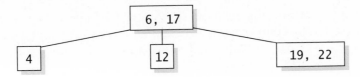

Step 1 of the pseudocode finds the first item in the root that is greater than or equal to the new entry 18. As you see, none of the root entries is greater than or equal to 18, so what does Step 1 do instead? From the pseudocode, you see that the index i will be set to 2 (the number of entries in the root node).

In Step 2 we notice that we have not found the new entry in the root, nor are we at a leaf. So we proceed to Step 2c, making a recursive call to insert 18 into subtree number 2, as shown here:

Insert 18 into this subset.

The recursive call finds a small subtree with just a root. Following Step 2b, the recursive call inserts the number 18 into the root of the subtree and then returns. After the recursive call returns, the entire tree looks like this:

When the recursive call returns, we carry out the rest of Step 2c, checking whether the root of the subtree now has too many entries. Indeed, the root of subset[2] now has three entries, which is one more than the allowed maximum. We must fix this problem child, but how? It seems that fixing the child may take quite a bit of work, so we will propose another private member function to carry out this work.

A Private Member Function to Fix an Excess in a Child

Here's the specification for the private member function that we have in mind:

```
template <class Item>
void Set<Item>::fix_excess(size_t i);
// Precondition: (i < child_count) and the entire B-tree is valid EXCEPT that
// subset[i] has MAXIMUM + 1 entries.
// Postcondition: The tree has been rearranged so that the entire B-tree is
// valid EXCEPT that the number of entries in the root of this set might be
// one more than the allowed maximum.
```

Looking at the specification, you can see that the function starts with a problem child. When the function finishes, the child no longer has a problem, although the *root* may now have a problem. The approach of the `fix_excess` function can be simply stated:

Fixing a Child with an Excess Entry

In order to fix a child with MAXIMUM + 1 entries, the child node is split into two nodes that each contain MINIMUM entries. This leaves one extra entry, which is passed upward to the parent.

Let's examine an example of this approach. In the example, suppose that MINIMUM is 2, so that the maximum number of entries in a node is 4 (which is 2*MINIMUM). We want to fix subtree number 1 (the shaded subtree) in this example tree:

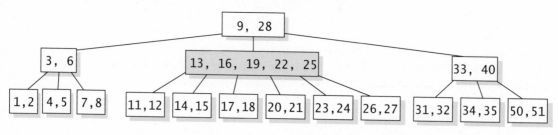

The approach taken by `fix_excess` is to split the problem node (with 2*MINIMUM + 1 entries) into two smaller nodes (with MINIMUM entries each). This leaves one entry unaccounted for, and that one extra entry will be passed upward to the parent of the split node. Therefore, the parent of the split node gains one additional child (from splitting the full node) and also gains one additional entry (the extra entry that is passed upward). In the example shown above, the result of the splitting is shown here:

The full node has been split into
two nodes, and the middle entry (19)
has been passed upward.

It is always the *middle* entry of the split node that moves upward. Also, notice that the children of the split node have been equally distributed between the two smaller nodes.

As another example of `fix_excess` in action, suppose that MAXIMUM is 2, and we have the problem child shown here:

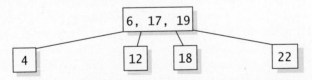

subset[2] has an
excess entry.

After calling `fix_excess(2)`, the problem child will be split into two nodes, with the middle entry passed upward, as shown here:

As you can see in this example, fixing the problem child can create a root with an excess entry—but that is all right because the postcondition of `fix_excess` permits the root to have an extra entry.

In your implementation of `fix_excess`, you will once again find the Appendix I toolkit useful.

Back to the Insert Member Function

We need to finish the discussion of the original insert function. By using the `loose_insert` function, the public `insert` function has just two steps:

```
// Pseudocode for the public insert member function
loose_insert(entry);
if (data_count > MAXIMUM)
        Fix the root of the entire tree so that it no longer has too many entries.
```

*pseudocode for
insert*

In this pseudocode, how do we "fix the root of the entire tree so that it no longer has too many entries"? The step can be accomplished in two parts. The first part copies all entries and child pointers from the root to a newly allocated node and clears out the root, leaving it with one child (which is the newly allocated node) and no entries. For example, suppose that we do a loose insertion, and then the B-tree looks like this (with MAXIMUM set to 2):

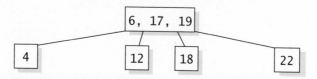

We will copy everything from the root to a new node and clear out the root. In the resulting tree, the root will have no entries, and everything else has moved down one level, as shown here:

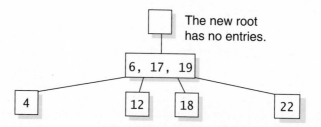

Once we have shifted things in this way, the problem is now with the child of the root. We can fix this problem by splitting the subset[0] of the root into two nodes and passing the middle entry upward. In fact, if you are careful in writing fix_excess, this splitting can be carried out by calling fix_excess(0). Care must be taken because this root has no entries, so fix_excess must be prepared to deal with such a situation. (If you take this approach, you should document the extended ability of fix_excess in its precondition.)

In this example, after splitting subset[0] we have the completely valid B-tree shown here:

B-trees gain height only at the root

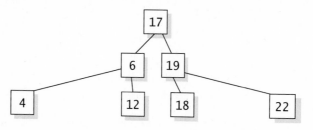

By the way, this growth at the root (within the insert member function) is the only point where a B-tree gains height.

Employing Top-Down Design

As you work on the project, keep in mind the top-down design that we have employed. As shown in Figure 11.5 (to the right), the original insert member function calls the private member function `loose_insert`. Both the ordinary insert and the loose insert functions call `fix_excess`. And at several points in the design we were able to use previous functions from the Appendix I toolkit.

FIGURE 11.5 Top-down Design for the `insert` Member Function

The `insert` function calls:
- `loose_insert`
- `fix_excess`

The `loose_insert` function is recursive and also calls:
- `fix_excess`
- various Appendix I functions

The `fix_excess` function calls:
- various Appendix I functions

Removing an Item from a B-tree

The `remove` member function of the set removes an entry from the B-tree. Most of the removal work will be accomplished with a private member function, `loose_remove`, which performs a "loose removal" that is analogous to the loose insertion. The looseness in `loose_remove` occurs because it is allowed to leave a root that has one entry too few. In other words, it might leave the root of the whole tree with zero entries (which is not permitted unless there are also no children), or it might leave the root of an internal subtree with fewer than `MINIMUM` entries. The specification of `loose_remove` is given here:

```
template <class Item>
void Set<Item>::loose_remove(const Item& target);
// Precondition: The entire B-tree is valid.
// Postcondition: If target was in the set, then it has been removed from
// the set; otherwise the set is unchanged. The entire B-tree is still valid
// EXCEPT that the number of entries in the root of this set might be one
// less than the allowed minimum.
```

Our complete remove function will first call `loose_remove`. Afterwards, if necessary, we can fix a root that may have been left with zero entries and one child. Thus, the remove pseudocode has just two short steps:

```
// Pseudocode for the public remove member function
loose_remove(target);
if ((data_count == 0) && (child_count == 1))
    Fix the root of the entire tree so that it no longer has zero entries.
```

pseudocode for remove

In this pseudocode, how do we "fix the root of the entire tree so that it no longer has zero entries"? For example, we might have a tree that looks like this:

Our solution for this problem is to first set a temporary pointer that points to the only child. Second, copy everything from the only child up to the root node. Finally, delete the original child. After this rearrangement, our tree will be one level shorter, as shown here:

B-trees lose height only at the root

This shrinking at the root (within the remove member function) is the only point where a B-tree loses height.

Now we are left with the task of designing the loose removal.

The Loose Removal from a B-tree

The private `loose_remove` function starts in the same way as the search and insert functions, by finding the first index i such that `data[i]` is greater than or equal to the target. Once we have found this index, there are four possibilities, shown here:

pseudocode for loose remove

// *Removing a target entry from a Set*

1. Make a local variable, i, equal to the first index such that `data[i] >= entry`. If there is no such index, then set i equal to `data_count`, indicating that none of the entries is greater than or equal to the target.

2. Deal with one of these four possibilities:

   2a. The root has no children, and we did not find the target: In this case, there is no work to do, since the target is not in the set.

   2b. The root has no children, and we found the target: In this case, remove the target from the data array, and return.

   2c. The root has children, and we did not find the target (see below).

   2d. The root has children, and we found the target (see below).

Cases 2c and 2d require further development.

Case 2c. In this case, we did not find the target in the root, but the target still might appear in `subset[i]`. We will make a recursive call:

```
subset[i]->loose_remove(target);
```

This call will remove the target from `subset[i]`, but we are then left with the problem that the root of `subset[i]` might have only `MINIMUM - 1` entries. If so, then we'll fix the problem by calling another private member function with the specification shown here:

```
template <class Item>
void Set<Item>::fix_shortage(size_t i);
// Precondition: (i < child_count) and the entire B-tree is valid EXCEPT that
// subset[i] has MINIMUM – 1 entries.
// Postcondition: The tree has been rearranged so that the entire B-tree is
// valid EXCEPT that the number of entries in the root of this set might be
// one less than the allowed minimum.
```

We'll look at the design of `fix_shortage` later.

Case 2d. In this case, we have found the target in the root, but we cannot simply remove it from the data array because there are children below (and removing an entry would thereby violate B-tree Rule 4 on page 501). Instead, we will go into `subset[i]` and remove the *largest* item in this subset. We will take a copy of this largest item and place it into `data[i]` (which contains the target). The total effect is the same as removing the target.

For example, suppose we have found the target 28 at `data[1]` in the root of this B-tree:

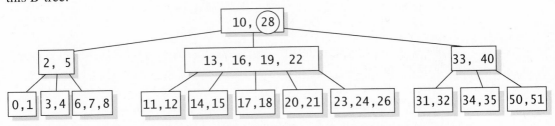

Our plan is to go into `subset[1]`, remove the largest item (the 26), and place a copy of this 26 on top of the target. After these steps, the B-tree no longer has the 28:

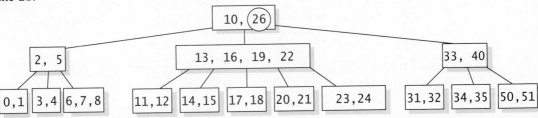

The combination of removing the largest item from subset[i] and placing a copy of the largest item into data[i] can be accomplished by calling another new private member function, remove_biggest, with a specification shown here:

```
template <class Item>
void Set<Item>::remove_biggest(Item& removed_entry);
// Precondition: (data_count > 0) and the entire B-tree is valid.
// Postcondition: The largest item in the set has been removed, and a copy
// of this removed entry has been placed in removed_entry. The entire
// B-tree is still valid, EXCEPT that the number of entries in the root of this
// set might be one less than the allowed minimum.
```

By using remove_biggest, most of Step 2d is accomplished with one function call:

```
subset[i]->remove_biggest(data[i]);
```

After this function call returns, we have deleted the largest entry from subset[i] and placed a copy of this item into data[i] (replacing the target). The only work that remains is to fix the possible shortage that may occur in the root of subset[i] (since the postcondition of subset[i]->remove_biggest allows for the possibility that the root of subset[i] ends up with MINIMUM - 1 entries). How do we fix such a shortage? We can use the same fix_shortage member function that we used at the end of Step 2c. Thus, the entire code for Step 2d is the following:

```
subset[i]->remove_biggest(data[i]);
if (subset[i]->data_count < MINIMUM)
    fix_shortage(i);
```

We have two more issues to deal with: the designs of fix_shortage and remove_biggest.

A Private Member Function to Fix a Shortage in a Child

four situations for the fix_shortage pseudocode

When fix_shortage(i) is called, we know that subset[i] has only MINIMUM - 1 entries. How can we correct this problem? There are four situations that you can consider:

Case 1 of fix_shortage: Transfer an extra entry from subset[i-1].
Suppose that subset[i-1] has more than the minimum number of entries. Then we can carry out these transfers:

   a. Transfer data[i-1] down to the front of subset[i]->data. Remember to shift over the existing entries to make room, and add one to subset[i]->data_count.

b. Transfer the final item of `subset[i-1]->data` up to replace `data[i-1]`, and subtract one from `subset[i-1]->data_count`.

c. If `subset[i-1]` has children, transfer the final child pointer of `subset[i-1]` over to the front of `subset[i]`. This involves shifting over the existing array `subset[i]->subset` to make room for the new child pointer at `subset[i]->subset[0]`. Also add one to `subset[i]->child_count`, and subtract one from `subset[i-1]->child_count`.

For example, let's call `fix_shortage(2)` for this tree (with `MINIMUM` set to 2):

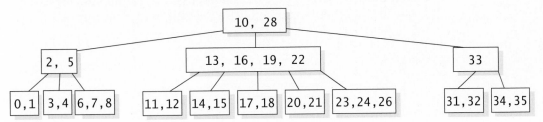

In this example, we need to fix `subset[2]`, which has only one entry. Following the steps outlined above, we can transfer an entry from `subset[1]`. This transferred entry is the 22, which gets passed up to `data[1]`, and the 28 (from `data[1]`) comes down to be the new first entry of the problem node. One child is also transferred from the end of `subset[1]` to the front of `subset[2]`, as shown here:

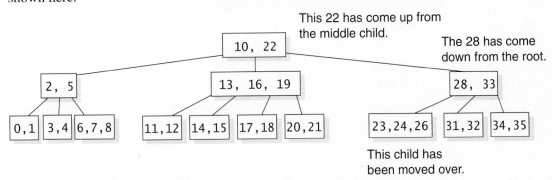

This 22 has come up from the middle child.

The 28 has come down from the root.

This child has been moved over.

Case 2 for `fix_shortage`: Transfer an extra entry from `subset[i+1]`.
Another possibility is to transfer an extra entry from `subset[i+1]`. The work is similar to what you have just seen for transferring an entry from `subset[i-1]`.

Case 3 for `fix_shortage`: Combine `subset[i]` with `subset[i-1]`.
Suppose that `subset[i-1]` is present (in other words, `i > 0`), but it has only `MINIMUM` entries. In this case, we cannot transfer an entry from `subset[i-1]`, but we can combine `subset[i]` with `subset[i-1]`. The combining occurs in three steps:

a. Transfer `data[i-1]` down to the end of `subset[i-1]->data`. This actually removes the item from the root, so shift `data[i]`, `data[i+1]`, and so on, leftward to fill in the gap. Also remember to subtract one from `data_count`, and add one to `subset[i-1]->data_count`.

b. Transfer all the items and children from `subset[i]` to the end of `subset[i-1]`. Remember to update the values of `subset[i-1]->data_count` and `subset[i-1]->child_count`. Also set `subset[i]->data_count` and `subset[i]->child_count` to zero.

c. Delete the node `subset[i]`, and shift `subset[i+1]`, `subset[i+2]`, and so on leftward to fill in the gap. Also reduce `child_count` by one.

For example, let's call `fix_shortage(2)` for this tree (with `MINIMUM` set to 2):

In this example, `subset[2]` is merged with its sibling to the left. During the merge, the 28 also is passed down from the root to become a new entry of the merged nodes. The result is the following tree:

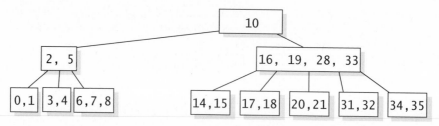

As you can see, this tree has too few entries in its own root, but that is okay because the postcondition of `fix_shortage` allows the root of the resulting tree to have one less than the required number of entries.

Case 4 for `fix_shortage`: Combine `subset[i]` with `subset[i+1]`.
Our fourth case is to combine the problem subset with `subset[i+1]`. The work is similar to what you have just seen for combining with `subset[i-1]`.

You now have enough information to write the `fix_shortage` member function. You should emphasize a clear logical structure to determine which of the four approaches is appropriate. Your implementation will be cleaner if you provide four new private member functions to do the actual work in each of the four cases.

Removing the Biggest Item from a B-tree

Our final member function has this specification:

```
template <class Item>
void Set<Item>::remove_biggest(Item& removed_entry);
// Precondition: (data_count > 0) and the entire B-tree is valid.
// Postcondition: The largest item in the set has been removed, and a copy
// of this removed entry has been placed in removed_entry. The entire
// B-tree is still valid, EXCEPT that the number of entries in the root of this
// set might be one less than the allowed minimum.
```

The work of `remove_biggest` is easy if the root has no children. In this case, we copy the last item of `data` into the reference parameter, `removed_entry`. Then we subtract one from `data_count`. That's all! We might be left with a node that has one less than the allowed minimum number of entries, but according to the postcondition, that is okay.

What if the root has children? If this case, we make a recursive call to remove the largest entry from the rightmost child. The recursive call is:

```
subset[child_count-1]->remove_biggest(removed_entry);
```

Notice the argument, `removed_entry`, that we use in the recursive call. This argument will be set equal to the item that is removed from the subtree. This is exactly what we need, and there is only one remaining problem. The recursive call might leave the root of `subset[child_count-1]` with one entry too few. How can we fix a child that has a shortage of entries? The `fix_shortage` function can fix such a node. So, after the recursive call, you should check the number of entries in the root of `subset[child_count-1]`. If the number of entries is less than `MINIMUM`, then call `fix_shortage(child_count-1)`.

Programming Tip: Write and Test Small Pieces

TIP

If you are implementing the entire set ADT, don't try to do the whole thing at once. Instead, you should write and test functions one at a time. In this project, you should also carry out a major testing after you have completed the `insert` and `contains` functions, and before you have started on any of the removal machinery.

When you start on the removal, draw a diagram of the top-down design that you are implementing.

Test pieces as soon as you can. This early testing can be aided by initially implementing all of your planned functions with a single line that simply prints the name of the function, indicating that the function has been activated. A single line such as this is called a **stub**. With stubs in place, you can test any function as soon as you have written the complete version. For example, as soon as you implement the remove function, you can test it. You know that it should call the `loose_remove` function, so you expect the `loose_remove` stub to print a message indicating that `loose_remove` has been called.

Throughout your implementation work, it will be useful if you can print some representation of a B-tree. We suggest that you temporarily add a public print function, similar to the function shown in Figure 11.6. (You may want to provide a fancier print function, similar to the backward in-order traversal for binary trees (see "A Useful Backward In-Order Traversal" on page 457).

In order for the output of the print function to be understandable, keep the value of MINIMUM small during testing—perhaps 1 or 2.

External B-trees

Programmers may use B-trees to ensure quick behavior from the fact that the trees are always balanced (all the leaves are at the same depth). If a balanced tree is your only objective, then the choice of the MINIMUM constant is

---

FIGURE 11.6   Implementing a Temporary Member Function That Prints a Set's B-tree

A Function Implementation

```
template <class Item>
void Set<Item>::print(int indent) const
// This is a temporary public function for use by the programmer who implements the Set
// class. The function prints a representation of the set's B-tree. The entries of the root node
// are printed with an indentation given by the parameter, and each subtree has an extra
// four spaces of indentation.
// Library facilities used: iostream.h (provides cout), and iomanip.h (provides setw)
{
    const int EXTRA_INDENTATION = 4;
    size_t i;

    cout << setw(indent) << ""; // Print indentation.

    // Print the data from the root.
    for (i = 0; i < data_count; i++)
        cout << data[i] << " ";
    cout << endl;

    // Print the subtrees.
    for (i = 0; i < child_count; i++)
        subset[i]->print(indent+EXTRA_INDENTATION);
}
```

not critical. Sometimes MINIMUM is simply 1, meaning that each node has one or two entries, and non-leaf nodes have *two or three* children. This situation is called a **2-3 tree,** which was proposed by John E. Hopcroft several years before B-trees were devised.

Sometimes B-trees become large—so large that the entire tree cannot reside in the computer's main memory at one time. For example, a residential phone book of the United States contains about 100 million entries. The set of entries can still be organized as a B-tree, but most of the nodes must be stored in slower secondary memory such as a hard drive or a CD-ROM. Typically, the root node is loaded into main memory, where it stays for the life of the program. But, non-root nodes must be loaded from the secondary memory whenever they are needed. This situation is called an **external B-tree.**

most of the nodes reside in slower secondary memory

A primary consideration with external B-trees is to reduce the total number of accesses to the secondary memory device. Therefore, the MINIMUM constant will be set quite large. With MINIMUM set to 1000, we can store more than one billion (10^9) entries with just the root and two levels below it. Because the root is always kept in memory, no search will ever require more than two nodes from the secondary memory device.

Another factor concerns the retrieval mechanism used by the secondary storage device. When a request is made to read from a hard disk or CD-ROM, there is a relatively long initial *access time* to position the disk's read head over the requested section of the disk. Once the head has been positioned, contiguous data can be read fairly quickly. This data is transferred in fixed-sized blocks, using a relatively high *sustained transfer rate*. The 8x CD-ROMs that are common today have an access time of about $1/10$ of a second. Once the head is positioned, the drive transfers about 1.2 million bytes per second. With this in mind, you need to ensure that each node is stored in a contiguous area of the disk—for if the node is spread out in several different areas, each area will require $1/10$ of a second access time to reposition the head.

Self-Test Exercises

5. Suppose MINIMUM is 200 for a B-tree. What is the maximum number of entries that a node may contain? What is the minimum number of entries that a non-root node may have? What is the maximum number of children that a node may have? What is the minimum number of children that a non-leaf, non-root node may have?

6. Suppose MINIMUM is 1000 for a B-tree. The tree has a root and one level of 1000 nodes below that. What is the minimum number of entries that this tree might have? What is the maximum?

7. Start with an empty B-tree, with MINIMUM set to 1. Enter the integers 1 through 10. Draw the resulting tree.

8. Remove the numbers 8, 3, and 6 from the tree that you created in the previous exercise. Draw the resulting tree after each removal.

11.3 TREES, LOGS, AND TIME ANALYSIS

The implementations in this chapter—heaps and B-trees—are efficient for a simple reason: The depth of the trees is kept small so that following a path from the root to a leaf does not examine too many nodes. In fact, we can make a strong statement relating the depth of a tree, and the worst-case time required for the operations we have implemented:

Worst-case Times for Tree Operations

The worst-case time performance for the following operations are all $O(d)$, where d is the depth of the tree:

1. Adding an entry in a binary search tree, a heap, or a B-tree.

2. Deleting an entry from a binary search tree, a heap, or a B-tree.

3. Searching for a specified entry in a binary search tree or a B-tree.

For example, consider adding an entry to a heap. The new entry is placed at the next available location of the heap at the deepest level, d. The priority of the new entry is then compared with its parent's priority, and the new entry might be swapped with its parent. In the worst case, this process continues, comparing the new entry with its parent and swapping, until the new entry reaches the root. In this worst case, the new entry had to be compared with its parent and swapped d times, where d is the depth at which the new entry began its life. Since one comparison and swap requires a fixed number of operations, the total number of operations in the algorithm is a fixed number times d, which is $O(d)$. You can carry out a similar analysis for each of the other operations listed above.

This could be the end of our story, except that time analyses for these operations are more useful if they are given in terms of the number of entries in the tree, rather than in terms of the tree's depth. In order to express the time analyses in these terms, we must first answer a secondary question: *What is the maximum depth for a tree with n entries?* We'll answer this question for binary search trees and heaps, leaving the case of B-trees for your exercises. Once this question is answered, we can provide worst-case time analyses in terms of the number of entries in a tree.

Time Analysis for Binary Search Trees

Suppose a binary search tree has n entries. What is the maximum depth the tree could have? A binary tree must have at least one node at each level. For example, a binary tree with depth 2 must have a root (at level 0), at least one child of the root (at level 1), and at least one child of the child (at level 2). If a tree has n nodes, then the first node may appear at the root level, the second node at level 1, the third node at level 2, and so on until the nth node which appears at depth $n-1$. So, a binary tree with n entries could have a depth as big as $n-1$.

What does this say about the worst-case time analysis of the binary search tree operations in terms of the number of entries in a tree? Here's the analysis:

Worst-case Times for Binary Search Trees

Adding an entry, deleting an entry, or searching for an entry in a binary search tree with n entries is $O(d)$, where d is the depth of the tree. Since d is no more than $n-1$, the operations are $O(n-1)$, which is $O(n)$ (since we can ignore constants in big-O notation).

Time Analysis for Heaps

In a heap, we can examine the relationship between depth and number of entries by first computing the smallest number of entries required for a heap to reach a given depth d. Remember that a heap is a complete binary tree so that each level must be full before proceeding to the next level. The first entry goes at level 0 (the root level). The next two entries must go at level 1, the next four entries at level 2, the next 8 entries at level 3, and so on. Let's present this information in a table.

Level	Number of nodes to fill the level
0	1 node
1	2 nodes
2	4 nodes
3	8 nodes
4	16 nodes
...	
d	2^d nodes

The values in the table are the maximum number of nodes that may occur at each level. Using the table, we can obtain the total number of nodes needed to reach level d:

Number of nodes needed for a heap to reach depth d is

$$(1 + 2 + 4 + \ldots + 2^{d-1}) + 1$$

The first part of the formula, up to 2^{d-1}, is the number of entries required to completely fill the first $d-1$ levels, and the extra "+ 1" at the end is required because there must be at least one entry in level d.

This formula can be simplified by shifting the +1 to the front:

Number of nodes needed for a heap to reach depth d is

$$1 + 1 + 2 + 4 + \ldots + 2^{d-1}$$

Why is this a simplification? Look at the start of the formula, which begins $1 + 1 \ldots$ Then combine the two 1's, like this:

$$1 + 1 + 2 + 4 + \ldots + 2^{d-1} \quad = \quad 2 + 2 + 4 + \ldots + 2^{d-1}$$

Now we have a formula that begins with two 2's, which can also be combined:

$$2 + 2 + 4 + \ldots + 2^{d-1} \quad = \quad 4 + 4 + \ldots + 2^{d-1}$$

Now we have a formula that begins with two 4's, and if we combine the 4's we get two 8's, and so on until we eventually end up with just $2^{d-1} + 2^{d-1}$. So:

Number of nodes needed for a heap to reach depth d is

$$= (1 + 2 + 4 + \ldots + 2^{d-1}) + 1$$
$$= 2^{d-1} + 2^{d-1}$$

This last formula, $2^{d-1} + 2^{d-1}$, is the same as 2^d, so we have the following result:

The number of nodes needed for a heap
to reach depth d is 2^d.

Expressed another way: The number of nodes in a heap is at least 2^d, where d is the depth of the heap.

This is certainly a simple formula, but in order to use it, we need to explain a bit about **base 2 logarithms**. For any positive number, x, the base 2 logarithm of x is an exponent r such that:

$$2^r = x$$

The number r in this equation is usually written $\log_2 x$. For example:

$$2^0 = 1, \text{ so that } \log_2 1 = 0$$
$$2^1 = 2, \text{ so that } \log_2 2 = 1$$
$$2^2 = 4, \text{ so that } \log_2 4 = 2$$
$$2^3 = 8, \text{ so that } \log_2 8 = 3$$
$$2^4 = 16, \text{ so that } \log_2 16 = 4$$
$$2^d = 2^d, \text{ so that } \log_2 2^d = d$$

The last line of this table is the key to our heap analysis. We know that in a heap the number of entries, n, is at least 2^d, where d is the depth of the heap. Therefore:

$$\log_2 n \geq \log_2 2^d \text{ (since } n \geq 2^d \text{)}$$

Since $\log_2 2^d = d$, this implies that:

$$\log_2 n \geq d.$$

This is the relationship that we need between the number of entries, n, and the depth of a heap. Here's the analysis:

Worst-case Times for Heap Operations

Adding or deleting an entry in a heap with n entries is $O(d)$, where d is the depth of the tree. Because d is no more than $\log_2 n$, the operations are $O(\log_2 n)$, which is $O(\log n)$ (since we can ignore log bases in big-O notation).

The time analysis for B-trees will also result in $O(\log n)$ time, as you'll be asked to show in Self-Test Exercise 10.

Omitting the subscript, 2, from $O(\log_2 n)$ may be a bit confusing, but to explain why the omission is valid, we need to look at logarithms in more depth. This look at logarithms will also give us a good understanding of the behavior that is expected from logarithmic algorithms, such as adding and deleting from a heap.

Logarithms

The definition of $\log_2 x$ is a number r such that $2^r = x$. The number 2 is called the **base of the logarithm**, and the definition extends to other bases. For example, $\log_{10} x$ is the number r such that $10^r = x$. Or consider base 16, where $\log_{16} x$ is the number r such that $16^r = x$.

Here are some specific examples for base 10:

$$10^0 = 1, \qquad \text{so that } \log_{10} 1 = 0$$
$$10^1 = 10, \qquad \text{so that } \log_{10} 10 = 1$$
$$10^{1.5} = \text{about } 32, \quad \text{so that } \log_{10} 32 = \text{about } 1.5$$
$$10^3 = 1000, \qquad \text{so that } \log_{10} 1000 = 3$$

From these examples, you can see why we said in Chapter 1 that the number of digits in a positive integer n is approximately $\log_{10} n$. You can work out a little table:

$$\text{For } n \text{ in the range 1 to 9,} \qquad 0 \leq \log_{10} n < 1$$
$$\text{For } n \text{ in the range 10 to 99,} \qquad 1 \leq \log_{10} n < 2$$
$$\text{For } n \text{ in the range 100 to 999,} \qquad 2 \leq \log_{10} n < 3$$
$$\text{For } n \text{ in the range 1000 to 9999,} \qquad 3 \leq \log_{10} n < 4$$

Extrapolating from this table, you can find a precise relationship between the number of digits in a positive integer and base 10 logarithms (using $\lfloor \log_{10} n \rfloor$ to indicate rounding down the logarithm to an integer):

The number of digits in a positive integer n is $\lfloor \log_{10} n \rfloor + 1$.

There is also a relationship between logarithms in one base and logarithms in another base:

For any two bases, a and b, and a positive number x:
$$(\log_b a) \times (\log_a x) = \log_b x$$

This equation is the reason why bases generally are omitted from big-O notation. For example, if an algorithm requires $\log_2 n$ operations, then that is the same as $4 \times \log_{16} n$ operations, since $\log_2 16$ is 4. In big-O notation, the multiplication by a constant (such as 4) is ignored, and this is why we write simply $O(\log n)$ rather than $O(\log_2 n)$.

Logarithmic Algorithms

Logarithmic algorithms are algorithms with worst-case time $O(\log n)$, such as adding and deleting from a heap. These algorithms have a characteristic time behavior:

Time Behavior of Logarithmic Algorithms

For a logarithmic algorithm, doubling the input size will make the time increase by a fixed number of new operations.

For example, consider adding a new entry to a heap with n entries. The algorithm may look at as many as $\log_2 n$ nodes. If we double the number of nodes to $2n$, then the algorithm may look at as many as $\log_2 2n$ nodes—but $\log_2 2n$ is just one more than $\log_2 n$. (For example, $\log_2 1024 = 10$, and $\log_2 2048 = 11$). So we can double the number of entries in a heap, and the process of adding a new entry requires us to examine only one extra node.

Self-Test Exercises

9. Evaluate the following logarithms:

$$\log_2 32 \qquad \log_5 125 \qquad \log_{16} 256$$

$$\log_{10} 100 \qquad \log_{37} 1 \qquad \log_9 81$$

10. Show that adding, deleting, and searching in a B-tree have worst-case time $O(\log n)$.

11. Use the definition of logarithms to show that $\log_2 2n$ is always just one more than $\log_2 n$.

CHAPTER SUMMARY

- A *heap* is a complete binary tree that follows the rule that the entry at any node is never less than any of its children's entries. Heaps provide an efficient implementation of priority queues.

- A *B-tree* is a tree for storing entries in a manner that follows six rules. The first two rules specify the minimum and maximum number of entries for each node. The third rule requires each node's entries to be sorted from smallest to largest. Rules 4 and 5 indicate how many subtrees a non-leaf node must have and provides an order on the elements of the subtrees. The last rule requires each leaf to be at the same depth.

- The tree algorithms that we have seen for binary search trees, heaps, and B-trees all have worst-case time performance of $O(d)$, where d is the depth of the tree.

- The depth of a heap or B-tree is never more than $O(\log n)$, where n is the number of nodes. Hence, the operations on these structures are also $O(\log n)$.

? Solutions to Self-Test Exercises

1. The priority queue class needs a private member variable that is an array. Each array component contains one item and the priority of that item, as shown in this struct definition:

```
template <class Item>
struct Component
{
    Item data;
    unsigned int priority;
};
```

Now we can write a priority queue definition that uses an array of 100 components. Our solution is based on the interface from Figure 8.13 on page 381, although we no longer need the HIGHEST constant. Here is the solution with a fixed-sized array:

```
template <class Item>
class PriorityQueue
{
public:
    // MEMBER CONSTANT
    static const size_t CAPACITY=100;
    // CONSTRUCTOR
    PriorityQueue( );
    // MODIFICATION MEMBER FUNCTIONS
    void insert(const Item& entry,
            unsigned int priority);
    Item get_front( );
    // CONSTANT MEMBER FUNCTIONS
    size_t size( ) const;
    int is_empty( ) const;
private:
    Component entries[CAPACITY];
    size_t used;
};
```

For the version with no fixed capacity, you can change the entries array to a dynamic array. You'll also need to add a copy constructor, an assignment operator, and a destructor.

2. With our insertion algorithm, you end up with this heap:

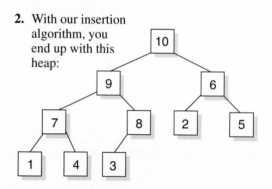

3. With our removal algorithm, you end up with this heap:

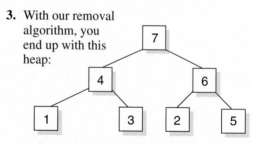

4. If we swap with the smaller child, then the larger child will still have a priority that exceeds its parent's priority.

5. The maximum number of entries that a node may contain is 400, although during an insertion we may temporarily have a node with 401 entries. The minimum number of entries that a

non-root node may have is 200, although during a removal we may temporarily have a node with 199 entries. The maximum number of children that a node may have is 401, although during an insertion, we may temporarily have a node with 402 children. The minimum number of children that a non-leaf, non-root node may have is 201, although during a removal we may temporarily have a node with 200 children.

6. The root has 999 entries, and each of the 1000 nodes at the next level has between 1000 and 2000 entries. Therefore, the total number of entries in the tree is between 1,000,999 entries and 2,000,999.

7. With our insertion algorithm, you end up with this B-tree:

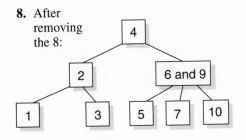

8. After removing the 8:

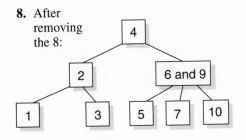

8. (continued)

After removing the 3:

After removing the 6:

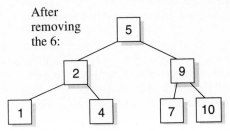

9. The logarithms are:

$$\log_2 32 = 5 \quad \log_5 125 = 3 \quad \log_{16} 256 = 2$$
$$\log_{10} 100 = 2 \quad \log_{37} 1 = 0 \quad \log_9 81 = 2$$

10. In all three functions, the number of total step is a constant times the height of the B-tree This height is no more than $\log_M n$, where M i the MINIMUM constant and n is the number o entries in the tree. Thus, the functions al require no more than $O(\log n)$ operations.

11. All logarithms in this solution are base 2:

$$2^{1 + \log n} = 2 \times 2^{\log n} = 2n = 2^{\log 2n}$$

Therefore, $1 + \log n = \log 2n$.

PROGRAMMING PROJECTS

1 Using a heap, implement the priority queue ADT from Section 8.4. The ADT should have a static constant member variable, CAPACITY, which is the maximum size of the heap (as in the solution to Self-Test Exercise 1). In order to have FIFO behavior for entries with equal priority, the array component should be a struct type with three member variables: (1) the entry itself, (2) the priority of the entry, and (3) the order in which the entry was added to the queue. For example, the first entry added has order number 1, the second entry has order number 2, and so on. When you are comparing two entries with equal priority, use the order number to "break the tie," (so that if two entries have the same priority number, then the one with the earlier order number will come out of the priority queue first). Give some thought to appropriate member variables for the priority queue itself. Naturally you'll need one member variable that is the array, but what else is needed with the approach we have outlined?

2 Repeat Project 1, with no predefined limit on the size of the heap. Use a dynamic array. Also, include a new member function with one parameter, an unsigned integer called level. The function returns the number of entries in the priority queue with priority greater than or equal to level.

3 Use a B-tree to implement the Set class from Figure 11.4 on page 503. Follow the programming tips from page 521.

4 The math.h facility provides a standard function ln(x), which returns the logarithm of x with a base that is approximately 2.71828. This base is written *e*, and the logarithms with this base are called **natural logarithms**. The number *e* may seem like a strange choice for the base of a logarithm, but the choice is motivated by the fact that natural logarithms are easy to approximate as the sum of a series. Anyway, in this project, you are to write a function:

```
double log(double base, double x);
```

The function returns the logarithm of x to the given base. Make use of the ln function and the formulas in Section 11.3.

12 Searching

His reasons are as two grains of wheat hid in two bushels of chaff: you shall seek all day ere you find them, and, when you have them, they are not worth the search.

WILLIAM SHAKESPEARE
The Merchant of Venice

Searching a list of values is a common computational task. An application program might retrieve a student record, bank account record, credit record, or any other type of record using a search algorithm. In this chapter, we present and analyze some of the most common (and some of the most efficient) methods of searching for a particular item. The algorithms include serial search, binary search, and search by hashing.

We also use the search algorithms to develop additional techniques for analyzing the running times of algorithms, particularly average-time analyses and the analysis of recursive algorithms.

12.1 SERIAL SEARCH AND BINARY SEARCH

Serial Search

Our starting point is the searching algorithm, shown in Figure 12.1. This algorithm, called a **serial search,** steps through part of an array one item at a time looking for a "desired item." The search stops when the item is found or when the search has examined each item without success. The technique is often used because it is easy to write and is applicable to many situations.

Serial Search—Analysis

The running time of the serial search is easy to analyze, but some care is needed to specify the precise kind of analysis. As always, we will count the number of "operations" required by the algorithm rather than measuring actual elapsed time. For searching an array, a common approach is to count one operation each time that the algorithm accesses an element of the array. With the serial search, the size of the array is one important factor in determining the number of array accesses—but even if we use a particular fixed array, the number of array accesses will still vary depending on precisely which target we are looking for. If the target is the first element in the array, then there will be only one array access. If the target is near the middle of the array, then the serial search accesses about half of the array elements.

FIGURE 12.1 | Serial Search Algorithm

Pseudocode for Serial Search

> // *Searches for a desired item in the n array elements starting at a[first]*

Set a `size_t` variable i to 0, and set a boolean variable found to false.

```
while ((i < n) && !found)
{
    if (a[first+i] is the desired item)
        found = true;
    else
        i++;
}

if (found)
    The desired item is in a[first+i].
else
    The desired item does not appear in the n items starting at a[first].
```

Usually when we discuss running times, we consider the "hardest" inputs, for example, a target that requires the algorithm to access the largest number of array elements. This is called the **worst-case** running time. For the serial search, the worst-case running time occurs when the target is not in the array. In this case, the algorithm accesses every element, and we have the following formula: *worst case*

Worst-Case Time for Serial Search

For an array of *n* elements, the worst-case time for serial search requires *n* array accesses.

With serial search, searches of an *n*-element array usually require fewer than *n* array accesses. Thus, the worst-case expression "*n* array accesses" makes serial search sound worst than it often is. An alternative is the **average-case** running time, which is obtained by averaging the different running times for all different inputs of a particular kind. For example, we can develop an expression for the average-case running time of serial search based on all the targets that are actually in the array. To be concrete in this first example, suppose that the array has ten elements, so that there are ten possible targets. If we are searching for the target that occurs at the first location, then there is just one array access. If we are searching for the target that occurs at the second location, then there are two array accesses. And so on, through the final target, which requires ten array accesses. In all, there are ten possible targets, which require 1, 2, 3, 4, 5, 6, 7, 8, 9, or 10 array accesses. The average of all these searches is: *average case*

$$\frac{1 + 2 + 3 + 4 + 5 + 6 + 7 + 8 + 9 + 10}{10} = 5.5$$

We can generalize this example so that the average-case running time of the serial search is written as an expression with part of the expression being the size of the array. Using *n* as the size of the array, this expression for the average-case running time is:

$$\frac{1 + 2 + \ldots + n}{n} = \frac{n(n+1)/2}{n} = (n+1)/2$$

The first equality in this formula is obtained from the formula that we developed on page 18. We can summarize the average-case running time for serial search:

Average-Case Time for Serial Search

For an array of *n* elements, the average-case time for serial search to find an element that is in the array requires (*n* + 1)/2 array accesses.

You may have noticed that both the worst-case time and the average-case time are $O(n)$ expressions, but nevertheless, the average case is about half the time of the worst case.

best case

A third way to measure running times is called **best-case** running time, and as the name suggests, it takes the most optimistic view possible. The best-case running time is defined as the smallest of all the running times on inputs of a particular size. For serial search, the best case occurs when the target is found at the front of the array, requiring only one array access:

Best-Case Time for Serial Search

For an array of *n* elements, the best-case time for serial search is just one array access.

Unless the best-case behavior occurs with high probability, the best-case running time generally is not used during an analysis.

Binary Search

Serial search is easy to implement, easy to analyze, and fine to use if you are only searching a small array a few times. However, if a search algorithm will be used over and over, it is worthwhile to find a faster algorithm. A dramatically faster search algorithm is sometimes available. The algorithm, called *binary search,* may only be used if the array is sorted. Here are three examples for which binary search is applicable:

- Searching an array of integers, where the array is sorted from the smallest integer (at the front) to the largest integer (at the end of the array).
- Searching an array of strings, where the strings are sorted alphabetically.
- Searching an array where each component is a `struct` containing information about an auto part, and the array is sorted by "part numbers" from the smallest to the largest.

For concreteness, we'll develop the algorithm for the first of these three cases (searching a sorted array of integers), but keep in mind that the same algorithm applies to any other kind of sorted array.

Our integer version of the binary search will be implemented with a function called `search`. The prototype for `search` requires six parameters. The first three parameters provide the array itself, the starting index of the portion of the array that we are searching, and the number of elements to search. The fourth parameter is the target that we are searching for. For example, consider:

```
search(b, 17, 10, 42, ...
```

This example shows the first four arguments needed to search for the number 42 occurring somewhere in the ten elements from `b[17]` through `b[26]`.

The fifth and sixth parameters are reference parameters, used to return the result of the search. The fifth parameter is a boolean value, indicating whether the target was found. If the target was found, then the sixth parameter indicates the index where the target occurs in the array. Here is the prototype:

```
void search(
    const int a[ ],
    size_t first,
    size_t size,
    int target,
    bool& found,
    size_t& location
);
// Precondition: The array segment starting at a[first] and containing size
// elements is sorted from smallest to largest.
// Postcondition: The array segment starting at a[first] and containing size
// elements has been searched for the target. If the target was present,
// then found is true, and location is set so that target == a[location].
// Otherwise found is set to false.
```

Binary Search—Design

Let us proceed to produce an algorithm to perform this search task. It will help to visualize the problem in concrete terms. Suppose that the list of numbers is a list of invalid credit card numbers, and it is so long that it takes a book to list them all. This is in fact how invalid credit card numbers are distributed to stores that do not have access to a computer. If you are a clerk and are handed a credit card, you must check to see if it is on the list and hence invalid. How would you proceed? Open the book to the middle and see if it is there. If not and it is smaller than the middle number, then work toward the beginning of the book. If it is larger than the middle number, work your way toward the back of the book. This idea produces our first draft of an algorithm:

```
if (size == 0)
    found = false;
else
{
    middle = index of the approximate midpoint of the array segment;
    if (target == a[middle])
        the target has been found at a[middle];
    else if (target < a[middle])
        search for the target in the area before the midpoint;
    else if (target > a[middle])
        search for the target in the area after the midpoint;
}
```

It is natural to use recursive calls for the two substeps that "search smaller lists," and that is what our implementation will do. As with any recursive function, we must ensure that the function terminates rather than producing infinite recursion. This insurance is provided by noting that each recursive call searches a shorter list, and when the list length reaches zero there can be no further recursive calls. This reasoning can be formalized as in Chapter 9 (see "Ensuring That There Is No Infinite Recursion" on page 415). Using the Chapter 9 technique, we see that the parameter size is a valid *variant expression*, with a *threshold* of zero. In other words, the size parameter is always reduced by at least one on each recursive call, and when size reaches zero, there is no further recursion.

Our complete implementation of the pseudocode is shown in Figure 12.2.

PITFALL

Pitfall: Common Indexing Errors in Binary Search Implementations

Binary search and similar array-based algorithms are notorious for having errors involving the array indices. Two of the most common problems are listed here:

Calculating the size of the array for the recursive call. The implementation in Figure 12.2 has two recursive calls. It's important to double-check your expression for the size of the array segment that is being searched in the recursive call. For example, one of our recursive calls searches the segment that occurs before a[middle]. This segment begins at a[first] going up to (but not including) a[middle]. How many entries are there in this segment? The answer is middle-first, which is the same as size/2, according to this calculation:

```
middle - first = (first + size/2) - first = size/2
```

In our recursive call, we use the expression size/2 for the argument that expresses the size of the array, since this expression conveys the idea that the recursive call searches about half of the original array.

You should carry out a similar calculation to verify that the number of elements after a[middle] is (size-1)/2. Hence, the size argument in our second recursive call is the expression (size-1)/2.

Ensuring that size_t values do not become negative. A second common error is writing a size_t expression that could end up with a negative value. For example, first, size, and middle might all be as small as zero, so it would be a mistake to write any of these expressions: first - 1, size - 1, middle - 1. We did not need any of these expressions, but it may be tempting to use these expressions in other implementations of binary search (particularly if you change the prototype so that the first and last indices are both parameters).

Avoid these possibly negative size_t values, as the runtime results are unpredictable.

FIGURE 12.2 The Binary Search Function

A Function Implementation

```
void search(
    const int a[ ],
    size_t first,
    size_t size,
    int target,
    bool& found,
    size_t& location
)
// Precondition: The array segment starting at a[first] and containing size elements is sorted
// from smallest to largest.
// Postcondition: The array segment starting at a[first] and containing size elements has been
// searched for the target. If the target was present, then found is true, and location is set so
// that target == a[location]. Otherwise, found is set to false.
// Library facilities used: stdlib.h
{
    size_t middle;

    if (size == 0)
        found = false;
    else
    {
        middle = first + size/2;
        if (target == a[middle])
        {
            location = middle;
            found = true;
        }
        else if (target < a[middle])
            // The target is less than a[middle], so search before the middle.
            search(a, first, size/2, target, found, location);
        else
            // The target must be greater than a[middle], so search after the middle.
            search(a, middle+1, (size-1)/2, target, found, location);
    }
}
```

Sample Results of `search(b, 2, 5, 42, ...)` **when b contains**

-7	3	8	39	42	63	70
[0]	[1]	[2]	[3]	[4]	[5]	[6]

found will be set to true;
location will be set to 4.

search.cxx   **FTP**

Binary Search—Analysis

We want to estimate the running time for the binary search algorithm given in Figure 12.2. The algorithm tests to see if the middle entry of the array has the target that we are looking for. If it does, the algorithm stops, returning the index of this middle entry. If our sought-after target is not in the middle of the array, the algorithm searches either the "half" above or the "half" below this midpoint. This narrows the search to about half of the array elements, then another recursive call can take it to half of that, then half of that, and so forth. The algorithm runs longest if the target is not in the array. If the target is not in the array, then eventually the algorithm will make a recursive call to search an array with zero elements. Of course, the target cannot occur in an empty array, so at that point the algorithm returns and tells us that the target could not be found. We want to analyze this algorithm for worst-case running time.

The binary search algorithm is a recursive algorithm so we need to compute the amount of time taken by all recursive calls and recursive calls of recursive calls etc. As in other cases, we will simply count the number of operations performed. The only operations mentioned in the algorithm are addition, subtraction, division, assignment, tests for equality or "less than," and the array access operation.

Let *n* be the number of elements in the array segment being searched (i.e., the value of size). We want to know how many operations the algorithm will perform in the worst case. As it turns out, the worst case is when the target is not in the array so we will assume that target is not in the array.

one operation

When the algorithm starts out, it tests to see if the array segment is empty (size == 0). This is a stopping case for the recursion. We'll charge one operation for this test for emptiness.

three more operations

After that, the algorithm computes the midpoint index as follows:

```
middle = first + size/2;
```

This adds an additional three operations, one each of division, addition, and assignment.

two more operations

Next the algorithm tests to see whether the target equals a[middle]. This requires one array access, and one application of ==, and so counts as two more operations.

another two operations

We are assuming that the target is not in the array. So the algorithm then goes on to do the comparison:

```
(target < a[middle])
```

This also requires 2 operations—one for the array access and one for the comparison.

ten more operations

The algorithm then makes a recursive call, which requires a few operations to provide the arguments. The exact number of operations depends on the way function calls are implemented, but ten operations should handle all the arithmetic and passing of arguments. And, of course, there will be the operations carried out by the recursive call, but we have not begun to worry about that yet.

If we total up all the operations used, we've estimated that the algorithm performs no more than 18 operations before each recursive call. The recursive call can produce another recursive call, which in turn produces another recursive call, which in turn produces another recursive call, until the procedure gets to a stopping case. Each of these recursive calls is preceded by 18 (or fewer) operations. The total number of operations is thus no more than 18 times the length of this chain of recursive calls plus the number of operations performed in the stopping case. Using the symbol $T(n)$ for the worst-case running time to search an array of n elements, we therefore have:

$T(n) = 18 \times$ (the length of the longest chain of recursive calls)
$+$
the number of operations performed in the stopping case

There are two possible stopping cases—when the size becomes zero, or when the target is found. Since the worst case is when the key is not in the array, we assume that the key is not found. The stopping case when the key is not found requires three operations (an array access, an equality test, and an assignment to found).

Thus, the running time function can be expressed by

$T(n) = 18 \times$ (the length of the longest chain of recursive calls) + 3

There is a standard term for the long phrase in parentheses, namely **the depth of recursive calls**:

Depth of Recursive Calls

The length of the longest chain of recursive calls in the execution of an algorithm is called the **depth of recursive calls** for that algorithm.

This definition allows us to replace the long phrase in our formula with this standard term and so obtain the slightly more compact formula:

$T(n) = 18 \times$ (the depth of recursive calls) + 3

Rather than compute the exact value for the depth of recursive calls, we will determine an upper bound approximation to the number of recursive calls. The figure we obtain may be slightly larger than the actual number of calls but will be a close approximation. This is common practice when analyzing running times. It is often easier to calculate an upper bound than it is to calculate the exact running time. As long as we use an upper bound so that we are estimating higher than the true value, then we will always be safe. This way our algorithm might turn out to be a bit faster than we thought, but never slower. Now let us calculate this upper bound on the length of the longest string of recursive calls.

The array contains n elements to be searched. Each recursive call is made on an array segment that contains, at most, half of the elements. Hence, to approximate the depth of recursive calls, all we need to do is determine how many times we can divide n in half, and then divide that half in half again, then divide that result in half yet again, and so on until the array is "all gone." The array is "all gone" when there are no entries to divide in half (that is, when size is zero). Thus:

Depth of Recursive Calls for Binary Search of an *n*-Element Array

The depth of recursive calls is, at most, the number of times that *n* can be divided by two, stopping when the result is less than one.

We can now estimate the number of operations performed by the binary search algorithm on an array with n elements. We know that the number of operations performed is at most

$$T(n) = 18 \times \text{(the depth of recursive calls)} + 3$$

$$= 18 \times \text{(the number of times that } n \text{ can be divided by two, stopping when the result is less than one)} + 3$$

Let us denote the second expression in parentheses by $H(n)$ and call it the **halving function.** In other words:

The Halving Function

The **halving function** *H*(*n*) is defined by *H*(*n*) = (the number of times that *n* can be divided by two, stopping when the result is less than one).

With this new definition, we can express our estimate of the running time for the binary search algorithm compactly. The worst-case running time is closely approximated by:

$$T(n) = 18\,H(n) + 3$$

To get a feel for how fast or slow this running time is, we must know a little about this function $H(n)$. As it turns out $H(n)$ is almost exactly equal to the base 2 logarithm of n, which is written $\log_2 n$. To be even more precise, for any positive integer n:

Value of the Halving Function

$H(n)$ = (the number of times that n can be divided by two, stopping when the result is less than one) has the value:
$$H(n) = \lfloor \log_2 n \rfloor$$

The symbols $\lfloor \ \rfloor$ mean that we round fractional numbers down to the next lowest whole number. For example, $\lfloor 3.7 \rfloor$ is 3. The notation $\lfloor \ \rfloor$ is called the **floor function**, and we have used it before in Chapter 1 when we noted that the number of digits in a positive integer n is $\lfloor \log_{10} n \rfloor + 1$. Since $H(n)$ is a whole number and $\log_2 n$ might include a fractional part, they cannot always be exactly equal, but the above equality means that $H(n)$ and $\log_2 n$ will never differ by more than one. Let's explore what this equality tells us about the running time of binary search.

For an array with n elements ($n > 0$), we have seen that the worst-case running time of the binary search algorithm is:

$$T(n) = 18\,H(n) + 3 = 18\,(\lfloor \log_2 n \rfloor + 1) + 3$$

If we throw out the constants, the result says that the worst-case running time is *logarithmic* (that is, $O(\log n)$).

Worst-Case Time for Binary Search

For an array of n elements, the worst-case time for binary search is logarithmic.

An algorithm with logarithmic running time is fast because the logarithm of n is much smaller than n. Moreover, the larger that n is, the more dramatic this difference becomes. For example, the base two logarithm of 2 is 1, the base two logarithm of 8 is 3, the base two logarithm of 64 is 6, the base two logarithm of a thousand is less than 10, and the base two logarithm of a million is less than 20.

This means that the binary search algorithm is very efficient. On an array with a thousand elements our binary search algorithm with a running time of $18\,(\lfloor \log_2 n \rfloor + 1) + 3$ will perform no more than 183 operations. Even with a million entries, the worst-case time is fewer than 400 operations.

binary search is an O(log n) algorithm

*average time is
also O(log n)*

We won't give a rigorous analysis of the average running time for binary search, but we can tell you that the average running time for actually finding a number is $O(\log n)$. It is not hard to see why this is true. We have already seen that, when a target is not found, the depth of recursion is $\lfloor \log_2 n \rfloor + 1$. In the worst case, even a found target requires a recursion depth of $\lceil \log_2 n \rceil$ (just one less than not finding a target). In some cases, the algorithm will not need that many recursive calls. If the sought-after target is found, the algorithm can terminate without additional recursive calls. Thus, on some inputs the depth of recursive calls will be 0, on others it will be 1, on others 2, and so forth up to $\lfloor \log_2 n \rfloor$. However, a more complete analysis would show that nearly half the keys in the array end up taking a recursion depth of $\lfloor \log_2 n \rfloor$. Even if the other half of the keys had no recursion at all, this would still result in an *average* recursion depth of one half of $\lfloor \log_2 n \rfloor$. Thus, the average number of recursive calls for finding a key is at least one half of $\lfloor \log_2 n \rfloor$ So, the average case can only save us a factor of ½ or less over the worst case. But constants like ½ do not matter in big-O expressions, therefore the average-case running time is $O(\log n)$, the same as the worst-case running time.

Self-Test Exercises

1. Reimplement the search function from Figure 12.2 on page 539 as a serial search. Use the pseudocode from Figure 12.1 on page 534, and make appropriate adjustments to the precondition/postcondition contract.

2. This exercise requires familiarity with template functions (Section 6.1). Rewrite the search function from Figure 12.2 on page 539 so that it is a template function. There is a template parameter for the type of the array's component.

3. Consider the search function from Figure 12.2 on page 539. Rewrite the function so that there is no `size` parameter. Instead, there is a parameter called `last`, which is the last index of the array segment that is being searched. Your precondition may require `first <= last`.

4. Compute the following values (H is the halving function): $H(1)$, $H(2)$, $H(4)$, $H(7)$, $H(8)$, $H(9)$.

12.2   OPEN-ADDRESS HASHING

In this section we will present another approach to storing and searching for values. The technique, called *hashing,* has a worst-case behavior that is linear for finding a target, but with some care, hashing can be dramatically fast in the average case. Hashing also makes it easy to add and delete elements from the collection that is being searched, providing an advantage over binary search (since binary search must ensure that the entire list stays sorted when elements are added or deleted).

Introduction to Hashing

The Sixth Column Tractor Company sells all kinds of tractors with various stock numbers, prices, and other details. They want us to store information about each tractor in an inventory so that they can later retrieve information about any particular tractor simply by entering its stock number. To be specific, suppose the information about each tractor is an object of the following form, with the stock number stored in the key field:

```
struct Tractor
{
    int key;            //  The stock number
    double cost;        //  The price, in dollars
    int horsepower;     //  Size of the engine
};
```

We call each of these objects a tractor **record.** Of course there might be other information in each tractor record, but this will do for our example.

If the stock numbers have values ranging from 0 to 49, we could store the records in an array of the following type, placing stock number i in location data[i]:

```
Tractor data[50]; // Array of 50 tractor records
```

The record for stock number i can be retrieved immediately since we know it is in data[i].

But what if the stock numbers do not form a neat range like 0...49. Suppose that we know there will be 50 or fewer different stock numbers, but that they will be distributed in the range 0 through 4999. We could use an array with 5000 components, but that seems wasteful since only a small fraction of the array would be used. It appears that we have no alternative but to store the records in an array with 50 elements and to use a serial search through the array whenever we wish to find a particular stock number. Things are not that bad. If we are clever, we can store the records in a relatively small array and yet retrieve particular stock numbers much faster than we would by serial search.

To illustrate the trick involved, suppose that an inside informer at the Sixth Column Tractor Company tells us that the stock numbers will be these:

```
0, 100, 200, 300, ... 4800, 4900
```

In this case, we can store the records in an array called data with only 50 components. The record with stock number i can be stored at this location:

```
data[i / 100]
```

With the aid of integer division, we can make do with the indexes 0 through 49, even though the numbers become as large as 4900. If we want stock number

700, we compute 700/100 and obtain the index 7. The record for stock number 700 is stored in array component data[7].

This general technique is called **hashing.** Each record requires a unique identifying value called its **key**. In our example, the key was the stock number that was stored in a member variable called key, but other, more complex keys are sometimes used. A function, called the **hash function,** maps key values to array indexes. Suppose we name our hash function hash. If a record has a key value of i, then we will try to store that record at location data[hash(i)]. Using the hash function to compute the correct array index is called **hashing the key to an array index.** The hash function must be chosen so that its return value is always a valid index for the array. The hash function may be either a declared C++ function or a simple arithmetic expression. In our example, hash(i) was this expression:

hash function

```
i / 100
```

collisions

In our example, every key produced a different index value when it was hashed. That is a perfect hash function, but unfortunately a perfect hash function cannot always be found. Suppose we change the example so that we no longer have stock number 400, but we have 399 instead. Then the record with stock number 300 will be placed in data[3] as before, but where will stock number 399 be placed? Stock number 399 is supposed to be placed in data[399/100]. In other words, the record for stock number 399 is supposed to be placed in data[3]. There are now two different records that belong in data[3]. This situation is known as a **collision.** In this case we could redefine the hash function to avoid the collision. But in practice, you do not know the exact numbers that will occur as keys, and therefore you cannot design a hash function that is guaranteed to be free of collisions (unless, perhaps, your insider at the tractor company has a lot of pull). Something must be done to cope with the tractor collisions.

Typically you do not know what numbers will be used as the key values, but you do know an upper bound on how many there will be. The usual approach is to use an array size that is larger than needed—later we will see formulas that indicate how many extra positions are needed. The extra array positions make collisions less likely. A good hash function will distribute the key values uniformly through the index range of the array. If the array indexes range from 0 to 99, then you might use the following hash function to produce an array index for a record with a given key:

```
key % 100
```

This hash function always produces a value in the range 0 to 99 (that is, the remainder when key is divided by 100).

dealing with collisions

One way of dealing with collisions is the algorithm given at the top of the next page.

// Basic storage by hashing algorithm

1. For a record with key value given by `key`, compute the index `hash(key)`.

2. If `data[hash(key)]` does not already contain a record, then store the record in `data[hash(key)]` and end the storage algorithm.

3. If the location `data[hash(key)]` already contains a record, then try `data[hash(key)+1]`. If that location already contains a record, try `data[hash(key)+2]`, and so forth until a vacant position is found. When the highest numbered array position is reached, simply go to the start of the array. For example, if the array indexes are 0...99, and 98 is the key, then try 98, 99, 0, 1, and so on, in that order.

This storage algorithm is called **open-address hashing,** or more simply **open addressing.** In open addressing, collisions are resolved by placing the item in the next *open* spot of the array. Open addressing requires that the array be initialized so that the program can test to see if an array position already contains a record. For example, if the key will always be a non-negative integer, the key field of each array element can be initialized to a negative number, perhaps −1. As long as the key field contains a negative number, the program knows that the array location does not contain a record.

The Table ADT—Specification

Storage by hashing forms the basis to implement a new container class called a table. A **table** is a container of records with operations for inserting, deleting, and locating records. This sounds a lot like a bag, but the difference is that each table operation is controlled by a single key field of the record rather than being controlled by the entire item value.

The `Table` class will actually be a template class that depends on the data type of the records that are being stored. We use the name `RecordType` for the name of these records, so the actual `Table` class definition will begin like this:

```
template <class RecordType>
class Table
{  ...
```

We place some requirements on the `RecordType`: It must have a public integer member called `key`, and this member holds the key of each record. Each key must be a non-negative integer, and two different records cannot have the same key.

We will implement the table using a hash function as we outlined above. When a table is implemented in this way, it is called a **hash table.** The next few paragraphs specify the five operations for our `Table` class.

The constructor. The `Table` class has a default constructor that creates a table with a capacity of 811 records. The number 811 will be defined as a static constant named CAPACITY in the Table class. There are several ways that we could allow for larger tables, but we will postpone that in order to focus on the table mechanism itself. So, a typical Table declaration using the Tractor data type would be as follows:

```
Table<Tractor> deere;  // Can hold up to 811 tractors
```

The insert function. The Table class has an insert function to place a new record into the table. There are two possible outcomes from an insertion:

- There might already be a record with the same key as the new record. In this case, the old record is replaced by the new record with the same key.
- If the new record has a key that is not already in the table, then the new record is added to the table.

The specification of the insert member function is shown here:

```
void insert(const RecordType& entry);
// Precondition: entry.key >= 0. Also if entry.key is not already a
// key in the table, then the table has space for another record
// (that is, size( ) < CAPACITY).
// Postcondition: If the table already had a record with a key
// equal to entry.key, then that record is replaced by entry.
// Otherwise entry has been added as a new record of the table.
```

The precondition requires that entry.key is a valid key (not negative), and if the key is a new key, then the table must not be already full (otherwise there won't be room for the new record).

The is_present and find functions. There are two constant functions called is_present and find. These functions search the table for a record with a particular key. Here are the specifications of the member functions:

```
bool is_present(int key) const;
// Postcondition: The return value is true if the table contains a record with
// the specified key. Otherwise the return value is false.
```

```
void find(int key, bool& found, RecordType& result) const;
// Postcondition: If the table contains a record with the specified key, then
// result is a copy of the record with that key, and found is true.
// Otherwise found is false, and the result contains garbage.
```

The remove function. This function removes a particular record from the table. Here is the specification of the member function:

```
void remove(int key);
// Postcondition: If a record was in the table with the specified key, then
// that record has been removed. Otherwise the table is unchanged.
```

The Table ADT—Design

Now we'll move on to the design and implementation of our `Table` class. The complete header file for this first version of our table is shown in Figure 12.3.

FIGURE 12.3 | Header File for the Table Template Class

A Header File

```
// FILE: table1.h
// TEMPLATE CLASS PROVIDED: Table<RecordType>
//    This class is a container template class for a Table of records.
//    The template parameter, RecordType, is the data type of the records in the Table. It may
//    be any of the built-in C++ types (int, char, etc.), or a class with a default constructor, a
//    copy constructor, an assignment operator, and an integer member variable called key.
//
// MEMBER CONSTANT for the Table<RecordType> template class:
//    static const size_t CAPACITY = _____
//       Table::CAPACITY is the maximum number of records that a Table can hold.
//
// CONSTRUCTOR for the Table<RecordType> template class:
//    Table( )
//       Postcondition: The Table has been initialized as an empty Table.
//
// MODIFICATION MEMBER FUNCTIONS for the Table<RecordType> class:
//    void insert(const RecordType& entry)
//       Precondition: entry.key >= 0. Also if entry.key is not already a key in the table, then
//       the Table has space for another record (that is, size( ) < CAPACITY).
//       Postcondition: If the table already had a record with a key equal to entry.key, then that
//       record is replaced by entry. Otherwise, entry has been added as a new record of the
//       Table.
//
//    void remove(int key)
//       Postcondition: If a record was in the Table with the specified key, then that record has
//       been removed. Otherwise the table is unchanged.
//
// CONSTANT MEMBER FUNCTIONS for the Table<RecordType> class:
//    bool is_present(int key) const
//       Postcondition: The return value is true if there is a record in the Table with the
//       specified key. Otherwise, the return value is false.
//
//    void find(int key, bool& found, RecordType& result) const
//       Postcondition: If a record is in the Table with the specified key, then found is true, and
//       result is set to a copy of the record with that key. Otherwise found is false,
//       and the result contains garbage.
```

(continued)

(FIGURE 12.3 continued)

```
//
//      size_t size( ) const
//          Postcondition: Return value is the total number of records in the Table.
//
// VALUE SEMANTICS for the Table<RecordType> template class:
//    Assignments and the copy constructor may be used with Table<RecordType> objects.
#ifndef TABLE1_H
#define TABLE1_H
#include <stdlib.h>       // Provides size_t
    template <class RecordType>
    class Table
    {
    public:
        // MEMBER CONSTANT -- See Appendix E if this fails to compile.
        static const size_t CAPACITY = 811;
        // CONSTRUCTOR
        Table( );
        // MODIFICATION MEMBER FUNCTIONS
        void insert(const RecordType& entry);
        void remove(int key);
        // CONSTANT MEMBER FUNCTIONS
        bool is_present(int key) const;
        void find(int key, bool& found, RecordType& result) const;
        size_t size( ) const { return used; }
    private:
        // MEMBER CONSTANTS -- These are used in the key field of special records.
        static const int NEVER_USED = -1;
        static const int PREVIOUSLY_USED = -2;
        // MEMBER VARIABLES
        RecordType data[CAPACITY];
        size_t used;
        // HELPER FUNCTIONS
        size_t hash(int key) const;
        size_t next_index(size_t index) const;
        void find_index(int key, bool& found, size_t& index) const;
        bool never_used(size_t index) const;
        bool is_vacant(size_t index) const;
    };

#include "table1.template" // Include the implementation.
#endif
```

table1.h   **FTP**

Invariant for the Table ADT. The records of the table are stored in an array called data, which is a private member variable. The number of array locations actually being used is stored in the private member variable used. Here is our complete invariant:

Invariant for the Table ADT

1. The number of records in the table is in the member variable used.

2. The actual records of the table are stored in the array data, with a maximum of CAPACITY entries. Each used spot in the array has a non-negative key. An unused record in the array has its key field set to the constant NEVER_USED (if it has never been used) or the constant PREVIOUSLY_USED (if it once was used but is now vacant).

The second rule of the invariant needs some discussion. We have restricted valid keys to be non-negative integers. So, any unused spot in the array can be indicated by using a negative key. It turns out that we'll gain some efficiency if we distinguish between two different kinds of negative keys. We will use the constant NEVER_USED (defined as −1) in the key field to indicate a location that has *never* held a record. On the other hand, the constant PREVIOUSLY_USED (defined as −2) in the key field indicates a location that once held a record that has since been removed. You'll see the purpose of NEVER_USED versus PREVIOUSLY_USED when we implement the find function.

Five private member functions. The table definition also has five private member functions. We think these five functions will be useful for the implementation, but they are not part of the public interface. We don't want other programmers to use these functions; they are just for our own use in implementing a specific kind of table—a hash table. We have used similar "helper" functions in the past (such as next_index for one of the queue classes in Chapter 8).

The first helper function is the hash function, called hash. The function takes a key (which is an *int*) and hashes the key to an array index.

The second helper function, called next_index, is used to step through the array one index after the other with wraparound at the end. The function call next_index(i) usually returns i + 1, with one exception. When i is equal to the last index of the array, next_index(i) returns the first index of the array (zero).

The third helper function, find_index, is intended to find the array index of a record with a particular key. The function call find_index(key, found, i) searches for a record with the specified key. If such a record is found, the function sets the reference argument found to true and sets i to the index of the record. Otherwise the function sets found to false and leaves i as garbage. This helper function is similar to the public find member function. The difference is that find returns a copy of the record with the specified key, whereas find_index returns the array index of the record that contains the specified key. The find_index function is useful for the implementor of the ADT because the implementor often needs to know where a particular record is located in the array. On the other hand, the programmer who uses the ADT doesn't need to know where a record is stored—in fact, that programmer doesn't even know that the records happen to be stored in an array.

The last two helper functions are boolean functions. The value of never_used(i) is true if data[i] has never been used (indicated by the NEVER_USED value in its key field). The value of is_vacant(i) is true if data[i] is not currently being used (indicated by any negative value in the key field).

Programming Tip: Using size_t Can Indicate a Value's Purpose

Can you tell that the return value of the hash function is intended to be used as an array index? Yes, you can—because the return value is a size_t value (rather than a mere *int*). In a similar manner, both the parameter and the return value of next_index are size_t values, because both of these items are array indexes. The parameters of find_index, never_used, and is_vacant follow the same practice.

We use size_t values for array indexes because doing so helps us easily identify the purpose of various values. Later, we could change the type of the keys to something other than an *int*, but each of the size_t values (used for array indexes and sizes) would remain size_t.

You should consistently use size_t for values that are array indexes or array sizes. This helps you quickly identify the purpose of a value. In the case of the hash table, you are using size_t for array indexes and array sizes, but you are using *int* for the key values. Later, if we change to a different type of key, it will be easy to see which things to change and which to leave alone.

The Table ADT—Implementation

The definition for the table template class has been written, and we know the ADT's invariant. The actual implementation is fairly straightforward because there is no use of dynamic memory. We'll discuss the functions one at a time.

The constructor. Most of the table constructor's work involves filling the key fields of each array component with NEVER_USED, to indicate that the locations are not now used and have never been used previously. The constructor will also set `used` to zero.

The `insert` member function. The insert member function uses two local variables: (1) A boolean variable, called `already_present`, is set to true or false to indicate whether there is already an entry with the same key as the new entry. (2) A `size_t` variable, called `index`, is set so that `data[index]` is the right location for the new entry. The complete pseudocode has three steps:

1. `find_index(entry.key, already_present, index);`

2. *if* `(!already_present)`
   2a. Check that the size of the array is less than its capacity.
   2b. Use a loop to set `index` so that `data[index]` is the first vacant location at or after `data[hash(entry.key)]`. If the loop reaches the end of the array, then it should continue searching at `data[0]`.
   2c. `used++;`

3. `data[index] = entry;`

This pseudocode is implemented in the top of Figure 12.4 on page 554. Notice that the loop in Step 2b uses this assignment statement:

```
index = next_index(index);
```

This assignment moves `index` to the next available array index, wrapping back to the start of the array when `index` reaches the last valid array index. Also notice how the insert works if there is already a record with the same key as the new entry. In this case, the new entry replaces the old record (and the private member variable `used` remains unchanged).

The `remove` member function. In our insert function, we made use of the helper function, `find_index`. This function also simplifies the remove function, which has only two steps in its pseudocode (using local variables `found` and `index`):

1. `find_index(key, found, index);`

2. *if* `(found)`
   Remove the entry by setting `data[index].key` to `PREVIOUSLY_USED` (indicating a spot that's no longer used), and subtract 1 from `used`.

The `remove` implementation appears in the bottom of Figure 12.4 on page 554.

FIGURE 12.4	Implementation of the `insert` and `remove` Functions for the Open-Address Hash Table

Two Function Implementations

```
template <class RecordType>
void Table<RecordType>::insert(const RecordType& entry)
// Library facilities used: assert.h
{
    bool already_present;    // True if entry.key is already in the table
    size_t index;            // data[index] is location for the new entry

    assert(entry.key >= 0);

    // Set index so that data[index] is the spot to place the new entry.
    find_index(entry.key, already_present, index);

    // If the key wasn't already there, then find the location for the new entry.
    if (!already_present)
    {
        assert(size( ) < CAPACITY);
        index = hash(entry.key);
        while (!is_vacant(index))
            index = next_index(index);
        used++;
    }

    data[index] = entry;
}


template <class RecordType>
void Table<RecordType>::remove(int key)
// Library facilities used: assert.h
{
    bool found;      // True if key occurs somewhere in the table
    size_t index;    // Spot where data[index].key == key

    assert(key >= 0);

    find_index(key, found, index);
    if (found)
    {   // The key was found, so remove this record and reduce used by 1.
        data[index].key = PREVIOUSLY_USED; // Indicates a spot that's no longer in use.
        used--;
    }
}
```

table1.template	**FTP**

The `find_index` function. We have pushed a substantial amount of work into the `find_index` function, which we will now implement. The function is responsible for finding the location in the array that contains a particular key value. Here is the full specification of the private member function:

```
void find_index(int key, bool& found, size_t& index) const;
// Precondition: key >= 0.
// Postcondition: If a record is in the table with the specified key, then
// found is true, and index is set so that data[index].key is the specified
// key. Otherwise found is false, and i is garbage.
```

The function begins by hashing the key value to an array index and assigning this index to its reference parameter, `i`. The function then uses a loop to advance `i` through the array until we find the key or we determine that the key is not in the array. If the loop finds the key, then the index `i` will be exactly at the spot where `data[i].key == key`, so the function can set `found` to true and return. On the other hand, if `data[i]` is not equal to `key`, then the function should set `found` to false before returning.

In our description of this work, just what does it mean to "determine that the key is not in the array"? One possibility is that we have examined every record in the array without finding the key. But sometimes it is possible to determine that the key is not in the array even though some records have not been examined. Recall that if there is a record with its key equal to the parameter `key`, then this record should be in position `hash(key)` or in the first available position after that. Our function starts searching at array index `hash(key)`. Should it ever encounter a position that has *never* held a record, then we have an interesting fact: If the key were ever inserted in the array, then it would have been inserted at or before this vacant spot. Hence, the function knows that it has looked at every place that the key could possibly occur. Therefore, in the `find_index` implementation, the loop terminates if it reaches a position that has never been used, as shown in this implementation of the loop (`count` is a local variable that keeps track of how many records we have examined):

```
count = 0;
i = hash(key);
while((count < CAPACITY) && (!never_used(i)) && (data[i].key != key))
{
    count++;
    i = next_index(i);
}
```

Notice that this technique for terminating the search cannot simply stop when it encounters a position that is *currently* vacant, but the loop must continue until it encounters a position that has *never* held a record.

The `find_index` implementation is shown as part of the complete implementation file in Figure 12.5. The figure also implements all the other member functions that we have not yet discussed.

An Implementation File

```
// FILE: table1.template
// TEMPLATE CLASS IMPLEMENTED: Table (See table1.h for documentation.)
// INVARIANT for the Table ADT:
//     1. The number of records in the Table is in the member variable used.
//     2. The actual records of the table are stored in the array data, with a maximum of
//        CAPACITY entries. Each used spot in the array has a non-negative key. Any unused
//        record in the array has a key field of NEVER_USED (if it has never been used) or
//        PREVIOUSLY_USED (if it once was used, but is now vacant).

#include <assert.h> // Provides assert
#include <stdlib.h> // Provides size_t

template <class RecordType>
Table<RecordType>::Table( )
// Library facilities used: stdlib.h
{
    size_t i;

    used = 0;
    for (i = 0; i < CAPACITY; i++)
        data[i].key = NEVER_USED;   // Indicates a spot that's never been used.
}

template <class RecordType>
void Table<RecordType>::insert(const RecordType& entry)
|| See the implementation in Figure 12.4 on page 554.

template <class RecordType>
void Table<RecordType>::remove(int key)
|| See the implementation in Figure 12.4 on page 554.

template <class RecordType>
bool Table<RecordType>::is_present(int key) const
|| See the solution to Self-Test Exercise 5 on page 567.

template <class RecordType>
void Table<RecordType>::find(int key, bool& found, RecordType& result) const
// Library facilities used: assert.h, stdlib.h
{
    size_t index;

    assert(key >= 0);

    find_index(key, found, index);
    if (found)
        result = data[index];
}
```

(continued)

(FIGURE 12.5 continued)

```
template <class RecordType>
inline size_t Table<RecordType>::hash(int key) const
// Library facilities used: stdlib.h
// Postcondition: The return value is the hash value for the given key.
{
    return (key % CAPACITY);
}


template <class RecordType>
inline size_t Table<RecordType>::next_index(size_t index) const
// Library facilities used: stdlib.h
// Precondition: index < CAPACITY.
// Postcondition: The return value is either index+1 (if this is less than CAPACITY) or zero
// (if index+1 equals CAPACITY).
{
    return ((index+1) % CAPACITY);
}


template <class RecordType>
void Table<RecordType>::find_index(int key, bool& found, size_t& i) const
// Library facilities used: stdlib.h
// Precondition: key >= 0.
// Postcondition: If a record is in the table with the specified key, then found is true and index
// is set so that data[index].key is the specified key. Otherwise found is false, and i is garbage.
{
    size_t count;  // Number of entries that have been examined

    count = 0;
    i = hash(key);
    while((count < CAPACITY) && (!never_used(i)) && (data[i].key != key))
    {
        count++;
        i = next_index(i);
    }
    found = (data[i].key == key);
}


template <class RecordType>
inline bool Table<RecordType>::never_used(size_t index) const
|| See the solution to Self-Test Exercise 6 on page 568.


template <class RecordType>
inline bool Table<RecordType>::is_vacant(size_t index) const
|| See the solution to Self-Test Exercise 6 on page 568.
```

| table1.template | **FTP** |

C++ *Feature:* Inline Functions in the Implementation File

Four of the five `Table` helper functions are short—just one line of code each. Because of their shortness, you might want to provide quicker execution by declaring the helper functions to be inline member functions. On the other hand, you could be unwilling to put the implementations of the functions in the header file (where we have previously put inline member functions). After all, a programmer who uses the `Table` class doesn't need to know about the helper functions and certainly doesn't need to see their implementations.

In such a case, you can get the best of both worlds by putting the implementations in the usual implementation file and including the keyword *inline* just before the function definition. For example, here is the start of one of the helper functions from the implementation file of Figure 12.5:

```
template <class RecordType>
inline size_t Table<RecordType>::hash(int key) const
```

The keyword *inline* causes most compilers to provide a faster implementation of the short function (by avoiding the actual function call and putting the code for the function body at each location where the function is called).

Remember, you do not normally provide documentation for a helper function in the header file. Instead, the documentation goes with the implementation in the implementation file, where it can help the programmer who is implementing the class.

Choosing a Hash Function to Reduce Collisions

We have used a simple hash function that hashes a given key to the array index:

```
key % CAPACITY
```

This kind of hash function depends on the remainder upon division, and is therefore called a **division hash function.**

With a division hash function, certain table sizes are better than others at avoiding collisions that arise in data taken from real examples. C.E. Radke's 1970 study suggests that a good choice is a table size that is a prime number of the form $4k+3$. For example, 811 is a prime number equal to $(4 \times 202) + 3$.

Although division hash functions are the most common, you may sometimes encounter data that produces many collisions regardless of the table size. In this case, you can try two other common kinds of hash functions:

- **Mid-square hash function:** The key is multiplied by itself. The hash function returns some middle digits of the result.
- **Multiplicative hash function:** The key is multiplied by a constant less than one. The hash function returns the first few digits of the fractional part of the result.

Double Hashing to Reduce Clustering

Consider what happens during an insertion with a collision. The insertion function moves forward from the original index until a vacant spot is found in the array. For example, suppose that a new key hashes to location 330, but this location is full. Then the insertion tries 331, then 332, then 333, and so on. Searching for a vacant spot in this manner is called **linear probing.**

There is a problem with linear probing. When several different keys are hashed to the same array location, the result is a small cluster of elements, one after another. As the table approaches its capacity, these clusters tend to merge into larger and larger clusters. This is the problem of **clustering.** If the key values happen to be consecutive numbers (such as a run of consecutive stock numbers in an inventory), then a "division hash function" makes clustering even worse. As clustering gets worse, insertions take longer because the insert function must step all the way through a cluster to find a vacant location. Elements are inserted farther and farther from their correct hashed index, and searches require more time.

The most common technique to avoid clustering is called **double hashing.** The technique uses a second hash function to determine how we move through an array to resolve a collision. To see how this works, let's call the original hash function `hash1`, and call the second hash function `hash2`. When an item is inserted, double hashing begins by hashing the key to an array index using `hash1`. If there is a collision, then we calculate `hash2(key)` using the result to tell us how far forward to move through the array in looking for a vacant spot. For example, suppose that a new key hashes to location 330, and that `hash2(key)` is 7. If location 330 is occupied, then we move forward 7 spots and try location 337. If 337 is also occupied, then we move forward another 7 spots to location 344, and so on.

As we are stepping through the array, adding `hash2(key)` to the index at each step, there are two considerations:

- The array index must not leave the valid range of 0 to `CAPACITY - 1`. We can keep the index in this range with the "%" operation. In particular, suppose that `i` is the index that we have just examined (with a collision). Then the next index to examine is:

    `(i + hash2(key)) % CAPACITY`

    For example, suppose that `CAPACITY` is 811, and `hash2(key)` is 14. If a new key hashes to spot 787, and there is a collision, then the next few spots that we will try are 801, then 4, then 18, then 32. Notice that the "4" is calculated as (801 + 14) % `CAPACITY`.

- As we step through the array, we must ensure that every array position is examined. With double hashing, this is a potential problem. We could come back to our starting position before we have examined every available location. There is an easy way to avoid this problem: Make sure that the array's capacity is *relatively prime* with respect to the value returned by hash2 (in other words, these two numbers must not have any common factors, apart from 1). One way to accomplish this is to choose CAPACITY as a prime number, and have hash2 return values in the range 1 through CAPACITY - 1. With this in mind, the preeminent computer scientist Donald Knuth suggests the following possibility:

1. Both CAPACITY and CAPACITY - 2 should be prime numbers. For example, 811 is prime and so is 809. (Two such primes, separated by 2, are called **twin primes**.)

2. hash1(key) = key % CAPACITY.

3. hash2(key) = 1 + (key % (CAPACITY-2)).

With our Table class from Figure 12.3 on page 549, double hashing can be incorporated in several ways. The easiest approach is to add another private member function to compute hash2, and change next_index to return:

```
(i + hash2(key)) % CAPACITY
```

This next_index function needs key as another parameter.

At this point, you know enough to implement open-address hashing with linear probing or with double hashing. We'll delay the analysis of hashing until after the presentation of *chaining*, which is another way to resolve collisions.

Self-Test Exercises

5. Write the table's is_present member function.

6. Write the two table helper functions: never_used and is_vacant. These functions appear in the implementation file of Figure 12.5 on page 556, but they are also inline functions (as described in the C++ Feature on page 558). Your implementations should include a precondition/postcondition contract. The never_used function returns true if data[index] has never been used. The is_vacant function returns true if data[index] is not currently being used.

7. Suppose that a hash table is full and you try to insert a new entry. What happens if the new entry's key is already in the table? What happens if the new entry's key is not already in the table?

8. In the implementation of the table's find_index function, the function may sometimes find a key field with a value of −2. Why does the function need to continue to search?

9. An empty hash table has a capacity of 100, and you insert 6 entries with keys 100, 0, 1199, 1299, 1399, and 2. Using linear probing and a division hash function, where will these entries be placed in the table? Where will they be placed with double hashing (with hash2(key) returning the value 1 + (key % 98)).

10. Write a quick program to determine whether there is a pair of twin primes between 1200 and 1250, with the upper prime having the form $4k+3$ for some k. With this information, can you suggest a good size for a hash table that uses double hashing and has a capacity around 1225?

12.3 CHAINED HASHING

In open-address hashing, a collision is handled by probing the array for an unused position. Each array component can hold just one entry. When the array is full, no more items can be added to the table. We could handle this problem by resizing the array and rehashing all the entries, placing each entry in a new larger array. But this would require a careful choice of the new size and probably require each entry to have a new hash value computed. A better approach is to use a different collision resolution method called chained hashing.

In **chained hashing,** also called **chaining,** each component of the hash table's array can hold more than one entry. As with all hashing, we still hash the key of each entry to obtain an array index. But if there is a collision, we don't worry too much. We simply place the new entry in its proper array component along with other entries that happened to hash to the same array index.

How does chaining place more than one entry in each component of the array? The answer is that each array component must have some underlying structure. For example, each component of the array could be a List (using the List ADT that we first implemented in Chapter 3). The most common structure that you will see for the array's components is to have each `data[i]` be a head pointer for a linked list. The nodes of the linked list each have an `Item` that is the `RecordType` of the table, as diagrammed here:

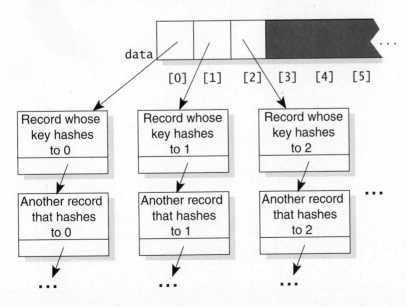

In this scheme, all the records that hash to location i are placed on the linked list, which has its head pointer stored in data[i]. To maintain the linked lists, we can use the template version of our linked list toolkit (from Section 6.4). With this approach, the Table class definition is shown in Figure 12.6.

In the figure we have included the file link2.h from Figure 6.7 on page 292 to provide the linked list toolkit. We also have defined a static member constant called TABLE_SIZE, which determines the size of the table's array. In our example, the size is 811, so that the data array consists of 811 head pointers for 811 linked lists. This array is declared as follows:

```
Node<RecordType> *data[TABLE_SIZE];
```

In other words, each list is a linked list of RecordType values. We used the name TABLE_SIZE rather than CAPACITY since "CAPACITY" suggests a limit to

---

FIGURE 12.6	Definition of the Table Template Class Using Chaining and the Linked List Toolkit

A Template Class Definition

```
#include "link2.h"          // Provides the Node type, from Figure 6.7 on page 292
template <class RecordType>
class Table
{
public:
    // MEMBER CONSTANT -- See Appendix E if this fails to compile.
    static const size_t TABLE_SIZE 811;
    // CONSTRUCTORS AND DESTRUCTOR
    Table( );
    Table(const Table& source);
    ~Table( );
    // MODIFICATION MEMBER FUNCTIONS
    void insert(const RecordType& entry);
    void remove(int key);
    void operator =(const Table& source);
    // CONSTANT MEMBER FUNCTIONS
    void find(int key, bool& found, RecordType& result) const;
    bool is_present(int key) const;
    size_t size( ) const { return total_records; }
  private
    Node<RecordType> *data[TABLE_SIZE];
    size_t total_records;
    // HELPER MEMBER FUNCTION
    size_t hash(int key) const;
};
```

Each component of the array is a head pointer for a linked list.

the number of entries—but in fact, the chaining hash table can hold more than `TABLE_SIZE` entries.

Our class definition has one other private member variable, `total_records`, which keeps track of the total number of records in all 811 linked lists. You can complete this implementation yourself.

Self-Test Exercises

11. Consider the chaining version of the table that we have described. What value will the constructor place in each component of `data`?

12. Write the insert member function for the chaining version of the table.

13. Use your insert function to place six items in a hash table with a table size of 811. Use the keys 811, 0, 1623, 2435, 3247, and 2.

14. In our new `Table` class, the array is still a fixed size. So why do we need the copy constructor, destructor, and overloaded assignment operator?

15. Suppose that the keys can be compared with the usual "less than" operator. Can you think of some advantage to keeping each linked list of the table sorted from smallest key to largest key?

12.4   TIME ANALYSIS OF HASHING

The worst-case for hashing occurs when every key gets hashed to the same array index. In this case, we may end up searching through all the items to find the one we are after—a linear operation, just like serial search. However, with some reasonable assumptions, the average time for a search of a hash table is dramatically fast, requiring us to examine just a handful of elements. This section provides the information needed for an average-time analysis of our three hashing methods.

The Load Factor of a Hash Table

The average-time performance of hashing is complex, particularly if deletions are allowed. However, Knuth's *The Art of Programming*, Volume 3, provides formulas that can guide our choice of hash-table algorithms. Knuth's most useful formulas provide the average number of table elements that must be examined during a successful search for a key. There are three different formulas for the three versions of hashing: open addressing with linear probing, open addressing with double hashing, and chained hashing.

These three formulas depend on how many items are in the table. When the table has many items, there are many collisions and the average time for a search is longer. With this in mind, we first define a fraction called the **load factor,** which is written α and defined by the formula at the top of the next page.

definition of the
load factor, α

$$\alpha = \frac{\text{Number of occupied table locations}}{\text{The size of the table's array}}$$

For open-address hashing, each array element holds at most one item, so the load factor can never exceed 1. But with chaining, each array position can hold many items, and the load factor might be higher than 1.

Average search time for open addressing (linear probing). Open-address hash tables with linear probing have just one hash function. Collisions are resolved by stepping forward, probing consecutive array elements. With linear probing, and no deletions, Knuth's formula for the average time of a successful search is:

Searching with Linear Probing

In open-address hashing with linear probing, a nonfull hash table, and no deletions, the average number of table elements examined in a successful search is approximately:

$$\frac{1}{2}\left(1 + \frac{1}{1-\alpha}\right)$$

This formula is not exact, but it is a good approximation when the load factor (α) is below 1. You might notice that the formula completely fails when α is 1, since there is then a division by zero. But, that situation would indicate a full hash table, and you should avoid getting close to full anyway. If you insist on a full hash table of n elements, Knuth shows that the average time for a successful search is approximately $\sqrt{n}\,(\pi/8)$ —but better yet, steer clear of full tables, and you can use the formula in the box above. In addition to a nonfull table, the formula's derivation also assumes that we have not deleted any items, and that the hash function does a good job of uniformly distributing all possible keys throughout the array (which is called **uniform hashing**).

As an example of how to use the formula, suppose that we plan to put 649 entries in a table with a capacity of 811. This provides a load average of 649/811, or about 80%. On average, we expect successful searches to examine three table elements, as shown here:

$$\frac{1}{2}\left(1 + \frac{1}{1-\alpha}\right) = \frac{1}{2}\left(1 + \frac{1}{1-0.8}\right) = 3.0$$

Average search time for open addressing (double hashing). You have seen that open-address hash tables with double hashing provide some relief from clustering. The result is a smaller average time, given by the following formula (which uses "ln" to denote the natural logarithm of a number):

Searching with Double Hashing

In open-address hashing with double hashing, a nonfull hash table, and no deletions, the average number of table elements examined in a successful search is approximately:

$$\frac{-\ln (1 - \alpha)}{\alpha}$$

As with the previous formula, this estimate is approximate. It depends on a nonfull hash table, no deletions, and using a hash function with uniform hashing.

You don't need to memorize the formula, but you should know how to use it along with the ln key on your calculator. For example, $\ln(0.2)$ is about -1.6, so with a load factor of 0.8 we expect to examine an average of two elements in a successful search, as shown here:

$$\frac{-\ln (1 - \alpha)}{\alpha} = \frac{-\ln (0.2)}{0.8} = \frac{1.6}{0.8} = 2$$

This is an improvement over the linear probing with the same load factor.

Average search time for chained hashing. With chaining, each element of the table's array is a head pointer for a linked list, and each of these linked lists may have several items. Therefore, the load factor may be higher than one in this formula:

Searching with Chained Hashing

In open-address hashing with chained hashing, the average number of table elements examined in a successful search is approximately:

$$1 + \frac{\alpha}{2}$$

Once again, this estimate is approximate, and it depends on using uniform hashing. Unlike the other two formulas, the chaining formula remains valid even with deletions.

FIGURE 12.7 Average Number of Table Elements Examined During a Successful Search

Load factor (α)	Open addressing with linear probing $\frac{1}{2}\left(1 + \frac{1}{1-\alpha}\right)$	Open addressing with double hashing $\frac{-\ln(1-\alpha)}{\alpha}$	Chained hashing $1 + \frac{\alpha}{2}$
0.5	1.50	1.39	1.25
0.6	1.75	1.53	1.30
0.7	2.17	1.72	1.35
0.8	3.00	2.01	1.40
0.9	5.50	2.56	1.45
1.0	Not applicable		1.50
2.0			2.00
4.0			3.00

With a load factor of 0.8, chained hashing expects to examine only 1.4 items during a successful search. Some other possible load factors are shown in Figure 12.7, where you can compare the average numbers for the three different hashing methods.

Self-Test Exercises

16. Suppose that you place 180 items in a hash table with an array size of 200. What is the load factor? For each of the three hash methods, what is the average number of table elements that you expect to have examined during a successful search?

17. You want to place 1000 elements in a hash table, and you'd like an average search to examine just two table elements. How big does the table's array need to be? Give separate answers for the three hash methods.

CHAPTER SUMMARY

- Serial search is quick to program but requires linear time to find an item in both the worst-case and the average case.

- Binary search works well on a sorted array of items, requiring O(log n) time in both the worst case and the average case. But as items are added or deleted, keeping the array in order may take considerable time (linear time for each insertion or deletion in the worst-case).

- Hash tables are a good strategy for storing and retrieving records. In fact, it would be perfect if there were no collisions.

- One way to deal with collisions is **open addressing.** This scheme handles collisions by placing the new entry in the first open location that is at or after the spot where the key hashes to. Two methods of searching for an open location are **linear probing** (which examines the array locations in consecutive order) and **double hashing** (which uses a second hash function to size of the steps that are taken through the array). Double hashing is the better method, because it avoids clustering.

- Another way to deal with collisions is **chaining.** In the chaining approach, each location of the hash table's array is able to hold multiple entries. A common way to implement hashing is for each array location to be a head pointer for a linked list of entries.

- The worst-case search time for a hash table is linear. But the average-case time is quite fast. Depending on the load factor and the precise method of hashing, the average case requires about two to five table elements to be examined during a successful search (see Figure 12.7 on page 566).

Solutions to Self-Test Exercises ?

1. The precondition is modified so that the array no longer needs to be sorted. Here's the code:

```
void search(
    const int a[ ],
    size_t first, size_t size,
    int target, bool& found,
    size_t& location
)
{
    size_t i;
    bool found;
    i = 0;
    found = false;
    while ((i < size) && !found)
    {
        if (a[first+i] == target)
        {
            found = true;
            location = first+i;
        }
        else
            i++;
    }
}
```

2. The following template prefix is placed before the function:
```
template <class Item, class SizeType>
```
In the implementation, change every occurrence of *int* to Item, and change the size_t parameters to SizeType. (See "Parameter Matching for Template Functions" on page 267 for an explanation of the need for the SizeType.)

3. The function is not difficult to write, but pay attention to the potential pitfalls from page 538.

4. $H(1)=1$, $H(2)=2$, $H(4)=3$, $H(7)=3$, $H(8)=4$, $H(9)=4$.

5. Here's the body of the implementation:
```
{
    bool found;
    size_t index;
    assert(key >= 0);
    find_index(key, found, index);
    return found;
}
```

6. Here is the `never_used` member function:
```
template <class RecordType>
inline bool Table<RecordType>::
never_used(size_t index) const
// Library facilities used: stdlib.h
// Precondition: index < CAPACITY.
// Postcondition: If data[index] has never
// been used, then the return value is true.
// Otherwise the return value is false.
{
  return
    (data[index].key == NEVER_USED);
}
```

Here is the `is_vacant` member function:
```
template <class RecordType>
inline bool Table<RecordType>::
is_vacant(size_t index) const
// Library facilities used: stdlib.h
// Precondition: index < CAPACITY.
// Postcondition: If data[index] is not now
// being used, then the return value is true.
// Otherwise the return value is false.
{
  return
    (data[index].key < 0);
}
```

7. If the key was already present, then the record with that key is overwritten. If the key was not already present, then the assertion tests whether `size( )` < CAPACITY is true, and this assertion fails, halting the program.

8. Suppose we start looking in the data array at some index, say 34, and we move forward until we find an unoccupied location. Perhaps this first unoccupied location is at index 36. If position 36 has a key of NEVER_USED, then that indicates that the position has never been used, and therefore no record with the given key appears in the array (since it would have been placed in this unused position, or perhaps in position 34 or 35 that we have already examined).

On the other hand, if position 36 has a key of PREVIOUSLY_USED, then this position has previously been used and since removed. In this case, it is possible that there is a record with the given key in the array at a position after `data[36]`. It might be after this position,

because at the time it was inserted, `data[36]` might have been in use.

9. For linear probing, the key/index pairs are: 100 at [0], 0 at [1], 1199 at [99], 1299 at [2], 1399 at [3], and 2 at [4]. For double hashing the key/index pairs are: 100 at [0], 0 at [1], 1199 at [99], 1299 at [25], 1399 at [27], and 2 at [2].

10. There is a twin prime pair at 1229 and 1231, which suggests that 1231 is a good table capacity.

11. NULL

12. We suggest that you first write a helper function with one parameter that is a key. The function returns a pointer to a node with the specified key (or returns NULL if there is no such node). Using this function (which we call `find_ptr`):
```
template <class RecordType>
void Table<RecordType>::
insert(const RecordType& entry)
{
  Node<RecordType> *cursor;

  cursor = find_ptr(entry.key);
  if (cursor == NULL)
  {
    list_head_insert
      (data[hash(entry.key)], entry);
    used++;
  }
  else
    cursor->data = entry;
}
```

13. The `data[0]` list will have the keys 0 and 811. The `data[1]` list will have the key 1623. The `data[2]` list will have the keys 2 and 2435. The `data[3]` list will have the key 3247. All other lists are empty.

14. The ADT does use dynamic memory (the linked lists).

15. If the lists are kept in order, then a search can stop as soon as it reaches a key that is greater than the target.

16. The load factor is 0.9 (i.e., 180/200). With linear probing, the expected average is 5.50; with double hashing, the expected average is 2.56; with chained hashing, the expected average is 1.45.

17. For linear probing, we need a load factor of 2/3, which requires a table capacity of 1500. For double hashing, we need a load factor of just less than 0.8, requiring a table capacity of about 1250. For chaining, we need a load factor of 2, requiring an array size of 500.

PROGRAMMING PROJECTS

1 Reimplement the binary search using a loop and no recursion. If you are familiar with template functions, then your implementation should be a template function that can search any array that is sorted from smallest to largest (using the < operator).

2 Use a binary search technique to rewrite the guess_game function from Figure 1.7 on page 23. The function may ask questions such as "Is your number bigger than 42?" Your result should have worst-case time of $O(\log n)$.

3 Use **double hashing** to reimplement the hash table from Figure 12.3 on page 549.

4 In our open-address hash tables, we have used linear probing or double hashing. Another probing method, which avoids some clustering, is called **quadratic probing.** The simplest version of quadratic probing works like this: Start by hashing the key to an array index. If there is a collision, then move to the next array index. If there is a *second* collision, then move forward *two* more spots through the array. After a *third* collision, we move forward *three* more spots, and so on. For example, suppose that a new key hashes to location 327, and this location is full. The next location that we try is 328. If 328 is a second collision, then we move two spots forward to location 330. If 330 is a third collision, then we move three spots forward to location 333. If our calculation of the next spot takes us beyond the end of the array, then we "wrap around" to the front of the array (similar to double hashing). In general, if data[i] is the location that has just caused a collision, and we have already examined count elements, then we increase i according to the assignment:

```
i = (i + count) % CAPACITY;
```

In this formula, the "% CAPACITY" causes the "wrap around" to the front of the array. In order for this approach to work correctly, the capacity must be a power of 2, such as $2^{10} = 1024$. Otherwise, the sequence of probes does not correctly examine all array items.

For this project, use quadratic hashing to reimplement the hash table from Figure 12.3 on page 549.

13 Sorting

A place for everything and everything in its place.

ISABELLA MARY BEETON
The Book of Household Management

One commonly encountered programming task is sorting a list of values. By way of examples, the list might consist of exam scores, and we may want to see them sorted from lowest to highest, or from highest to lowest; the list might be a list of words that we have misspelled, and we may want to see them in alphabetical order; the list might be a list of student records, and we may want them sorted by student number or alphabetically by student name. In this chapter we present and analyze a number of different sorting algorithms.

To maintain a sharp focus on the sorting algorithms, we will only consider arrays of integers and design algorithms to sort the integers into the order smallest to largest. However, if you are familiar with templates (Chapter 6), then you may easily adapt the algorithms to sort arrays of values of other types, or to sort values according to other ordering relations. Other adaptations are also possible. For example, one common way of ordering records is to choose one special field, which is then called the **key field**, and to sort the records according to that key field. Using a key field, we could sort a list of student records by student number

sorting by key value

(with the student number serving as the key field). We could sort the same records alphabetically by student name (with the student name serving as the key field).

13.1 QUADRATIC SORTING ALGORITHMS

In this section we develop and implement two algorithms to sort a list of numbers into increasing order.

Selectionsort—Specification

We have an array of integers that we wish to sort into order from smallest to largest. To be concrete, we'll use this prototype and precondition/postcondition contract:

```
void selectionsort(int data[ ], size_t n);
// Precondition: data is an array with at least n components.
// Postcondition: The elements of data have been rearranged so
//   that data[0] <= data[1] <= ... <= data[n-1].
```

Selectionsort—Design

One way to design an algorithm is to rely on the definition of the problem. In this case the problem is to sort an array, such as `data`, from smallest to largest. That means rearranging the values so that `data[0]` is the smallest, `data[1]` the next smallest, and so forth up to `data[n-1]`, which is the largest. That definition yields an outline for a straightforward algorithm (`i` is a local variable):

```
for (i = 0; i < n; i++)
    Put the next smallest element in location data[i].
```

This approach finds the smallest element, then the next smallest, and so on, placing the items in `data[0]`, `data[1]`, ... as they are found. We can also work the approach the other way, finding the largest item, then the second largest, and so on:

```
for (i = n-1; i >= 0; i--)
    Put the next largest element in location data[i].
```

There are many ways to realize either of these general approaches. The details can be developed using two arrays and copying the elements from one array to the other in sorted order. However, one array is both adequate and economical, and so we decide to develop the algorithm using only one array. To help in exploring the problem, we will use the concrete example shown at the top of the next page.

data

10	8	6	2	16	4	18	11	14	12
[0]	[1]	[2]	[3]	[4]	[5]	[6]	[7]	[8]	[9]

Consider sorting this array with a pencil and eraser according to the second version of the pseudocode that we have outlined (finding and placing the largest element, then the next largest, and so on).

We begin by searching the array for the largest element, and we find this largest element at `data[6]`, which is the 18. We next want to set the final element of the array equal to this value of 18. In doing so, we must be careful to not lose the original value of 12 that was stored in array location `data[9]`. A simple assignment statement like the following would destroy the 12:

```
data[9] = data[6]; // No good: destroys the original data[9].
```

The algorithm must not simply destroy the original value 12 that was in the final spot of the array. Fortunately we have an array location in which to store it. We can place it in the location that used to have the largest element. In other words, we actually want to "swap" the largest element with the final element of the array. After the swap, the array looks like this:

The values of `data[6]` and `data[9]` have simply been swapped. A similar thing is done with the second-largest value of the array. We find this second largest value (the 16 at `data[4]`) and swap it with the next-to-last element of the array (`data[8]`), resulting in this array:

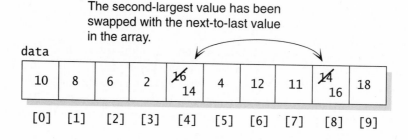

The entire array can be sorted by a series of swaps such as these. Any sorting algorithm that is based on swapping elements is referred to as an **interchange sort**.

The simplest interchange sorting algorithm, which we have been describing, is called **selectionsort**. The algorithm is a refinement of our previous pseudo-code, as shown here:

```
for(i = n-1; i > 0; i--)
    swap(data[i], data[suitable index]);
```

These two lines of pseudocode have two refinements from the original pseudo-code. First, we are using the `swap` function that we previously wrote as part of the item toolkit of Figure 6.3 on page 274 (`itemtool.h`). The function inter-changes the values of its two arguments. As the second refinement, notice that the loop executes only `n-1` times, stopping as soon as `i` drops to zero. There is no need to execute the loop with `i` equal to zero because when `i` reaches zero, all the larger elements are already in their correct spots. Therefore, `data[0]` must already have the smallest element.

All that remains is to calculate the expression "suitable index." When the loop considers `data[i]` and looks for a suitable value to interchange, the indexed variables with indexes above `i` already contain the correct values for a sorted array. So the sought-after index is the index of the largest of the remaining ele-ments `data[0]`, `data[1]`, ... `data[i]`. There are `i+1` of these elements to exam-ine, searching for the index of the largest one. Moreover, we are in the nice situation of already having a function that finds the index of the largest item from the front part of the array. The function `index_of_maximal` is also part of the item toolkit of Figure 6.3 on page 274. The function has two arguments: an array and a `size_t` value specifying how many elements to search from the front of the array. To calculate the index of the largest element from the first `i+1`, we can use the highlighted expression in this further refinement of our code:

```
for (i = n-1; i > 0; i--)
    swap(data[i], data[index_of_maximal(data, i+1)]);
```

Selectionsort—Implementation

The complete sorting algorithm is implemented by the function `selectionsort`, which is shown in Figure 13.1, along with a main program that demonstrates the function sorting some user-entered numbers.

In the implementation, you will notice that `i` and `n` are both `size_t`, so we have added an extra if-statement to handle the case of "sorting an empty array" (the case where `n` is zero). In this case, the function has no work to do (there are no elements to sort), but since `size_t` values may not be negative, we must avoid the assignment `i = n-1`.

FIGURE 13.1   Selectionsort

A Program

```
// FILE: select.cxx
// An interactive test program for the selectionsort function

#include <iostream.h>   // Provides cout and cin
#include <stdlib.h>     // Provides EXIT_SUCCESS, size_t
#include "itemtool.h"   // Provides swap, index_of_maximal from page 274

// PROTOTYPE of the function used in this test program:
void selectionsort(int data[ ], size_t n);
// Precondition: data is an array with at least n components.
// Postcondition: The elements are rearranged so that data[0] <= data[1] <= ... <= data[n-1].

int main( )
{
    const char BLANK = ' ';
    const size_t ARRAY_SIZE = 10;   // Number of elements in the array to be sorted
    int data[ARRAY_SIZE];           // Array of integers to be sorted
    int user_input;                 // Number typed by the user
    size_t number_of_elements;      // How much of the array is used
    size_t i;                       // Array index

    // Provide some instructions.
    cout << "Please type up to " << ARRAY_SIZE << " positive integers. ";
    cout << "Indicate the list's end with a zero." << endl;

    // Read the input numbers.
    number_of_elements = 0;
    cin >> user_input;
    while ((user_input != 0) && (number_of_elements < ARRAY_SIZE))
    {
        data[number_of_elements] = user_input;
        number_of_elements++;
        cin >> user_input;
    }

    // Sort the numbers, and print the result with two blanks after each number.
    selectionsort(data, number_of_elements);
    cout << "In sorted order, your numbers are: "<< endl;
    for (i = 0; i < number_of_elements; i++)
        cout << data[i] << BLANK << BLANK;
    cout << endl;

    return EXIT_SUCCESS;
}
```

(continued)

(FIGURE 13.1 continued)

```
void selectionsort(int data[ ], size_t n)
// Library facilities used: itemtool.h, stdlib.h
{
    size_t i;

    if (n > 0)
    {
        for (i = n-1; i > 0; i--)
            swap(data[i], data[ index_of_maximal(data, i+1) ]);
    }
}
```

Sample Dialogue

```
Please type up to 10 positive integers. Indicate the list's end with a zero.
80  10  50  70  60  90  20  30  40 0
In sorted order, your numbers are:
10  20  30  40  50  60  70  80  90
```

| select.cxx | FTP |

Selectionsort—Analysis

We want to analyze the worst-case running time for the selectionsort algorithm that we implemented as the function `selectionsort` shown in Figure 13.1. Let us use *n* for the number of items to be sorted. In the function `selectionsort`, *n* is the value of the `size_t` parameter n.

In outline form, the main work of the selectionsort algorithm is given here:

```
for (i = n-1; i > 0; i--)
    swap(data[i], data[suitable index]);
```

When i is equal to n-1, then `data[suitable index]` is the largest element in the array; when i is equal to n-2, then `data[suitable index]` is the second-largest element in the array, and so forth.

How many operations are performed by the above for-loop? The answer is not easy. Many of the operations are hidden. The loop control variable, i, is compared to zero at the start of each loop iteration. The swap function uses some number of assignment operations, and the calculation of the "suitable index" requires some work. The value of i is decremented at the end of each loop iteration. We could determine the precise number of operations for each of these subtasks in the loop. However, that is more detail than we need. We are only looking for a big-*O* approximation, which means that we do not need the exact values for constants. This will simplify our analysis significantly.

During each iteration of the loop, there is some constant number of operations in managing the loop control variable, and there is some constant number of operations involved in the call to the swap function. So *the number of operations in each loop iteration is the sum:*

some constant + the cost of finding the suitable index

Since there are n–1 loop iterations, the total count of the number of operations performed is given by the product:

$(n - 1) \times$ (some constant + the cost of finding the suitable index)

To change this into a nice formula expressed in terms of n, we need to determine the cost of finding the "suitable index."

As it turns out, when the algorithm is looking for the value to place in location data[i], the "suitable index" is the index of the largest of the values

data[0], data[1], ..., data[i]

The selectionsort algorithm uses a function that determines the location of this largest element and thereby the value of the "suitable index." This function, called index_of_maximal, looks at each of the above array elements and performs some constant number of operations with each of them. Since i can be as large as n–1, in the worst case, the subalgorithm will need to look at all n array elements from data[0] to data[n-1] and perform a constant number of operations on each one. Hence, our estimate of the number of operations to find this "suitable index" is *at most a constant times n.*

Putting this information together, we see that the total count of the number of operations performed in the selectionsort is this:

Total $= (n - 1) \times$ (some constant + the cost of finding the suitable index)

$\leq (n - 1) \times$ [some constant + (some other constant) $\times n$]

Now we need to estimate the quantity:

$(n - 1) \times$ [some constant + (some other constant) $\times n$]

If you multiply this out, there will be an n^2 term, an n term, and a constant term without any n. Thus, the number of operations performed is:

$n^2 \times$ (some new constant)
+
$n \times$ (some other new constant)
+
(yet another new constant)

This is our estimate of the worst-case run time for selectionsort. Because we are doing a big-O analysis, we can ignore the constants and only consider the highest exponent of n. Hence, we see that the worst-case running time for selectionsort is $O(n^2)$.

The above analysis of the running time for selectionsort did not depend on the initial values in the array. The selectionsort algorithm performs the same number of operations no matter what values are in the array that it sorts. Thus, the average-case running time (and even the best-case running time) is the same as the worst-case running time.

Selectionsort Running Time

The worst-case running time, the average-case running time, and the best-case running time for selectionsort are all quadratic.

Programming Tip: **Rough Estimates Suffice for Big-O**

TIP

We have just computed big-O expressions for the worst-case running time of the selectionsort algorithm. Notice that when we performed the big-O analyses, we did not compute exact formulas for the running times. For example, when we estimated the number of operations in one iteration of the primary loop used in the algorithm, we decided that the algorithm performed the following number of operations in each loop iteration:

some constant + the cost of finding the suitable index

Notice that we never computed the exact value of "some constant." Because big-O expressions are only accurate to "within a constant multiple," the exact value of the constant does not matter. If we want only a big-O expression, there is no reason to spend time computing an exact value for this constant.

Insertionsort

Another simple and natural sorting algorithm is based on the following illustration of sorting an array that contains this list of ten integers:

```
( 8,  2,  5,  3, 10,  7,  1,  4,  6,  9 )
```

One way to proceed is to take the numbers one at a time and build up another sorted list of values. The first number is 8, so make a list that contains only the one number 8. That is certainly a sorted list. Next take the 2 and combine it with the 8 to obtain a longer sorted list, namely (2, 8). Next, add the 5 to obtain the list: (2, 5, 8).

If you keep adding numbers to the list, you will eventually obtain a sorted list containing all the numbers. The original list decreases by one on each iteration, and the list we are building increases by one on each iteration. The progress of this process is shown here for the example list:

( )　　(8, 2, 5, 3, 10, 7, 1, 4, 6, 9)

(8)　　(2, 5, 3, 10, 7, 1, 4, 6, 9)

(2, 8)　　(5, 3, 10, 7, 1, 4, 6, 9)

(2, 5, 8)　　(3, 10, 7, 1, 4, 6, 9)

(2, 3, 5, 8)　　(10, 7, 1, 4, 6, 9)

(2, 3, 5, 8, 10)　　(7, 1, 4, 6, 9)

(2, 3, 5, 7, 8, 10)　　(1, 4, 6, 9)

(1, 2, 3, 5, 7, 8, 10)　　(4, 6, 9)

(1, 2, 3, 4, 5, 7, 8, 10)　　(6, 9)

(1, 2, 3, 4, 5, 6, 7, 8, 10)　　(9)

(1, 2, 3, 4, 5, 6, 7, 8, 9, 10)　　( )

With the insertionsort, your first thought might be to use an additional array and copy values from one array to the other. The numbers in the left-hand lists in our drawings above would be in one array, and the numbers in the right-hand lists would be in the other array. But, if you look carefully at the drawings, you will see that one list grows at exactly the same rate that the other list shrinks. So we need only one array. If we have ten numbers, we need only ten positions. One list can be kept at the front of the array and the other at the back of the array.

We can redraw the progress of the insertionsort in a way that makes it evident that one array is sufficient. At the start of the insertionsort, we have the same ten-element array that we have been working with:

data

8	2	5	3	10	7	1	4	6	9
[0]	[1]	[2]	[3]	[4]	[5]	[6]	[7]	[8]	[9]

We have called the array data. The first component, data[0], is shaded to indicate that even at the start, the front part of the array—with only the one shaded item—can be viewed as a tiny sorted array on its own. The first actual work will be to insert the second element (data[1], which is a 2) into the tiny sorted array, increasing the "sorted part" of the array to encompass two elements, as shown here:

data

2	8	5	3	10	7	1	4	6	9
[0]	[1]	[2]	[3]	[4]	[5]	[6]	[7]	[8]	[9]

So, at this point, the first two elements (2, 8) form a small sorted list, and we still need to insert the remaining elements (5, 3, 10, 7, 1, 4, 6, 9). After the insertion of the 5, we have the situation shown here:

data

2	5	8	3	10	7	1	4	6	9
[0]	[1]	[2]	[3]	[4]	[5]	[6]	[7]	[8]	[9]

The insertion process continues, taking the next element from the unsorted side of the array and inserting it into the sorted side of the array. Each insertion increases the size of the sorted side and decreases the unsorted side until the entire array is sorted.

All we need to do now is convert these ideas into C++ code. In fact, part of the work is already done in the itemtool toolkit that we developed on page 274. That toolkit has a template function with the following specification:

```
template <class Item, class SizeType>
void ordered_insert(Item data[ ], SizeType n, Item entry);
// Precondition: data is a partially filled array containing n items sorted
// from small to large. The array size is large enough to hold at least one
// more item.
// Postcondition: data is a partially filled array containing the n original
// items plus the new entry. These items are still sorted from small to
// large.
```

As an example of how to use the function, suppose that data[0] through data[i-1] are the sorted part of the array, and we are now ready to insert the next element, data[i]. This next insertion is accomplished with this function call:

```
ordered_insert(data, i, data[i]);
```

After this function call, the sorted part of the array encompasses one more element, now stretching from data[0] through data[i]. The entire insertionsort can be accomplished with this loop:

```
for (i = 1; i < n; i++)
    ordered_insert(data, i, data[i]);
```

You can incorporate this loop into the actual insertionsort function yourself (see Self-Test Exercise 3 on page 583).

Insertionsort—Analysis

We'll analyze the insertionsort in a slightly different manner, determining how many times the algorithm must access an element of the array—either for a comparison, or for a swap of some sort. For many sorting algorithms, such as insertionsort, the count of array accesses is proportional to the total number of operations. Therefore, the final big-O analysis comes out the same.

We start by asking how many array accesses are required to insert just one new element with a function call ordered_insert(data, i, data[i]). If you analyze the ordered_insert implementation from Figure 6.3 on page 276, you will see that the function starts by comparing the new element to the final element from the sorted portion of the array. After this comparison, the algorithm works backward through the array until it finds the correct spot to insert a new element. In the worst case, the algorithm could compare and shift each element of the array once, and therefore the total number of array accesses is limited to a constant times n. In fact, the call of ordered_insert(data, i, data[i]) may need significantly fewer than $O(n)$ accesses as this function call uses only the first i elements of the array rather than all n. But $O(n)$ operations is a good overestimate because it is easy to express and easy to work with.

So, the insertion of one new element takes $O(n)$ time, and there are n elements to insert. Thus the total time for n separate insertions is no more than this:

Total $= n \times$ (the number of operations in an $O(n)$ algorithm)

$\quad\quad = n \times$ (some constant times n)

$\quad\quad =$ some constant times n^2

$\quad\quad = O(n^2)$

This analysis shows one important trick to remember:

Analysis for Quadratic Time

An $O(n)$ process that is performed n times results in a quadratic number of operations ($O(n^2)$).

In the case of insertionsort, we actually perform $n-1$ insertions rather than n, but the time for $n-1$ insertions is also quadratic.

Our analysis has used one major overestimation. We assumed that each insertion required the ordered_insert to examine the full n elements of the array, but some insertions require the examination of far fewer elements. Will a more accurate estimate reduce the time analysis? The answer is no. A precise analysis of the worst-case running time still results in a quadratic formula. To see this, suppose that all the original elements are far from their correct places. In fact, these elements might be completely backwards, as shown here:

data

10	9	8	7	6	5	4	3	2	1
[0]	[1]	[2]	[3]	[4]	[5]	[6]	[7]	[8]	[9]

In this case, the first insertion must insert the 9 in front of the 10, resulting in this array:

data

9	10	8	7	6	5	4	3	2	1
[0]	[1]	[2]	[3]	[4]	[5]	[6]	[7]	[8]	[9]

The next insertion must insert the 8 in front of everything else. And then the 7 is inserted, again at the front. With the elements starting out backwards, each insertion must compare and shift all the elements in the currently sorted part of the array, placing the new element at the front. So, for an insertionsort to work on a completely backwards array requires these comparisons and shifts:

1 compare and shift to insert the 1st element
+
2 compares and shifts to insert the 2nd element
+
3 compares and shifts to insert the 3rd element
+
. . .
+
n–1 compares and shifts to insert the $(n–1)^{st}$ element

The total number of compare and shifts is thus $1 + 2 + 3 + . . . + (n–1)$. You can use a technique similar to Figure 1.5 on page 18 to evaluate this sum. The result is $n(n–1)/2$, which is $O(n^2)$. So the worst case for insertionsort is indeed quadratic time, the same as selectionsort.

The analysis of the average-case running time for insertionsort is essentially the same as that for the worst case. The only difference is that a single insertion will, on the average, stop after accessing half of the elements from the sorted side, rather than accessing them all. This means that the average-case running time is half that of the worst-case running time, but we know that a constant multiple, such as ½, does not affect a big-O expression. Thus, the average-case running time for insertionsort is quadratic, the same as the worst-case running time.

On the other hand, the best-case running time for insertionsort is much better than quadratic. In particular, suppose that the array is *already sorted* before we begin our work. This is certainly an advantage, though the advantage does not help all sorting algorithms. For example, starting with a sorted array does not help selectionsort, which still requires quadratic time. But starting with a sorted array does help insertionsort. In this case, each insertion of a new element will examine only a single element from the array. This single-element examination is carried out once to insert each new element, and the result is an $O(n)$ time.

You probably think that starting with an already sorted array does not happen too often, and perhaps you are right. But frequently an array is *nearly* sorted—perhaps a few new elements are out of place. Insertionsort is also quite quick for nearly sorted arrays.

Here is a summary of insertionsort times:

Insertionsort Running Time

Both the worst-case running time and the average-case running times are quadratic. But the best-case (when the starting array is already sorted) is linear, and the algorithm is also quick when the starting array is nearly sorted.

Self-Test Exercises

1. The `selectionsort` function in Figure 13.1 on page 574 sorts integers into increasing order. How would you change the function so that it sorts integers into decreasing order?

2. The `selectionsort` function in Figure 13.1 on page 574 sorts integers into increasing order. How would you change the function so that it sorts an array of strings into alphabetical order? Assume that the strings are objects of a class called `String`, which can be compared with the usual "less than" operator. All strings consists of only lower-case letters.

3. Give a complete function implementation for insertionsort. It will be short and will call `ordered_insert` (from the item toolkit in Figure 6.3 on page 274).

13.2 RECURSIVE SORTING ALGORITHMS

Divide-and-Conquer Using Recursion

Let's start with an explicit statement of a recursive design technique that we have used a few times in the past. The technique, called **divide-and-conquer,** is applicable to many problems. Here's the idea: When a problem is small, simply solve it. When the problem is large, divide the problem into two smaller subproblems, each of which is about half of the original problem. Solve each subproblem with a recursive call. After the recursive calls, extra work is sometimes needed to combine the solutions of the smaller problems, resulting in a solution to the larger problem.

Divide-and-conquer can work in slightly different ways, perhaps having more than two subproblems or having subproblems with unequal size, but the basic approach—two subproblems with roughly equal size—works best.

Applied to sorting, divide-and-conquer results in the following pattern:

> **Key Design Concept**
>
> *Divide-and-conquer works best with two equally sized subproblems, each of which is solved with a recursive call.*

The Divide-and-Conquer Sorting Paradigm

1. Divide the elements to be sorted into two groups of equal (or almost equal) size.

2. Sort each of these smaller groups of elements (by recursive calls).

3. Combine the two sorted groups into one large sorted list.

As an illustration, we can see how these three steps will sort a small array. The first step divides the array into two equally sized groups, as shown in this cut:

| 9 | 12 | 31 | 25 | 5 | 8 | 20 | 2 | 3 | 6 |

After the cut, we have two smaller arrays, with five elements each. These smaller arrays can separately be sorted with recursive calls, providing this result:

| 5 | 9 | 12 | 25 | 31 |

| 2 | 3 | 6 | 8 | 20 |

When the recursive calls return, the two half-arrays need to somehow be put together into one sorted array, as shown here:

| 2 | 3 | 5 | 6 | 8 | 9 | 12 | 20 | 25 | 31 |

We will present two recursive sorting functions based on this divide-and-conquer paradigm. But first there is a C++ feature that we will discuss to make the recursive calls easier.

++ FEATURE

C++ Feature: Specifying a Subarray with Pointer Arithmetic

Our sorting functions will require recursive calls to sort various portions of the array. This raises an interesting problem regarding the arguments of a sorting function. As an example of the problem, look at the specification of one of our sorts:

```
void selectionsort(int data[ ], size_t n);
// Precondition: data is an array with at least n components.
// Postcondition: The elements of data have been rearranged so
// that data[0] <= data[1] <= ... <= data[n-1].
```

Is it possible to use this function to sort only *part* of an array? Certainly we can sort the *first part* of an array. For example, suppose that data is an array of ten integers. This function call will sort the first five elements of data:

```
selectionsort(data, 5);
```

This function call will rearrange the elements data[0] through data[4] so that the values are smallest to largest. But can we use the function to sort the second part of the array (from data[5] through data[9]) or a middle piece (such as data[2] through data[6])? The answer is yes, but we'll need a C++ feature called *pointer arithmetic.*

To illustrate pointer arithmetic, we'll continue with our array, data, of ten integers. Suppose that data has these values:

data

9	12	31	25	5	8	20	11	3	6
[0]	[1]	[2]	[3]	[4]	[5]	[6]	[7]	[8]	[9]

For any value i from 0 to 9, the expression data[i] refers to *one* of the ten components. For example, data[5] refers to the value 8 in the above array. This is not new. But another use of the index i is new: For any value i from 0 to 9, the expression (data + i) refers to the small array that starts at data[i] and continues to the end of the array. For example, (data + 5) refers to that part of data that begins at data[5] and includes 8, 20, 11, 3, 6. A small array, which is actually part of a larger array, is called a **subarray.** The expression (data + 5) is an example of **pointer arithmetic**, which allows a programmer to combine a pointer or an array with integer values. Pointer arithmetic has many interesting uses, but we'll only use it for this one purpose of *specifying a subarray.*

Consider the subarray (data + 5). This is part of the complete data array, containing the last five elements of data. Moreover, (data + 5) can be used just like any other five-element array. Here are some examples:

```
cout << (data + 5)[0]; // Prints the 8
cout << (data + 5)[2]; // Prints the 11
(data + 5)[1]++;       // Adds one to the array element
```

The third statement, (data + 5)[1]++, adds one to the [1] element of the subarray, increasing it from 20 to 21. After this statement, the data array has these values:

data

9	12	31	25	5	8	21	11	3	6
[0]	[1]	[2]	[3]	[4]	[5]	[6]	[7]	[8]	[9]

Notice that (data + 5)[1] is the [1] element of the subarray, but it is also the [6] element of the whole array. So changing (data + 5)[1] will actually change data[6]. In other words: *A subarray is always part of a complete array. Changing the subarray will change the complete array.*

Have you figured out why we wanted subarrays in the first place? Using a subarray, we can make a function call that sorts *part* of an array. Here are two examples:

```
selectionsort((data + 5), 4); // Sorts data[5] through data[8]
selectionsort((data + 2), 5); // Sorts data[2] through data[6]
```

For example, the second function call sorts five elements starting at data[2]. With subarrays in hand, we can develop our two recursive sorting algorithms.

Specifying Subarrays with Pointer Arithmetic

Suppose that data is an array with at least n elements. For any integer i from 0 to n, the expression (data + i) refers to the subarray that begins at data[i] and continues to the end of the array.

In the subarray, (data + i)[0] is the same as data[i]; (data + i)[1] is the same as data[i+1]; and so on.

A subarray is always part of a complete array. Changing the subarray will change the complete array.

Mergesort

The most straightforward implementation of the divide-and-conquer approach to sorting is the **mergesort** algorithm. The mergesort algorithm divides the array near its midpoint, sorts the two half-arrays by recursive calls to the algorithm, and then merges the two halves to get a new sorted array of elements. The final "merging" step of the process will require some thought, so we'll postpone that part of the implementation by assuming that we have a separate function to carry out the merging. The prototype for the separate merging function is shown here:

```
void merge(int data[ ], size_t n1, size_t n2);
// Precondition: data is an array (or subarray) with at least n1 + n2
// elements. The first n1 elements (from data[0] to data[n1-1]) are sorted
// from smallest to largest, and the last n2 (from data[n1] to
// data[n1 + n2 - 1]) are also sorted from smallest to largest.
// Postcondition: The first n1 + n2 elements of data have been rearranged
// to be sorted from smallest to largest.
// NOTE: If there is insufficient dynamic memory, then new_handler is
// called.
```

FIGURE 13.2 | Mergesort

A Function Implementation

```
void mergesort(int data[ ], size_t n)
// Precondition: data is an array with at least n components.
// Postcondition: The elements of data have been rearranged so
// that data[0] <= data[1] <= ... <= data[n-1].
// NOTE: If there is insufficient dynamic memory, then new_handler is called.
// Library facilities used: stdlib.h
{
    size_t n1;  // Size of the first subarray
    size_t n2;  // Size of the second subarray

    if (n > 1)
    {
        // Compute sizes of the subarrays.
        n1 = n / 2;
        n2 = n - n1;

        mergesort(data, n1);         // Sort from data[0] through data[n1-1]
        mergesort((data + n1), n2);  // Sort from data[n1] to the end

        // Merge the two sorted halves.
        merge(data, n1, n2);
    }
}
```

This function calls merge, which uses dynamic memory, so we must indicate the possibility of failure.

The two subarrays are sorted with recursive calls.

merge.cxx   **FTP**

This merge function will be used as the last step of our mergesort. Notice that the merge function will use some dynamic memory, so there is a possibility of failure that we have indicated in the specification. Can you predict where the dynamic memory will come into play? You'll see the answer shortly, but for now, examine the mergesort function in Figure 13.2.

The stopping case for mergesort's recursion is when the array to be sorted consists of only one element. In this stopping case, there is no work to do because a single element does not need to be "rearranged." On the other hand, if there is more than one element, then the mergesort function carries out these steps:

1. Calculate the sizes of the two subarrays. The first size, n1, is approximately half of the entire size (calculated by n/2, using integer division). The second size, n2, is whatever is left over (calculated by n - n1).

2. Use recursive calls to sort the two subarrays. Notice that the second recursive call, mergesort((data + n1), n2), uses pointer arithmetic to specify the subarray that begins at data[n1].

3. Finally, a call to the merge function combines the two sorted halves.

The operation of the merge function has some issues that we discuss next.

The Merge Function

The algorithm for the merge function uses a second temporary array that we will call temp. Elements will be copied from the array data to the array temp in such a way that the array temp is correctly sorted. (After that, the values are simply copied back to the array data.) The merging algorithm uses the precondition that the two halves of the array (data[0] through data[n1 - 1], and data[n1] through data[n1 + n2 -1]) are each sorted. Since they are both sorted, we know that data[0] contains the smallest element in the first half, and data[n1] contains the smallest element in the second half. Therefore, we know that the smallest element in the *entire* array is either data[0] or data[n1]. The algorithm compares these two elements and copies the smallest one to position temp[0]. The algorithm then somehow marks the copied element as being "already copied." For example, suppose that data contains ten integers. After the first one is copied to temp, we might have this situation:

	[0]	[1]	[2]	[3]	[4]	[5]	[6]	[7]	[8]	[9]
data	5	9	12	25	31	2	3	6	8	20

	[0]	[1]	[2]	[3]	[4]	[5]	[6]	[7]	[8]	[9]
temp	2	?	?	?	?	?	?	?	?	?

The drawing has a thick black line to separate the two halves of the data array. In this example, the 2 (at the front of the second half) is smaller than the 5 (at the front of the first half), so this 2 is copied to the front of the temporary array. We marked the 2 as "already copied" by shading it in the diagram. In the actual algorithm, we'll keep track of which items have been copied by maintaining three size_t variables:

```
size_t copied;    // Number of elements copied from data to temp
size_t copied1;   // Number copied from the first half of data
size_t copied2;   // Number copied from the second half of data
```

All three local variables are initialized to zero in the merge function. Each time that we copy an element from the first half of data to the temporary array, we add one to both `copied` and `copied1`. Each time that we copy an element from the second half of `data` to the temporary array, we add one to both `copied` and `copied2`. So, after copying the 2 in the above example, `copied` and `copied2` will both be 1, but `copied1` remains zero.

The merge algorithm proceeds by looking at the next uncopied elements from each half of the `data` array. The smaller of these two elements is copied to the next spot in the temporary array. In our example, we would next compare the 5 (from the first half) to the 3 (the next uncopied element from the second half). Since the 3 is smaller, we copy the 3 to the next spot in `temp` array, as shown here:

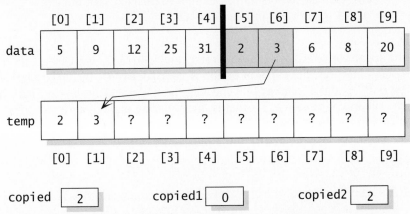

At this point we have copied a total of two elements (since `copied` is 2). Both of the copied elements came from the second half (since `copied1` is 0 and `copied2` is 2).

The next step of the algorithm will compare the 5 (from the first half) to the 6 (from the second half). The 5 is lower, so it gets copied to the temporary array, as shown here:

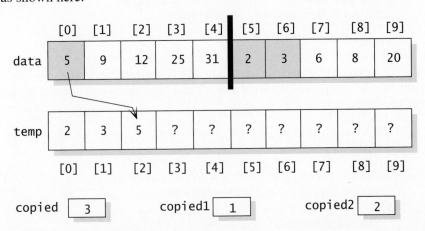

The loop proceeds in this way, moving through the two array halves. With this idea, we can write our first version of the pseudocode, as shown at the top of the next page.

1. Initialize `copied`, `copied1`, and `copied2` to zero.

2. *while* (both halves of the array have more elements to copy)
   if (the next element of 1st half is <= the next element of the 2nd half)
   {

       Copy the next element of 1st half to the next spot in `temp`.
       Add 1 to both `copied` and `copied1`.

   }
   else
   {

       Copy the next element of 2nd half to the next spot in `temp`.
       Add 1 to both `copied` and `copied2`.

   }

Using the local variables `copied`, `copied1`, and `copied2`, we can refine the pseudocode a bit. The "next spot in temp" is `temp[copied]`; the "next element in the 1st half" is `data[copied1]`. And the "next element in the 2nd half" is part of the subarray (`data + n1`)—that is, the subarray that begins at `data[n1]`. In fact, the element that we want to examine from the second half is the element (`data + n1`)`[copied2]`, as shown in this refinement:

1. Initialize `copied`, `copied1`, and `copied2` to zero.

2. *while* (both halves of the array have more elements to copy)
   if (`data[copied1]` <= `(data + n1)[copied2]`)
   {

       `temp[copied]` = `data[copied1]`;
       Add 1 to both `copied` and `copied1`.

   }
   else
   {

       `temp[copied]` = `(data + n1)[copied2]`;
       Add 1 to both `copied` and `copied2`.

   }

In our actual implementation, the two assignment statements can be modified to also add 1 to `copied` and to the appropriate one of the other two local variables (`copied1` or `copied2`). The modified assignment statements make use of the ++ operator, as shown here:

1. Initialize `copied`, `copied1`, and `copied2` to zero.

2. *while* (both halves of the array have more elements to copy)
   if (`data[copied1]` <= `(data + n1)[copied2]`)
       `temp[copied++]` = `data[copied1++]`;
   else
       `temp[copied++]` = `(data + n1)[copied2++]`;

Using an index such as `copied++` has the effect of using the *current* value of the variable `copied` as the index and *afterwards* adding 1 to the variable. (If we wanted to add 1 before using the index, we would write `++copied` instead of `copied++`).

This part of our algorithm works fine as long as neither half of the array runs out of elements. However, eventually one of the two halves will run out of elements. For our example, this will occur after we copy the last element (20) from the second half of the `data` array to the temporary array, as shown here:

At a point like this, we want to copy the elements remaining in the nonempty half into the temporary array. This yields the following final version of our pseudocode for the `merge` function:

1. Initialize `copied`, `copied1`, and `copied2` to zero.

2. *while* (both halves of the array have more elements to copy)
   if (data[copied1] <= (data + n1)[copied2])
       temp[`copied++`] = data[`copied1++`];
   else
       temp[`copied++`] = (data + n1)[`copied2++`];

3. Copy any remaining entries from the left or right subarray.

4. Copy the elements from `temp` back to `data`.

This pseudocode translates to the C++ function shown in Figure 13.3 on page 592. The only additional items deal with allocating the memory for the temporary array. This temporary array is a dynamic array containing `n1 + n2` elements. At the end of the function, the dynamic array is released via the *delete* operator.

FIGURE 13.3   A Function to Merge Two Sorted Arrays

A Function Implementation

```
void merge(int data[ ], size_t n1, size_t n2)
// Precondition: data is an array (or subarray) with at least n1 + n2 elements. The first n1
// elements (from data[0] to data[n1 - 1]) are sorted from smallest to largest, and the last n2
// (from data[n1] to data[n1 + n2 - 1]) also are sorted from smallest to largest.
// Postcondition: The first n1 + n2 elements of data have been rearranged to be sorted from
// smallest to largest.
// NOTE: If there is insufficient dynamic memory, then new_handler is called.
// Library facilities used: stdlib.h
{
    int *temp;          // Points to dynamic array to hold the sorted elements
    size_t copied  = 0; // Number of elements copied from data to temp
    size_t copied1 = 0; // Number copied from the first half of data
    size_t copied2 = 0; // Number copied from the second half of data
    size_t i;           // Array index to copy from temp back into data

    // Allocate memory for the temporary dynamic array.
    temp = new int[n1+n2];

    // Merge elements, copying from two halves of data to the temporary array.
    while ((copied1 < n1) && (copied2 < n2))
    {
        if (data[copied1] < (data + n1)[copied2])
            temp[copied++] = data[copied1++];              // Copy from first half.
        else
            temp[copied++] = (data + n1)[copied2++];  // Copy from second half.
    }

    // Copy any remaining entries in the left and right subarrays.
    while (copied1 < n1)
        temp[copied++] = data[copied1++];
    while (copied2 < n2)
        temp[copied++] = (data+n1)[copied2++];

    // Copy from temp back to the data array, and release temp's memory.
    for (i = 0; i < n1+n2; i++)
        data[i] = temp[i];
    delete [ ] temp;
}
```

merge.cxx   **FTP**

Dynamic Memory Usage in Mergesort

During a mergesort, our `merge` function will be called many times. A complete analysis would show that a mergesort of an *n*-element array makes $O(n)$ calls to the `merge` function. Each call to `merge` allocates a temporary dynamic array, uses the array, and then releases the array. With some computers, this repeated allocation and release of dynamic memory takes a significant amount of execution time. A solution to the problem is given in Programming Project 6 on page 618.

Mergesort—Analysis

A complete analysis of mergesort's running time is beyond the scope of this book, but we can give the final result and hint at its derivation. First the result:

Mergesort Running Time

The worst-case running time, the average-case running time, and the best-case running time for mergesort are all $O(n \log n)$.

As usual, *n* is the number of items to be sorted. Let us try to motivate this formula. In the case of the mergesort, the algorithm performs similarly on all inputs; so our motivation will apply to both the worst-case, average-case, and best-case running times. Let's diagram the first few levels of recursive calls made by a typical mergesort:

original array of n elements

Two recursive calls sort subarrays with n/2 elements.

Four recursive calls sort subarrays with n/4 elements.

and so on. . .

At the top level, we make two recursive calls to sort subarrays with *n*/2 elements each. At this level, we call `merge` once to merge those two *n*/2 arrays into a single *n* element array. At the second level, each *n*/2 array is broken into two *n*/4 arrays. At this level there will be two `merge` calls, each of which merges a pair of $n/4$ arrays to create the two $n/2$ arrays. Continuing this pattern, you will see a total of these calls to `merge`:

At the top level, 1 call to `merge` creates an array with n elements
+
At the next level, 2 calls to `merge` to create two $n/2$ arrays
+
At the next level, 4 calls to `merge` to create two $n/4$ arrays
+
At the next level, 8 calls to `merge` to create two $n/8$ arrays
+

. . .

The pattern continues until we cannot further subdivide the arrays (because we have only a single element).

At each level of the pattern, the *total* work done by merging is $O(n)$. For example, at the top level we have one `merge` call to create an array with n elements, and the number of operations in this one call is proportional to n. At the next level, there are two `merge` calls, but each of the calls does work that is proportional to $n/2$, so again the *total* work done at that level is $O(n)$. At the next level we have four `merge` calls that each do work that is proportional to $n/4$. And so on.

Each level does *total* work proportional to n. So the total cost of the mergesort is given by this formula:

(some constant) $\times n \times$ (the number of levels in the pattern)

The size of the array pieces is halved on each step down the pattern. So the number of levels in the pattern is approximately equal to the number of times that n can be divided by two, stopping when the result is less than or equal to one. That number of "halvings" is closely approximated by $\log_2 n$ (the base 2 logarithm of n). Therefore, mergesort appears to perform the following number of operations:

(some constant) $\times n \times \log_2 n$

As a big-O formula, we can throw out the multiplicative constant and also the constant 2 in the base of the logarithm. So the time is $O(n \times \log n)$. This time of n multiplied by a logarithm of n is usually written more simply as $O(n \log n)$, pronounced "big-O of $n \log n$."

Our analysis has not been formal, but it is the correct answer, and a rigorous demonstration would follow the same outline as our intuitive explanation.

FIGURE 13.4

Value of $n \log_2 n$ versus n^2

n	$n \log_2 n$	n^2
2	2	4
8	24	64
32	160	1024
128	896	16,384
512	4608	262,144
2048	22,528	4,194,304

Mergesort has a worst-case running time of $O(n \log n)$ operations, which is faster than the $O(n^2)$ running times for the selectionsort and insertionsort algorithms. But, how much faster is it? We can get a feel for the difference by comparing the function $n \log_2 n$ with n^2. The table in Figure 13.4 gives some representative values for comparison. As you can see by studying the table, an $n \log_2 n$ running time is substantially faster than an n^2 running time, particularly if the array to be sorted is large.

Mergesort for Files

The mergesort algorithm is not actually a good choice for sorting arrays. The quicksort and heapsort, which we will describe in a moment, are better because they don't require a temporary array for the merge step. However, mergesort can be modified to sort a file, even if the file is too large to fit in the largest possible array. In the mergesort of a file, the file is divided into several pieces, and each piece is sorted (perhaps with a recursive call of the mergesort function). The sorted pieces are then merged into a single sorted file, and the separate pieces can be removed.

With this use of mergesort, the separate file pieces get smaller and smaller with each recursive call. Eventually, a piece gets small enough to fit into an array. At this point, the piece should be read into an array and sorted using quicksort or heapsort.

Quicksort

We developed the mergesort algorithm as a special case of a general sorting technique that is called divide-and-conquer sorting. In this section we will develop another sorting algorithm based on this same basic divide-and-conquer approach. This sorting algorithm is called **quicksort**, first devised by the computer scientist C. A. R. Hoare. It is similar to mergesort in many ways. It divides the elements to be sorted into two roughly equal groups, sorts the two groups by a recursive call, and combines the two sorted groups into a single array of sorted values. However, the method for dividing the array in half is much more sophisticated than the simple method we used for mergesort. On the other hand, the method for combining these two groups of sorted elements is trivial compared to the method used in mergesort. In mergesort the division is trivial and the combining complicated. With quicksort the division is complicated and the combining is trivial.

pivot element

The basic idea of quicksort is simple: Suppose you know some particular value that belongs in the middle of the array, or at least the approximate middle of the array. We will call this value the **pivot element,** or simply, the **pivot.** Suppose we somehow put this pivot element into its correct location in the array, somehow put all the values less than or equal to the pivot in array positions before the pivot, and somehow put all the values greater than the pivot in array positions after the pivot element. At this point we have not sorted the values less than the pivot element, we simply placed them, in any order, in array positions before the pivot element. Similarly, we have not yet sorted the values greater than the pivot, but we simply placed them, in any order, in array positions after the pivot element.

After this initial moving of array elements, we have moved the array closer to being sorted. We know that the pivot element of the array is in the correct position. We also know that all other values are in the correct segment of the array, either the segment before the pivot element or the segment after the pivot element. However, although we know they are in the correct segment, those segments are still not sorted. One way to proceed is to sort the two segments separately. This works because we know that all values in the first segment are less than all values in the second segment, so no value ever needs to move from one segment to the other. How do we sort the two segments? These are smaller versions of the original sorting task, and so we can sort the two smaller array segments by recursive calls. If we continue to divide the array into smaller portions in the way we outlined, we will eventually get down to array segments of size one and we can use that as a stopping case (requiring no work).

The above idea is sound except for one problem. How do we find a pivot element and its correct final position in the sorted array? There is no obvious way to quickly find the midpoint value until after the array is sorted. Our solution will be to take an arbitrary array value and use it as the pivot element. As a result, we may not be dividing the array exactly in half, but as long as we do divide it into smaller pieces, our algorithm will eventually sort the array. We perform the subtask of dividing the array elements with a function called `partition`. The `partition` function chooses some arbitrary pivot element, places it at the correct index position, and divides the remaining array elements as we have described. The function will not necessarily do those three things in that order, but it will do them all. The function prototype and specification is as follows:

```
void partition(int data[ ], size_t n, size_t& pivot_index);
// Precondition: n > 1, and data is an array (or subarray) with at least n
// elements.
// Postcondition: The function has selected some "pivot value" that occurs
// in data[0]...data[n-1]. The elements of data have then been
// rearranged and the pivot index set so that
//     -- data[pivot_index] is equal to the pivot;
//     -- each item before data[pivot_index] is <= the pivot;
//     -- each item after data[pivot_index] is > the pivot.
```

We will formulate our sorting algorithm as a recursive function called quicksort, which makes a call to the partition function. After the partitioning, the array and the pivot index look like this:

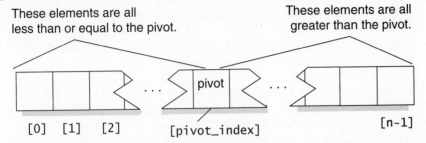

After the partition, our quicksort function makes two recursive calls. The first recursive call sorts the elements before the pivot element, from data[0] to data[pivot_index - 1]. The second recursive call sorts the elements after the pivot element, from data[pivot_index + 1] to data[n - 1]. The recursive calls are part of the quicksort implementation in Figure 13.5. We still need to derive the code for the partition function.

FIGURE 13.5   Quicksort

A Function Implementation

```
void quicksort(int data[ ], size_t n)
// Precondition: data is an array with at least n components.
// Postcondition: The elements of data have been rearranged so that
// data[0] <= data[1] <= data[2] <= ... <= data[n-1].
// Library facilities used: stdlib.h
{
    size_t pivot_index;  // Array index for the pivot element
    size_t n1;           // Number of elements before the pivot element
    size_t n2;           // Number of elements after the pivot element

    if (n > 1)
    {
        // Partition the array, and set the pivot index.
        partition(data, n, pivot_index);

        // Compute the sizes of the subarrays.
        n1 = pivot_index;
        n2 = n - n1 - 1;

        // Recursive calls will now sort the subarrays.
        quicksort(data, n1);
        quicksort((data + pivot_index + 1), n2);
    }
}
```

quick.cxx   **FTP**

The Partition Function

Since we have no information about the values in the array, all values have an equal probability of being the value that belongs in the middle of the array. Moreover, we know that the algorithm will work no matter what value we use for the pivot element. So, we arbitrarily choose the first array element to use as the pivot element. (On page 603 we discuss why this is not always the best choice and propose a method to fix the problem.)

The `partition` function will move all the values that are less than or equal to this pivot element toward the beginning of the array, that is, toward positions with lower numbered indexes. All values that are greater than this pivot element are moved the other way, toward the tail end of the array, with higher numbered indexes. Because the pivot element is not necessarily the value that belongs at the exact midpoint position of the array, we do not know where the dividing line between the two array portions belongs. Hence, we do not know how far forward we need to move elements less than or equal to the pivot element, nor do we know how far toward the end of the array we must move elements that are greater than the pivot element. We solve this dilemma by working inward from the two ends of the array. We move smaller elements to the beginning of the array, and we move larger elements to the tail end of the array. In this way we obtain two segments—one segment of smaller elements growing to the right from the beginning of the array, and one segment of larger elements growing to the left from the tail end of the array. When these two segments meet, we have correctly partitioned the array. The correct location for the pivot element is at the boundary of these two segments.

Starting at the beginning of the array, the algorithm passes over smaller elements at the beginning of the array until it encounters an element that is larger than the pivot element. This larger element is not in the correct segment and must somehow move to the tail end segment. Starting at the tail end of the array, the algorithm passes over larger elements at that end of the array until it encounters an element that is smaller than (or equal to) the pivot element. This smaller element is not in the correct segment and must somehow move to the beginning segment. At that point we know that the elements in the two segments up to, but not including, these out-of-place elements are in the correct segment of the array. If we switch these two out-of-place elements, we will know that they also are in the correct portion of the array. Using this technique of locating and switching incorrectly placed elements at the ends of the array, our algorithm proceeds to continually expand the segment at the beginning of the array and the segment at the tail end of the array, until these two segments meet.

For example, suppose the following represents our array:

40	20	10	80	60	50	7	30	100	90	70
[0]	[1]	[2]	[3]	[4]	[5]	[6]	[7]	[8]	[9]	[10]

We choose the first value, 40, as our pivot element. Starting at the beginning of the array, we look for the first element that is greater than the pivot. That is the 80. Starting from the other end we look for the first value that is less than or equal to the pivot. That is the 30. We use two variables called `too_big_index` and `too_small_index` to hold the indexes of these two array elements. After finding the two out-of-place elements, the array can be represented as follows:

40	20	10	80	60	50	7	30	100	90	70
[0]	[1]	[2]	[3]	[4]	[5]	[6]	[7]	[8]	[9]	[10]

too_big_index [3]   too_small_index [7]

The two shaded elements are in incorrect segments of the array. If we interchange them, the array will be closer to being divided correctly. After the exchange the array will contain these elements:

40	20	10	30	60	50	7	80	100	90	70
[0]	[1]	[2]	[3]	[4]	[5]	[6]	[7]	[8]	[9]	[10]

too_big_index [3]   too_small_index [7]

We now repeat the process. Continuing from the places we left off, we increment `too_big_index` until we find another element larger than the pivot; we decrement `too_small_index` until we find another element less than or equal to the pivot element. This changes the values of the two index variables as shown here:

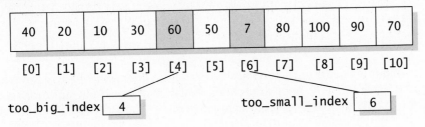

40	20	10	30	60	50	7	80	100	90	70
[0]	[1]	[2]	[3]	[4]	[5]	[6]	[7]	[8]	[9]	[10]

too_big_index [4]   too_small_index [6]

Exchanging these two elements places them in the correct array portions and yields the following array value:

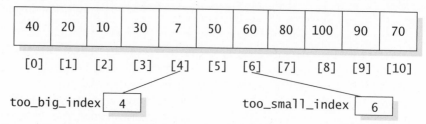

If we continue to look for elements to exchange, we will increment the too_big_index until it reaches the element that contains 50, and we will decrement the too_small_index past the element 50 to the index of the element 7. At this point the two indexes have crossed each other, as shown here:

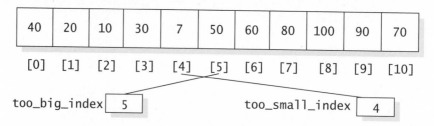

Once the indexes cross each other, we have partitioned the array. All elements less than or equal to the pivot element of 40 are in the first five positions. All elements greater than the pivot element of 40 are in the last six positions. However, the pivot is not yet at the dividing point between the two parts of the array. At this point, the correct spot for the pivot will always be at the location given by the variable too_small_index. The reason is because the too_small_index has just hit the tail end of the first of the two array segments.

So, we exchange the values of data[0] and data[too_small_index]. After moving the pivot element, the array configuration is as follows:

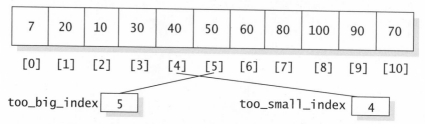

In addition to the local variables too_small_index and too_big_index, our pseudocode for the complete partition function will also have a local variable called pivot to hold a copy of the pivot element. The array itself is called data, and the total number of elements is n. The precondition guarantees that n is at least 2. Here is the pseudocode:

```
void partition(int data[ ], size_t n, size_t& pivot_index)
// Precondition: n > 1, and data is an array (or subarray)
// with at least n elements.
// Postcondition: The function has selected some "pivot value"
// that occurs in data[0]...data[n-1]. The elements of data
// have then been rearranged and the pivot index set so that
//     -- data[pivot_index] is equal to the pivot;
//     -- each item before data[pivot_index] is <= the pivot;
//     -- each item after data[pivot_index] is > the pivot.
```

1. Initialize values:
   ```
   pivot = data[0];
   too_big_index = 1;        // Index of first item after pivot
   too_small_index = n-1;    // Index of last item
   ```

2. Repeat the following until the two indexes cross each other (in other words, keep going while `too_big_index <= too_small_index`):

   2a. `while too_big_index` has not yet reached n, and `data[too_big_index]` is less than or equal to the pivot, move `too_big_index` up to the next index.

   2b. `while data[too_small_index]` is greater than the pivot, move `too_small_index` down to the previous index.

   2c. `if (too_big_index < too_small_index)`, then there is still room for both end portions to grow toward each other, so swap the values of `data[too_big_index]` and `data[too_small_index]`.

3. Move the pivot element to its correct position:

   3a. `pivot_index = too_small_index;`

   3b. Move `data[pivot_index]` (which still contains a value that is less than or equal to the pivot) to `data[0]` (which still contains the pivot).

   3c. `data[pivot_index] = pivot;`

Quicksort—Analysis

We want to estimate the running time of quicksort from Figure 13.5 on page 597. As always, *n* will be the number of items to be sorted, and we will express our running times in terms of *n*. In the best situation, the analysis of quicksort is much like our mergesort analysis from page 593. In this situation, each partition places the pivot element in the precise middle of the current subarray so that each recursive call sorts about half of the current subarray, as shown here:

The total work carried out by the partitions on each level is $O(n)$, so that the total time for quicksort is

(some constant) $\times n \times$ (the number of levels in the pattern)

In the ideal case, with the pivot element near the middle of each subarray, the number of levels is about $\log_2 n$ (just like the mergesort analysis). This results in a running time of $O(n \log n)$, which is the *best* that quicksort can manage.

But sometimes quicksort is significantly worse than $O(n \log n)$. In fact, the worst time behavior occurs when the array is already sorted before calling quicksort. In this case, the first element is smaller than everything else. Because we have been using the first element for the pivot, the pivot element is smaller than everything else. This causes a miserable partition, with everything to the right of the pivot, as shown here:

In this situation, the recursive call to sort the right-hand subarray has a lot of work to do. It must sort $n{-}1$ elements. Even worse, when the recursive call does its own partitioning, its pivot element will be the smallest of its $n{-}1$ elements, and again a bad partitioning occurs. The recursive call at the next level will have to sort $n{-}2$ elements. This pattern of bad partitions continues with recursive calls to sort $n{-}3$, $n{-}4$, and so on right down to 1. The total work done by all these recursive calls is proportional to the familiar sum: $n + (n{-}1) + (n{-}2) + (n{-}3) + \ldots + 1$.

What's the big-O analysis for this sum? It is $O(n^2)$ (see Figure 1.5 on page 18). So the *worst*-case running time for quicksort is quadratic.

Despite a poor worst-case time, quicksort generally is quite good. In fact, the average time (which we won't develop) turns out to be $O(n \log n)$. This is the same as mergesort, and we have the bonus of not needing to allocate an extra array for the merging process.

Quicksort Running Time

The worst-case running time of quicksort is $O(n^2)$. But the average-case running time, and the best-case running time for quicksort are both $O(n \log n)$. Obtaining a good running time requires the choice of a good pivot element.

Quicksort—Choosing a Good Pivot Element

Our analysis of running times points out that the choice of a good pivot element is critical to the efficiency of the quicksort algorithm. If we can ensure that the pivot element is near the median of the array values, then quicksort is very efficient. One technique that is often used to increase the likelihood of choosing a good pivot element is to choose three values from the array and then use the middle of these three values as the pivot element. For example, if the three values chosen from the array are 10, 107, and 53—then 53 would be used as the pivot element. One possibility for the three values is to use the first array value, the last array value, and the value in the array position nearest to the midpoint of the array. However, with our particular partitioning pseudocode, using these three values actually has poor performance when the array starts in reverse order. A better choice is to use three randomly selected values from the array.

Several other common techniques to speed up quicksort are discussed in the Self-Test Exercises and Programming Projects.

Self-Test Exercises

4. Suppose that `data` is an array of 1000 integers. Write a single function call that will sort the 100 elements `data[222]` through `data[321]`.

5. Which recursive sorting technique always makes recursive calls to sort subarrays that are about half the size of the original array?

6. In quicksort, what kind of time performance is obtained when the good "splitting" of arrays continues for all recursive calls? What time performance occurs if there is bad splitting, so that many recursive calls reduce the array size by only one?

7. The `quicksort` function in Figure 13.5 on page 597 produces its worst-case running time when the array is already sorted. Suppose you know that the array might already be sorted or almost sorted. How should you modify the algorithm for quicksort?

stopping recursion before the subarrays get too small

8. One problem with both of our recursive sorting algorithms is that the recursion continues all the way down until we have a subarray with only one entry. The one-entry subarray is our stopping case. This works fine, but once the size of the subarrays becomes fairly small, a lot of time is wasted making more and more recursive calls. To fix this problem, actual implementations usually stop making recursive calls when the size of the array becomes small. The definition of "small" can vary, but experiments have shown that somewhere around 15 entries is a good choice for small arrays. For this exercise, modify the recursive quicksort algorithm so that any small array is sorted using insertion sort, and the process of partitioning and making recursive calls is done only for arrays that are not small.

13.3 AN *O*(*N* LOG *N*) ALGORITHM USING A HEAP

Heapsort

Both mergesort and quicksort have an average-case running time that is $O(n \log n)$. Mergesort also has a worst-case running time that is $O(n \log n)$, whereas the worst-case running time for quicksort is $O(n^2)$. That makes mergesort sound preferable to quicksort. However, mergesort requires more storage since it requires an extra array. In this section we present a sorting algorithm, called *heapsort*, that combines the time efficiency of mergesort and the storage efficiency of quicksort. Like mergesort, heapsort has a worst-case running time that is $O(n \log n)$, and like quicksort it does not require an additional array.

heapsort is an interchange sorting algorithm

Like selectionsort, heapsort is an interchange sorting algorithm that works by repeatedly interchanging pairs of array elements. Thus, heapsort needs only some small constant amount of storage in addition to the array that holds the items to be sorted. Heapsort is similar to selectionsort in another way as well. Selectionsort locates the largest value and places it in the final array position. Then it locates the next largest value and places it in the next-to-last array position, and so forth. Heapsort uses a similar strategy, locating the largest value, then the next largest, and so on. However, heapsort uses a much more efficient algorithm to locate the array values to be moved.

the array is made into a heap

Heapsort works by first transforming the array to be sorted into a *heap*. This notion of a heap is the same data structure that was used in Section 11.1 to implement a priority queue. As a quick review, here is the definition of a heap:

Heap Review
(From Section 11.1)

A **heap** is a binary tree where the entries of the nodes can be compared with a total order semantics. In addition, these two rules are followed:

1. The entry contained by a node is greater than or equal to the entries of the node's children.

2. The tree is a complete binary tree, so that every depth except the deepest must contain as many nodes as possible; and at the deepest level, all the nodes are as far left as possible (see "Complete Binary Trees" on page 427).

A heap is a *complete* binary tree, and we have an efficient method for representing a complete binary tree in an array. This representation was first shown in Section 10.2, following these rules:

- Data from the root of the complete binary tree goes in the [0] component of the array.

- The data from depth one nodes is placed in the next two components of the array.

- We continue in this way, placing the four nodes of depth two in the next four components of the array, and so forth. For example, a heap with ten nodes can be stored in a ten-element array, as shown here:

Location of the data
for a complete
binary tree, as stored
in an array

To be more precise about the location of data in the array, we have these rules:

1. The data from the root always appears in the [0] component of the array.
2. Suppose that the data for a nonroot node appears in component [i] of the array. Then the data for its parent is always at location [(i-1)/2] (using integer division).
3. Suppose that the data for a node appears in component [i] of the array. Then its children (if they exist) always have their data at these locations:

   Left child at component [2i+1]

   Right child at component [2i+2]

With these facts in mind, we can easily state the general idea that underlies the heapsort algorithm. We start with an array of values to be sorted. The heapsort algorithm treats the array values as if they were values in a complete binary tree using the three rules listed above. That much is easy since any array of n values represents some complete binary tree with n nodes.

first, the array is made into a heap

The first step of the heapsort algorithm is to rearrange the values in the array so that the corresponding complete binary tree is a heap. In other words, we rearrange the array so that the corresponding complete binary tree follows the heap storage rule: *The value contained in a node is never less than an entry from one of the node's children.* For example, suppose that the array begins with these ten values:

21	35	22	27	23	45	42	19	4	5
[0]	[1]	[2]	[3]	[4]	[5]	[6]	[7]	[8]	[9]

This array can be interpreted as representing the complete binary tree shown here:

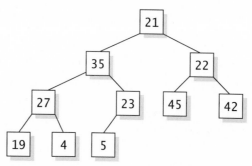

Of course, this complete binary tree is *not* a heap—for example, the data in the root's left child (35) is larger than the data in the root (21). So, the first step of the heapsort is to rearrange the array elements so that the corresponding complete binary tree is a heap.

For the ten-element example that we have just seen, the first step of the heap-sort might rearrange the array so that the elements are in the following order:

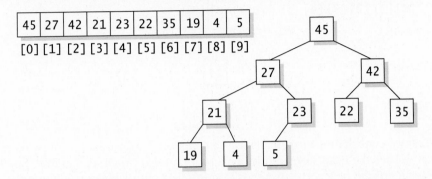

45	27	42	21	23	22	35	19	4	5
[0]	[1]	[2]	[3]	[4]	[5]	[6]	[7]	[8]	[9]

After the rearrangement of the array elements, the corresponding complete binary tree is a heap, and to aid your visualization, we have drawn the corresponding tree beside the array. But keep in mind that the only place that the numbers are stored is in the array. The tree is just our visualization of how those elements are structured. In a moment, we'll provide the details of how the rearrangement into a heap occurs, but first let's look at the rest of the heapsort algorithm.

Recall that the largest value in a heap is stored in the root, and that in our array representation of a complete binary tree, the root node is stored in the first array position. Thus, since the array represents a heap, we know that the largest array element is in the first array position. To get the largest value into the correct array position, we simply interchange the first and the final array elements. After interchanging these two array elements, we know that the largest array element is in the final array position, as shown here:

find the largest element, and move it to the end of the array

5	27	42	21	23	22	35	19	4	45
[0]	[1]	[2]	[3]	[4]	[5]	[6]	[7]	[8]	[9]

The dark vertical line in the array separates the "sorted side" of the array (on the right) from the "unsorted side." Moreover, the unsorted side (on the left) still represents a complete binary tree, which is *almost* a heap, as shown at the top of the next page.

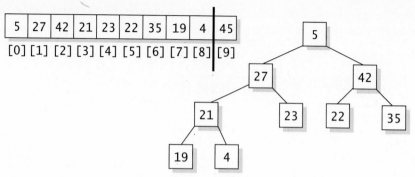

fix the heap

When we consider the *unsorted* side as a complete binary tree, it is only the root that violates the heap storage rule. This root is smaller than its children. So, the next step of the heapsort is to reposition this one out-of-place value in order to restore the heap. In Section 11.1 we discussed this process of restoring the heap by repositioning the out-of-place root. The process, called *reheapification downward*, begins by comparing the value in the root with the value of each of its children. If one or both children are larger than the root, then the root's value is exchanged with the larger of the two children. This moves the troublesome value down one level in the tree. For our example, the out-of-place value (5) is exchanged with its larger child (42), as shown here:

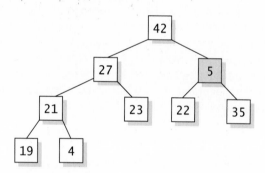

Of course, this "exchange" of values actually occurs within the array that represents the heap, so that the array now looks like this:

In this example, the 5 is still out of place, so we will once again exchange it with its largest child, resulting in the array (and heap) shown here:

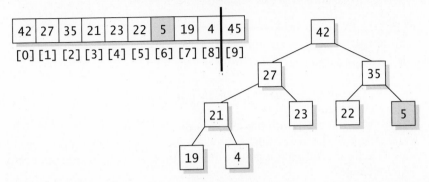

Keep in mind that only the unsorted side of the array must be maintained as a heap. In general, the reheapification continues until the troublesome value reaches a leaf or it reaches a spot where it is no larger than its children.

When the unsorted side of the array is once again a heap, the heapsort continues by exchanging the largest element in the unsorted side with the rightmost element of the unsorted side. For our example, the 42 is exchanged with the 4, as shown here:

4	27	35	21	23	22	5	19	42	45
[0]	[1]	[2]	[3]	[4]	[5]	[6]	[7]	[8]	[9]

As you can see, the "sorted side" now has the two largest elements, and the unsorted side is once again *almost* a heap, as shown here:

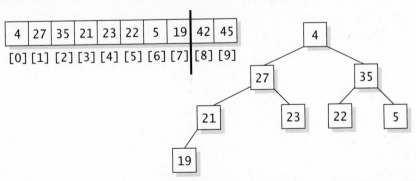

Only the root (4) is out of place, and that may be fixed by another reheapification downward. After the reheapification downward, the largest value of the unsorted side will once again reside at location [0], and we can continue to pull out the *next* largest value.

Here is the pseudocode for the heapsort algorithm that we have been describing:

```
// Heapsort for the array called data with n elements
```

1. Convert the array of *n* elements into a heap.
2. `unsorted = n; // The number of elements in the unsorted side`
3. `while (unsorted > 1)`
   ```
   {
       // Reduce the unsorted side by one.
       unsorted--;
       Swap data[0] with data[unsorted].
   ```
   The unsorted side of the array is now a heap with the root out of place.
   Do a reheapification downward to turn the unsorted side back into
   a heap.
   ```
   }
   ```

The implementation of this pseudocode is shown in Figure 13.6. In the implementation, we use two functions, `make_heap` and `reheapify_down`, which we will discuss next.

FIGURE 13.6   Heapsort

A Function Implementation

```
void heapsort(int data[ ], size_t n)
// Precondition: data is an array with at least n components.
// Postcondition: The elements of data have been rearranged so
// that data[0] <= data[1] <= ... <= data[n-1].
// Library facilities used: itemtool.h (from page 274), stdlib.h
// NOTE: The implementation also uses two functions make_heap and reheapify_down, which
// are discussed in the text.
{
    size_t unsorted;

    make_heap(data, n);

    unsorted = n;

    while (unsorted > 1)
    {
        unsorted--;
        swap(data[0], data[unsorted]);
        reheapify_down(data, unsorted);
    }
}
```

Making the Heap

At the start of the heapsort algorithm, we must rearrange the array elements so that they form a heap. This rearrangement is accomplished by calling a function with the following specification:

```
void make_heap(int data[ ], size_t n);
// Precondition: data is an array with at least n elements.
// Postcondition: The elements of data have been rearranged so that the
// complete binary tree represented by this array is a heap.
```

There are two common ways to build an initial heap from the array. One method is relatively easy to program, and we will show that method here. A second, more efficient method requires more difficult programming that we will outline in Programming Project 5 on page 617.

The simple approach to make_heap builds the heap one element at a time, starting at the front of the array. Initially we start with just one element, and this one element forms a small heap of one node. For example, we might start with the array shown here:

21	35	22	27	23	45	42	19	4	5
[0]	[1]	[2]	[3]	[4]	[5]	[6]	[7]	[8]	[9]

the first array element forms a heap with one node

In this array, the area to the left of the vertical bar can be viewed as a heap with just one node, and the area to the right is still a jumble of random values.

The make_heap algorithm adds the array nodes to the heap one at a time. In our example, we will next add the 35 to the heap, resulting in the following configuration. In this illustration, we have drawn both the array and the state of the heap that is formed from the elements to the left of the vertical bar.

21	35	22	27	23	45	42	19	4	5
[0]	[1]	[2]	[3]	[4]	[5]	[6]	[7]	[8]	[9]

As you can see, just adding the node in this way does not actually create a heap because the newly added node (35) has a value that is larger than its parent. However, we can fix this problem by pushing the out-of-place node upward until it reaches the root or it reaches a place with a larger parent. This process of pushing a new node upward is called *reheapification upward*. We have seen reheapification upward before, in Section 11.1. In that section, reheapification upward was used whenever a new item was added to the priority queue (which was represented as a heap).

The pseudocode for `make_heap` uses reheapification upward, as shown here (with two local `size_t` variables called i and k):

```
// Making a heap from an array called data with n elements
for (i = 1; i < n; i++)
{
   k = i; // The index of the new entry
   while (data[k] is not yet the root, and data[k] is bigger than its parent)
       Swap data[k] with its parent, and reset k to be the index of its parent.
}
```

The complete implementation of this pseudocode as the function `make_heap` is left up to you. The readability of your implementation can be improved if you also implement another function called `parent`, as shown here:

```
inline size_t parent(size_t k)
// Precondition: k > 0.
// Postcondition: The function assumes that k is the index of an array
// element, where the array represents a complete binary tree. The return
// value is the index of the parent of node k, using the formula from
// Rule 3 on page 606.
// Library facilities used: stdlib.h
{
    return (k-1)/2;
}
```

Whenever k is an index of an element in the array and k is not zero, the value of `parent(k)` is the array index of the parent of `data[k]`. You can use this function whenever you need to calculate the index of the parent of a node.

inline function

By the way, you may have noticed the keyword *inline* at the front of the `parent` function. This keyword has the same effect that we have seen before for inline member functions, causing the compiler to make the function calls a bit faster by putting the actual code for the function body at each location where the function is called. We suggest that you use inline functions for any one-line function that returns the value of a simple formula.

Reheapification Downward

We have one more function to implement, the reheapification downward, with this specification:

```
void reheapify_down(int data[ ], size_t n);
// Precondition: n > 0, and data is an array with at least n elements. These
// elements form a heap, except that data[0] may be in an incorrect
// location.
// Postcondition: The data values have been rearranged so that the first
// n elements of data now form a heap.
```

The function works by continually swapping the out-of-place element with its largest child, as shown in this pseudocode:

```
// Reheapification downward (for a heap where the root is out of place)
size_t current;         // Index of the node that's moving down
size_t big_child_index; // Index of current's larger child
bool heap_ok;           // Will become true when heap is correct

current = 0;
heap_ok = false;

while ((!heap_ok) && (the current node is not a leaf))
{
```
Set `big_child_index` to be the index of the larger child of the `current` node. (If there is only one child, then `big_child_index` will be set to the index of this one child.)

```
    if (data[current] < data[big_child_index])
    {
```
Swap data[current] with data[big_child_index].
```
        current = big_child_index;
    }
    else
        heap_ok = true;
}
```

The swapping stops when the out-of-place element reaches a leaf, or when the out-of-place element is larger than both of its children. If you implement this function, use two auxiliary functions (`left_child` and `right_child`) to compute the indexes of the left and right child of a node.

Heapsort—Analysis

Let us count operations for the worst-case running time for the heapsort algorithm. As usual, we take the problem size *n* to be the number of items to be sorted. If you look back at the implementation from Figure 13.6 on page 610, you will see that the total number of operations can be given as this sum:

(The operations to build the initial heap)
+
(The operations to pull the items out of the heap one at a time)
+
(Some fixed number of operations for a few other assignments)

In order to refine this formula, we must calculate the number of operations to build the initial heap and the number of operations required when an element is pulled out of the heap.

Building the initial heap. To build the heap we add the items one at a time, using reheapification upward to push the new item upward until it reaches the root or it reaches an acceptable spot (where the parent has a larger value). Since we actually add $n-1$ elements (rather than n), the total time is this:

$$(n - 1) \times \text{(number of operations for one reheapification upward)}$$

The maximum number of operations for one reheapification upward is a constant times the depth of the heap. In Section 11.3, we showed that the depth of a heap is no more than $\log_2 n$. Therefore, the worst-case time for building the heap is the following:

$$(n - 1) \times \text{a constant} \times (\log_2 n)$$

Removing the constants from this formula results in an $O(n \log n)$ running time to build the initial heap.

Pulling the items out of the heap. Once the initial heap is built, we pull the items out of the heap one at a time. After each item is removed, we perform a reheapification downward. We pull out a total of $n-1$ items, and the number of operations in each reheapification downward is never more than a constant times the depth of the tree. Therefore, pulling all the items out of the tree also requires $(n - 1) \times$ a constant $\times (\log_2 n)$ operations, which is an $O(n \log n)$ running time.

worst case for heapsort

Total time for heap sort. We can now give a final estimate for the worst-case running time for the entire heapsort algorithm. Building the initial heap requires $O(n \log n)$ operations, and then pulling the items out of the heap requires another $O(n \log n)$ operations. You might be tempted to write that the sum of all this work is $O(2n \log n)$, and you would be right. But remember that multiplication by a constant (such as 2) can be ignored in big-O notation, so in fact the entire algorithm from start to finish requires $O(n \log n)$ operations.

average case for heapsort

Although we won't give a derivation, it turns out that the average-case running time for heapsort is also $O(n \log n)$, the same as the worst-case running time.

Heapsort Running Time

The worst-case running time and the average-case running time for heapsort are both $O(n \log n)$.

Self-Test Exercise

9. How would you modify the heapsort algorithm so that it sorts integers into decreasing order rather than increasing order?

CHAPTER SUMMARY

- All the sorting algorithms presented in this chapter apply to any type of values sorted according to any reasonable ordering relation. The array values do not need to be integers.

- In the divide-and-conquer sorting method, the values to be sorted are divided into two approximately equal groups, the groups are sorted by a recursive call, and then the two sorted groups are combined into the final sorted list. Mergesort and quicksort are two examples of divide-and-conquer sorting algorithms.

- Selectionsort and insertionsort have quadratic running times in both the worst case and the average case. This is comparatively slow. However, if the arrays to be sorted are short, or if the sorting program will only be used a few times, then they are reasonable algorithms to use. Insertionsort is particularly good if the array is nearly sorted beforehand.

- Mergesort and quicksort are much more efficient than selectionsort and insertionsort. They each have an average-case running time that is $O(n \log n)$. If you need to sort a large number of long lists, it would be worth the extra effort of coding and debugging one of these more complicated algorithms.

- Mergesort has the advantage that its worst-case running time is $O(n \log n)$, but it has the disadvantage of needing to allocate a second array to use in the merging process.

- Quicksort has the disadvantage of a quadratic worst-case time. However, with some care in the pivot selection process, we usually can avoid this bad time. Quicksort can be further improved by stopping the recursive calls when the subarrays become small (around 15 elements). These small subarrays can be sorted with an insertionsort.

- Heapsort works by creating a heap from all the array elements and then pulling the largest element out of the heap, then the next largest, and so on. The worst-case and average-case running times for heapsort are both $O(n \log n)$.

Solutions to Self-Test Exercises ?

1. Write a new function, `index_of_minimal`, that returns the index of the smallest element of an array. Use this new function instead of `index_of_maximal` in the selectionsort in Figure 13.1 on page 574.

2. To sort strings, change each declaration of the array to an array of strings rather than an array of integers. Alternatively, if you are familiar with template functions (Chapter 6), you could implement the selectionsort as a template

function that depends on the underlying type of items in the array. This underlying type could be any type with a copy constructor, an assignment operator, and with the comparison operators defined as a total order.

3. Here is one solution:
```
void insertionsort
(int data[ ], size_t n)
{
    size_t i;

    for (i = 1; i < n; i++)
        ordered_insert(data,i,data[i]);
}
```

4. `quicksort((data + 222), 100);`

5. Mergesort always makes recursive calls to sort subarrays that are about half the size of the original array, resulting in $O(n \log n)$ time.

6. When there is good splitting in quicksort, the resulting time is $O(n \log n)$. When there is bad splitting in quicksort, the result can be quadratic time.

7. See "Quicksort—Choosing a Good Pivot Element" on page 603.

8. Your new quicksort function should have an `if` statement that tests whether (n <= 15). If so, then call insertionsort; otherwise, proceed as in the original quicksort.

9. Change the heap rule so that the value in every node is less than or equal to its children. Modify `make_heap` to build this new kind of heap by changing the test in the while-loop to this:
```
(k>0 && data[k] < data[parent(k)])
```

In `reheapify_down`, change the series of if-statements so that they find the index of the smaller child. If this smaller child is less than the current node, then swap the current node with the smaller child and continue. Otherwise, the heap is okay.

PROGRAMMING PROJECTS

1 If you are familiar with template functions (Chapter 6), then rewrite one of the sorting functions as a template function. You may choose selectionsort, insertionsort, mergesort, quicksort, or heapsort. For example, with selection-sort you would have the specification shown here:
```
template <class Item, class SizeType>
void selectionsort
(Item data[ ], SizeType n);
// Precondition: data is an array with at
// least n components.
// Postcondition: The elements of data
// have been rearranged so that
// data[0] <= data[1] <= ... <= data[n-1].
// NOTE: Item may be any of the C++ built-in
// types (int, char, etc.), or any class with a
// copy constructor, an assignment operator,
// and the six comparison operators forming a
// total order semantics.
```

2 Redo the insertion sort algorithm so that the values are inserted into a linked list rather than an array. This eliminates the need to move other values when a new value is inserted, since your algorithm can simply insert a new node where the new value should go. Analyze your algorithm to obtain a big-O expression of the worst-case running time. Code your algorithm to produce a complete C++ program that reads in a list of ten integers, sorts the integers, and then writes out the sorted list. Your program should allow the user to repeat the process and sort another list until the user says he or she wants to exit the program.

3 One of the advantages of mergesort is that it can easily be adapted to sort a linked list of values. This is because the algorithm retrieves the values from the two lists being merged in the order that they occur in the lists. If the lists are linked lists, then that algorithm can simply move down the list node after node. With heapsort or quicksort the algorithm needs to move values from random locations in the array so they do not adapt as well to sorting a linked list. Write a program that sorts a linked list of integers using mergesort. The program will read the integers into a linked list and then sort the linked list using mergesort. This will require additional linked lists, but you should use linked lists, not arrays, for all your list storage.

4 Rewrite quicksort so that there are no recursive calls. The technique is to use a stack to keep track of which portions of the array still need to be sorted. Whenever we identify a portion of the array that still needs to be sorted, we will push two items onto the stack: (1) the starting index of the array segment, and (2) the length of the array segment. The entire quicksort can now work as follows (with no recursion):

1. Push 0 and n onto the stack (indicating that we must sort the n-element array segment starting at data[0]).

2. *while* (the stack is not empty)

   2a. Pop a size n and a starting index i off the stack. We must now sort the n-element array segment starting at data[i]. To do this sort, first call:
   partition(data+i,n,pivot_index)

   2b. If the area before the pivot index has more than one element, then we must sort this area. This area begins at data[i] and has pivot_index elements, so push i and pivot_index onto the stack.

   2c. If the area after the pivot index has more than one element, then we must sort this area. This area begins at
   data[i + pivot_index + 1]
   and has (n - pivot_index - 1) elements, so push (i + pivot_index + 1) and (n - pivot_index - 1) onto the stack.

With this approach, in the worst case, the stack must be nearly twice as big as the array that's being sorted. This worst case occurs when we keep pushing two-element array segments onto the stack. However, there is a modification that reduces the maximum stack size. When you do steps 2b and 2c, make sure

that the *larger* array segment gets pushed onto the stack first. With this modification, the maximum necessary stack size is just $2\log_2 n$. With this in mind, you can use a stack with a fixed size—for example, a 100-element stack is enough to sort an array with 2^{50} elements.

5 The discussion on page 611 shows our algorithm for building the initial heap in the heapsort algorithm. The algorithm is reasonably efficient, but we can be even more efficient. The more efficient algorithm uses a function that creates a heap from a subtree of the complete binary tree. This function has the following specification:

```
void heapify_subtree(
  int data[ ],
  size_t root_of_subtree,
  size_t n
);
// Precondition: data is an array with at least
// n elements, and root_of_subtree < n. We will
// consider data to represent a complete
// binary tree, and in this representation the
// node at data[root_of_subtree] is the root of
// a subtree called s. This subtree s is already
// a heap, except that its root might be out of
// place.
// Postcondition: The subtree s has been
// rearranged so that it is now a valid heap.
```

You can write the heapify_subtree function yourself. Using this function, you can make an entire *n*-element array into a heap with the algorithm:

```
for (i = (n/2); i > 0; i--)
  heapify_subtree(data, i-1, n);
```

For example, with *n*=10, we will end up making the following sequence of calls:

```
heapify_subtree(4);
heapify_subtree(3);
heapify_subtree(2);
heapify_subtree(1);
heapify_subtree(0);
```

It turns out that this method is actually $O(n)$ rather than $O(n \log n)$.

For this project, reimplement make_heap, as outlined above.

6 On page 593, we discussed problems with the dynamic memory usage of mergesort. One solution to the problem is to rewrite the mergesort according to the following specification:

```
void mergesort(
    int data[ ],
    size_t first_index,
    size_t last_index,
    int temp[ ]
);
// Precondition: data[first_index] through
// data[last_index] are array elements in no
// particular order. The temp array has
// locations temp[first_index] through
// temp[last_index].
// Postcondition: The elements
// data[first_index] through data[last_index]
// have been rearranged so that they are
// ordered from smallest to largest. The array
// elements temp[first_index] through
// temp[last_index] have been used as
// temporary storage and now contain a
// copy of data[first_index] through
// data[last_index].
```

14 Software Reuse with Derived Classes

*It is indeed a desirable thing to be well descended, but
the glory belongs to our ancestors.*

PLUTARCH
Morals

Often you will find yourself with a class that is *nearly* what
you require, but not quite. Perhaps the class that you require needs alterations to
one or two of the member functions of an existing class, or maybe an existing
class just needs a few extra member functions. Object-oriented languages provide support for this situation by allowing programmers to easily create new
classes that acquire most of their properties from an existing class. The original
class is called the **base class** (or *parent* class, or *ancestor* class, or *superclass—*
the lingo isn't entirely stabilized), and the new, slightly different class is the
derived class (or *child* class, or *descendant* class, or *subclass*).

The first section of this chapter provides an introduction to derived classes.
The next two sections show two detailed programming examples, including an
illustration of how many of our previous ADTs might have benefited from using
a derived class.

14.1 DERIVED CLASSES

One of the exercises in Chapter 2 was a `Clock` class to keep track of one instance of a time value such as 9:48 P.M. (see Self-Test Exercise 13 on page 57). One possible definition for this class is shown in Figure 14.1 on page 621. Now suppose you're writing a program with various kinds of clocks: 12-hour clocks, 24-hour clocks, alarm clocks, grandfather clocks, cuckoo clocks, maybe even a computer clock. Each of these things is a `Clock`, but each of these also has additional properties that don't apply to clocks in general. For example, a `CuckooClock` might have an extra function, `is_cuckooing`, that returns true if its cuckoo bird is currently making noise. How would you implement a `CuckooClock`, which is a `Clock` with one extra `is_cuckooing` member function?

One possible solution uses no new ideas: Modify the original `Clock` definition by adding an extra member function, `is_cuckooing`. With this solution, the `CuckooClock` definition looks a lot like the ordinary `Clock`. The only changes are the highlights shown here:

```
class CuckooClock
{
public:
    // CONSTRUCTOR
    CuckooClock( );
    // MODIFICATION MEMBER FUNCTIONS
    void set_time(int hour, int minute, bool morning);
    void advance(int minutes);
    // CONSTANT MEMBER FUNCTIONS
    int get_hour( ) const;
    int get_minute( ) const;
    bool is_morning( ) const;
    bool is_cuckooing( ) const;
private:
    | We don't care what private implementation is used.
};
```

Can you think of some potential problems with this solution? Problems occur when a program has a `CuckooClock` but also has an ordinary `Clock` and perhaps other kinds of clocks as well. We'll end up writing a separate class definition for each different type of clock. Even though all of these have similar or identical constructors and member functions, we'll still end up repeating the member function implementations for each different kind of clock.

FIGURE 14.1   The Clock Class

Documentation for the Clock Class

```
// CONSTRUCTOR for the Clock class:
//    Clock( )
//       Postcondition: The clock is set to 12:00 (midnight).
//
// MODIFICATION MEMBER FUNCTIONS for the Clock class:
//    void set_time(int hour, int minute, bool morning)
//       Precondition: 1 <= hour <= 12, and 0 <= minute <= 59.
//       Postcondition: The clock's time has been set to the given hour and minute (using usual
//       12-hour time notation). If the third parameter, morning, is true, then this time is from
//       12:00 midnight to 11:59 A.M. Otherwise this time is from 12:00 noon to 11:59 P.M.
//
//    void advance(int minutes)
//       Postcondition: The clock has been moved forward by the indicated number of minutes.
//       Note: A negative argument moves the clock backward.
//
// CONSTANT MEMBER FUNCTIONS for the Clock class:
//    int get_hour( ) const
//       Postcondition: The value returned is the current hour using a 12-hour clock.
//
//    int get_minute( ) const
//       Postcondition: The value returned is the current minute on the clock.
//
//    bool is_morning( ) const
//       Postcondition: If the clock's time lies from 12:00 midnight to 11:59 A.M. (inclusive),
//       the function returns true; otherwise it returns false.
//
// VALUE SEMANTICS for the Clock class:
//    Assignments and the copy constructor may be used with Clock objects.
```

Class Definition

```
class Clock
{
public:
    // CONSTRUCTOR
    Clock( );
    // MODIFICATION MEMBER FUNCTIONS
    void set_time(int hour, int minute, bool morning);
    void advance(int minutes);
    // CONSTANT MEMBER FUNCTIONS
    int get_hour( ) const;
    int get_minute( ) const;
    bool is_morning( ) const;
private:
    ‖ For this example, we don't care what private implementation is used.
};
```

clocks.h   FTP

The solution to the clock problem is a new concept, called **derived classes**, described here:

Derived Classes

Derived classes use a concept called inheritance. In particular, once we have a class, we can then declare new classes that contain all of the members of the original class—plus any extras that you want to throw in. This new class is called a **derived class** of the original class. The original class is called the **base class**. And the members that the derived class receives from its base class are called **inherited** members.

How to Declare a Derived Class

In the definition of the derived class, the name of the derived class is followed by a single colon, the keyword *public*, and then the name of the base class. For example, suppose that we want to declare a derived class CuckooClock using the existing Clock class as the base class. The beginning of the CuckooClock class definition would then look like this:

```
class CuckooClock : public Clock
{
    ...
```

This definition indicates that every CuckooClock is also an ordinary Clock. The primary consequence is that all of the public members of an ordinary Clock are *immediately available as public members* of a CuckooClock. These members are said to be **inherited** from the Clock.

public base class versus private base class

In the clock example, we used the keyword *public*, which creates a **public base class.** An alternative is to use the keyword *private* instead of *public*, resulting in a **private base class**. With a private base class, all of the public members of an ordinary Clock are immediately available as *private* members of a CuckooClock. In both cases—public base class or private base class—it is the public members of the Clock that are accessible to the CuckooClock. In some sense, the private members of the Clock are also present in a CuckooClock—they must be present because some of the public members make use of the private members. But, these private members cannot be directly accessed in a CuckooClock, not even by the programmer who implements a CuckooClock. This is why we did not even list the Clock's private members in Figure 14.1 on page 621.

For future reference, you should know that there is a third kind of member called a **protected member**. In most respects, a protected member is just like a private member, but the programmer of a derived class has direct access to protected members. None of our examples will use protected members.

FIGURE 14.2 The CuckooClock Is Derived from the Ordinary Clock

A Derived Class Definition

```
class CuckooClock : public Clock
{
public:
    bool is_cuckooing( ) const;
};
```

The definition could be added to the same header file that contains the Clock class, or be placed anywhere else that has access to the Clock class.

A Function Member Implementation

```
bool CuckooClock::is_cuckooing( ) const
{
    return (get_minute( ) == 0);
}
```

The new member function is in an implementation file.

clocks.h and clocks.cxx   **FTP**

Now, let's finish our CuckooClock definition and see how it can be used in a program. Our complete CuckooClock is shown in Figure 14.2. As you can see, a CuckooClock has one extra public member function: a boolean function called is_cuckooing, which returns true when the clock's cuckoo is making noise. In the implementation of is_cuckooing, you can see that our cuckoos make noise whenever the current minute of the time is zero. In this implementation, we use the ordinary clock function, get_minute, to determine whether the current minute is zero.

Once the CuckooClock definition is available, a program may declare CuckooClock objects using all the public Clock member functions and also using the new is_cuckooing function. In this usage, there are some special considerations for the constructors, the destructor, and the assignment operator. We'll discuss these considerations over the next few pages.

The Automatic Constructors of a Derived Class

A derived class may declare its own constructors, or it may use the automatic default constructor and the automatic copy constructor that are provided for every C++ class. Later we will examine the case of derived classes with their own declared constructors, but for the cuckoo clock, the automatic constructors are sufficient. We get the following automatic constructors.

The automatic default constructor. If we don't declare *any* constructors for a derived class, then C++ will automatically provide a default constructor. This default constructor will carry out two steps: (1) activate the default constructor for the base class (to initialize any member variables that the base class uses), then (2) activate default constructors for any new member variables that the derived class has, but the base class does not have.

For example, our cuckoo clock has an automatic default constructor that is activated in an object declaration such as this:

```
CuckooClock noisy;
```

The `CuckooClock`'s automatic default constructor will activate the ordinary `Clock` default constructor for `noisy`, initializing any private member variables of the ordinary clock. Remember, these private member variables are present in any cuckoo clock, and therefore they must be initialized even though there is no way to directly access these member variables.

The automatic copy constructor. If a derived class does not define a copy constructor of its own, then C++ will automatically provide a copy constructor. This copy constructor is similar to the automatic default constructor in that it carries out two steps: (1) activate the copy constructor for the base class (to copy any member variables that the base class uses), then (2) activate copy constructors for any new member variables that the derived class has but the base class does not have. The copy constructors that are activated in Steps 1 and 2 may themselves be automatic copy constructors, or they may be specially written to accomplish correct copying of dynamic data structures.

Using a Derived Class

We now know enough to write a bit of code that uses a derived class. For example, here is a bit of code that declares a cuckoo clock, advances the cuckoo clock some number of minutes, and then prints a message about whether the cuckoo clock is currently cuckooing:

```
CuckooClock noisy;
int minutes;

cout << "How many minutes should I advance the clock? ";
cin >> minutes;
noisy.advance(minutes);

if (noisy.is_cuckooing( ))
    cout << "Cuckoo cuckoo cuckoo." << endl;
else
    cout << "All's quiet on the cuckoo front." << endl;
```

The key feature is that a cuckoo clock may use ordinary clock member functions (such as `advance`), and it may also use the new `is_cuckooing` function. The inheritance is accomplished with little work on our part. We only need to write the body of `is_cuckooing`; none of the ordinary clock functions need to be rewritten for the cuckoo clock.

FIGURE 14.3	Implementation of the Less Than Operator for Clocks

A Function Implementation

```
bool operator < (const Clock& c1, const Clock& c2)
// Postcondition: Returns true if the time on c1 is earlier than the time on c2
// over a usual day (starting at midnight); otherwise returns false.
{
    // Check whether one is morning and the other is not.
    if (c1.is_morning( ) && !c2.is_morning( ))
        return true;
    else if (c2.is_morning( ) && !c1.is_morning( ))
        return false;

    // Check whether one is 12 o'clock and the other is not.
    else if ((c1.get_hour( ) == 12) && (c2.get_hour( ) != 12))
        return true;
    else if ((c2.get_hour( ) == 12) && (c1.get_hour( ) != 12))
        return false;

    // Check whether the hours are different from each other.
    else if (c1.get_hour( ) < c2.get_hour( ))
        return true;
    else if (c2.get_hour( ) < c1.get_hour( ))
        return false;

    // The hours are the same, so check the minutes.
    else if (c1.get_minute( ) < c2.get_minute( ))
        return true;
    else
        return false;
}
```

clocks.cxx	**FTP**

There's another advantage to derived classes: An object of the derived class may be used at any location where the base class is expected. For example, suppose we overload the "less than" operator to compare the times on two clocks, as shown in Figure 14.2. We can use this relational operator to compare two ordinary clocks, but we can also compare any of the clock's derived classes. For example, consider the code at the top of the next page.

```
CuckooClock sunrise, your_time;
int minutes;

sunrise.advance(60 * 6); // Set the sunrise for 6 A.M.
cout << "How many minutes do I advance your clock?" << endl;
cin >> minutes;
your_time.advance(minutes);

if (sunrise < your_time)
    cout << "That's before sunrise!" << endl;
else
    cout << "That's not before sunrise." << endl;
```

In fact, we can even use the "less than" operator to compare an ordinary Clock with a CuckooClock, or to compare two objects from different derived classes.

Any functions that you write to manipulate a clock will also be able to manipulate all of the clock's derived classes. Without descendant types, we would need to write a separate function for each kind of clock that we want to manipulate.

The Automatic Assignment Operator for a Derived Class

If a derived class does not define its own assignment operator, then C++ will automatically provide an assignment operator. This automatic assignment operator is similar to the automatic constructors, carrying out two steps: (1) activate the assignment operator for the base class (to copy any member variables that the base class uses), then (2) activate the assignment operator for any new member variables that the derived class has but the base class does not have. The assignment operators that are activated in Steps 1 and 2 may themselves be automatic assignment operators, or they may be specially written to accomplish correct copying of dynamic data structures.

Assignments are also allowed from a derived class to the base class, for example:

```
Clock ordinary;
CuckooClock fancy;

fancy.advance(60);
ordinary = fancy;
```

Advance the fancy clock to 1 A.M. and assign the ordinary clock to equal the fancy clock.

The assignment `ordinary = fancy` is permitted because a cuckoo clock (such as fancy) can be used at any point where an ordinary clock is expected. Therefore, the assignment will activate the assignment operator for an ordinary clock (using fancy as if it was just an ordinary clock).

On the other hand, an assignment in the other direction, `fancy = ordinary`, is *forbidden* because an object of the base class (the ordinary clock) cannot be used as if it were an object of the derived class (the cuckoo clock).

Allowed:	Forbidden:
When a base class is public, an object of a derived class may be used as if it were an object of the base class.	But an object of the base class cannot usually be used as if it were an object of the derived class.

The Automatic Destructor of a Derived Class

Before we proceed to more examples of derived classes, we'll throw in one last automatic feature. If a class does not have a declared destructor, then C++ provides an automatic destructor that carries out two steps: (1) the destructors are called for any member variables that the derived class has, but the base class does not have, then (2) the destructor is called for the base class. Notice that an automatic destructor works differently than an automatic constructor: An automatic destructor first activates the destructors for member variables and then activates the destructor for the base class. But an automatic constructor first activates the constructor for base class, and then activates the constructors for member variables.

Overriding Inherited Member Functions

Frequently, a derived class needs to perform some member function different from the way the base class does. For example, the original clock provides the current hour via get_hour, using a 12-hour clock. Suppose we want to implement a derived class that provides its hour on a 24-hour basis, ranging from 0 to 23. The new clock can be defined as a derived class called Clock24. The Clock24 class inherits everything from the ordinary clock, but it provides a new get_hour member function. This is called **overriding** an inherited member function.

To override an inherited member function, the derived class uses a new prototype for the overridden function, as shown here:

```
class Clock24 : public Clock
{
public:
    int get_hour( ) const; // Overridden from the Clock class
};
```

Now we are free to define a new implementation of Clock24::get_hour. Within this implementation, we can use any of the ordinary clock functions, and we can even use the get_hour member function from the ordinary clock. The *use the scope resolution operator to call the original version of the function*

notation for using the ordinary clock's `get_hour` function is to place the scope resolution operator, `Clock::`, in front of the function call. So, when we write `Clock::get_hour( )`, we are activating the original clock's `get_hour` function. Here's the complete implementation of `Clock24::get_hour`:

```
int Clock24::get_hour( ) const
{
    int ordinary_hour;

    ordinary_hour = Clock::get_hour( );
    if (is_morning( ))
    {
        if (ordinary_hour == 12)
            return 0;
        else
            return ordinary_hour;
    }
    else
    {
        if (ordinary_hour == 12)
            return 12;
        else
            return ordinary_hour + 12;
    }
}
```

   TIP

Programming Tip: Make the Overriding Function Call the Original

In the example of the `Clock24::get_hour` function, the first action of the overriding function is to call the original function. Almost always, the overriding function will call the original function to do some of its work. Frequently the call to the original function will be the *first* action of an overriding method.

Several features of derived classes remain to be seen, such as derived classes that require new private member variables. These considerations will arise in the examples from the next three sections of this chapter.

Self-Test Exercises

1. Design and implement a derived class called `DaylightClock`. A daylight clock is like a clock except that it has one extra boolean member function to determine whether it is currently daylight. Assume that daylight stretches from 7 A.M. through 6:59 P.M.

2. Suppose a derived class does not declare any constructors of its own. What constructors is it given automatically?

3. Describe the actions of the automatic assignment operator and the automatic destructor for a derived class.

4. Design and implement a derived class called `NoonAlarm`. A noon alarm object is just like a clock, except that whenever the `advance` function is called to advance the clock forward through 12 o'clock noon, an alarm message is printed (by the advance member function).

14.2 SIMULATION OF AN ECOSYSTEM

There are many potential uses for derived classes, but one of the most frequent uses comes from the is-a relationship. "A is-a B" means that each A object is a particular kind of B object. For example, a cuckoo clock is a particular kind of clock. Some other examples of is-a relationships for living organisms are shown in Figure 14.4. The relationships are drawn in a tree called an **object hierarchy** tree. In this tree, each base class is placed as the parent of its derived classes.

A is-a B means that A is a particular kind of B

FIGURE 14.4   An Object Hierarchy

Programming Tip: When to Use a Derived Class

Look at each line in the object hierarchy tree (Figure 14.4 on page 629). For each child and its parent, does it make sense to say "A is a B"? Whenever it makes sense to say "A is a B," consider implementing the class for A as a derived class of B. This lets the new A class benefit from inheriting all of B's public members.

Implementing Part of the Organism Object Hierarchy

We will implement four classes from the object hierarchy tree of living organisms, and use these four classes in a program that simulates a small ecosystem. The four classes that we will implement are:

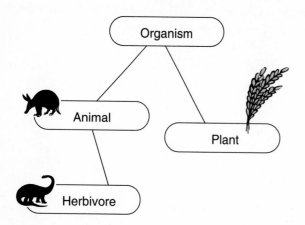

- A general class, called Organism, that can be used by a program to simulate the simplest properties of organisms, such as being born, growing, and eventually dying.

- Two classes that are derived from an Organism. The classes, called Animal and Plant, can do everything that an ordinary organism can do—but they also have extra abilities associated with animals and plants.

- The final class, called Herbivore, is derived from the animal class. It is a special kind of animal that eats plants.

Keep in mind that the derived classes might have new member variables as well as new member functions.

The Organism Class

At the top of our object hierarchy tree is a class called Organism. Within a program, every organism is given an initial size, measured in ounces. Each organism is also given a growth rate, measured in ounces per week. A program that wants to simulate the growth of an organism will start by specifying an initial size and growth rate as arguments to the organism's constructor. Throughout the computation, the program may call a member function named simulate_week, which causes the organism to simulate the passage of one week in its life—in other words, activating simulate_week makes the organism grow by its current growth rate. The Organism class has a few other member functions specified in Figure 14.5 on page 631, and a usage of the Organism class is shown in Figure 14.6 on page 632.

FIGURE 14.5 Documentation for the Organism Class

Documentation for the Organism Class

```
// CLASS PROVIDED: Organism
//     An Organism object can simulate a growing organism such as a plant or an animal.
//
// CONSTRUCTOR for the Organism class:
//     Organism(double init_size = 1, double init_rate = 0)
//         Precondition: init_size >= 0. Also, if init_size is 0, then init_rate is also zero.
//         Postcondition: The organism being simulated has been initialized. The value returned
//         from get_size( ) is now init_size (measured in ounces), and the value returned from
//         get_rate( ) is now init_rate (measured in ounces per week).
//
// MODIFICATION MEMBER FUNCTIONS for the Organism class:
//     void simulate_week( )
//         Postcondition: The size of the organism has been changed by its current growth rate.
//         If the new size is less than zero, then the actual size is set to zero rather than to a
//         negative value, and the growth rate is also set to zero.
//
//     void assign_rate(double new_rate)
//         Postcondition: The organism's growth rate has been changed to new_rate
//         (measured in ounces per week).
//
//     void alter_size(double amount)
//         Postcondition: The given amount (in ounces) has been added to the organism's current
//         size. If this results in a new size less than zero, then the actual size is set to zero
//         rather than to a negative value, and the growth rate is also set to zero.
//
//     void death( )
//          Postcondition: The organism's current size and growth rate have been set to zero.
//
// CONSTANT MEMBER FUNCTIONS for the Organism class:
//     double get_size( ) const
//          Postcondition: The value returned is the organism's current size (in ounces).
//
//     double get_rate( ) const
//          Postcondition: The value returned is the organism's current growth rate (in oz/week).
//
//     bool is_alive( ) const
//          Postcondition: If the current size is greater than zero, then the return value is true.
//          Otherwise the return value is false.
//
// VALUE SEMANTICS for the Organism class:
//     Assignments and the copy constructor may be used with Organism objects.
```

organism.h FTP

FIGURE 14.6   Sample Program from the Movie, *The Blob*

A Program

```
// FILE: blob.cxx
// This small demonstration shows how the Organism class is used.
#include <iostream.h>        // Provides cout and cin
#include <stdlib.h>          // Provides EXIT_SUCCESS
#include "organism.h"        // Provides the Organism class

int main( )
{
    Organism blob(20.0, 100000.0);
    int week;

    // Untroubled by conscience or intellect, the Blob grows for three weeks.
    for (week = 1; week <= 3; week++)
    {
        blob.simulate_week( );
        cout << "Week " << week << ":" << " the Blob is ";
        cout << blob.get_size( ) << " ounces." << endl;
    }

    // Steve McQueen reverses the growth rate to -80000 ounces per week.
    blob.assign_rate(-80000.0);
    while (blob.is_alive( ))
    {
        blob.simulate_week( );
        cout << "Week " << week << ":" << " the Blob is ";
        cout << blob.get_size( ) << " ounces." << endl;
        week++;
    }

    cout << "The Blob (or its son) shall return." << endl;
    return EXIT_SUCCESS;
}
```

Sample Dialogue

Can anyone stop
the Blob?!

```
Week 1: The Blob is 100020 ounces.
Week 2: The Blob is 200020 ounces.
Week 3: The Blob is 300020 ounces.
Week 4: The Blob is 220020 ounces.   ←
Week 5: The Blob is 140020 ounces.
Week 6: The Blob is 60020 ounces.
Week 7: The Blob is 0 ounces.
The Blob (or its son) shall return.
```

Steve McQueen comes to
the rescue at the end of
week 3!

blob.cxx   **FTP**

The `Organism` class has functions to assign a new growth rate, to alter the organism's current size by a specified amount, and to return information about the organism's current size and growth rate. Also notice that the constructor has default arguments (one ounce for the initial size and zero ounces per week for the initial growth rate); therefore the constructor may be used with no arguments (that is, a default constructor).

The organism class is not hard to implement, and we'll leave its implementation up to you. But we will give one example of using the organism class. Movie buffs may recall the 1958 film, *The Blob*. The Blob came to Earth from outer space at a mere 20 ounces, but "untroubled by conscience or intellect," it absorbs anything and anyone in its path. Without giving away the whole plot, let's suppose that the Blob grows at the astonishing rate of 100,000 ounces per week for three weeks. Then our hero (Steve McQueen) manages to reverse its growth to a rate of negative 80,000 ounces per week. A program to simulate the movie plot is shown in Figure 14.6 on page 632. The program assumes that the `Organism` class is implemented with a header file called `organism.h`.

The Animal Class: A Derived Class with New Private Member Variables

Now we want to implement a class that can be used to simulate an animal. Since an animal *is-an* organism, it makes sense to declare the `Animal` class as a derived class of the `Organism`. In our design, an animal is an organism that must consume a given amount of food each week to survive. If a week has passed and the animal has consumed less than its required amount of food, then death occurs. With this in mind, the `Animal` class will have two new private member variables, which are not part of the `Organism` class, as shown in the private part of this partial definition:

```
class Animal : public Organism
{
public:
    || We discuss the animal's public members in a moment.
private:
    double need_each_week;
    double eaten_this_week;
};
```

the derived class has two new private member variables

The first new member variable, `need_each_week`, keeps track of how many ounces of food the animal must eat each week in order to survive. The second new member variable, `eaten_this_week`, keeps track of how many ounces of food the animal has eaten so far this week.

When a derived class has some new member variables, it will usually need a new constructor to initialize those member variables. This is the first example that we have seen where a derived class has a new constructor rather than using the automatic constructors that were described on page 623. A new feature arises when a derived class has a new constructor, so we will discuss this feature now.

How to Provide a New Constructor for a Derived Class

When a derived class has a new constructor, the prototype for the new constructor appears in the public portion of the class definition, just like any other constructor. In the case of the animal, the new constructor will have three arguments. The first two arguments are the same as the arguments for any organism, providing the initial size and the initial growth rate. The third argument will indicate how much food the animal needs, in ounces per week. Thus, the start of the animal's public section is given here:

```
class Animal : public Organism
{
public:
    Animal(double init_size = 1, double init_rate = 0, double init_need = 0);
    We'll discuss the other public members in a moment.
private:
    double need_each_week;
    double eaten_this_week;
};
```

The constructor has no argument for eaten_this_week, since we plan to have that member variable initialized to zero, indicating that a newly constructed animal has not yet eaten.

The work of the animal's constructor is easy enough to describe: The first two arguments must somehow initialize the size and growth rate of the animal; the last argument initializes need_each_week; the value of eaten_this_week is initialized to zero. But how do we manage to use init_size and init_rate to initialize the size and growth rate of the animal? Most likely the size and growth rate are stored as private member variables of the Organism class, but the animal has no direct access to the organism's private member variables.

The C++ language provides a solution to this problem, called the **member initialization list.** The member initialization list is an extra line in the constructor of a derived class. The purpose is to *call the constructor of the base class.* The details of using the member initialization list are given in Figure 14.7 on page 635.

Here is the implementation of our animal constructor, with the member initialization list highlighted:

```
Animal::Animal(double init_size, double init_rate, double init_need)
: Organism(init_size, init_rate)
// Library facilities used: assert.h
{
    assert(init_need >= 0);
    need_each_week = init_need;
    eaten_this_week = 0;
}
```

FIGURE 14.7 Using the Member Initialization List to Call the Constructor of the Base Class

---

The Member Initialization List

In a derived class constructor, the member initialization list is used to call the constructor of the base class. The rules are as follows:

1. The member initialization list appears in the implementation of a constructor. It appears after the closing parenthesis of the parameter list and before the opening bracket of the implementation's body.

2. The member initialization list begins with a colon, followed by the name of the base class, and then a list of arguments for the base class constructor. These arguments appear in parentheses, like any other argument list.

3. When the derived class constructor is called, the constructor for the base class will be activated before anything else is done.

4. If a base class constructor is not activated in the member initialization list, then the default constructor for the base class will automatically be activated before any of the rest of the derived class constructor is executed.

Example:
```
Animal::Animal(double init_size, double init_rate, double init_need)
 : Organism(init_size, init_rate)
 {
     need_each_week = init_need;
     eaten_this_week = 0;
 }
```

By the way, in the `Animal` class definition, we will provide each of the parameters with a default argument, so that this constructor can be used as a default constructor for the animal.

The member initialization list actually serves several purposes and can appear in any constructor—derived class or not. We will use the list only in the constructor of a derived class, where the purpose is to call the constructor of the base class. Figure 14.7 shows the rules for using the member initialization list in this way.

The Other Animal Member Functions

The animal has four new member functions that deal with eating, and the `simulate_week` member function must also be overridden. The four new functions are called `assign_need`, `eat`, `still_need`, and `total_need`. The prototypes for all these member functions are shown in this `Animal` definition:

```
class Animal : public Organism
{
public:
    // CONSTRUCTOR
    Animal(double init_size = 1, double init_rate = 0, double init_need = 0);
    // MODIFICATION MEMBER FUNCTIONS
    void assign_need(double new_need);
    void eat(double amount);
    void simulate_week( ); // Overridden from the Organism class
    // CONSTANT MEMBER FUNCTIONS
    double still_need( ) const;
    double total_need( ) const { return need_each_week; }
private:
    double need_each_week;
    double eaten_this_week;
};
```

We'll discuss each of these member functions now.

The `assign_need` function. This member function has this prototype:

```
    void assign_need(double new_need);
```

The member function is activated when a simulation needs to specify how much food an animal must eat to survive a week. For example, if `spot` is an animal that needs 30 ounces of food to survive a week, then `spot.assign_need(30)` is activated. During a simulation, the food requirements may change, so that `assign_need` can be activated several times with different arguments.

The eat function. Whenever the animal, `spot`, eats `m` ounces of food, the member function `spot.eat(m)` records this event. Here's the prototype of the member function:

```
    void eat(double amount);
```

The amount of food that has been eaten during the current week is stored in a private member variable, `eaten_this_week`. So, activating `eat(m)` will simply add `m` to `eaten_this_week`.

Overriding the `simulate_week` function. The animal must do some extra work in its `simulate_week` member function. Therefore, it will override the organism's `simulate_week` function. The animal's `simulate_week` will first activate `Organism::simulate_week` to carry out whatever work an ordinary organism does to simulate one week. Next, the animal's `simulate_week` determines whether the animal has had enough food to eat this week. If `eaten_this_week` is less than `need_each_week`, then `death` is activated. Also, `eaten_this_week` is reset to zero to restart the recording of food eaten for the animal's next week.

Here's some example code to show the coordination of the new methods. It begins by declaring a 160-ounce animal `spot` (perhaps a cat). Spot is not currently growing (since `init_rate` is zero in the constructor), but she does require 30 ounces of food per week:

```
Animal spot(160, 0, 30);

spot.eat(10);
spot.eat(25);
spot.simulate_week( );
if (spot.is_alive( ))
    cout << "Spot lives!\n";
else
    cout << "Spot has died.\n";

spot.eat(10);
spot.eat(15);
spot.simulate_week( );
if (spot.is_alive( ))
    cout << "Spot lives!\n";
else
    cout << "Spot has died.\n";
```

Spot catches a 10-ounce fish and steals 25 ounces of chicken from the kitchen.

Spot still lives at the end of her first week.

Spot catches another 10-ounce fish, but gets only 15 ounces of chicken this week.

Sadly, Spot dies at the end of her second week.

Two constant functions. The last two animal member functions are constant functions called `total_need` and `still_need`. The `total_need` function returns the total amount of food that the animal needs in a week, and the `still_need` function returns the amount of food that the animal still needs in the current week (which is the total need minus the amount already eaten).

The complete documentation and definition for the animal appears in Figure 14.8. The documentation and class definition could be placed in the same header file as the `Organism` class (`organism.h`), and the member function implementations would then appear along with the organism member functions in `organism.cxx`. Alternately, the animal class could have a separate header file and a separate implementation file. If the animal files are separate, then `organism.h` must be given in an include directive in the animal files.

FIGURE 14.8 │ The Animal Class

Documentation for the Animal Class

```
// CLASS PROVIDED: Animal
//     Animal is a derived class of the Organism class. All the Organism public member functions
//     are inherited by an Animal. In addition, an Animal has these extra member functions:
//
// CONSTRUCTOR for the Animal class:
//     Organism(double init_size = 1, double init_rate = 0, double init_need = 0)
//         Precondition: init_size >= 0, and init_need >= 0. If init_size is 0, then init_rate is zero
//         too.
//         Postcondition: The organism being simulated has been initialized. The value returned
//         from get_size( ) is now init_size (measured in ounces), the value returned from
//         get_rate( ) is now init_rate (measured in ounces per week), and the animal must eat
//         at least init_need ounces of food each week to survive.
//
// MODIFICATION MEMBER FUNCTIONS for the Animal class:
//     void assign_need(double new_need)
//         Precondition: new_need >= 0.
//         Postcondition: The animal's weekly food requirement has been changed to new_need
//         (measured in ounces per week).
//
//     void eat(double amount)
//         Precondition: amount >= 0.
//         Postcondition: The given amount (in ounces) has been added to the amount of food
//         that the animal has eaten this week.
//
//     void simulate_week( )  -- overridden from the Organism class
//         Postcondition: The size of the organism has been changed by its current growth rate.
//         If the new size is less than zero, then the actual size is set to zero rather than to a
//         negative value, and the growth rate is also set to zero. Also, if the animal has eaten
//         less than its required need over the past week, then death has been activated.
//
// CONSTANT MEMBER FUNCTIONS for the Animal class:
//     double still_need( ) const
//         Postcondition: The return value is the ounces of food that the animal still needs to
//         survive the current week (which is the total need minus the amount eaten so far).
//
//     double total_need( ) const
//         Postcondition: The return value is the total amount of food that the animal needs to
//         survive one week (measured in ounces).
//
// VALUE SEMANTICS for the Animal class:
//     Assignments and the copy constructor may be used with Animal objects.
```

(continued)

(FIGURE 14.8 continued)

Class Definition

```
class Animal : public Organism
{
public:
    // CONSTRUCTOR
    Animal(double init_size = 1, double init_rate = 0, double init_need = 0);
    // MODIFICATION MEMBER FUNCTIONS
    void assign_need(double new_need);
    void eat(double amount);
    void simulate_week( ); // Overridden from the Organism class
    // CONSTANT MEMBER FUNCTIONS
    double still_need( ) const;
    double total_need( ) const { return need_each_week; }
private:
    double need_each_week;
    double eaten_this_week;
};
```

Implementation of the Member Functions

```
Animal::Animal(double init_size, double init_rate, double init_need)
: Organism(init_size, init_rate)
// Library facilities used: assert.h
{
    assert(init_need >= 0);
    need_each_week = init_need;
    eaten_this_week = 0;
}

void Animal::assign_need(double new_need)
// Library facilities used: assert.h
{
    assert(new_need >= 0);
    need_each_week = new_need;
}

void Animal::eat(double amount)
// Library facilities used: assert.h
{
    assert(amount >= 0);
    eaten_this_week += amount;
}
```

(continued)

(FIGURE 14.8 continued)

```
void Animal::simulate_week( )
{
    Organism::simulate_week( );
    if (eaten_this_week < need_each_week)
        death( );
    eaten_this_week = 0;
}

double Animal::still_need( ) const
{
    if (eaten_this_week >= need_each_week)
        return 0;
    else
        return need_each_week - eaten_this_week;
}
```

organism.h and organism.cxx   **FTP**

The next derived class that we'll build is a class to simulate a plant. The plant class is derived from an organism, and it has one extra method—but the work is left up to you in the next few Self-Test Exercises.

Self-Test Exercises

5. Draw an object hierarchy diagram for various kinds of people.

6. Declare a new class called Plant, which is derived from an organism and has one extra member function:

   ```
   void nibbled_on(double amount);
   // Precondition: 0 <= amount <= get_size( ).
   // The plant's size has been decreased by amount. If this reduces
   // the size to zero, then death is activated.
   ```

   Suppose fern is a plant. Activating fern.nibbled_on(m) corresponds to some beast eating m ounces of fern. Notice that nibbled_on differs from the existing alter_size method, since in the nibbled_on function, the amount is removed from the size (rather than added), and there is also a strict precondition on the amount eaten.

   Your Plant class should have one constructor with the same parameters as the organism constructor. The plant's constructor merely calls the organism constructor (in the member initialization list). The actual body of the plant constructor has no lines (though you may want to put a comment indicating that "the plant constructor does no work except calling the organism constructor"). Provide default arguments of zero for both parameters so that the plant constructor can be used as a default constructor.

7. Write a function with one argument, which is a bag of *pointers* to plants, as shown in this prototype:

> *double* `total_mass(Bag<Plant*>& collection);`

This uses the bag template class from `bag5.h` in Figure 6.8 on page 298. This version of the bag included an internal iterator, making it easy to process all the items in the bag, one after another. The function should calculate and return the mass of all the plants that are pointed to by pointers in the bag. You may assume that none of the pointers are null.

The Herbivore Class

We're almost ready to start designing a simulation program for a small ecosystem. The ecosystem will be a small pond containing weeds and weed-eating fish. The weeds will be modeled by the `Plant` class from Self-Test Exercise 6 on page 640, and the fish will be a new class that is derived from the animal class that we have just completed.

The new class for the fish, called `Herbivore`, is an animal that eats plants. This suggests that an herbivore should have one new member function, which we call `nibble`. The member function will interact with a plant object that the herbivore is nibbling, and this plant object is a parameter to the new member function. Here is the specification we have in mind:

> *void* `Herbivore::nibble(Plant& meal);`
> `// Postcondition: eat(amount) and meal.nibbled_on(amount) have both been`
> `// activated. The amount is usually half of the plant, but it will not be`
> `// more than 10% of the herbivore's weekly need nor more than the amount`
> `// that the animal still needs to eat to survive this week.`

For example, suppose that `carp` is an herbivore, and `bushroot` is a plant. If we activate `carp.nibble(bushroot)`, then `carp` will eat some of `bushroot`, by activating two other functions: (1) its own `eat` member function, and (2) the `bushroot.nibbled_on()` function.

The `nibble` function follows a few rules about how much of the plant is eaten. The rules state that `carp.nibble(bushroot)` will usually cause `carp` to eat half of `bushroot`, but a single nibble will not eat more than 10% of the animal's weekly need nor more than the amount that the animal still needs to eat in order to survive the rest of the week. In an actual model, these rules would be derived from behavior studies of real herbivores.

The complete herbivore documentation is shown in Figure 14.9, along with the class definition and the implementation of the herbivore's member functions.

FIGURE 14.9 The Herbivore Class

Documentation for the Herbivore Class

```
// CLASS PROVIDED: Herbivore
//     Herbivore is a derived class of the Animal class. All the Animal public member functions
//     are inherited by an Herbivore. In addition, an Herbivore has these extra member
//     functions:
//
// CONSTRUCTOR for the Herbivore class:
//     Herbivore(double init_size=1, double init_rate=0, double init_need=0)
//         Same as the Animal constructor.
//
// MODIFICATION MEMBER FUNCTIONS for the Herbivore class:
//     void nibble(Plant& meal)
//         Postcondition: eat(amount) and meal.nibbled_on(amount) have been activated. The
//         amount is usually half of the plant, but it will not be more than 10% of the
//         herbivore's weekly need nor more than the amount that the animal still needs to eat to
//         survive this week.
//
// VALUE SEMANTICS for the Herbivore class:
//     Assignments and the copy constructor may be used with Herbivore objects.
```

Class Definition

```
class Herbivore : public Animal
{
public:
    // CONSTRUCTOR
    Herbivore(double init_size=1,  double init_rate=0,  double init_need=0);
    // MODIFICATION MEMBER FUNCTIONS
    void nibble(Plant& meal);
};
```

Implementation of the Member Functions

```
Herbivore::Herbivore(double init_size, double init_rate, double init_need)
: Animal(init_size, init_rate, init_need)
{
    // No work is done here, except calling the animal constructor.
}
```

(continued)

(FIGURE 14.9 continued)

```
void Herbivore::nibble(Plant& meal)
{
    const double PORTION = 0.5;        // Eat no more than this fraction of plant
    const double MAX_FRACTION = 0.1;   // Eat no more than this fraction of weekly need
    double amount;                     // How many ounces of the plant will be eaten

    // Set amount to some portion of the plant but no more than a given maximum fraction
    // of the total weekly need and no more than what the herbivore still needs to eat this
    // week.
    amount = PORTION * meal.get_size( );
    if (amount > MAX_FRACTION * total_need( ))
        amount = MAX_FRACTION * total_need( );
    if (amount > still_need( ))
        amount = still_need( );

    // Eat the plant.
    eat(amount);
    meal.nibbled_on(amount);
}
```

organism.h and organism.cxx **FTP**

The Pond Life Simulation Program

A simulation program can use objects such as our herbivores to predict the effects of changes to an ecosystem. We'll write a program along these lines to model the weeds and fish in a small pond. The program stores the pond weeds in a bag of plants. To be more precise, we have a bag of *pointers* to plants. For example, suppose the pond has 2000 weeds with an initial size of 15 ounces each and a growth rate of 2.5 ounces per week. Then we will create a bag of 2000 pointers to plants, as shown here:

```
const size_t MANY_WEEDS = 2000;  // Number of weeds in the pond
const double WEED_SIZE   =   15; // Initial size of each weed (ounces)
const double WEED_RATE   =  2.5; // Weed growth rate (ounces/week)
size_t i;                        // Loop control variable
Bag<Plant*> weeds;

for (i = 1; i <= MANY_WEEDS; i++)
    weeds.insert( new Plant(WEED_SIZE, WEED_RATE));
```

Let's start our explanation of this code with the highlighted expression *new* Plant(WEED_SIZE, WEED_RATE). This expression uses the *new* operator to allocate a new plant object. After the type name, `Plant`, we have an argument list (WEED_SIZE, WEED_RATE). This is the form of *new* that allocates a new plant using a constructor with two arguments WEED_SIZE and WEED_RATE. We have not seen this form of *new* too often, because our prior programs have not needed to allocate new objects that require a particular constructor. But using *new* in this way will be common in your later programming, so you might want to go back and review the forms of *new* in Figure 4.1 on page 144.

Anyway, the statement `weeds.insert(`*new* `Plant(WEED_SIZE, WEED_RATE))` is executed 2000 times in the above code. Each of the 2000 allocations results in a pointer (returned by the *new* operator), and these 2000 pointers are inserted into the `weeds` bag.

Our simulation has a second bag, called `fish`, which is a bag of pointers to herbivores. Initially, we'll stock the fish bag with 300 full-grown fish.

With the pointers in the bags, our simulation may proceed. Throughout the simulation, various fish nibble on various plants. Each week, every weed increases by its growth rate (stated as 2.5 ounces/week in the above code). Some weeds will also be nibbled by fish, but during our simulation no weed will ever be completely eaten, so the weeds never die, nor do we ever create new weeds beyond the initial 2000. On the other hand, the number of fish in the pond may vary throughout the simulation. When a fish dies (because of insufficient nibbling), the pointer to that fish is removed from the fish bag. New fish are also born each week at a rate that we'll explain in a moment. For now, though, you should be getting a good idea of the overall simulation. Let's lay out these ideas precisely with some pseudocode:

// *Pseudocode for the pond life simulation*

1. Allocate a bunch of new plants, and put the pointers to these new plants in a bag of plant pointers called `weeds`. The exact number of weeds, their initial size, and their growth rate are determined by constants called MANY_WEEDS, WEED_SIZE, and WEED_RATE.

2. Allocate a bunch of new herbivores, and put the pointers to these new herbivores in a bag of herbivore pointers called `fish`. The number of fish and their initial size are determined by constants INIT_FISH and FISH_SIZE. In this simple simulation, the fish will not grow (their growth rate is zero), and their weekly need will be their initial size times a constant called FRACTION.

3. For each week of the simulation, we will first cause some randomly selected fish to nibble on randomly selected weeds. On average, each fish will nibble on AVERAGE_NIBBLES weeds (where AVERAGE_NIBBLES is yet another constant in our program). After all these nibbles, we will activate `simulate_week` for each fish and each weed. Dead fish will be removed from the fish bag. At the end of the week, we will give birth to some new fish. The total number of new fish is the current number of fish times a constant called BIRTH_RATE. To simplify the simulation, we will have the new fish born fully grown with a growth rate of zero.

At the end of each week (simulated in Step 3), our program prints a few statistics. These statistics show the number of fish that are currently alive and the total mass of the weeds.

Our program implementing the pseudocode is given in Figure 14.10. The top of the program lists the various constants that we have mentioned, from MANY_WEEDS to BIRTH_RATE. After the constants, we list prototypes for two functions that we found useful in the implementation. One of the functions, called pond_week, carries out the simulation of one week in the pond, as described in Step 3 of the pseudocode. The other function, total_mass, computes the total mass of all the plants in the bag of weeds.

We discuss a few of the implementation details starting on page 648.

FIGURE 14.10	The Pondlife Simulation

A Program

```
// FILE: pondlife.cxx
// A simple simulation program to model the fish and weeds in a pond

#include <iostream.h>   // Provides cin, cout
#include <iomanip.h>    // Provides setw
#include <stdlib.h>     // Provides EXIT_SUCCESS, size_t
#include "bag5.h"       // Provides a Bag template class
#include "organism.h"   // Provides Herbivore, Plant classes

// PROGRAM CONSTANTS
const size_t MANY_WEEDS    = 2000;  // Number of weeds in the pond
const double WEED_SIZE     =   15;  // Initial size of each weed, in ounces
const double WEED_RATE     =  2.5;  // Growth rate of weeds, in ounces/week
const size_t INIT_FISH     =  300;  // Initial number of fish in the pond
const double FISH_SIZE     =   50;  // Maximum fish size, in ounces
const double FRACTION      =  0.5;  // A fish must eat FRACTION times its size
                                    // during one week or it will die.
const int    AVERAGE_NIBBLES = 30;  // Average number of plants nibbled by
                                    // a fish over one week.
const double BIRTH_RATE    = 0.05;  // At the end of each week, some fish have
                                    // babies. The total number of new fish born is
                                    // the current number of fish times the
                                    // BIRTH_RATE (rounded down to an integer).
```

(continued)

(FIGURE 14.10 continued)

```
// PROTOTYPES for the functions used in the program:
void pond_week(Bag<Herbivore*>& fish, Bag<Plant*>& weeds);
// Precondition: weeds.size( ) > 0.
// Postcondition: On average, each fish has nibbled on AVERAGE_NIBBLES plants, and then
// simulate_week has been activated for each fish and each weed. Any fish that died are
// removed from the fish bag, and then BIRTH_RATE * fish.size( ) new fish have been added to
// the fish bag.

double total_mass(Bag<Plant*>& collection);
// Postcondition: The return value is the total mass of all the plants in the collection.


int main( )
{
    Bag<Herbivore*> fish;              // A bag of pointers to our fish
    Bag<Plant*> weeds;                 // A bag of pointers to our weeds
    unsigned int many_weeks;           // Number of weeks to simulate
    size_t i;                          // Loop control variable

    // Initialize the bags of fish and weeds.
    for (i = 0; i < INIT_FISH; i++)
        fish.insert(new Herbivore(FISH_SIZE, 0, FISH_SIZE * FRACTION));
    for (i = 0; i < MANY_WEEDS; i++)
        weeds.insert(new Plant(WEED_SIZE, WEED_RATE));

    // Get number of weeks, and format the output.
    cout << "How many weeks shall I simulate? ";
    cin >> many_weeks;
    cout.setf(ios::fixed);
    cout << "Week     Number    Plant Mass" << endl;
    cout << "      ·     of Fish    (in ounces)" << endl;

    // Simulate the weeks.
    for (i = 1; i <= many_weeks; i++)
    {
        pond_week(fish, weeds);
        cout << setw(4) << i;
        cout << setw(10) << fish.size( );
        cout << setw(14) << setprecision(0) << total_mass(weeds);
        cout << endl;
    }

    return EXIT_SUCCESS;
}
```

(continued)

(FIGURE 14.10 continued)

```cpp
void pond_week(Bag<Herbivore*>& fish, Bag<Plant*>& weeds)
{
    size_t i;
    size_t many_iterations;
    Herbivore *fish_ptr;
    Plant *weed_ptr;

    // Have randomly selected fish nibble on randomly selected plants.
    many_iterations = AVERAGE_NIBBLES * fish.size( );
    for (i = 0; i < many_iterations; i++)
    {
        fish_ptr = fish.grab( );
        weed_ptr = weeds.grab( );
        fish_ptr->nibble(*weed_ptr);
    }

    // Simulate the weeks for the fish.
    fish.start( );
    while (fish.is_item( ))
    {
        fish.current( )->simulate_week( );
        if (fish.current( )->is_alive( ))
            fish.advance( );
        else
        {
            delete fish.current( );
            fish.remove_current( );
        }
    }

    // Simulate the weeks for the weeds.
    for (weeds.start( ); weeds.is_item( ); weeds.advance( ))
        weeds.current( )->simulate_week( );

    // Create some new fish, according to the BIRTH_RATE constant.
    many_iterations = int(BIRTH_RATE * fish.size( ));
    for (i = 0; i < many_iterations; i++)
        fish.insert(new Herbivore(FISH_SIZE, 0, FISH_SIZE * FRACTION));
}

double total_mass(Bag<Plant*>& collection)
{
    double answer;

    answer = 0;
    for (collection.start( ); collection.is_item( ); collection.advance( ))
        answer += collection.current( )->get_size( );
    return answer;
}
```

pondlife.cxx **FTP**

Pondlife—Implementation Details

our bags require a grab function and an internal iterator

The implementations of pond_week and total_mass are at the end of Figure 14.10. These implementations show that our bags require a few features that were not present in all of the bag implementations. In particular, we need the ability to grab a random item out of a bag and the ability to step through the items of a bag one at a time (an internal iterator). The best bag for these purposes is one of our bags from Chapter 6 (with a header file bag5.h in Figure 6.8 on page 298).

The use of the internal iterator is particularly important. For example, within the pond_week function, we activate simulate_week for each plant by using the internal iterator to step through the weeds one at a time, as shown here:

```
// Simulate the weeks for the weeds.
for (weeds.start( ); weeds.is_item( ); weeds.advance( ))
    weeds.current( )->simulate_week( );
```

A similar loop steps through the fish, simulating one week for each fish and removing dead fish.

why we are storing pointers in the bags

The implementation of the simulation also answers a question that may have been on your mind: Why do our bags store *pointers* to plants and *pointers* to herbivores, rather than merely storing plants and herbivores directly? The answer is that storing pointers allows us to retrieve a pointer from the bag and then manipulate the actual object that the pointer points to. On the other hand, if we stored actual plant objects and herbivore objects in the bags, then the bag access functions would permit us to retrieve *copies* of these objects, and we could manipulate the *copies* of the objects—but the actual objects themselves would remain in the bag unchanged.

TIP

Programming Tip: When to Use a Container Class of Pointers

When you use a container class, such as a bag, ask yourself two questions:

- Do the container class functions provide mere copies of the objects?
- Will I need to manipulate the actual objects rather than copies of the objects?

If both answers are *yes*, then you should probably use a container of pointers, such as our bag of pointers to plants and our bag of pointers to herbivores.

Using the Pond Model

No doubt you have noticed that our pond model is not entirely rooted in reality. For example, each fish is born full grown and does not continue to grow. Some extensions to make the model more realistic are given in the Programming Projects of this chapter. Nevertheless, even our simple program illustrates the principles of simulation programs. Let's look at one way that a simulation program such as ours could be used.

Suppose that your friend Judy owns a pond with 2000 weeds, about 15 ounces each. And perhaps the pond is too choked with weeds for Judy's taste. One way to control the weeds is to introduce a weed-eating species of fish, and the pond life program can help us predict what will happen when a certain number of fish are put in the pond. For example, suppose we have a species of fish where the program's constants (Figure 14.10 on page 645) are accurate. When we run the program with these constants, the output in Figure 14.11 occurs.

Actually, if you run the program, you may get slightly different output because of the use of the random factor in the bag's grab function. What does the program predict will happen in the pond if we introduce 300 of this kind of fish? Each output line gives the fish population and the plant mass at the end of one more week. The model predicts that the mass of the weeds will decrease fairly rapidly. This is followed by a period of some oscillation in both the fish and plant populations, including a rather catastrophic week for the fish when their population drops from 359 to 144. Sudden declines such as this are observed in real ecosystems when a species is allowed to expand, limited only by its food supply.

This kind of model can provide predictions as well as testing theories of interactions in an ecosystem. It's also important to remember that any predictions are only as accurate as the underlying model.

Heap Warnings

The pondlife program requires a fairly large heap—enough room for about 6000 double numbers, plus room for the bags of pointers. For example, the Borland 4.5 C++ for DOS is unable to provide sufficient heap memory unless you use the "huge memory model" (-mh option on the compile line). If you receive abnormal program termination with your pondlife program, it is probably due to an insufficient heap size.

FIGURE 14.11 Mergesort

Sample Dialogue

How many weeks shall I simulate? **38**

Week	Number of Fish	Plant Mass (in ounces)
1	315	27500
2	330	24625
3	346	21375
4	363	17725
5	379	13654
6	359	9286
7	144	6462
8	109	7960
9	112	10245
10	117	12445
11	122	14520
12	128	16470
13	134	18270
14	140	19920
15	147	21420
16	154	22745
17	161	23895
18	169	24870
19	177	25645
20	185	26220
21	194	26595
22	203	26745
23	213	26670
24	223	26345
25	234	25770
26	245	24920
27	257	23795
28	268	22374
29	281	20674
30	292	18656
31	306	16356
32	313	13720
33	301	10984
34	244	8689
35	189	7812
36	163	8225
37	161	9176
38	164	10159

Self-Test Exercises

8. Write code to declare a bag of pointers to organisms. Put ten new organisms in the bag, with an initial size of 16 ounces and a growth rate of 1 ounce per week. Grab five random organisms, and alter their growth rates to 2 ounces per weed. Finally, calculate the total of all the organisms' growth rates, and print the result.

9. In the previous exercise, you started with ten organisms growing at 1 ounce per week. Five random organisms had their growth rates changed to 2 ounces per week, so you might think that the total of all the organisms' rates would be 5*1 + 5*2, which is 15. But when we ran the program, the total was only 14. Why?

10. When should you use a container class of pointers to objects rather than a container of the actual objects?

11. Design and implement a new class derived from the animal class. The new class, called `Carnivore`, has one new member function with the prototype shown here:

```
void Carnivore::chase(Animal& prey, double chance);
```

When `chase(prey, chance)` is activated for some carnivore, the carnivore chases the prey. The probability of actually catching the prey is given by the parameter `chance` (which should lie between 0 and 1—for example 0.75 for a 75% chance). If the prey is actually caught, then this will also activate the carnivore's `eat` member function and (sadly) activate the prey's `death` member function.

Note: You can use the standard library `rand` function to determine whether the animal is caught, as shown here:

```
if (rand( )/double(RAND_MAX) < chance)
{
    ‖ Code for catching and eating the prey
}
```

14.3 USING DERIVED CLASSES FOR ADTS

Many ADTs from previous chapters can be implemented as derived classes, resulting in less programming and less debugging—an all around good way to reuse previous work. For example, consider the stack ADT from Section 7.1. Many of the stack operations are similar to the list ADT that you first implemented in Section 3.2, and later revised in Section 5.4.

Now suppose that you have implemented a list class with a header file `list3.h` and the documentation shown in Figure 14.12. This is a template version of the list class, and we don't really care exactly how it is implemented—in fact, perhaps some other programmer implemented this list, and we don't have access to the implementation details.

FIGURE 14.12 | Documentation for a List Template Class

Documentation for a Header File

```
// FILE: list3.h
// TEMPLATE CLASS PROVIDED: List<Item> (a container class for a List of items)
//     The template parameter, Item, is the data type of the items in the List.
//     It may be any of the C++ built-in types (int, char, etc.), or a class with a default
//     constructor, an assignment operator, and a copy constructor.
//
// CONSTRUCTOR for the List<Item> template class:
//   List( )
//       Postcondition: The List has been initialized as an empty list.
//
// MODIFICATION MEMBER FUNCTIONS for the List<Item> template class:
//   void start( )
//       Postcondition: The first item on the List becomes the current item (but if the List is
//       empty, then there is no current item).
//
//   void advance( )
//       Precondition: is_item returns true.
//       Postcondition: If the current item was already the last item on the List, then there is
//       no longer any current item. Otherwise, the new current item is the item immediately
//       after the original current item.
//
//   void insert(const Item& entry)
//       Postcondition: A new copy of entry has been inserted in the List before the current
//       item. If there was no current item, then the new entry has been inserted at the front of
//       the List. In either case, the newly inserted item is now the current item of the List.
//
//   void attach(const Item& entry)
//       Postcondition: A new copy of entry has been inserted in the List after the current
//       item. If there was no current item, then the new entry has been attached to the end of
//       the List. In either case, the newly inserted item is now the current item of the List.
//
//   void remove_current( )
//       Precondition: is_item returns true.
//       Postcondition: The current item has been removed from the List, and the item after
//       this (if there is one) is now the new current item.
//
// CONSTANT MEMBER FUNCTIONS for the List<Item> template class:
//   size_t size( ) const
//       Postcondition: The return value is the number of items on the List.
//
```

(continued)

(FIGURE 14.12 continued)

```
//    bool is_item( ) const
//        Postcondition: A true return value indicates that there is a valid current item
//        that may be retrieved by activating the current( ) member function (listed below).
//        A false return value indicates that there is no valid current item.
//
//    Item current( ) const
//        Precondition: is_item( ) returns true.
//        Postcondition: The item returned is the current item on the List.
//
// VALUE SEMANTICS for the List<Item> template class:
//    Assignments and the copy constructor may be used with List<Item> objects.
//
// DYNAMIC MEMORY USAGE by the List<Item> template class:
//    If there is insufficient dynamic memory, then the following functions call new_handler:
//    insert, attach, the copy constructor, and the assignment operator.
```

list3.h **FTP**

Our question is this: *Is there some way that the template list class can be used to quickly implement a new stack class?* Yes. A new `Stack` class can be implemented as a derived class, using the `List` class as the base class. The plan is for the stack to push and pop items from only one end of the list, ignoring many of the other features of a list. But wait! The list has many public member functions that implement these "other features." We would like to use the list as a base class, but we don't want all of the list's public member functions to also be public functions of the stack. The solution is to use a *private* base class, which we'll describe now.

Private Base Classes

Until now, our derived classes have used the keyword *public* before the base class. For example, at the start of the CuckooClock class we wrote this:

```
class CuckooClock : public Clock ...
```

The effect of the keyword *public* is that the public members of the base class are inherited as *public* members of the derived class.

An alternative is to use the keyword *private* before the base class, as shown in the start of this class definition:

```
class B: private A ...
```

In this example, all of the public members of the base class A are inherited as *private* members of the derived class B. The base class is called a **private base class.**

Public Base Class vs. Private Base Class

With a public base class, all the public members of the base class are inherited as *public* members of the derived class.

With a private base class, all the public members of the base class are inherited as *private* members of the derived class.

When we implement the new `Stack` class as a derived class, the `List` class will be a private base class. Therefore, `start`, `advance`, `insert`, and the other list member functions will all be private member functions of the new `Stack` class. The `Stack` class can use those private member functions to implement its own push and pop operations, always working at the front of the list. Since both the list and the stack are template classes, the start of the new stack definition looks like this:

```
template <class Item>
class Stack : private List<Item> ...
```

In this definition of the `Stack` template class, the base class is `List<Item>`. In other words, our stack of items will be implemented as a list of items. Now let's look at the implementation of the new stack as a derived class.

a derived class and a base class may both be template classes

What the Derived Class Gets for Free

The derived stack class gets several things automatically from its base class:

- Constructors: The stack has an automatic default constructor, which activates the list's default constructor. The stack has an automatic copy constructor, which activates the list's copy constructor.

- Assignment operator: The stack has an automatic assignment operator, which activates the list's assignment operator.

- Destructor: The stack has an automatic destructor, which activates the list's destructor.

If necessary, we could override any or all of these, but in the case of the stack we merely say "thank you" to the list and take all four automatic functions.

Pitfall: Compiler Problems with a Template Base Class

PITFALL

When the base class is a template class, some compilers have problems generating the automatic constructor, assignment operator, and destructor. The result is a message, usually during the link step, indicating that certain symbols cannot be found. You should read your compiler documentation to see how to force the base class operations to be generated. A typical solution is to declare at least one object of the base class and use the assignment operator at least once with this object.

Pushing and Popping for the Derived Stack Class

A stack has two member functions to push an item onto a stack and pop the top item from the stack. The start of the stack definition gives the push and pop prototypes shown here:

```
template <class Item>
class Stack : private List<Item>
{
public:
    // MODIFICATION MEMBER FUNCTIONS
    void push(const Item& entry);
    Item pop( );
    ...
```

Our plan is to push new items onto the front end of the list using the list's `insert` member function. The list's current item will always be at the front of the list, so that a pop operation can be carried out with the other list member functions. With this plan, the push and pop can be implemented as shown here:

```
template <class Item>
void push(const Item& entry)
{
    insert(entry);
}

template <class Item>
Item pop( )
{
    Item answer;

    answer = current( );
    remove_current( );
    return answer;
}
```

Notice that within the implementations, the private member functions of the base class can be called just like any other private member function. It may help to keep in mind that our implementation means that a stack *is-a* list, so that the stack's member functions may use all the usual list members.

Exempting Inherited Members from the Effect of a Private Base Class

Let's consider the list's `size` member function. The `size` function returns the number of items in the list. It would be useful for a stack to have this function as a *public* member function. After all, a programmer who uses a stack might need to know how many items are in the stack. The problem is that `size` is one of the list's member functions, and the List class is a *private* base class. Therefore, size is not normally available as a *public* stack member function. Fortunately, C++ permits a programmer to change an individual member of a private base class into a public member of the derived class. The syntax for making the change requires us to simply list the full name of the individual member in the public portion of the derived class. For example, size is changed to a public member of the derived Stack class by using the highlighted line here:

```
template <class Item>
class Stack : private List<Item>
{
public:
    // MODIFICATION MEMBER FUNCTIONS
    void push(const Item& entry);
    Item pop( );
    // CONSTANT MEMBER FUNCTIONS
    List<Item>::size; // size function is obtained from the List
    ...
```

Notice that we have to write the full name of the member function, including the scope resolution operator `List<Item>::`, but we do not need to list the function's return type or parameter list. The technique is called **exempting** the inherited members from the effects of a private base class. Exempting is permitted only with *public* members of the base class; there is no way to change a private member of the base class into a public member of the derived class.

Exempting Inherited Members from the Effect of a Private Base Class

The public members of a private base class are usually inherited as *private* members of the derived class. But, individual public members of the base class may be declared as public members of the derived class. The technique, called **exempting** the inherited member, requires the full name of the exempted member to be listed in the public section of the derived class definition.

Example:
```
template <class Item>
class Stack : private List<Item>
{
public:
    ...
    List<Item>::size;
    ...
```

The Derived Stack Class—Putting Together the Pieces

The documentation and definitions for the derived stack class are shown in Figure 14.13. The only functions that we haven't previously discussed are the stack's is_empty and peek functions, which are implemented in the figure.

FIGURE 14.13   The Derived Stack Class

Documentation for a Header File

```
// FILE: stack3.h
// TEMPLATE CLASS PROVIDED: Stack<Item> (a stack of items)
//    The template parameter, Item, is the data type of the items in the Stack.
//    It may be any of the C++ built-in types (int, char, etc.), or a class with a default
//    constructor, an assignment operator, and a copy constructor.
//
// CONSTRUCTOR for the Stack<Item> template class:
//    Stack( )
//      Postcondition: The Stack has been initialized as an empty Stack.
//
// MODIFICATION MEMBER FUNCTIONS for the Stack<Item> template class:
//    void push(const Item& entry)
//      Precondition: size( ) < CAPACITY.
//      Postcondition: A new copy of entry has been pushed onto the Stack.
//
//    Item pop( )
//      Precondition: size( ) > 0.
//      Postcondition: The top item of the Stack has been popped and returned.
//
// CONSTANT MEMBER FUNCTIONS for the Stack<Item> template class:
//    size_t size( ) const
//      Postcondition: Return value is the total number of items in the Stack.
//
//    bool is_empty( ) const
//      Postcondition: Return value is true if the Stack is empty.
//
//    Item peek( ) const
//      Precondition: size( ) > 0.
//      Postcondition: Return value is the top item on the Stack (but the Stack is unchanged).
//
// VALUE SEMANTICS for the Stack<Item> template class:
//    Assignments and the copy constructor may be used with Stack<Item> objects.
//
// DYNAMIC MEMORY USAGE by the Stack<Item> template class:
//    If there is insufficient dynamic memory, then the following functions call new_handler:
//    push, the copy constructor, and the assignment operator.
```

(continued)

(FIGURE 14.13 continued)

Class Definition

```
template <class Item>
class Stack : private List<Item>
{
public:
    // MODIFICATION MEMBER FUNCTIONS
    void push(const Item& entry);
    Item pop( );
    // CONSTANT MEMBER FUNCTIONS
    bool is_empty( ) const { return size( ) == 0; }
    Item peek( ) const;
    List<Item>::size; // size function is obtained from the List
};
```

Implementation of the Member Functions

```
template <class Item>
void push(const Item& entry)
{
    insert(entry);
}


template <class Item>
Item pop( )
// Library facilities used: assert.h
{
    Item answer;

    assert(size( ) > 0);
    answer = current( );
    remove_current( );
    return answer;
}


template <class Item>
Item peek( )
// Library facilities used: assert.h
{
    Item answer;

    assert(size( ) > 0);
    answer = current( );
    return answer;
}
```

stack3.h and stack3.template   **FTP**

Self-Test Exercises

12. What is the difference between a public base class and a private base class?

13. Suppose that you are implementing a derived class called `Tribble`. The base class, called `Willis`, is a private base class with a public member function. This member function has the prototype `void drink(int i);` How can you make `drink` be a public member function of `Tribble`? (To read more about Willis, you'll have to track down *Red Planet* by Robert A. Heinlein.)

14. Implement a new member function of the stack class. The function has one parameter, `i`, and the precondition requires the stack to contain at least `i` items. The function returns the item that is `i` positions from the top of the stack. For example, an argument of 1 will return the top item, an argument of 2 returns the item under the top, and so on.

15. Which would be easier: to implement a bag as a derived class of the list, or to implement the list as a derived class of the bag?

CHAPTER SUMMARY

- Object-oriented programming supports the use of *reusable components* by permitting new *derived classes* to be declared, which automatically *inherit* all members of an existing base class.

- All members of a base class are inherited by the derived class, but only the nonprivate members of the base class can be accessed by the programmer who implements the derived class. This is why most of our examples of base classes do not specify the precise form of the private members of the base class.

- The connection between a derived class and its base class can often be characterized by the *is-a* relationship. For example, an herbivore *is-a* particular kind of animal, so it makes sense to implement `Herbivore` as a derived class of the `Animal` base class.

- When you implement a new class, ask yourself whether the new class is an example of an existing class with slightly different capabilities or extra capabilities. In these cases, the new class can be implemented as a derived class of the existing class.

FURTHER READING

This chapter has introduced the concept of derived classes and inheritance, which is a central concept for OOP programming. In your future programming, further extensions of inheritance are likely to be important. For example, C++

permits **multiple inheritance,** where a single derived class inherits members from several base classes.

Another aspect of inheritance that we have not covered is the notion of a **virtual member function.** These are member functions that can be overridden by a derived class in a special manner. The special manner guarantees that an activation of the virtual member function will always activate the correct version of the function—even if that version of the function was unavailable at the time the activation was compiled.

To learn more about inheritance, multiple inheritance, and virtual member functions, you can consult a comprehensive C++ language guide such as *C++ Primer* by Stanley B. Lippman.

Solutions to Self-Test Exercises ?

1. The definition for the derived class is shown here, along with the implementations of the new member function:

```
class DaylightClock : public Clock
{
public:
    bool is_day( ) const;
};

bool DaylightClock::is_day( ) const
{
    if (is_morning( ))
        return (get_hour( ) >= 7);
    else
        return (get_hour( ) < 7);
}
```

2. The derived class receives an automatic default constructor (which calls the default constructor for the base class and then calls the default constructor for any member variables of the derived class). The derived class also receives an automatic copy constructor (which calls the copy constructor for the base class and then calls the copy constructor for any member variables of the derived class).

3. The automatic assignment operator calls the assignment operator for the base class and then calls the assignment operator for any member variables of the derived class. The automatic destructor first calls the destructor for any member variables of the derived class, and then calls the destructor for the base class.

4. The NoonAlarm overrides the advance member function of the ordinary clock. Here is one solution:

```
class NoonAlarm : public Clock
{
public:
    void advance(int minutes);
};

void NoonAlarm::advance(int minutes)
// Library facilities used: iostream.h
{
    int until_noon;

    // Calculate number of minutes until
    // noon.
    if (is_morning( ))
        until_noon =
            60 * (12-get_hour( ))
            - get_minute( );
    else if (get_hour( ) != 12)
        until_noon =
            60 * (24 - get_hour( ))
            - get_minute( );
    else
        until_noon =
            60 * 24
            - get_minute( );
```

```
    // Maybe print an alarm message.
    if (minutes > 0)
        if (minutes >= until_noon)
            cout << "Alarm!";

    // Call the base member function.
    Clock::advance(minutes);
}
```

5.

Person — Youth — Adult, Youth — Baby

6. The Plant definition is:
```
class Plant : public Organism
{
public:
    // CONSTRUCTOR
    Plant(double init_size = 0,
          double init_rate = 0);
    // MODIFICATION FUNCTIONS
    void nibbled_on(double amount);
};
```

The member functions are implemented here:

```
Plant::Plant(double init_size,
             double init_rate)
: Organism(init_size, init_rate)
{
    // All work is done by the Organism
    // constructor.
}


void Plant::
nibbled_on(double amount)
// Library functions used: assert.h
{
    assert(amount >= 0);
    assert(amount <= get_size( ));
    alter_size(-amount);
}
```

7. See the solution in Figure 14.10 on page 647. Notice that the bag cannot be a constant parameter since the bag's internal iterator is used.

8. Here is one solution:
```
Bag<Organism*> blobs;
int i;
double answer;
Organism *random_ptr;

for (i = 1; i <= 10; i++)
    blobs.insert(new Organism(16, 1));

for (i = 1; i <= 5; i++)
{
    random_ptr = blobs.grab( );
    random_ptr->assign_rate(2);
}

answer = 0;
for (blobs.start( );
     blobs.is_item( );
     blobs.advance( ))
    answer +=
        blobs.current()->get_rate();

cout << answer << "total of rates\n";
```

9. The random grab function must have selected one organism twice (and three other organisms were selected once each).

10. See the programming tip on page 648.

11. We'll leave some of this to you, but here is the new member function:
```
void Carnivore::chase
(Animal& prey, double chance)
// Library functions used: assert.h, stdlib.h
{
    assert(chance >= 0);
    assert(chance <= 1);
    if (chance > 0)
        if (rand()/double(RAND_MAX)
                            < chance)
        {
            eat(prey.get_size( ));
            prey.death( );
        }
}
```

12. See the box on page 653.

13. In the public section of the Tribble definition, put the line: Willis::drink;

14. Here is one implementation:
```
template <class Item>
Item Stack<Item>::get(size_t i)
// Library facilities used: assert.h, stdlib.h
{
    size_t count;
    Item answer;

    assert(i > 0);
    assert(i <= size( ));

    for (count=1; count<i; count++)
        advance( );

    answer = current( );
    start( );
    return answer;
}
```

15. The easy task is to implement a bag as a derived class, with the list as the base class.

PROGRAMMING PROJECTS

1 A *set* is like a *bag*, except that a set does not allow multiple copies of any element. If you try to insert a new copy of an item that is already present in a set, then the set simply remains unchanged. For this project, implement a set as a new class that is derived from one of your bags. Your implementation should override only the insert member function.

2 Rewrite the pond life program from Figure 14.10 on page 645 so that the values declared at the start of the program are no longer constant. The program's user should be able to enter values for all of these constants. Also, extend the program so that the fish are more realistic. In particular, the fish should be born at a small size and grow to some maximum size. Each fish should also have a weekly food requirement that is proportional to its current size.

3 Extend the Organism object hierarchy from Section 14.2 so that there is a new class Carnivore as described in Self-Test Exercise 11 on page 650. Use the hierarchy in a model of life on a small island that contains shrubs, geese that eat the shrubs, and foxes that eat the geese. The program should allow the user to vary the initial conditions on the island (such as number of foxes, the amount of food needed to sustain a fox, and so on).

4 Implement a bag template class as a derived class of a list. Use the list from Figure 14.12 on page 651. The bag should have all of the operations from Figure 6.8 on page 298.

15 Graphs

So many gods, so many creeds,
So many paths that wind and wind,
When just the art of being kind
Is all this sad world needs.

ELLA WHEELER WILCOX
The World's Need

15.1 GRAPH DEFINITIONS

15.2 GRAPH IMPLEMENTATIONS

15.3 GRAPH TRAVERSALS

15.4 PATH ALGORITHMS

     CHAPTER SUMMARY

     SOLUTIONS TO SELF-TEST EXERCISES

     PROGRAMMING PROJECTS

Graphs are the most general data structure in this text. In fact, it's fair to say that graphs are the ultimate commonly used data structure. Many of the data structures that you will study in the future can be expressed in terms of graphs. This chapter provides an introduction to graphs and their algorithms, including the implementation of a graph class in C++.

15.1 GRAPH DEFINITIONS

A graph, like a tree, is a nonlinear data structure consisting of nodes and links between the nodes. In the trees that we have already seen, the nodes are somewhat orderly: The root is linked to its children, which are linked to their

662

children, and so on to the leaves. But in a graph, even this modicum of order is gone Graph nodes may be linked in any pattern—or lack of pattern—dependent only upon the needs of an application.

Graphs occur in several varieties. We'll start with the simplest form: *undirected graphs*.

graphs occur in several varieties, the simplest of which is an undirected graph

Undirected Graphs

An undirected graph is a set of nodes and a set of links between the nodes. Each node is called a **vertex**, each link is called an **edge**, and each edge connects two vertices. Undirected graphs are drawn by putting a circle for each vertex and a line for each edge. For example, here is a drawing of an undirected graph with five vertices and six edges:

Often we'll need to refer to the vertices and edges of a graph, and we can do this by writing names next to each vertex and edge. For example, the following graph has vertices named v_0, v_1, v_2, v_3, and v_4, whereas its edges are named e_0, e_1, e_2, e_3, e_4, and e_5 :

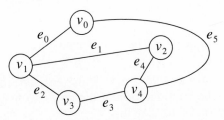

In a drawing such as this, the actual placement of the vertices and edges is unimportant. The only important points are which vertices are connected and which edges are used to connect them. So, when you are feeling like a contortionist, you might draw the above graph differently:

in a drawing, the placement of the vertices and edges is unimportant

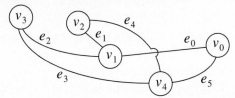

This is the same as the previous graph—we have just drawn it differently.

Here's a formal definition of these graphs:

Undirected Graphs

An **undirected graph** is a finite set of "vertices" together with a finite set of "edges." Both sets might be empty (no vertices and no edges), which is called the **empty graph**.

Each edge is associated with two vertices. We sometimes say that the edge **connects** its two vertices. The order of the two connected vertices is unimportant, so it does not matter whether we say "This edge connects vertices u and v," or "This edge connects vertices v and u."

An edge is even allowed to connect a single vertex to itself—we'll see examples of this later, and we'll also see several different variants of graphs. Many applications will require additional data to be attached to each vertex or to each edge, but even without these extras, we can give the flavor of a graph application with an example.

PROGRAMMING EXAMPLE: Undirected State Graphs

As an example of a problem where graphs are useful, we'll look at a little game. To start the game, you place three coins on the table in a line, as shown here:

      The start of the game

At the start of the game, the middle coin is "tails" and the other two are "heads." The goal is to change the configuration of the coins so that the middle coin is heads and the other two are tails, like this:

      The goal of the game

Now, this wouldn't be much of a game without a few good rules. Here are the rules:

1. You may flip the middle coin (from heads to tails or vice versa) whenever you want to.
2. You may flip one of the end coins (from heads to tails or vice versa) only if the other two coins are the same as each other (both heads or both tails).

You are not allowed to change the coins in any other way, such as shuffling them around. But within these rules you may flip coins. For example, if you start with the position *head-tail-head*, then the first rule allows you to flip the middle coin resulting in three heads:

     From the start position,
flip the middle coin.

If you play the game for a while, you'll soon figure out how to get from the starting position (*head-tail-head*) to the goal position (*tail-head-tail*) within the limits of the rules. But our *real* goal is to figure out how a graph can aid in solving this kind of problem—even if the rules were beyond human manageability. The graph we'll use is called an undirected state graph, which is a graph where each of the vertices represents one of the possible configurations of the game. These configurations are called "states," and the coin game has eight states ranging from head-head-head to tail-tail-tail. Therefore, these eight states are the vertices of the state graph for the coin game. Figure 15.1 shows each vertex as a large oval so that we have room inside the oval to draw the state of the coins. Two vertices of the undirected state graph are connected by an edge whenever it is possible to move back and forth between the two states using one of the rules. For example, Rule 1 allows us to move between head-head-head and head-tail-head, so one of the edges in the graph goes from the topmost state in Figure 15.1 (head-head-head) to the state directly below it (head-tail-head). Figure 15.1 shows a total of eight edges: The four vertical edges come from Rule 1, and the four diagonal edges come from Rule 2. You may have noticed a curious fact about our rules: Whenever it is possible to move from one state to another (such as moving head-head-head to head-tail-head), it is also possible to move in the other direction (such as head-tail-head to head-head-head). If you

a graph may represent the legal moves in a game

FIGURE 15.1 Undirected State Graph for the Coin Game

study the rules, you will see that this is true. The way we have drawn the edges reflects this symmetry. The edges are drawn as line segments connecting two vertices, with no indication as to which direction a movement must proceed. In this game, if an edge connects two vertices v_0 and v_1, then a movement is permitted in both directions, from v_0 to v_1, or from v_1 to v_0. This property of the coin game is the reason why we may use an undirected state graph. Later, we will see more complex games where movements might be permitted in only one direction, and hence we will need more complex graphs.

Once we know the undirected state graph, the game becomes a problem of finding a path from one vertex to another, where the path is only allowed to follow edges. According to our rules, we need to find a path from the vertex *head-tail-head* to the vertex *tail-head-tail*, and one such path consists of edges 1 through 5, highlighted here:

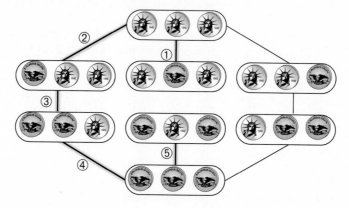

The coin game is a small problem, and the state graph isn't vital to the solution. But the important idea of the example goes beyond this small game:

Graphs in Problem Solving

Often, a problem can be represented as a graph, and the solution to the problem is obtained by solving a problem on the corresponding graph.

Because of this wide applicability of graphs, we will study many different kinds of graphs, exploring how to implement the graphs and how to solve problems such as "Is there a path from here to there?" The rest of this section shows the kinds of graphs we'll study and some of the problems that we'll solve.

Directed Graphs

The graphs we have seen so far are all *undirected*, which means that each edge connects two vertices with no particular orientation or direction. An edge just connects two vertices—there is no "first vertex" or "second vertex." But there is another kind of graph called a *directed graph*, where each edge has an orientation connecting its first vertex (called the edge's **source**) to its second vertex (the edge's **target**). Here is the formal definition of a directed graph:

Directed Graphs

A **directed graph** is a finite set of "vertices" together with a finite set of "edges." Both sets might be empty (no vertices and no edges), which is called the **empty graph**.

Each edge is associated with two vertices, called its **source** and **target** vertices. We sometimes say that the edge **connects** its source to its target. The order of the two connected vertices *is* important, so it *does* matter whether we say "This edge connects vertex *u* to vertex *v*," or "This edge connects vertex *v* to vertex *u*."

Directed graphs are drawn as diagrams with circles representing the vertices and *arrows* representing the edges. Each arrow starts at an edge's source and has the arrowhead at the edge's target, for example:

One application of directed graphs is a state graph for a game where reversing a move is sometimes forbidden. For such a game, the state graph might have an edge from a source v_1 to a target v_2 but *not* include the reverse edge from v_2 to v_1. This would indicate that the game's rules permit a move from state v_1 to state v_2, but not the other way around. For example, we could use a large state graph to represent the different states in a game of tic-tac-toe. Two of the many possible states are shown at the top of the next page, with a directed edge between them.

Two states in the state graph for tic-tac-toe

There is a directed arrow between these two states, since it is possible to move from the first state to the second state (by placing an O), but it is not possible to move the other direction (since once an O is placed, it may not be removed).

More Graph Terminology

Loops. A **loop** is an edge that connects a vertex to itself. In the diagrams that we've been using, this is drawn as a line (or arrow) with both ends at the same location. The highlighted edges at the left of these two graphs are both loops:

Path. A **path** in a graph is a sequence of vertices, $p_0, p_1, \ldots p_m$, such that each adjacent pair of vertices p_i and p_{i+1} are connected by an edge. In a directed graph, the connection must go from the source p_i to the target p_{i+1}.

Multiple edges. In principle, a graph may have two or more edges connecting the same two vertices in the same direction. These are called **multiple edges**. In a diagram, each edge is drawn separately, for example:

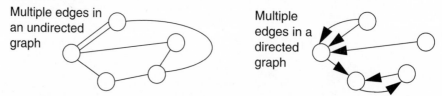

Multiple edges in an undirected graph

Multiple edges in a directed graph

Note that the two edges at the bottom of the directed graph are not multiple edges because they connect the two vertices in different directions. Many applications do not require multiple edges. In fact, many implementations of graphs do not permit multiple edges. Throughout the graph implementations of this chapter, we will specify which implementations permit multiple edges and which implementations forbid them.

Simple Graphs. The simplest of graphs have no loops and no multiple edges. Appropriately enough, these graphs are called **simple** graphs. Many applications require only simple directed graphs, or even simple undirected graphs.

Airline Routes Example

Let's examine a directed graph that represents the flights of a small airline called Crocodile Airlines. Each vertex in the graph is a city, and each edge represents a regularly scheduled flight from one city to another. Crocodile's complete collection of flights is shown in Figure 15.2. Notice that the graph is directed; for example, it's possible to fly from Darwin to Canberra on a nonstop flight but not the other way around.

airline routes form a directed graph

   The point of expressing the flights as a graph is that questions about the airline can be answered by carrying out common algorithms on the graph. For example, a sheep farmer might wonder what is the fewest number of flights required to fly from Black Stump to Melbourne. This is an example of a *shortest path* problem that we will solve in Section 15.4. With a small graph such as Figure 15.2, you can probably see that the shortest path from Black Stump to Melbourne consists of four edges, but a manual examination might not suffice for a larger graph.

FIGURE 15.2   Crocodile Airlines Routes

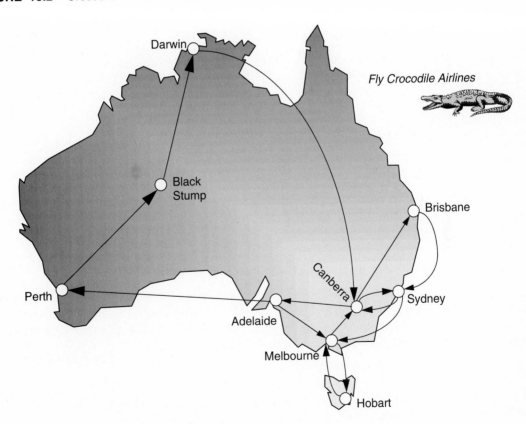

Self-Test Exercises

1. How many vertices and edges does the graph in Figure 15.2 have? How many loops? How would you interpret a loop in this graph?

2. Is Figure 15.2 a simple graph? Why or why not?

3. Suppose we have four coins in the coin game instead of just three. At the start of the game, the coins are in a line, with the two end coins heads and the other two coins tails. The goal is to change the configuration so that the two end coins are tails, and the other two coins are heads. There are three rules for this game: (1) Either of the end coins may be flipped whenever you want to. (2) A middle coin may be flipped from heads to tails only if the coin to its immediate right is already heads. (3) A middle coin may be flipped from tails to heads only if the coin to its immediate left is already tails. Your mission: Draw the directed state graph for this game, and determine whether it is possible to go from the start configuration to the goal. Why does the graph need to be directed?

15.2 GRAPH IMPLEMENTATIONS

"I could spin a web if I tried," said Wilbur, boasting. "I've just never tried."

E. B. WHITE
Charlotte's Web

Different kinds of graphs require different kinds of implementations, but the fundamental concepts of all graph implementations are similar. We'll look at several representations for one particular kind of graph: directed graphs in which loops are allowed. Some of the representations allow multiple edges, and some do not. In each of the representations, the vertices of the graph are named with numbers 0, 1, 2, ..., so that we may refer to each vertex individually by saying "vertex 0," "vertex 1," and so on.

Representing Graphs with an Adjacency Matrix

Let's start with a directed graph with no multiple edges. The graph's edges may be represented in a square grid of boolean (true/false) values, called the graph's *adjacency matrix*. The top of the next page shows an example of a graph with four vertices and its adjacency matrix.

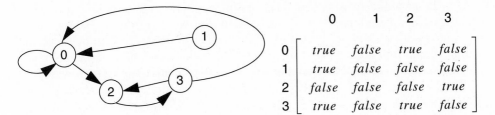

Each component of the adjacency matrix indicates whether a certain edge is present. For example, is there an edge from vertex 0 to vertex 2? Yes, because true appears at row 0 of column 2. But is there also an edge from vertex 2 to vertex 0? No, because false appears at row 2 of column 0. The general rule for using an adjacency matrix is given here:

a true component at row i and column j indicates an edge from vertex i to vertex j

---

Adjacency Matrix

An **adjacency matrix** is a square grid of true/false values that represent the edges of a graph. If the graph contains *n* vertices, then the grid contains *n* rows and *n* columns. For two vertex numbers *i* and *j*, the component at row *i* and column *j* is true if there is an edge from vertex *i* to vertex *j*; otherwise the component is false.

Using a Two-Dimensional Array to Store an Adjacency Matrix

In C++, an adjacency matrix can be stored in a **two-dimensional array** in which every component has two indexes rather than the usual one index. Programmers usually view a two-dimensional array as a grid of elements, where the first index provides the row number of a component, and the second index provides the column number of a component. In a declaration of a two-dimensional array, the number of rows is given in square brackets, followed by the number of columns (also in square brackets). For example, a program might require a two-dimensional array of double numbers with 12 rows and 8 columns, as declared here:

in a two-dimensional array, every component has two indexes

```
double budget[12][8];
```
Declaring a two-dimensional array with 12 rows and 8 columns.

Within the program, the individual components of the two-dimensional array can be accessed by providing both indexes. For example, we can assign the value 3.14 to row number 2 and column number 6 with this assignment statement:

```
budget[2][6] = 3.14;
```

As with an ordinary array, the index numbers begin with zero, so our `budget` has rows numbered from 0 to 11, and columns numbered from 0 to 7.

For an adjacency matrix, we use a two-dimensional array with one row and one column for each vertex of the graph. The components of the array are boolean true/false values. For example, the adjacency matrix for a graph with four vertices can be stored using this declaration of a two-dimensional array:

```
bool adjacency_matrix[4][4];
```

The location `adjacency_matrix[i][j]` contains true if there is an edge from vertex *i* to vertex *j*. A false value indicates no edge. Edges of a graph can be added (by placing true in a location of the matrix) or removed (by placing false). Once the adjacency matrix has been set, an application can examine locations of the matrix to determine which edges are present and which are missing.

Representing Graphs with Edge Lists

Again, suppose we have a directed graph with no multiple edges. Such a graph can be represented by creating a linked list for each vertex. Here's an example:

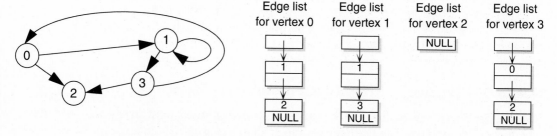

To understand the example, look at the linked list for vertex number 0. This list contains 1 and 2, which means that there is an edge from vertex 0 to vertex 1, and a second edge from vertex 0 to vertex 2. In general, the linked list for vertex number *i* is a list of vertex numbers following this rule:

Linked List Representation of Graphs

A directed graph with *n* vertices can be represented by *n* different linked lists. List number *i* provides the connections for vertex *i*. To be specific: For each entry *j* in list number *i*, there is an edge from *i* to *j*.

Loops are allowed in this representation; for example, look at the list for vertex 1 in the edge lists given above. Number 1 appears on this list itself, so there is an edge from vertex 1 to vertex 1 in the graph. We may also have vertices that are not the source of any edge—for example, vertex 2 in the graph above. Since vertex 2 is not the source of any edge, the edge list for vertex 2 is empty. If we allow the same element to appear more than once on the list, then multiple edges could also be allowed. But often, multiple edges are not allowed.

In a graph with *n* vertices, there are *n* edge lists. The head pointers for the *n* edge lists can be stored in an array of *n* head pointers. When we need to determine whether an edge exists from vertex *i* to vertex *j*, we check to see whether *j* appears on list number *i*.

Representing Graphs with Edge Sets

Another implementation of graphs requires a previously programmed implementation of a set ADT. For example, suppose that we have declared `Set` as a template class capable of holding a set of items. Presumably, the set class has operations to insert an item, check whether an item is in the set, remove an item, and so forth. To represent a graph with 10 vertices, we can declare an array of 10 sets of integers, as shown here:

```
Set<int> connections[10];
```

Using this representation, a set such as `connections[i]` contains the vertex numbers of all of the vertices that vertex *i* is connected to. For example, suppose that `connections[3]` contains the numbers 1 and 2. In this case, there is an edge from vertex 3 to vertex 1, and another edge from vertex 3 to vertex 2.

Which Representation Is Best?

If the space is available, then an adjacency matrix is easier to implement and generally easier to use than edge lists or edge sets. But sometimes there are other considerations. For example, how often will you be doing each of these operations:

1. Adding or removing edges
2. Checking whether a particular edge is present
3. Iterating a loop that executes one time for each edge with a particular source vertex *i*

The first two operations require only a small constant amount of time with the adjacency matrices. But in the worst case, both (1) and (2) require $O(n)$ operations with the edge list representation (where *n* is the number of vertices). This worst case occurs when the operation must traverse an entire edge list, and that edge list might contain as many as *n* edges. With edge sets, both (1) and (2) might also require $O(n)$ operations—but this time could be cut to $O(\log n)$ by using a fast set representation such as B-trees from Section 11.2.

On the other hand, the edge lists are efficient for the third operation. With an edge list, the third operation can be carried out by simply stepping through the list one element at a time. The time required is $O(e)$, where e is the number of edges that have vertex i as their source. A good set ADT should also provide the operations to step through the elements of the set one at a time. In this way, both edge lists and edge sets are likely to require just $O(e)$ operations to step through the edges with a particular source vertex. But with an adjacency matrix, the act of stepping through the edges with source vertex i requires each entry in row i to be examined. This traversal of the entire row is necessary just to see whether each entry is true or false. This always requires $O(n)$ time, where n is the number of vertices.

In general, your choice of representations should be based on your expectations as to which operations are most frequent. The availability of a previously programmed set ADT may also affect your choice. One last consideration is the average number of edges originating at a vertex. If each vertex has only a few edges (a so-called **sparse** graph), then an adjacency matrix is mostly wasted space filled with the value false.

PROGRAMMING EXAMPLE: Labeled Graph ADT

Now we'll implement an ADT for directed graphs with no multiple edges. This first ADT has only a few member functions; for example, there is no way to remove vertices. The simple form of the first Graph class provides a sharp focus on graphs and their algorithms.

With our Graph class, each graph is initially created with no vertices and no edges. There is a member function to add new vertices. For an n-vertex graph, these vertices are always numbered from zero to $n-1$. Once a graph has some vertices, other functions add or remove edges. Each graph has a maximum number of vertices specified by the constant Graph::MAXIMUM. We could avoid a maximum number of vertices by using dynamic memory, but doing so introduces complications that we leave for the Programming Projects in this chapter.

When we implement the graph, the number of vertices will be stored in the member variable named many_vertices, which may be anywhere from zero to MAXIMUM. A graph's edges are stored in an adjacency matrix, which is implemented as the two-dimensional boolean array called edges. The edges array has MAXIMUM rows and MAXIMUM columns, but keep in mind that we might not be using all of this array. For example, if many_vertices is 3, then we will only use the nine components ranging from edges[0][0] to edges[2][2].

Our Graph class will have one extra feature: The vertices will have information attached to them in the same way that we attached information to tree nodes. For example, in the airline route graph of Figure 15.2 on page 669, each vertex is associated with a city name. The addition of information at each vertex makes the graph a **labeled graph**, and the information itself is called a vertex's **label**. Of course, the information might be any data type—integers, doubles, strings, you-name-it—which suggests that an ADT for labeled graphs should be implemented as a template class, with the type of the labels determined by a template parameter.

The labels of the vertices will be stored in a private member variable named labels, which is an ordinary one-dimensional array. The label for vertex number i will be stored in labels[i]. Thus, our graph definition has a total of three member variables, listed in the private section shown here:

```
template <class Item>
class Graph
{
public:
    // MEMBER CONSTANTS
    static const size_t MAXIMUM = 20;
    We'll discuss the member functions in a moment.
private:
    bool edges[MAXIMUM][MAXIMUM];
    Item labels[MAXIMUM];
    size_t many_vertices;
};
```

If your compiler does not permit initialization of static constants, see Appendix E.

Member Functions to Add Vertices and Edges

When a graph is initialized with the constructor, it has no vertices and no edges. At any time, the current number of vertices can be obtained from a constant member function named size. Thus, a newly constructed graph g has g.size( ) equal to zero.

Two member functions, add_vertex and add_edge, allow us to add new vertices and edges, with these specifications:

```
void add_vertex(const Item& label);
// Precondition: size( ) < MAXIMUM.
// Postcondition: The size of the Graph has been increased by adding
// one new vertex. This new vertex has the specified label and no edges.

void add_edge(size_t source, size_t target);
// Precondition: (source < size( )) and (target < size( )).
// Postcondition: The Graph has all the edges that it originally had, and
// also has another edge from the specified source to the specified target.
// (If this edge was already present, then the Graph is unchanged.)
```

For example, the following four statements create the two-vertex graph shown at the top of the next page. In this graph, vertex number zero (v_0) contains the *double* number 3.14, and vertex number one (v_0) contains the double number 2.17:

```
Graph<double> t;
```

```
t.add_vertex(3.14);  // Adds vertex number 0, with data of 3.14
t.add_vertex(2.17);  // Adds the next vertex, with data of 2.17
t.add_edge(1, 0);    // Adds an edge from vertex 1 to vertex 0
```

As you can see from the example, the add_vertex member function of the Graph class requires an argument, which is the label of the newly added vertex.

Labeled Graph ADT—Overloading the Subscript Operator

Once a graph is created, we want to access its vertex labels by using the usual "square bracket" notation from C++. For example, suppose that g is a ten-vertex labeled graph. In order to print the label of vertex 3, we would like to write this:

```
cout << g[3];
```

When used this way, the square brackets are called the **subscript operator.**

We also want the subscript operator to allow assignments and other changes to the labels. For example, suppose that g's labels are integers. We want to be able to change the label of a vertex with a simple assignment statement such as this:

```
g[3] = 42;◄————Change the label of vertex 3 to 42.
```

In C++, we can overload the subscript operator to behave in exactly this way. The overloading of the subscript operator is accomplished with the highlighted prototype in the following complete class definition:

```
template <class Item>
class Graph
{
public:
    ...
    Item& operator [ ] (size_t vertex);
    ...
```

In this definition, you can see the prototype for the overloaded subscript operator. We have overloaded the subscript operator for other classes (such as the String class from Section 4.5), but the Graph subscript operator has a new feature, listed third in this list:

- The subscript operator may be overloaded only as a member function. It is not possible to overload the subscript operator as a nonmember function.

- When the subscript operator is called for an object, the square brackets are placed after the object name, and the arguments appear inside the brackets. For example, `g[3]` activates the subscript operator for the object g, using 3 as the single argument.
- We want to use the subscript operator both for obtaining the current value of a label and for changing a label such as the assignment statement `g[3] = 42`. Because of this, the return value of the subscript operator may not be simply `Item`. A return value of `Item` would permit us to get a current value, but it would not provide any way to change a label. The alternative is a return type of `Item&`, placing the "reference symbol &" after the type name. This technique is called a **reference return value,** which we explain next.

Reference Return Values

A member function may have a *reference return value*, which is obtained by placing the reference symbol & after the return type of the function. The return value of such a function is usually a private member variable, or part of a private member variable of the object. A reference return value may be used like any other return value, such as assigning it to a variable printing the value, or using the value in some other way. But, in addition, a reference return value has a special property:

Reference Return Values

When a function has a reference return value, the calling program may call the function and use the result just like a variable. Any changes to this variable will alter the actual variable specified in the function's return statement.

As an example, consider our overloaded subscript operator, which has a reference return value, as shown by the symbol & in the prototype:

```
Item& operator [ ] (size_t vertex);
```

For a graph g, an expression such as `g[3]` allows us to directly alter a vertex label. Here are two examples:

```
g[3] = 42;    // Assign the value 42 to the label of vertex 3.
cin >> g[7];  // Read the label of vertex 7 from standard input.
```

As another example, suppose that we have double numbers for our labels, and we wish to cut each label in half. We could first define a halving function, shown here:

```
void halve(double& r)
{
    r = r/2;
}
```

With the halving function in hand, we can move through the labels of a graph g, cutting each label in half, as shown here:

```
size_t v;

for (v = 0; v < g.size( ); v++)
    halve(g[v]);
```

The key point is that changes made to g[v] will affect the actual variable that is returned by the subscript operator, and this actual variable is part of the private member variable, labels, which stores the graph's labels.

The implementation of the overloaded subscript operator is shown here:

```
template <class Item>
Item& Graph<Item>::operator [ ] (size_t vertex)
// Library facilities used: assert.h
{
    assert(vertex < size( ));

    return labels[vertex];
}
```

The return statement, return labels[vertex], indicates that any changes that the calling program makes directly on the return result will actually change the component labels[vertex] in the private member variable labels.

Labeled Graph ADT—Implementation

The header file and implementation file for the graph ADT are given in Figures 15.3 and 15.4. In addition to the member functions that we have already mentioned, there is also a function to remove an edge from a graph, and a function to determine whether a particular edge exists.

FIGURE 15.3 Header File for the Graph Class

A Header File

```
// FILE: graph.h
// TEMPLATE CLASS PROVIDED: Graph<Item> (a class for labeled graphs)
//     The vertices of an n-vertex graph are numbered from zero to n–1. Each vertex has a
//     label of type Item. It may be any of the C++ built-in types (int, char, etc.), or any
//     class with a default constructor and an assignment operator. The graph may not have
//     multiple edges.
//
// MEMBER CONSTANTS for the Graph<Item> template class:
//     static const size_t MAXIMUM = _____
//        Graph::MAXIMUM is the maximum number of vertices that a Graph can have.
//
// CONSTRUCTOR for the Graph<Item> template class:
//     Graph( )
//        Postcondition: The Graph has been initialized with no vertices and no edges.
//
// MODIFICATION MEMBER FUNCTIONS for the Graph<Item> template class:
//     void add_vertex(const Item& label)
//        Precondition: size( ) < MAXIMUM.
//        Postcondition: The size of the Graph has been increased by adding one new vertex.
//        This new vertex has the specified label and no edges.
//
//     void add_edge(size_t source, size_t target)
//        Precondition: (source < size( )) and (target < size( )).
//        Postcondition: The Graph has all the edges that it originally had, and it also has
//        another edge from the specified source to the specified target. (If this edge was
//        already present, then the Graph is unchanged.)
//
//     void remove_edge(size_t source, size_t target)
//        Precondition: (source < size( )) and (target < size( )).
//        Postcondition: The Graph has all the edges that it originally had except for the edge
//        from the specified source to the specified target. (If this edge was not originally
//        present, then the Graph is unchanged.)
//
//     Item& operator [ ] (size_t vertex)
//        Precondition: vertex < size( ).
//        Postcondition: The return value is a reference to the label of the specified vertex.
```

(continued)

(FIGURE 15.3 continued)

```
//
// CONSTANT MEMBER FUNCTIONS for the Graph<Item> template class:
//    size_t size( ) const
//       Postcondition: The return value is the number of vertices in the Graph.
//
//    bool is_edge(size_t source, size_t target) const
//       Precondition: (source < size( )) and (target < size( )).
//       Postcondition: The return value is true if the Graph has an edge from source to target.
//       Otherwise the return value is false.
//
// VALUE SEMANTICS for the Graph<Item> template class:
//    Assignments and the copy constructor may be used with Graph<Item> objects.

#ifndef GRAPH_H
#define GRAPH_H
#include <stdlib.h>   // Provides size_t

    template <class Item>
    class Graph
    {
    public:
        // MEMBER CONSTANTS
        static const size_t MAXIMUM = 20;
        // CONSTRUCTOR
        Graph( ) { many_vertices = 0; }
        // MODIFICATION MEMBER FUNCTIONS
        void add_vertex(const Item& label);
        void add_edge(size_t source, size_t target);
        void remove_edge(size_t source, size_t target);
        Item& operator [ ] (size_t vertex);
        // CONSTANT MEMBER FUNCTIONS
        size_t size( ) const { return many_vertices; }
        bool is_edge(size_t source, size_t target) const;
    private:
        bool edges[MAXIMUM][MAXIMUM];
        Item labels[MAXIMUM];
        size_t many_vertices;
    };

#include "graph.template" // Include the implementation.
#endif
```

If your compiler does not permit initialization of static constants, see Appendix E.

This special operator allows access to the vertex labels. It is discussed further in the text.

graph.h   **FTP**

FIGURE 15.4	Implementation File for the Graph Class

An Implementation File

```
// FILE: graph.template
// TEMPLATE CLASS IMPLEMENTED: Graph<Item> (See graph.h for documentation.)
// This file is included in the header file and not compiled separately.
// INVARIANT for the Graph ADT:
//     1. The number of vertices in the Graph is stored in the member variable many_vertices.
//        These vertices are numbered from 0 to many_vertices-1.
//     2. edges is the adjacency matrix for the Graph (with true in edges[i][j] to indicate an
//        edge from vertex i to vertex j).
//     3. For each i < many_vertices, labels[i] is the label of vertex i.

#include "assert.h"     // Provides assert
#include "stdlib.h"     // Provides size_t

template <class Item>
void Graph<Item>::add_vertex (const Item& label)
// Library facilities used: assert.h, stdlib.h
{
    size_t new_vertex_number;
    size_t other_number;

    assert(size( ) < MAXIMUM);
    new_vertex_number = many_vertices;
    many_vertices++;
    for (other_number = 0; other_number < many_vertices; other_number++)
    {
        edges[other_number][new_vertex_number] = false;
        edges[new_vertex_number][other_number] = false;
    }
    labels[new_vertex_number] = label;
}

template <class Item>
void Graph<Item>::add_edge(size_t source, size_t target)
// Library facilities used: assert.h, stdlib.h
{
    assert(source < size( ));
    assert(target < size( ));

    edges[source][target] = true;
}
```

(continued)

(FIGURE 15.4 continued)

```
template <class Item>
void Graph<Item>::remove_edge(size_t source, size_t target)
// Library facilities used: assert.h, stdlib.h
{
    assert(source < size( ));
    assert(target < size( ));

    edges[source][target] = false;
}


template <class Item>
Item& Graph<Item>::operator [ ] (size_t vertex)
// Library facilities used: assert.h, graph.h, stdlib.h
{
    assert(vertex < size( ));

    return labels[vertex];
}


template <class Item>
bool Graph<Item>::is_edge(size_t source, size_t target) const
// Library facilities used: assert.h, stdlib.h
{
    assert(source < size( ));
    assert(target < size( ));

    return edges[source][target];
}
```

graph.template   **FTP**

An Iterator Class for The Neighbors of a Vertex

Programming with graphs will be easier if we provide an additional class. The class, called NeighborIterator, allows us to easily step through the neighbors of a vertex in a graph. The neighbor iterator is a template class, with a definition that begins like this:

```
template <class Item>
class NeighborIterator
{
public:
    // CONSTRUCTOR
    NeighborIterator(const Graph<Item>& g);
    ...
```

As you can see, when a neighbor iterator is constructed, it must be provided with a graph g. The constructor "attaches" the neighbor iterator to the graph g, and thereafter a programmer may ask the iterator to step through the neighbors of a vertex of g one at a time. There are four member functions that cooperate to provide the mechanism of stepping through neighbors. The four functions are listed here:

```
template <class Item>
class NeighborIterator
{
public:
    // CONSTRUCTOR
    NeighborIterator(const Graph<Item>& g);
    // MODIFICATION MEMBER FUNCTIONS
    void restart(size_t source);
    void advance( );
    // CONSTANT MEMBER FUNCTIONS
    size_t current( ) const;
    bool done( ) const;
    ...
```

When we want to step through the neighbors of a vertex *v*, we begin by activating restart(v). After this activation, the current function will return the lowest-numbered neighbor of vertex *v*. When we want to step to the next neighbor, we activate the advance function. We can keep calling current to get the next neighbor number, and activating advance to move to the next neighbor—until done returns true. At this point, with done returning true, we have run out of neighbors and should no longer call current or advance. However, we can call restart to start the process all over again.

As an example, suppose that australia is a graph with String labels and at least four vertices (using our String class from Section 4.5). The following code will print the vertex numbers of all of the neighbors of vertex 3:

```
NeighborIterator<String> flights(australia);
for (flights.restart(3); !flights.done( ); flights.advance( ))
    cout << flights.current( ) << endl;
```

Some slightly different code will print the *labels* of the neighbors of vertex 3:

```
NeighborIterator<String> flights(australia);
for (flights.restart(3); !flights.done( ); flights.advance( ))
    cout << austrailia[flights.current( )] << endl;
```

The documentation and implementation of the neighbor iterator is shown in Figure 15.5. These may be placed in the graph.h and graph.template files along with the Graph class, or they may be placed in a separate file of their own.

FIGURE 15.5 │ The Neighbor Iterator Template Class

Class Documentation

```
//   TEMPLATE CLASS PROVIDED: NeighborIterator<Item>
//      Neighbor Iterator is an external iterator class that allows you to step through the
//      neighbors of a vertex in a Graph. The Item is the same as the Graph's Item.
//
//   CONSTRUCTOR for the NeighborIterator<Item> class:
//      NeighborIterator(const Graph<Item>& g)
//         Precondition: g.size( ) > 0.
//         Postcondition: The neighbor iterator has been attached to Graph g, and restart(0) has
//         been activated.
//
//   MODIFICATION MEMBER FUNCTIONS for the NeighborIterator<Item> class:
//      void restart(size_t source)
//         Precondition: (source < graph_size( )).
//         Postcondition: The neighbor iterator has been restarted, so it will now step
//         through all the neighbors of the specified source vertex. At this point, if source has at
//         least one neighbor, then current( ) returns the lowest-numbered neighbor, and done( )
//         returns false. If source has no neighbors, then done( ) returns true, and current( ) must
//         not be called.
//
//      void advance( )
//         Precondition: done( ) returns false.
//         Postcondition: If current( ) is already providing the highest-numbered neighbor of the
//         source vertex, then done( ) is set to return true, and current( ) should no longer be
//         called. Otherwise, current( ) is set so that it returns the next-lowest-numbered
//         neighbor of the source vertex, and done( ) still returns false.
//
//   CONSTANT MEMBER FUNCTIONS for the NeighborIterator<Item> class:
//      size_t current( ) const
//         Precondition: done( ) returns false.
//         Postcondition: The return value is the current neighbor of the source vertex.
//
//      bool done( ) const
//         Postcondition: The return value is true if the iterator has already visited all neighbors
//         of the specified source vertex. In this case, the current( ) function may not be called.
//         On the other hand, a false return value means that it is valid to call the current( )
//         function.
//
//      size_t graph_size( ) const
//         Postcondition: The return value is the number of vertices of the attached Graph.
//
//   VALUE SEMANTICS for the NeighborIterator class:
//      Assignments and the copy constructor may be used with NeighborIterator<Item> objects.
```

(continued)

(FIGURE 15.5 continued)

Template Class Definition

```
#include <stdlib.h>  // Provides size_t

template <class Item>
class NeighborIterator
    {
    public:
        // CONSTRUCTOR
        NeighborIterator(const Graph<Item>& g);
        // MODIFICATION MEMBER FUNCTIONS
        void restart(size_t source);
        void advance( );
        // CONSTANT MEMBER FUNCTIONS
        size_t current( ) const;
        bool done( ) const;
        size_t graph_size( ) const { return graph_ptr->size( ); }
    private:
        size_t my_source;
        size_t my_target;
        const Graph<Item> *graph_ptr;
    };
```

Implementation of the Member Functions

```
//  INVARIANT for the NeighborIterator ADT:
//  1. graph_ptr is a pointer to the graph that is attached to the neighbor iterator.
//  2. We are stepping through the neighbors of one vertex, and this vertex number is stored
//     in the member variable my_source.
//  3. If we have already stepped through all the neighbors of my_source, then my_target is
//     equal to graph_size( ). Otherwise, my_target is equal to the current neighbor.

template <class Item>
NeighborIterator<Item>::NeighborIterator(const Graph<Item>& g)
// Library facilities used: assert.h
{
    assert(g.size( ) > 0);
    graph_ptr = &g;
    restart(0);
}
```

(continued)

(FIGURE 15.5 continued)

```
template <class Item>
void NeighborIterator<Item>::restart(size_t source)
// Library facilities used: assert.h, stdlib.h
{
    assert(source < graph_size( ));

    my_source = source;
    my_target = 0;
    while ((my_target < graph_size( )) && !graph_ptr->is_edge(my_source, my_target))
        my_target++;
}

template <class Item>
void NeighborIterator<Item>::advance( )
// Library facilities used: assert.h
{
    assert(!done( ));

    do
        my_target++;
    while((my_target < graph_size( )) && !graph_ptr->is_edge(my_source, my_target));
}

template <class Item>
size_t NeighborIterator<Item>::current( ) const
// Library facilities used: assert.h, stdlib.h
{
    assert(!done( ));

    return my_target;
}

template <class Item>
bool NeighborIterator<Item>::done( ) const

// Library facilities used: assert.h, stdlib.h
{
    return (my_target == graph_size( ));
}
```

graph.h and graph.template **FTP**

How the Neighbor Iterator Works

A neighbor iterator has a private member variable called `graph_ptr`. When the neighbor iterator's constructor is called, the `graph_ptr` is set to point at the attached graph. Later, when we need to know information about the graph, we can obtain that information through `graph_ptr`. For example, suppose we need to know whether two vertices, `my_source` and `my_target`, are connected by an edge. The expression to determine this is:

```
graph_ptr->is_edge(my_source, my_target)
```

This expression occurs as part of the `restart` and `advance` member functions.

Programming Tip: Use External Iterators

TIP

Our neighbor iterator was implemented as a *class* that is separate from the Graph class. This separate implementation is called an **external iterator**. This differs from previous approaches, such as our bag iterator in Section 6.5. That bag iterator was an **internal iterator,** which means that the ability to "step through" an object is provided by *member functions of the object* itself.

An external iterator is more flexible than an internal iterator. For example, we can attach several different neighbor iterators to a single graph. Each of these neighbor iterators may be responsible for a different task, and each can step through a different part of the graph. Multiple iterators such as this are not possible with an internal iterator.

Self-Test Exercises

4. Write a new Graph member function to remove the highest-numbered vertex from a graph.

5. We have assumed that there are no multiple edges in a graph, and therefore we could store simple true/false in the adjacency matrix. Describe how adjacency matrixes might be used even if the graphs do have multiple edges.

6. Compare and contrast the adjacency lists and edge lists.

7. What is the difference between an external iterator and an internal iterator? Describe an advantage of an external iterator.

8. Suppose that g is a graph with integer labels. What is the label of vertex 3 at the three points marked here? Assume that the statements are executed one after another, and i is an integer variable.

```
g[3] = 42;  // Point 1
i = g[3];   // Point 2
i = 43;     // Point 3
```

15.3 GRAPH TRAVERSALS

In the chapter on trees, we saw three different binary tree traversals. Each traversal visits all of a binary tree's nodes and does some processing at each node. The three traversals had similar recursive implementations, with the distinguishing factor being whether a node was visited before, after, or in between its two children. A graph vertex doesn't have children like a tree node, so the tree traversal algorithms are not immediately applicable to graphs. But there are two common ways of traversing a graph. One of the methods (breadth-first search) uses a queue to keep track of vertices that still need to be visited, and the other method (depth-first search) uses a stack. The depth-first search can also be implemented recursively in a way that does not explicitly use a stack of vertices.

This section discusses the two traversal algorithms in a general way and then provides implementations of the algorithms to traverse a Graph object (using the Graph class (Figure 15.3 on page 679) and the NeighborIterator (Figure 15.5 on page 684). Both of the traversal algorithms have the same underlying purpose: to start at one vertex of a graph (the "start" vertex), process the information contained at that vertex, and then move along an edge to process a neighbor. When the traversal finishes, all of the vertices that can be reached from the start vertex (via some directed path) have been processed.

when the traversal finishes, all of the vertices that can be reached from the start vertex have been processed

A traversal algorithm must be careful that it doesn't enter a repetitive cycle—for example, moving from the start vertex to a neighbor, from there to the neighbor's neighbor, and possibly from there back to the starting point and back to the same neighbor, and back to the same neighbor's neighbor, and so on. To prevent this potential "spinning your wheels," we will include an ability to *mark* each vertex as it is processed. If a traversal ever returns to a vertex that is already marked, then reprocessing is not done. If we are drawing the graphs, then we might indicate a marked vertex by shading it. For example, suppose a traversal starts at vertex 0 of this graph:

The traversal begins by processing vertex number 0. We don't really care what kind of processing occurs—maybe the labels are printed out, or perhaps there is more complicated processing. When we implement the traversal, the processing will be done by a function that is given as an argument to the traversal function, similar to the tree traversals in Figure 10.11 on page 465. In any case, there will be some processing of vertex number 0, and then we will mark it as processed, looking like this:

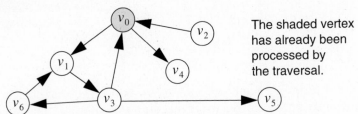

The shaded vertex has already been processed by the traversal.

The progress of a traversal after the start vertex depends on the traversal method being used. We'll start by looking at how a depth-first search proceeds.

Depth-First Search

After processing vertex 0, a depth-first search moves along a directed edge to one of vertex 0's neighbors. In our example, there are two possibilities: moving to vertex 1 (along the edge from 0 to 1) or to vertex 4 (along the edge from 0 to 4). In our example, it is not possible to move from vertex 0 to 3, or from vertex 0 to 2, because the edges go in the wrong direction. So the traversal has a choice: Move to vertex 1 or move to vertex 4. Right now we won't worry about exactly how the choice is made—let's just assume that the next vertex processed is vertex 1. After processing vertex 1, the picture looks like this:

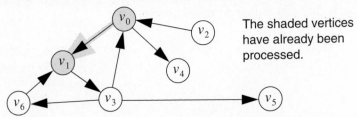

The shaded vertices have already been processed.

In the drawing we have highlighted the edge from vertex 0 to vertex 1 to indicate the intuitive notion of "moving from one vertex to another."

From here, the traversal moves to one of vertex 1's neighbors. You may think of vertex 1 as being at the "leading edge" of the depth-first traversal. It is the vertex that has most recently been processed, and so we will continue pushing forward from vertex 1, moving to one of vertex 1's unprocessed neighbors. In this example, there is only one unprocessed neighbor to consider, vertex 3. So we will move to vertex 3 and process it. At this point, we have processed three of the vertices, as shown at the top of the next page.

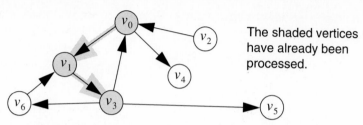

The shaded vertices have already been processed.

to prevent going around in circles, never move forward to a marked vertex

One of vertex 3's neighbors is vertex 0—but vertex 0 has already been marked as previously processed. So, to prevent the traversal from going around in circles, we will not move from 3 back to 0. In general, *we will never move forward to a marked vertex, (since it has already been processed).* But we will move to vertex 3's other neighbors (vertices 5 and 6). Suppose we move to vertex 5 first. After processing vertex 5, the picture looks like this:

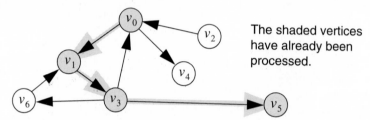

The shaded vertices have already been processed.

Since vertex 5 has no neighbors, the depth-first traversal cannot proceed forward any farther. Instead, the traversal comes back to see if the previous vertex—vertex 3—has any more unmarked neighbors:

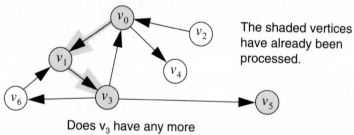

The shaded vertices have already been processed.

Does v_3 have any more
unmarked neighbors?

In this drawing, you can see that four vertices have been processed. And the "leading edge" of the search has pulled back to vertex v_3. Does v_3 have any more unmarked neighbors where the search can proceed? Yes—v_6 is an unmarked neighbor of v_3, so again the search plunges forward, along the edge from v_3 to v_6. Vertex 6 is processed, giving the picture at the top of the next page.

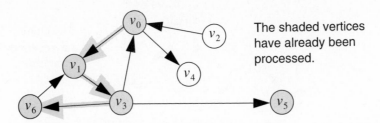

The shaded vertices have already been processed.

What now? Vertex 6 does have a neighbor—vertex 1—but v_1 has already been marked. So, since vertex 6 has no *unmarked* neighbors, the traversal again backs up to see if v_3 has any more unmarked neighbors. After the backup, we have this situation:

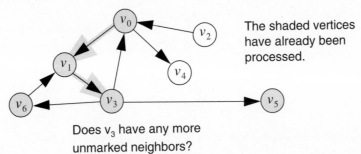

The shaded vertices have already been processed.

Does v_3 have any more unmarked neighbors?

Vertex 3 has no more unmarked neighbors (thank goodness!). So back we go to the previous vertex—vertex 1—to check whether it has any unmarked neighbors:

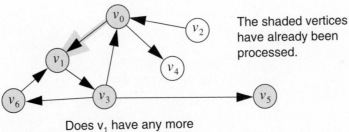

The shaded vertices have already been processed.

Does v_1 have any more unmarked neighbors?

You can see that the leading edge of the search is now at v_1, and that v_1 has no more unmarked neighbors, so back we go to vertex 0, to see if it has any unfinished business. This situation is drawn at the top of the next page.

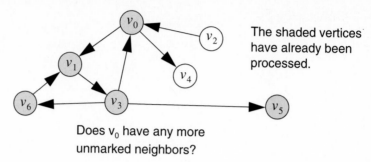

The shaded vertices have already been processed.

Does v_0 have any more
unmarked neighbors?

From vertex 0 we can still travel to the unmarked vertex 4 and process it, as shown here:

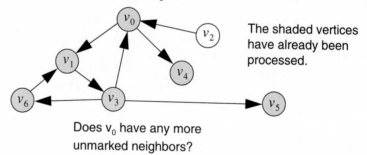

The shaded vertices have already been processed.

Vertex 4 has no neighbors, so we back up once more to vertex 0:

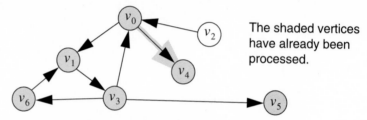

The shaded vertices have already been processed.

Does v_0 have any more
unmarked neighbors?

*some vertices
are not
processed
because they
can't be
reached from
the start vertex*

Vertex 0 has no more unmarked neighbors—and since this was the starting point there is no place left to back up to. That's the end of the traversal.

In this example, vertex 2 was never processed because there was no path from the start vertex (vertex 0) to vertex 2. A traversal only processes those vertices that can be reached from the start vertex.

There's one other important point about a *depth-first* search: From the start vertex, the traversal proceeds to a neighbor and from there to another neighbor and so on—always going as far as possible before it ever backs up. In describing this behavior, it seems as if there's a lot to keep track of: where we start, where we go from there, and where we go from there. But the actual implementation can use recursion to keep track of most of these details in a simple way. We'll tackle that recursive implementation after looking at an alternative method: breadth-first search.

Breadth-First Search

A breadth-first search uses a queue to keep track of which vertices might still have unprocessed neighbors. The search begins with a starting vertex, which is processed, marked, and placed in the queue. For example, suppose we are processing this graph with vertex 0 as our starting point, so that vertex 0 is the first vertex to be processed, marked, and placed into the queue:

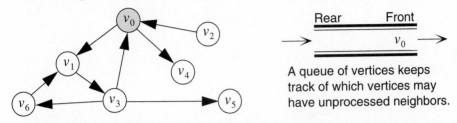

A queue of vertices keeps track of which vertices may have unprocessed neighbors.

Once the starting vertex has been processed, marked, and placed in the queue, the main part of the breadth-first search begins. This consists of repeatedly carrying out the following steps:

1. Remove a vertex, v, from the front of the queue.
2. For each unmarked neighbor, u of v: Process u, mark u, and then place u in the queue (since u may have further unprocessed neighbors).

These two steps are repeated until the queue becomes empty. Let's look at our example to see how these two steps are carried out when vertex 0 is at the head of the queue. The vertex 0 is removed from the queue, and we note that it has two unprocessed neighbors: vertices 1 and 4. Vertices 1 and 4 will each be processed, marked, and placed in the queue. Let's assume that vertex 1 is placed in the queue first, and then vertex 4. (The queuing could also occur the other way, with vertex 4 placed first; the algorithm is correct either way.) After 1 and 4 are in the queue, the situation looks like this:

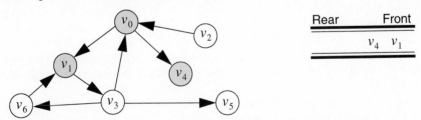

Since the queue still has entries, we repeat the two steps again: Remove the front entry (vertex 1), process and mark any unmarked neighbors of vertex 1, and enter these neighbors into the queue. The only unmarked neighbor of vertex

1 is vertex 3, so after processing, marking, and entering vertex 3, the situation looks like this:

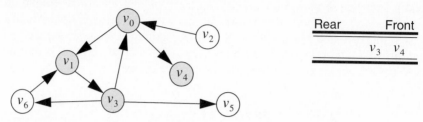

Next we remove vertex 4 from the front of the queue. Since vertex 4 has no neighbors, no new entries are processed or placed in the queue. The situation is now:

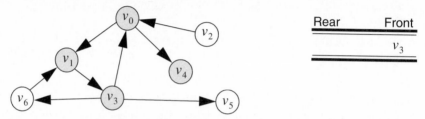

Vertex 3 comes out of the queue next. It has two unmarked neighbors (vertices 5 and 6) which are processed, marked, and placed in the queue, like this:

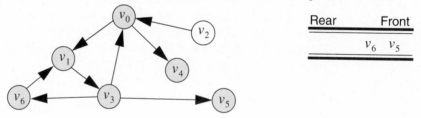

Notice that vertex 0 (which is also a neighbor of vertex 3) does not get reprocessed because it is already marked.

the effects of breadth-first and depth-first search are similar—only the order of processing vertices differs

At this point, we remove vertex 5 from the front of the queue, but it has no unmarked neighbors to worry about. We then remove vertex 6 from the queue. It also has no unmarked neighbors. The queue is finally empty, which ends the breadth-first search.

The effect of the breadth-first search is similar to the depth-first search: Vertices 0, 1, 3, 4, 5, and 6 have all been processed since they could all be reached from the starting point (vertex 0). Vertex 2 was not processed since there is no directed path from vertex 0 to vertex 2. However, the breadth-first search processes the vertices in a different order than the depth-first search. The breadth-first search first processed vertex 0, then processed the neighbors of the start point (1 and 4), then processed *their* neighbors (vertex 3), and so on. This contrasts with a depth-first search that processed the vertices 0, 1, 3 and 5 to start with (in that order).

You should now be able to carry out depth-first and breadth-first searches by hand on a directed graph. Next we will specify and implement the two searches as template functions that can be applied to any labeled graph.

Depth-First Search—Implementation

One way to implement a depth-first search is with the following template function:

```
template <class Process, class Item, class SizeType>
void depth_first(Process f, Graph<Item>& g, SizeType start);
// Precondition: start is a vertex number of the labeled graph g.
// Postcondition: A depth-first search of g has been executed, starting at
// the start vertex. The function f has been applied to the label of each
// vertex visited by the search.
```

In this prototype, the parameter g may be any Graph. For example, g could be a graph with integer labels, so that the actual type of g is Graph<*int*>. The parameter f is a function with one argument. The argument must be the same data type as the labels of the graphs. During a search, each time a vertex v is reached, that vertex is "processed" by calling f with the label of v as the actual argument to f.

For example, suppose that we have the following function to print integer values, as shown here:

```
void print_int_line(int value)
{
    cout << value << endl;
}
```

With this function in hand, we can carry out a depth-first search of a graph g, starting at vertex 0, and print all the values that we encounter. The function call for the search is as follows:

```
depth_first(print_int_line, g, 0);
```

The implementation of depth_first uses an array of boolean values declared as a local variable of the function, shown here:

```
bool marked[g.MAXIMUM];
```

This array has one component for each possible vertex of the graph g, and its purpose is to keep track of which vertices have been marked as visited by the search. In general, for a vertex number v, the component marked[v] is true if v has already been visited by the search, and false otherwise. The complete pseudocode for `depth_first` is short:

pseudocode for depth-first search

1. Check that the start vertex is a valid vertex number of the graph.
2. Set all the components of `marked` to false.
3. Call a separate function to actually carry out the search.

You may be wondering, "Why call separate function in Step 3? Why can't we just carry out the search in the body of the `depth_first` function itself?" Good question. The answer is that we plan to use recursion: The start vertex is processed and then recursive calls are made to process each of the start vertex's neighbors. Further recursive calls are made to process the neighbors' neighbors, and so on. So, if the work were carried out in the body of the `depth_first` function, each time a recursive call is made, we would do Step 2—clearing the `marked` array—and . . . oops! Clearing the marked array at every recursive call will definitely lead to trouble.

The new function, executed in Step 3, will be called `rec_dfs` with this prototype:

```
template <class Process, class Item, class SizeType>
void rec_dfs(
    Process f,
    Graph<Item>& g,
    SizeType v,
    bool marked[ ]
);
// Precondition: g is a labeled graph that is being traversed by a depth-
// first search. For each vertex x, marked[x] is true if x has already been
// visited by this search; otherwise marked[x] is false. The vertex v is an
// unmarked vertex that the search has just arrived at.
// Postcondition: The depth-first search of g has been continued through
// vertex v and beyond to all the vertices that can be reached from v via a
// path of unmarked vertices. The function f has been applied to the label
// of each vertex visited by the search, and each such vertex x has also
// been marked by setting marked[x] to true.
```

Now let's examine the body of the `rec_dfs` function. The first task is to mark and process the vertex v. After this we will examine each of vertex v's neighbors. Each time we find an unmarked neighbor we will make a recursive call to continue the search through that neighbor and beyond. The phrase "and beyond" is important because if a neighbor has another unmarked neighbor, then there will be another recursive call at that level, and so on until we reach a vertex with no unmarked neighbors. This description of `rec_dfs` is implemented in the top of Figure 15.6, and the actual `depth_first` function is implemented at the bottom of the figure.

FIGURE 15.6	Depth-First Search

Function Implementations

```
template <class Process, class Item, class SizeType>
void rec_dfs(Process f, Graph<Item>& g, size_t v, bool marked[ ])
// Precondition: g is a labeled graph that is being traversed by a depth-first search. For each
// vertex x, marked[x] is true if x has already been visited by this search, otherwise marked[x]
// is false. The vertex v is an unmarked vertex that the search has just arrived at.
// Postcondition: The depth-first search of g has been continued through vertex v and beyond
// to all the vertices that can be reached from v via a path of unmarked vertices. The function
// f has been applied to the label of each vertex visited by the search, and each such vertex x
// has also been marked by setting marked[x] to true.
// Library facilities used: graph.h, stdlib.h
{
    NeighborIterator neighbors(g);

    marked[v] = true;    // Mark vertex v
    f(g[v]);             // Process the label of vertex v with the function f

    // Traverse all the neighbors, looking for unmarked vertices:
    for (neighbors.restart(v); !neighbors.done( ); neighbors.advance( ))
    {
        if (!marked[neighbors.current( )])
            rec_dfs(neighbors.current( ));
    }
}


template <class Process, class Item, class SizeType>
void depth_first(Process f, Graph<Item>& g, size_t start)
// Precondition: start is a vertex number of the labeled graph g.
// Postcondition: A depth-first search of g has been executed, starting at the start vertex.
// The function f has been applied to the label of each vertex visited by the search.
// Library facilities used: graph.h, stdlib.h
{
    bool marked[g.MAXIMUM];
    size_t i;

    assert(start < g.size( ));

    for (i = 0; i < g.size( ); i++)
        marked[i] = false;

    rec_dfs(f, g, start, marked);
}
```

searches.template **FTP**

Breadth-First Search—Implementation

The breadth-first search is implemented with a queue of vertex numbers. The start vertex is processed, marked, and placed in the queue. Then the following steps are repeated until the queue is empty: (1) remove a vertex, *v*, from the front of the queue, and (2) for each unmarked neighbor *u* of *v*: process *u*, mark *u*, and then place *u* in the queue (since *u* may have further unprocessed neighbors).

These steps are implemented in Figure 15.7.

FIGURE 15.7 | Breadth-First Search

Function Implementation

```
template <class Process, class Item, class SizeType>
void breadth_first(Process f, Graph<Item>& g, size_t start)
// Precondition: start is a vertex number of the labeled graph g.
// Postcondition: A breadth-first search of g has been executed, starting at the start vertex.
// The function f has been applied to the label of each vertex visited by the search.
// Library facilities used: assert.h, graph.h, stdlib.h, queue2.h (from Figure 8.11 on page 372)
{
    bool marked[g.MAXIMUM];
    size_t v;
    size_t next;
    NeighborIterator neighbors(g);
    Queue<size_t> vertex_queue;    // The queue is from Figure 8.11 on page 372.

    assert(start < g.size( ));

    for (v = 0; v < g.size( ); v++)
        marked[v] = false;

    marked[start] = true;
    f(g[start]);
    vertex_queue.insert(start);
    do
    {
        v = vertex_queue.get_front( );
        // Mark and process v's unmarked neighbors, and place them in the queue.
        for (neighbors.restart(v); !neighbors.done( ); neighbors.advance( ))
        {
            next = neighbors.current( );
            if (!marked[next])
            {
                marked[next] = true;
                f(g[next]);
                vertex_queue.insert(next);
            }
        }
    }
    while (!vertex_queue.is_empty( ));
}
```

searches.template **FTP**

Self-Test Exercises

9. Do a depth-first search of the Australia graph (Figure 15.2 on page 669), starting at Sydney. List the order in which the cities are processed. Do the same for a breadth-first search.

10. Suppose you are doing a breadth-first search of a graph with *n* vertices. How large can the queue get?

11. What kind of search occurs if you replace breadth-first search's queue with a stack?

15.4 PATH ALGORITHMS

Determining Whether a Path Exists

Frequently, a problem is represented by a graph, and the answer to the problem can be found by answering some question about paths in the graph. For example, a network of computers can be represented by a graph, with each vertex representing one of the machines in the network, and each edge representing a communication wire between two machines. The question of whether one machine can send a message to another machine boils down to whether the corresponding vertices are connected by a path.

Either breadth-first search or depth-first search may be used to determine whether a path exists between two vertices *u* and *v*. The idea is to use *u* as the start vertex of the search and proceed with a breadth-first or depth-first search. If the vertex *v* is ever visited, then the search may stop and announce that there is a path from *u* to *v*. On the other hand, if *v* is never visited, then there is no path from *u* to *v*.

Graphs with Weighted Edges

Often we need to know more than just *"Does a path exist?"* In the network example described above, each edge represents a communication wire between machines. Such a wire might have a "cost" associated with using the wire. The cost could be the amount of energy required to use the path, or perhaps the amount of time required for the wire to transmit a message, or even a dollars-and-cents cost required to use the wire to send one message. In any case, there could be many paths from one vertex to another, and we might want to find the path with the lowest total cost (that is, the path with the lowest possible sum of its edge costs).

This kind of question can be solved by using a graph where each edge has a non-negative integer value attached to it, called the **weight** or **cost** of the edge.

Here's an example of a graph with edge weights:

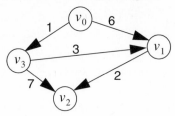

the shortest path between two vertices is the path with lowest total cost

In this example, there are several paths from vertex v_0 to vertex v_2. The path with the lowest total cost traverses the edge from v_0 to v_3 (with a cost of 1), then from v_3 to v_1 (with a cost of 3), and finally from v_1 to v_2 (with a cost of 2). The total cost of this path is $1 + 3 + 2$, which is 6. There is a path with fewer edges (such as the path from v_0 to v_1 to v_2), but no other path has a lower total cost. The path with the lowest total cost is called the **shortest path**. (If you think of the weights as distances, then the term *shortest path* will sound like a sensible term.) The problem of finding the shortest path between two vertices of a graph occurs often in computer science (such as the network example) and in applications (such as finding the shortest driving distance between two points on a road map).

Here is a summary of the concepts we have introduced:

Weighted Edges and Shortest Paths

A **weighted edge** is an edge together with a non-negative integer called the edge's **weight**.

The **weight of a path** is the total sum of the weights of all edges in the path. (Note: The weight of the empty path, with no edges, is always zero.)

If two vertices are connected by at least one path, then we can define the **shortest path** between two vertices. This is the path that has the smallest weight. (There may be several paths with equally small weights, in which case each of the paths is called "smallest.")

Shortest Distance Algorithm

In this section we will present an efficient algorithm called *Dijkstra's algorithm* (named for computer scientist Edsgar Dijkstra, who proposed the algorithm) for finding the shortest path between two vertices. Throughout the section we will use graphs with weighted edges where each weight is a non-negative integer. We will use pseudocode rather than a particular language such as C++.

We start with a problem that's simpler than actually finding the shortest path from one vertex to another. We'll concentrate on simply finding the *weight* of the shortest path—in other words the smallest possible sum of edge weights along a path from one vertex to another. This weight is called the *shortest distance.*

Dijkstra's algorithm actually provides more information than just the shortest distance from one vertex to another. In fact, the algorithm provides the shortest distance from a starting vertex (which we call `start`) to *every* vertex in the graph. The algorithm uses an integer array called `distance`, with one component for each vertex in the graph. Here is the algorithm's goal:

we'll actually find shortest distances rather than shortest paths

---

Goal of the Shortest Distance Algorithm

The goal is to completely fill the distance array so that for each vertex v, the value of `distance[v]` is the weight of the shortest path from `start` to v.

We'll illustrate how the algorithm works with this small graph:

The starting vertex is v_0.

The algorithm begins by filling in one value in the distance array. We fill in zero for the component that is indexed by the `start` vertex itself, indicating that the weight of the shortest path from the `start` vertex to the `start` vertex itself is zero. This is correct since the empty path exists from the `start` vertex to itself. At this point, the distance array has one known value:

	0	?	?	?	?	?
distance	[0]	[1]	[2]	[3]	[4]	[5]

At this point we have one correct value, `distance[0]`. In the other locations we will write a value based on what we know so far. Because we don't know too much, our initial values won't be too accurate, but that's okay. In fact, the values that we fill in will all be *infinity*, represented by the symbol ∞. The distance array, with mostly ∞, is shown at the top of the next page.

In an actual implementation, we would use some special integer value for ∞. For example, we could use −1 and make sure that all the rest of our programming always treats an occurrence of −1 as if it were infinity.

Now we are ready to do some processing that will steadily improve the values in the distance array. We begin with an observation about the initial values that we've placed in the distance array: These initial values are actually correct, *if we are only permitting the empty path and ignoring all other paths*. In other words, if the empty path is the only path that we are permitting, then there is a path from the start vertex to itself (namely the empty path with weight zero). But there is no way to get from the start vertex to any other vertex, and the fact that there is no path is represented by ∞ in the distance array.

the algorithm gradually improves the values in the distance array

Of course, permitting *only* the empty path is an overwhelming restriction. The key to the algorithm is in gradually relaxing this restriction, allowing more vertices to appear in permitted paths. As more and more vertices are allowed, we will continually revise the distance array so that its values are correct, *for paths that only pass through allowed vertices*. By the end of the algorithm, all vertices are allowed, and the distance array has values that are entirely correct.

The idea we have described needs some refinement. How are newly allowed vertices selected? How do we keep track of which vertices are currently allowed? How is the distance array revised to permit the newly allowed vertices to appear in a path? These questions are addressed in the following list of three steps for the complete algorithm:

Step 1. Fill in the distance array with ∞ at every location with the exception of distance[Start], which is assigned the value zero.

Step 2. Initialize a *set* of vertices, called allowed_vertices, to be the empty set. Throughout the algorithm a *permitted path* is a path that starts at the start vertex, and where each vertex on the path (except perhaps the final vertex) is in the set of allowed vertices. The final vertex on a permitted path does not need to be in the allowed_vertices set. At this point, allowed_vertices is the empty set, so the only permitted path is the empty path without any edges. (This empty path does contain one vertex, the start vertex. But since this vertex is the *final* vertex on the path, the vertex is not required to be in the allowed vertices set.)

Step 3. The third step is a loop. Each time through the loop we will add one more vertex to allowed_vertices and then update the distance array so that all the allowed vertices may appear on paths. Here's a brief summary of the loop:

```
//  Loop in Step 3 of the shortest distance algorithm:
//  n is the number of vertices in the graph

for (allowed_size = 1; allowed_size <= n; allowed_size++)
{
    //  At this point, allowed_vertices contains allowed_size - 1 vertices,
    //  which are the allowed_size - 1 closest vertices to the start vertex.
    //  Also, for each vertex v, distance[v] is the shortest distance from the
    //  start vertex to vertex v, provided that we are only considering
    //  permitted paths  (i.e., paths where each vertex except the final
    //  vertex must be in allowed_vertices).
```

Step 3a. Let next be the closest vertex to the start vertex that is not yet in the set of allowed vertices (if several vertices are equally close, then you may choose next to be any of them).

Step 3b. Add the vertex next to the set `allowed_vertices`.

Step 3c. Revise the distance array so that the new vertex (next) may appear on permitted paths.

```
}
```

The loop's computation hinges on the condition written just before Step 3a. The condition indicates that the `allowed_vertices` set actually contains the `allowed_size-1` vertices that are *closest* to the start vertex. The condition also indicates that `distance[v]` is always the shortest distance from the start vertex to vertex v, provided that we are only considering permitted paths (that is, paths where all vertices except the final vertex must be in the set of allowed vertices). This condition is true the first time the loop is entered, and it is also true at the start of each subsequent iteration. The responsibility of the three steps—3a, 3b, and 3c—is to ensure that the condition remains valid at the start of each iteration. Let's examine the three steps in some detail.

Step 3a. This step must determine which of the *unallowed* vertices is closest to the start vertex. There is a simple rule for choosing this vertex:

How to Choose the Next Vertex in Step 3a

In Step 3a, we will always choose the unallowed vertex that has the *smallest* current value in the distance array. (If several vertices have equally small distances, then we may choose any of them.)

For example, suppose we reach Step 3a, and we have this situation:

	0	2	10	17	∞	8
distance	[0]	[1]	[2]	[3]	[4]	[5]

In this example, the two shaded vertices, 0 and 1, are already in the set of allowed vertices.

Since vertices 0 and 1 are already in the allowed set, we may not choose them as the next vertex. Among the other vertices, vertex 5 has the smallest current value in the distance array (the value is 8). So, we would choose vertex 5 as the next vertex. In the answer to Self-Test Exercise 12, we will explain precisely *why* this rule works, but for now it is sufficient to know that this is the correct way to select the next vertex.

Step 3b. In this step we "add the vertex `next` to the set `allowed_vertices`." The implementation of this step depends on how the set of allowed vertices is represented. One possibility is to implement `allowed_vertices` as a set of vertex numbers, using an ADT for a set of integers. In this case, Step 3b merely inserts `next` into the set

Step 3c. Finally, we must revise the distance array so that the newly allowed vertex, `next`, is permitted on a path from the start vertex to another vertex. An example will explain the necessary revisions. Suppose that vertices 0, 1, and 5 are already in the `allowed_vertices` set, and that we have just added vertex 2 as our next vertex, as shown here:

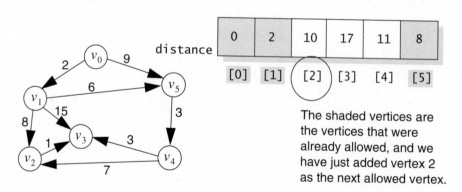

The shaded vertices are the vertices that were already allowed, and we have just added vertex 2 as the next allowed vertex.

Since we have just added vertex 2 as a newly allowed vertex, we must now update the distance array to reflect the fact that vertex 2 may now appear on paths.

For example, `distance[3]` is currently 17. This means that there is a path from the start vertex to vertex 3 that only uses vertices 0, 1 and 5, and that has a length of 17. Here's the key question: *If we also allow vertex 2 to appear on a path from the start vertex to vertex 3, can we obtain a distance that is smaller than 17?* A smaller distance might be possible by taking a two-part path, shown here:

The first part of the path goes from the start vertex v_0 to the newly allowed vertex v_2 . . .

. . . and the second part of the path consists of one more edge from the newly allowed vertex v_2 to vertex v_3.

This path has two parts: the part from the start vertex to vertex 2, followed by the part that has the single edge from vertex 2 to vertex 3. The total weight of this path is:

`distance[3]` + (weight of the edge from vertex 2 to vertex 3)

In our example, this sum is 11, which is smaller than the current "best distance to vertex 3." Therefore we should replace `distance[3]` with this smaller sum. We must also create similar two-part paths for each of the other unallowed vertices, and if the two-part path is smaller than the current distance, then we modify the distance array. This provides the following refined pseudocode for Step 3c:

Step 3c. Revise the distance array so that the new vertex (next) may appear on permitted paths. The integer n is the number of vertices; v and sum are local integer variables, as shown in this code:

```
for (v = 0; v < n; v++)
    if ((v is not an allowed vertex)  and (there is an edge from next to v))
    {
        sum = distance[next] + (weight of the edge from next to v);
        if (sum < distance[v])
            distance[v] = sum;
    }
```

Notice that we do not consider a possible new smaller distance to vertices that are already allowed vertices. That is because these vertices are all closer to the start vertex than next is, so that `distance[next]` is going to be larger than the shortest distance to any of these vertices.

Also, when we are creating the new two-part paths, we only consider the case where the second part of the path is a *single edge* from next to the end vertex. The reason for this is that a longer path from next to the end vertex would have to pass through other allowed vertices, meaning that we have a path that goes from the start vertex, through next, through *another* allowed vertex, and finally to the end vertex. But such a path will always be shorter by avoiding the next vertex altogether—just go from the start vertex to that other allowed vertex (using the shortest path) and then to the end vertex. Such a path, which does not go through the next vertex, is already permitted. We don't need to consider such a path again—we need only consider new paths that pass through the next newly allowed vertex.

The complete pseudocode for the algorithm is shown in Figure 15.8. The main loop actually stops at the number of vertices minus 1 because at that point there is only one unallowed vertex, and this must be the farthest vertex from the start vertex so that no shortest paths can go through this farthest vertex.

We'll execute the algorithm on our example graph. Here's the situation after initializing the distance array:

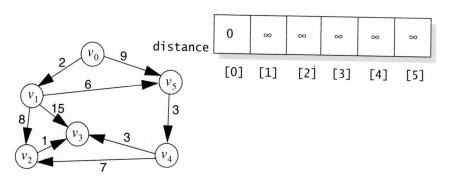

At this point, the set of allowed vertices is empty, and we will enter the main loop for the first time. In Step 3a, the value of next is set to vertex 0 (since distance[0] is the smallest value in the distance array). We then look at each unallowed vertex v with an edge from vertex 0 to vertex v. These are vertices 1 and 5, so we check to see whether we need to revise distance[1] and distance[5]:

- distance[0] + (the weight of the edge from 0 to 1) is 2. Since this is smaller than the current value of distance[1], we replace distance[1] with 2.

- distance[0] + (the weight of the edge from 0 to 5) is 9. Since this is smaller than the current value of distance[5], we replace distance[5] with 9.

FIGURE 15.8   Dijkstra's Shortest Distance Algorithm

Pseudocode

Input. A directed graph with positive, integer edge weights and n vertices. One of the vertices, called start, is specified as the start vertex.

Output. A list of the shortest distances from the start vertex to every other vertex in the graph.

The algorithm uses an array of n integers (called distance) and a set of vertices (called allowed_vertices). The variables v, allowed_size, and sum are local integer variables. There is some special value (∞) that we can place in the distance array to indicate an infinite distance (which means there is no path).

Step 1. Initialize the distance array to contain all ∞, except distance[start], which is set to zero.

Step 2. Initialize the set of allowed vertices to be the empty set.

Step 3. Compute the complete distance array:

```
for (allowed_size = 1; allowed_size < n; allowed_size++)
{
    // At this point, allowed_vertices contains allowed_size - 1 vertices, which are the
    // allowed_size - 1 closest vertices to the start vertex. Also, for each vertex v, distance[v]
    // is the shortest distance from the start vertex to vertex v, provided that we are only
    // considering permitted paths (i.e., paths where each vertex except the final vertex must
    // be in allowed_vertices).
```

Step 3a. Let next be the closest vertex to the start vertex, which is not yet in the set of allowed vertices (if several vertices are equally close, then you may choose next to be any of them).

Step 3b. Add the vertex next to the set allowed_vertices.

Step 3c. Revise the distance array so that the new vertex (next) may appear on permitted paths:

```
    for (v = 0; v < n; v++)
        if ((v is not an allowed vertex)  and (there is an edge from next to v))
        {
            sum = distance[next] + (weight of the edge from next to v);
            if (sum < distance[v])
                distance[v] = sum;
        }
}
```

Step 4. Output the values in the distance array. (Each distance[v] is the shortest distance from the start vertex to vertex v.)

At this point, the distance array is as shown below (with the allowed vertices shaded):

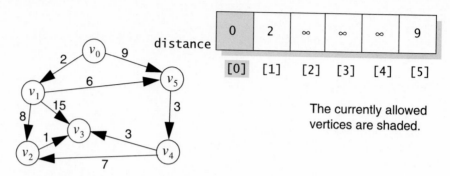

distance

0	2	∞	∞	∞	9
[0]	[1]	[2]	[3]	[4]	[5]

The currently allowed vertices are shaded.

The second time we enter the main loop, the value of next is set to vertex 1 (since distance[1] is the smallest value of the unallowed vertices). We then look at each unallowed vertex v with an edge from vertex 1 to vertex v. These are vertices 2, 3, and 5, so we check to see whether we need to revise distance[2], distance[3], and distance[5]:

- distance[1] + (the weight of the edge from 1 to 2) is 10. Since this is smaller than the current value of distance[2], we replace distance[2] with 10.

- distance[1] + (the weight of the edge from 1 to 3) is 17. Since this is smaller than the current value of distance[3], we replace distance[3] with 17.

- distance[1] + (the weight of the edge from 0 to 5) is 8. Since this is smaller than the current value of distance[5], we replace distance[5] with 8.

At this point, the distance array is:

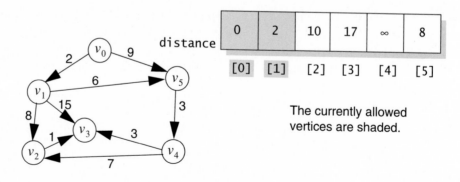

distance

0	2	10	17	∞	8
[0]	[1]	[2]	[3]	[4]	[5]

The currently allowed vertices are shaded.

The third time we enter the main loop, the value of `next` will be set to vertex 5 (since `distance[5]` is the smallest value of the unallowed vertices). We then look at each unallowed vertex v with an edge from vertex 5 to vertex v. Vertex 4 is the only vertex that is the target of an edge from vertex 5, so we check to see whether we need to revise `distance[4]`:

- `distance[5]` + (the weight of the edge from 5 to 4) is 11. Since this is smaller than the current value of `distance[4]`, we replace `distance[4]` with 11.

At this point, we have this situation:

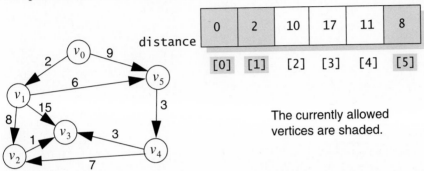

The currently allowed vertices are shaded.

The fourth time we enter the main loop, the value of `next` will be set to vertex 2 (since `distance[2]` is the smallest value of the unallowed vertices). We then look at each unallowed vertex v with an edge from vertex 2 to vertex v. Vertex 3 is the only such vertex, so we check to see whether we need to revise `distance[3]`:

- `distance[2]` + (the weight of the edge from 2 to 3) is 11. Since this is smaller than the current value of `distance[3]`, we replace `distance[3]` with 11.

At this point, the situation is:

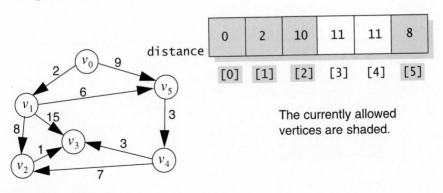

The currently allowed vertices are shaded.

The fifth time we enter the main loop, the value of next will be set to either vertex 3 or vertex 4 (since both distance[3] and distance[4] are 11). It doesn't matter which one we choose, so let's choose vertex 4. We then look at each unallowed vertex v with an edge from vertex 4 to vertex v. This is only vertex 3, so we check to see whether we need to revise distance[4]:

- distance[4] + (the weight of the edge from 4 to 3) is 14. Since this is *larger* than the current value of distance[3], we do not replace distance[3].

At this point, we are nearly done:

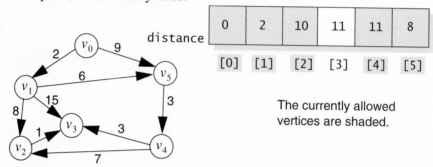

distance

0	2	10	11	11	8
[0]	[1]	[2]	[3]	[4]	[5]

The currently allowed vertices are shaded.

The main loop of the algorithm now stops. We don't need to process that last unallowed vertex (3), since it is the farthest vertex from the start vertex. For each vertex v, the value of distance[v] is the shortest distance from the start vertex (vertex 0) to v.

Shortest Path Algorithm

We have shown how to compute the *weight* of the shortest path from a start vertex to each other vertex in a graph. But how can we compute the actual sequence of vertices that occurs along the shortest path? It turns out that Dijkstra's shortest distance algorithm contains enough information to actually print the shortest path from the start vertex to any other vertex, provided that we keep track of one extra piece of information:

Predecessor Information for Shortest Paths

For each vertex v, we will keep track of which vertex was the next vertex when distance[v] was given a new smaller value. We will keep track of these values in an array called predecessor, so that for each vertex v, predecessor[v] is the value of next at the time when distance[v] was given a new smaller value. (Note: predecessor[start] does not need to have a value, since distance[start] is never updated.)

The predecessor information is easy to keep track of. Each time that we update distance[v] with the assignment `distance[v] = sum` , we must also update predecessor[v] with this assignment:

```
predecessor[v] = next;
```

When the algorithm finishes, the value of distance[v] is the weight of the shortest path from the start vertex to vertex v. Or distance[v] might be ∞, indicating that there is no path from the start vertex to vertex v. But when distance[v] is not ∞, we can actually print out the vertices on the shortest path from the start vertex to vertex v, using the following method:

```
// Printing the vertices on the shortest path from the start vertex to v:
// Vertices are printed in reverse order, starting at v, and going to start.

vertex_on_path = v; // The last vertex on the path
cout << vertex_on_path << endl; // Print the final vertex.
while (vertex_on_path != start)
{
    vertex_on_path = predecessor[vertex_on_path];
    cout << vertex_on_path << endl;
}
```

In other words, the last vertex on the path to v is vertex v itself. The next-to-last vertex is predecessor[v]. And the vertex before that is obtained by applying predecessor to the next-to-last vertex—and so on, right back to the start vertex. As indicated, this algorithm, manages to print the vertices in reverse order, from vertex v back to the start vertex.

Self-Test Exercises

12. When we select the next vertex in the shortest distance algorithm, we need to select the unallowed vertex that is closest to the start vertex. How is this selection done?

13. Consider the graph that we have been using throughout this section, except change the weight of the edge that goes from 0 to 5. Its new weight is 4. Go through the entire algorithm to compute the new distance array.

14. Compute the complete predecessor array for the previous exercise, and use it to find the actual shortest path from vertex 0 to vertex 3.

CHAPTER SUMMARY

- Graphs are a flexible data structure with many occurrences in computer science and in applications. Many problems can be solved by asking an appropriate question about paths in a graph.

- There are several different kinds of graphs: undirected graphs (where edges have no particular orientation), directed graphs (where each edge goes from a source vertex to a target vertex), graphs with loops (i.e., an edge connecting a vertex to itself), graphs with multiple edges (i.e., more than one edge may connect the same pair of vertices), labeled graphs (where each vertex has an associated label), and graphs with weighted edges (where each edge has an associated number called its weight).

- There are two common ways to implement a graph: an adjacency matrix or edge lists. The different implementations have different time performance for common operations such as determining whether two vertices are connected.

- There are two common ways to traverse a graph: depth-first search and breadth-first search.

- Dijkstra's algorithm provides an efficient way to determine the shortest path from a given start vertex to every other vertex in a graph with weighted edges.

? Solutions to Self-Test Exercises

1. The airline route graph has nine vertices, 14 edges, and no loops. A loop would be an excursion flight that takes off and lands at the same city.

2. It is simple (no loops, no multiple edges).

3. Your state graph should have 16 vertices and 48 directed edges. (There are 32 edges from Rule 1, and eight edges each from Rules 2 and 3.) It is possible to go from the start state to the goal state in four moves.

4. The function need only subtract 1 from the member variable `size( )`.

5. The adjacency matrix, a, could be a two-dimensional array of unsigned integers with `a[i][j]` storing the number of edges from vertex i to vertex j.

6. This is an open-ended question, but your answer should consider space requirements for each representation, and time requirements for common operations.

7. An internal iterator is implemented with member functions of the class that has items to step through. An external iterator is implemented as a separate class that can be "attached" to the object that has items to step through. An external iterator has the advantage that many different iterators can be active simultaneously on the same object.

8. At point 1, the label is 42. At point 2, the label is still 42, and the integer variable i is also 42. At point 3, the i has changed to 43, but the label is still 42. (In order to change the label, the change must be made to g[3] itself.)

9. Traversals sometimes make choices about which vertex to visit next. When we have such a choice, we will visit the vertex that is alphabetically first, giving these two orders: *Depth-first:* Sydney, Canberra, Adelaide, Melbourne, Hobart, Perth, Black Stump, Darwin, Brisbane. *Breadth-first:* Sydney, Canberra, Melbourne, Adelaide, Brisbane, Hobart, Perth, Black Stump, Darwin.

10. If *n* is 1, then the queue needs room for only one vertex. If *n* is more than 1, then the queue will never have more than *n*-1 entries. Here is why: The start vertex is only in the queue once (by itself), and then we remove the start vertex from the queue. Each other vertex is placed in the queue at most once, so the largest queue needed would occur if all *n*-1 vertices are neighbors of the start vertex.

11. A depth-first search

12. From among the unallowed vertices, we select the vertex with the smallest current value in the distance array. This works because the current distance array contains the correct distance values if we are only permitting allowed vertices, and the currently allowed vertices are the n-1 closest vertices. Therefore, the shortest path to the nth closest vertex must pass through only currently allowed vertices, and therefore the distance array contains the correct value for that n^{th} closest vertex.

13. The new final distance array: (0, 2, 10, 10, 7, 4).

14. The new shortest path to vertex 3: vertex 0 to vertex 5, vertex 5 to vertex 4, vertex 4 to vertex 3.

PROGRAMMING PROJECTS

1 Consider our Graph objects from Figure 15.3 on page 679. These graphs have a maximum number of vertices, determined by the static constant Graph::MAXIMUM. This constant determines the number of rows and columns of the adjacency matrix, and the size of the array for the labels. These two arrays are declared in the highlighted lines of the Graph definition:

```
template <class Item>
class Graph
{
public:
    // MEMBER CONSTANTS
    static const size_t MAXIMUM = 20;
    ...
private:
    bool edges[MAXIMUM][MAXIMUM];
    Item labels[MAXIMUM];
    size_t many_vertices;
};
```

There are several ways to change edges to a dynamic array, which can grow and shrink as vertices are added and removed. This project describes one approach for you to carry out. The approach is to eliminate the static constant, and change the private member variables as shown here:

```
template <class Item>
class Graph
{
public:
    // MEMBER CONSTANTS
    static const size_t MAXIMUM = 20;
    ...
private:
    bool **edges;
    Item *labels;
    size_t allocated;
    size_t many_vertices;
};
```

The array of labels has been changed to an ordinary dynamic array. But what is the meaning of the declaration `bool **edges`? This declaration says that edges is more than a pointer to a boolean value; in fact, it is a *pointer to a pointer* to a boolean. A "pointer to a pointer" can be made to act like a two-dimensional array. For example, suppose that we want `edges` to act like an array with *n* rows and *n* columns. Using a `size_t` variable i, we could write this code to allocate the needed memory:

```
edges = new (bool*)[n];
for (i = 0; i < n; i++)
    edges[i] = new bool[n];
```

In this code, the first statement has an interesting effect. The statement `edges = new (bool*)[n]` makes `edges` point to an array of *n* pointers. The for-loop then makes each of these pointers point to a dynamic array of *n* boolean values. After the for-loop, we can use `edges` just as if it was an *n* by *n* two-dimensional array of boolean values. For example, we could fill the entire "array" with *false* using the loop shown here (i and j are both `size_t` variables):

```
for (i = 0; i < n; i++)
    for (j = 0; j < n; j++)
        edges[i][j] = false;
```

For example, with *n* equal to three, then the above code constructs the dynamic arrays shown below. The key point is that with this structure, we can use `edges` as if it was a two-dimensional array.

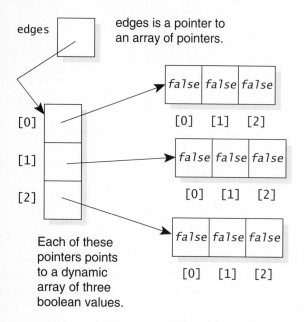

edges is a pointer to an array of pointers.

Each of these pointers points to a dynamic array of three boolean values.

For this project, rewrite the `Graph` class so that

`edges` is implemented as we have described. You should also add another private member variable called `allocated`. The value of `allocated` is the number of rows and columns in `edges`. This number must be no less than the actual number of vertices (which is still stored in the private member variable `many_vertices`).

Your implementation should include a constructor with one argument. This argument is a `size_t` value that specifies the initial allocation for the number of rows and columns in the adjacency matrix. There should also be a `resize` function to allow a programmer to explicitly change the allocation. If `add_vertex` is called and the matrix is already full, then `add_vertex` should call `resize` to allocate a larger adjacency matrix.

2 Use edge lists to reimplement the `Graph` class from Figure 15.3 on page 679. There should be no limit to the number of vertices. Also rewrite the `NeighborIterator` class so that it works efficiently with your new `Graph` class. The new `NeighborIterator` will need to be a friend class of the new `Graph` class.

3 Implement a new template class that is derived from the `Graph`. The new class should permit both edges and vertices to have labels.

4 Implement a function with three arguments: a graph, a starting vertex number, and an ending vertex number. The function determines whether there is a directed path from the starting vertex to the ending vertex.

5 Implement a new class for graphs with weighted edges. Use the ordinary `Graph` class as a base type for your implementation. After implementing the new class, provide two extra functions to implement Dijkstra's shortest distance and shortest path algorithms.

6 Write a program to help a traveler plan the shortest traveling path from one city to another. The program should read a file of data containing a list of cities and a list of roads connecting the cities. Each road has a distance attached to it. Allow the user to enter queries of the form "City1, City2" and have the program print the shortest sequence of roads to travel from City1 to City2.

7 Write a program to help you make better social connections. The program should read a file of data containing a list of people in your community and a list of who-knows-who. Allow the user to enter various queries about which people know each other, such as "How many people does Harry know?" or "Is there anyone that both Harry and Cathy know?"

Appendix A
ASCII Character Set

Most implementations of C++ provide the standard ASCII (American Standard Code for Information Interchange) character set as the first 128 characters. Characters 0 through 31 and 127 are standard signals to control devices such as a printer.

Your programming should not depend on the ASCII characters being present. However, the language does guarantee that the integer codes for the digits '0' through '9' will be numerically ordered and consecutive. So, for example, '0'+3 must be the character '3'.

0	null '\0'	22	syn	44	comma	66	B	88	X	110	n
1	soh	23	etb	45	minus	67	C	89	Y	111	o
2	stx	24	can	46	period	68	D	90	Z	112	p
3	etx	25	em	47	/	69	E	91	[	113	q
4	end transmission	26	sub	48	0	70	F	92	\	114	r
5	enquire	27	escape	49	1	71	G	93	]	115	s
6	acknowledge	28	fs	50	2	72	H	94	^	116	t
7	ring a bell '\a'	29	gs	51	3	73	I	95	underscore	117	u
8	backspace '\b'	30	rs	52	4	74	J	96	back quote	118	v
9	tab '\t'	31	us	53	5	75	K	97	a	119	w
10	new line '\n'	32	blank	54	6	76	L	98	b	120	x
11	vertical tab '\v'	33	!	55	7	77	M	99	c	121	y
12	form feed '\f'	34	"	56	8	78	N	100	d	122	z
13	carriage return '\r'	35	#	57	9	79	O	101	e	123	{
14	so	36	$	58	:	80	P	102	f	124	|
15	si	37	%	59	;	81	Q	103	g	125	}
16	dle	38	&	60	<	82	R	104	h	126	~
17	dc1	39	single quote	61	=	83	S	105	i	127	delete
18	dc2	40	(	62	>	84	T	106	j		
19	dc3	41	)	63	?	85	U	107	k		
20	dc4	42	*	64	@	86	V	108	l		
21	nak	43	+	65	A	87	W	109	m		

Appendix B
Further Big-O Notation

Formal Definition of Big-*O*

Throughout the text, we analyze the running times of algorithms in terms of the size of an algorithm's input. For example, in Section 12.1 we developed a binary search algorithm to search an array of n elements, looking for a specified target. On page page 543, we saw that the maximum number of operations for the binary search is given by the formula:

$$T(n) = \text{the maximum number of operations to search an } n\text{-element array}$$
$$= 18 \left(\lfloor \log_2 n \rfloor + 1 \right) + 3$$

Big-*O* notation is a way of analyzing a function such as $T(n)$. The analysis throws away some information about the function, but keeps other information that is most relevant to determining algorithm performance. In an informal way, you know enough to examine the function $T(n)$ for the binary search; you can "throw out the constants" and conclude that $T(n)$ is a $O(\log n)$ function.

In general, when we examine a function, such as $T(n)$, the big-*O* analysis results in some simpler expression, such as $\log n$. The simpler expression is also a function of n. If we call this $F(n)$, then a typical big-O analysis provides a result of the form "$T(n)$ is a $O(F(n))$ function." In mathematical terms, this kind of result has a precise definition as follows:

Formal Definition of Big-*O*

When we say that "$T(n)$ is a $O(F(n))$ function," we mean that there is some fixed number that we call the *threshold*, and some constant multiplier that we call c, such that:

Whenever $n \geq threshold$, then $T(n) \leq cF(n)$.

For example, consider the function $T(n) = 3n^2 + 9n$. Some arithmetic shows that whenever $n \geq 5$, then $3n^2 + 9n \leq 4n^2$. Therefore, using a threshold of 5, and a constant multiplier of 4, we can see that

$$3n^2 + 9n \text{ is a } O(n^2) \text{ function.}$$

The graph to the right illustrates the meaning of a big-*O* expression. Notice that before the *threshold*, either of the two functions may be larger; anything can happen before this threshold value. But once *n* exceeds the threshold, the function *cF(n)* is always greater than *T(n)*. Also notice that it is *c* multiplied by *F(n)*, and not simply *F(n)*, that we are comparing to *T(n)*.

So, the graph illustrates the fact that "*T(n)* is a *O(F(n))* function."

If not used with some care, big-*O* expressions can grossly misrepresent the true running time of an

algorithm. For example, if an algorithm runs in *O(n)* time, then we could also say that it runs in *O(n²)* time (since any function that is below a constant times *n* will also be below the same constant times *n²*). But of course, it would be silly to say that an algorithm runs in *O(n²)* time, when we know that it runs in *O(n)* time. When a programmer gives a big-*O* time, he or she usually means that it is a "good" big-*O* expression.

What Big-*O* Expressions Indicate

Big-*O* expressions are admittedly crude, but they do contain some information. A big-*O* analysis will not distinguish between a running time of 4*n*+3 and a running time of 100*n*+50, but it will let us distinguish between some running times and determine that some algorithms are faster than others. Look at the graphs of the four functions to the right. Notice that all three *O*(n) functions

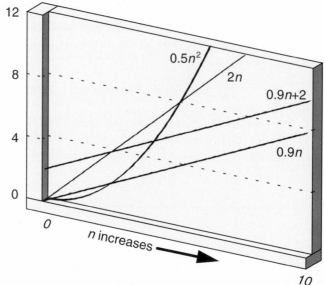

eventually fall below the $O(n^2)$ function. This leads us to an important big-O principle:

Big-O Comparison of Algorithms

Suppose that two different algorithms perform the same task with different big-O times. With a sufficiently large input, the algorithm with the better big-O analysis will perform faster.

What exactly does it mean when we say "with a sufficiently large input"? Does this mean that an input size of $n=100$ will result in a faster time from the algorithm with the better big-O? Or does it require $n=1000$, or maybe even $n=1,000,000$? Unfortunately, a big-O analysis does not tell us *how big* the input needs to be in order for the better big-O time to result in a faster algorithm. All that's known is that larger and larger inputs will *eventually* result in a faster time for the algorithm with the better big-O time.

Appendix C
Precedence of Operators

This table gives the precedence of C++ operators. Operators in higher boxes have higher precedence than operators in lower boxes. Unary operators and the assignment operator are done right to left when operators have the same precedence. For example x = y = z means x = (y = z). Other operators that have the same precedence are done left to right. For example, x - y - z means (x - y) - z.

High Precedence

Low Precedence

Operators		Description
`: :`		Scope resolution operator

`.` `->`
`[ ]` `( )`
`++` `--`
		Member selection operators
		Array indexing and function call
		Postfix increment/decrement

`++` `--`
`!`
`~`
`unary +` `unary -`
`*`
`&`
`new` `delete`
`sizeof`
		Prefix increment/decrement
		Not
		Bitwise not
		Unary plus and minus
		Dereferencing operator
		Address of
		Memory allocation/deallocation
		Size in bytes

`->*` `.*`		Member pointer selection
`*` `/` `%`		Multiplication and division Remainder upon division
`+` `-`		Binary addition and subtraction
`<<` `>>`		Shift operators
`<` `<=` `>` `>=`		Less than; less than or equal Greater than; greater than or equal
`==` `!=`		Equal and not equal
`&`		Bitwise and
`^`		Bitwise exclusive or
`|`		Bitwise or
`&&`		Boolean and
`||`		Boolean or
`? :`		Conditional operator

`=`
`+=` `-=` `*=` `/=` `%=`
`<<=` `>>=` `&=` `|=` `^=`
		Assignment operators

`,`		Comma operator

Appendix D
Compiling, Linking, and Running Programs

Many C++ compilers provide an easy-to-use interface, including an editor (allowing you to create or edit programs) with simple buttons that you click to compile and run your programs. Other C++ compilers provide a "command line" mode. With a command line compiler, you use your favorite editor program to create or edit programs, and after a program is created you type one or more commands to compile, link, and run the program.

This appendix provides the details of compiling, linking, and running programs for two popular command line compilers:

- **The GNU Project C++ Compiler**, produced by Free Software Foundation, Inc., and widely available on machines that use the Unix® operating system.
- The **Borland® C++ Compiler**, produced by Borland International, Inc., for IBM-compatible PCs running the DOS operating system. With this compiler, you may prefer to use the interactive interface, but you may also use it as a command line compiler, typing your command at the DOS prompt. A simpler version of this compiler is available as **Turbo® C++ for DOS.**

Compiling

Both command line compilers can compile any ".cxx" file on its own. The act of compiling creates an **object file,** which contains low-level machine instructions corresponding to your C++ code. By the way, these machine instructions are usually specific for a given type of machine. For example, you cannot create an object file for an IBM-compatible PC, and expect the object file to work on a Sun Workstation.

Anyway, the general command to compile a ".cxx" file with the GNU and Borland command line compilers are shown here:

Compiling with GNU

```
g++ -Wall -c filename.cxx
```

Compiling with Borland

```
bcc -w -c -P filename.cxx
```

In both commands, the `filename.cxx` may be any ".cxx" file that you want to compile. The minus signs in the commands provide various options. For example, -Wall (in GNU) and -w (in Borland) ask the compiler to provide all possible warning messages. The -c option specifies "compilation only" (rather than combining compiling and linking). In the Borland command, the -P option indicates that the file contains C++ code (rather than mere C code). For the Borland compiler, a file extension of ".cpp" is assumed to have C++ code, but other extensions, such as ".cxx", require the -P option.

The GNU command will compile `filename.cxx`, creating an object file named `filename.o`. The Borland command will compile `filename.cxx`, creating an object file named `filename.obj`.

A program that is split between several ".cxx" files can be compiled with a single command, placing all the file names at the end of the command line. Or, you may give separate commands to compile each piece of the program. For example, consider the demonstration program `demo2.cxx` from Figure 2.7 on page 56. This program makes use of `throttle.cxx`, so we must create two object files with the commands shown here:

Compiling with GNU

```
g++  -Wall  -c  throttle.cxx
g++  -Wall  -c  demo2.cxx
```

Compiling with Borland

```
bcc  -w  -c  -P  throttle.cxx
bcc  -w  -c  -P  demo2.cxx
```

If you are using an older compiler that does not support the *bool* data type, then these command lines need a modification. We'll discuss this modification in detail in Appendix E; for now you should know that these highlighted options must be added in order to provide simple boolean values:

Compiling with GNU compilers that do not have the bool type

```
g++  -Wall  -c  -Dbool=int  -Dfalse=0  -Dtrue=1  throttle.cxx
g++  -Wall  -c  -Dbool=int  -Dfalse=0  -Dtrue=1  demo2.cxx
```

Compiling with Borland compilers that do not have the bool type

```
bcc  -w  -c  -P  -Dbool=int  -Dfalse=0  -Dtrue=1  throttle.cxx
bcc  -w  -c  -P  -Dbool=int  -Dfalse=0  -Dtrue=1  demo2.cxx
```

With the GNU compiler, these commands produce two object files, `throttle.o` and `demo2.o`. The Borland compiler produces object files `throttle.obj` and `demo2.obj`. Once the object files are present, you can move to the next step: linking the pieces together.

Linking

Before you can run a program, you must link the different object files together. The general form of the linking commands for GNU and Borland are shown here with an example:

Linking object files with GNU

```
g++  file1.o file2.o  ...   -o  filename
```

Example:
```
g++  demo2.o  throttle.o  -o  demo2
```

Linking object files with Borland

```
bcc  file1.obj file2.obj  ...
```

Example:
```
bcc  demo2.obj  throttle.obj
```

The result of these commands is an executable file that can be run on your machine. In the case of the GNU compiler, the name of the executable file is explicitly given by the `-o` `filename` option at the end of the command. In the example, we have called the executable file `demo2`, so after the GNU linking step you would find a file named `demo2` (with no file extension). If you forget the `-o` option, then GNU places the executable in a file with the peculiar name "`a.out`".

The name of the executable file does not need to be specified for the Borland compiler. This compiler automatically uses the name of the first object file, changing the file extension to ".exe". In the example given on the previous page, the executable file created by the Borland compiler will be demo2.exe.

Running a Program

Once the executable file has been created, it can be run by typing the filename (without any extension). In both of the examples shown above, you can run the demo2 program by typing the command:

```
demo2
```

This will run the demo2 program with standard input from the keyboard and standard output to the monitor.

You can also run a program with standard input taken from a file (rather than the keyboard), or run the program with standard output sent to a file (rather than the monitor). To **redirect input,** use the option "< infile" when you run the program (where infile is the name of the file that provides the input). To **redirect output,** use the option "> outfile" when you run the program (where outfile is the name of the file where you want the output sent). For example, to run the demo2 program with input from a file called data and output to a file called results, you would give the command:

```
demo2  <data  >results
```

Linking with the math.h Library

If you use the math.h library, the GNU compiler requires -lm to be listed during the link step, after all the object files. For example, if the demo2 program used the math library, then we would link with the example command shown below:

Linking object files with GNU (math library needed)

```
g++  file1.o file2.o ...    -lm   -o  filename
```

Example if the demo2 program used the math library:
```
g++  demo2.o  throttle.o  -lm -o  demo2
```

The "-lm" option stands for "link math" (so make sure that you use the letter "l" rather than the digit one "1").

Specifying an Include Directory

Both the GNU and Borland compilers allow you to specify a particular directory where #include files can be found. The option is specified by -Idirectory . For example, we keep many of our header files in a directory named c:\source\headers, so with the Borland compiler we have:

```
bcc -Ic:\source\headers -w -c -P demo2.cxx
```

Appendix E
Dealing with Older Compilers

The boolean data type and static member constants are not supported by older compilers. This appendix shows how these two features can be simulated in any C++ compiler. We also provide a note about using template classes in older compilers.

If Your Compiler Does Not Have the bool Data Type

The *int* data type can simulate the new *bool* data type. The simulation is most easily carried out by placing these three definitions in your own header file called bool.h:

```
#define bool int
#define false 0
#define true 1
```

Any program that uses the *bool* type should include your bool.h. If you are using a command line compiler, such as the GNU compiler or the Borland® compiler described in Appendix D, then you may incorporate the three definitions directly in your compilation command. For example, using the GNU compiler to compile throttle.cxx, you would use the highlighted definitions shown here:

```
g++  -Wall  -c  -Dbool=int  -Dfalse=0  -Dtrue=1  throttle.cxx
```

The use of these three definitions is not perfect because it does not allow the compiler to detect type errors that may arise from unintentional mixing of *int* and *bool* values. Nevertheless, the definitions provide a quick solution that works all the time.

If Your Compiler Does Not Have Static Member Constants

We have made extensive use of static member constants, particularly in container classes. For example, our first bag from Chapter 3 had the static member constant shown here at the start of the Bag class definition:

```
class Bag
{
public:
    // TYPEDEF and MEMBER CONSTANTS
    static const size_t CAPACITY = 30;
    ...
```

The bag's CAPACITY constant determines the maximum number of elements that can be placed in a bag. What should you do if your compiler does not permit static member constants? There are two common solutions:

1. You may use an ordinary constant declaration, prior to the class definition. In the case of the Bag we would write:

```
const size_t BAG_CAPACITY = 30;
class Bag
{
    ...
```

   With this approach, you should use a more descriptive name such as BAG_CAPACITY, rather than merely CAPACITY. Otherwise you may find yourself with several ADTs, each of which wants to define its own CAPACITY, and these names will conflict with each other.

2. For integer values, you may use an *enum* definition within a class definition. An *enum* definition is allowed to assign integer values to a whole set of identifiers, but you can use it to create a name for just a single integer value. In our Bag example, we would write:

```
class Bag
{
public:
    enum { CAPACITY = 30 };
    ...
```

   The keyword *enum* appears before the list of values that you want to define, and the list itself is enclosed in curly brackets. After this definition, the name Bag::CAPACITY is defined to have the integer value 30. Although this is not the intended use of an *enum* definition, the result is the same as using a static member constant.

Older Compilers May Not Fully Support Templates

Older compilers, particularly those before 1995, did not always fully support template functions and template classes. The problems generally occur when several different ".cxx" files use the same template function or template class. In this case, each ".cxx" file compiles okay on its own, but "duplicate definition" errors occur when the separate object files are linked together. You'll need to check the documentation on your compiler to find the best way to solve this problem.

Appendix F
Input and Output in C++

This appendix is primarily for students with a background in C programming, but with little or no C++ programming. In the appendix we provide details of the C++ approach to reading from standard input, writing to standard output, and reading/writing files.

Writing to Standard Output

The **insertion operator** (written <<) is used to write a value to an output stream such as the standard output device (usually the monitor screen). For example, if i is an integer variable, then the following statement writes its value to the standard output:

```
cout << i;
```

In this statement, cout stands for the "console output," and is defined as part of the header file iostream.h. You may write several items at once by chaining together a sequence of insertion operators. For example, if i, j, and k are integer variables, then the following statement first writes i, then j, and finally k to the standard output:

```
cout << i << j << k;
```

Writing the End of a Line

There are two ways to write the end of a line to an output stream. You may simply write the newline character '\n', or you may write the special object called endl (which is part of iostream.h). For example:

```
cout << '\n';
cout << endl;
```

What's the difference between these two statements? The main difference deals with the fact that output is often written to a special place called a **buffer,** rather than to the actual output device. When the buffer becomes full, the output is "flushed" from the buffer to the actual output device. Such buffering can cause problems if a program crashes before the buffer is flushed. The buffer may contain some output that never shows up on the output device. To avoid this problem, whenever you write the endl object, the output buffer is automatically flushed. However, simply writing the newline character does not automatically flush the output buffer.

Setting the Field Width of an Output Item

The **field width** of an output item is the preferred number of output characters to be used when the item is printed. For example, if you print the number 123 with a field width of eight, the result will be five blank spaces followed by the digits 123 for a total of eight characters. If the output item won't fit in the specified field width, then more characters may be used. For example, if you print the number 123 with a field width of only two, then the entire number 123 is still printed (even though this requires three characters rather than just two). If you define the field width to be zero, the item will be printed using the minimum possible number of characters.

How do you define the field width for an output item? One method is to use a special "manipulator" named `setw`, which is part of `iomanip.h`. The `setw` manipulator is called like a function, with one argument that is the desired field width. This manipulator is placed in the output statement just before the item to be printed. For example, to print the number 123 with a field width of eight, you may write the statement:

```
cout << setw(8) << 123; ←────── uses setw from iomanip.h
```

The `setw` function may be used with the standard output device (`cout`), or with other output devices that you will use later. Keep in mind that `setw` affects the field width of only the next item to be printed.

Justification of the Output and Showing Plus Signs on Positive Numbers

When output occurs with a wide field width, each output item is padded with spaces to bring the total number of characters up to the required field width. For example, when the number 123 is printed with a field width of eight, the complete output will consist of five spaces followed by the three digits of 123. If you don't specify otherwise, the item is printed on the far right of the field width, with any padding spaces before the item. You can control the placement of the item by calling the `setf` function to set the "control flags" of an output device such as `cout`. This function is called with the syntax shown in these three examples:

```
cout.setf(ios::right;     ios::adjustfield); // Item appears on right side of field
cout.setf(ios::left;      ios::adjustfield); // Item appears on left side of field
cout.setf(ios::internal;  ios::adjustfield); // "Internal" spaces (described below)
```

Once the justification is set with the `setf` function, it remains in effect for all subsequent outputs until it is reset to some other value. The `ios::internal` setting causes numbers to be printed with the + or - sign as the first output character, but the remainder of the number appears on the right side of the field width. (In order to force a number to be printed with a + sign, you will have to call `cout.setf(ios::showpos);` When you no longer want the + signs to print, you may call `cout.unsetf(ios::showpos)`.)

By the way, you can see that `setf` and `unsetf` are both member functions of the `cout` output stream. They are defined in `iostream.h` and may be used with any output stream. The arguments, such as `ios::left`, are also defined in the header file `iostream.h`.

Format of Float and Double Numbers

The format for printing *float* and *double* numbers is also controlled by the setf functions. Here are three examples:

```
cout.setf(ios::fixed,      ios::floatfield);
cout.setf(ios::scientific, ios::floatfield);
cout.setf(0,               ios::floatfield);
```

Fixed-point notation. The first example, using ios::fixed, causes numbers to be printed in *fixed-point notation,* which is the common way of writing numbers with a decimal point. For example, the number 19¼ will be printed as 19.25.

Scientific notation. The second example, using ios::scientific, causes numbers to be printed in *scientific notation* consisting of a number times some power of ten. For example, the large number 1.8×10^{16} will be printed as 1.8e16. The letter e indicates the exponent.

Automatic notation. The third form, using the number 0 as the argument, causes C++ to select the format that it thinks is best for a number (either fixed-point or scientific notation).

   If you don't specify one of the three formats, then C++ uses the automatic format. Once a format is set, it remains in place for all subsequent outputs.

Precision of Float and Double Numbers

Output streams have a precision function with one integer argument to determine how many digits are printed for each number. For example, this statement sets the precision to 12:

```
cout.precision(12);
```

(An alternative is `cout << setprecision(12);`, using setprecision from iomanip.h.) With a precision of 12, the fixed-point and scientific notations will both have 12 digits of accuracy after the decimal point. The automatic notation will have a total of 12 significant digits. Once you set the precision, it stays in effect for all subsequent outputs.

   When the fixed-point notation is used, trailing zeros and the decimal point are not always printed. For example, the *double* number 123.0 will be printed as 123 (with no decimal point). With a precision of 12, the number 19¼ will be printed with no trailing zeros, resulting in 19.25 (rather than 19.250000000000). You may force the decimal point and trailing zeros for fixed-point numbers with the function call cout.setf(ios::showpoint). You may revert to the usual method of fixed-point numbers with the function call cout.unsetf(ios::showpoint). As usual, these functions may be used with any output stream (not just with cout).

Reading from Standard Input

The **extraction operator** (written >>) is used to read a value from an input stream such as the standard input device (usually the keyboard). For example, if i is an integer variable, then the following statement reads an integer value from the standard input, and stores the result in i:

```
cin >> i;
```

In this statement, `cin` stands for the "console input," and is defined as part of the header file `iostream.h`. You may read several items at once by chaining together a sequence of extraction operators. For example, if `i`, `j`, and `k` are integer variables, then the following statement first reads `i`, then `j`, and finally `k` from the standard input:

```
cin >> i >> j >> k;
```

There are several details that you should be aware of regarding the extraction operator:

1. If the standard input device is a keyboard, then usually nothing is read until the user presses the return key. This gives the user a chance to use the backspace key to correct mistakes before pressing the return key.

2. When the extraction operator reads a data value, it starts by skipping any "white space" that occurs in the input. This white space consists of any blanks, tabs, and newline characters. Skipping the white space occurs even if you are reading a character value, which means that the extraction operator cannot be used to read a character if the value that you want to read might be a blank or other white space.

3. The extraction operator reads the input until the end of the input value is reached. The end of the value occurs by reaching any character that is not part of the input value. This "ending character" is called the **delimiter,** and the delimiter is not actually read. For example, suppose that `i` is an integer variable, `c` is a character variable, and we execute the statement:

   ```
   cin >> i >> c;
   ```

   The program's user might type the following input (followed by the return key):

   42xyz

   With this input, the number 42 will be assigned to `i`, and the character `'x'` is assigned to `c`. The characters `'y'` and `'z'` remain in the input, perhaps to be read at a later time.

Reading a Null-Terminated String

You may use the extraction operator to read a null-terminated string. For example:

```
char message[100];
cin >> message;
```

In this case, the extraction operator skips any initial white space and reads characters into `message` until more white space is encountered. For example, suppose that the program's user types the following input line (followed by the return key):

The quick brown fox jumps over the lazy dog.

The statement `cin >> message` will skip any initial white space, read the characters **The**—ending when the blank is encountered after the **e.** The blank itself is not read. The three characters that were read are placed in `message`, with a null terminator after the third character. There is no checking to ensure that the array is large enough to hold the characters that were read.

Bad Input

Sometimes a user provides illegal data for an input operation. For example, the program might be reading an integer, but the user types the word **quick.** Whenever bad data is encountered, the input stream is marked as **bad input.** Once the input stream is bad, any subsequent attempts to read from the input stream will *have no effect!* Nothing is read, no variable values are assigned.

You may use the name of an input stream as a boolean expression to test whether the stream is bad. A bad stream results in a false expression; a device that is still good results in a true expression. For example:

```
if (cin)
    cout << "Input is still good." << endl;
else
    cout << "Input is bad." << endl;
```

Three More Functions: `get`, `ignore`, and `peek`

Many other input functions are part of `iostream.h`. We'll describe three of the most useful functions. The first function, called `get`, has several forms, including a form that simply reads the next input character. For example, suppose that `c` is a character variable. The following statement reads the next character from the standard input, and assigns the read value to `c`:

```
cin.get(c);
```

Notice that `get` is called as a member function of the `cin` object. How does `cin.get(c);` differ from `cin >> c;`? The answer is that `get` always reads the next character without skipping white space; on the other hand, the `>>` operator skips white space before reading the next character.

Another member function, called `ignore`, allows you to read and discard the next input character. With `cin`, the function is called as shown here:

```
cin.ignore( ); // Read the next character from cin, and discard this character.
```

Another member function, called `peek`, allows you to look at the next available character without actually reading it. For example, the following code checks to see whether the next character is the letter `'X'`:

```
if (cin.peek( ) == 'X')
    cout << "I am about to read an X from the standard input." << endl;
```

The `peek` function always returns the next input character without skipping white space. As another example, this code will read and discard characters until the input stream becomes bad, or a newline character is reached:

```
while (cin  &&  (cin.peek( ) != '\n'))
    cin.ignore( );
```

Here is one more example of a function that reads and discards characters until the input stream becomes bad or a non-white space character is reached. The function makes use of a boolean function, called isspace, to determine whether a character is white space:

```
void eat_white( )
// Postcondition: Characters have been read from standard input until the input stream
// becomes bad, or a non-white space character is reached.
// Library facilities used: ctype.h (provides isspace)
{
    while (cin  &&  isspace(cin.peek( )))
        cin.ignore( );
}
```

Detecting the End of a File

It is possible for the standard input to be connected to a file of characters. In this case, a program must be able to detect when the end of the input file has been reached. When the last actual character of the file has been read, the peek function returns a special constant named EOF (which is part of iostream.h). For example:

```
if (cin.peek( ) == EOF)
    cout << "There is nothing more to read." << endl;
```

One warning: The peek function does not return the EOF constant until all characters of the file have been read—including any blanks or newline characters that may appear after the last piece of actual data. For example, suppose that the standard input is a file of integers. We want to read and add up all these integers until the end of file is reached. The correct way to process the input file is shown here (using the eat_white function, written above):

```
int sum = 0;  // The sum of all the numbers that we read
int next;     // The next number that we read

eat_white( ); // Skip any white space at the front of the file.
while (cin  &&  (cin.peek( ) != EOF))
{
    cin >> next;
    eat_white( );
    sum += next;
}

cout << "The total of all numbers is: " << sum << endl;
```

The special EOF character at the end of a file can be read by the usual get function. After this character is read, the input stream is marked as bad.

Writing or Reading a Text File

So far, we have shown output and input using the standard streams cout and cin. A program can also create its own streams, connecting these streams to files. Such a program must include both iostream.h and fstream.h, and proceed as follows:

Opening a file. For writing, a program should declare a variable of type ofstream. For reading, a program should declare a variable of type ifstream. Once the variable is declared, it can be connected to an actual file with the open member function, as shown here:

Opening an Output File:

```
#include <iostream.h>
#include <fstream.h>

ofstream outfile;

outfile.open("results");
```

Opening an Input File:

```
#include <iostream.h>
#include <fstream.h>

ifstream infile;

infile.open("data");
```

The argument to the open function is the name of the file that you wish to write. In our output example, this argument is the constant string "results", so we will be writing a file named results. Our input example is reading text from a file named data. The argument to the open function may also be a string variable, or any other string expression.

Checking for failure. Sometimes, when you open a file, the open operation fails. For example, opening a file for writing can fail if the computer's disk is already full. Opening a file for input will fail if the specified file cannot be found. If the open operation fails, then the stream will be marked as "bad." You may use the name of a stream as a boolean expression to test whether the stream is bad. A bad stream results in a false expression; a device that is still good results in a true expression. Thus, after opening a file, you should check for possible failure. A simple approach uses the assert function (from assert.h), as shown here:

Check for Failure of an Output File:

```
#include <iostream.h>
#include <fstream.h>
#include <assert.h>

ofstream outfile;

outfile.open("results");
assert(outfile);
```

Check for Failure of an Input File:

```
#include <iostream.h>
#include <fstream.h>
#include <assert.h>

ifstream infile;

infile.open("data");
assert(infile);
```

Using the `ofstream` or `ifstream`. Once an `ofstream` is open, you may use it in the same way that you have used `cout`. For example, using `outfile` (opened as shown above), you may write:

```
outfile << "This sentence will be written to the file." << endl;
```

Once an `ifstream` is open, you may use it in the same way that you have used `cin`. For example, suppose that `infile` (opened above) contains lines of digits. You can read the next integer in the input file, storing the result in an integer variable `i`, as shown here:

```
infile >> i;
```

Closing a file. When you are done writing or reading a file, you should activate the `close` member function of the `ofstream` or `ifstream`. This function has no arguments, as shown here:

Closing an Output File:

```
#include <iostream.h>
#include <fstream.h>
#include <assert.h>

ofstream outfile;

outfile.open("results");
assert(outfile);

...Statements that use outfile...

outfile.close( );
```

Closing an Input File:

```
#include <iostream.h>
#include <fstream.h>
#include <assert.h>

ifstream infile;

infile.open("data");
assert(infile);

...Statements that use infile...

infile.close( );
```

Closing a file releases any resources that the file implementation uses. If output buffering is used, then closing an output file also flushes the output buffer.

Appendix G
Selected Library Functions

Functions from <ctype.h> to Manipulate Characters

Note: The actual arguments of these functions may be integers, which are converted to characters.

```
bool isalpha(char c);  // Returns true if c is a letter from 'A' to 'Z' or from 'a' to 'z'.
bool isdigit(char c);  // Returns true if c is a digit  from  '0'  to  '9'.
bool isspace(char c);  // Returns true if c is a blank, tab, newline, or carriage return.
char tolower(char c);  // If c is an upper-case letter, then the function returns the equivalent
                       // lower-case letter. Otherwise c is returned unchanged.
char toupper(char c);  // If c is a lower-case letter, then the function returns the equivalent
                       // upper-case letter. Otherwise c is returned unchanged.
```

Random Number Facility from <stdlib.h>

```
int rand( );                      // Successive calls to rand( ) return a sequence of
                                  // pseudorandom numbers in the range 0 to RAND_MAX.
void srand(unsigned int seed);    // The seed for the pseudorandom number generator
                                  // has been set to the specified value.
const int RAND_MAX;               // The largest return value from the rand function.
```

Functions from <string.h> to Manipulate Null-Terminated Strings

```
char* strcat(char target[ ], const char source[ ]);
    // A copy of the null-terminated string source is copied to the end of the null-terminated
    // string target. The function returns a pointer to the first character of target.
int strcmp(const char s1[ ], const char s2[ ]);
    // Compares two null-terminated strings. A negative return value indicates s1 < s2; a zero
    // return value indicates that s1 == s2; a positive return value indicates s1 > s2.
char* strcpy(char target[ ], const char source[ ]);
    // Copies the null-terminated string source to the null-terminated string target. The function
    // returns a pointer to the first character of target.
size_t strlen(const char s[ ]);
    // The return value is the length of s (a null-terminated string).
char* strchr(const char s[ ], char c);
    // The return value is a pointer to the first occurrence of c in the null-terminated string s (or
    // the NULL pointer if c does not appear in s).
int strpos(const char s[ ], char c);
    // The return value is the first index i such that s[i] = c (or –1 if c does not appear in the
    // null-terminated string s).
char* strstr(const char s[ ], const char sub[ ])
    // Returns a pointer to the first occurrence of the substring sub in the string null-terminated
    // string s (or the NULL pointer if sub does not appear in s).
```

Appendix H
A Toolkit of Useful Functions

Header File

```
// FILE: useful.h
// PROVIDES: A toolkit of useful functions for random numbers and displays.
//
// FUNCTIONS in the toolkit:
//    double random_fraction( )
//        Postcondition: The return value is a random real number in the closed interval [0..1]
//        (including the endpoints).
//
//    double random_real(double low, double high)
//        Precondition: low <= high.
//        Postcondition: The return value is a random real number in the closed interval [low..high]
//        (including the endpoints).
//
//    void display(double x)
//        Postcondition: The function has written one line of output to the standard output, with a
//        vertical bar in the middle. If x is positive, then approximately x stars are printed to the
//        right of the vertical bar. If x is negative, then approximately -x stars are printed to the
//        left of the vertical bar. If the absolute value of x is more than 39, then only 39 stars
//        are printed. Examples:
//        display(8) prints:                                      |********
//        display(-4) prints:                               ****|
//
//    void eat_line( )
//        Postcondition: Up to next newline has been read and discarded from cin.
//
//    bool inquire(const char query[ ])
//        Precondition: query is a null-terminated string of characters.
//        Postcondition: query has been printed, and a one-line response read from the user.
//        The function returns true if the user's response begins with 'Y' or 'y', and returns false if
//        the user's response begins with 'N' or 'n'. (If the response begins with some other letter,
//        then the query is repeated.)

#ifndef USEFUL_H
#define USEFUL_H

    double random_fraction( );
    double random_real(double low, double high);
    void display(double x);
    void eat_line( );
    bool inquire(const char query[ ]);

#endif
```

(continued)

Implementation File

```
// FILE: useful.cxx
// IMPLEMENTS: A toolkit of functions (See useful.h for documentation.)

#include <assert.h>    // Provides assert
#include <ctype.h>     // Provides toupper
#include <iostream.h>  // Provides cout, cin, get
#include <stdlib.h>    // Provides rand, RAND_MAX
#include "useful.h"

void display(double x)
// Library facilities used: iostream.h, stdlib.h
{
    const char STAR = '*';
    const char BLANK = ' ';
    const char VERTICAL_BAR = '|';
    const int  LIMIT = 39;
    int i;

    if (x < -LIMIT)
        x = -LIMIT;
    else if (x > LIMIT)
        x = LIMIT;

    for (i = -LIMIT; i < 0; i++)
    {
        if (i >= x)
            cout << STAR;
        else
            cout << BLANK;
    }
    cout << VERTICAL_BAR;
    for (i = 1; i <= LIMIT; i++)
    {
        if (i <= x)
            cout << STAR;
        else
            cout << BLANK;
    }
    cout << endl;
}

double random_fraction( )
// Library facilities used: stdlib.h
{
    return rand( ) / double(RAND_MAX);
}
```

(continued)

```
double random_real(double low, double high)
// Library facilities used: assert.h
{
    assert(low <= high);
    return low + random_fraction( ) * (high - low);
}

void eat_line( )
// Library facilities used: iostream.h
//
{
    char next;

    do
        cin.get(next);
    while (next != '\n');
}

bool inquire(const char query[ ])
// Library facilities used: ctype.h, iostream.h
{
    char answer;

    do
    {
        cout << query << " [Yes or No]" << endl;
        cin >> answer;
        answer = toupper(answer);
        eat_line( );
    }
    while ((answer != 'Y') && (answer != 'N'));
    return (answer == 'Y');
}
```

useful.h and useful.cxx **FTP**

Appendix I
A Toolkit of Useful Template Functions

This is an expansion of the "item toolkit" from Chapter 6. It is available by FTP as the two files `items.h` and `items.template`.

Header File

```
// FILE: items.h
// PROVIDES: A toolkit of template functions for manipulating items.
//
// TEMPLATE FUNCTIONS in the linked list toolkit:
//     template <class Item>
//     Item maximal(Item a, Item b)
//         Postcondition: Returns the larger of a and b.
//         Note: Item may be any type with the > operator and a copy constructor.
//
//     template <class Item>
//     void swap(Item& x, Item& y)
//         Postcondition: The values of x and y have been interchanged so that y now has the
//         value of x, and vice versa. Note: Item may be any type with an assignment operator
//         and a default constructor.
//
//     template <class Item, class SizeType>
//     size_t index_of_maximal(const Item data[ ], SizeType n)
//         Precondition: data is an array with at least n items, and n>0.
//         Postcondition: The return value is the index of a maximal item from data[0] to data[n-1].
//         Note: Item may be any type with the < operator defined.
//         SizeType may be any of the integer or const integer types.
//
//     template <class Item, class SizeType>
//     void ordered_insert(Item data[ ], SizeType n, Item entry)
//         Precondition: data is a partially filled array containing n items sorted from small to
//         large. The array size is large enough to hold at least one more item.
//         Postcondition: data is a partially filled array containing the n original items plus the new
//         entry. These items are still sorted from small to large.
//         Note: Item may be any type with an assignment operator and the >= operator defined.
//         SizeType may be any of the integer or const integer types.
//
```

(continued)

```
//    template <class Item, class SizeType>
//    size_t first_ge(const Item data[ ], SizeType n, const Item& entry)
//        Precondition: data is a partially filled array containing n items sorted from
//        small to large.
//        Postcondition: The return value i is the first location such that data[i] >= entry.
//        If there is no such location, then the return value is n.
//        Note: Item may be any type with the >= operator defined.
//        SizeType may be any of the integer or const integer types.
//
//    template <class Item, class SizeType>
//    void attach_item(Item data[ ], SizeType& n, const Item& entry)
//        Precondition: data is a partially filled array containing n items. The array size is large
//        enough to hold at least one more item.
//        Postcondition: data is a partially filled array containing the n original items plus the new
//        entry at the end. The value of n has been increased by one.
//        Note: Item may be any type with an assignment operator.
//        SizeType may be any of the integer or const integer types.
//
//    template <class Item, class IndexType, class SizeType>
//    void insert_item(Item data[ ], IndexType i, SizeType& n, Item entry)
//        Precondition: data is a partially filled array containing n items, 0 <= i <= n, and the array
//        size is large enough to hold at least one more item.
//        Postcondition: data is a partially filled array containing the n original items plus the new
//        entry. The new entry appears at data[i], and the original entries from data[i] onward
//        have all been shifted up one spot. The value of n has also been increased by one.
//        Note: Item may be any type with an assignment operator.
//        SizeType and IndexType may be any of the integer or const integer types.
//
//    template <class Item, class SizeType>
//    void detach_item(Item data[ ], SizeType& n, Item& entry)
//        Precondition: data is a partially filled array containing n items, and n > 0.
//        Postcondition: n has been decremented by one, so that data can now be considered a
//        partially filled array with one less item. A copy of this removed item is now in the
//        parameter entry.
//        Note: Item may be any type with an assignment operator.
//        SizeType may be any of the integer or const integer types.
//
//    template <class Item, class IndexType, class SizeType>
//    void delete_item(Item data[ ], IndexType i, SizeType& n, Item& entry)
//        Precondition: data is a partially filled array containing n items, and n > 0.
//        Postcondition: The item that was originally at data[i] has been removed from the partially
//        filled array by shifting data[i+1]... down one spot. The value of n has been decremented
//        by one, so that data can now be considered a partially filled array with one less item.
//        A copy of the removed item is now in the parameter entry.
//        Note: Item may be any type with an assignment operator.
//        SizeType and IndexType may be any of the integer or const integer types.
//
```

(continued)

```
//   template <class Item, class SizeType>
//   void merge(Item data1[ ], SizeType& n1, Item data2[ ], SizeType& n2)
//       Precondition: data1 is a partially filled array containing n1 items, and data2 is a partial-
//       ly filled array containing n2 items. The array data1 also has room for n2 more items.
//       Postcondition: All items have been copied from data2 to the end of data1.
//       The value of n1 has been increased by n2, and n2 has been set to zero.
//       Note: Item may be any type with an assignment operator.
//       SizeType may be any of the integer or const integer types.
//
//   template <class Item, class SizeType>
//   void split(Item data1[ ], SizeType& n1, Item data2[ ], SizeType& n2)
//       Precondition: data1 is a partially filled array containing n1 items, and data2 is a partial-
//       filled array containing n2 items. The array data2 also has room for n1/2 more items.
//       Postcondition: The final n1/2 items have been copied from data1 to the end of data2. The
//       value of n2 has been increased by n1/2, and n1 has been reduced by this same amount.
//       Note: Item may be any type with an assignment operator.
//       SizeType may be any of the integer or const integer types.

#ifndef ITEMS_H
#define ITEMS_H
#include <stdlib.h> // Provides size_t

    // FUNCTIONS for the items toolkit
    template <class Item>
    Item maximal(Item a, Item b);

    template <class Item>
    void swap(Item& x, Item& y);

    template <class Item, class SizeType>
    size_t index_of_maximal(Item data[ ], SizeType n);

    template <class Item, class SizeType>
    void ordered_insert(Item data[ ], SizeType n, Item entry);

    template <class Item, class SizeType>
    void attach_item(Item data[ ], SizeType& n, const Item& entry);

    template <class Item, class IndexType, class SizeType>
    void insert_item(Item data[ ], IndexType i, SizeType& n, Item entry);

    template <class Item, class SizeType>
    void detach_item(Item data[ ], SizeType& n, Item& entry);

    template <class Item, class IndexType, class SizeType>
    void delete_item(Item data[ ], IndexType i, SizeType& n, Item& entry);

    template <class Item, class SizeType>
    void merge(Item data1[ ], SizeType& n1, Item data2[ ], SizeType& n2);

    template <class Item, class SizeType>
    void split(Item data1[ ], SizeType& n1, Item data2[ ], SizeType& n2);

#include "items.template" // Include the implementations.
#endif
```

(continued)

An Implementation File for Template Functions

```
// FILE: items.template
// IMPLEMENTS: The template functions of a small toolkit to manipulate items (see items.h).
// This is an expansion of the smaller toolkit from Chapter 6.
// Note that this file is not compiled on its own. Instead, this file is included in items.h.

#include <assert.h>      // Provides assert
#include <stdlib.h>      // Provides size_t

template <class Item>
Item maximal(Item a, Item b)
{
    if (a > b)
        return a;
    else
        return b;
}

template <class Item>
void swap(Item& x, Item& y)
{
    Item temp;

    temp = x;
    x = y;
    y = temp;
}

template <class Item, class SizeType>
size_t index_of_maximal(const Item data[ ], SizeType n)
// Library facilities used: assert.h, stdlib.h
{
    size_t answer;
    size_t i;

    assert(n > 0);
    answer = 0;

    for (i = 1; i < n; i++)
    {
        if (data[answer] < data[i])
            answer = i;
        // data[answer] is now biggest from data[0] to data[i].
    }

    return answer;
}
```

(continued)

```
template <class Item, class SizeType>
void ordered_insert(Item data[ ], SizeType n, Item entry)
// Library functions used: stdlib.h
{
    size_t i;

    for (i = n; (i > 0) && (data[i-1] > entry); i--)
        data[i] = data[i-1];

    data[i] = entry;
}
```

```
template <class Item, class SizeType>
size_t first_ge(const Item data[ ], SizeType n, const Item& entry)
// Library functions used: stdlib.h
{
    size_t i;

    for (i = 0; (i < n) && !(data[i] >= entry); i++);

    return i;
}
```

```
template <class Item, class SizeType>
void attach_item(Item data[ ], SizeType& n, const Item& entry)
{
    data[n++] = entry;
}
```

```
template <class Item, class IndexType, class SizeType>
void insert_item(Item data[ ], IndexType i, SizeType& n, Item entry)
{
    size_t shift_index;

    for (shift_index = n; shift_index > i; shift_index--)
        data[shift_index] = data[shift_index-1];
    data[i] = entry;
    n++;
}
```

```
template <class Item, class SizeType>
void detach_item(Item data[ ], SizeType& n, Item& entry)
{
    entry = data[--n];
}
```

(continued)

```
template <class Item, class IndexType, class SizeType>
void delete_item(Item data[ ], IndexType i, SizeType& n, Item& entry)
{
    size_t shift_index;

    entry = data[i];
    for (shift_index = i+1; shift_index < n; shift_index++)
        data[shift_index-1] = data[shift_index];

    n--;
}
```

```
template <class Item, class SizeType>
void merge(Item data1[ ], SizeType& n1, Item data2[ ], SizeType& n2)
{
    size_t i;

    for (i = 0; i < n2; i++)
        data1[n1 + i] = data2[i];
    n1 += n2;
    n2 = 0;
}
```

```
template <class Item, class SizeType>
void split(Item data1[ ], SizeType& n1, Item data2[ ], SizeType& n2)
{
    size_t i;
    size_t new_size1;

    new_size1 = n1 - n1/2;

    for (i = 0; i < n1/2; i++)
        data2[n2 + i] = data1[new_size1 + i];

    n2 += n1/2;
    n1 = new_size1;
}
```

items.h and items.template   **FTP**

Appendix J
Fundamental Style Guide

This appendix outlines three of our fundamental style guidelines. A program called `standard.cxx` is available to help you check whether your programs meet these guidelines. For information on obtaining the program, see "Supplements Via Internet" on page xii.

Specifications with Preconditions and Postconditions

Each of our function's *behavior is specified with a precondition/postcondition contract.*

- For a function that is provided as part of a toolkit, the contract appears in a comment at the top of the toolkit's header file.

- For a member function of a class that is provided with a header file and implementation file, the contract appears in a comment at the top of the class's header file.

- For a function that is implemented and used only in a ".cxx" file, the contract appears with the function's implementation in the ".cxx" file.

Capitalization

Variable names and *function names* are written with all lower-case letters. If the name consists of several words, then these words are separated by an underscore (such as `eat_white`).

Declared constants and member constants of a class are written with all upper-case letters. If the name consists of several words, then these words are separated by an underscore (such as `MANY_COLUMNS`). However, constant function parameters are written with lower-case letters (just like any other parameter).

New class names are written with an initial upper-case letter, and the rest lower case. If the name consists of several words, then each word is capitalized and there are no underscores (such as `PriorityQueue`).

Indentation

- Any statements grouped between brackets (`'{'` and `'}'`) are indented four spaces. The brackets themselves appear on separate lines with no extra indentation. The only exceptions are the keywords *public*, *private*, or *protected* (in a class definition), which appear on lines by themselves with the same indentation as the brackets.

- In a loop or conditional statement with a one-line body (i.e., no brackets), the one line appears on a line by itself with four spaces of indentation beyond the loop or conditional statement.

- The statements that follow a case label of a switch statement are written with at least four spaces of indentation beyond the case label.

Index

DATA STRUCTURES
AND OTHER OBJECTS USING C++

Michael Main, University of Colorado at Boulder
Walter Savitch, University of California, San Diego

Where will you be ten years from now? How will a course in data structures help you? Perhaps you will be a software engineer writing large software in specialized areas such as computer graphics. The authors of such programs, today and in the future, require a ready knowledge of proven methods for representing data.

For example, the graphics program that generated the cover of this book uses a collection of three-dimensional objects—and a programmer must use the knowledge of data structures to make decisions on how to represent such collections. As a programmer, you must also possess an unshakable understanding of fundamental programming techniques and algorithms to manipulate the data structures. The graphics program is again a good example, using recursion to generate beautiful fractal patterns, and using efficient sorting algorithms in the process of removing hidden objects.

With many accessible examples, this book provides the knowledge of data representations and algorithms in a way that will be immediately useful to you with C++. This book also focuses on foundational material that will continue to be useful to you over the next ten years and beyond.

Data Structures and Other Objects Using C++ provides:
- a balanced approach to data structures and object-oriented programming
- early, self-contained coverage of key C++ and object-oriented programming topics
- a solid foundation in specifying, designing, implementing, and using simple container classes, lists, stacks, queues, trees, and more
- accessible coverage of fundamental topics such as container classes, pointers and linked lists, time
- extensive appendice
  come

Access the latest informa
site: http://www.aw.co

ADDISON-WESLEY

Addison-Wesley is an impri
of Addison Wesley Longma